DESIGNING GREAT BEERS

The Ultimate Guide to Brewing Classic Beer Styles

Ray Daniels

brewers
publications

A Division of the
Brewers Association
Boulder, Colorado

Brewers Publications
A Division of the Brewers Association
PO Box 1679, Boulder, CO 80306-1679
(303) 447-0816; Fax (303) 447-2825
www.beertown.org

Printed in the United States of America
10 9 8

ISBN-13: 978-0-937381-50-2
ISBN-10: 0-937381-50-0

Library of Congress Cataloging-in-Publication Data

Daniels, Ray.
        Designing great beers / Ray Daniels.
            p. cm.
        Includes bibliographical references and index.
        IBSN 0-937381-50-0 (alk. paper)
            1. Beer.   2. Brewing.   I. Title.
    TP577.D26 1996
    663'.42—dc20   96-30660
                                                           CIP

Technical Editor: Paul Farnsworth
Book Project Editor: Theresa Duggan
Copy Editor: Dianne Russell
Cover Designer: Randy Mosher/Randy Mosher Design
Interior Designer: Wendy Lyons

To my wife, Laura, for her patience and forbearance with all beery things.

BEER

It is the drink of men who think
And feel no fear nor fetter —
Who do not drink to senseless sink,
But drink to think the better.

— Anonymous

CONTENTS

FIGURES

TABLES

ACKNOWLEDGMENTS

Project	Designing Great Beers
	Brewers Publications
Project No.	61766

No book is possible without the help of many individuals. In this case, all of the people who helped out were knowledgeable about and interested in beer, and that made working with them all the more pleasant.

I must start by thanking Steve Castleman of California's Maltose Falcons. Steve suggested to me and to Brewers Publications that a book like *Designing Great Beers* would be a worthy undertaking. I also thank his wife, Maribeth Raines, who shared her time and expertise with me.

Two other people who profoundly affected this book, also deserve early mention. The first is Randy Mosher. His unselfish sharing of all that he knows, not only with me but with anyone interested in beer, has catalyzed many of the accomplishments made by brewers associated with the Chicago Beer Society. Without him, neither this book nor my own understanding of beer would be what it is today. While you will find his name mentioned frequently in the text and credits, his influence extends much further. The second is my technical editor, Paul Farnsworth. His in-depth scientific knowledge and practical brewing experience, in both Britain and the United States, brought valuable objectivity to the manuscript. Through more than twenty years of writing for publication, I have worked with a lot of editors. I only wish all of them had been as careful and constructive as Paul.

Next, I'll thank the U.S. postal service for (again) clearly demonstrating that private or electronic means should be used for all important communications. In August 1993, I wrote a proposal for this book and sent it

to Elizabeth Gold, Publisher of Brewers Publications. She sent a letter back expressing interest in the project, but I never got it. Thinking that there was no interest in the book, I turned my attention to other priorities. When I saw Elizabeth the following April, she surprised me by saying, "How's the book going?" My reply, "What book?" I'm sure was no less surprising to her. By the time we sorted everything out and I started work on the book, it had been over a year since my original proposal.

The first place I went for information was the library at the Siebel Institute in Chicago, which has an extensive catalog of both current and historical brewing literature. Bill Siebel was kind enough to allow me regular access to this treasure trove. For more than a year, many others at Siebel, including Linda Peek, Jackie Kelly, and Maureen Miller, also assisted me. The school's brewer-turned-registrar, Christopher Bird, served as host during many of my visits and was constantly supportive and helpful.

Not long after my visits to Siebel began, I wound up enrolling in their ten-week diploma course on brewing. Work on my brewery project had hit an unexpected snag, and so it seemed like a good time to invest in a little formal brewing education. Of course, the book benefited from this experience as well; my fellow classmates contributed unique perspectives on brewing that furthered my understanding of beer science and practice.

The faculty at Siebel is fantastic. Many of the lectures and informal discussions contributed either directly or indirectly to this book. I want to thank Dr. Joe Power for taking the time to talk with me on many occasions about technical issues, Klaus Zastrow for helping me decode old German brewing texts as well as imparting his knowledge of beer history and brewing science, Paul Smith for his comprehensive insight into the issues of beer color and specialty malts, Jim Helmke for sharing his vast expertise in modern brewing science, and Ilse Shelton for further training my palate. I also want to thank Kurt Duecker of Schreier Malt for providing me and my classmates with a thorough understanding of the malting process and its relationship to finished beer quality. Finally, under sponsorship from Bill Siebel, the Siebel laboratory ran a couple of IBU analyses for me to help provide data for the hop section of this book. This contribution was greatly appreciated.

Of course, Siebel was not my only resource. A number of others shared their time and expertise with me on hop issues alone, including Max L. Deinzer at Oregon State University, and fellow brewers Mark Garetz, Glenn Tinseth, and Al Korzonas.

Many people provided guidance and advice during my research of beer color. In addition to Joe Power and Paul Smith of Siebel, I received valuable input from Keith Thomas of Brewlab at the University of Sunderland in England, food technologist Terri Paeschke, Marianne Gruber at Briess Malting, and also Ilse Shelton and Jim Helmke at Siebel. Thanks also to Greg Noonan for steering me toward a needed correction after the color material was published in *Brewing Techniques*.

During a trip to England while writing the style sections, I learned a good deal from both brewers and beer drinkers. Geoff Cooper shared his knowledge of British styles over a number of pints, as did others, including Mr. Barry Pepper. Mark Dorber, landlord of the White Horse Pub, shared his knowledge of cellarmanship as well as a few tips on sources of historical brewing books. Keith Thomas facilitated further discovery of the British styles through a series of conversations.

During the London trip, I spent a good deal of productive time talking with James Spence of the American Homebrewers Association® about beer styles. James later arranged for me to acquire a copy of the *500 Bier Aus Aller Welt* series from Charlie Papazian's library. A big thanks to both Charlie and James for that resource.

In addition to the Siebel collection, I studied many other old brewing texts. I was able to acquire a number of these for my personal collection thanks to book collector Steve Presley and beer history buff Pete Slosberg. Of course, several references came from the personal library of Randy Mosher.

Others who helped include Steve Hamburg, Dennis Davison, Chris Nemeth, Todd McGuiness, and Dan McConnell.

The Association of Brewers has contributed to this book in various ways. Thanks to Karen Barela and the AHA for contributing the second-round entry forms for analysis and to Bill Simpson for making copies of those forms. Thanks to the Great American Beer Festival® and the Institute for Brewing Studies for conducting events that allowed me to learn more about beers and brewing methods in the United States today.

Before closing, let me thank the small but efficient staff of Brewers Publications. Publisher Elizabeth Gold, for her patience while I sorted out my conflicting priorities and for generously understanding the changes in scope of this project that evolved during its writing. In the spirit of the Association of Brewers, Theresa Duggan and Kim Adams have been fun to work with as they contributed their own special skills.

Finally, I want to thank my parents, Jon and Phyllis Daniels, for nurturing my interest in the fields of science and journalism. For more than twenty rewarding years, my life and my work have been defined by the intersection of these two fields. This book is but one fruit of the seeds they have sown.

— Ray Daniels

INTRODUCTION

Project   Designing Great Beers
          Brewers Publications

Project No.   61766

For the most part, brewing is a series of mundane tasks. From the smallest homebrewer to the biggest commercial producer, the essential brewing tasks are repeated over and over, with each batch that's brewed. In reality, what makes brewing different from making potato chips or silicon chips is simply the finished product.

Brewers like to drink beer, of course. But what really gets a brewer out of bed in the morning is the chance to create something new and to share it with the world. At big breweries, only a select few brewers ever get to create a new beer; sometimes the task is farmed out to a consultant. It's not surprising, then, that those who work at large breweries occasionally envy the small brewer and even the homebrewer.

Small brewers are oftentimes presented with the opportunity to create new recipes. Once the beer is done, they receive immediate feedback from their customers and often from other brewers as well. Although a portion of the feedback is verbal, more significant indicators are how well and how quickly a beer sells. For those whose livelihood depends upon the production of good beers, every new recipe must be carefully planned and executed to achieve the desired results.

Homebrewers often develop a new recipe every time they brew. Faced with few economic pressures, they can brew solely for pleasure. Many start in a haphazard way — throwing in a handful of this and an ounce of that — but after a few batches, most homebrewers learn more about the culture of beer. This might start with a bit of tasting and reading about great beers or entering some beers in homebrew competitions. With these events, the homebrewer acquires a new motivation to achieve something with his or her brews: to impart a special flavor, to produce a specific style, or to copy an outstanding commercial example.

Thus all brewers who formulate their own recipes have a common need for information that will help them produce good beers. Helping you achieve your brewing goals is what *Designing Great Beers* is all about.

This book is divided into two parts that cover two types of information necessary for recipe formulation. Part one discusses what various ingredients can do for you and gives you tools to help you achieve your brewing goals. Part two examines specific beer styles to help you understand how they are defined and what special ingredients or techniques must be used to brew a representative example.

Among the tools included in part one, you'll find both ingredient catalogs and formulas. The catalogs provide you with resources for understanding the flavor effects of various malts, hops, yeasts, and water salts. These general references are valuable sources of information, no matter what type of beer you are making.

The formulas will help you to hit target values for qualities such as bitterness and gravity in your beer. If basic algebra makes your knees shake, you might find the text introducing these formulas a bit tedious, but don't forsake the formulas themselves. They can — and will — help you brew better beer.

Wherever possible, I have translated formulas into tables that allow you to look up a number instead of calculating it. In most cases, the look-up method will give an answer every bit as good as an exact calculation.

Part two has a wealth of information about fourteen major style categories, from pale ale to Pilsener and from brown ale to bock. Studying a style provides important information that will guide you in the process of recipe formulation.

Each chapter in part two includes a style characteristics chart like the one shown in table 0.1. These charts present a shorthand definition of the style. As a starting point, this type of definition helps you to begin creating a recipe from scratch by allowing you to specify many of the details that describe what you are trying to achieve with the beer.

Despite the usefulness of such descriptions, they tell little about the actual ingredients and techniques used in making the style. For this reason, the style chapters in part two also outline the ways each style typically has been made, both now and in the past. This information goes a long way in helping you understand how brewers actually achieve the flavors of their beers. Finally, to assist you with your own formulations, each chapter includes analyses of contemporary recipes to show you how other brewers produce a particular style of beer.

Using the resources, discussions, and tools available in this book, and with a blank sheet of paper, you can write a recipe for the beer of your dreams. In the process, you'll probably flip back and forth between part one and part two, collecting information on the style you want to produce in part two and consulting the resource charts and calculation guides in part one. This process reflects the reality of recipe formulation, and I think you'll find it easy to jump back and forth between the two parts — and even between chapters within the parts.

Today, both homebrewers and a number of small commercial breweries use malt extract in their formulations. I know from my own experience as a homebrewer and as a homebrew judge that beers containing extract can be every bit as outstanding as

Table 0.1
Example of a Style Characteristics Chart

Scottish Ale Light (60/-)

Original gravity	1.035
Bitterness	9–20
BU:GU ratio	0.3–0.55
Hop flavor and aroma	None to low
Color (SRM)	8–17
Apparent extract	1.006–1.010
Alcohol (volume)	3–4
Esters	None to low
Diacetyl	Low to medium

those made from grain alone. As a result, the use of extract will be considered and addressed throughout this book, beginning with a chapter on extract in part one.

Finally, you will not find a lot of instruction on brewing techniques in this book — nothing on mashing, aerating, transferring, and so on. Most of these techniques are learned when brewing your first few batches, and more advanced techniques (e.g., decoction mashing) are too involved to cover during the discussion of the formulation process. Instead, you'll find a guide to essential brewing techniques in appendix 1. It lists the areas critical to brewing and provides information on where to learn more about them.

A good understanding of basic brewing techniques allows you to produce beers from the recipes created by others. What *Designing Great Beers* provides are tools you need to go beyond borrowed recipes to creating and perfecting your own great beers. It also will give you the tools needed to tailor the recipes of others to your own brewing equipment and processes.

You'll find great satisfaction in mastering recipe design. This is, after all, the creative part of brewing. Once the recipe is written, it's time for the work and the waiting. And, if you are going to invest your time and energy in brewing, you should produce a product that meets your expectations. *Designing Great Beers* will help you do this so that you get more satisfaction, enjoyment, and perhaps even more relaxation from brewing.

Cheers and good brewing!

PART ONE

1 | SIX STEPS TO SUCCESSFUL BEER

In part one, I focus on the recipe formulation process. To provide a structure for these discussions, I have broken the process into the following six steps:

1. Identify and characterize the beer you want to make.
2. Determine malt and extract bill.
3. Determine water quantity and chemistry.
4. Determine hop bill.
5. Select yeast and fermentation plan.
6. Ascertain finishing issues, including clarification and carbonation.

To think through the recipe formulation process, all six elements in the proper order must be considered. Of course, in many situations you won't make specific decisions about all these questions, you'll just follow your normal practice. But if you want to think about copying a classic style or matching the flavor of a wonderful beer you have enjoyed, each step will need to be considered.

Let's review the six steps so that the issues are clear.

Six Steps to Successful Beer

1. Identify your goal and characterize the desired beer. This includes the style of beer to be brewed, commercial example to be copied, ingredient to experiment with, and so on. To characterize your beer, determine the following:
- How much finished beer will you make?
- Will an ale, lager, or specialty yeast be used?
- What is the original gravity target or range?
- What is the approximate bitterness level desired (in IBUs)?
  What approximate color is desired?
- What malt characteristics are appropriate or desired?
- What hop flavor and aroma characteristics are desired?
- What special ingredients (fruit, spices, syrups, etc.) will be included, and how will they be added?

2. Determine the malt and extract bill, both character and quantity.
- What base malt or extract will be used?
- What specialty malts will be used; what proportion of the mash will they constitute?
- What type of mash program will be required?
To set quantity, calculate backwards from target gravity to grain and extract bill. Hit your target gravity during brewing.

3. Consider water and water treatment.

7

- What is the character of the starting water?
- What concentrations of minerals are desired for the style?
- What treatment regimen is required to achieve these mineral concentrations?
- What impact will these additions have on mash chemistry?
- Any other adjustments needed for mash chemistry?
- What volume of water is required?

4. Determine the hop bill, both character and quantity.
- What hop aroma is desired (source and type of hops to be used)?
- What hop flavor is desired (source and type of hops to be used)?
- What hop bitterness is desired?

To determine flavor hop additions, calculate likely IBU impact. Subtract flavor hop IBUs from total IBU target; calculate needed bittering hops.

5. Determine a fermentation plan.
- What yeast will be used?
- How much yeast will be required for pitching?
- What fermentation temperature will be used? How will temperature be controlled and monitored?
- What fermentation vessel will be used? Airlock or blowtube?
- Will a diacetyl rest be needed?
- Will lagering be employed?

6. Consider clarification and carbonation.
- Does the beer need to be ready by a specific date?

- What clarification methods will you use (Irish moss in boil, filtration after fermentation, cold settling, other clarifying agents)?
- How will you carbonate and serve the beer?
- What quantity of priming sugar or pressure of CO_2 will be required to achieve the desired level of carbonation?

The first step — identifying exactly what you want to achieve in a beer — can be quite challenging. There are so many intriguing possibilities that it can be hard to focus on the goals for a single beer. But focus you must so that you can continue the exciting journey from the first thought (or taste!) of a beer you want to emulate to a finished beer that you are happy with.

Certainly a bit of experimentation will be needed in the brewery, but before you get to that stage, some research can be quite useful. And that, my fellow brewer, is why I have included the information in part two, which details the characteristics and brewing particulars of many different popular styles, reducing the amount of time you must spend thumbing through brewing books and collecting information before you can accurately reproduce either a current or historical beer style.

But before you get to the specific styles, you need to be thoroughly familiar with the tools available and the processes required for recipe formulation. The following chapters in part one deal with various aspects of the six steps to successful beer, starting with the process of setting goals.

Imagine a blank piece of paper. Imagine that you are going to write down a beer recipe on that sheet of paper. How do you decide what to write? If your purpose is just to "make a beer," then the job is pretty easy. Just write down "malt extract, water, yeast." Every homebrewer has made beer this way, and the product is drinkable (usually). But, of course, you want to do something more.

Maybe you just tasted a great beer that you would like to duplicate. Or perhaps you have noticed that other brewers manage to get a lot more hop flavor in their pale ales. Or maybe you have been reading Michael Jackson's *The New World Guide to Beer*, and you are fascinated with Düsseldorf-style altbier. Or perhaps you are ready to experiment more with beer ingredients, to understand the real impact of chocolate malt or decoction mashing. All these motivations provide an important starting point for the brewing process — a goal. Only by knowing where you want to go can you actually hope to arrive there.

So the first thing you need to establish is a goal, a target. If you want, write it down at the top of the recipe to help you better remember what you're aiming for. Examples might include:

• Brew an authentic Pilsener beer
• Copy Guinness stout
• Experiment with rye

Now that you have an overall goal, fill in a few specifics. Every beer can be defined by certain characteristics, starting with specific gravity, color, and bitterness. These three items can be numerically defined for every beer. Descriptions in part two provide appropriate ranges for each style, and the formulas in part one provide the tools needed to hit those target values.

In addition to these objectively definable characteristics, a beer has other traits that must be recorded descriptively, such as aroma. Do you smell malt or hops in the aroma? What is the character of that aroma? Spicy? Coffeelike? Other traits include flavor, head retention, and finish.

The more carefully you define what you want in a beer, the more you can tailor the recipe and the brewing process to achieve those ends. One of the greatest tools you can use to help define a beer is established style descriptions. The whole concept of styles and their definition is an important one, so let's discuss them here.

Beer Styles

A beer style comes into being when several brewers, often in close geographic proximity to each other, create beers that share a similar set of distinctive traits. These traits include body, alcohol content, bitterness, color, and flavor profile. In the end, the traits of a style incorporate the variation seen from brewer to brewer while still defining a formulation that is generally distinguishable from other styles of beer.

Perhaps the most important function of style is beer flavor. The use of a single word, such as "stout," gives you an immediate idea of what a beer will be like without going through a long description like, "it's a 1.045 original gravity opaque black ale with roasted malt or coffeelike notes, a hint of diacetyl, and a rich, creamy head." This shorthand is very useful for communication between brewers, retailers, and consumers. It allows brewers to tell others what they have brewed without long, drawn-out explanations. It allows servers to tell consumers about a menu of products in an equally efficient manner. And finally, it allows consumers to pinpoint the beers they want to drink.

I often equate styles in beer to breeds in dogs. Every dog or beer is different, but those within the same breed or style have a set of common characteristics. If your dog doesn't meet the characteristics of its breed, people may confuse it for some other breed. Likewise, a beer that lacks the key characteristics of its designated style may be confused for another style.

In competition, dogs are judged by breed; beers are judged by style. Judges consider the full range of the category and try to find the entry that best exemplifies it. If you have the world's most wonderful dog (or beer), but it does not fit within the confines of its category, it is not going to win. (Yes, there are wonderful mongrel beers too!)

Brewing to meet a style's specifications will ensure that your beer is well received by consumers and judges alike. After all, if you subdue the IBUs (International Bitterness Units) on a pale ale or put a ton of aroma hops in your stout, people will be surprised. The point of putting a style label on a beer is not to dash expectations, but to meet them.

When you brew something that's a little different, you can use a modifier or two with the style name to let people know what they're getting. Descriptions like "strong mild" and "American-hopped alt" extend the shorthand language of styles in useful ways. Then, if enough brewers make beer in that style, the shorthand itself may become a new style designation as we have seen with American brown ale.

While styles are important, they are not the be-all and end-all of brewing. Keep your mind (and mouth) open to good beer. A good Pilsener doesn't have to taste exactly like Pilsener Urquell, and a good stout doesn't have to taste exactly like Guinness.

By studying styles, you gather valuable input for the recipe formulation process. Part two provides you with the kind of research and data that accomplished brewers gather when formulating a new recipe. By using this research, as well as your own knowledge of a style, you can devise a good set of goals for your brewing efforts. Once those goals are established, you are ready to devise the details of the recipe by identifying specific ingredients and determining exactly how much of each is needed. With that in mind, chapter 3 begins the discussion of fermentable ingredients along with a look at malt extract.

Project	Designing Great Beers
	Brewers Publications
Project No.	61766

3 MALT EXTRACTS

Malt extracts are a subject of some controversy in the brewing world, no matter what kind of brewing you are doing. Many purists turn up their noses at extracts and refuse to use them for any purpose in their finished beers. However the ranks of experienced and award-winning brewers include many who, by chance or by choice, use extract as a significant source of fermentable material in their beers.

Most homebrewers start out making beers from extract kits, and many continue to make fine extract-based beers as they gain more experience. Extract breweries are also found in commercial settings. A recent survey by the Institute for Brewing Studies found that 5 percent of the country's brewpubs have extract brewing systems, some of which are supplemented by a portion of grain.[1]

Among homebrewers, the use of extract is inevitable and, indeed, other sources bear this out. Among winners of the annual American Homebrewers Association® National Homebrew Competition, the use of malt extract is common. Four of the seven Homebrewers of the Year between 1988 and 1994 used extract in their recipes, and all but one used 5 pounds or more.[2] Similarly, as late as 1994, the First Place recipes from the twenty-four individual style categories included nine (38 percent) that used extract extensively.

While observing the prevalence of extract in these winning recipes, we must also note that virtually *none was made from extract only.* Only two winning recipes were made with no grain, an herb beer and a lambic.[3] (No doubt other flavors made up for the lack of grain-malt character.)

Data on winning beers demonstrate that you can make great beer using extract as the base for your creation; however they also tell us that grain plays an important role in virtually every beer recipe. You can certainly make drinkable beer from nothing but extract, but to make truly wonderful beer, you will want to add some grain to the mix.

How much grain is enough? Well, ultimately that depends upon the recipe and the style you are brewing. In general, however, 25 to 67 percent of the gravity of your beer should come from grain. That equates to 2½ to 5 pounds for a 5-gallon batch of 1.045 to 1.048 beer. The low end of this range can be extracted using a grain bag, but in the long run, you'll be better off buying or building a small device for conducting appropriate-sized mashes. (See Conducting a Mini-mash in appendix 1 for sources you can consult on this subject.)

Of course, there are a number of issues beyond quantity that bear on your use of extracts. As you become a more experienced brewer, you will want to consider these issues and the implications they will have on your selection, storage, and use of extract. I present them here for education and reference.

Characteristics of Malt Extract

The one authoritative study conducted on malt extracts as they apply to small-scale brewing in North America provides substantial data and some astounding findings but fails to provide data on specific brands of extract.[4] This study, conducted at the University of Saskatchewan, evaluated forty-four light lager malt extracts purchased at homebrewing stores, and compared them to the wort produced by one of Molson's breweries.

Several studies were performed using these extracts. First, a 1.048 wort was made with each extract, and all were fermented with the same yeast. In addition, several common physical and chemical analyses were performed and a detailed evaluation of the carbohydrate content of each extract was completed using high-performance liquid chromatography (HPLC).

The type and distribution of sugars, or carbohydrates, contained in malt extract distinguish it from other fermentables (such as corn sugar). Extracts with a sugar profile substantially different from those acquired from freshly mashed grain are likely to have different fermentation and taste characteristics. (See the discussion of sugar chemistry in chapter 5.)

The findings of the study include the following:

- The color of wort made from extract was substantially darker than the color of wort from the commercial brewery. Although the extracts were called light lager, the authors considered the color too dark for the lager style.
- "Ninety-three percent of the malt extracts had demonstrably slower fermentation rates than the standard (com-

mercial) wort." The range of fermentation time for the extracts was 45 hours (1.9 days) to 173 hours (7.2 days). The authors report that this most likely was due to low levels and low utilization of free amino nitrogen, a critical component for yeast metabolism.

- Several worts would not ferment lower than 1.020 (5.1 °P), while others fermented to less than 1.006 (1.3 °P). This could have resulted from the wide variation in the nonfermentable class of carbohydrates called dextrins, which ranged from 11 percent to 42 percent among the extracts.
- From the carbohydrate analysis, the authors state that less expensive non-malt syrups (corn syrup, glucose syrup, etc.) had been added to many of the extracts. In some cases, products contained only a fraction of the desirable maltose, maltotriose, and dextrin carbohydrates found in normal worts. Less desirable glucose and sucrose fractions constituted two to eight times the expected portion of some extracts. Since many of the products were labeled as all malt, this finding indicates some disturbing possibilities about the extracts sold to both home and commercial brewers.

As mentioned earlier, this study did not identify the manufacturers or packagers of these products, which creates a further problem. While some of the extracts were close to fresh wort in their composition, they cannot be identified; therefore, *all* malt extracts become somewhat suspect.

Another problem with the study is that it lacked a longitudinal component, where products from one manufacturer were evaluated from batch to batch over time. This would indicate if variations seen in the study reflect practices of specific manufacturers or simply the reality of malt extract production.

Without additional information, the only reasonable course of action is to select and use a limited number of extract products that have provided good results in the past. To help you do that, let's discuss the three key issues to consider when selecting an extract: color, and fermentability and flavor.

Color

Malt extracts are prone to darkening during production and storage.[5] The production of extract requires wort be concentrated to an original gravity of 1.400 to 1.450.[6] This means that a great deal of water must be removed by evaporation. Even though this usually is done under vacuum to reduce the required temperature, the wort is heated for a long period of time, which drives the formation of melanoidins.[7] Also, extracts that contain higher than normal concentrations of simple sugars may be more prone to darkening during storage, as simple sugars are more readily converted to color pigments via the browning reactions.[8]

In addition, color reactions continue, albeit at a much slower rate, once the syrup is packaged.[9] Water is required for the browning reactions, and recent literature indicates that liquid malt extract contains the optimal amount of water for these reactions to occur.[10]

As a result, liquid extract that spends a long time in storage — whether it be at the distributor's warehouse, on the retailer's shelf, or in the brewer's cabinet — will have darkened considerably. To keep this to a minimum, buy popular products from successful retailers. Products that look like they have been around for a while should probably be avoided; if possible, inquire about product freshness.

Because they lack the moisture needed to promote browning reactions, dry extracts, when kept dry and cool, are not prone to darkening during storage.[11] For this and other reasons, they may be preferred for many homebrewing applications.

Finally, though all worts darken during boiling, personal experience indicates that those made from extract seem to darken more quickly. Thus, it may be worthwhile to limit the boil time (some sources support this suggestion).[12]

Fermentability and Flavor

The fermentability and flavor produced by extract are influenced by its chemical composition. Many color substances and associated products produced during storage can impact flavor.[13] Some authors have referred to the off-flavor produced by old extract as having a "sherry-like oxidized quality."[14] This is another reason to avoid old and light extracts that produce a dark wort.

Since homebrewers have no way to evaluate the chemical composition of their extracts, they can rely only on their own experience and tests or those of others. Homebrewers also can examine extract recipes that win awards in homebrew competitions — those most popular with good brewers and homebrew judges. Discussions with homebrewers experienced with malt extract also can be helpful.

Of course, the flavor of your extract can best be assessed by taste tests. Using the extract test described below, you can assess the flavors produced by several different extracts using the same yeast. At the same time, you will gather information about the fermentability these products yield.

Before I discuss the test method, let's review a technique called apparent attenuation, which measures the fermentability of a wort. Simply stated, apparent attenuation is the difference between the original gravity (OG) and the final gravity (FG) divided by the original gravity. This gives a decimal result that, when converted to a percentage, gives the apparent attenuation value. This can be calculated by the following equation:

$$A = (OG - FG) / (OG - 1) \times 100$$

OG and FG are specific gravities at the beginning and end of fermentation. With extracts, apparent attenuation values may range between 50 and 80 percent, but most fall in the range of 55 to 65 percent.

The extent of fermentation is an important factor in defining many beer styles, as it affects the alcohol level and body, or mouthfeel. The percent of apparent attenuation indicates how much of the original gravity of the wort has been fermented. That which is fermented will yield alcohol; thus, the higher the attenuation, the higher the alcohol content for a given original gravity. The gravity that is not fermented remains in the finished beer, providing body and mouthfeel. Thus, the lower the attenuation level, the greater the body and mouthfeel will be.

In grain brewing, you can manipulate a mash to produce a wort that will have a higher or lower rate of apparent attenuation, but you can't manipulate malt extract in a similar way. Instead, you have to control extract fermentability through selection of the specific product you buy.

The Saskatchewan study points out the wide range of fermentability found in extracts. Your challenge is to identify the level of fermentability provided by the extracts you work with so that you can select an extract according to the character you want in the finished beer. The easiest way to do this is by running an extact test.

The Extract Test

The basic idea of an extract test is to make a small batch of beer to evaluate its flavor and fermentability before you brew a full batch. This procedure involves a bit of work; therefore, it's best applied when you work with a new type of extract.

Basic procedure: (1) make a 1-quart batch of beer using just 5 to 6 ounces of liquid extract or 4 to 5 ounces of dry extract (this doesn't need to be boiled for long — ten or fifteen minutes will do); (2)

when cool, take an OG reading and pitch with an ample quantity of yeast — preferably the yeast you use most often; (3) when fermentation is complete, chill the beer in your refrigerator to help drop the yeast out of suspension; (4) measure the final gravity and calculate the apparent attenuation (see page 13); and (5) taste the "beer" to assess the flavor of the extract.

For best results, take very careful specific gravity (SG) measurements. This means take the reading with the sample cooled to as close to 60 °F (15.5 °C) as possible, both before and after fermentation. Also, read the hydrometer correctly. (The hydrometer reading should be observed at the *top* of the small meniscus that forms around the hydrometer shaft.) While this might seem simple, I did it incorrectly for nearly six years!

To ensure full fermentation of the sample wort and to speed the process, pitch an excess of yeast. In my experiments, I use one 7-gram packet of dry ale yeast in 1 gallon of wort. The resulting fermentation starts within two hours or less and is usually done within twenty-four hours. If you want to use liquid yeast for this test, simply consider this a yeast starter and pitch one or two swollen pouches of liquid yeast into your quart of wort. When the experiment is finished, you can save the yeast in the refrigerator (for up to three weeks) to use in your next full-scale batch.

Using this technique, you can begin to better understand the differences between available extracts. After a few tests, you should be able to identify one or two extracts that give good flavor and predictable results. I tested several brands of extract using this method; the results are shown in table 3.1.

Substitution of Extract for Grain

The remainder of this book primarily focuses on all-grain approaches to recipe development. But take heart! If you are mainly an extract brewer, you still can make virtually every beer that is discussed. The key is intelligent substitution of malt extract for some of the grains in the recipes.

Generally, extract substitution focuses on what is referred to as the base malt in the recipe. This is the malt that constitutes the majority of the grist — usually under a name such as lager, Pilsener, pale ale, two-row, or six-row malt.

Substitutions can be made in proportion to the base malt removed, or they can be determined a bit more precisely through extract calculations, such as those shown in chapter 5.

For a straight substitution, put in a fixed amount of extract for every pound of base malt taken out of the recipe. The amount of extract you add, like most things in brewing, depends on a couple of considerations: (1) dry extract is more concentrated than syrup, so you would add less; and (2) depending on the source of the recipe, you might need to vary the substitution rate based upon the extract efficiency assumed by the recipe to begin with.

As shown in table 3.2, if an extract efficiency of 65 percent is assumed, substitute about ½ pound of dry or ⅔ pound of syrup extract for 1 pound of grain. If an 80 percent rate is assumed, add more extract: about ¾ pound of syrup or ⅔ pound of dry extract. Most recipes formulated for home or small breweries assume extraction rates of 65 to 75 percent, so use of the 70 percent values would be a good starting point. If this initial assumption is way off, you can adjust the overall gravity during the boil as described in chapter 6.

Table 3.1
Light, Unhopped Malt Extract Test Worts

Sample°	Fermentability (%)	Color	Flavor
Laaglander Dried (Light)	44.4	Amber	C2, O1
Northwestern (Dry, Gold)	57.1	Amber	M1, C1, S1
Munton & Fisons Light Syrup	57.5	Lt. Amber	C1, O1
158 °F (70 °C) Mash of Two-Row Malt	57.8	Pale-Gold	O3*
Munton & Fisons Spray-Dried (Light)	59.5	Pale-Gold	S1, M1, O1
John Bull Unhopped Light Syrup	60.4	Amber	M1, S2, O2
Alexander's Pale Syrup	61.9	Golden	C1, O1
Northwestern Syrup (Gold)	61.8	Amber	M2, C1, S1
Coopers Unhopped Light Syrup	64.1	Amber	S2, C2, O1
Corn Sugar	88.6	N/A	N/A

Note: The above results show the range of results you might encounter in evaluating malt extract. These determinations are based upon a single sample of each product and do not necessarily demonstrate the characteristics normally observed with these products. Flavor was assessed by two experienced Beer Judge Certification Program (BJCP) national judges. Common descriptors are given, followed by an intensity ratings. The 158 °F (70 °C) mash and pure corn sugar provide references for the low and high levels of fermentability.

Flavor Key	Flavor Intensity
C = Caramel	1 = Faint or slight, not always detectable
S = Sweet	2 = Clearly present, but not strong or overwhelming
M = Malt	3 = Strong to overwhelming
O = Off-flavor	

* This fermentation had a distinct off-flavor indicating contamination, but the attenuation level turned out as expected.

If you don't know what efficiency to assume for the grains, *don't worry!* You can add the lower amounts to begin with. Once this is done, you can live with the results and things will be fine, or you can adjust the overall gravity during the boil as described in chapter 6.

The total portion of the base malt you can replace with extract depends upon the beer style. A light-colored beer, such as a Munich helles, which relies on malt for the primary flavor component, will not tolerate much extract. To get both the color and the flavor required for good results, the majority of the total extract must come from a grain mash.

As the target color of the beer gets darker, it generally can sustain larger proportions of extract without detrimental effects. The same is true of beers where hops or spices are the primary flavor components. Good hoppy American pale ales, for instance, can be quite good when made from a recipe that contains a large amount of extract. Also, beer with strong yeast-derived flavors, such as weizen, can be made with a larger portion of extract than grain.

My general guideline is that every 5-gallon batch should include 3 to 5 pounds of grain. Ideally, this should include the specialty grain as well as some base malt, all processed in a minimash.

A perfect place to use extract is in high gravity beers. Almost any beer with an intended OG above 1.060 (15 °P) can incorporate extract without any detrimental effects. When you review winning recipes for styles such as doppelbock and barley wine, it is unusual to find one that does not include extract. These recipes usually start with a regular mash of about 10 pounds of grain to get the gravity up to 1.050 or so, then rely on the extract to provide the rest. Using this technique, even brewers with relatively modest mashing capability can produce good high gravity beers.

Extract Types

When you start looking at the names on extract labels, it can be a bit dizzying. You have to decide between dry and syrup; you have to pick a color (ultralight, light, amber, dark, etc.). Along the way, you run into hopped and unhopped varieties and something called diastatic malt extract (DME). Then there are kits, labeled only by beer style, such as stout or Scotch ale. This multitude of choices is enough to drive anyone to embrace all-grain brewing!

When selecting extract: I prefer a simple and practical approach. For almost all applications, I use light malt extracts. These usually are labeled as light, gold, pale, or some similar term. This comparative label distinguishes these products from darker-colored varieties sold under the same brand name and bearing labels such as amber and dark.

If you want color (and the resulting flavor) in your beer, you will be much happier with the results you get using specialty grains to augment light extract as the base

Table 3.2
Malt Extraction Substitution Rates

Type	Assumed Mash Efficiency:	65%	70%	75%	80%
Syrup		0.63	0.68	0.73	0.78
Dry		0.52	0.56	0.60	0.64

Note: Quantities are in pounds of malt extract per pound of grain replaced.

ingredient. The darker extracts are intended only for the simplest types of brews and, I believe, are best left to true beginners who are brewing their first three or four batches.

As a rule, I use dry or powdered extract, for two reasons. First, my use for extract rarely calls for a complete package; instead, a specific amount needs to be measured out — ¾ pound here, 4½ pounds there. In these cases, dry extract products are easier to handle. You can measure them accurately with little fuss and reseal them to use again later. Because of their high viscosity and intense stickiness, syrups tend to be more difficult to handle and store. Second, dry extracts do not darken during storage the way syrups do, which makes their color and flavor more predictable. Also, dry extracts tend to be packaged in clear plastic pouches, so you can see the condition of the product before you buy or use it. I often find that opening a can of syrup is a bit like opening a present wrapped in a shirt box. Even though you have a basic idea of what is inside, what you actually get can still be a surprise — and not always a pleasant one. Even when packaged in opaque foil bags, dry malts are more predictable.

Having expressed a strong preference for dry malts, I will note that in the extract tests summarized in table 3.1, I found that the syrup products generally had a slightly better flavor. Thus, when using large amounts of extract, you might choose a better-tasting syrup for the majority and employ dry extract for fine tuning. For instance, for 5 gallons of beer at a gravity of 1.053, you might use two 3-pound cans of syrup plus 1 pound of dry extract. If you choose this route, go with fresh, reliable products.

A handy specialty extract (usually in dry form) is the combined wheat-malt type. These usually contain 45 to 65 percent wheat and the rest regular malted barley. When added to the results of a small mash of wheat and malt and fermented with a proper weizen yeast, such extracts are capable of producing a very drinkable and reasonably authentic weizen.

DME also can be useful in certain settings. DME contains diastase, the malt enzymes that convert starch into fermentable sugar. It can be used when specialty grains or adjuncts, such as corn or rice, are extracted, without any base malts to provide enzymes. At present, however, these products do not appear to be widely used by homebrewers.

No matter which extract you use, there are several brands to choose from. There are real differences between brands that can have a considerable affect on the finished beer. Ideally, you should run an extract test on a new brand before using it, as described previously.

Summary of Extract Brewing Guidelines

- Use light extracts only. Add color and flavor through the use of specialty malts.

- Use dry extracts. They allow accurate measurement, ease of handling, and convenient storage of partially used containers.

- Use liquid extracts for high-volume brewing and when the flavor quality of syrup is clearly better than that of dry malt alternatives.

- Run extract tests on products that are new to you in order to assess their fermentability and flavor.

Summary of Extract Brewing Guidelines (continued)

- Select and use a limited number of extracts so that you can rely on the results achieved from your brews.

- Avoid all-extract brews; include at least some specialty grains in every batch.

- For best results, extract should supplement the proceeds of a mash that contributes 25 to 67 percent of the gravity of the beer. For 5 gallons, this equates to 3 to 5 pounds of grain per batch.

- As the color and flavor of the beer get lighter, the amount of extract must be reduced and grain increased in order to achieve good results.

- Beers dominated by hops, spices, dark grains, and even strong yeast-derived flavors (e.g., weizen) can employ a greater amount of extract.

- Supplement a full mash with extract to reach the higher gravities required by styles such as bock, strong ale, barley wine, and imperial stout.

4 FLAVOR AND AROMA FROM FERMENTABLES

Project	Designing Great Beers
	Brewers Publications
Project No.	61766

Malt flavors in beer are influenced by more than just the amount of malt you add to the recipe — a fact that is obvious to anyone who has ever used crystal, chocolate, black, or other specialty malts. So, before I discuss calculating the malt bill, let's examine malted barley and other ingredients that can provide fermentable sugars in beer.

You could get years of brewing pleasure simply exploring the flavors of malt. First, there are base malts (pale ale and Pilsener malts) that generally make up 80 to 100 percent of the mash. The combination of varieties and products available to brewers from maltsters across Europe and North America provide at least two dozen alternatives to explore.

When it comes to specialty malts, the variety is even greater. A single maltster can produce as many as ten different crystal or caramel malt products. And, if you think that a 40 °L crystal from one maltster provides the same flavor as that from another, you'll be pleasantly surprised at how much difference there can be! Other specialties include Munich, Vienna, chocolate, and black malts. Then you have the unusual products like brown malt, mild malt, Special "B," Victory, Special Roast, rauch malt, peat-smoked malt, and many others (see figure 4.1).

If those aren't enough, you can tackle grains other than barley. Wheat is so common that many classic styles can't be made without it. Then there are oats, rye, sorghum, rice, corn, and, yes, quinoa. (Quinoa is a small, round, ivory-colored food grain grown in Chile and Peru.) You can put all of these in beer, so, sooner or later, you'll probably try each of them.

What you get from all these choices is a cornucopia of malt (and other grain) flavors. Whether you brew with extract or not, you'll have fun exploring and enjoying the flavors these products contribute to your beer.

Understanding malt flavors also will help you create beers intended to meet certain style characteristics. You'll find that most styles (and all great commercial beers) have a characteristic grain bill that you must understand in order to approximate the flavor of the beer.

This chapter discusses the types of malts available and their typical uses. The descriptions will help you understand malt more fully so that you can explore and create knowledgeably. As you review these different types of malt, remember that you don't have to brew with them to get a sense for their flavors. Just grab a pinch, throw it in your mouth, and chew! This is especially useful when comparing similar products from different vendors, such as pale malts, crystal malts, and so on.

Base Malts

- Pale ale, lager, Pilsener, two-row, and six-row.
- Constitute 80 to 100 percent of the mash for most styles.
- For some styles, includes wheat, Munich, or Vienna malt.
- For authentic results, use malts from the country where the style originates.

Specialty Malts

- All products not included in the base malt category.
- Provide character through flavor, body, and color.
- Examine part two to determine which grains to include and what proportions or amounts to use.

Barley-based Brewing Ingredients

Aromatic malt: A color malt that undergoes special steeping and germination procedures and is kilned up to 240 °F (115 °C). Much like a darker Munich malt, it provides a high degree of malt aromatics with a color of about 20 °L. It contains low levels of enzymes but can self-convert if given enough time (twenty-five minutes in laboratory settings).

Amber malt: This type of malt was commonly used by brewers from the late 1700s to mid-1800s, especially in making porters. It can be reproduced today by toasting pale malt in an oven, as described in chapter 22.

Biscuit malt: A roasted malt, colored to about 25 °L, much lower than chocolate or brown malt. It provides a slightly burned, biscuitlike flavor and light brown color. It contains no enzymes.

Black barley: Darker than roast barley, it has a sharp, acrid flavor that may be used in stouts. It contains no enzymes.

Black malt (also called black patent malt, sometimes roasted malt): Malted barley that has been kilned at a high temperature. It may be found in small quantities in styles such as Scotch ales and in larger quantities in porters. In quantity, it contributes a dry, burned bitterness with an ashlike character. Many brewers use it for coloring the beer, as it imparts little color to the head. It contains no enzymes.

Brown malt: A roasted product that is lighter than chocolate malt, rarely produced by maltsters today. Used in bitter and mild ales, sweet stouts, and London porters, it contributes a light, biscuitlike dry flavor. It contains no enzymes. It can be reproduced by toasting pale malt in an oven, as described in chapter 23.

Brumalt: See Honey malt.

Chocolate malt: Malted barley that has been kilned at a high temperature to a rich brown color. Flavors are sometimes described as sharp and acrid, while others find it imparts a nutty, toasted quality in both aroma and flavor. It is often found in porters and some stouts, brown ales, and dunkels. It contains no enzymes.

Crystal/Caramel/Carastan: These names are used interchangeably for products made in the same general way, although some maltsters use different terms for color values. The terms CaraVienna and CaraMunich can be used to describe different colors of crystal malts. The lightest malt made by the crystal process is CaraPils, which may also be called dextrin malt or light carastan. (See also Dextrin malt.)

Typically, crystal malts have color ratings between 20 and 120 °L, in 10° units. The flavor imparted depends upon the maltster and, to some degree, the color level. The flavors imparted to the beer may include caramel, toffee, nutty, and/or biscuitlike. These malts also contribute body and mouthfeel. Because of the broad range of colors and flavors offered, these malts appear in many styles of ales and lagers. They contain no enzymes.

Dextrin malt (also called CaraPils, sometimes light carastan): This light-colored (about 10 °L) crystal malt product contributes mostly body, with little flavor or color impact, and may be used in light beers, such as Pilseners. Generally, the kernel is very hard and glassy. It contains no enzymes.

Flaked barley: This is an adjunct that can be added directly to the mash tun. Flaked barley imparts a grainy flavor and assists in head formation and retention. It is used in

bitters and, in higher proportions, in milds and stouts.[1]

Honey malt: A light-colored (18 to 20 °L) European malt with an intense maltiness.

Mild malt: A lightly toasted malt with enough diastatic power to serve as the base malt. It is used predominantly in mild ales and has a slight nutty flavor.

Munich malt: This is a pale malt that is kilned at temperatures just above those used for pale malt to provide body and rich maltiness. Often described as sweet and mellow, this malt lacks the flavors associated with crystal malts. The color may be gold to reddish amber. It lacks the enzymes of pale

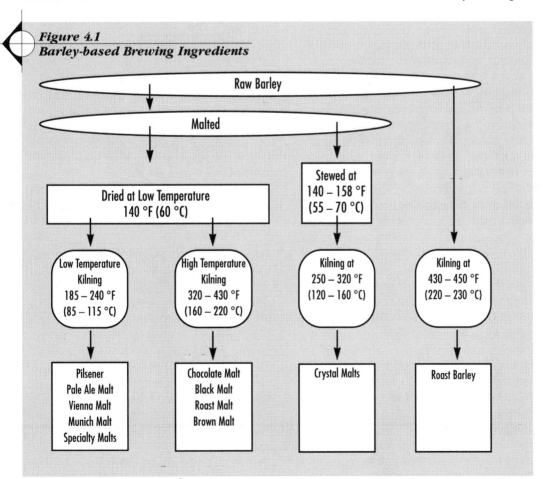

Figure 4.1
Barley-based Brewing Ingredients

Raw Barley

Malted

Dried at Low Temperature 140 °F (60 °C)

Stewed at 140 – 158 °F (55 – 70 °C)

Low Temperature Kilning 185 – 240 °F (85 – 115 °C)

High Temperature Kilning 320 – 430 °F (160 – 220 °C)

Kilning at 250 – 320 °F (120 – 160 °C)

Kilning at 430 – 450 °F (220 – 230 °C)

Pilsener
Pale Ale Malt
Vienna Malt
Munich Malt
Specialty Malts

Chocolate Malt
Black Malt
Roast Malt
Brown Malt

Crystal Malts

Roast Barley

or Pilsener malt but has adequate diastatic activity to convert its own starch during mashing. In Vienna, Märzen, Oktoberfest, and some bock formulations, it may account for most of the grist. Small amounts may be used to add malt character to other styles as well.

Peat malt: Like rauch malt, this is a smoked malt, but the smoke comes from a peat fire. It may be used in interpretations of Scottish-style ales. It should contain adequate enzymes for self-conversion, although it is usually used in combination with base malt.

Rauch malt: A relatively pale malt that has been smoked over a wood fire. It provides the characteristic smoked flavor of Bamburg-style rauchbier and other specialty smoked products. Smokiness may vary from batch to batch, depending on the amount of time that has passed since manufacture.

Roast barley: This is unmalted barley that has been roasted to near-black at a high temperature. It gives a definite coffeelike roast flavor when used in quantity, primarily in stouts. It can also impart a dry bitterness. As a coloring agent, it will produce a brown head as well as a very dark beer when used in quantity. It is sometimes used in very small quantities in Pilseners and some red beers to provide color adjustment. It contains no enzymes.

Special Roast: Described by the maltster as "double malted," this product gives a dark orange color and a biscuitlike flavor. It may be used as a flavor malt in a variety of styles.

Torrified barley: Unmalted barley that has been heated until it pops. Similar in flavor to flaked barley, but drier. Favored by commercial brewers as an aid to lautering, it also adds body.[2]

Victory malt: Described by the maltster as "double processed" providing increased

color and a toasted flavor sometimes described as "warm." It may be used in pale ales at 5 to 15 percent of the mash.

Vienna malt: Produced in the same way as Munich malt with similar applications. It is lighter in color than Munich malt, which gives it a gold to orange effect. It contains adequate enzymes for conversion of its own starch.

Additional Brewing Grains

Wheat malt: Although the color rating of wheat, at 2.5 to 3.5 °L, equals that of base malts, it contributes less color to the finished beer, perhaps because is has no husk. This lack of husk contributes some challenges in mashing and lautering, where runoffs may become slow or stuck.

Wheat malt accounts for the majority of the grist in German wheat beers, including Berliner weisse, Bavarian weizen, dunkel weizen, and weizenbock. Because it improves head formation and retention, it is often added in small quantities (1 to 5 percent) to a wide variety of styles. Unmalted wheat is a major component in Belgian-style white (wit) beers and is traditionally used in lambics. Its flavor is a sort of malty spiciness, especially under the influence of weizen yeasts.

Oats: Contribute creaminess and oiliness. High oil and fat content cause a problem whenever oats are processed in any quantity, and they make malting nearly impossible. Often used in Belgian-style white (wit) beer, where it makes up 10 to 11 percent of the grist. In oatmeal stout, it accounts for about 22 percent of grist.[3] Some brewers use malted (and unmalted) oats to help counteract the harshness brought on by hard water.[4] Unmalted oats tend to produce a haze.

Rye: Malted, flaked, and torrified rye products are available. Light in color (2 to 4 °L) rye helps to create a creamy head and an oiliness that can become extreme when used in high quantities. It lends a dryness to any recipe and, when used in quantity, has an aroma and flavor reminiscent of ripe apples or calvados, an apple brandy. Some describe it as spicy. High in beta glucans and pectins, as are wheat and oats, it can cause problems in mashing and lautering when used in quantities greater than 20 or 30 percent of the total grist.

Sorghum: Has a high tannin (polyphenol) content. It tends to create cloudy beers, so much so, in fact, that sorghum beer (indigenous to southern Africa) is known as "opaque beer." The beers made with this grain are most often described as "sour," but that may be due more to the action of lactic acid bacteria than to the flavors contributed by the grain.[5] In recent years, large commercial producers in Africa have managed to make crystal-clear light lagers from this grain.[6]

Rice: Doesn't contribute much flavor, if any, although it can contribute to dryness and thereby accentuate the flavor of the hops. It mostly contributes additional sugars for conversion into alcohol and is more neutral than corn. It is used in American- and Japanese-style lagers, with the most often-cited example being Budweiser. The use of both rice and corn in these beers was adopted, in part, to help dilute the high protein levels of six-row American lager malt.

Wild rice: Contributes a sweet, nutty flavor.[7] Expense prohibits its use in significant quantities.

Corn: Reported to give a mellow, corny flavor to beers,[8] especially those with delicate flavor profiles, but, like rice, it contributes mostly to increased alcohol production. This grain is degerminated before processing to remove the oily embryo. Flakes do not require boiling before addition to the mash. It is used in some English bitters and pale ales and some American-style lagers.

Special Fermentables

If you are adding fermentables other than malt, you must consider how you will use them and how they will be expressed in the finished beer. Many special items, such as fruit, honey, and molasses, can be added to beer. You can get a lot of good

Table 4.1
Chemical Composition of Brewing Grains

Grain	Cellulose (fiber)	Starch & Carbohydrates	Lipids & Fats	Protein	Other
Barley	5.7	71.0	2.5	11.8	7.1
Wheat	2.9	76.0	2.0	14.5	5.0
Rye	2.4	74.0	2.0	13.5	8.2
Oats	12.4	61.0	6.1	13.4	5.9
Maize (corn)	2.0	69.2	3.9	8.7	1.2
Rice	2.3	81.0	0.5	9.0	0.4
Sorghum	2.3	70.7	3.0	10.9	2.1

Source: J. S. Hough, D. E. Briggs, R. Stevens, T. W. Young, Malting and Brewing Science, vol. 1, 2d ed., (London: Chapman and Hall, 1982), 225.

information on how these ingredients behave in beer by talking to other home-brewers. Another good source is **Zymurgy,** which has had a couple of special issues dealing with nonstandard ingredients (Summer 1992 has information on adding fruit; Special Issue 1994 has information on adding other ingredients). To get you started, the remainder of this chapter provides an overview of the issues that relate to brewing with special fermentables.

Sugars and Syrups

Yeast ferments sugar to produce alcohol and CO_2. Therefore, it would seem that any sugar would make a perfectly fine addition to beer. But sugar is not one chemical compound, but many different compounds. In addition, many common sources of sugar include not only the sugar, but some portion of nonfermentable compounds as well. Let's look at the things you should consider when using these sources of fermentable material.

Sugar Chemistry

In its simplest form, a sugar is a ringed structure made up of carbon, oxygen, and hydrogen molecules. Common brewing sugars are hexoses, so named because their rings have six members — five carbons and one oxygen. A sixth carbon is attached to the side of the ring at one corner. The simplest sugars consist of a single hexose ring and are called monosaccharides. These include glucose, fructose, galactose, and mannose. The configuration of the oxygen and hydrogen atoms attached to each carbon, as well as other slight structural variations, determine the identity of each of these simple sugar molecules.

When two monosaccharides join together, they form a two-ringed sugar known as a disaccharide. The monosaccharides involved and their configuration determine the character of these sugars. The three disaccha-

rides commonly found in food are sucrose, maltose, and lactose. Sucrose is a combination of glucose and fructose, maltose is a combination of two glucose molecules, and lactose is a combination of glucose and galactose. The first two, sucrose and maltose, are fermentable by yeast; lactose is not.

Finally, there are trisaccharides — strings of three monosaccharides joined together. The primary molecule of interest here is maltotriose, which consists of three joined glucose molecules. Maltotriose is fully fermentable by all beer yeast, whereas the trisaccharides melitose (also known as raffinose and melitriose) can only be fully fermented by lager yeast.

When monosaccharides are joined into rings of four or more sugars, the resulting molecules are called dextrins. These are not fermentable by beer yeast.

While yeast can ferment a wide variety of sugars, the production of beer with a typical "beer" flavor requires a certain balance of these various sugars. Typically, maltose is the most prevalent sugar in wort, accounting for about 40 percent of the total carbohydrates.

Only three other mono- or disaccharides are found in wort in significant quantities — glucose, fructose, and sucrose. Together they usually account for less than 15 percent of the total carbohydrates in wort. If their proportions increase dramatically, the yeast's ability to process maltose may be lost or diminished. When this happens, the wort will not be fully fermented, and a variety of problems will ensue.

Thus, when adding processed sugars of any kind, do so in moderation. Remember that the old Prohibition recipe that called for a lot of table sugar gave a very cidery product. If you add too much processed sugar to any beer, this same flavor will be a part of your finished product.

Flavor Components

When looking at alternative sources of fermentable material, remember that the fermentable sugars give you no direct flavor impact. After all, they are fermented into alcohol and CO_2. (The cidery flavor that comes from adding too much sugar is the result of yeast function and does not come from the sugar itself.)

The sources of flavor contributed by sugars and syrups come from the unfermented components. These may include unfermentable sugars, such as lactose, and substances other than sugars that come from the raw material.

Most of the available sugars have little in the way of flavor components. They have been processed and refined so that they contain little except for fermentable sugar. Examples include:

Table sugar   →   Sucrose
Corn sugar   →   Glucose
Candi sugar   →   Sucrose
Invert sugar   →   Glucose and fructose
Corn syrup   →   Glucose

In general, these sugars should be avoided or restricted as they add little, if anything, to the character of the beer. If used, they should be limited to no more than 10 percent of the total fermentable material in the recipe.

In order to get some real flavor from a sugar or syrup, it must contain some portion of impurities. The impurities from beet sugar are not desirable, so typically the attractive flavors in processed sugar come from sugar cane. Honey may be another source of flavorful impurities. Alternately, flavor may be created as the result of the heating used to concentrate a sugar solution, for instance when maple syrup is produced.

Brewing Sugars

Here is a list of potentially flavorful sugars that can be used in brewing. Most should be used sparingly until you become familiar with the character they impart in the beer. All contain fermentable mono- or disaccharides, which can disrupt fermentation if used in excess. In addition, some are strongly flavored and can easily overwhelm the character of the beer. Again, I suggest no more than 10 percent of the fermentables come from a sugar source.

Brown sugar: Consists of sucrose crystals covered with molasses.[9] The molasses itself provides the flavor, and the darker it gets, the more flavorful it will be.

Caramel: Caramel is formed when sugar is heated to very high temperatures (400/204 °F/ °C). It can provide both flavor and color. You might experiment with the candy type sold in stores, but who knows what they contain. Alternately, you can make up some of your own from corn syrup or table sugar.[10]

Honey: Honey is naturally a highly concentrated form of sugar, and it includes a number

Table 4.2
Honey Varieties

Mild and Aromatic	Stronger Flavored	To Be Avoided
Clover	Buckwheat	Eucalyptus
Alfalfa	Heather	
Orange blossom		
Sage		
Mixed wildflower		

of impurities that can contribute a distinct flavor and aroma to a beer. Because of its flavor components, it can be used for almost any portion of the fermentables in a beer (although at a certain point you are making mead rather than beer). It requires special handling for best results. (See sidebar, Brewing with Honey.)

Lactose: Known as milk sugar, this substance is not fermentable by brewing yeasts and therefore will remain in the finished beer to provide some residual sweetness. Traditionally, lactose is used in the production of sweet stouts, and thereby dubbed milk stout.

Maple syrup: The sap that runs from maple trees contains only about 2 percent solids (mostly sugar), and therefore must be concentrated before use. This is done by boiling off water to bring the concentration of solids up to about 66 percent. As you can imagine, this requires quite a bit of boiling, and in the process, a portion of the sugars are caramelized. Caramelization provides much of the characteristic flavor of maple syrup.

The sugar in maple syrup is mostly sucrose. In addition, most commercial products are a blend of one part maple syrup plus four to six parts corn syrup.[11] Since corn syrup is mostly glucose, it offers little in the way of flavor components. Instead, try getting some raw or unblended maple syrup that has not been diluted in this manner.

Molasses: When raw sugar cane is processed into sugar, molasses is the residue. This contains the impurities from the sugar cane that are not wanted in refined sugar. As a result, it also contains the most flavor of all the available sugars and syrups. Three grades can be found — light, medium, and blackstrap. The lighter grades are more highly fermentable (90 percent) with fewer flavor components, while the blackstrap grades will be less fermentable (50 to 60 percent) with a much higher flavor impact.[12] One cup in 5 gallons gives a discernible flavor.

Palm sugar: A dark, highly flavored product derived from the sap of palm trees.[13] Its flavors and impact on beer are unknown, but if you check out some Asian specialty stores, you might be able to find some to experiment with.

Raw sugar: Raw sugar is reported to be 97 percent sucrose,[14] so it should be highly fermentable and contain little in the way of flavor-producing impurities. If you want to experiment, look for the darkest stuff you can find.

Treacle (also known as British molasses): There are various colors and grades, as with molasses.

Turbinado sugar: A form of raw cane sugar sometimes found in the United States. See comments on raw sugar for additional information.

Fruit: In addition to the many fermentable ingredients discussed in this chapter, fruit is sometimes used in making beer (quantities and methods are discussed in chapter 19).

Sidebar: Brewing with Honey

Honey has become a popular brewing adjunct in recent years, with even the bigger breweries getting into the act. Still, there is a lot of room for experimentation by home and craft brewers.

Honey consists of about 95 percent fermentable sugars, including glucose, fructose, sucrose, and maltose.[15] When compared to an equal amount of malt, a honey addition will reduce the body of the beer you are making and increase the alcohol content. Also, honey does not contain the essential nitrogen nutrients needed by yeast. Thus, if you experience sluggish fermentation, you should think about adding yeast nutrients.

The National Honey Board says that adding between 3 and 11 percent will provide a "very subtle honey character to a standard pale ale or lager." Levels up to 30 percent "should be distinctly noticeable, and stronger hop flavors, caramelized or roasted malts, spices, or other adjuncts should be carefully considered when formulating recipes." The board considers any beverage that derives more than 30 percent of its fermentable materials from honey to be a beverage other than beer.

As for honey varieties, most are fairly mild and can be used in the proportions described in the previous paragraph without further caution. Stronger honeys, such as buckwheat and heather, may require some adjustments for an equivalent flavor impact. Finally, eucalyptus honey should be avoided, as even in small proportions it is said to impart a distinct medicinal bitterness.

Unlike most other sugar sources, honey contains many living organisms. It contains yeast and bacteria and also diastatic enzymes. At the same time, the flavors and aromas of honey are delicate and easily driven off by boiling. These two facts create a dilemma in the use of honey. On the one hand, you don't want to add honey to your beer without sanitizing it and deactivating the enzymes; on the other hand, why add it at all if you are going to drive off the flavors by boiling?

The National Honey Board recommends the following process:

1. Dilute your honey to the gravity of your wort with water.
2. Conduct a hold for two and one-half hours at 176 °F (80 °C) under a CO_2 blanket.
3. Add this preparation directly to the fermenting beer at high kraeusen.

While this exact procedure may be a bit impractical in some settings, you can see the type of compromise you are faced with when handling honey. You may decide just to boil it in your wort for a few minutes as that will probably do the trick, even though you will lose some flavor components. Whatever you do, *don't* add unpasteurized honey directly to your cool wort — you will have problems if you do.

For further information, call the National Honey Board in San Francisco (800-356-5941) and ask for their publication about using honey in beer. It includes additional information and several recipes.

5 CALCULATING THE MALT BILL

Project	Designing Great Beers
	Brewers Publications
Project No.	61766

The malt bill is the heart of any beer. It plays a key role in a number of characteristics of the finished beer, including flavor, color, body, and alcohol content. When finished, the malt bill should list the identity and weight of all fermentable materials used in the beer.

When preparing the malt bill, keep in mind the flavor attributes desired in the beer. Decide in advance the approximate portion of the total grist to be provided by each ingredient. For instance, in an authentic Bavarian weizen, wheat makes up about two-thirds, or 67 percent, of the total malt bill; a pale or Pilsener malt makes up the remaining one-third.

Once you have decided on the proportions, you'll need to know the total amount of malt needed to make the quantity of beer you desire. This is where some basic calculations are useful.

First Things First

To determine the total amount of malt (or other fermentable materials) needed for a recipe, you need to know four things.

1. *Target gravity:* A given value for the particular style or beer that you are trying to achieve. For a weizen, for instance, the target range is 1.048 to 1.056. (12 to 14 °P).

2. *Finished volume of beer to be produced:* Determined by your brewing system, as represented by the finished volume of beer you intend to produce; for example, if you are making 5 gallons, you may have 5.5 gallons in the kettle at the end of the boil.

3. *Fermentable ingredients and their approximate proportions:* Create a list of malts and other fermentable materials you will use in the recipe. Then, decide approximately what portion of the total extract or gravity should come from each ingredient. Both the selection of ingredients and their proportions depend upon the style being brewed or the specific ingredients you have decided to work with. (Part two examines these issues for a number of beer styles.) For the weizen example, the two ingredients will be wheat malt and pale malt; the proportions will be 67 and 33 percent.

4. *Efficiency of extraction for the ingredients that you use:* This figure may be 100 percent in special cases, but it usually runs in the 60 to 80 percent range. The special cases where efficiency equals 100 percent are those where nongrain fermentable materials are added directly to the boil kettle or fermenter and are not subjected to the mashing process. Malt extract is an example of this, honey is another. When making your

calculations, it's important to remember this difference in utilization. Otherwise, you will wind up with a much higher gravity than you expected.

Determining mash efficiency can be challenging. Ideally, it is based on past brewing experience with your system; but, for a number of reasons, you may not have established an extract efficiency value for your system. (See sidebar, on page 33.)

If you are just starting out or if you have never calculated this number, don't worry. Most home and craft brewers usually get between 65 and 80 percent efficiency from their mash and lauter procedures. For your initial calculations, it's best to start low, at 68 percent or even 65 percent. If you get better yield than this, you can adjust the gravity of your brew later in the brewing process. For our weizen example, we will assume an efficiency of 68 percent.

Also, extract efficiency will vary from batch to batch, even on the same system. Changes in recipe or in the basic raw materials themselves can cause these differences. (Chapter 6 discusses how to correct for variations in your extraction efficiency during the brewing process.)

Determining the Grain Bill

Once you have established your parameters, it's time to crunch some numbers. Using three easy steps, you can calculate the total amount of extract needed for the batch, the amount that should come from each source, and the actual amount of each type of grain needed in the recipe. But first, you need to understand the concept of gravity units, or GUs.

Most calculations in this book that involve beer gravity use GUs, which are simply the nonzero digits to the right of the decimal place in a specific gravity (SG) reading. Mathematically, you can convert an SG reading to GUs by subtracting 1 and multiplying by 1,000 as shown in the following equation:

$$GU = (SG - 1) \times 1,000$$

Thus, 1.050 equals 50 GUs; 1.038 equals 38, and 1.105 equals 105. Pretty simple stuff, I hope you'll agree. The equation simply shows you the math; I don't expect you'll need it, unless you are writing a computer program to do your calculations for you.

If you work in degrees Balling or Plato, you can substitute either reading at any time with the GU measure. Also, barrels can be substituted for gallons, as long as you do it consistently.

Now let's look at the three steps of calculating your bill of fermentable materials.

1. *Determine the total amount of extract needed for the batch.* This is equal to the final volume of beer multiplied by the gravity. For our weizen example, we'll shoot for a final gravity of 1.052, or 52 GUs. This is then multiplied by the 5.5-gallon volume. Thus

$$52 \times 5.5 = 286 \text{ GU of total gravity}$$

This total gravity tells you how much extract you need to get from all of the fermentable ingredients used in this brew. In addition, this number will serve as a means for monitoring and hitting the target gravity of the beer during the brewing process.

2. *Calculate the amount of extract that should come from each fermentable source.* Previously, you decided the proportions of each malt you will use in the recipe. Now that you know the total extract you need, it is a simple matter to multiply that total by the relative proportions of each ingredient. This will tell you the extract required from each ingredient. Thus

Ingredient gravity =
Ingredient (% of total grist) x Total gravity

For example wheat malt:

0.67 x 286 = 191 GU of ingredient gravity

And for pale malt:

0.33 X 286 = 95 GU of ingredient gravity

3. *Calculate the number of pounds of each ingredient needed.* To determine this, divide the ingredient gravity (GU) by the amount of extract that can be gotten from each pound of malt. Thus

$$\text{Lbs. needed} = \frac{\text{Ingredient gravity}}{\text{Gravity per lb. malt}}$$

Gravity per pound of malt is, in turn, the product of two factors: (1) mash efficiency, as discussed previously, and (2) a number that represents the ideal, or maximum extract, that might be derived from the particular grain in question. This maximum extract is driven by the accessible starch content of the grain as a percentage of total grain weight.[1]

Figures for the maximum extract available from specific malts can be read from a table of common extract values (table 5.1). This table gives the expected extract for each type of malt in specific gravity per pound, per gallon. If all of the extract derived from mashing 1 pound of grain were contained in 1 gallon of water, it would have an OG in the range given.

Since the values in table 5.1 represent the maximum extract potential of each grain, they must be adjusted to reflect the extract that you are likely to get during your brewing process. This is where the mash efficiency number comes in. Simply multiply the value from table 5.1 by the mash efficiency to get the effective gravity you can expect from each type of malt.

Let's go through this process for the weizen recipe. We know the ingredient gravity is 191, calculated with

Ingredient gravity =
Ingredient (% of total grist) x Total gravity

Next, determine gravity per pound of malt by multiplying the potential extract value (from table 5.1) by your expected mash efficiency (as a decimal)

Gravity per lb. of malt =
(Value from table 6) x Mash efficiency

For example, the table 5.1 value for malted wheat is 1.037 to 1.040; use 1.038, or 38 after converting it to GUs. Mash efficiency (calculated previously) was 68 percent. Putting it all together, divide the ingredient gravitiy (as calculated in step 2) by the product of potential extract (from table 5.1) and expected mash efficiency (expressed as a decimal). Thus

191 ÷ (38 x 0.68) = 7.39

or (more simply)

191 ÷ 38 ÷ 0.68 = 7.39

So, for this recipe, you need 7⅓ pounds of wheat malt!

To determine how much pale malt you will need, use the same equation. Thus

95 ÷ 36 ÷ 0.68 = 3.88

We have successfully calculated the complete malt bill for a weizen beer recipe.

Because I had to explain a lot of things along the way, it probably seemed complicated. In reality, it's quite simple and wonderfully quick. Once you go through it once or twice, you'll find you can do it without even looking at the book.

A Second Example

Let's run through one more example. This time, with a honey wheat recipe. The fermentables will include wheat (20 percent), two-row malt (60 percent), and honey (20 percent). Since volumes and efficiencies don't change much from batch to batch,

Table 5.1
Extract Potential of Fermentable Materials

Specifications for a series of common craft-brewing malts, extracts, and adjuncts. They are sorted into two types of materials: (1) those that must be mashed or extracted, and (2) those that can be directly added to the boiling kettle.

Mash Ingredients	Extract Potential
Standard Ingredients	**1 lb. in 1 gallon**
Chocolate/black/roast	1.025–1.030
Crystal and Cara malts	1.033–1.035 (darker = lower extract)
Munich/Vienna/mild/biscuit	1.035–1.036
Pale or Pilsener malt	1.035–1.037
Other Ingredients	
Corn	1.037–1.039
Oats	1.033
Rye malt	1.029
Wheat (malted)	1.037–1.040
Wheat/rye (unmalted raw or flakes)	1.036
Boil Kettle Fermentables*	
Cane sugar	1.046
Corn sugar	1.037
Dry extract	1.045
Honey	1.030–1.035
Liquid extract	1.037–1.039
Maple syrup	1.030
Molasses	1.036

* Add directly to kettle, efficiency factor = 1.00.

we'll use the same assumptions given before: 5.5 gallons and 68 percent efficiency. The target gravity will be a bit lower: 1.044, or 44 GU. Ready to calculate?

1. *Total gravity*
   5.5 gal. x 44 = 242 GU

2. *Proportion amounts*
   Wheat: 242 x 0.20 = 48.4 GU
   Honey: 242 x 0.20 = 48.4 GU
   Two-row: 242 x 0.60 = 145 GU

3. *Pounds needed*
   Wheat: 48.4 ÷ 38 ÷ 0.68 = 1.87
   Honey: 48.4 ÷ 33 ÷ 1.00 = 1.46
   Two-row: 145 ÷ 36 ÷ 0.68 = 5.92

Now wasn't that quick? I even added a third item to the bill of fermentables, and it still went fast.

Did you notice what happened with the honey? Even though both the wheat and the honey make up 20 percent of the extract, you wind up with different weights for the two ingredients. The difference is extraction. The wheat gets mashed and the honey doesn't. As a result, I use an extract efficiency of 100 percent, or 1.00, when doing the calculations for honey. This also would be true for malt extract and other items listed in the third section of table 5.2.

Accuracy in Potential Extract

You may notice that the numbers given in table 5.1 show a range for each type of malt. This is the result of natural variation in the available supplies of malted barley and other fermentable ingredients. In larger commercial settings, the number for potential extract would be determined by a laboratory mash on the actual lot of malt being used. Maltsters perform this analysis on every lot and supply the information to breweries and large distributors who buy their products. (If you have access to this information [usually reported as a percentage], appendix 2 shows how to precisely determine the specific gravity of your potential extract.)

The ranges given in table 5.1 provide the highest level of accuracy you will be able to achieve without the laboratory analysis figures. This is important to remember because you can find other published sources that give more precise extract figures associated with specific types of malt (e.g., Belgian Pilsener malt quoted at 1.037). Such figures are a bit misleading. They do not indicate the batch-to-batch or year-to-year variation found even in products that come from a single maltster. (See table 5.1 for some examples.)

The ranges given in table 5.1 should constantly remind you that the *actual* potential extract of the malt you are working with may fall anywhere within that range.

Continuing the Process

This chapter has presented the process for calculating the bill of fermentable materials before you brew. These calculations help you hit your brewing targets by providing a prebrew review of what you want to happen. However, as in life, the best-laid plans often go awry.

For a variety of reasons, you can expect the actual brew to turn out a bit differently than you had planned. I have already discussed the range of potential extract seen in malts between suppliers and between years, so you know that the calculations might be off by a percent or two. In addition, the value used for extract efficiency may turn out to be different from what actually is encountered.

For all these reasons, your efforts to manage the brewing process cannot end with the completion of the brewing calculations. In the next chapter, I discuss how some simple steps during the brewing process can help you follow through on your calculations and achieve your brewing goals.

Table 5.2
Variation in the Potential Extract of Brewing Malts

Grain	Coarse, as is, Extracts* 1990 (%)	1994 (%)	Wort Gravity (GU), 1 lb./gal. 1990 (%)	1994 (%)
European pale ale	76.2	78.6	35.2	36.3
European Pilsener	75.4	78.1	34.8	36.0
U.S. two-row	79.6	77.2	36.8	35.6

Note: GU = (specific gravity - 1) x 1000
* See appendix 2 for a detailed discussion of this measure.

Sidebar Calculating Mash Efficiency

The efficiency of your mash is equal to the total gravity you actually get in your wort, divided by the potential gravity available from your grains. This can be expressed as

$$\text{Efficiency} = \frac{\text{Total gravity of wort}}{\text{Total potential gravity of grains}}$$

From here, it is simply a matter of determining the two total gravity numbers so that you can complete the calculation. For simplicity, both measures can be expressed as gravity units (GU).

Total gravity of the wort is equal to GU multiplied by volume. This may be determined any time after mash runoff is completed and before any other fermentable materials, such as extract, honey, and so on, have been added to the wort. Obviously, the accuracy of this figure will depend on the accuracy of your specific gravity and volume readings, so you should determine these values at a time when you can read both items most accurately. (See table 6.1 in chapter 6 for temperature correction of SG.)

To determine the total gravity of the grain, you basically reverse the third calculation involved in determining the grain bill. The two important differences are: (1) completely exclude any non-mashed materials, and (2) eliminate the efficiency factor.

Let's look at how these calculations would work for a pale ale using 8 pounds of pale ale malt and ½ pound of crystal malt.

After the mash, the brewer collected 6 gallons of wort at 1.036 SG. This gives a total gravity of wort of 216: 1.036 = 36 GU; 36 GU x 6 gal. = 216.

The total potential gravity of the grains is equal to the sum of the total potential gravity for each grain, which is equal to the weight in pounds multiplied by potential extract. For the pale ale recipe:

Pale ale malt: 8 lbs. x 36 GU = 288 GU
Crystal malt: 0.5 lb. x 32 GU = 16 GU
Total: 304 GU

Now, using the original equation

$$\text{Efficiency} = \frac{\text{Total gravity of wort}}{\text{Total potential gravity of grains}}$$

Efficiency is then

216 ÷ 304 = 0.71 (71%) efficiency

6 Hitting Target Gravity

Project	Designing Great Beers
	Brewers Publications
Project No.	61766

Hitting the gravity you plan for your brew is important because it will affect your happiness with the beer you produce. The OG affects the amount of alcohol in the beer and also influences your perception of the balance between its maltiness and bitterness. If you decide to make a 1.045 beer with 35 IBUs of bitterness but the beer only winds up with an OG of 1.035, you will have made a very different beer from the one you set out to create.

I have found that target gravity can be hit to within 0.005 SG easily and to within 0.002 SG without much difficulty when the techniques outlined in this chapter are used. They rely on measurements and adjustments during the course of brewing — generally in the time after the mash and before the addition of the first hops. Let's look at how to measure gravity during the brewing process and also at how to take some corrective steps, if necessary.

Assessing Gravity During Brewing

The calculations in the last chapter show what the expected gravity of your recipe should be when the brewing is completed. But don't wait until the end of the brewing process to find out if you really hit it or not, for you may be considerably off the mark and suddenly facing several problems that might not be easily rectified.

To avoid this, evaluate the total gravity during the brewing process and use it as a guide in adjusting the wort to the exact gravity you want. Remember that total gravity is the product of wort volume multiplied by its measured gravity in gravity units. As an equation, it is stated thus:

Total gravity = GU x Volume$_{gallons}$

An important characteristic of total gravity is that it doesn't change as you boil or dilute your wort. The only way to change the total gravity is to add fermentable materials such as malt extract, honey, or sugar to the wort. Knowing this, you can begin to get a handle on what the finished gravity of the beer will be long before the boil is finished and usually before it begins.

To assess total gravity, measure both the gravity and volume of your beer or wort. Often you will need to do this with hot wort that is in a boiling pot or any container other than a fermenter.

For measuring gravity, a hydrometer will be perfectly suitable. If you don't have one, it's time to invest the ten bucks. And in order to pinpoint OG, a thermometer will help you correct the specific gravity of hot wort samples.

You can assess the specific gravity of hot wort at temperatures up to boiling, but it is usually preferable to draw a sample and measure it at a lower temperature. Glass hydrometers dropped into boiling wort can break, and plastic hydrometer tubes may soften or even melt in such heat.

Stir the wort well before sampling (the runoff tends to stratify, with the first, heaviest fluid at the bottom and later, lighter fluid at the top). Unless it is an unusual one, your hydrometer tube will hold about 6 ounces of fluid; so draw about a cup of wort from the sample vessel.

If the sample is boiling, let it cool in the measuring cup — you can even pop it in the freezer for a few minutes if you desire. Wort running out of a lauter tun will usually have cooled to no more than 150 °F (66 °C) by the time you sample it, so you needn't worry about cooling it first.

If your thermometer will fit down the side of the hydrometer tube while you take a specific gravity reading, you can read temperature and gravity at the same time. If you have a large thermometer, take a temperature reading in the hydrometer tube before you insert the hydrometer to check the specific gravity. After you read the specific gravity, put the thermometer in the hydrometer tube again for a second temperature check. The average of these two values will be the temperature you should use in adjusting the specific gravity.

Table 6.1 provides gravity correction factors for temperatures up to boiling in 10-degree (F) increments. Choose the temperature closest to your temperature readings and add the corresponding figure to the SG reading to get the actual SG of the wort. For example:

First temperature reading: 128 °F (53 °C)
Gravity reading: 1.042
Second temperature reading: 126 °F (52 °C)

From these data, you can estimate that the actual temperature during the hydrometer reading was about 127 °F (53 °C) — or about one-third of the way between 130 °F (54 °C) and 120 °F (49 °C). Add the adjustment factor for 130 °F (54 °C) to get 1.042 + 0.013 = 1.055 corrected specific gravity. Alternatively, reduce the correction factor by 0.001 to reflect the temperature reading at 127 °F (53 °C).

Measuring volume is easy if your brewing vessels are calibrated. Most people don't buy calibrated pots, but if you're in the market for a big pot anyway, some restaurant pots are calibrated on the inside by quarts or gallons to make this kind of measurement easy. But you will need to calibrate your equipment in some way. This involves pouring measured amounts of water into each of your brewing pots and sparge collection vessels to quantify them in gallons. If you mark them on the inside, the marks will wash away in your first brew. Better to mark on the outside. On plastic vessels this is easy to do, because you can see the liquid level.

Table 6.1
Gravity Correction Chart

Temp °F	(°C)	Add SG	Temp, °F	(°C)	Add SG
80	(27)	0.002	140	(60)	0.016
90	(32)	0.004	150	(66)	0.018
100	(38)	0.006	160	(71)	0.022
110	(43)	0.008	170	(77)	0.025
120	(49)	0.010	190	(88)	0.033
130	(54)	0.013	212	(100)	0.040

Note: Specific gravity is based on the density of a liquid at 60 °F. When gravity is read at warmer temperatures a correction factor must be added to the value you read on the hydrometer.

For measuring and marking metal pots, use a wooden-spoon handle for help. Pour the amount of water you want to measure into the pot. Lower the handle of the spoon until it barely touches the water. With your thumb, mark the spot on the handle that is level with the rim of the pot. Now move the handle to the outside of the pot, keeping your thumb in place and lining it up with the outside rim. Mark the pot, perhaps by etching it in some way, at the point or end of the spoon handle, which will correspond to the water level inside the pot. You'll need to repeat this process for each measurement level you want to record.

To avoid marking your pots altogether, use a calibrated stick, spoon, or rod that either hangs from the top edge of the pot or can be set against the bottom of the pot when you need to take a measurement. Mark various volumes on this instrument and use it in the way automobile oil dipsticks are used.

One final issue is the expansion and contraction of wort at various temperatures. Water of a given weight occupies 4 percent more volume at boiling point than at 60 °F (16 °C). Thus, if your method of measurement allows you the precision to account for this, you may want to do so. In practice, however, few systems can account for this effect accurately.

Using Total Gravity Values

To see how you might use total gravity values, let's use an all-grain example. At the end of your mash, you run off sweet wort that will go into the boil pot. For an all-grain brew, the volume of runoff will be greater than your expected finished volume. During the boil, water evaporates, and the total gravity of the wort is concentrated into a smaller volume of water. By knowing the volume and gravity of the starting wort and the expected final volume of the boil, you can tell what the gravity of the wort will be at the end of the boil. Thus:

$$\text{Total gravity}_{(\text{beg. of boil})} = \text{Total gravity}_{(\text{end of boil})}$$

Because this is true, you can also say that

$$GU_{(\text{beg.})} \times \text{Volume}_{(\text{beg.})} = GU_{(\text{end})} \times \text{Volume}_{(\text{end})}$$

This restates total gravity in terms of the factors that determine it. If you now divide both sides of this equation by volume (end), you get an equation for estimating the final gravity of the brew. Thus

$$\frac{GU_{(\text{beg.})} \times \text{Volume}_{(\text{beg.})}}{\text{Volume}_{(\text{end})}} = GU_{(\text{end})}$$

Say you have 8 gallons of runoff from the mash. The specific gravity of this wort is 1.038. You plan to boil long enough to yield 5.5 gallons of finished beer. Because the total gravity will not change during the boil, you can calculate the finishing gravity of the boil:

$$(38 \text{ GU} \times 8 \text{ gallons}) \div 5.5 \text{ gallons} = 55.3 \text{ GU}$$

This calculation tells you that this wort will have a gravity of 1.055 when boiled down to 5.5 gallons.

In this example, I have set the terms "beginning" and "end" according to a specific brewing process that starts with excess volume and reduces it during the boil. In practice, other definitions of beginning and end can be used to suit your own brewing practices. For example, you may have a boiling pot that is big enough to contain only 4 gallons of wort. At the end of the boil you chill the wort, add it to the fermenter, and then top off the fermenter with water to achieve a final volume of 5 gallons. In this case, "beginning" would be the volume and gravity of the wort in your boil pot, and "end" would be the volume and gravity of the liquid in your fermenter.

If you begin your boil with 4 gallons of wort with a specific gravity of 1.060, what will the specific gravity of the wort be once it is added to the fermenter and diluted to 5 gallons? Use the same equation:

$$[GU_{(beg.)} \times Volume_{(beg.)}] \div Volume_{(end)} = GU_{(end)}$$

but define "beginning" as the conditions in the boil pot and "end" as those in the fermenter. Thus

$$[60 \times 4] \div 5 = 48 \text{ GU or } 1.048$$

Hitting Target Gravity

Once you have assessed the total gravity of your wort, you can determine whether the original gravity at the volume you intended to make is what you planned. If it is not, you can then make adjustments to hit that gravity.

To adjust the original gravity of your finished beer, you can take three or maybe four courses of action.

If the gravity is *lower than* your target, you can: (1) boil longer to produce a smaller volume of finished beer that has the gravity you want, or (2) add sufficient malt extract to bring the gravity up to the expected value.

If the gravity is *higher than* your target, you can: (1) produce a larger volume of beer so that the finished beer has the gravity you desire, or (2) remove a portion of the wort from the boil pot and use it for another purpose, such as for yeast starters or a separate small batch of beer.

When working on gravity adjustment, it is easiest to think in terms of total gravity. Say you are brewing 6 gallons of bock beer for which you want an OG of 1.068. Multiplying that (6 × 68), you find that you need a total gravity of 408 GU.

If you perform a mash that gives you a total gravity of 355 GU, you are 53 GU short of where you need to be. If you want to adjust with extract, you'll need to know how much extract it will take to reach your target gravity.

To find the weight of extract needed, divide the difference between your target gravity and the actual total gravity by the extract/pound value for the type of extract you will use. Thus

$$Extract_{(lbs.)} = \frac{[(\text{Target GU} \times \text{Target vol.}) - (GU \times Vol.)_{from\ mash}]}{(\text{Extract/lb./gal. value})}$$

or more simply:

$$Extract_{(lbs.)} = \frac{(\text{Total Gravity}_{Target} - \text{Total Gravity}_{from\ mash})}{(\text{Extract/lb. value})}$$

Generally, the extract potential for dry extract is 45 GU per pound, and for liquid extract it is about 38 GU per pound (see table 5.1 in chapter 5). If you want to calculate the amount of dry extract needed to bring your 6-gallon batch of bock to the desired gravity, follow this formula:

$$\begin{aligned} Extract_{lbs} &= (408 \text{ GU} - 355 \text{ GU}) \div 45 \text{ GU/lb.} \\ &= 53 \text{ GU} \div 45 \text{ GU/lb.} \\ &= 1.2 \text{ lbs.} \end{aligned}$$

For liquid malt extract, simply divide 53 GU by 38 GU per pound to get 1.4 pounds.

Use the same calculation to determine the right amount of extract to add when you use specialty grains or a minimash but rely on extract for the bulk of the fermentable material.

To determine what volume of beer you would have if you boiled the mash proceeds to a gravity of 1.068, simply divide the total gravity of the mash runoff by the desired gravity units, in this case 68. Thus

$$355 \div 68 = 5.22 \text{ gal.}$$

If you are willing to give up ¾ gallon of finished product, you can still hit your target gravity. The full equation for this would be:

$$Volume_{final} = (GU \times Vol.)_{from\ mash} \div \text{Target GU}$$

If you have too much gravity (lucky you!), use this same equation to find out how much more beer you'll need to make to hit your target gravity. Thus, if you did a small mash and supplemented it with three cans of malt extract, you might find that the total gravity of the wort in the boil pot is 470. Divide that by 68 to find that you can make 6.9 gallons of wort with an OG of 1.068.

Additional Thoughts on Working with Gravity

I hope the detailed equations provided after the examples are becoming superfluous by now. In order for you to use these concepts to your advantage, they need to become intuitive so that you can quickly determine what is going on with your brew and adjust it accordingly.

Basically, you are working with just two terms: specific gravity (as expressed in gravity units) and volume. Multiply them and you get total gravity. Because total gravity doesn't change during the boil, you can predict the gravity you will have at the end of the boil by assuming the final volume, or vice versa.

Let's look at two more examples, one for extract brewing and one for all-grain brewing. Both start simply and become more complicated.

Extract Example

Let's say you plan a beer with a starting gravity of 1.042. Following a minimash of 3 pounds of grain, you have 2 gallons of runoff at 1.034. This equals a total gravity of 68 GU, and your final target for 5.5 gallons of finished wort is 231 GU (5.5 gallons x 42 GU). Thus, you need 231 GU – 68 GU, or 163 GU, from the extract.

If you are using liquid extract, find the number of pounds you need by dividing 163 GU by 38 GU per pound to get 4.2 pounds. The liquid extract you have is in

3-pound containers, and you don't want to leave a partially used container sitting around. So, you decide you'll use dry extract, and you calculate that it would require 163 GU ÷ 45 GU per pound, or 3.6 pounds. But you only have 2.5 pounds of dry extract on hand. Now you have two problems: You don't want to use part of a can of liquid extract, and you don't have enough dry extract to do the job.

Finally, you hit upon the solution: You'll add one can of syrup and then just enough dry extract to hit the desired gravity. This sounds like a great idea, but first you need to determine how much dry extract to add. You can do this using a tally method:

Target total gravity: 231 GU	231 GU
Less minimash: 68 GU	- 68 GU
Still need: 163 GU	163 GU

Then the next step is

GUs needed:	163 GU
Less 1 can extract:(3 lbs. x 38 GU/lb.)	- 114 GU
Still need	49 GU

And finally

49 GU ÷ 45 GU/lb. of dry extract = 1.1 pounds

Start with the target total gravity of 231 GU, subtract the results of the minimash, which is 68 GU, then subtract the gravity contributed by the malt syrup (3 pounds x 38 GU per pound), 114 GU. This leaves 49 GU to pick up from the dry extract, with a rating of 45 GU/pound. And 49 divided by 45 equals 1.1 pounds of dry extract. Voila! You have exactly the gravity you need to hit your objective.

Mash Example

One way to use these equations is in making multiple batches of beer from a single mash. Here's how it might work. Let's say you want to make an old ale at

1.075 and a pale ale at about 1.052 from the same mash. You would like to make 5 gallons of each. Let's begin by calculating the total gravity for each beer:

Old ale: 5 gallons x 72 GU = 375 GU
Pale ale: 5 gallons x 52 GU = 260 GU

From this you can determine that the combined total gravity needed to make both beers will be 375 GU + 260 GU, or 635 GU.

Let's assume you mash 20 pounds of grain and run off 12 gallons of wort into two vessels. The first contains 6.5 gallons at 1.068, the second contains 5.5 gallons at 1.023. The total gravity of this runoff is

(6.5 gal. x 68 GU) + (5.5 gal. x 23 GU) = 568 GU

This leaves you somewhat short of the 635 GU total you need. You quickly determine that you can make both beers simply by adding 1.5 pounds of dry extract:

$$\frac{(635 \text{ GU target} - 568 \text{ GU obtained})}{45 \text{ GU/lb. of extract}} = 1.5 \text{ lbs.}$$

Now the question is how to divide up the first and second runnings. If you use all of the first runnings for the old ale you will probably have problems because the total gravity in the first runnings is 442 GU, and the old ale requires a total gravity of only 375 GU. The second runnings have a total gravity of 127 GU, and even after adding malt extract (1.5 pounds at 45 GU per pound for total gravity of 67.5 GU) you will only have a total gravity of 194.5 GU, well short of the 260 GU you want.

You have already calculated the amount of extract needed to achieve the desired total gravity for both brews, and the amount

over on the old ale is equal to the amount under on the pale ale. This difference is equal to about 65 or 67 GU. Since the first runnings have a gravity of 68 GU, this difference is equal to almost exactly 1 gallon of the first runnings.

Thus, the material you would add to the boil kettle for each batch could be as follows:

Old ale: 5.5 gal. of first runnings
Total gravity = 5.5 x 68 or 374

Pale ale: 5.5 gallons of second runnings
Total gravity = 5.5 x 23 or 126.5

1.0 gallon of first runnings
Total gravity = 1 x 68 or 68

1.5 pounds of dry malt extract
Total gravity = 1.5 45 or 67.5

Total gravity in the pale ale brewpot:
126.5 + 68 + 67.5 = 262

Conclusion

The concepts of gravity units and total gravity can help you maintain control of the brewing process. By using them, you can brew accurately, and your resulting beers will more closely match your original intentions.

In addition, these concepts allow you flexibility in your brewing. Using them, you can easily vary your process yet achieve predictable results. Change your final boil volume, make two beers from one mash, borrow extract from one source and loan it to another — it's fun, it's exciting, and it's all part of small-scale brewing.

7 BEER COLOR

Project	Designing Great Beers
	Brewers Publications
Project No.	61766

The color of beer has gotten little attention in the brewing literature over the past forty or so years. The basic techniques for assessing and quantifying color in beer were established in the 1940s and early 1950s, and since that time little additional discovery has taken place.

The science of beer color deals only with ingredients and finished products and makes little attempt to predict the color of a beer based upon its recipe and process. This is easy enough to understand: At least a dozen factors influence color, and none are reliable, precise predictors of finished beer color.

Of course, the demands placed on color by the big brewers (for whom most research is conducted) are quite different from those made by the craft brewer. Most commercial brewers make the same product day after day, year after year.[1] Because they produce the same recipe all the time, they have little need to predict the likely color of a new recipe formulation — and when they do, it is all worked out in the pilot brewery.

The big breweries do place very demanding color specifications on their finished beers. The allowable variation is less than 0.1 °SRM (Standard Reference Method) in many cases — a level below the lab-to-lab variability inherent in the measuring techniques.[2]

To achieve such close tolerances, most big breweries cheat a bit. Coloring beers made from dark malts are often added to batches in small quantities to increase the color of the finished product. For this reason, the color specification for most commercial beers is darker than what the raw ingredients would normally yield. In addition, blending batches is commonly done to ensure the consistency of commercial beers along a variety of parameters, and color can often be adjusted this way.

With craft brewers, and especially homebrewers, the brewer's needs with regard to color are quite different. First, craft brewers demand less reproducibility in their finished product and are generally satisfied when final color falls within a range rather than right on a specific SRM reading.

Second, the most common methods of control used by bigger brewers are generally not available on the home and small brewery scale. Certainly the production of "pilot," or test brews, that are not intended for sale or consumption is virtually unknown with craft brewers. In addition, craft brewers have less opportunity to smooth out variations through blending.

Thus, what craft brewers need is to (1) understand the factors that influence color formation in beer, including the practical implications, and (2) devise a system that can be used in recipe formulation to

Figure 7.1
Yellow-Red Proportions of Beers, Malts, and Caramels

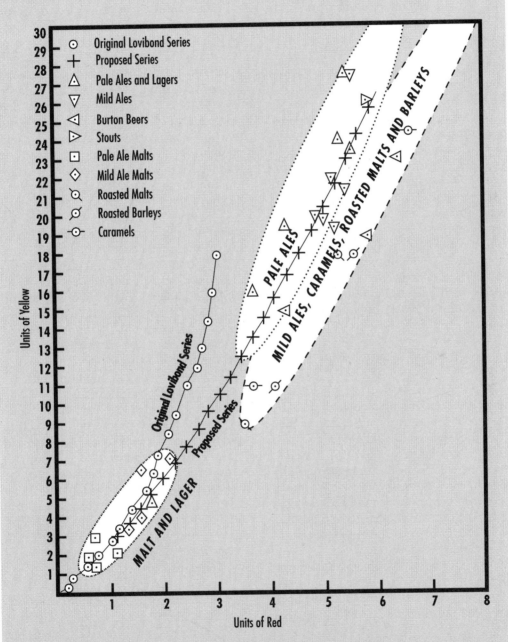

Source: L. R. Bishop, "Proposed Revision of the Lovibond 52 Series of Glass Slides for the Measurement of the Colour of Worts and Beers." Journal of the Institute of Brewing 56, (1950), 377. *Used with permission.*

estimate the color that can be expected from a particular recipe.

In this chapter I discuss the standards used for measuring beer color both with and without laboratory instruments. This will ensure that subsequent references (e.g., 10 °L) will have some meaning for the reader. This will also provide small brewers with techniques that can be used to quantitatively evaluate the colors of their own beers at minimal expense.

Following the discussion of measurement standards, I examine the chemistry of beer color and discuss the implications for controlling color. I look at practical brewing aspects of color, including the areas of the brewing process that affect the color of the finished product, and at a specific set of steps you can take to lighten or darken color if you wish.

Finally, I examine techniques for predicting the finished color of a beer and discuss how, to a limited extent at least, you can predict the colors of your own beers from readily available data.

Systems for Quantifying Beer Color

The determination of beer and wort colors has been troublesome in the malting and brewing industries for at least one hundred years. Half a dozen techniques — each giving different results — have been used to assess the color of beer during the past fifty years. To make matters worse, at least two of these methods have been used at one time by brewers in North America and Europe, making for further variation in comparisons of beer color.

One of the big problems facing the assessment of beer and wort color is the broad range of colors found in finished beer. One need only compare a "light" beer to a Guinness to appreciate this point. In addition, hues of both red and yellow contribute to the color of beer at all points along this scale.[3] One difficulty is that the relative contribution of red and yellow to the finished

color changes from beer to beer (see figure 7.1).[4] To make matters worse, these proportions do not necessarily remain constant when beer is diluted with water.[5]

These challenges have led to many changes in the measurement of beer color over the years. The original Lovibond system was created in 1883 by J. W. Lovibond,[6] and at least in some implementations it used a system of colored slides, which would be assembled in combinations until a color that matched that of the beer was found. We still find the term *Lovibond* in use today, and methods for determining color can be traced back to the original system.

For several decades, visual comparison between a beer or wort sample and a colored-glass standard was the basis for assigning color values (see figure 7.2). For some time, a standard called the "Series 52 Lovibond Scale" was used by brewers. This was a set of colored glass standards corresponding to Lovibond numbers and containing the hues thought to be most prevalent in beer. This system attempted to capture both the yellow-red balance and the overall intensity of color with a single standard at each Lovibond rating.

Widespread use of this method had a number of drawbacks. First, color blindness is somewhat common, affecting about 8 percent of males and 5 percent of females.[7] Readings made by a person with some degree of color blindness may be inaccurate. Second, the standards themselves turned out to vary from laboratory to laboratory,[8] and certain inconsistencies could be found even within a single set of standards, for instance, where the color of two standards labeled with different values would turn out to be identical.[9]

Other standards and photometer calibration methods were developed, based upon iodine and potassium dichromate, but none proved ideal.[10]

Of course, all this predated the arrival of affordable, reliable spectrophotometers. These instruments allow accurate control

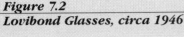

Figure 7.2
Lovibond Glasses, circa 1946

Source: E. H. Vogal, F. H. Schwaiger, H. G. Leonhardt, and J. A. Merten. The Practical Brewer: A Manual for the Brewing Industry (Master Brewers Association of America, 1946), 176. Courtesy of The Practical Brewer.

of light so that a single wavelength can be selected from the spectrum of visible light (which has a range of about 400 to about 700 nanometers [nm]),[11] passed through a sample, and the degree of transmission, or absorbance, measured. When this tool became available to brewers in the 1940s and early 1950s, a great deal of research was done with it on both sides of the Atlantic. However, this research led to different results in Europe than it did in the United States.

The American Society of Brewing Chemists (ASBC), based upon work done by Beyer, Stone, and a subcommittee of the society, identified a method of direct color determination that provided a good correlation with visual methods. They noted a much lower level of variation between operators and sites with the instrumental method than with the visual technique.[12] Thus, in 1950 the ASBC subcommittee on color recommended adoption of a "standard reference color method" based upon spectrophotometer readings for the determination of beer color. This method is the same one used today in the United States for determining Standard Reference Method, or SRM, color. Despite this, one will often still see "Lovibond" applied to SRM results.

In Europe, a researcher used the spectrophotometer as a tool for improving upon the visual Series 52 Lovibond standards. Once this was done, studies showed a good correlation between visual and instrumental methods, and the European Brewing Convention (EBC) adopted the new system of *visual* standards as their analytical method. The EBC color value of a beer using this system was quite different from that of the SRM color value for the same beer. Thus, the techniques and terminology of American and European brewers diverged, and it would take twenty-five years before they began to come together again.

To confuse matters further, the British Institute of Brewing (IOB) adopted a spectrophotometric method using an entirely different wavelength (530 nm) than that used by the EBC or the Americans. This was resolved finally in 1991, when the IOB formally revised their standards to include the EBC measurement technique as discussed next. [13]

Measuring Color in the Lab

In the United States, the SRM is the standard method for determining beer color, as adopted by the American Society of Brewing

Chemists. This technique was originally set up to approximate the Lovibond scale and is now used as the basis for assigning Lovibond ratings to grains as well as for determining the actual color of finished beer.

The ASBC method uses a spectrophotometer to assess the amount of light absorbed by beer in a ½-inch glass cuvette when illuminated with light at the specific wavelength of 430 nm. The SRM color rating is equal to ten times this absorbance value. Absorbance is measured on a logarithmic scale, and on most spectrophotometers the maximum value that can be read (corresponding to 99 percent absorbance) is 2.0. This introduces some problems with evaluation of beers that are darker than 20 °SRM, as we will discuss later in this chapter.

The other major system of measuring beer color is the EBC method. This technique reads absorbance in a smaller, 1-centimeter (10-millimeter) cuvette, but at the same wavelength as is used by the SRM. To get the final color value using the EBC method, multiply the absorbance by twenty-five.[14]

This technique was adopted relatively recently in Europe;[15] previously the EBC used a method that read absorbance at a longer wavelength of 530 nm.[16] The absorbance reading thus obtained was the EBC color rating. The current technique (reading at 430 nm) can be directly compared to the ASBC method as follows:

SRM x 1.97 = EBC

or

EBC ÷ 1.97 = SRM

In general, a factor of two can be applied for an approximate translation between the two systems.

If you are looking at older values for EBC color — measurements made before 1990 — be cautious in making any comparisons with SRM color. Due to the varying color measurement techniques in use in the past, the results may not be directly comparable to current SRM values.

Visualizing the Standards

Serious beer drinkers and brewers need to understand how these precise quantitative measures relate to the types of color they actually see in beer. After all, knowing that a beer has an SRM color of 10 doesn't do you much good if you don't know what a 10 should look like!

A variety of charts that provide descriptions of SRM color are available.[17] However, few state the conditions under which the beers are to be observed. This is important, because visual perception of beer color depends upon many factors, including the diameter and depth of the glass used for viewing and the source and character of the light by which it is viewed. Also, I find many of the descriptors used in these charts confusing.

At the risk of repeating these errors, table 7.1 gives qualitative descriptions for the range of SRM colors based on the use of the standard American Homebrewers Association (AHA) beer judging cup. The cup generally contains 1 to 2 inches of beer when color is observed. The best light is sunlight reflected off a sheet of white paper; other bright but diffused light sources may also be used.

These descriptions are based on analysis of the various style guidelines published by the Association of Brewers.[18] Well-known beers are given as examples to provide some visual reference for the descriptions.

Measuring Beer Color for Home and Small Brewers

Knowing that the big boys assess beer color with a spectrophotometer is fine, but it doesn't do the average homebrewer or craft brewer much good. Of course, you

Table 7.1
SRM Values and Beer Color

Description	SRM Color	Example
Very pale	2–3	Budweiser (2)
Pale	3–4	Molson Export Ale (4)
Gold	5–6	
Amber (brownish yellow)	6–9	
Deep amber/light copper	10–14	Whitbread Pale Ale (11)
Copper (reddish brown)	14–17	
Deep copper/light brown	17–18	Michelob Dark (17)
Brown	19–22	Salvator (21)
Dark brown	22–30	
Very dark brown	30–35	
Black	30+	
Black, opaque	40+	Most stouts

could send your beer to one of the beer laboratories for a color analysis. For ten to fifteen dollars, you would find out the exact SRM color of the beer to a tenth of a degree. But that isn't very practical — or necessary. What's needed is an easy, reliable way to assess the color of a finished beer when you're sitting in the comfort of your own home or brewery.

This chapter describes not one but several approaches to this challenge. All use a system of comparison where the unknown sample (your beer) is visually compared to a standard or standards of known SRM value. All of these require certain standard procedures. These procedures include:

- Pour an inch or two of beer into a clear plastic cup or standardized glass container labeled with the identity of that beer. (The container used and the level of beer should be approximately the same in every instance.)

- Pour to maximize foaming, then swirl the beer a few times to release additional gas. Repeat as necessary.

- When the beer has no visible gas bubbles, you are ready to begin.

- Compare standards and unknowns in front of a sheet of white paper illuminated with daylight or a high-intensity lamp.

Standards

Let us see what options you have for establishing standards to read your beers against. The first method — using a hand-held card — is very quick and easy but requires a specific tool. The others — using beers — are a bit more involved, but may be more convenient. Differences in red-yellow balance are found in each system, so no one approach is perfect.

The first system uses a commercially available card made with photographic film to provide standards for nine different ratings ranging from 3 to 19 °SRM.[19] The card was created by homebrewer Dennis Davison for comparison with beers contained in the standard American Homebrewers Association beer judging cup, mentioned above.

To use the Davison guide, pour about 1 inch of beer into the cup and then hold the cup and the card side by side in front of a source of diffuse daylight (see figure 7.3). The values of the nine color panels in SRM degrees are 3, 4.5, 6, 7.5, 9, 11, 14, and 19. By comparing the color of your beer to the transparent color panels on the card, you can determine the color of your beer to within about 1 °SRM.

I have used this card extensively during my research and have found that it provides a reasonably accurate result very quickly. The difficulties I have encountered involve the qualitative aspects of some of the panels (red-yellow balance) and the challenges of interpolating values that lie between the standard panels — especially in the 11 to 14 range. Nonetheless, I found the correlation between this method and instrumental readings to be very high.

If you don't have access to the Davison guide, you can use any one of a number of methods that rely upon commercial beers as color standards. One such method, described by George Fix,[20] compares the unknown beer to dilutions of Michelob Classic Dark. I have difficulty finding Michelob Classic Dark in my area, so I have devised a similar technique using the German doppelbock Salvator.

Dilutions of dark beer do not appear to produce linear results. Thus, you must read the SRM value of the diluted standard off a curve, as shown in figure 7.4. If Michelob Dark is easier for you to find, table 7.2 shows the dilutions needed for a good set of standards

Occasionally you may want to read a number of beers in one session. Assuming you don't have access to the Davison card, you will want to prepare a set of beer-based standards that cover a broad range of SRM colors to use for comparison. This will allow you to read each sample fairly quickly and will also ensure that you have a common standard for all of the data you generate.

The first approach you can take is to assemble a group of beers that have well-documented color values and use them as standards. Using the data provided in table 7.1 in addition to data from other sources, you can assemble a set of several beers that will provide you with a reasonable "standard curve" from which you can read the colors of your beers. I find that Budweiser, Molson Export Ale, Bass Ale, and either Michelob Dark or Salvator give a reasonable set of standards.

Another approach to making standards is to set up a series of dilutions of a dark beer in a fashion similar to the Fix test mentioned above. Table 7.2 shows the ratios to use in making standards from either Michelob Dark or Salvator.

Figure 7.3
Assessing Beer Color Using the Davison Guide

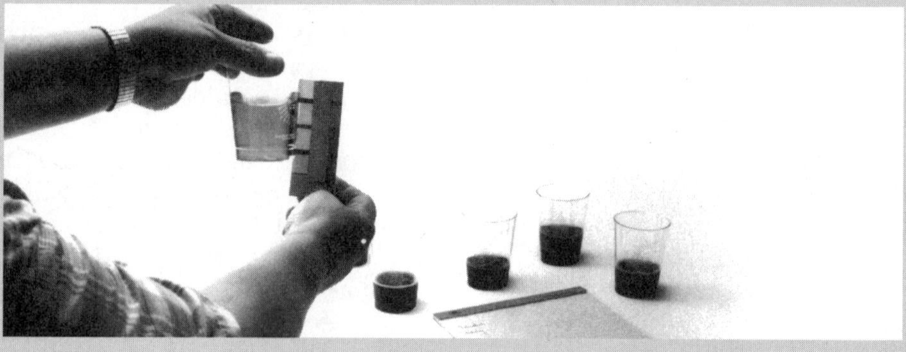

Photo courtesy of Dennis Davison, 1996.

Table 7.2
Creating SRM Color Standards Using Michelob Dark and Salvator

Amount of distilled water (mL) per 20 mL of Michelob Dark	SRM value standard	Amount of distilled water (mL) per 20 mL of Salvator	SRM value standard
0	17	0	21
10	15	15	15
25	12.5	24	12.5
40	10	40	10
70	7	60	7.5
100	5	120	5
250	2		

If you find the making of these dilutions a bit too tedious, you can make a good set of standards from mixtures of just three different beers. In contrast to dilutions with water, intermixtures of some beers are very close to linear. Thus, using Salvator (SRM 21), Bass (SRM 9.8), and Spaten Club Weiss (SRM 4.6), you can create a full set of color standards. (Note: Dilutions of Salvator with Club Weiss are not linear.)

Table 7.3 gives a simple way to do this that requires no complicated mixing. Each beer is used undiluted and then mixed half and half (1:1) with another. These standards provide good coverage of the whole range of SRM values from 2 to 20.

You need only 2 to 4 ounces of each standard if you use AHA cups for making the comparisons. That means you'll have plenty of Salvator and Club Weiss left over to enjoy as you measure the colors of your beers!

This section has presented a number of techniques for easily measuring beer color. All of the standards and dilutions

Figure 7.4
SRM Values for Salvator Dilutions

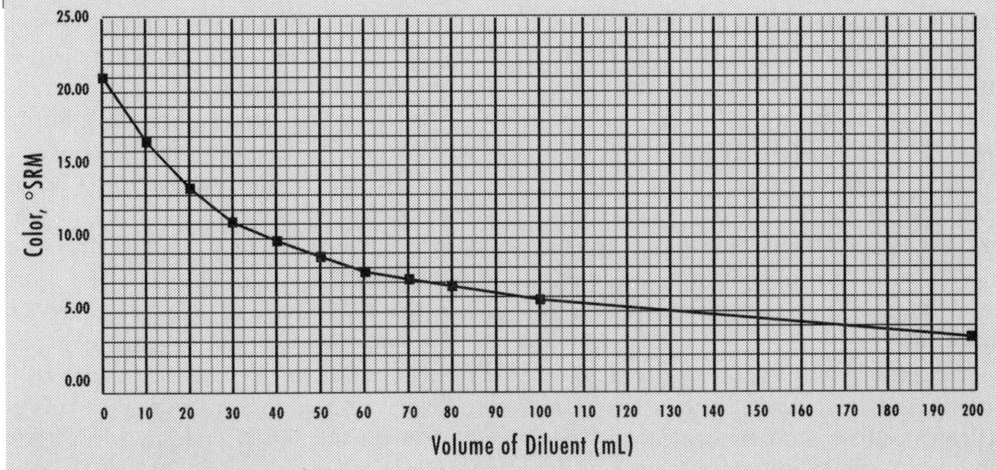

Note: Twenty mL of Salvator plus the amount of distilled water shown on the horizontal axis will produce a solution with the color value indicated by the curve.

Table 7.3
Creating SRM Color Standards Using Beer Combinations

Beer or Beer Combination	SRM Value
Salvator (undiluted)	21
Half Salvator, half Bass	15.4
Bass	9.8
Half Bass, half Club Weiss	7.2
Club Weiss	4.6
Half Club Weiss, half distilled water	2.3

have been checked by photometer to ensure that they provide accurate results. Be aware, however, that even commercial beers can vary — or even change by intention. If something doesn't seem right, double check it using a different method or a different beer as a standard.

Assigning Color for Very Dark Beers

The scales cited in the previous section allow you to read beers up to 17 or 21 °SRM before you run out of standards with which to compare the beer. Thus, these systems leave out most porters, all stouts, and a variety of Scotch ales, bocks, milds, and even some weizenbocks.

The logical solution is to dilute these darker beers so that they fall below 17 or 21 and can be read within the scale of the standards. But beware! Diluting dark beers lands you on a slippery slope of beer confusion. The problem is that, incredible as it may seem, beer does not always follow Beer's Law. In brief, this law states that there is a linear relationship between the concentration of a solution and the amount of light it absorbs when read in a spectrophotometer.[21]

Over the years, several writers have asserted that beer obeys Beer's Law. Unfortunately, these studies appear to have examined a very limited portion of the beer-color universe. It appears that Beer's Law does hold true for beers with a final color of less than 5 or perhaps 10 °SRM. This can be demonstrated by checking the color of various dilutions of a beer on a spectrophotometer and comparing them to the expected (i.e., linear, Beer's Law) results. Figure 7.5 shows that Spaten Club Weiss, with an initial color of 4.6 °SRM, does in fact give a linear dilution profile and thus complies with Beer's Law.

However, more highly colored beers do not appear to comply with Beer's Law when diluted with water.[22] Figure 7.6 shows dilutions of six dark beers. The absorbance readings (indexed for the figure) given by these beers diverge substantially from the linear profile predicted by Beer's Law. These results agree with the data that Fix presents on Michelob Dark and its lack of linearity. As can be seen in these samples, even the nonlinearity is not consistent between samples.

This failure of some beers to comply with Beer's Law is important because it affects the color values assigned to beers with a color above 20 °SRM. In the lab, color is determined by multiplying the spectrophotometer reading by 10. But since the maximum absorbance that can be read on many of these instruments is 2.0, any beer darker than 20 must generally be diluted or read in a smaller cell. (This is also true in the visual systems.) In either case, Beer's Law must be applied to give the final reading. Thus, a failure in Beer's Law means that the assigned color of a

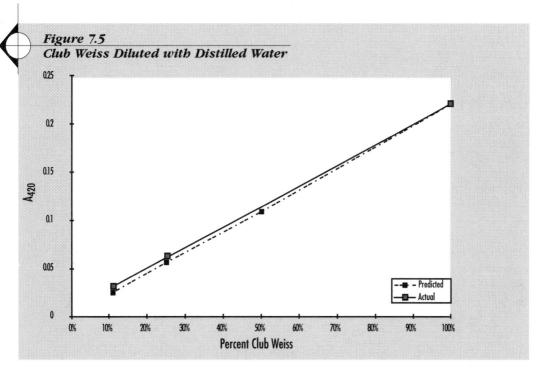

Figure 7.5
Club Weiss Diluted with Distilled Water

dark beer may vary according to the dilution (or cell size) that is selected.

In figure 7.6, the color of Porter 132 after using Beer's Law to correct for the dilutions could be assigned different values after each dilution, as shown in table 7.4.

The physical or chemical phenomenon responsible for this behavior has not been characterized in the beer literature.[23] However based upon other investigations into the failure of Beer's Law, it has been postulated that the melanoidin pigment compounds in beer form complexes when present at high concentrations. After dilution, the complexes dissociate into products that absorb more light than the complexes themselves.[24]

Despite these problems with dilution, several sources have confirmed that it is common practice in beer laboratories to dilute dark beers or worts and determine color by assuming that Beer's Law does hold true.[25]

The only guidance on this practice provided by the ASBC is a statement that the ideal range for reading absorbance would be 0.187 to 0.699, because this area provides the highest accuracy of readings. This would suggest that any beer of more than 7 °SRM might be diluted before being read — although not all labs or technicians will follow this practice. Unless a standard dilution is employed, a single beer may receive different readings from different labs or even from the same lab on different days. Anyone trying to control color on any beer with more than a smidgen of color should be aware of this possibility.

All of these data suggest that when assessing the color of dark beers by either visual or photometric methods, one needs to select a standard dilution factor and stick with it. The results of such readings may be surprising — some of the stouts I read would have colors in excess of 100 °SRM by this method. Despite this, a series of such readings will at least provide a meaningful basis for comparison and for process control (if this is desired) by increasing reproducibility from reading to reading.

In my work, I have used a one-to-eleven dilution factor for both photometer

Figure 7.6
Dilutions of Dark Beer

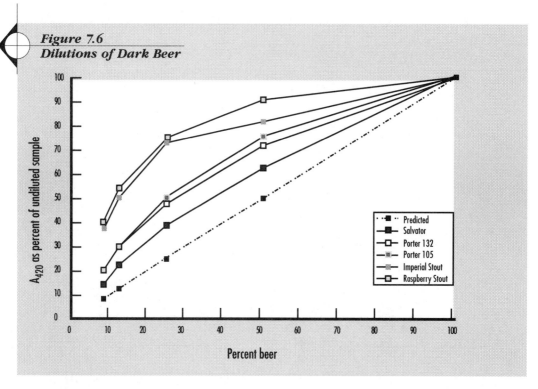

Legend:
- Predicted
- Salvator
- Porter 132
- Porter 105
- Imperial Stout
- Raspberry Stout

Y-axis: A_{420} as percent of undiluted sample

X-axis: Percent beer

and visual readings of dark beers, and this seems to work reasonably well. A typical dilution would be 4 mL of beer to 44 mL of distilled water. The color value given by this solution would then be multiplied by 12 (the total number of parts) to give the color of the undiluted beer.

The Chemistry of Beer Color

Now that you have a good understanding of color and how it can be measured in beer, you can begin the process of considering how to control the level of color in your own beers. To do this, you must first start with a bit of chemistry so that you understand the origins and causes of beer color.

Three areas of chemistry have been identified with potential bearing on beer color.[26] These include:

1. Maillard, or browning, reactions that produce both color pigments and flavor compounds

Table 7.4
Color Values after Dilution of Porter 132

Dilution	Final SRM
undiluted	28.0*
1:1	40.4
1:3	54.0
1:7	65.6
1:11	68.4

*This undiluted beer was read in a 10-mm cell at A_{420}, as all of my photometer readings were. It gave an absorbance of 1.650.

Figure 7.7
Basic Food Chemistry

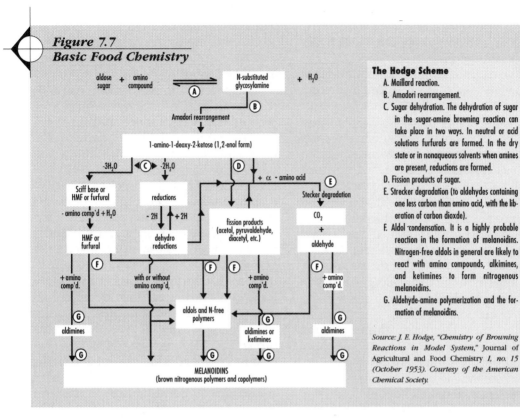

Source: J. E. Hodge, "Chemistry of Browning Reactions in Model System," Journal of Agricultural and Food Chemistry I, no. 15 (October 1953). Courtesy of the American Chemical Society.

The Hodge Scheme

A. Maillard reaction.

B. Amadori rearrangement.

C. Sugar dehydration. The dehydration of sugar in the sugar-amine browning reaction can take place in two ways. In neutral or acid solutions furfurals are formed. In the dry state or in nonaqueous solvents when amines are present, reductions are formed.

D. Fission products of sugar.

E. Strecker degradation (to aldehydes containing one less carbon than amino acid, with the liberation of carbon dioxde).

F. Aldol condensation. It is a highly probable reaction in the formation of melanoidins. Nitrogen-free aldols in general are likely to react with amino compounds, alkimines, and ketimines to form nitrogenous melanoidins.

G. Aldehyde-amine polymerization and the formation of melanoidins.

2. Caramelization products
3. Oxidation products

Maillard Reactions

The Maillard reactions are by far the most important source of color in beer. They account for the formation of color in the production of malt and also during the production of beer itself.

Formation of browning products commences with reactions between sugars (glucose, fructose, maltose, etc.) and amino acids (the building blocks of proteins). A variety of pathways may then be followed, and the colored end-products are nitrogen-containing polymers called *melanoidins*. Figure 7.7 provides an idea of the complexity of these reactions.

Melanoidins were described by Maillard in 1912, and their formation occurs in virtually every heated food product from toast to hamburgers.[27] Despite this, scientists still know little about their chemical formation or structure.[28] The latest food science research holds that the color-causing melanoidins themselves have no aroma or flavor.[29] Despite this, the browning reactions are a primary source of aroma and flavor for beer and food through intermediary compounds and minor end-products.[30] Thus, the conditions that lead to color also lead to flavor, although the exact products and proportions will vary based on the conditions of the reaction environment.[31]

Most "malt" flavors are attributable to these browning-reaction products, and a wide variety of flavors may result from them, as shown in table 7.5. When combined with certain amino acids, maltose is reportedly able to produce some unusual aromas, such as those typical of beef broth, baked ham, stale potato, and horseradish.[32]

Melanoidins may have a more direct flavor influence in finished beer. When melanoidins are oxidized during wort production, they contribute to beer staling through the oxidation of higher alcohols into aldehydes during beer storage.[33]

The melanoidin raw materials — sugars and amino acids — occur in ample concentrations in beer worts. The production of color compounds consumes only a small fraction of these ingredients during the production of beer.[34] One study measured the amounts lost as 8.6 percent of the total amino acids and 3.8 percent of the sugars.[35] Within the population of amino acids, certain specific members (e.g., threonine) seem to be preferentially consumed,[36] and some sources suggest that the basic amino acids react most readily.[37] Among the sugars, maltose appears to play the major role in the formation of color compounds, followed by fructose and glucose.[38]

The exact products formed by the Maillard reactions are affected by a number of variables, including time, temperature, water content, and pH. They do not require the presence of oxygen.[39]

Time and temperature are the most significant variables in many settings, and different combinations of time and temperature produce different sets of end products.[40] If you remember that these reactions affect the production of malt as well as beer, this helps to explain the differences in both color and flavor between different types of malt — even between different crystal malts that have supposedly been treated in very similar ways. Also, formation of browning products is rapid at

temperatures of 212 °F (100 °C) or higher,[41] so that the length of time wort is boiled will have a direct influence on the production of color.

To proceed, the browning reactions require the presence of water. Water concentration affects the speed and mix of end products produced by these reactions. The most rapid formation of Maillard-reaction products occurs where water is present in relatively small quantities, such as in dried or evaporated food products.[42] Malt extract syrup falls within the ideal range for the formation of these color and flavor products.[43] Obviously, beer worts are made up mostly of water. Thus the Maillard or browning reactions are allowed to occur, but they move forward at a slower rate than would be possible under other circumstances.

Alkaline conditions (high pH) hasten browning reactions,[44] although they can take place under both alkaline and acidic conditions.[45] Some researchers have shown that in beer a change in wort pH from pH 5.57 to pH 6.44 can produce dramatic changes in wort color during the boil, from 5.9 °L to 15.6 °L.[46]

Other Possible Contributors to Beer Color

Although Maillard-reaction products are the major source of color for beer, other sources have a significant impact.

The oxidation of polyphenols is probably the second most significant source of

Table 7.5
Flavors Attributable to Maillard Browning Reaction Products

Chocolate	Burnt	Caramel
Rye bread	Toasted	Bready
Musty	Fruity aromatic	Maple syrup
Violets	Rose perfume	Burnt protein
Buttery	Rock candy	Sweet

Source: F. A. Lee, Basic Food Chemistry, 2d ed., (Westport, Conn.: AVI Publishing Company, Inc., 1983), 298-299.

color formation in beer. Polyphenols are sometimes referred to as tannins and may be derived from malt husks and from hops. They are multiringed structures that can react with oxygen to contribute redbrown colors in beer.[47] If you boil hops alone in water rather than in wort for an hour or so you can usually see this effect.

Contemporary beer research into phenol oxidation focuses on staling and haze properties of the reaction products rather than on the color contribution they make.[48] Nonetheless, many sources note the darkening of color that attends oxygenation of worts and beers at any stage of production.[49] Thus, reduction of polyphenol levels and reductions in wort oxidation can help to reduce color formation from this source. These issues will be of particular importance to those brewers who wish to produce very light-colored finished beers.

Caramelization is a chemical process that affects sugars subjected to temperatures of about 400 °F (200 °C) or greater.[50] Unlike melanoidin formation, this reaction as it occurs in beer does not involve nitrogen-containing compounds.[51] (Although commercial production of the now-outlawed caramel coloring did utilize ammonia.[52])

Caramelization occurs in the boil but to a limited extent in most cases and may be accentuated by the shape of the brew kettle and the method of heating.[53] Longer boils and higher-gravity wort will increase the amount of caramelization produced. Increased pH has been shown to accelerate the process as well.[54]

Naturally occurring pigments of barley and hops such as flavins, anthocyanins, and *carotenes* have been examined as a potential source of color in beer, but they appear to play little if any role in the color of the finished product.[55]

Brewer Control Points for Beer Color

Both ingredients and process may have effects upon the development of beer color. Any effort to understand the outcome of color in a particular beer and to control that end point must consider all of the possible effects from these two areas.

Ingredients

Malts and malt extracts are the ingredients that have the greatest effect on beer color. The range of color contributed by malts is indicated by the Lovibond ratings of commonly used products, which may range from 1.2 °L for a Pilsener malt to more than 600 °L for black malt or roasted barley. These colors are almost exclusively contributed by melanoidins and result from kilning of the malt, especially at temperatures above 200 °F.

Unfortunately, malt color does not correlate well with the actual color of the finished beer.[56] A number of reasons for this can be found, stemming from the Congress mash procedure used in determining malt color. In this laboratory mash procedure distilled water is employed, and the wort is not boiled before the color is read. The use of distilled water changes the water chemistry and therefore the pH of the mash; elimination of the boil dramatically reduces the development of color-contributing melanoidins. As a result, dramatic differences will be seen between malt color and the color of a finished beer.

Malt extracts can be purchased in several different color designations, such as light, amber, and dark. Because there are no standards for the measurement of color in extracts, these designations indicate only the relative color contribution of the fresh products when compared to other products made by the same maltster. Many factors affect the actual color of the wort obtained from an extract, including the extract manufacturing process, the actual chemical composition, and the conditions of storage. Furthermore, variation in color from batch to batch of a similarly labeled product from the same maltster has been observed by most brewers experienced with extracts. All of these factors make it very difficult to predict the color contribution of extract to a finished beer.

Recently some extract manufacturers have begun placing a color value on the product label. Although I assume this has been determined by a standardized process, I don't know of a published protocol for such a determination. Nonetheless, if you use the same brand of extract regularly, those numbers — if determined on a batch-to-batch basis — can help you predict the expected outcome of your current brew. Clearly, this is a trend that should be encouraged among all malt extract suppliers.

Color can also be influenced by hops. Hops contain a great deal of polyphenol, which will darken beer color. In addition, they contribute very small quantities (2 percent by weight) of reducing sugars that can participate in Maillard browning reactions.

Some studies showing that a boil conducted with pale, fresh hops will produce lighter colored beer than a boil conducted with older, darker hops.[57] In this situation, wort boiled two hours without hops had a color of 5.1 °L; when boiled for a similar period with fresh, pale hops the color was 5.9 °L; and when boiled with old hops, the color was 6.15 °L. For most home- and craft-brew settings, such a difference will be inconsequential.

Unless you want to rely upon distilled hop extracts, it is generally impractical to boil wort without hops. Thus, color contribution from this source cannot be entirely avoided. However, steps can be taken to reduce the total amount of polyphenols contributed by hops. For instance, the use of hop pellets reduces the total hop bulk added to the boil and should result in reduced polyphenol contribution. Also, the use of high alpha-acid hops for bittering applications will reduce hop mass for the hop additions that have the longest exposure to the boiling wort.

For most styles of craft-brewed beer, the color difference contributed by hops are probably of little concern. Unless you are shooting for a finished beer color of 5 °SRM or less, a difference of 1 °L will probably go completely unnoticed.

Another ingredient that affects color formation is the water used for malting and brewing. Carbonate water, because of its high alkalinity, promotes the development of color compounds to a great degree. It hastens melanoidin formation, increases the extraction of polyphenols from husks and hops, and increases caramelization. Thus, brewers who want to produce light-colored beers must take care to remove or neutralize carbonates from water that is used for mashing and sparging.

Processes

At least one large brewing company (headquartered in Colorado) prohibits many of the "cheats" commonly used by its competitors in order to control the color of their products. As a result, the maltsters and brewers who work for this company must become quite adept at controlling the process parameters that affect color. Although a number of sources contributed to the information contained in this section, I want to thank Coors veteran Paul Smith for the thorough review of this subject he presented through his lectures and notes at the Siebel Institute.

The brewing processes with the greatest impact on color formation are those involved in processing grains and producing wort.[58] Included are grain grinding, mashing, grist transfers, wort handling, boiling, and cooling. Some steps in fermentation and finishing also play a role in color production. The following paragraphs review an extensive list of factors that affect color, and these are summarized in table 7.6.

For beers with an expected color of greater than 5 or 6 °SRM, many of these steps will not have much effect. But in the attempt to produce a very pale-colored beer

— especially one that does not rely on corn or rice adjuncts — closer attention should be paid to all aspects of the process that can affect color.

Grain Selection and Handling

Specialty grains with color ratings of 10 °L or greater obviously have a dramatic effect on color production in a beer. Later, we will address ways of estimating the beer color that may be produced with these ingredients. In this section we will focus more on the use of base malts (Pilsener, pale ale, etc.), which make up the majority of the grist.

The quantity and destruction of the barley husk is a key consideration in the color obtained from base malts. Color-producing polyphenols come primarily from the husk. Thus, the quantity of husk is obviously important. Also, the release of polyphenols from the husk is increased by breaking and grinding.

To reduce the presence of polyphenols in the wort, the brewer may select base malts with thinner, lighter husks. This may generally be done by selecting two-row rather than six-row barley varieties. Some large brewers use a blend of the two types.

To reduce breakage of the husk, we must look at the grain grinding and handling processes. Breweries that have six-roller mills can achieve this goal with few compromises; however, this is rarely applicable to small craft brewers and certainly not to homebrewing. Thus, where color reduction is a priority, coarser grinds are preferred, because they will produce fewer husk particles than fine grinds.

One alternative available to small brewers, even at home, is wet-conditioning the

---

Table 7.6
Factors That Can Reduce Color Formation in Pale Beers

Factor	Practical Implication
Decreased malt nitrogen content	Select malts low in total and soluble nitrogen
Thinner husk, less husk mass	Select two-row malt varieties
Less husk breakage	Wet milling or wet conditioning of grain before grinding; coarse grinds rather than fine grinds
Increase adjunct usage	Use of corn, rice, wheat to dilute color of malt
Lower mash pH	Add calcium salts to mash water to ensure proper mash pH
Reduced mash time	Single-infusion mash, rapid conversions
Reduced aeration of mash	Minimize agitation; use low velocity, etc.
Low extraction of polyphenols	Keep sparge temperature below 167 °F (75 °C); treat sparge water to ensure appropriate pH or stop runoff at or below wort pH of 6.0
Reduced aeration of wort	Minimize splashing during collection, transfer, etc., of hot wort
Reduced hop mass	Use pellet hops, high alpha varieties
Short boil time	Know your evaporation rates, control volumes to avoid overly long boils
Gentler boil	Use steam jackets or coils on kettle rather than direct fire
Increased break formation	Use Irish moss; allow proper settling and separation or whirlpooling of break material before transferring or pitching
Rapid chilling of wort	Minimize stand time of finished hot wort before chilling
Increased yeast mass	Always pitch ample yeast; provide ample oxidation before pitching
Filter the finished beer	Remove turbidity by filtration

grain before grinding. This involves misting the malt with an amount of water equal to 1 to 2 percent of the malt by weight. When this is done about fifteen to thirty minutes before grinding it softens the husk and reduces husk breakage. Because it helps to keep husks intact, this technique may also improve lautering efficiency.

Finally, all conveying and mixing activities should be evaluated for their potential to cut or shear the husks. These steps present few problems for homebrewers, but small commercial breweries should consider a couple of issues. First, screw-auger conveyors should be kept as short as possible both before and after grinding the grain. If mash agitators are used, they should be designed to reduce shear and should always be operated at low speeds.

Another factor worth considering when color reduction is critical is the total nitrogen content of the malt. The amino acid precursors for Maillard reactions are one component of total and soluble nitrogen. Therefore, any reduction in nitrogen can aid in reducing these reactions and in subsequent color production. Of course, these same amino acids are critical to yeast growth during fermentation, and care must be taken to maintain prefermentation levels at appropriate values.

Mash and Sparge Considerations

During mashing and sparging, concern with the extraction of husk polyphenols continues, and new concerns arise about activities that can oxidize these compounds into their color-producing form.

With regard to extraction, pH is a major issue. Increased pH enhances polyphenol extraction during mashing and sparging. Water chemistry should be evaluated to ensure that adequate calcium salts are added to offset any carbonate present in the water. Generally, mash pH should be 5.7 or lower; anything above 5.9 is clearly problematic.

As mash time increases, polyphenol extraction will rise. This indicates that mashes should be kept to a minimum schedule when color is critical. To achieve this, single infusions may be employed. An iodine test can help you to begin the mash-out as soon as possible.

Decoction mashes, because of their length and the actual boiling of a mash portion, tend to produce darker worts, although the flavor compounds produced by decoction play a key role in the character of beer styles such as bocks.[59]

Sparge conditions can also conspire to extract polyphenols from the mash. Sparges above 167 °F (75 °C) will increase polyphenol extraction, as can uncompensated alkalinity in the water. The pH of every mash will rise after a certain period of sparging. Brewers should avoid oversparging; one method is to stop collecting wort when the pH rises above 6.0.

As grain processing draws to a conclusion, concerns over polyphenol extraction come to an end. However, even before this happens, you must begin to worry about oxidizing those polyphenols that have been extracted into their color-producing form. This issue involves what is commonly referred to as hot-side aeration.

Any exposure of the mash or wort to air results in rapid uptake of oxygen by the polyphenols. Some exposure to air is inherent in the process, because it is not practical or even desirable to conduct these operations in an oxygen-free environment. The main concerns are with operations that generate unnecessary aeration during the mixing and transfer of the mash and during the collection and transfer of the wort.

Mash stirring introduces the first opportunity for hot-side aeration. In most small-scale settings stirring is done by hand. In general, stirring should be limited to the minimum required to maintain uniform and ideal mash temperatures. During this phase, brewers should stir gently and avoid splashing. Stirring should never create a vortex that sucks air into the mash.

These same concerns apply where motorized mash mixers are used. Mash mixers should turn slowly and, where possible, should be set to run periodically rather than continuously. At no time should a mash mixer create a vortex in the mash.

Any transfer between the mash tun and the lauter vessel should be done in a way that reduces splashing and the potential for drawing air. In general, such transfers should be avoided, if possible, in the home setting. In commercial breweries, lauter vessel inlets should be placed at or near the bottom of the vessel.

Aerating the hot mash and wort is an acknowledged source of color and staling compounds in beer.[60] Brewers should evaluate the procedures used from mashing to wort cooling to ensure that sources of aeration, such as splashing and overly aggressive stirring, are minimized. In advanced setups, pumps can be a source of unwanted aeration if they generate frothing in the hot wort or introduce air by cavitation. Gravity-based transfer arrangements minimize this concern — even if they are sometimes a little harder on the back.

Brewers should also take steps to reduce aeration during the collection of the wort. This requires minimization of splashing into the boil kettle and at intermediate points such as during transfer through the collection grant.

Wort Boiling and Separation

Boiling is an important step in color development for all beer and is the primary source for light beers, which may acquire fully two-thirds of their color during the boil.[61] Table 7.7 shows data on the color changes from barley to beer.

Boiling provides a good environment for development of the melanoidin compounds that constitute the primary factor in beer color. The length and vigor of the boil, as well as any subsequent standing time of the finished hot wort, contribute to formation of these products and deepening of the beer color.

Of course, vigorous boiling accomplishes a number of other goals in beer production, and generally it should not be cut down below the customary sixty to ninety minutes because of concerns over color formation.

Hops are added during the boil, and they provide another source of polyphenols that can be extracted into the wort. High wort pH will increase this extraction. If color reduction is critical, hop mass may be reduced by the use of pellets or high-alpha hop varieties, especially for the bittering hop additions. Just keep in mind the potential flavor impact of such decisions.

Caramelization can also occur to an appreciable degree during the boil. Direct-flame heating and kettle design may increase the degree of caramelization encountered in different settings. The caramelization associated with long boils is a desirable characteristic in styles such as Scotch ale, where caramelization produces a different malt flavor than that produced by crystal malts.[62]

After the boil ends, rapid cooling of the wort will also help to reduce color formation. In home settings this is best achieved through the use of an immersion chiller that quickly drops the temperature of the entire wort. This is more of an issue for commercial-sized breweries where whirlpooling requires the wort to remain hot for up to an hour after the boil is completed. Furthermore, the pumping and swirling involved will inevitably introduce additional air into the hot wort.

Despite this, delays in wort cooling may not be entirely negative with regard to color if a good hot break is formed and if a good separation of trub and wort is achieved. Break material carries color-forming compounds, so effective removal should help to reduce color slightly.

Counterflow chillers are commonly used in craft breweries and are also often

Table 7.7
Color from Barley to Beer

Sample	Color (SRM)
Barley	1.2
Malt	1.4
Wort, preboil	2.8
Wort, postboil	5.3
Beer	4.4

Source: Adapted from S. Laufer, "Factors Influencing Color of Beer and Ale," The American Brewer 74, no., 5 (1941): 20–24.

found in home setups. During the use of such chillers, a portion of the wort stands for some time before it is chilled. The key to reduced color production at this stage is appropriate sizing of the cooling system to ensure rapid processing of the knock-out volume.

Fermentation and Finishing

Color is reduced during fermentation, conditioning, and filtration primarily by precipitation or removal of color compounds[63] (see table 7.7).

Color reduction during fermentation depends upon final yeast mass, and therefore upon proper pitching rates and yeast growth. The use of an adequate starter, plus proper aeration and sufficient free amino nitrogen, should produce optimal reduction in color during fermentation. Of course, these are also the conditions required for proper management of the fermentation in any case.

The color reduction that occurs during fermentation may change with yeast strain. Fix reports that some sources claim differences in the amount of color lost during fermentation based upon the yeast strain employed.[64]

Since color compounds reside in the cold break, timely separation of your beer from the trub deposited in the primary fermenter will help to create a slightly lighter product.[65]

Also, in advanced settings, the "lightening" effects of filtering (at one micron or smaller) may result from removal of turbidity as well as of actual color pigments. A clear beer will appear lighter in color than the same beer suffering from turbidity, even though no color compounds have been removed.[66]

Some large brewers have employed activated carbon filters to remove actual pigment compounds from beer, but from a practical point of view there is little else a small brewer can affect related to lightening factors.

Predicting Beer Color During Recipe Formulation

Finished beers display colors that range from ghostly pale to opaque black. When people talk about beer styles, color plays a definite role: Each style has an ideal color range. And, when judges — or consumers — evaluate beer, color is one of the first criteria they use, whether consciously or unconsciously. All of this is evidence that color has a strong "halo" effect on the drinker's impression of the beer.

For all these reasons, it is important for the brewer to be able to predict and control the color of the finished beer. It turns out, however, that this is a tall order. As the previous sections illustrate, there are wide variations in ingredients and in the procedures that affect color. These variations are apparent not only from brewery to brewery but also from batch to batch at the same brewery. As a result of these variables, there are no tools that will allow you to predict color with accuracy. And since accuracy is what the big brewers are interested in, there is seldom any discussion of color prediction in the beer literature. Nonetheless, small brewers who routinely create new recipes need ways to evaluate the probable color of a beer before it is brewed. Let's review the few tools available to the small brewer and discuss practical applications.

The Basics: Malt Color Units

As discussed in earlier sections, malt color is but one factor that influences the finished color of a beer. Nonetheless, it is a major factor, and in most settings it will be the most variable component.

The total malt color in a recipe can be quantified fairly simply using a measure called Malt Color Units, or MCU. This calculation provides the brewer with a relative measure of the amount of color being contributed by the grains in the recipe.

For each malt, we would calculate the following:

MCU = (Lovibond rating x pounds) ÷ gallons

Where Lovibond rating equals the Lovi-bond rating as marked on the package or as supplied from a table of common values, such as table 7.8. Pounds equals the number of pounds of that grain in the recipe. Gallons equals the number of finished gallons of beer you will have in the fermenter. The MCU color for a complete recipe is the sum of the MCUs for each of the malts included in the recipe.

Thus, a 5-gallon pale ale with 8 pounds of pale malt and 2 pounds of 40 °L crystal malt would have:

Pale malt:	(8 x 2.5) ÷ 5 =	4
Crystal:	(2 x 40) ÷ 5 =	16
MCU total:		20

The use of extracts creates problems when estimating MCU, because few of the extract packages are marked as to color. Thus, we have no reliable way of assigning MCU values for most extracts. To make matters worse, tests with extracts labeled "light" and "gold" show fairly wide variation in the finished color of the beer (see table 7.9). Thus, any assumed value would be subject to fairly broad variation.

Finally, extract syrup darkens during storage due to a slow but steady progression of Maillard reactions. Thus, even extract from a single batch may develop a different color if enough time has passed since the initial use. As with most issues related to extract, your knowledge of and experience with a particular brand is the best source of information.

Making Sense of MCUs

The biggest drawback to the calculation of MCUs is that they do not correlate to any known system of color measurement. Most style specifications and published data on commercial beers give color in SRM. What brewers need is some way to correlate MCU with SRM so that they can predict the color of a finished beer before it is brewed.

Unfortunately, attempts to correlate these two measures run into the problems we have been discussing throughout this chapter. Although MCUs are an important part of color, other variables have a strong influence, especially in the range of 2 to 10 °SRM.

In an attempt to address this issue I have studied various sources and made color measurements on a range of beers for which I have recipes. The results of these studies are summarized in figure 7.8. This figure shows two lines, each derived from a different set of data that relates MCUs to SRM. The solid line is based upon published information about commercial beers; the broken line comes from data on homebrewed beers. Figure 7.8 also shows the data points used in

Table 7.8
Common Color Values for Base and Specialty Malts

Malt Type	SRM (or Lovibond)
Pilsener, lager	1.2–1.9
Pale ale	2.2–2.7
Vienna	4–6
Munich	7–14
Chocolate	300–450
Black patent	500–1100
Roasted barley	500–800
Crystal malt	10–120
CaraPils, dextrin	2–3

calculating the homebrew line. As you can see, there is considerable variation between the actual and predicted color values at most points along the scale. Thus, any use of these equations should be undertaken with caution and a clear understanding that actual results may vary considerably.

A more qualitative comparison of MCU to color may be all that is needed in most settings. Table 7.10 incorporates the information from the above equations and my studies to give a reasonable correlation of MCU to SRM color. For most craft brewers these guidelines — tempered in time with experience — will provide a practical and adequate guide to color in recipe formulation.

As with the quantitative methods, this chart is not without its imperfections. First,

you will notice some overlap between the SRM values. This is done to reflect the variability that can occur from brewer to brewer and from batch to batch. For example, if you want to target 9 to 10 °SRM, you might use as few as 8 MCUs or as many as 15. You will have to decide which end to err on based upon your overall priorities and the other parameters of the recipe.

Second, you will notice the note attached to the 1 to 10 range for MCUs and SRM. At this low end of the scale, the MCU and SRM values can be very close to each other — a recipe with 4 MCUs may give a value of almost 4 °SRM. In this range, it is ultimately the process that drives much of the color formation. If you want to make very pale beers — or if you feel that your light

Table 7.9
Variation in Color among "Light" Malt Extracts

Color	Extract brand
Pale golden	Mash of two-row European malt
Pale golden	Munton & Fisons spray-dried malt extract (Light)
Golden	Alexander's Pale malt extract syrup
Light amber	Munton & Fisons light syrup (unhopped)
Light amber	Laaglander dried malt extract
Amber	John Bull unhopped light syrup
Amber	Coopers unhopped light syrup
Amber	Northwestern malt extract syrup, gold
Amber	Northwestern malt extract — dry, gold

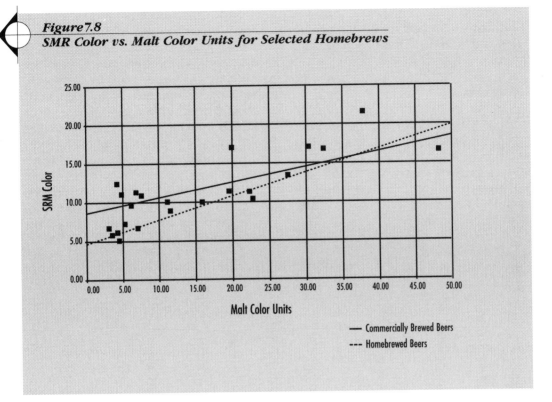

Figure 7.8
SMR Color vs. Malt Color Units for Selected Homebrews

Malt Color Units

— Commercially Brewed Beers
--- Homebrewed Beers

Table 7.10
An Approximate Correlation of SRM to MCU

MCU	SRM	Color
1–10	1–10	Pale to light amber*
11–20	8–12	Amber to dark amber
21–30	11–15	Dark amber to copper
31–40	14–17	Copper
41–50	17–20	Light brown to brown
50–85	20–30	Brown to black
>85	>30	Black to opaque

Actual color is very process-dependent.

beers are coming out darker than you would like — carefully review the process factors listed earlier in this chapter to help you achieve your objective.

Conclusion

This chapter has covered the issues relevant to understanding, predicting, and controlling beer color for small brewers. Like most of beer chemistry, the factors that determine beer color are complex and highly interdependent with other considerations in the brewing process.

Most experienced brewers develop an intuitive sense for beer color that helps to guide them in their recipe formulation decisions. However, brewers periodically face situations where they want to pay special attention to color-related issues. When these situations arise, a full understanding of the methods used for assessing and controlling color will be a valuable part of the brewer's store of knowledge. In addition, small brewers routinely formulate new recipes with the intention of achieving specific finished product characteristics. Here prediction of color becomes an important part of the overall creative process.

8 WATER

Project	Designing Great Beers
	Brewers Publications
Project No.	61766

On the face of it, water is incredibly simple stuff. But the use of water in brewing is a subject that could fill at least one book, maybe two. You'll probably be glad to hear that I don't intend to cover this subject exhaustively. A number of good sources can give you the basics about water chemistry, and I'll leave you to pursue that information as it interests you. However, note that the various minerals and salts found in water can accentuate beer flavors or contribute undesirable flavor components and therefore do contribute significant features to beer formulation. The sidebar Water: The Key Constituents briefly covers flavor issues related to water chemistry. It appears later in this chapter.

Most of this chapter focuses on two or three issues of importance in formulating a recipe. The first is determining the total quantity of brewing water you will need. Next is the issue of pH, and I will review a relatively simple calculation for predicting it in your mash. Finally, I will cover the essential calculations necessary when brewing salts are added to your water or mash.

The information on pH and salt additions will be of greatest benefit if you know the composition of your brewing water. If you have not done so previously, you should arrange to get a full analysis. Most municipal water departments will send one to you if you call and ask for it. If you are using a well or other private water source, you may have to purchase a water analysis from an independent laboratory by mail.

How Much Water Is Enough?

For years I didn't bother calculating how much water I needed for a brew. I would just heat some water, treat it, and use however much I needed. Of course, I sometimes ran short and had to quickly prepare more. I finally learned my lesson and prepared a lot of water in advance. When it came time to sparge, I just pumped and pumped water, collecting everything that came out. Then I usually had twice as much wort as I needed. This led to long boils and wasted time and energy.

I learned at last how to calculate the amount of water I would actually need. This saves time by making the whole brewing process more efficient. Then, too, I can calculate my water-salt additions in advance to match the quantity of water. All of this avoids confusion and crisis and makes the brewing day a lot more pleasant.

Those are some pretty good reasons for calculating water quantity. But if you're like me, you just won't do it if it is too complicated. Let's see if I can keep it simple.

The total quantity of water you need for brewing includes five variables. The first one is the finished beer! If you are making 5 gallons of beer, you've got to use at least 5 gallons of water. Beyond the final wort volume, all the other water you add is lost somewhere in the process. Generally, these losses can be categorized into four areas. They are:

• water trapped in the spent grains
• water evaporated during the boil
• water left behind in equipment, hoses, etc.
• shrinkage of the hot wort as it cools

Let's go through each of these items, discussing how each would be calculated, before I provide an overall example.

During mashing, the grains absorb a lot of water that cannot be drained out in the lauter tun. As it turns out, the weight of the water trapped in the grains is predictable. The total weight of the spent grain mass is 20 percent grain and 80 percent water.

Simple, right? The only thing you have to remember is that the weight of the grain after mashing is *not* the same as the weight of the grain that went into the mash. During mashing, sugar and protein is extracted from the grains, and that leaves them as shadows of their former selves. Although you can calculate this more precisely for

each batch if you really want to, it is safe to assume that the postmash grain mass is about 40 percent of the weight of the grain you added.[1]

So, if you mash 10 pounds of grain, it will weigh about 4 pounds when you are finished. Since this 4 pounds is 20 percent of the weight of the spent grains, the weight of the water will equal four times the weight of the grain (80 percent divided by 20 percent equals 4). Thus, you will lose 4×4 pounds, or 16 pounds, of water in the spent grains. Since water weighs about 8 pounds per gallon, this equals 2 gallons.

After you do this calculation once or twice, it can become second nature. But I know that many people don't get to brew as often as they would like, so table 8.1 indicates water loss based upon the weight of the mashed grain. If you work with larger amounts of grain (or simply prefer to use an equation rather than a table), you can use the following equations to predict the amount of water retained by the grains.

Grain weight in lbs. x 0.2 = *Gallons* of water retained by grains

Grain weight in lbs. x 0.0064 = *Barrels* of water retained by grains

Table 8.1
Gallons of Water Lost in Spent Grains

Pounds of Grain Mashed	Gallons of Water Lost	Pounds of Grain Mashed	Gallons of Water Lost
3	0.675	15	3.250
4	0.875	16	3.500
5	1.000	17	3.675
6	1.300	18	4.000
7	1.500	19	4.125
8	1.750	20	4.330
9	2.000	21	4.500
10	2.125	22	4.750
11	2.375	23	5.000
12	2.500	24	5.250
13	2.750	25	5.500
14	3.000		

Evaporation losses are usually calculated on the basis of an accepted hourly rate of evaporation, multiplied by the length of the boil. For homebrewers, this can vary rather widely depending upon the amount of wort boiled and the heat source used. If you want a more exact number to represent water loss due to evaporation, you can perform an experiment to determine the actual rate of evaporation on your system. In the meantime, you can work with the figure of 5 percent per hour, which is based upon the experience of large breweries.[2]

By the way, if you plan a decoction mash, don't forget to figure in some additional water to account for evaporation during the boiling parts of the decoction.

The amount of water left in equipment is a figure you can probably determine on a one-time basis. This is the stuff left in the bottom of a vessel, in tubing, or mixed up with debris that you can't move to the next step in the process. In many homebrew setups this number is pretty close to zero. But before you assume that, think about your process step by step, remembering where you find leftover liquid as you go through a brew. In larger setups, you may want to collect all your losses during one brew in order to develop a good estimate of this number.

In my homebrew setup there are two main areas of water loss. First, my mash/lauter tun has a substantial dead space below the wort outlet, which accounts for about ½ gallon of loss during each brew. Next, I lose about 2 quarts of sparge water in the holding bucket that I pump from and in the tubing that runs to the mash tun. Based on these two sources of water loss, I add an extra gallon to my water needs for every batch.

We also need to account for losses in trub and hop debris, but here it makes more sense to adjust the volume you target at the end of the boil. Although my fermenters are generally 5-gallon carboys, I try to hit 5.5 to 6 gallons at the end of the boil. This way, when the wort is chilled and I have siphoned the clear wort off the trub and hop debris, I get the right amount of wort to fill my fermenter. This explains why I generally formulate my recipes as a 5.5- or 6-gallon batch size.

Finally, shrinkage accounts for some water loss. This is the change in density, and therefore volume, when water cools from boiling to 68 °F (20 °C). This value is 4 percent.

Now that I have accounted for all the types of water loss, let's calculate the total volume of water required for 5 gallons of pale ale made with 8.5 pounds of grain. My target final volume is 5.5 gallons at the end of a ninety-minute boil.

Batch size:	5 gallons
Final boil volume:	5.5 gallons
	(Trub and hop debris losses.)
Shrinkage:	Divide by 0.96
	(Shrinkage during cooling.)
Evaporation:	Divide by 0.925
	[1 – (evap. rate x boil length)]
Equals:	
Runoff volume:	6.2 gallons
	(Volume in kettle when boil starts.)
Equipment losses:	Add 1 gallon
	(System value.)
Spent grain:	Add 1.875
	(From table 8.1.)
Total water required:	9.075 gallons

Once you have this figure, you can easily determine the distribution between mashing and sparging: Multiply your grain weight by the ratio of water with which you will mash. In this case, I'll use 1.33 quarts/pound, which equals 2.8 gallons of mash water. If your mash tun has a false bottom, as mine does, you'll need to add enough water to fill the space below the false bottom.

In my case, this volume is 1 gallon, so I would use 3.8 gallons of water in the mash process. The remainder of the water — about 5.25 gallons in this case — will be needed for sparging in order to ensure that I get adequate volume in the boil kettle.

This procedure is really quite simple and will prevent a lot of confusion during brewing. To make it as easy as possible, I have included a blank work sheet at the end of this chapter.

Predicting Mash pH

As was mentioned earlier, the subject of water chemistry is too vast to get into here. Indeed, the subject of pH alone is too large to tackle in any depth. What I do want to pass along is an equation that can be used to evaluate your likely mash pH based upon simple information about your water supply. It not only allows you to predict but also to adjust this parameter without worrying about other aspects of the water. Let's start with just one paragraph of "theory."

Brewing chemists recognize that three compounds commonly found in water affect mash pH. The first is bicarbonate (HCO_3^-), often referred to as temporary hardness, or alkalinity. This raises the pH of the water. Two other ions, specifically calcium (Ca^{++}) and magnesium (Mg^{++}) serve to lower the pH. Even though there are a lot of other charged particles in water, their changing concentrations have no noticeable effect on mash pH

The effects of these three components on pH were integrated by Kolbach into an equation for residual alkalinity.[3] Using this tool, we can predict the likely pH of a mash. In practice, residual alkalinity allows us to determine how much the pH of our mash will differ from a mash made with distilled water — that is, water with no bicarbonate, calcium, or magnesium ions.

The equation requires inputs available from a water analysis and expressed in parts per million (ppm), which is equal to

milligrams per liter (mg/L). Once residual alkalinity is calculated, it must be converted to a relative pH value. Basically, 10 degrees of residual alkalinity (degrees of German hardness, to be exact) equals 0.3 pH unit.

The equation starts with the mash pH achieved with distilled water (pH 5.8) and then adjusts it for the effects of the three constituents. When all this is combined into one equation for expected pH, it looks like this:

Full Equation: $pH = 5.8 + (0.028 \times [(\text{Total Alk}_{(ppm\ CaCO_3)} \times 0.056) - (Ca_{(ppm\ Ca)} \times 0.04) - (Mg_{(ppm\ Mg)} \times 0.033)])$

At the end of this chapter is a worksheet that takes you through each of these steps.

When I calculate this equation for Chicago tap water, I get a value of 5.9. In actual experience this is the value I usually measure, although it sometimes dips to 5.8 or rises to 6.0.

The recommended value for mash pH is in the range of 5.8 to 5.2,[4] and I generally try to shoot for around 5.5. The expected pH value for Chicago water tells me that if I just mash pale malt, I'm going to be way off the mark.

You can apply this equation to your own water to determine your expected mash pH. You will then have some idea of how much attention needs to be paid to pH adjustment during brewing.

Correcting pH

Three possible actions can be taken to correct mash pH. They are: specialty grain additions, calcium and magnesium salt additions, and using other water treatments.

Even in fairly modest amounts, specialty malts (crystal, roast, etc.) can drop the pH up to 0.5. In my experience, if 10 percent of the grist is crystal malt, the mash pH drops by 0.3. At 20 percent, the pH drops by 0.5. Many recipes have enough specialty malt that I don't need to worry about further reductions of the mash pH.

For lighter-colored beers, the use of calcium salts such as calcium sulfate and (my favorite) calcium chloride can help to adjust the pH. Using the calculations shown in the section on salts, calculate the parts per million of calcium being added by the salt and add this figure to the amount of calcium in your water in the equation for predicting mash pH. This will give you a good idea of the impact of the salt addition on pH.

Finally, if you are desperately off the mark on your desired mash pH, you may have to take some other measures to get your pH where it should be. I would recommend that you consider changing your source water in some way, either by diluting it with distilled water or by boiling it to remove some alkalinity. If these measures fail, you may add some food-grade acid to the mash — but go easy, the stuff is usually quite concentrated, and it is easy to add too much.

Salt Additions

In part two of this book, I discuss the levels of various water ions commonly found in examples of the classic beer styles. In addition, you can see from the sidebar on key water constituents that most water salts may have an impact on flavor depending on their concentration in a beer.

To adjust the quantities of different ions for specific brews, you may want to add brewing salts. The most common one is gypsum or calcium sulfate. Others include calcium chloride, magnesium sulfate, sodium chloride, and calcium carbonate.

Because salts play an important role in recipe formulation, this section discusses the correct ways to calculate the amount of each ion that is added when individual brewing salts are used. As you begin the calculations, it is important to remember two points: (1) the concentration of the individual ions is not equal to the concentration of the overall salt, and (2) parts per million (ppm) is equal to milligrams per liter (mg/L).

1. *The concentration of the individual ions is not equal to the concentration of the overall salt.* For instance, if you add 100 parts per million of gypsum to your beer, you do not get 100 parts per million of calcium as a result. Calcium represents only a fraction of the total weight of gypsum, so the parts per million of calcium added will be a fraction of the total salt added. Table 8.2 shows the percentage represented by each ion in each of the major salts.

2. *Parts per million (ppm) is equal to milligrams per liter (mg/L).* This provides the linkage between the way you talk about water (ppm) and the way you measure water salts (milligrams).

Let's solve a problem using this knowledge. If I am brewing the pale ale from the

Table 8.2
Water Salts and Their Ions

Common Name	Scientific Name	Molecular Formula	Weight	Major Ions (% of Total Molecular Weight)	
Gypsum	Calcium Sulfate	$CaSO_4 \cdot 2H_2O$	172	Ca = 23%	SO_4 = 56%
	Calcium Chloride	$CaCl_2 \cdot 2H_2O$	146	Ca = 27%	Cl = 48%
Epsom salts	Magnesium Sulfate	$MgSO_4 \cdot 7H_2O$	246	Mg = 10%	SO_4 = 39%
Chalk	Calcium Carbonate	$CaCO_3$	100	Ca = 40%	CO_3 = 60%
Table salt[a]	Sodium Chloride	NaCl	58	Na = 40%	Cl = 60%

[a] *Any table salt used in beer should be noniodized. Try the rock salt that is sold for making homemade ice cream.*

Table 8.3
Concentrations Produced by Salt Additions

Salt Addition	Ion Concentrations (ppm)							
	Calcium, when added to:				Sulfate, when added to:			
Gypsum	2.5 gal.	5 gal.	7.5 gal.	10 gal.	2.5 gal.	5 gal.	7.5 gal.	10 gal.
0.25 oz. (7 grams)	169	85	57	43	413	207	138	104
0.5 oz. (14 grams)	339	170	113	85	825	415	276	207
0.75 oz. (21 grams)	508	256	170	128	1238	622	414	311
1 oz. (28 grams)	678	341	227	170	1651	830	552	415
	Calcium, when added to:				Choride, when added to:			
Calcium Chloride	2.5 gal.	5 gal.	7.5 gal.	10 gal.	2.5 gal.	5 gal.	7.5 gal.	10 gal.
0.25 oz. (7 grams)	199	100	67	50	354	178	118	89
0.5 oz. (14 grams)	398	200	133	100	707	356	237	178
0.75 oz. (21 grams)	597	300	200	150	1061	533	355	267
1 oz. (28 grams)	796	400	266	200	1415	711	473	356
	Magnesium, when added to:				Sulfate, when added to:			
Epsom Salts	2.5 gal.	5 gal.	7.5 gal.	10 gal.	2.5 gal.	5 gal.	7.5 gal.	10 gal.
0.25 oz. (7 grams)	74	37	25	19	287	144	96	72
0.5 oz. (14 grams)	147	74	49	37	575	289	192	144
0.75 oz. (21 grams)	221	111	74	56	862	433	288	217
1 oz. (28 grams)	295	148	99	74	1149	578	385	289
	Sodium, when added to:				Chloride, when added to:			
Table Salt[a]	2.5 gal.	5 gal.	7.5 gal.	10 gal.	2.5 gal.	5 gal.	7.5 gal.	10 gal.
1 grams	42	21	14	11	63	32	21	16
3 grams	126	63	42	32	189	95	63	48
5 grams	221	106	70	53	316	159	106	79
25 oz. (7 grams)	295	148	99	74	442	222	148	111
	Calcium, when added to:				Carbonate, when added to:			
Chalk	2.5 gal.	5 gal.	7.5 gal.	10 gal.	2.5 gal.	5 gal.	7.5 gal.	10 gal.
1 gram	42	21	14	11	63	32	21	16
3 grams	126	63	42	32	189	95	63	48
5 grams	211	106	70	53	316	159	106	79
25 oz. (7 grams)	295	148	99	74	442	222	148	111

Shaded boxes indicate concentrations that may give negative flavor effects.
[a] Any table salt used in beer must be noniodized.
Note: ppm = parts per million, also mg/L.

previous example and I want to add 100 parts per million of calcium, how much gypsum should I add? Remember that the pale ale recipe calls for 9.075 gallons of water.

I want to add 100 parts per million, which is equal to 100 milligrams per liter. If I multiply this by the number of liters of water I need to treat, I will know the weight of calcium that is required.

9.075 gal. = 34.4 L

34.4 L x 100 mg/L = 3,440 mg of calcium required

To determine the amount of gypsum required, divide by the calcium ion percentage in gypsum, which is 23 percent (from table 8.2).

3,440 mg ÷ 0.23 = 14,956 mg

And since 1,000 mg equals 1 gram, this equals about 15 grams, or about ½ ounce.

You can also calculate this from the other direction. For instance, you may wonder how many parts per million of chloride would be added if 1 ounce of calcium chloride was added to 5 gallons of water.

One ounce equals 28.3 grams, or 28,350 milligrams, and 5 gallons equals 18.9 liters. Therefore, I have added 1,500 ppm (28,350 mg ÷ 18.9 L) of calcium chloride to this water.

Since chloride equals 48 percent of the calcium chloride molecular weight, I have added 720 ppm (1,500 x 0.48) of chloride. (That's a lot!)

To make this process a bit easier, table 8.3 shows the ion concentrations that result from various salt additions to various volumes of brewing water.

The ultimate purpose of salt additions is to match your brewing water to that of some classic brewing center such as Munich, Pilsen, or Burton. Though such calculations may seem tedious, the good news is that you only have to do them once. Unless your source water varies a lot, you can develop a water treatment plan for each classic water type and then use it over and over again in your recipes.

Water: The Key Constituents

H_2O: This is water, pure and unblemished. Such a pure form is not found in nature.

Ca: Calcium. Primary contributor to hardness of water. It also plays a critical role in mashing and brewing chemistry. For flavor purposes, acceptable levels are 5 to 200 parts per million.

Mg: Magnesium. The secondary mineral of hardness. It is an enzyme cofactor and yeast nutrient. Accentuates beer flavor at 10 to 30 parts per million and contributes astringent bitterness when present in excess. If present in quantities of more than 125 parts per million, it is a diuretic and cathartic.

Na: Sodium. Contributes sour salty taste that can accentuate beer flavors at reasonable levels. Poisonous to yeast and harsh-tasting when in excess. Usual levels are 2 to 100 parts per million.

Fe: Iron. Contributes metallic, bloodlike, or inky flavor. Levels should be less than 0.3 parts per million.

HCO_3^-: Bicarbonate or carbonate (CO_3^{-2}). Usually expressed as alkalinity in water reports. It is a strong alkaline buffer, which raises pH. Contributes harsh, bitter flavor.

SO_4: Sulfate. Produces a dry, fuller flavor, some sharpness. It is strongly bitter above 500 parts per million but is characteristic of some British ales.

Cl: Chloride. As part of table salt (NaCl), chloride enhances beer flavor and palate fullness. It increases perception of sweetness, or mellowness. Increases beer stability and improves clarity. Usual levels are 1 to 100 parts per million in light beers. Can go up to 350 parts per million in beers greater than 1.050 in gravity.

pH: A twelve-point log scale that measures the acidity or alkalinity of a solution. A 7 is neutral or balanced. Lower numbers (1–6) are acidic; higher numbers (8–12) are alkaline, or basic.

Hardness: Expressed as total ions contributing to hardness. Hardness minus alkalinity equals permanent hardness.

Chlorine: The hydrated, or dissolved, form (HOCl) is used to help sanitize public water supplies. This stuff is bad news in beer. It can impart a swimming-pool-like flavor or smell to a finished brew, can corrode stainless steel equipment, and can combine with organic substances to produce plasticlike or medicinal chlorine-phenol complexes.

Sidebar: Residual Hardness Worksheet Full Equation

Full Equation: 5.8 + (0.028 x [(Total Alk$_{(ppm\ CaCO_3)}$ x 0.056) – (Ca$_{(ppm\ Ca)}$ x 0.04) – (Mg$_{(ppm\ Mg)}$ x 0.033)])

To complete this calculation for any water, begin by providing the appropriate values for each constituent in column A as described below.

	A	B
Total alkalinity in ppm or mg/L of CaCO₃:	_____ x 0.056 =	_____ (1)
Calcium content in ppm or mg/L of Ca:	_____ x –0.04 =	_____ (2)
Magnesium content in ppm or mg/L of Mg:	_____ x –0.033 =	_____ (3)

Sum of column B, lines (1), (2), and (3): _____ (4)

Multiply line 4 by 0.028: x 0.028 =

pH adjustment value (product of line (4) x 0.028): _____ (5)

Add to the mash pH achieved with distilled water: + 5.8 =

Mash pH predicted with your water (sum of line (5) + 5.8) : _____ (6)

Water Volume Calculation Worksheet

Batch size:	_____ gallons	
Trub and hop debris losses; add:	_____ gallon	*(0.5 to 1 gallon)*
Final boil volume:	_____ gallons	*(trub and hop debris losses)*
Shrinkage;	divide by 0.96	*(accounts for 4% shrinkage)*
Evaporation; divide by:	_____	*(= 1 – [evap. rate × boil length])*
Equals runoff volume:	_____ gallons	*(volume when boil starts)*
Equipment losses: add	_____ gallon	*(your system value)*
Spent grain losses: add	_____ gallon	*(from table 8.1)*
Total water required:	_____ gallons	

9 USING HOPS AND HOP BITTERNESS

Project	Designing Great Beers
	Brewers Publications
Project No.	61766

Although beer (or something like it) has been around for five or six thousand years, the use of hops is a relatively new feature of our favorite beverage, dating back only five hundred years or so.

Before hops were applied to the making of beer, brewers used a variety of plants, herbs, and potions to counter the sweetness of fermented malt beverages. At one point, a substance called "gruit" was used. It contained a secret mixture of herbs and spices known only to the nobles who controlled the making of beer. (There is more on this subject in chapter 14.)

Although the first recorded use of hops was in A.D. 736, they didn't really catch on as a regular ingredient in beer until the 1500s.[1] After some initial skirmishes over their adoption, hops became widely accepted, and now they constitute part of the definition of beer.

Hops are a wonderful resource for the brewer. They provide bitterness to counteract the sweetness of malt, thus making the beverage more palatable. They also provide some antibacterial properties that at one time increased the safety and potability of beer. Today this quality still aids in the preservation of beer. And hops contribute to head stabilization and kettle break formation.[2]

Hops also contribute more than just bitterness. Although it seems almost incred-ible that a single element of one plant could do so much, hops also contribute appealing flavors and aromas to beer when handled in the proper way by the brewer.

Beyond the variety of flavors that can be created with hops, one must also consider the many varieties of hops available — each with a different overall effect when used in various ways. Given the dozens of varieties already available and the many new hops being bred, it becomes clear that hops are indeed a source of tremendous richness and variety in beer flavor.

If you make "American Pilsener" for one of the big brewers, this diversity of hop choices may be more of a curse than a blessing — variety and consistency do not go hand in hand. But for home- and craft brewers, the diverse selection of available hops offers new opportunities to explore, experiment, and create wonderful beers.

As usual, whether you are trying to match your favorite commercial beer or just exploring the effects of some new variety of hops, it helps to know something about how hops affect the flavor of beer. Both chemically and in practice we can divide the effects of hops into two areas: (1) bittering, and (2) flavor and aroma. In the chapters that follow, I explore the use of hops for these purposes. In each case, I discuss how hops contribute their effects and issues pertaining to the selection of hops for a specific purpose. Finally, I present a detailed practical discussion of how hops are used for each application, including methods for quantifying the effects of your hops. We will begin in this chapter by considering the issues related to hop bitterness.

Hop Bitterness

Hops are the green flowers of a vine known as *Humulus lupulus*. In the United States, hops grow primarily in the northwest states of Washington, Oregon, and Idaho, with much of the crop focused in the Yakima Valley of Washington. They grow on wire trellises reaching 18 feet into the air. In August and September, when they are harvested, the vines are cut and brought to the grower's processing facility. Machinery plucks the hop cones from the vines and sorts them from leaves and other debris before sending them to huge drying houses. There, warm air is passed through the hops for up to twenty-four hours to remove the majority of the moisture from them. These dried hops are then baled and sent to hop brokers for distribution. The dried hops consist of a number of elements, as shown in table 9.1.

When it comes to the bittering character of hops, brewers are most interested in the total resins, which can be further characterized as soft and hard resins (see figure 9.1).

The alpha acids that appear in the soft-resin portion of the hop are of greatest interest to brewers because they provide the bulk of the bittering properties. The alpha acids include three specific compounds: humulone, cohumulone, and adhumulone.

During wort boiling, these alpha acids undergo a structural change known as *isomerization* to create the bittering compounds found in finished beers. These bittering compounds are known collectively as iso-alpha acids. Chemically, there is one for each of the original alpha acids: iso-humulone, iso-cohumulone, and iso-adhumulone.

The beta acids can also undergo isomerization during the boil to form bittering compounds, but in practice they contribute little to the bittering of most beers because they are poorly soluble in wort. In addition, other soft and hard resins can contribute bitter characteristics, even though their potency is a third to a tenth of that found in the iso-alpha acids.[3] Because alpha acids deteriorate during storage, these secondary bittering compounds can begin to play a more important role with aged hops.

The production of bittering iso-alpha acids during brewing is generally proportional to the amount of total alpha acids present in the hops added to a recipe. However, the quantity of alpha acids in a hop can vary considerably, from as low as

Table 9.1
Composition of Hops

Hops Components	Percentage
Vegetative material (cellulose, lignin, etc.)	40
Proteins	15 (0.1 amino acids)
Total resins	15
Water	10
Ash	8
Lipids, wax, pectin	5
Tannins	4
Monosaccharides	2
Essential oils	0.5–2

Figure 9.1
Profile of Hop Resins

I. Soft Resins
        A. Alpha acids (2% to 16% of total hop weight)
            1. Humulone
            2. Cohumulone
            3. Adhumulone
        B. Beta acids: lupulone, colupulone and adlupulone
        C. Uncharacterized soft resins
II. Hard Resins

2 percent to nearly 16 percent of the total weight of the hop.

This variation in alpha acids of 2 to 16 percent could occur between hop varieties, within a single variety from year to year, and between regions and growers in the same year depending upon agricultural conditions. Perhaps the only predictable thing about alpha acids is that their range within a specific hop variety is somewhat limited and generally characteristic of the variety. For instance, Tettnanger hops usually fall near the range of 4 to 5 percent, and Chinook hops generally run around the 12 to 14 percent range. (Figure 9.2 shows the characteristic alpha acid levels of a number of common hop varieties.)

When buying hops, you have probably noticed that the label includes a statement of the alpha acid content. If you don't see the alpha acids stated on the label, or if only a range is given, you would be well advised to buy your hops elsewhere. Alpha acid content is a critical part of producing a beer with a known character; it is the starting point for formulating a recipe that will meet your expectations with regard to total bitterness.

Bitterness in Beer

The bitterness in a finished beer is measured by a system of International Bitterness Units, or IBUs. Often, you will see this referred to simply as BUs.

The IBU is a measure of the concentration of iso-alpha acids, in parts per million, in the finished beer. Specifically, one IBU is equal to 1 milligram of iso-alpha acid per liter of beer. In practice, brewers drop all references to weight and quantity and just talk about the BUs in a beer.

American "light" lagers generally have the lowest BU levels of most commercially produced beers, with values in the 8 to 12 IBU range — very close to the taste threshold for bitterness.[4] By contrast, English pale ales may have up to 45 IBU in beers of about the same gravity as many American lagers.[5]

Of course, the bigger the beer, the more malt sweetness there is to be balanced. Thus, in high-gravity beers, you can see much higher bitterness levels, sometimes reaching up into the 80 to 100 IBU range for imperial stouts and barley wines.

Other methods for quantifying hop bitterness have been used in the brewing literature, including homebrewers bittering units (HBU) and alpha acid units (AAU). The sidebar at the end of this chapter discusses the meaning of these terms and their conversion into IBU.

As I have mentioned, beer styles can be characterized by a number of parameters; one is the level of bitterness found in the finished beer. Table 9.2 gives the typical bitterness levels for a number of beer styles. In addition, I discuss the bitterness levels appropriate for each style in part two of this book.

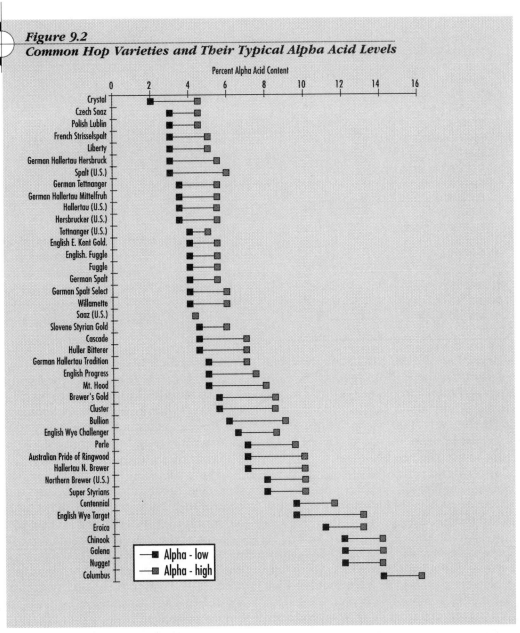

Figure 9.2
Common Hop Varieties and Their Typical Alpha Acid Levels

Controlling Bitterness in Beers

From available style information, you can get an idea of how many IBU should be present in the finished beer. For instance, if you are going to make a Bohemian Pilsener, you know that you will need about 35 to 45 IBU of bitterness. The question is how to go about achieving this goal.

Later in this chapter I review equations that can be used to estimate the IBUs you will achieve in a beer. However, the results that the equations provide are just *estimates*. More than a dozen factors affect the translation of alpha acids in hops into iso-alpha acids in finished beer. Thus, in reality no equation or set of equations can tell you the exact IBU level you have

Table 9.2

Bitterness Levels for Some Classic Beer Styles

Barley Wine	50 – 100	Classic Dry Stout	30 – 40
English Brown Ale	15 – 25	Sweet Stout	15 – 25
American Brown Ale	25 – 60	Bock	20 – 30
Mild Ale	10 – 24	Dopplebock	17 – 27
English Pale Ale	20 – 40	Munich Dunkel	16 – 25
India Pale Ale	40 – 60	Schwarzbier	22 – 30
American Pale Ale	20 – 40	Dortmund/Export	23 – 29
American Wheat	05 – 17	Munich Helles	18 – 25
English Bitter	20 – 35	Bohemian Pilsener	30 – 40
English Special	28 – 46	German Pilsener	35 – 45
English Extra Special	30 – 55	Vienna	22 – 28
Scottish Light	09 – 20	Märzen/Oktoberfest	22 – 28
Scottish Heavy	12 – 20	Altbier	25 – 48
Scottish Export	15 – 25	Kölsch	20 – 30
Porter	20 – 40	California Common	35 – 45
English Old Ale	25 – 40	Weizen	10 – 15
Strong Scotch Ale	25 – 35		

achieved in your beer. This same problem plagues the use of HBU and AAU. Even if they add the same amount of alpha acids, two different brewers are likely to get very different levels of IBU in the finished beers.

Despite shortcomings in the methods used to quantify hop bitterness, we still use them because we have few other options. Still, it is important to remember that the calculations produce estimates and not actual IBU measurements.

To really know the level of bitterness present in a beer, you must have a laboratory analysis performed. In large-scale brewing, laboratory analysis of IBUs is a common tool for the brewer. But this is only the beginning of the steps that must be taken to hit the IBU specification for a finished beer.

At the beginning of a new hop crop (or a new recipe), the amount of hops needed to achieve the desired IBU level is set based upon test batches made in the pilot brewery. Then, to ensure consistency, the big brewers purchase huge lots of hops and blend them to provide a uniform source over the course of a year. Furthermore, virtually all big brewers blend beer

from different fermenters before bottling. This allows them to even out the fluctuations in bitterness from batch to batch so that every gallon is virtually identical. Finally, they might add liquid hop preparations containing concentrated iso-alpha acids to further adjust the bitterness.

Using all these techniques, all this work, and all this money, the big guys only control their bitterness to within plus or minus 2 IBU![6] Given that the average level of bitterness might be something like 15 IBUs, that represents an allowable variation of 13 percent in the bitterness of the product. The reason they don't sweat over the IBU inside that range is because the human palate can't detect the difference. Studies have shown that the detection threshold for bitterness is about 5 IBU.[7] And that is for beers in the 10 to 15 IBU range. Among home and craft brewers, the sensitivity is usually even *less* because we are used to more bitter beers.[8]

Of course home and craft brewers rarely have the luxury of running a laboratory analysis on a finished beer. Furthermore, the practice of blending is seldom seen, and ingredients often vary widely from batch to batch. As a result, small brewers cannot hope to achieve the level of accuracy or reproducibility seen in mass-produced beers. The first time you brew a recipe you are lucky to hit within 5 BUs of your target bitterness.

Fortunately for the small brewer, the palate's poor sensitivity to bitterness and the brewer's inability to control it closely pretty much cancel each other out. Thus, if you adopt a *consistent* brewing process that minimizes variation in the factors influencing bitterness, you can produce beers that fall close enough to your desired target that neither you nor any consumer or judge will be able to tell the difference.

Factors Affecting IBU Levels

Unfortunately, not all the alpha acids added to beer show up in the finished product as bittering iso-alpha acids. The majority are lost during the brewing process due to their limited solubility in wort and the slow rate of isomerization. "Utilization" is the term used to describe the extent to which this conversion of alpha acids to iso-alpha acids takes place. Typical utilization values range from 0 to 40 percent depending upon a variety of circumstances.

Small brewers tend to think of utilization in terms of each individual hop addition. Some folks from big breweries don't understand this. They use a single utilization factor for all hop additions, no matter how long the boil. They can afford to do this because they don't rely on their calculations to control hop bitterness in the way small brewers do. In addition, they don't often use the levels of finishing hops employed by craft brewers. There is a wide variation in utilization by hop addition, from 0 percent for dry hopping[9] to greater than 35 percent for long-boiled bittering hops.

In the last section I emphasized the need for a consistent brewing process if you want to accurately predict IBUs. In my own experiments I have seen the hop utilization for a sixty-minute boil vary by as much as 100 percent — from 17 percent in one case to 35 percent in another — when measured by laboratory analysis. The differences were attributable almost entirely to process factors, most of which can be identified but not entirely quantified. Thus, any use of calculations to predict IBUs must be preceded by an understanding of the factors that may influence your actual results. This section reviews these factors.

In considering the issue of IBUs, it is important to remember that this is a measure of the *concentration* of iso-alpha acids in your beer. As such, it is very much dependent upon accurate measurement of your hops and your finished volume of beer.

First, you have to hit the final volume of your wort accurately. This means having some form of measurement in place, whether it be a calibrated brew pot or just marks on a fermenter showing the volume at various levels. After all, if you are just guessing, you're likely to be off by ¼ to ½ gallon (or barrel), and that is a 5 to 10 percent error right there.

A hop scale can make a big difference, too. Spring-type kitchen scales are fairly inaccurate when measuring hops at one ounce or less, with errors of up to 50 percent possible. Use of a digital scale that reads in hundredths of an ounce (0.01), or tenths of a gram, will provide much greater accuracy.

The bottom line on these kinds of things is not that you should go out and spend a couple hundred dollars on new equipment just to improve the accuracy of your efforts. The real point is to keep in mind the variation introduced by these factors and remember that the accuracy of your calculations begins to erode immediately if you don't pay attention to careful measurement during the brewing process.

Let's look at the process factors that affect utilization. The biggest influence may be the length of time the hops are boiled.

At a ten-minute boil, you get about 10 percent utilization; at sixty minutes, you get in the neighborhood of 30 percent. Values for times in between these two vary in a non-linear manner (see figure 9.4).

Another potential influence on alpha acid utilization is the deterioration of the alpha acids by aging during storage. In a small number of hop varieties the actual alpha acid content may be 50 percent *less* than it was at the time of harvest if the hops are stored improperly. Deterioration is re-tarded by oxygen-barrier packaging and cold storage. When these practices are followed, the actual deterioration during the course of a year will be less than 25 percent for most hops, and therefore, I believe, not worth worrying about. (This issue is discussed in greater detail at the end of this chapter.)

The form of hops used (whole or pellets) is believed to play a role in utilization. During pellet manufacturing, the hops are crushed and subjected to some oxidation and heating, and these factors may affect the speed of isomerization. In addition, when added to boiling wort, pellets rapidly dissolve into small pieces that make the alpha acids readily available for isomerization.

Depending upon which authority you consult, the difference in utilization between whole hops and pellet products may range from 25 percent to undetectable. Based upon a limited number of data points, my own experimental data indicate that a significant difference does occur.

The gravity of the wort in the boil pot also has an effect on utilization. Generally, higher-gravity beers show lower levels of utilization. The difference in utilization between a 1.040 wort and one at 1.080 can be as much as 15 percent. Given that the hop levels for a 1.080 beer may go up to 60 or even 80, a 15 percent difference would amount to 10 IBU.

In a similar vein, as you add increasing amounts of hops to the boil, utilization levels drop. This happens because the solubility of alpha acids in wort is limited. Once you reach a certain level, the addition of more hops achieves less and less.

Although wort pH doesn't appear to dramatically affect production of iso-alpha acids, a high pH can affect the perception of bitterness in the beer. High-pH worts produce a harsh bitterness that increases perceived bitterness and that most people find objectionable. If your water has a high pH (>7.5) or significant carbonate levels (above 50 parts per million), you may see this effect.

A number of factors that can affect hop utilization are related to the kettle boil. Many of these factors are difficult to quantify, such as the vigor of the boil, the extent of hot and cold break, and even the shape of the boil vessel. All affect utilization to some extent. Because these factors are very specific to individual brewing setups, they have not been quantified in the brewing literature.

Two other factors related to boil conditions have been quantified. First, because water boils at a lower temperature at higher elevations, altitude must be considered if you are brewing above 3,000 feet or so. Second, the vigor with which your hops are boiled will be reduced if you use a hop bag, and thus utilization will decrease.

Fermentation factors can affect the amount of iso-alpha acids that remain in finished beer in a number of ways. Many have to do with yeast, which plays a role in precipitating iso-alpha acids from the beer. The amount of yeast pitched and the extent of yeast growth during fermentation affect this precipitation. For instance, one source indicates that a variation of 50 percent in the yeast pitching rate (a common occurrence with small brewers) can produce a change of up to 40 percent in the final bitterness of the beer.[10]

This effect may be linked to yeast growth, which is affected not only by pitching rate but by the original gravity of the wort, the levels of nitrogen nutrients present, the extent of aeration before pitching, and the temperature of the fermentation.

Other factors during fermentation may also affect the loss of bitterness. If you use a blowoff tube or skim the kraeusen off your beer during fermentation, you can lose as much as 15 percent of the IBU.[11] Also, the separation of trub and spent hops from the wort prior to fermentation will have an impact.

After fermentation, aging and clarification practices will affect the extent to which not only bitterness but also other hop components will survive into finished beer. Any filtration will remove some bitterness and flavor components. For small commercial brewers, changes in filtration technique or media can change the extent of such removals and may require reformulation of proven recipes. The addition of clarifying agents such as gelatin or PVPP may have a similar effect.

If this litany of variables tempts you to throw up your hands in despair, don't. I mention all these factors not to discourage you but to make sure you understand that a lot of things other than your calculations can have an impact on bitterness. You can still do a good job of estimating and brewing to a target bitterness level. But when you do have a batch of beer that seems significantly off target, you should know to look at these other factors and not just for errors in your calculations.

Calculating Bitterness Units: The Simple Approach

International bitterness units are expressed as the parts per million of iso-alpha acid that occur in beer. In metric units, this conveniently works out to be the number of milligrams (mg) per liter.

We can easily determine the amount of alpha acid added to each beer just by multiplying the weight of hops added by the alpha acid percentage. To find the amount that winds up in the finished beer we just multiply this by a utilization rate. Thus, a basic equation for determining IBU is simple.

What is more difficult is determining the proper utilization factor. Simply stated, utilization tells us what percent of the alpha acids added appear as iso-alpha acids in the finished beer. The real trick to accurately estimating the IBUs you will get from a recipe comes in using the proper utilization factor in your calculations. A later section of this chapter discusses this issue in detail.

The basic equation for estimating the IBU you will get from a recipe is shown below. Since IBUs are equal to milligrams of iso-alpha acid per liter of beer, the equation is designed to convert the available information into those terms. The top part of the equation starts by quantifying iso-alpha acid, multiplying the weight of the hops (in ounces) by the utilization factor, then by the alpha acid concentration. The final element in the numerator is a correction factor that converts the units of the equation into milligrams per liter. The bottom part of the equation deals with volume, starting with the finished volume in gallons and including a correction factor that relates to wort gravity. (More on this below.) Thus, the basic equation looks like this:

$$IBU = \frac{W_{oz.} \times U\% \times A\% \times 7,489}{(V_{gal.} \times C_{gravity})} \qquad \text{(IBU \#1)}$$

Where:

$W_{oz.}$ = Weight of hops in ounces.

$A\%$ = Alpha acid level of hop as a decimal (e.g., 7% = 0.07).

$U\%$ = Percent utilization, again as a decimal. As a starting point, you can determine the utilization for each hop addition on the basis of the number of minutes the hops are boiled, as shown in table 9.3.

$V_{gal.}$ = Volume of final wort in gallons. This should be equal to the greater of either the final volume in your boil kettle or the total volume of wort in your fermenter before the yeast is added. (See examples.)

$C_{gravity}$ = Correction for worts that have a gravity above 1.050 *during boiling*. This includes every beer with a target original gravity of greater than 1.050, but it also includes most situations where you boil a concentrated wort that is then diluted in the fermenter. (See examples.) When the gravity of the boil is less than 1.050, then the correction factor is equal to 1.0. (The factor can never be less than 1.0.) The correction factor is calculated as follows:

$$C_{gravity} = 1 + [(G_{boil} - 1.050) \div 0.2]$$

The G_{boil} equals the specific gravity of the wort in the boil kettle. For example, for a beer with a boil gravity of 1.090, $C_{gravity}$ = 1.2.

If you do all this in metric units, it becomes a bit easier, since the conversion factor becomes 1,000.

$$IBU = \frac{W_{grams} \times U\% \times A\% \times 1,000}{(V_{liters} \times C_{gravity})} \quad (IBU\#2)$$

Table 9.3 provides some basic utilization values that any homebrewer can use as a starting point for estimating bitterness. They are based upon professional data as well as general homebrewing experience. If you notice that your results consistently differ, then it is time to customize the utilization values for your brewing conditions, beginning with the procedures described in the advanced section.

Any recipe that includes more than one hop addition will require you to perform this calculation for each addition, as you can see in the example below. Let's work through it.

Start with a pale ale with original gravity of 1.048, using 1 ounce of 12.5 percent alpha acid, whole Chinook hops for sixty minutes, and 0.5 ounce of 4.4 percent alpha-acid whole Cascade hops for fifteen minutes. The full volume will be boiled, and the target finished volume is 6 gallons.

Calculate the IBU generated by each hop addition separately. First, the Chinook, for which the variables would have the following values:

$W_{oz.}$ = 1.0
$A\%$ = 0.125
$U\%$ = 0.24
$V_{gal.}$ = 6.0
$C_{gravity}$ = 1

Thus

$$IBU = \frac{1 \times 0.24 \times 0.125 \times 7,489}{(6.0 \times 1)} = 37.4$$

Table 9.3
Basic Hops Utilization Values

Boil Time (minutes)	Whole-Hop Utilization (%)	Pellet-Hop Utilization (%)
Dry hop	0	0
0 to 9	5	6
10 to 19	12	15
20 to 29	15	19
30 to 44	19	24
45 to 59	22	27
60 to 74	24	30
75 or longer	27	34

Sources: These values are based my own tests and experience as well as a number of published sources, of which Randy Mosher's "Hop-Go-Round" was the most significant.

For the Cascade addition, the variables would be

W_{oz} = 0.5
$A\%$ = 0.044
$U\%$ = 0.12
$V_{gal.}$ = 6.0
$C_{gravity}$ = 1

$$IBU = \frac{0.5 \times 0.12 \times 0.044 \times 7,489}{(6.0 \times 1)} = 3.3$$

Total IBU for this recipe: 37.4 (from Chinook) + 3.3 (from Cascade) = 40.7.

Let's do one more example, this time with an English bitter that is being boiled at 3 gallons for dilution to 5 gallons in the fermenter. The gravity target is 1.040, so the gravity in the boil pot will be 1.066. (Remember: 5 gallons at 40 GU divided by 3 gallons . . .). Let's assume one hop addition, 1.5 ounces of 6.5 percent alpha acid Willamette hops, forty-five minutes before the end of the boil.

First, the gravity correction:

$$C_{gravity} = 1 + [(1.066 - 1.050) \div 0.2] = 1.08$$

Now the other variables look like this:

$W_{oz.}$ = 1.5
$A\%$ = 0.065
$U\%$ = 0.269
$V_{gal.}$ = 5.0

$$IBU = \frac{1.5 \times 0.269 \times 0.065 \times 7,489}{(5.0 \times 1.08)} = 36.4$$

Using this basic equation you can estimate IBU quite accurately — if the utilization values used are accurate for your brewery. Because the utilization values capture many characteristics of your brewing equipment and process, they can vary considerably from brewer to brewer. If the basic utilization values shown above don't give you accurate results over two or three

brews, then you may need to customize them for your own situation by increasing or decreasing the utilization values.

Determining the Weight of Hops Required

If you want to turn this equation around and determine the weight of a specific hop required to give you a specific IBU level, you can do that, too.

In ounces and gallons:[12]

$$W_{oz.} = \frac{V_{gal} \times C_{gravity} \times IBU}{U\% \times A\% \times 7489} \quad (IBU\#3)$$

In grams and liters:[13]

$$W_{grams} = \frac{V_{liters} \times C_{gravity} \times IBU}{U\% \times A\% \times 1000} \quad (IBU\#4)$$

Calculation of the Complete Hop Bill

These equations should only be used for deciding the quantity of bittering hops (those boiled thirty minutes or longer) included in your recipe. Hops boiled for less than thirty minutes will have a greater impact on flavor than on bitterness. Therefore, you should not use these IBU formulas to make your decisions about hop levels for flavoring. The quantity of essential oil contained in flavoring hops is much more important in determining the amount added to a recipe than is the alpha acid content. Furthermore, alpha acids and essential oils occur and deteriorate independently of each other. In short, if you look at a recipe that has 5 IBU of Cascade hops boiled for ten minutes and try to match that on an IBU basis, you may get some surprises.

Although you won't use the IBU formulas to decide on the quantity of flavor hops, you must still run the flavor hops through the calculations so you know how much bitterness you are getting from them. The proper approach to formulation of the overall hop bill includes four steps:

1. Decide on your target IBU's level.
2. Determine the amounts of flavor and aroma hops to be added. (See the next chapter and style data in part two.)
3. Determine the IBU's contributed by the flavor hops, if any, using equation IBU#1 or IBU#2, as discussed in this chapter. (You can skip the correction factors and just use the basic formula for these calculations. Any errors in total IBUs will be minimal.) Subtract the late-hop addition IBUs from the total quantity of IBUs desired for the recipe.
4. Use equation IBU#3 or IBU#4 to determine the quantity of bittering hops needed to produce the remaining IBU for the recipe.

Here's an example to illustrate this process. Let's assume you are making an American pale ale in the spirit of Anchor's Liberty Ale, using 5.2 percent alpha acid Cascade hop pellets throughout with additions at two, ten, twenty, and sixty minutes before the end of the boil. You are making 6 gallons and shooting for a total of 45 IBU. Original gravity will be 1.060.

You know your total IBU target, so the first thing you have to do is decide upon the aroma hops and calculate their contribution to overall IBU.

The Cascade hops are pretty aromatic, so we can probably use just a half-ounce for the first two additions, then bump it up to one full ounce for the twenty-minute addition.

The gravity correction factor for all these calculations will be the same, as follows:

$$C_{gravity} = 1 + [(1.060 - 1.050) \div 0.2] = 1.05$$

To calculate the IBU contributions of the late additions, use the equation above IBU#1:

$$IBU = \frac{W_{oz.} \times U\% \times A\% \times 7,489}{(V_{gal.} \times C_{gravity})}$$

Then, for the three late-hop additions, you get the following results:

Two minutes, 0.5 ounce:

$$IBU = \frac{0.5 \times 0.06 \times 0.052 \times 7,489}{(6 \times 1.05)}$$

Ten minutes, 0.5 ounce:

$$IBU = \frac{0.5 \times 0.15 \times 0.052 \times 7,489}{(6 \times 1.05)} = 4.5 \text{ IBU}$$

Twenty minutes, 1.0 ounce:

$$IBU = \frac{1 \times 0.19 \times 0.052 \times 7,489}{(6 \times 1.05)} = 11.7 \text{ IBU}$$

Total IBU from late-hop additions is 18 IBU.

1.8 + 4.5 + 11.7 = 18 IBU

Now, using equation IBU#3, determine how many ounces of hops to add at sixty minutes in order to get to the total target of 45 IBU:

$$W_{oz.} = \frac{V_{gal.} \times C_{gravity} \times IBU}{(U\% \times A\% \times 7,489)}$$

In the calculation, I use the term (45-18) for IBU to indicate the target of 45 IBU minus the 18 added by the late additions. The calculation is:

$$W_{oz.} = \frac{6 \times 1.05 \times (45 - 18)}{(0.30 \times 0.052 \times 7,489)} = 1.45 \text{ oz.}$$

Thus, we will add about 1.5 ounces of Cascade hops sixty minutes before the end of the boil. This, along with the other additions, will yield the approximate target IBUs.

Issues in Selection of Bittering Hops

The selection of bittering hops is significantly influenced not only by the level of alpha acids contained by the hops but also by the types of alpha acids present. (See figure 9.2 for typical hop alph acid values.)

On the one hand, higher alpha acid levels provide higher IBU per ounce of hops, which can improve both economy and convenience. On the other hand, the composition of the alpha acids — and even the hop oils — can affect the flavor contributed by boiling hops.

Some brewers believe that an IBU is an IBU, no matter where it comes from. But even long boils cannot eliminate characteristic effects of some varieties of hops on the overall flavor of a beer. For example, a beer I made recently with Chinook hops had just one addition, made sixty minutes before the end of the boil. The resulting beer had a very noticeable — and almost overwhelming — piney/resinous flavor from the hops. Garetz also reports that Chinook bittering hops leave a detectable character in beers.[14]

Other evidence that bitter hops affect flavor comes to us from the hopping approaches used in some classic beers such as Bohemian (or Czech) Pilseners, Munich beers, and even bocks. These beers rely on "aroma" hops at all stages of the boil,[15] even though these hops typically have fairly low alpha acid content. The reason for this seems clear: Any other hop would impart a different (and less desirable) character to the finished beer.

Even when none of the typical hop flavors can be associated with a particular boiling hop, some brewers feel that the character of the bitterness itself is affected. One possible explanation is the alpha acid cohumulone, believed by many brewers to impart a "harsh" bitterness to beers.[16] In this respect, hop varieties with high cohumulone values are considered undesirable by some brewers.

However, the utilization of cohumulone has been shown to be slightly better than that of the other two alpha acids, so some brewers actually prefer high cohumulone values because of the increased IBU they provide. As a result of these observa-

tions both for and against cohumulone, most hop brokers now test and publish the cohumulone values of their hops. As to its actual effect, you will have to make up your own mind.

A chart showing average or typical cohumulone values for forty-one varieties of hops is shown in figure 9.3. You will note that the proportion of cohumulone in traditional "aroma" hops, such as Hallertau, Tettnanger, and Saaz, is generally about one-half that found in the high-alpha bittering hops such as Bullion, Brewer's Gold, Chinook, Galena, and Eroica. This may explain some of the differences in bittering character imparted by these hop varieties.

In the next chapter, on hop flavor and aroma, I discuss the factors that seem to determine the characteristic flavors contributed by different hop varieties. In addition, I present a section describing all the different varieties of hops. This information may help you evaluate the potential or perceived flavor effects of bittering hops. Recall the beer I made with Chinook hops, mentioned above; the tables and figures in the next chapter show that Chinook has a very high average content of hop oil — the source of most hop flavoring compounds. I don't know if that explains the residual taste imparted after a sixty-minute boil, but it certainly is one possible influence.

If you are brewing a classic style of beer, hop selection can be guided by the traditional practices of commercial brewers. German, British, and American brewmasters tend to have fairly fixed opinions about what hops are suitable for their beers. As a first cut at a new style, these traditions can provide excellent guidance. You can find information of this type in part two of this book, where individual beer styles are discussed.

Advanced Topics in Bitterness

Earlier in this chapter I presented a formula and utilization values that can be

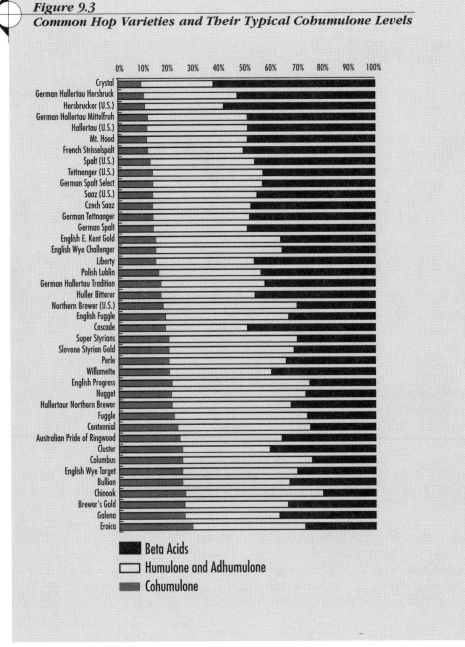

Figure 9.3
Common Hop Varieties and Their Typical Cohumulone Levels

- ■ Beta Acids
- □ Humulone and Adhumulone
- ■ Cohumulone

used as a starting point for any small brewer in calculating IBUs. However, as I mentioned in the section on factors that affect alpha acid utilization, no one set of figures will be appropriate for all brewers or even for every batch of beer brewed by the

same brewer. This section looks at some advanced issues that you may want to consider as your comfort with brewing calculations increases.

The three topics to be considered are: (1) customizing hops utilization for your brewery, (2) correcting for hop concentration, and (3) understanding hop deterioration. Under the right circumstances, each can be important to your overall IBU calculations.

Customizing Utilization for Your Brewery

The utilization values given earlier in table 9.3 reflect a reasonable average utilization for small-scale brewers. In practice, most brewers will experience somewhat different levels, and if those differences become noticeable you may want to customize your utilization values. Table 9.4 gives alternate values that may be useful in doing this.

To use table 9.4, you first need to make a simple test beer following your normal procedures. The test beer should be a normal-sized batch for you and should have a gravity of less than 1.050, preferably about 1.040. It should have just one hop addition at sixty minutes before the end of the boil. You must pay special attention to measurement of weight, volume, and boil time. Finally, you must assess the IBU in the finished beer through either a laboratory or taste analysis.

A lab analysis will cost you the equivalent of three to four bags of malt extract, but it will give you a solid answer. The taste analysis can be accomplished for the cost of one bag of extract, and though it may be more fun, the results will be far less accurate.

In either case, the analysis will tell you the number of IBU in the finished beer. Divide this by the mg/L of alpha acid added to the boil and you have your utilization for that boil length. Based upon this, you can choose an alternate set of utilization values from table 9.4.

Table 9.4 is designed to prevent you from driving yourself crazy by calculating every hop addition down to the minute. (Remember, people can't taste a difference

of less than 5 IBU.) Thus, it breaks the boil down into seven time groupings and gives an average utilization value for any hop addition that falls within that time. (The values for each line of the chart have been determined by adjustment of the values given in table 9.3 in proportion to the sixty-minute utilization value.)

Correction for Hop Concentration

Home- and small craft brewers who constantly brew new recipes may want to consider one or two additional variables that will be recipe-specific. The first of these is hop concentration.

Ultimately, the level of iso-alpha acids formed during the boil depends upon the quantity of alpha acids dissolved in the wort during the boil. The catch is that the solubility of alpha acids in wort is limited. Simply adding more and more hops does not produce a linear increase in the amount of bitterness produced. To account for this effect, a correction factor has been formulated. The denominator (bottom) of the IBU equation should be multiplied by the correction factor. As you can see from table 9.5, this factor is material for many situations where the full wort is not boiled and in all cases where the target IBU level is greater than 50.

Table 9.5 gives values for a range of target IBUs and boil factors. The boil factors relate the volume boiled to the final volume for those who boil less than their finished volume. For instance, a boil factor of 3.5:5 means that your boil volume will be about 3.5 gallons and you plan to add 1.5 gallons of water to the fermenter to make up the total batch volume of 5 gallons. If you brew 10-gallon batches, you can multiply by two to find the appropriate factor. Thus, 2.5:5 becomes 5:10.

This hop concentration factor should be included for every boiling hop addition that you make. If you are doing this all by hand, table 9.4 will be helpful. If you set

Table 9.4
Customized Hop Utilization Values

Utilization of 60-minute whole hop boil %	Whole Hops %						
	0 to 9 §	10 to 19 §	20 to 29 §	30 to 44 §	45 to 59 §	60 to 69 §	> 69 §
15	3	8	10	13	15	16	18
16	4	9	11	13	16	17	19
17	4	9	11	14	17	18	20
18	4	10	12	15	17	19	21
19	4	10	13	16	18	20	23
20	4	11	13	17	19	21	24
21	5	11	14	17	20	22	25
22	5	12	14	18	21	23	26
23	5	12	15	19	22	24	27
24	5	13	16	20	23	25	28
25	5	13	16	21	24	26	29
26	6	14	17	21	25	27	30
27	6	14	18	22	26	28	32
28	6	15	18	23	27	29	33
29	6	15	19	24	28	30	34
30	6	16	19	25	28	31	35
31	7	16	20	25	29	32	36
32	7	17	21	26	30	33	37
33	7	17	21	27	31	34	38
34	7	18	22	28	32	35	39
35	8	18	23	29	33	36	41
36	8	19	23	29	34	37	42
37	8	19	24	30	35	38	43
38	8	20	24	31	36	39	44
39	8	20	25	32	37	40	45
40	9	21	26	32	38	41	46

If you know the hop utilization resulting from a 60-minute boil of whole hops using your brewing system, you can estimate the utilization at all other points in the boil from this table. Read the 60-minute boil figure at the leftmost column, then read across to find the column with the hop type and boil length you need. The utilization for the boil appears as a percentage.

§ *Length of boil in minutes*

these calculations up in a computer, it will be more useful to understand the original math as developed by Mark Garetz,[17] so here is the equation:[18]

$$HCF = \frac{([Final\ vol. \div Boil\ vol.] \times Desired\ IBU)}{260} + 1$$

Alpha Acid
Deterioration During Storage

Another issue discussed by brewers is the deterioration of alpha acids during hop storage and the effect this has on hop bittering properties. Alpha acids deteriorate over time, and this deterioration may reach

Table 9.4 *continued*
Customized Hop Utilization Values

Utilization of 60-minute whole hop boil %	**Pellet Hops %**						
	0 to 9§	10 to 19§	20 to 29§	30 to 44§	45 to 59§	60 to 69§	> 69§
15	4	11	14	17	20	21	25
16	5	11	14	18	20	22	26
17	5	12	15	19	21	23	27
18	5	12	16	20	22	24	28
19	5	13	16	21	23	25	29
20	5	13	17	22	24	26	30
21	6	14	18	22	25	27	32
22	6	14	18	23	26	28	33
23	6	15	19	24	27	29	34
24	6	16	20	25	28	30	35
25	6	16	20	26	29	31	36
26	7	17	21	26	30	32	38
27	7	17	22	27	31	33	39
28	7	18	22	28	32	34	40
29	7	18	23	29	33	35	41
30	7	19	24	30	34	36	42
31	8	19	24	31	34	37	43
32	8	20	25	31	35	38	45
33	8	20	26	32	36	39	46
34	8	21	26	33	37	40	47
35	8	21	27	34	38	41	48
36	9	22	28	35	39	42	49
37	9	22	28	36	40	43	50
38	9	23	29	36	41	44	52
39	9	23	29	37	42	45	53
40	10	24	30	38	43	46	54

If you know the hop utilization resulting from a 60-minute boil of whole hops using your brewing system, you can estimate the utilization at all other points in the boil from this table. Read the 60-minute boil figure at the leftmost column, then read across to find the column with the hop type and boil length you need. The utilization for the boil appears as a percentage.

§ *Length of boil in minutes*

a point where it is worth considering. Although I find this is rarely the case in craft brewing, let us examine the issues involved.

The rate of deterioration is dependent upon several factors: (1) hop variety, (2) storage temperature, (3) packaging (exposure to air), and (4) passage of time.

You may recall an earlier mention that compounds other than alpha acids play a role in bitterness. As alpha acids deteriorate, these compounds increase somewhat, in part balancing out the loss of alpha acids. This leads to a discussion of whether hopping rates should be determined on the

Table 9.5
Hop Concentration Factor

Desired IBU	1:1*	4:5*	3.5:5*	3:5*	2.5:5*
5	1.02	1.02	1.03	1.03	1.04
10	1.04	1.05	1.05	1.06	1.08
15	1.06	1.07	1.08	1.10	1.12
20	1.08	1.10	1.11	1.13	1.15
22	1.08	1.11	1.12	1.14	1.17
24	1.09	1.12	1.13	1.15	1.18
26	1.10	1.13	1.14	1.17	1.20
28	1.11	1.13	1.15	1.18	1.22
30	1.12	1.14	1.16	1.19	1.23
32	1.12	1.15	1.18	1.21	1.25
34	1.13	1.16	1.19	1.22	1.26
36	1.14	1.17	1.20	1.23	1.28
38	1.15	1.18	1.21	1.24	1.29
40	1.15	1.19	1.22	1.26	1.31
45	1.17	1.22	1.25	1.29	1.35
50	1.19	1.24	1.27	1.32	1.38
55	1.21	1.26	1.30	1.35	1.42
60	1.23	1.29	1.33	1.38	1.46
65	1.25	1.31	1.36	1.42	1.50
70	1.27	1.34	1.38	1.45	1.54
75	1.29	1.36	1.41	1.48	1.58
80	1.31	1.38	1.44	1.51	1.62

*Boil Factor (boil volume:fermenter volume)

basis of the fresh alpha acid levels or on the basis of the actual values at the time of use.

In practice, big breweries appear to hop on the basis of the fresh-hop alpha acid level.[19] To help them in this task, there is a spectrophotometric technique that has produced an index of deterioration in hops.[20] This allows breweries to determine the fresh-hop alpha acid level when they know the current level of alpha acids in the hops.

Some authors claim, based upon taste tests with aged hops, that no adjustment for alpha acid loss need ever be made.[21] Other studies have concluded that an adjustment would be in order when total alpha acids dropped to less than 65 percent of their original value.[22] This second study looked very closely at perceived bitterness as the levels of alpha acids declined, and I believe it represents the most sensible approach to dealing with hop utilization.

My own experience with adjusting for alpha acid deterioration also indicates that adjustments are generally unnecessary for small-scale brewers. Let's see why.

The index of deterioration equation can be modified to predict the deterioration of alpha acids in hops over time.[23] Let's assume that the hops are sealed in barrier packaging or an airtight jar but are not free from oxygen. Table 9.6 lists several possible storage temperatures and the resulting levels of deterioration that might be encountered.

If stored at room temperature (68 °F, 20 °C), the alpha acid remaining in many hop varieties will drop below 65 percent.

Figure 9.4
Shape of the Hop Utilization Curve

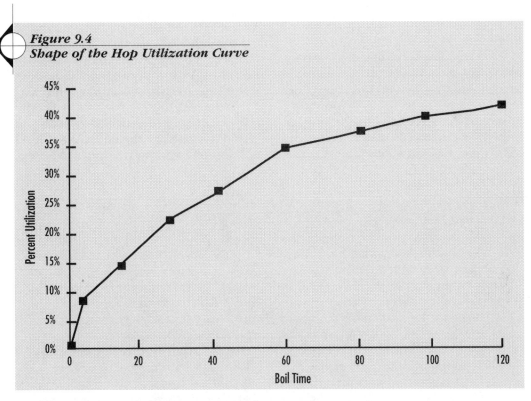

However, hops are rarely stored at room temperature for any length of time. These days everyone in the hop-supply chain, from brokers all the way down to retailers, generally stores hops under cold conditions. (If your supplier doesn't, find a new one!) Once the hops are at home or in the brewery, you should pop them in the freezer or cooler for safekeeping.

Only one hop (Liberty) has worse storage properties than Cascade, so you can see that when properly stored (at 20 °F or lower), hops rarely fall below 75 percent of their original alpha acid level over the course of a year. (This holds true for unpackaged hops held in a broker's cooler for a year, as well.) In addition, remember that even though alpha acid levels may have dropped somewhat, hops still contain other bittering compounds that may increase with age. Thus, hop bittering capacity can be adequately predicted by

Table 9.6
Percentage of Alpha Acids Remaining in Hops after One Year

	68°	34°	20°	5°
Cascade	35	65	74	81
Mt. Hood	41	69	77	84
Tettnanger	44	71	79	85
Fuggle	50	75	82	87
N. Brewer	65	84	88	92
Galena	78	90	93	95

°*Storage Temperature (F)*

the fresh alpha acid levels that appear on the package.

Of course, you will find some hops that are more than a year old, especially in the fall months before the new crop begins to arrive. In these cases, you should be sure to purchase hops that have been properly packaged and stored. For aroma hops (like Cascade and Liberty), this means packages that have been purged of oxygen either by vacuum or by inert gas in addition to being protected by an oxygen-barrier package. And, of course, the colder the storage the better.

Following these guidelines, it is difficult to imagine a situation where you would need to use the deteriorated level of hop alpha acids in your calculations.

Sidebar
AAU and HBU

Several homebrewing authors in the past have utilized simplified systems for expressing the level of bitterness in their beers. These systems bypassed the calculation of IBU by simply looking at the amount of alpha acid added to the beer at a specific time. These systems, known as Alpha Acid Units and Homebrew Bittering Units, are essentially equivalent. They are defined as the percentage of alpha acid present in the hop times the number of ounces. Thus, 1 ounce of 4.4 percent Tettnanger hops will have an HBU/AAU value of 4.4, while 0.5 ounce represents 2.2 AAU/HBU, and 1.5 ounces represents 6.6 HBU/AAU. Thus

AAU/HBU = % alpha acid content x oz. of hops

The main drawback of these systems is that they look only at the inputs to the process instead of at the final result, which is what IBU represents. The main ingredient missing is the length of the time the hops are boiled, so this must be stated separately for AAU and HBU. In addition, they do not address utilization differences that may occur between the author's brewing setup and those employed by users of the recipe.

To convert AAU or HBU measurements into IBU, you need to know the timing of the additions. When you know how long each addition is boiled, it is a simple matter of plugging all the variables into the equation to find the total IBUs.

Project	Designing Great Beers
	Brewers Publications
Project No.	61766

10 FLAVOR AND AROMA HOPS

In addition to providing bitterness, hops can contribute a wonderful variety of flavors and aromas to beer. However, the chemistry of hop flavor and aroma is anything but straightforward, and as a result, the brewer's ability to predict and control these effects — at least quantitatively — is quite limited.

In this chapter, I examine the ways hops impart flavor and aroma to beer. I also look closely at different hop varieties and their characteristics so that you can judge which ones may provide the flavors you desire. Finally, I discuss practical issues in creating desired hop effects.

The Chemistry of
Hop Flavor and Aroma

As noted in the chapter on hop bitterness, bittering properties come from the soft resins that generally account for less than 15 percent of the hop mass. Flavor and aroma come from an even smaller component — the essential oils. These can account for as little as 0.5 percent of the hop mass and up to as much as 3 percent in some varieties in some instances.

More than 250 chemical compounds that appear in beer have been traced to essential oils. Only a few dozen are believed to play a major role in hop flavor and aroma, but many more may contribute to the over-

all effect. Let's briefly review the major classes of essential oils, as shown in figure 10.1.

Hydrocarbons: This group accounts for up to 80 percent of hop oil in fresh hops. The key members of this group are terpenes and susquiterpenes, including:

• Myrcene
• Humulene
• Caryophyllene
• Farnesene

These compounds are highly volatile and rarely survive in their native form when boiled, but they are believed to contribute to the fresh hop flavor associated with dry hopping. More important, they react with oxygen during storage and boiling to create the second class of oils, called oxygenated hydrocarbons.

Oxygenated hydrocarbons: This class accounts for many of the potent flavor compounds associated with late hop additions. They are largely the oxidation products of the hydrocarbons that occur in hop oil. Important examples include humulene epoxide I, II, and III; humulenol; caryophyllene epoxide; linalool and geranyl acetate.

Sulphur-containing hydrocarbons: This small class of compounds includes products

Figure 10.1
An Overview of Hop Oil Constituents

I. Hydrocarbons

    A. Oxygen-free terpenes

        1. Monoterpenes (contain 2 isoprene units)

          a.Aliphatic

            i. Myrcene

            ii. Isobutene

            iii. Ocimene

          b. Cyclic

            i. Alpha- (and beta-) pinene

        2. Sesquiterpenes (3 isoprene units)

          a. Aliphatic

            i. Farnesene

          b.Cyclic

            i. Humulene

            ii. Caryophyllene

        3. Diterpenes

          a. Aliphatic

            i. Dimyrcene

    B. Other oxygen-free compounds: isoprene

II. Oxygenated substances (polar)

    A. Oxygenated terpenes (terpenoids, sesquiterpenoids)

        1. Epoxides

          a. Myrcene epoxide

          b. Farnesene epoxide

          c. Humulene epoxide

          d. Pinene epoxide

          e. Caryophyllene epoxide

         2. Alcohols

          a. Linalool

          b. Myrcenol

          c. Pinenol

          d. Farnesenol

          e. Caryophyllenol

          f. Humulenol

          g. Nerol (from myrcene)

        3. Aldehydes

          a.Geraniol

        4. Ketones

          a.Humuladienone

        5. Acids

          a. Myrcenic acid

        6. Esters

          a.Geranyl acetate

    B. Other oxygenated products

        1. Alcohols

        2. Aldehydes

        3. Ketones

        4. Acids

        5. Esters

        6. Lactones

    C. Terpenes containing oxygen and sulphur

        1. Epoxides: 8,9-epithiohumulene

    D. Other compounds containing oxygen and sulphur

        1. Esters: S-methyl hexanothioate

III. Oxygen-free sulphur compounds

    A. Dimethyl trisulphide

Note: Compounds named are examples only and do not constitute a complete list of hop oil constituents.

created by the combination of the hydrocarbons with sulphur. The chemical classifications include episulfides, thio-esters, and polysulfides. The polysulfides in particular are associated with unpleasant aromas and flavors such as those of cooked vegetables, onions, skunk, rubber, and sulphur. Some of the compounds have flavor thresholds of as low as 0.3 parts per billion.

The formation of these compounds is accelerated by heat, but most break down or evaporate in boiling wort. Hop additions made very late in the boil are the most likely to result in the production of these compounds in quantities that could be detected in finished beer.

The Flavors of Hop Compounds

Hop researchers believe that no one compound is responsible for the aroma and flavor effects of hops. Instead, these sensations are created by a group of flavor-active components that may act individually as well as synergistically. In this section I review the main compounds believed to have flavor impact in beer and discuss how each comes about. This will help you understand what you want in your beer and how to achieve it.

The compounds I focus on in this section have appeared repeatedly in the brewing literature as key components of hop flavor or aroma. Most data available to craft brewers on the specific flavor and aroma compounds present in hops relate to the four key hydrocarbons of myrcene, humulene, caryophyllene, and farnesene. In this section I look at the contributions made by these compounds, their oxidation products, and selected other hydrocarbons.

Myrcene: In many varieties of hops, myrcene constitutes the largest component of hop oil. This compound is described as having a greater flavor intensity than humulene, and it is frequently characterized as pungent.[1]

The portion of total oil accounted for by myrcene can range from 20 percent to 65 percent, depending upon the variety of hop. Myrcene levels tend to be low in the "noble-type" hops (e.g., Saaz, Tettnanger) and in other hops prized for their aroma characteristics (e.g., East Kent Goldings, Fuggles) and is often higher in hops used primarily for bittering (e.g., Brewer's Gold, Nugget, Galena).

Myrcene itself rarely survives into finished beer unless the hops are added at the very end of the boil or used as a dry hop. However, a number of other important flavor compounds are closely related to myrcene and are believed to occur in finished beer as oxidation or degradation products of myrcene. Included are linalool, geraniol, geranyl acetate and geranyl isobutyrate.[2] These compounds contribute aromas or flavors usually described as floral.[3] Linalool in particular has been found to have a logarithmic relationship with floral flavor in beer. The linalool oxides (1 and 2) have been highly correlated with European hop flavor.[4] Other myrcene degradation products include nerol and citral, which are believed to contribute citrus or piney impressions.[5]

Humulene: Brewers associate humulene with a delicate and refined flavor that is often described as elegant.[6] Aroma hops, including the "noble-type" hops, generally have levels of humulene that equal or exceed that of myrcene. The oil of Saaz hops, for instance, typically consists of 40 percent to 45 percent humulene and only 20 percent to 25 percent myrcene. In typical bittering hop varieties such as Cluster, Bullion, and Galena, humulene accounts for 15 percent or less of the total oil.

Like myrcene, humulene is unlikely to appear in finished beer unless the hops are added at the very end of the boil or are used as a dry hop addition.[7] However, humulene degrades into a variety of oxidation products that survive into finished beer and play important roles in beer flavor and aroma.[8] These products include: humulene epoxides (I, II, and III), humulene diepoxides (A, B, and C), humulenol II, humulol, and humuladienone.

These degradation products form naturally over time in stored hops[9] and at an accelerated rate when heated.[10] They contribute a character that is generally described as herbal or spicy.[11] In particular, the mono- and diepoxides have been strongly associated with the "spicy" characteristic.[12] Humulol has a certain correlation with European hop character.[13]

Caryophyllene and farnesene: The last two hop oil hydrocarbons that are commonly analyzed in fresh hops are caryophyllene and farnesene. These two account for a minor portion of the total oil. Caryophyllene ranges from about 5 percent to 15 percent across all hop varieties, with some tendency toward high values in aroma hops and lower values in bittering hops. Farnesene accounts for less than 1 percent of the total oil in most hop varieties but can be as much as 20 percent of the total in some of the aroma hops. Spalt, Tettnanger, Lublin, and Fuggle all display significant farnesene levels. (See table 10.5 for a list of hops with typical farnesene levels greater than 1 percent of total oil.) The flavors associated with farnesene and its oxidation products are not well characterized.

Caryophyllene has been found in finished beer, most likely as the result of dry hopping.[14] However, the flavor characteristics of caryophyllene are not commonly known. Two flavor-active oxidation products, caryophyllene oxide (or epoxide) and caryolan-1-ol, commonly occur.[15] Caryophyllene epoxide is associated with the herbal/spicy character,[16] and caryolan-1-ol with European hop character.[17]

Other Hydrocarbons: Several additional hydrocarbons occur in native hops and appear to play a role in beer flavoring.

These include: delta- and gamma-cadinene, alpha-muurolene, and beta-selinene. These compounds play roles in the citrus-piney aromas and flavors derived from hops.[18]

Table 10.1 summarizes hop flavors and their corresponding compounds.

Achieving Hop Flavor and Aroma Goals

In working with hops, you can use a number of different tools to achieve the effects you desire. These include selection of hop varieties, timing of hop additions, storage and aging of hops, and amount of hops used.

When you first brew a style, the safest approach is to follow the practices of the brewers who created it. If you brew an English ale, use English hops; for a German lager, use German hops. Furthermore, some styles are associated with a specific variety of hops. Bohemian Pilseners, for instance, rely on Saaz hops throughout. In these cases you are well advised to follow the classic practice — at least at first.

Of course, experimentation and variation are the hallmarks of home- and craft brewing. Some hops, for instance the prized Hallertau Mittelfruh from Germany, simply aren't available in U.S. supply channels. Other times, domestically grown versions of a hop (Tettnanger or Saaz for instance) may be the ones available when you do your shopping. And if economy is important, the domestic varieties are usually less expensive.

Finally, hop scientists are a bit like home- and craft brewers themselves. They love to tinker and create. As a result, a number of new hop varieties are always being evaluated and introduced to the market. Some of these are bred to emulate the characteristics of a classic European hop. For example, when Hallertau Mittelfruh was grown in the U.S. hop yards, it simply did not turn out like the original in Europe. As a result, three new U.S. hops — Mt. Hood,

Table 10.1
Hop Flavors and Their Related Compounds

Flavor	Compound	Source
Spicy		
	Humulene epoxides	Humulene oxidation products
	Humulene diepoxides	
Herbal or European		
	Humulol	Humulene oxidation product
	Linalool oxides	From linalool
Floral or Flowery		
	Linalool	Myrcene oxidation products
	Geraniol	Myrcene oxidation products
	Geranyl acetate	Myrcene oxidation products
	Geranyl isobutyrate	Myrcene oxidation products
Citrus and Piney		
	Citral	From Myrcene
	Nerol	From Myrcene
	Limonene	From Myrcene
	Cadinenes	Hydrocarbons native to hops
	Beta-Selinene	Hydrocarbons native to hops
	Alpha-Muurolene	Hydrocarbons native to hops

Liberty, and Crystal — have been introduced to more closely match the character of this European classic.

It is up to home and craft brewers to try new hops to see what they are like. You have the opportunity to use them to create new beer flavors and maybe even classic styles. In the course of experimentation, you may want to consider both the qualitative and quantitative characteristics of the hop. In addition, you will want to consider how to apply it in your recipe. The remainder of this chapter addresses these issues.

Selection and Use of Flavor and Aroma Hops

Both the character and degree of hop flavor and aroma produced in a beer can be controlled by the brewer. The control points are selection of the hop variety to be used and determination of how the hop will be processed during brewing. Generally, character hops are selected from among the low-alpha aroma or "noble-type" hop varieties.[19] Processing options generally call for a short period of boiling in the wort or for steeping the hops in the beer during aging.

Let's examine the processes of selection and use in further detail.

Selection

The selection of aroma hops is particularly important to the brewer because of the significant flavor impact the chosen variety of hop can have on the flavor of the beer produced.

Generally, those hops to be added in the final thirty minutes of the boil are chosen from among the varieties regarded as aroma hops. Typical examples include varieties such as Hallertau, Tettnanger, Saaz, Goldings, Fuggle, Cascade, and Willamette.

Although almost all these hops have been selected by brewers for use as aroma hops because they produce pleasant flavors and aromas in beer, they also share certain physical traits. These traits are as follows:

- Low alpha acid content (less than 5 or 6 percent)
- Low myrcene oil content (less than 50 percent of total oil)
- Low cohumulone alpha acid content
- Alpha acid to beta acid ratio near 1.0
- Generally poor storage characteristics
- Generally medium oil content (0.5 to 1.5 percent)
- Some also note a high humulene to caryophyllene ratio, and values above 3 are supposedly required for "noble-type" status.

The safest way to choose an appropriate hop for a beer is to evaluate the traditions of the style you are brewing. Some styles have very specific traditions, such as the use of Saaz in Bohemian Pilseners and of East Kent Goldings in English pale ales. In such cases, the use of another hop variety may result in a beer that, although pleasing, would not be identifiable as an example of the style you intended to make.

Other styles have less rigorous requirements with regard to hop character. In these cases, almost any aroma hop from the country where the style originates can be used. For instance, German lagers generally may be made using Hallertau, Hersbruck, Tettnanger, or Spalt hops in the finish. The style reviews in part two of this book discuss the hop varieties commonly used for each style of beer.

Thus, where tradition exists to guide you, hop selection can be fairly easy. But when it is time to experiment or improvise, traditions are meaningless. At times like that you must go back to the chemistry of the hop to understand what kind of results you may expect. Also, looking at

related families of hops may be useful.

In the first part of this chapter, I examined hop oils and their relationships to various hop flavors. This section presents data on different hop varieties and their typical oil profiles.

When substituting one variety for another, you may want to look for oil profiles that are similar. Although hops with similar oil profiles won't necessarily give identical flavor profiles, they will most likely produce similar effects. When experimenting with a new hop, you can compare its oil profile to that of other hops with which you are familiar to get an understanding of the character this hop may produce.

Tables 10.2 to 10.5 and figures 10.2 to 10.3 provide data about forty-one varieties of hops from various areas of the world. The values used in these tables and figures are averages for each variety based upon data supplied by hop brokers and hop growers' associations.

Table 10.2 shows the total oil as a percentage of total hop mass and then lists the individual hop oils as a percentage of total oil, ranked according to percentage of oil from lowest to highest.

Figures 10.2 and 10.3 are stacked-bar charts that sort hop varieties according to percentage of humulene and myrcene content from highest to lowest. The proportions of other hop oils present are also shown.

Tables 10.3 and 10.4 show the ratios of humulene to myrcene and humulene to caryophyllene and show the balance between each set of flavor-influencing oils for the listed hop varieties. Table 10.5 lists all hop varieties with significant farnesene levels, ranked by percentage of total hop weight. The similarities between some well-known aroma varieties are clear in this table.

Although these tables and figures provide a number of interesting insights into the character of various hops, they fail to provide information about the floral and citrus flavors produced by compounds

Table 10.2
Hop Oil Content and Character (ranked by total oil content)

Variety	Oil content as % of Whole Hop	Percentage of Total Oil				
		Myrcene	Humulene	Caryophyllene	Farnesene	Other
Czech Saaz	0.55	22.5	42.5	11.0	13.0	10.0
Saaz (U.S.)	0.60	37.0	23.0	7.0	–	33.0
Tettnanger	0.60	40.5	20.5	6.5	6.5	25.0
Cluster	0.60	50.0	16.5	6.5	0.5	26.0
Slovene Styrian Gold	0.75	30.0	36.0	10.0	3.5	20.0
French Strisselspalt	0.75	25.0	20.0	9.0	0.5	45.0
German Spalt Select	0.75	20.0	20.0	9.0	20.0	30.0
Spalt (U.S.)	0.75	45.0	15.0	5.0	12.5	22.0
English E. Kent Gold	0.80	23.0	45.0	14.0	0.5	17.0
Hallertau (U.S.)	0.80	39.5	34.0	11.0	0.5	14.0
Perle	0.80	50.0	30.5	11.0	0.5	7.0
German Tettnanger	0.80	22.5	22.5	8.0	14.0	32.0
German Spalt	0.80	20.0	21.5	12.5	12.5	33.0
English Progress	0.90	32.5	43.5	13.5	0.5	09.0
Liberty	0.90	37.5	37.5	10.5	0.5	13.0
Hersbrucker (U.S.)	0.90	45.0	25.0	7.5	0.5	21.0
Super Styrians	0.90	58.0	12.0	5.0	–	24.0
Polish Lublin	0.95	30.0	37.5	10.0	11.0	11.0
Fuggle (U.S.)	0.95	45.0	23.0	8.0	4.5	19.0
German Hallertau Mittelfruh	1.00	32.0	40.0	11.0	–	16.0
German Hallertau Hersbruck	1.00	20.0	20.0	9.5	0.5	49.0
English Fuggle	1.05	26.0	37.5	12.0	6.0	17.0
Galena	1.05	57.5	12.5	4.0	0.5	24.0
Eroica	1.05	60.0	0.5	9.5	0.5	28.0
Mt. Hood	1.15	60.0	20.0	8.5	0.5	10.0
Cascade	1.15	52.0	13.0	4.5	6.0	23.0
German Hallertau Tradition	1.20	22.5	50.0	12.5	0.5	13.0
Huller Bitterer	1.20	51.0	09.0	5.0	–	34.0
Willamette	1.25	50.0	25.0	7.5	5.5	11.0
Crystal	1.25	52.5	21.0	6.0	0.5	19.0
English Wye Challenger	1.35	36.0	28.5	9.0	2.0	23.0
English Wye Target	1.40	63.0	11.0	5.0	–	20.0
Brewer's Gold	1.50	65.0	12.0	5.0	–	16.0
Australian Pride of Ringwood	1.50	37.5	05.5	7.5	0.5	48.0
Nothern Brewer (U.S.)	1.75	55.0	25.0	7.5	0.5	10.0
Columbus	1.75	35.0	20.0	10.0	0.5	33.0
Hallertau Northern Brewer	1.85	32.5	27.5	9.0	0.5	29.0
Centennial	1.90	50.0	14.0	6.5	0.5	27.0
Nugget	1.95	55.0	17.0	8.5	0.5	17.0
Chinook	2.00	37.5	22.5	10.0	0.5	28.0
Bullion	3.20	64.0	12.0	8.0	–	13.0

such as linalool, geraniol, citral, and so on. I have been unable to find a published catalog of these compounds by hop variety, but a number of partial sources exist.

Unfortunately, the data on these flavor characteristics are not entirely straightforward. The levels tend to change from year to year, even in the same variety. In addition, the aging of the hops tends to increase the presence of these compounds in some cases while decreasing them in others.[20]

Changes in Hop Aroma Potential During Aging

Foster and Nickerson[21] have classified twenty hop varieties according to the stability of their hop aroma compounds during aging. They identified four main groups. Two groups change little during aging: in Kirin, Challenger, and Target the aroma compounds start at high levels and remain at high levels over time; in Nugget, Cluster, Perle, Columbia, and Olympic aroma compounds start low and remain low over time.

The other two groups show changes in hop aroma potential as the result of aging. The first group begins with high levels of these compounds, but they decline with age; in the second group, aroma compounds start low and actually increase with age. The members of these two groups, as identified by Foster and Nickerson, are shown in table 10.6.

The findings in table 10.6 provide some important information about using hops. First, some hops actually improve with age. Thus, mild aging of hops may be desirable to achieve the best aroma/flavor character. (In the papers I have reviewed, aging techniques that gave favorable results included 90 °F/32 °C for nineteen days, six months at ambient temperatures, and refrigerated for one year.)

Second, many of the hops that improve with age are the traditional aroma hops. This study looked at only twenty hop varieties and, with the exception of

Cascade, all the aroma hops wound up in the group that improves with age.

I must state that I have no experience with the intentional "aging" of hops before they are used. But the fact that hop character can increase with age is widely documented and would make an excellent area for experimentation.[22] Furthermore, it can help us to understand the differences that sometimes occur when we use a particular hop in different beers and seem to get different results.

Whether or not you choose to age your hops, table 10.7 provides some useful information about the spicy, floral, and citrus character of some hop varieties in both fresh and aged form. Figure 10.4 provides some information about the flavors associated with a small number of hop varieties. Although these two studies allow comparison of only a limited number of hop varieties, there are, unfortunately, no broader studies of hop character available in the beer literature.

Uses of Aroma Hops

Once you have selected an aroma hop for use in your beer, you'll need to make more decisions. You will have to decide how the hops will be added and how much to add. Let's begin with a look at your options for adding late hops and then examine the flavor effects these options may have.

Brewers have three options in adding aroma/flavor hops to a beer. These include:

- Boiling, generally for a short period — from as little as two minutes to no more than thirty minutes.

- Steeping, by addition to the kettle after the boil is completed or through the use of a hop back or grant, where hot wort is passed through a bed of hops.

- Dry hopping, where the hops are added to the beer during fermentation or aging.

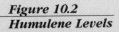

Figure 10.2
Humulene Levels

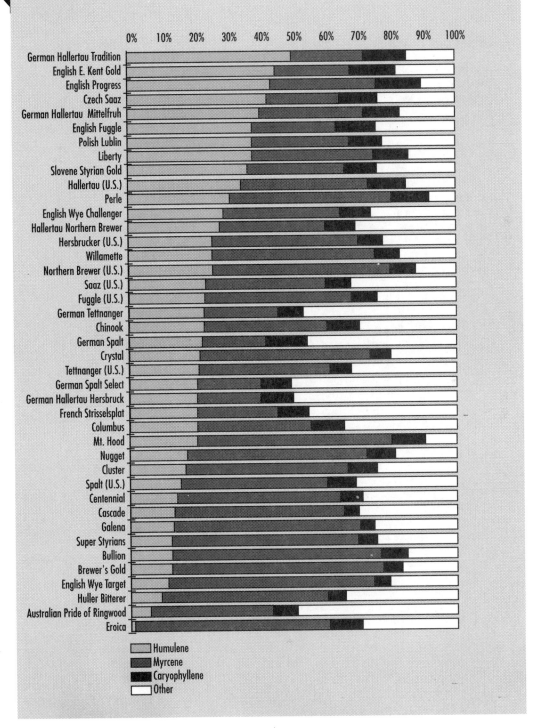

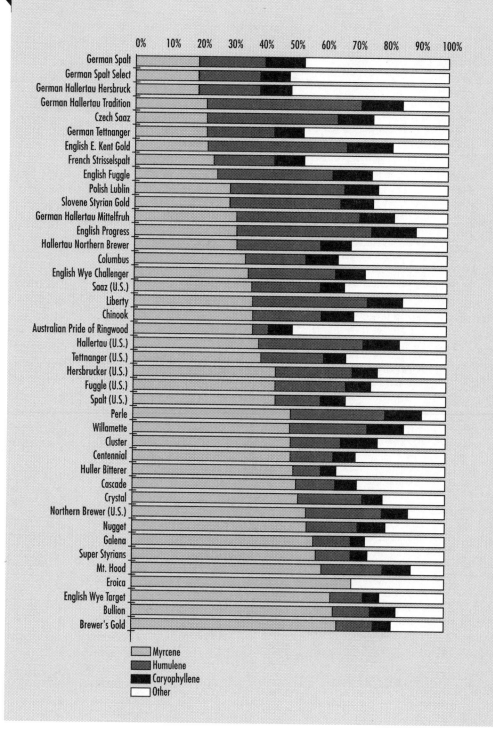

Figure 10.3
Myrcene Levels

Table 10.3
Ratios of Humulene to Myrcene
(ranked from highest to lowest)

Hop Variety	Humulene to Myrcene Ratio
German Hallertau Tradition	2.22
English E. Kent Gold	1.96
Czech Saaz	1.89
English Fuggle	1.44
English Progress	1.34
German Hallertau Mittelfruh	1.25
Polish Lublin	1.25
Slovene Styrian Gold	1.20
German Spalt	1.08
German Tettnanger	1.00
German Hallertau Hersbruck	1.00
German Spalt Select	1.00
Liberty	1.00
Hallertau (U.S.)	0.86
Hallertau Northern Brewer	0.85
French Strisselspalt	0.80
English Wye Challenger	0.79
Saaz (U.S.)	0.62
Perle	0.61
Chinook	0.60
Columbus	0.57
Hersbrucker (U.S.)	0.56
Fuggle (U.S.)	0.51
Tettnanger (U.S.)	0.51
Willamette	0.50
Northern Brewer (U.S.)	0.45
Crystal	0.40
Mt. Hood	0.33
Spalt (U.S.)	0.33
Cluster	0.33
Nugget	0.31
Centennial	0.28
Cascade	0.25
Galena	0.22
Super Styrians	0.21
Bullion	0.19
Brewer's Gold	0.18
Huller Bitterer	0.18
English Wye Target	0.17
Australian Pride of Ringwood	0.15
Eroica	0.01

Each of these techniques will produce a different flavor and aroma in the finished beer. Furthermore, the length of time the brewer chooses to boil (or to dry hop) will also affect the flavor obtained.

The effects of hop additions across these techniques can be detected in either the flavor or the aroma of the hops. To produce a pronounced hop aroma generally requires dry hopping, or the use of larger amounts of steeped hops. Hops that are boiled generally have a greater impact on flavor and produce rather little aroma, especially as the boil time increases. In addition, although thirty minutes is a traditional cut-off point for flavor hops, many hops will contribute detectable flavor characteristics even when boiled for sixty minutes or longer.

Hop research indicates that the flavors produced by dry hopping are quite different from those that result from addition during the boil.[23] Late-hopped additions have been characterized as more floral, fragrant, and less grassy than dry-hopped additions. Other studies use different terminology, stating that late-hopped beers show more "estery-fruity" and "fruity-citrus" character than their dry-hopped counterparts.[24] Generally, dry-hopped flavor is more like that of fresh hops than is a late-hop addition, and the dry-hopped beer may be more spicy or resinous.[25]

The reasons for these differences relate to the chemistry of hop oil and brewing. Many hop oil components are highly volatile, meaning they vaporize at low temperatures and will be driven off during boiling.[26] Except when dry hopping is employed, most native hop oil compounds are not found in finished beer.[27] Thus, very short boil times, steeping, and dry hopping serve to increase the amount of fresh hop oil constituents that appear in the wort and the subsequent beer.[28]

Although fresh oils may be lost during the boil, other flavor-active compounds not found in fresh hops are formed during the boil. This results when oil components

Table 10.4
Ratios of Humulene to Caryophyllene (ranked from highest to lowest)

Hop Variety	Humulene to Caryophyllene Ratio
German Hallertau Tradition	4.00
Czech Saaz	3.86
Polish Lublin	3.75
German Hallertau Mittelfruh	3.70
Slovene Styrian Gold	3.60
Liberty	3.57
Crystal	3.50
Saaz (U.S.)	3.40
Hersbrucker (U.S.)	3.33
Willamette	3.33
Northern Brewer (U.S.)	3.33
English Progress	3.22
English E. Kent Gold	3.21
English Wye Challenger	3.17
Tettnanger (U.S.)	3.15
English Fuggle	3.13
Galena	3.13
Hallertau (U.S.)	3.09
Hallertau Northern Brewer	3.06
Spalt (U.S.)	3.00
Cascade	2.89
Fuggle (U.S.)	2.88
German Tettnanger	2.81
Perle	2.77
Cluster	2.54
Super Styrians	2.50
English Wye Target	2.40
Mt. Hood	2.35
Brewer's Gold	2.30
Chinook	2.25
French Strisselspalt	2.22
German Spalt Select	2.22
Centennial	2.15
German Hallertau Hersbruck	2.11
Columbus	2.00
Nugget	2.00
Huller Bitterer	1.90
German Spalt	1.72
Bullion	1.50
Australian Pride of Ringwood	0.73
Eroica	0.05

undergo oxidation and other changes during boiling to create new flavor compounds.[29] Studies have found that the oxidation products that produce spicy hop flavors are well extracted into the wort during boiling.[30] Also, formation of floral compounds such as linalool (and its oxides) and geraniol are accelerated during the boil,[31] and these compounds survive well into the finished product.[32] Thus, the differences between dry-hopping and late hopping spring not only from the loss of volatile compounds but also from the creation of new flavors.

Unfortunately, the results from late hop additions can be somewhat inconsistent. You have already seen that the composition of the essential oils changes over time with many hops and that the amount of oil varies from year to year even in the same hop variety. In addition, hop compounds can be scrubbed away by the steam of the boil and the CO_2 that escapes during fermentation. As a result, any change in evaporation rate or fermentation temperature can affect hop character in the finished beer.[33]

In achieving optimal flavor and aroma with hop additions, whole hop products appear to be more desirable than pellets. Data show that the hop oil content of hop pellets decreases dramatically even during storage at temperatures below 32 °F (0 °C).[34] In addition, grinding and pelletizing may oxidize hop oils.[35] This oxidation may provide a little of that "aging" quality, discussed earlier and may be an asset if you factor it into your thinking.

Finally, of course, hop oil compounds (including all the oxidation products) appear to decline — in some cases dramatically — in bottled beer stored at room temperature.[36] Data on beers stored for two months showed that the flowery/floral compounds such as linalool and geraniol declined only modestly (11 to 12 percent), while the herbal and spicy compounds humulenol II and humulene diepoxide A dropped precipitously (66 to 84 percent).[37]

Table 10.5
Farnesene Analysis
(sorted by farnesene content as a percentage of total hop weight)

Variety	Total Oil as % of Hop Weight	Farnesene as % of Whole Oil	Farnesene as % of Hop Weight
German Spalt Select	0.75	20.0	**0.15**
German Tettnanger	0.80	14.0	**0.11**
Polish Lublin	0.95	11.0	**0.10**
German Spalt	0.80	12.5	**0.10**
Spalt (U.S.)	0.75	12.5	**0.09**
Czech Saaz	0.55	13.0	**0.07**
Cascade	1.15	6.0	**0.07**
Willamette	1.25	5.5	**0.07**
English Fuggle	1.05	6.0	**0.06**
Fuggle (U.S.)	0.95	4.5	**0.04**
Tettnanger (U.S.)	0.60	6.5	**0.04**
English Wye Challenger	1.35	2.0	**0.03**
Slovene Styrian Gold	0.75	3.5	**0.03**

Note: Those hop varieties not listed generally do not contain significant amounts of farnesene.

From a practical point of view, what all this means is that each different addition of late hops *will* have a different effect on the flavor of the finished product. Part of the joy of brewing is experimenting with these different techniques to see which ones, with which hops, provide the character you most want in your finished beer.

If you want hop aroma, you should definitely do some dry hopping. I recommend addition of the hops not to the primary fermentation but to the secondary fermenter or serving vessel. This has several effects. First, hops in the primary fermenter, especially whole hops, tend to make a big mess. If you use a blowoff tube, it will get plugged with hops, and you'll likely wind up with a gusher that puts beer on your ceiling and many square feet of surrounding area. Also, if you try to repitch your yeast, it will be full of hop debris.

Second, unboiled hops carry bacteria, wild yeast, and other undesirable organisms into the beer.[38] By adding the

Table 10.6
Hop Varieties That Show Changes in Hop Aroma Potential During Aging

Start High — End Low	Start Low — End High
Cascade	Hersbrucker
Galena	Tettnanger
Brewer's Gold	Fuggle
	Hallertau Mittelfruh
	Willamette
	Styrian Goldings
	Record

Table 10.7
Relative Concentrations of Hop Flavor and Aroma Compounds

	Oxidation Products (Spicy)		Citrus Products		Floral Products	
	Fresh	Aged	Fresh	Aged	Fresh	Aged
Highest level/gm of alpha acid	Cascade	Herbrucker	Kirin II	Kirin II	Kirin II	Kirin II
	Galena	Tettnanger	Wye Challenger	Wye Challenger	Cascade	Hersbrucker
	Wye Challenger	Fuggle	Wye Target	Wye Target	Hersbrucker	Tettnanger
	Fuggle	Record	Brewer's Gold	Eroica	Wye Challenger	Blisk
	Eroica	Kirin II	Cascade	Record	Tettnanger	Eroica
	Styrian	Wye Challenger	Eroica	Blisk	Eroica	Wye Target
	Tettnang	Blisk	Fuggle	Galena	Fuggle	Wye Challenger
	Record	Styrian	Tettnanger	Hersbrucker	Wye Target	Record
	Kirin II	Hallertau Mittelfruh	Willamette	Fuggle	Galena	Fuggle
	Wye Target	Willamette	Galena	Tettnanger	Blisk	Galena
	Brewer's Gold	Eroica	Nugget	Brewer's Gold	Brewer's Gold	Hallertau Mittelfruh
	Cluster	Wye Target	Hersbrucker	Nugget	Record	Cascade
	Willamette	Brewer's Gold	Record	Willamette	Hallertau Mittelfruh	Styrian
	Hallertau Mittelfruh	Galena	Perle	Hallertau Mittelfruh	Nugget	Nugget
	Hersbrucker	Cluster	Hallertau Mittelfruh	Cluster	Cluster	Willamette
	Olympic	Nugget	Styrian	Perle	Styrian	Brewer's Gold
	Nugget	Cascade	Cluster	Styrian	Willamette Gold	Cluster
	Columbia	Columbia	Olympic	Olympic	Perle	Perle
	Blisk	Perle	Blisk	Cascade	Columbia	Olympic
Lowest level/gm of alpha acid	Perle	Olympic	Columbia	Columbia	Olympic	Columbia

Relative Concentration of Flavor Compounds

From: R. T. Foster, and G. B. Nickerson, "Changes in Hop Oil Content and Hoppiness Potential (Sigma) During Hop Aging," ASBC Journal 43, no. 3 (1985): 127–135.

hops after primary fermentation, you have already allowed formation of alcohol in the beer to help fight off these contaminants. Thus, study of this practice concludes that it is microbiologically safe, especially after three days of fermentation.[39]

For creating hop flavor, you can start with a simple five-minute boil and work from there. My favorite recipes (I love hop flavor) often include three or even four hop additions in the last twenty minutes of the boil.

Finally, you have the steeping option. It has not been discussed very much in the literature, but it seems to provide results that are more similar to dry hopping than to a boil of five minutes or longer. Since the wort is not boiling during the steep, fewer volatile compoundss are lost and fewer of the boil-derived flavor compounds will be formed. In short, steeping provides a way to get some aroma character without the process challenges of dry hopping.

Quantitative Considerations

Realistically speaking, small brewers have few tools to predict the quantity of hop aroma or flavor they will get in a finished beer. Neither alpha acids nor hop oil as a percentage of hop weight have proven to provide effective control.

A number of more sophisticated systems have been proposed, but most are

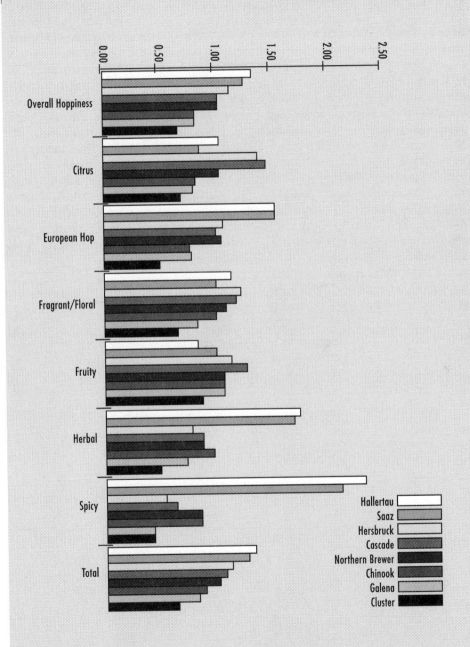

Figure 10.4
Indexed Taste Panel Perceptions of Hop Flavor

Source: T. L. Peppard, S. A. Ramus, C. A. Witt, K. J. Siebert, "Correlation of Sensory and Instrumental Data in Elucidating the Effect of Varietal Differences on Hop Flavor in Beer," ASBC Journal 47, no. 1 (1988): 18–26.

based upon costly chromatography techniques that will not soon be within the reach of the craft brewer.[40]

If you *really* want control of your late-hop character, the only solution discussed in the literature that can be achieved without expensive instrumental analysis is the use of hop extracts.[41] These extracts (different from the isomerized alpha acid extracts) contain the flavor and aroma compounds of specific varieties of hops in a concentrated liquid form. You can add them to taste in a finished beer and then reproduce your results in the future based upon the concentration of hop oil extract per gallon of beer. Of course these extracts are a bit pricey, and I don't think they are all that much fun to use. Few self-respecting craft brewers would be caught using this for anything other than experimentation.

Beyond this, you will have to be satisfied with rough estimates based upon your own experience and the success of others.

Generally, a 5-gallon batch of beer will require late-hop kettle additions in amounts varying from 0.25 ounces to 1 full ounce per addition. Dry hop amounts may be higher, say 1 to 2 ounces per 5 gallons. Each of the style chapters in part two of this book contain data on the average sizes of these additions in successful formulations.

If these amounts don't give you enough impact, make more additions. If the addition of 0.5-ounce at five minutes didn't give you the level of intensity you were looking for, try using a full ounce next time. If the flavor wasn't quite what you wanted, maybe you should add 0.5-ounce at twenty minutes as well. If these don't do it, maybe you need another addition at ten minutes, too. As I mentioned earlier, three, four, maybe even five hop additions can be made for flavor and aroma.

11 | HOP VARIETY CHARACTERISTICS

Project   Designing Great Beers
             Brewers Publications

Project No.   61766

Alsace: Hops grown in the Alsace area of France; may be either Strisselspalt or a strain called Elsasser. Sometimes used by big brewers but not usually seen in the U.S. market.

Aquila: Middle alpha variety previously grown in the United States, but as of 1994 this hop is no longer in production.

Banner: Middle alpha U.S. variety with rapidly declining production.

Bramling Cross: Considered an aroma hop, this English variety was bred as a replacement for Goldings and was very popular at one time in the United Kingdom. Little else is known about this hop.

Brewer's Gold: An old variety; it was released in 1934. It is interchangeable with Bullion and has a virtually identical chemical makeup. Like Bullion, it lacks stability in storage. Good breeding stock: It was a parent to Galena. It is highly bitter and not recommended for flavor or aroma applications.

Bullion: Sibling of Brewer's Gold from Wye College, University of London. Released in 1938, it is a cross of Goldings with American hops and is very unlike Goldings. Highly bitter; not recommended for flavor or aroma applications. Once very popular, it has experienced a decline since the late 1970s. The soft resins exhibit poor stability: Although its aroma can be aromatic and pleasant on the vine, it becomes harsh and pungent soon after picking.

Cascade: Released in 1972, its breeding included being crossed with Fuggle. It keeps poorly and requires cold storage immediately after baling. Although "coarse" compared to European aroma hops, it delivers very nice spicy/citrus flavors in beers. Anchor™ Liberty™ Ale is reportedly made exclusively with this hop. It can impart a grapefruit flavor, especially when aged before use. One taste-panel study rated Cascade higher than imported Saaz, Hallertau, and Hersbruck varieties for citrus and fruity flavors and placed it near the other three for the fragrant/floral flavor.[1]

Centennial: A cross of Brewer's Gold and an unknown USDA variety. It is a middle alpha hop with a citrus floral aroma character.

Challenger (English): Britain's second most popular hop as of the early 1990s, it is reputed to provide good aroma and is employed at all stages of brewing, including dry hopping. It has moderate alpha acid levels. Released in 1968, it is a cross of Northern Brewer with disease-resistant strains.

Chinook: Bred from Brewer's Gold, a Goldings variety, and wild hops, this variety has a distinct character in all applications. I find it piney and resinous even when boiled for sixty minutes. As a result of this distinct character, some people will not use this hop for any purpose. Bitterness tends toward the harsh side, and in flavor and aroma applications it is definitely overwhelming. I would recommend experimenting with this hop in a carefully controlled batch of beer before you use it to produce a "show" beer.

Cluster: Once the dominant U.S. hop, it is believed to be the oldest American variety still grown. Probably derived from native American hops or perhaps a cross with European varieties brought by settlers. It has few attractive features. I have never used this hop and see no motivation for doing so!

Columbus: A new variety of super-alpha hop, with alpha acids reported to be in the 14 to 16 percent range. No qualitative information is available at time of publication. Oil ratios are typical of high alpha hop.

Columbia: A general-purpose hop with a mild English flavor.

Comet: Cross of an old English variety called Sunshine and a wild male, it has a pungent "wild American" aroma. Some sources list it as "not recommended." Need I say more?

Crystal: A triploid developed from German Hallertau with contributions from Cascade, Brewer's Gold, and others. It has a flowery, perfumelike character that complements pale lagers.

East Kent Goldings (England): A fine English aroma hop that is generally preferred over Fuggle for finish and dry hopping. The Golding strain has been around for more than two hundred years and has contributed to the character of several other hop varieties.

Eroica: Released in 1980, this is a sibling of Galena. It has a better aroma than some high alpha hops but is recommended only for bittering applications, especially for English ales. Its storage properties are similar to Talisman, better than Bullion, not as stable as Galena or Clusters.

Fuggle: This variety has been in the United States since the latter half of the 1800s. Its aroma is described as "pronounced, somewhat spicy, not pungent." It is normal to have some seeds in the cone. When baled, these hops store fairly well.

Fuggle (English): One of Britain's most popular hops, this variety has been extensively used for finishing and aroma in dark ales. Its production in the United Kingdom has declined from 80 percent to 10 percent of the total hops crop since 1950.

Galena: This was the first commercially grown premium alpha hop developed in the United States. Released in 1972, by 1985 it was the second most widely grown. Developed from open pollination of Brewer's Gold. It has good storage properties and is reported to have an "English" flavor that can be pungent and very bitter.

Hallertau Hersbruck (German): German aroma hop with a spicy, somewhat floral character. It rates slightly higher than Hallertau or Saaz for citrus and fruity flavor; somewhat lower for herbal and spicy character.[2]

Hallertau Mittelfruh (German): Some consider this the king of all hops, the noblest of the "noble-type" hops. Used in German-style Pilseners to impart the refined, high-quality hop flavor and aroma they require. It is in decline due to growing problems and will soon be replaced by new German aroma varieties such as Hallertau Tradition. Attempts to grow it in the United States have been thwarted by poor yield. It is rarely seen in homebrew settings. It has been rated high in herbal, spicy, and European hop characteristics in taste-panel tests.[3]

Hallertau Tradition (German): A descendant of Hallertau Mittelfruh, it was bred for disease resistance. Released in 1991, it is reportedly undergoing expansion in German growing areas where it may at least partially replace Mittelfruh and Hersbruck. Too early for qualitative analysis.

Hallertau (U.S.): A German "noble-type" hop variety grown in the United States. Not the same as the European versions, but it is fairly clean and neutral with some spicy and floral character.

Hersbrucker (U.S.): Same variety as that grown in Germany.

Huller Bitterer: A German bittering hop rarely seen in U.S. distribution channels.

Liberty: An aroma hop bred from Hallertau Mittelfruh and released in the United States in 1991. Initial reviews report that it has an excellent aroma similar in character to the fine German hops.

Lublin (Polish): A fine aroma hop sometimes mentioned in the same breath with Saaz, from which it was bred. It meets the technical criteria for a "noble-type" hop. It was unavailable in the West prior to the opening of the Iron Curtain and is still rarely seen on the U.S. scene.

Magnum: A German hop grown on an increasing number of acres in the Hallertauer region.

Mt. Hood: A relatively new hop, it was released in the U.S. in 1989, bred from German Hallertau seedlings. Similar to German Hallertau and Hersbrucker in flavor and aroma, it is gaining popularity in German-style lagers brewed by American microbrewers.

Northdown (English): A Northern Brewer derivative reportedly with good flavor and aroma, it has replaced Northern Brewer in many U.K. applications and is said to be used throughout the brewing process, including dry hopping (according to the Campaign for Real Ale, or CAMRA).

Northern Brewer: A medium to high alpha hop now mostly grown in Germany. This was an early hybrid hop developed in England as a good general-purpose variety. It has an acceptable aroma profile. Reportedly the only hop used in Anchor Steam®.

Nugget: A cross between Brewer's Gold (⅝), East Kent Goldings (¹⁄₁₆), and Bavarian (¹⁄₃₂). It has good storage properties and sharp bitterness but little else to recommend it.

Olympic: Released in 1983, it is a cross of Brewer's Gold (¾), Fuggle (³⁄₃₂), EKG (¹⁄₁₆), and Bavarian (¹⁄₃₂). Extremely bitter.

Orion: A German middle alpha bitter hop reported to have a very good bitter quality.

Omega (English): A bittering hop that was introduced in the mid-1980s. Used by the Courage brewing company in some recipes.

Perle (German): A Northern Brewer cross with more alpha than other German varieties but a similar European aroma. According to Miller, "Excellent flavor, aroma not quite as fine as Hallertau, but still good. Recommended for all lagers except Pilsener."[4]

Pride of Ringwood (Australian): A cross between wild Tasmanian hop and English "Pride of Kent." It has relatively high alpha acid levels and is reasonably stable in storage but is considered coarse in aroma. Released in 1965, at which time it was the highest-alpha-acid hop in the world. It has accounted for 90 percent of the Australian crop and is associated with the well-known Foster's lager.

Progress (English): Introduced in 1966 as a wilt-tolerant Fuggle replacement and bred from Whitbread's Golding Variety. It is an aroma hop that is rapidly losing popularity and dying out; it was released just before brewers started placing increased emphasis on high alpha acid content.

Saaz (Czech): A true "noble-type" hop in anyone's book. Fine aroma and flavor. The prototypical hop for Pilseners. Taste-panel tests rate it higher than other European and American varieties for herbal, spicy, and European hop flavors but lower than other aroma hop varieties for citrus character.[5]

Spalt (German): A fine German aroma hop that some call noble. Spalt Spalter is somewhat in decline, but other varieties such as Spalt Select are taking over its role. It has a fairly delicate, fine aroma. Not often seen in U.S. homebrew channels, but it is available. Nice addition to an American lager.

Spalt (U.S.): Same variety as that grown in Germany, though some differences are to be expected due to variances in agricultural conditions.

Spalt Select (German): Released in 1991, bred to emulate the fine aroma character of Saaz, Tettnanger, and Spalt. It is too soon for any meaningful information to be available.

Strisselspalt (French): The major aroma hops of the Alsace area of France, near Strasbourg. Well accepted as a good aroma hop around the world, it is similar to Hersbruck in profile but is preferred by some breweries. Rarely seen in U.S. homebrew channels.

Styrian Goldings (Slovene): Bred from English Fuggles hops, this is a well-known aroma variety from the former Yugoslavia. It has a sharper flavor and aroma than German hops. May be found in both ales and lagers.

Talisman: A bittering hop related to Cluster but with a somewhat better aroma character. Released in 1965.

Target (English): An important high alpha acid British hop accounting for 40 percent of the U.K crop. Recommended for bittering only.

Tettnanger (German): A "noble-type" German hop, it provides a fine character that includes a unique mix of spicy, herbal, and flowery characteristics.

Tettnanger (U.S.): The same variety as that grown in Germany but with some differences in character.

Whitbread Golding Variety: A hybrid aroma hop that is classed as a Fuggle substitute. Not seen in the United States.

Willamette (U.S.): Bred from Fuggles in the United States and released in 1976. Provides an American-grown alternative to the English aroma hops. Seedless.

Yeoman (English): Introduced in 1980, similar to Target, with a more mellow aroma. Considered a bittering hop, suitable for lagers.

Zenith (English): Considered a bittering hop, even though it is high in oils with a "fairly good" aroma (according to Campaign for Real Ale). It is rarely used in commercial brewing and is not seen in the United States.

12 YEAST AND FERMENTATION

Project	Designing Great Beers
	Brewers Publications
Project No.	61766

It is no exaggeration to say that yeast makes the beer. The fruit of your brewing labor is, after all, only wort before the yeast goes to work. More important, the particular yeast you choose to add to the wort will determine what your beer will taste like just as much as any other ingredient you add.

Skeptical? Next time you brew, split off one gallon from the rest of your finished wort. Pitch that gallon with a different yeast from the one used in your main fermentation. For even more fun, split the whole batch into five 1-gallon batches and pitch each with a different yeast. Believe me, you will be amazed at the differences.

For several years now I have helped to organize a competition where we give about two dozen brewers a fixed kit of ingredients with which to brew a beer. It includes malt and hops,[1] but the brewer gets to pick the yeast. And guess what? No two beers are ever even remotely similar.

Although even the biggest brewers will buy the same malt their competitors use, they would never dream of using the same yeast. Indeed, they guard their yeast strain as if it were a fabulous diamond. Even some craft brewers have acquired or "developed" unique strains that they are reluctant to share with others.

At the same time, it can be ridiculously easy to get a new brewing yeast. You can purchase dry or liquid yeast from at least a half-dozen different suppliers, many of whom offer more than a dozen alternatives. These sources alone present many ale, lager, weizen, Belgian, lambic, wine, champagne, and mead yeasts, as well as other microorganisms that will ferment wort. (The only drawback to these sources is that the amount of yeast supplied is rarely adequate for fermenting a 5-gallon batch of homebrew, much less a 10-barrel commercial batch. More on this when I discuss pitching volumes.)

And you can collect and grow your own yeast. Fishing in the bottom of a bottle-conditioned beer often yields an interesting find. Or you may get to know one of the serious homebrewers who have developed a yeast bank with scores of yeast strains.

The bottom line is this: Yeast makes the finished beer what it is, and there are many options to choose from.

Two factors make identifying yeast a bit confusing. First, yeast don't wear name tags; and second, they change.

Unlike hops or malt, which you can often identify just by basic sensory evaluation, different yeast strains are difficult to distinguish from one another without sophisticated techniques such as chromosome mapping.[2] Even basic laboratory techniques, such as growing the yeast on plates or examining it under the microscope, often won't allow you to distinguish between two ale or two lager yeasts.

This difficulty in identifying yeast strains creates a number of problems for brewers. If you have more than one yeast in your brewery, you have to keep them strictly separated and carefully labeled. Any confusion or contamination will result in unexpected results in the flavor of finished beer.

If you reuse the same yeast over a long period, its very character may change. This is because the conditions of fermentation, harvest, and storage exert selection pressures on the yeast.[3] The specific members of the strain that like the conditions they are subjected to will thrive while others die out. As a result, you may wind up with a population that is very much different from what you started with.

As a result of these changes, two cultures of yeast that are supposed to be the same can produce different results. Let me give you an example.

At one point I decided to work on making a good weizen. The key, I knew, was as much in the yeast as in the recipe itself. In order to evaluate the available weizen yeasts, I decided to make 10 gallons of wort and split it into several batches, which I would pitch with different weizen yeasts.

I collected three different yeasts — two from different commercial suppliers and one from a yeast bank. Then I consulted a friendly midwestern "yeast rancher" to see what he knew about the individual strains. He was familiar with each one and believed they all had come from the same original pure German weizen yeast culture. Faced with this news, I changed one of the three yeasts to an alternate and carried on with the test.

Given what I had been told, I was confident that two of the three batches would taste the same. The finished results, however proved more different than I could have imagined. The two yeasts that were supposed to be the same gave noticeably different results. (Not surprisingly, the third yeast

was quite different from either one of the supposedly "matched" pair.) Although there are several possible explanations for this phenomenon, it seems likely that these two samples had undergone some changes in character somewhere between their common origins and my basement brewery.[4]

From this example you can see that until you know the character of a yeast, it is difficult to predict exactly how the resulting beer will taste. Fortunately, there is a good deal of data available on yeasts that can help you in the recipe formulation process.

In the remainder of this chapter I look at two aspects of yeast character, including both qualitative and quantitative factors. First, I will look at the parameters of yeast character that are commonly discussed and provide an overview of available yeast strains. Then, I consider the factors that affect yeast performance and therefore affect the flavor of a beer. I also discuss how to determine the amount of yeast you should pitch into your wort.

Yeast Characteristics and Strains

When brewers consider yeast, they usually look at a handful of parameters. These parameters help them decide which yeast to select for a specific use. In addition, they help to tell the brewer how the yeast should be handled during fermentation. In the paragraphs below, I have arranged five parameters in their order of importance for the recipe formulation process. Let's review them and get a sense of each one.

1. *Type:* The brewing yeasts are typically divided into three groups — labeled ale, lager, and weizen. The members of each group are related both in terms of their actual performance and in terms of their genetic structure.[5] There are also an increasing number of non-Saccharomyces wort fermenters available on the market. The selection of type is the first criteria you must apply when deciding upon a yeast.

2. *Flavor Character:* As mentioned above, individual strains of yeast within the same type produce very different flavor profiles. Depending upon the yeast, the resulting beer may be malty, hoppy, fruity, sulphur-like, woody, mineral, sweet, dry, neutral, or clean. Knowing what to expect from the strain you select is important to understanding the finished beer.

3. *Attenuation:* This is the extent to which the yeast ferments the sugars in the wort. For any specific mix of wort sugars, each strain will show a characteristic degree of fermentation. Some beer styles call for higher or lower than normal attenuation. Although you can find data given in percentages, it is usually enough to know this trait in general terms, such as low, medium, or high.

4. *Optimal Fermentation Temperature:* This tells the temperature that should be targeted during fermentation. If you are planning to ferment at ambient conditions in your house, you had better know if the yeast you are considering only works best at 62 °F (17 °C).

5. *Flocculation:* Flocculation is the clumping of yeast cells into grapelike clusters near the end of fermentation. Because the large clusters settle to the bottom of the fermenter faster than individual yeast cells do, the extent of flocculation determines how quickly the beer will clear. Highly flocculent yeast settle out quickly and produce a nice clear product. Although I can't remember ever using this as a selection criteria, it is nice to know what to expect. Beers with low-flocculation yeast may have to be fined or filtered to get them clear.

The Common Brewing Yeast Strains

Based upon typical yeast parameters, you can begin to characterize the different strains of yeast available to brewers. I have divided the ale and lager types into a number of strains that are commonly available. In doing this, I have tried to avoid using the commercial labels of a single supplier. On some occasions I found that two suppliers use the same name for very different yeasts. To know how these strains compare with the offerings of your favorite supplier, you'll need to compare the suppliers' descriptions with those offered in these profiles.

Ale Yeasts

Ale yeasts are probably the original beer producers used by people for more than five millennia. They ferment at warmer temperatures than lager yeasts and tend to collect at the top of the fermenter and are therefore called top-fermenting yeasts. Thanks to the long heritage of ale brewing, there is a vast array of different ale yeasts available.

American: Produces a clean, smooth character sometimes described as neutral. The classic American yeast ferments well even at temperatures down to the mid-50s °F (about 13 °C). Medium attenuation is typical. Flocculation is low to medium. It is generally regarded as an all-purpose yeast.

Belgian: Yeasts falling under this description generally produce a fairly high fruity, estery character that may include some clove or phenolic notes. They often have a high alcohol tolerance. Medium to high in both attenuation and flocculation. Belgian yeasts are sometimes labeled Abbey or Trappist.

British: At the moment, there are more than a dozen British ale yeasts available. About half seem to fit into some definable subgroup, and the others are unique. You'll have to study and experiment to find the ones you like best, but my general groupings will at least give you an idea of the different characteristics you are likely to find.

Examples of the first two groups will be found under those names, but the others are sold under variations of the name British Ale, often distinguished only by an item number.

- *Whitbread* is a tart, crisp, clean, well-balanced, fast-starting yeast. Its optimum fermentation is at 70 °F (21 °C), but it is tolerant of colder temperatures. It has medium attenuation and flocculation.
- *London* yeasts produce a mineral character with slight diacetyl or woody notes, a crisp/tart impression, and medium attenuation and flocculation. They like to ferment at 65 to 68 °F (18 to 20 °C).
- *Woody* yeasts are low-attenuating; they produce woody or oaklike flavors as part of an overall complex malt profile.
- *Full-bodied* yeasts provide a balance of classic ale fruitiness and are noted for their well-rounded, full-bodied character.
- *Classic* yeasts, some of which reportedly come from classic old English breweries, produce a clean, well-balanced product with some fruity esters.
- *Scottish* yeast provides a malty accent with low attenuation and will ferment at temperatures as low as 55 °F (13 °C) to simulate the cold fermentation practices of the Scottish brewers.

Canadian: Provides a clean, lightly fruity, complex finish. It is high in attenuation and flocculation and produces light-bodied beers. Good for lighter ales, including cream ale, bitter, and even pale ale.

German: Two very different strains of yeast may be found among those described as German yeasts. One gives a very dry, clean result, while the other gives a very much sweeter, maltier product.

- The *dry strain* ferments dry and crisp, leaving a complex yet mild flavor. It produces an extremely rocky head and ferments well down to 55 °F (13 °C). Flocculation is high and attenuation is medium to high. It is described by some as an "old" German ale yeast, and many use this for alt beers.
- The *sweet strain* produces full body, complex flavor, and spicy sweetness. It has low to medium attenuation and high flocculation. Its optimal fermentation temperature is 68 to 70 °F (20 to 21 °C). It is often described as an alt beer yeast, but the attenuation level laid is a bit too low for the style.

Kolsch: Good attenuation gives beers fermented with this type of yeast a crisp, clean finish. Malt character comes through well, and some fruity character is usually apparent. It can ferment at temperatures as low as the mid-50s °F (about 12 °C).

Irish: Two of the three yeasts I found under this description were highly attenuative yeasts intended for producing a classic dry Irish stout. A third example, although it's currently more popular, is a very low attenuator that is widely recommended for dark beers, including most stouts. Slight woody or diacetyl notes are common with both strains. Good stouts can be made with either of these yeasts, although you should be aware that the low attenuator tends to produce very high levels of diacetyl in high-gravity beers. The low attenuator is best for porters and Scotch ales.

Lager Yeasts

Lagers emerged from the German brewing traditions, where the selection pressures of cold-climate brewing brought these chill-loving yeasts to the fore. Typical fermentation temperatures for lagers are quite a bit cooler than are those for ales, in the range of 45 to 55 °F (7 to 13 °C). They typically ferment some sugars that ale yeasts do not and tend to produce a smoother, cleaner character in the finished beer.

American: Although you might expect to find examples of the yeasts used by big American brewers under this name, that is not always the case. Still, most examples produce a clean, crisp beer with a slight fruity character. High attenuation and medium flocculation are common. The one outlier in this category gives a woody character and produces a lot of diacetyl with medium attenuation and flocculation. Make sure you get the one you want!

California: This is a specialty yeast used to re-create the "California Common" style of brewing that is still practiced by Anchor Brewing Company. It ferments warmer than a normal lager yeast (up to 66 °F, 19 °C) and provides a malty profile that exhibits some fruitiness. Medium attenuation and high flocculation.

Bohemian: These yeasts provide the character seen in the classic Pilsener Urquell. Typically they produce a smooth, full-bodied beer with good malty character and a clean finish. Fairly low attenuation, medium flocculation.

Pilsen: A few suppliers provide a strain under this name in addition to their Bohemian lager yeast. This strain tends to be drier and crisper than the Bohemian and may be more appropriate to German Pilseners.

Bavarian: General-purpose lager yeasts that deliver rich, full-bodied flavor with the emphasis firmly on malt. Medium flocculation and attenuation. Although it can be a bit of a slow starter, it is generally good for all malt-balanced lager styles.

Munich: German yeast used for medium-bodied lagers and bocks. Produces a very smooth, soft overall impression while still providing a subtle complexity. Can be a bit fussy in fermentation and may produce a hint of sulphur when fresh. These yeasts bring out hop character more than the Bavarian strains. Medium attenuation and medium flocculation.

Danish/North German: These yeasts produce a crisp, clean effect that accentuates hop character. Low flocculation, medium attenuation, fairly forgiving. Optimal temperature is 48 °F (9 °C). Good for general pale lagers.

Weizen

Most suppliers offer at least one German wheat beer yeast, sometimes under the name *Saccharomyces delbruckii*. Most Ph.D.s tell me that by definition *Sac. delbruckii* is not capable of fermenting maltose and therefore is not used in beer of any kind. A few suggest that there is no species with this name. In fact, weizen yeasts are just funky examples of regular *Sac. cerevisiae*. Genetically they are quite distinct from both ale and lager yeasts,[6] so it is easy to understand the dramatically different flavor they produce in a beer.

These yeasts give significant ester and phenolic notes, with the two most common flavors being banana and clove. Depending upon the strain selected, the fermentation temperature used, and the wort composition, you can influence the balance of these two flavors from an extreme of either one to some balance of the two. Some suppliers offer a blend of weizen yeast with a regular ale yeast that downplays these classic weizen yeast flavors.

These yeasts typically do not flocculate well and are often left in the product, giving a hazy, cloudy effect. Attenuation is medium.

Neither Belgian nor Berliner wheat beers are made with these yeasts. Instead, they require other specialty yeasts, or in the case of Berliners, a bacterial culture.

Non-Saccharomyces Fermenters

Brettanomyces bruxellensis: A component of Belgian lambic-style brewing and also reported in Berliner weisse, this yeast provides a rich, earthy aroma and an acidic finish. Generally used in combination with other yeast or bacteria.

Brettanomyces lambicus: A wild yeast strain used in Belgian lambics. It contributes a flavor described as horsey or like old leather. Works slowly and may take a year or more to express the desired flavor. May be added to any ale to simulate that nineteenth-century "old ale" effect.

Pediococcus damnosus: This is a common brewery bacterium that most brewers avoid like the plague. It can produce diacetyl but when included purposely it is for the lactic acid effect it contributes with long aging. Primarily used in lambics.

Factors Affecting Yeast Performance

When you select a yeast for certain flavor characteristics, you may be surprised to find that they are not as pronounced as you had hoped. On other occasions you may find that the character of a yeast seems to have changed since the last time you used it when brewing.

A number of factors can influence the actual flavors produced by a yeast during fermentation. Many of them relate to the rate of growth and replication the yeast undergoes during fermentation. Although factors such as fermenter geometry and yeast strain play a role, the chief factors to concern the brewer are the temperature of fermentation, the composition of the wort, oxygen levels, and the quantity of yeast pitched into the wort.[7]

Yeasts change their metabolism according to the temperature of their environment. When this occurs, the chemical products they produce during fermentation can shift, altering the flavor of the beer that results. I mentioned one example of this in the differences observable in weizen yeast character. Another example

most brewers know is the increase in fruity character that occurs when almost any yeast is fermented at a temperature above the yeast's optimal range.

When I talk about the composition of the wort with regard to yeast metabolism, it really doesn't matter which specialty malts were added or how long you boiled your hops. What you need to focus on are the nutrients utilized by the yeast, namely sugar, oxygen, and nitrogen.

The wort from most mashes contains a fairly small percentage of simple sugars (glucose and fructose) and sucrose with large proportions of maltose and other di- and trisaccharides. Many homebrewers know from experience that if you add a lot of simple sugar to a beer, the flavor can take on a distinct — sometimes assertive — ciderlike flavor.

By the same token, inadequate amounts of oxygen or nitrogen can stunt yeast growth, leading to aborted or flawed fermentations and poor flavor results.

These three features of the wort are very difficult to measure in a small brewery, but by following good brewing practices, you can usually rest assured that you have proper wort composition. As I mentioned previously, the sugar profile is driven by your malt-to-adjunct ratio. As it turns out, the nitrogen nutrients (called free amino nitrogen, or FAN) also come mostly from malt. Thus, two of the three nutrients are dependent upon the use of adequate quantities of malt in your recipe.

In general, if you are using more than 10 percent raw sugar or more than 25 percent nonbarley adjuncts, you may have a problem. One way to solve it is with yeast nutrients that can be added to the boil, or even — if you are desperate — to the fermentation.

Oxygen is another essential nutrient for the yeast. This is why you aerate the wort before pitching.

Yeast use oxygen to build cell-membrane components that are essential to replication.

These cell-wall building blocks (unsaturated fatty acids and sterols) are often found in wort and can sustain yeast growth even when present at very low levels.[8] Thus, even when oxygen is not present in adequate amounts, proper yeast growth can occur. In this scenario, wort oxygen levels may be more important to the long-term viability of the yeast — and that is an issue only if it is going to be repitched more than one or two times. A second effect of poor aeration can be higher than normal ester production by the yeast.[9]

Despite all we know about yeast metabolism, there are still many questions and debates about how much aeration is needed for a successful fermentation. It appears that most yeast require a minimum of 5 parts per million of oxygen in the wort[10] but that some yeast show no change in performance when levels rise above 6 parts per million.[11] On the other hand, experiments with lager yeast show that some strains achieve optimal performance only at levels of 10 to 12 parts per million of oxygen.[12] What is clear is that different strains of yeast have different requirements for oxygen.[13]

To complicate this further, it is known that, using air, the maximum oxygenation levels achievable are 8.5 parts per million in a 1.040 wort and 7.9 parts per million in a 1.070 wort.[14] In practice, the splashing used by most homebrewers no doubt achieves a level of aeration that is somewhat lower. Nonetheless, many homebrewers achieve excellent fermentation and produce superlative beers. The preceding paragraphs suggest several reasons why this occurs, and ample pitching rates may also help.

Professional practice on this issue varies. To increase wort oxygen levels, a number of small breweries use oxygen to aerate their worts, but I'm told that big breweries generally just use air. And lest you think the use of pure oxygen can be undertaken without any risks, you should know that excessive oxygenation can lead to excess yeast growth and reduced ethanol production.[15] (Some would consider this a minor consequence and rightly point out that excessive oxygenation levels may be difficult to achieve, even with oxygen.)

Although special equipment can be used for aeration with either air or oxygen, splashing into the fermenter is still the most widely practiced homebrew technique. One time you might consider more aggressive aeration techniques is with higher-gravity worts. The solubility of oxygen decreases with the increasing gravity of your wort, as indicated above. Here, a second racking step can be completed, in effect repeating the splashing achieved upon transfer from the boiling pot.

Of course, if you are having problems with fermentation, you can take steps to increase oxygenation of your worts using more aggressive aeration techniques and even oxygen. However, it can be much easier to increase the amount of yeast pitched.

Pitching Rates

As a general rule, homebrewers pitch far less yeast to their worts than they should. Evidence of this comes from the standard packages of yeast sold for homebrewing use. They generally contain only a small percentage of the total yeast population needed to achieve recommended pitching rates.

On a commercial scale, good brewing practice calls for pitching no less than 10 million yeast cells per milliliter of wort.[16] That's approximately 200 billion yeast cells in a 5-gallon batch. This minimum amount is intended for "normal" gravity worts, and those with higher OG will need even more yeast. The standard rule of thumb for worts of all gravities is this: 1 million yeast cells per degree Plato per milliliter of wort. (For purposes of this calculation, you can assume that degrees Plato are equal to specific gravity divided by four.)

Although lower pitching rates can be used successfully, this rate is recommended by a number of sources, even for ale fermentations.[17]

If you perform this calculation on a variety of wort sizes and gravities, you will find that the recommended pitching range is between 200 and 400 billion yeast cells for a 5-gallon batch.

Knowing this is fine, but the real question is: How are you going to get that many yeast cells, anyway? As we'll see in the paragraphs below, most yeast sources used by small brewers don't supply anywhere near this number of yeast cells. As a result, some reduced pitching rate must often be accepted. A reduced rate that is achievable and gives good results is a total of 10 to 20 billion yeast cells for 5 gallons of beer.[18] Let's call this the homebrew pitching rate and consider it to be the absolute minimum that should be pitched. Let's look at how you have to treat the various forms of yeast to get them to an optimal pitching level.

Yeast generally comes in three forms: dry, liquid slurry, or grown on a slant. Each provides a progressively smaller number of yeast cells per package. Let's look at how these sources can provide an adequate amount of yeast for pitching.

Dry yeast have the potential to provide the greatest number of yeast cells for pitching into a wort. Good brewing practice guidelines call for 0.5-gram of dry yeast per liter of normal strength wort.[19] Thus, for a 5-gallon (19 liter) batch, you would need 9.5 grams of yeast.

Most of the foil packets of dry yeast sold for homebrewing contain 7 grams of yeast, and some contain as much as 14 grams. I counted a sample recently and found 20 billion cells per gram of dried yeast material. Thus, a 7-gram packet should deliver 140 billion cells, which is just about right for a 5-gallon batch.

The biggest question with dried yeast is viability. Although drying helps to preserve the yeast during shipping and stor-

age, poor conditions can lead to extensive deterioration. To ensure that you are getting the most from dry yeast, check the storage conditions at your retailer and "proof" your yeast before use as described in various introductory texts on homebrewing. But even with dry yeast that is not in the best condition, you should get 10 to 20 percent viability, and that will meet the alternate homebrew pitching rate.

Liquid yeast cultures offer the brewer a wide variety of fresh yeast from which to choose. Two styles of liquid culture may be offered to homebrewers. In one, the package includes both yeast and starter wort that can be mixed together to increase the total cell count and to make the yeast ready for pitching. The second style includes just the yeast in a liquid medium, and the user is expected to make his or her own starter to prepare the yeast for pitching.

One popular brand of liquid yeast that has been available for a number of years is Wyeast. The manufacturer claims to deliver about 2.5 billion cells per package after the package has expanded. My own counts on several packages gave results close to this, with only one falling below the 1 billion mark. A couple were at 5 billion or slightly higher. Still, amounts in this range are one hundred times less than the commercial pitching rate and a quarter to an eighth of the minimum homebrew pitching rate.

To compensate for this, you should make a starter to increase the total yeast count for pitching. It could take as much as 11 liters (almost 3 gallons) of starter to get the commercial cell count for a 5-gallon batch, so you may be better off shooting for the homebrew pitching rate. Starting with 2.5 billion cells in 50 milliliters of wort, you can get the total count up to about 20 billion cells with 1 quart of starter.[20]

Finally, we come to yeast slants. A "slant" is a small test-tube-like vessel containing agar. The portion of the agar near the top of the test tube is sloped diagonally across the tube so that the surface area is much greater than the cross-section of the tube. Once yeast is grown on the agar surface, it can be easily stored and transported. Rather than provide a liquid slurry of yeast, some suppliers simply provide a slant of the yeast, which can be grown up to pitching volume.

When a slant is grown up to pitching volumes, one manufacturer says that a good number for estimating cell counts is 50 million cells per milliliter of starter. Following this rule, you need about 4.5 liters (about 1.2 gallons) of starter to generate the commercial pitching rate for a 5-gallon batch. Here again, a starter of about 1 quart should deliver the minimum yeast count needed for a good fermentation.

Although I occasionally make a 1-gallon starter from either a slant or a liquid yeast culture, the excess fluid constitutes a significant diluent in the final beer. If I plan far enough ahead, I will chill the gallon of starter in the refrigerator after fermentation is complete and then separate the beer from the yeast slurry on the bottom. This slurry can be pitched directly or roused with a few cups of wort an hour or two before you pitch.

The richest source of yeast for pitching is the bottom of your fermenter. If you can arrange to brew every few weeks, you can repitch the yeast from a prior batch and meet the commercial pitching rates with no problem. The length of time that you can store yeast this way will vary depending upon the yeast strain, storage temperature, and original condition of the yeast. Practical guidelines usually say to reuse the yeast within one week.[21] Another source tells me that the loss of viability is about 25 percent per week, so if you have enough yeast, you might get by with two or three weeks.[22]

As for quantity, an old brewery rule of thumb calls for 1 pound of yeast slurry per barrel of wort.[23] That equates to 0.5-ounce (by weight) per gallon, or 2.5 ounces (by weight) per 5-gallon batch. This, in turn, appears equal to about 1 fluid ounce per gallon, or about 5 to 6 fluid ounces for a 5-gallon batch.[24]

Table 12.1 provides a summary of the yeast concentration data, including recommended pitching amounts.

Table 12.1
Summary of Yeast Pitching Guidelines

| Yeast Type | Quantity of Yeast Cells | | Pitching Guidelines | | |
	From Source	In Starter	Per Gallon	In 5 Gallons	Notes
Dry	20 billion/g	—	1.9 g	9.5 g	From package
Slurry*	1.5 billion/mL	—	0.5 oz. (weight)	2.5 oz. (weight)	From prior batch
			1.0 oz. (volume)	5–6 oz. (volume)	From prior batch
Liquid	50–100 million/mL	20 million/mL	1 qt.	1.2 gal.	Optimal starter
			1 c.	1 qt.	Minimum starter
Slant	—	20–50 million/mL	1 qt.	1.2 gal.	Optimal starter
			1 c.	1 qt.	Minimum starter

*Yeast slurry harvested from the bottom of a fermenter.

PART TWO

13 INTRODUCTION TO PART TWO: THE STYLE CHAPTERS

Project	Designing Great Beers
	Brewers Publications
Project No.	61766

In part one of *Designing Great Beers*, I reviewed recipe formulation issues common to all recipes, for instance, the character of different malts and hops and the calculations required to manage specific gravity and bitterness.

In part two, I discuss recipe formulation issues related to the brewing of specific styles of beer. Each chapter examines one style or several closely related styles. In these chapters, you'll find both historical information and contemporary brewing approaches. I think you will find both types of information will stimulate your thinking about how a style might be brewed. This, in turn, broadens the number of ways in which you might approach each style and serves ultimately to enrich your understanding of the style today.

The history section in each chapter varies considerably depending on the longevity and popularity of the style. In some cases, such as wheat beers and Scottish ales, we can only trace the barest skeleton of a trail leading from the style's creation to today's interpretations. In other cases, such as porter or Vienna/Oktoberfest, we have a rich trove of cultural, business, and technical history related to the style.

Commercial Examples

Flavor descriptions and quantitative parameters help to define the style, and commercial examples available in the United States are cited in each chapter for the benefit of those who wish to conduct direct sensory research.

For information more directly applicable to the recipe formulation process, wherever possible I provide detailed data on the ingredients and methods currently used by commercial brewers. In doing this, I have relied heavily on two sources for raw data. For ales, the key source was Roger Protz's *The Real Ale Drinker's Almanac*.[1] It provides data on hundreds of beers made by British brewers, including gravity, bitterness, grist composition, and hop bill. Without this data as a starting point, many of the analyses of commercial beers that are included in the ale chapters would not have been possible.

For lagers, I could find no source as detailed as Protz's fine work. What I did find, however, was a long series of laboratory analyses published as nearly fifty articles in the German brewing journal *Brauindustrie* during the 1980s.[2] These studies were conducted by Professor Anton Piendl of the famous Weihenstephan brewing institute, and they covered five hundred beers from one hundred different countries. Just collecting these studies was quite a challenge. It would have proven impossible if Charlie Papazian had not had one complete set of the articles under lock and key in his library.

My thanks to him both for having the foresight to collect them years ago and for sharing them with me for this project.

Recipe Data

After a review of the available commercial information, each chapter looks at the recipe formulations used by accomplished homebrewers. This data comes from what has undoubtedly been the world's largest homebrew competition, the National Homebrew Competition (NHC) conducted each year by the American Homebrewers Association (AHA).

The recipes I selected for analysis were those that made it to the second round of judging during two years, 1993 and 1994. Each year, the three thousand or so entries in the NHC undergo first-round judging in four to six different regions of the country. The judges at these regional competitions pick the three best beers in each style category to send on to the second round. In the second round, held about six weeks after the first, judges evaluate the twelve to fifteen beers from each style that have been forwarded by the regions. At this second round of judging, the first-, second-, and third-place winners in each style for the entire competition are selected.

There are some pros and cons to using judged entries as the basis for any characterization of a style. One of the biggest advantages is that the beers are judged blind, so judges do not know the brewer or the recipe while they are tasting the beer. This means that their decisions about the quality and character of the beer are based solely upon sensory evaluation.

On the other hand, we know that no matter how much we try to make judging an objective process, it still contains a significant subjective component. Still, the judges that participate in the NHC have been tested on their knowledge of brewing and beer styles. Furthermore, they are generally the most experienced people in

the United States at judging classic styles of beer.

One reason that I chose to analyze all the second-round beers was to minimize the effects of judge subjectivity. Two to four judges in each region participate in selecting the beers that will be forwarded to the second round. Because of this, the collection of second-round beers for each style generally represents the input of ten to fifteen judges, or nearly as many judges as we have beers.

I took one further step in using data from two different years of the competition. This increased the amount of data available for analysis and further diluted the influence of individual judges on the character of that data.

In the end, I had fifteen to thirty recipes for each style, and the profiles that they presented generally matched very well with the technical characteristics of the style, and often with the commercial data as well. In cases where anomalies occur — such as the nearly universal acceptance of American hops in what should be English-style India pale ales — it is clear that a wide group of beer judges feel this is the proper approach to the style today.

Terminology

In analyzing both the commercial and the NHC second-round data for each style, I generated some standard charts regarding malt and hop usage. A couple of the terms used in these analyses bear further explanation.

The malt analyses are divided into two sections, called "incidence" and "proportion" (see the table 14.5 on page 146). The incidence data tells you how often brewers include a particular type of grain or fermentable in their recipe. Proportion tells you how much of the ingredient is used in those recipes that include it.

Simply stated, incidence is the frequency with which a particular malt is found in recipes for a certain style. If you looked at eight pale ale recipes and found that six contained crystal malt and two did not, you could say that the incidence of crystal malt in these recipes is six out of eight or 75 percent.

Proportion refers to the amount of a particular grain added to a recipe relative to the total quantity of grain used. If a recipe has 1 pound of crystal malt and 7 pounds of pale ale malt, the proportion of crystal malt is 1 pound divided by 8 pounds, or 12.5 percent.

The proportion sections give three figures for each major fermentable ingredient: an average as well as a minimum and a maximum (listed as Range %). All values are given as percentages. The total number of recipes included in the proportion analysis is noted at the bottom of the table. At times the number of recipes included in the proportion analysis may differ from the number used in the incidence analysis. This occurs because some recipes provided a list of ingredients without giving the amounts used.

The proportion figures for each ingredient are based only on the recipes that included that particular ingredient. Thus, the average proportion figure tells you the mean percent contributed by an ingredient among the recipes that used that ingredient. Likewise, the minimum proportion tells you the smallest amount included in any recipe that used that ingredient. Thus, if you find a reading of "0 percent" for the minimum proportion, you know that at least one recipe included this ingredient in an amount that equaled less than 0.5 percent of the total grist weight.

In using these analyses, look at incidence charts to decide which grains to include in your recipe. Then, having made that decision, look at the proportion data to help you decide how much of each ingredient to use.

In addition to the malt and hop analyses, most chapters include information on the yeast strains used in the NHC second-round beers. In most cases, strain names are given without reference to a specific commercial product. These strain names are based on the descriptions listed in the chapter on yeast (chapter 12) in part one of this book.

Specific Measures

Most of the quantitative data provided in these chapters will be easily understood by brewers of all levels. Only two specific measures that I have used require further explanation. The first of these is fairly widely used; the second I pressed into service for purposes of these analyses.

The first measure is apparent attenuation. This is a measure of the extent to which a wort is fermented, and it is based on original and terminal gravity readings. When expressed as a percentage, the difference between the original and final gravity readings divided by the original gravity equals apparent attenuation. Here's a quick example: A pale ale with OG of 1.048 gives a reading of 1.012 before bottling. The apparent attenuation equals 75% as determined by

$$(48 - 12) \div 48 = 36 \div 48 = 0.75$$

Note that the OG reading is first converted to gravity units, or GUs. The same calculation can be performed directly on gravities read on the Balling or Plato scale. For this example, OG is 12, TG is 3, and apparent attenuation (AA%) is equal to

$$(12 - 3) \div 12 = 9 \div 12 = 0.75$$

As you read through the style chapters, you'll see that apparent attenuation is an important characteristic in understanding styles.

The second measure I adopted for these analyses is a ratio of bitterness to original gravity. This measure helps you understand the real balance of a style with just one number. The old English brewers accomplished a similar goal by stating the "pounds of hops per quarter of malt" used in their recipes. A figure like this is particularly helpful when you are looking at styles where original gravity can vary considerably, such as old ales or the whole family of bitters and pale ales.

When listed, this measure is referred to as "BU:GU ratio," and it usually has a value between 0.20 to 1.20. It is calculated by dividing IBU by original gravity expressed in gravity units. Here's an example: A pale ale with an original gravity of 1.050 contains 40 IBU. The BU:GU ratio is 0.80, determined by dividing 40 IBU by 50 gravity units (GU).

Concerning bitterness, I should mention that the IBU figures for the homebrew recipes were calculated by me during analysis using the values listed in table 9.3 (chapter 9). If you have determined the proper levels of utilization for your own system, you may want to adjust the target bitterness levels accordingly. On the other hand, if you use the values shown in chapter 9, you'll be adding the same quantities of alpha acid to your recipes that the average homebrewer did in making his or her successful recipe.

14 THE BARLEY ALES OF GERMANY

Project	Designing Great Beers
	Brewers Publications
Project No.	61766

For those of us who live in the United States, the styles known as kölsch and alt remain something of an enigma. Few examples can be found among either imported or craft-brewed fare. And when examples *are* found, debate inevitably arises about their authenticity compared to the "real" German examples. As we will see, the alt style seems particularly susceptible to such debates.

With regard to this supposed authenticity of styles, we often turn to history for guidance. But in this case, the passage of time has left few clues regarding the character or evolution of these styles. Ales have probably been brewed continuously in Germany for many centuries, but the barley-based ale styles we know today may not have been formulated until the last one hundred years.

A German text on top-fermented beers published in 1938 (*Obergärige Biere und ihre Herstellung*) makes no mention of the names kölsch and alt.[1] Instead, we find a listing for "Obergärige Lagerbier,"[2] which has characteristics like those recognized for alt and kölsch. This phrase literally means "top-fermented lager beer," and it is reportedly the name under which alt beer is commonly sold in Düsseldorf brewpubs even today.[3]

This odd mix of brewing descriptors captures the essence of these styles. They are fermented using an ale — or top-fermenting — yeast. But following fermentation, they undergo a period of aging, or lagering, at cool temperatures. The resulting beer has a flavor profile with characteristics of both a lager and an ale.

According to this German source on top-fermented beers, this style did not really appear until about 1898 to 1900. At this time a small revival in the popularity of top-fermented beers led to the development of this style, which the source describes as being more suited to the demands of consumers[4] — who, of course, were all accustomed to drinking nothing but lager beer.

The application of lagering to the ale styles may have been prompted by consumer desire for a lagerlike flavor profile. But the timing of this development also makes some sense from a technology perspective, for refrigeration was becoming fairly commonplace in breweries by the end of the 1800s. Thus, development of the styles as we know them today appears to have resulted from an intersection of consumer tastes, brewing technology, and brewer innovation.

Still, we cannot discard the centuries of brewing history that preceded development of these contemporary styles. Many events influenced the course of ale brewing in Germany, creating the conditions that allowed for creation of alt and kölsch at the appropriate time. We get some hint

Table 14.1
Analysis of Münster Altbier (1883)

OG	12.25
TG	1.30
Attenuation	89.4%
ABW	4.45%
Lactic acid	0.372%

of this in the single analysis of Münster altbier that is available from the nineteenth century (see table 14.1).[5]

The level of attenuation in this beer is remarkably high, but contemporary alts and kölsch beers also show high attenuation levels. The gravity level is also quite similar to today's product — which is remarkable considering the age of this data.

The feature that most distinguishes this beer from contemporary examples is the high level of acidity. Lagers and present-use ales from the late 1800s show lactic acid levels of 0.060 to 0.180. By comparison, the level in this altbier is similar to that of Berliner weisse, thus we could expect it to have quite an acidic flavor.

Acidic sourness is an accepted characteristic in some beer styles and clearly has its roots in historical production practices. But whereas this acidity has survived in the German Berliner weisse, it has been eliminated from the kölsch and alt beers. In the case of the former, the acidic flavor seems to have been desired by the brewers; however, in the case of the latter, the sourness may have been unintentional. In evidence of this, we have a quote from one Jacobus Theodorus Tabernaemontanus in the year 1613.

In some cities of the Rhine a beer is made now, and it is a pity that good fruit is spoiled in such manner; the people derive only half the benefit from it, for the reason that before a cask is half emptied, the other half has spoiled and has become sour. The cause of this is that not enough malt is used and too much water, and that it is not boiled, not to speak of the fraud that instead of hops some take willow leaves, others kaminvuss, in order to color the beer.[6]

Although we can't read too much into this quote, both Cologne and Düsseldorf are located along the Rhine, and their beers might have been the subject of this observation. Furthermore, the same stubbornness that kept ale brewing alive in the region slowed the adoption of hops and caused various spices to be used instead. Without the protective bitterness of hops, souring of the finished beer was no doubt a common occurrence. To fully appreciate these influences requires a brief review of the history of brewing in Cologne.

Brewing in Cologne

Founded by the Romans, Cologne was raised to the status of a free city in A.D. 949. Cologne is nearly equidistant from London and Munich and from its earliest history had commercial relations with London that may have influenced its brewing practices.[7]

By the 1200s, brewing was a major activity in Cologne, and a brewers guild was represented on the town council formed in 1396. At this time, hops had come into use in most parts of present-day Germany, but a substance called *gruit* was still used to flavor beer in the Cologne region. Gruit is defined by Arnold as "the macerated or crushed aromatic substances used in brewing instead of hops."[8] Its continued use in the face of competition from hops was the subject of nearly three hundred years of struggle in and around Cologne.

It seems the gruit trade was controlled by the Archbishop of Cologne, who refused to relinquish the requirement that all beer — both commercial and private — must contain the requisite dose of his secret recipe. This resistance to hops would continue through most of the fifteenth century, but hops would eventually win out. Still, gruit remained a part of the brewing culture for many years, and the term *Gruitherren* was an honorific title for brewers in the region through the nineteenth century.

This resistance to hops may have spawned some of the resistance to lager beers, that next challenged the powerful brewers of Cologne. In 1603 and again in 1698, a "mandate against the brewing of bottom-fermented beer" was enforced in the city proper. Arnold provides details as follows.

The young master brewer has to swear, according to the formula of the oath of August 12, 1698, "that you prepare your beer, as of old, from good malt, good cereals, and good hops, well boiled, and that you pitch it with top-yeast, and by no means with bottom yeast, no 'Tollbier,' raw wort, no noxious herbs, no matter of what name."[9]

This passage formed a sort of *Reinheitsgebot* for ale brewers of the day. It appears to correct the faults attributed to Rhine beers by Tabernaemontanus by requiring the use of hops, by ensuring that the wort is "well boiled," and by prohibiting the use of any "noxious herbs" that might be used to adulterate the brew. (If London brewers of the same period had taken such an oath, porter would have been quite a different drink for much of its history!)

The word *Tollbier* in this passage simply means lager beer. Brewers who made lager were banished outside of the town walls, and the citizens of Cologne would

have to leave the city to enjoy it. (Ah, the romance of the forbidden!) Despite decrees against such behavior (both the brewing and the drinking), this clandestine lager economy continued for nearly two centuries. In 1750, the ale brewers in the city were still trying to eliminate the brewing of lager beers.[10] However, not long after, they gave in and began to brew lagers themselves.

The brewers' oath of 1698 may also be the source of the term "alt" as applied to the ale styles of Germany. In German, *alt* means "old." The oath binds brewers to prepare their beer "as of old." The guidelines given for this "old" method are clear and relevant for brewers even today. Thus it is not surprising that a German brewer making top-fermented beers according to this formula might dub the result an "alt" beer.

Of course, today we associate the alt style more closely with Düsseldorf than with Cologne. The related but pale-colored kölsch takes its name from the German of Cologne, which is Köln. The development of this pale alternative is almost certainly a twentieth century invention, although data about formulations and even malt characteristics have proven difficult to find. Indeed, I have not found a single reference to either of these styles by their current names prior to 1980. Though I'm sure there must be other references in the post–World War II German literature that I have not had time to find, none of the general brewing or beer references of the twentieth century even hint at the existence of barley-based ale styles.

Contemporary Alt and Kölsch

Given the scant history available on alt and kölsch, we must treat them almost as if they were delivered fully developed to the beer world within the last few decades. Fortunately, there is some significant data available about these styles that allow us to establish a pretty good set of technical parameters. By doing this, we can establish a better system for determining what constitutes an authentic example of the style when we find beers under the alt and kölsch names in the United States.

The primary source for the data on these styles is the work of Professor Anton Piendl in the series entitled *500 Bier Aus Aller Welt* (500 Beers from All Over the World) that appeared in the German trade magazine *Brauindustrie* during the 1980s. Professor Piendl completed separate articles on each style, from which I extracted twenty-two altbier profiles and nine kölsch profiles, as presented below. In addition, I found another article on altbier published in 1980, which included analyses of a dozen different examples of the style and provided some useful insights into brewing techniques.

As the alt style seems to be the older of the two, let's take a look at it first. Quite a number of brewers throughout Germany market beers that carry the name alt. Not surprisingly, they span a broad range of characteristics — although chiefly with regard to their bitterness. The current AHA description of the style calls it Düsseldorf-style alt beer, and most people regard that town as the source of the authentic examples of the style. Thus, let us take the alts from Düsseldorf as our starting point in examining the style.

From Prof. Piendl's work, I found profiles of five Düsseldorf alts by the following names: Düssel Alt, Gatzweilers Alt, Frankenheim Alt, Schlosser Alt, and Uerige Alt.

The average profile of these five (see table 14.2) shows us a style with average original gravity, high attenuation, assertive but not extreme bitterness, a deep copper color, and ester levels that fall between those typically found in lagers and those found in ales.

Among these five, the most unique is Zum Uerige Alt, a beer some cite as a prototype of the style. At 50 IBU, this beer is intensely bitter yet wonderfully refreshing. In truth, however, Zum Uerige is as much an outlier from the average Düsseldorf alt as are the watered-down industrial versions of the style produced by the big breweries in Munich. In short, bitterness is a hallmark of the style, but it need not be extreme to be accurate.

As you look across the full range of alt beers produced in Germany, bitterness provides the key point of difference. Listed below are the analytical values for Uerige Alt, the group of five Düsseldorf-brewed alts (including Uerige) and then two groups of alts made by breweries outside Düsseldorf. The first "outside" group includes beers that are substantially similar to the Düsseldorf alts — in fact you'll see that there is very little variation in the analytical data. The second group of "outside" beers are those that are substantially different from the Düsseldorf group — most dramatically with regard to bitterness (see table 14.2).

These four groups of beer are remarkably similar in every respect except bitterness. Uerige — and perhaps one or two similar examples — form a class of their own. From there, BUs drop while all else

Table 14.2
Analytical Values of Düsseldorf-Brewed Alts

Beer or Group	OG	SG	Apparent Atten.%	ABW%	BUs	Color (EBC)	Acetate Esters
Zum Uerige	11.8	1.047	78	3.70	48	33	NA
Düsseldorf-made Alts	11.7	1.047	80	3.84	33	34	28
Others, like Düsseldorf	11.8	1.047	79	3.83	31	37	25
Others, not like Düsseldorf	11.8	1.047	80	3.87	25	38	32

stays virtually the same: gravity, attenuation, alcohol, even color, and esters vary little. By contrast, the BUs drop at least one complete flavor threshold (5 BUs) between the Düsseldorf-style beers and those not like the Düsseldorf beers. This final group includes one beer with BU as low as 12 and another — commonly seen in the United States as Pinkus Müller Alt — at 18. These beers clearly do not represent the Düsseldorf style of alt beer.

Among the beers that are like those brewed in Düsseldorf are Rhenania Alt, Waldschloss Alt, Diebels Alt, König-Alt, and Hannen Alt. This group of beers has the following BU:GU ratios: 0.70 average, 0.56 minimum, and 1.00 maximum.

Beyond bitterness, two other features of Alt beer should be noted by brewers. First is the high level of attenuation seen across the style. Average attenuation of these beers approaches 80 percent, meaning that a beer with an original gravity of 1.047 should have a final gravity of 1.010 to 1.008. Achieving this effect will require attention to both the mash process and yeast selection.

Second, the deep color of alt beer is achieved through the use of specialty malts for a portion of the grist. Though some commercial producers use caramel for coloring beers, most will add a portion of Munich malt and even some small amounts of black malt in order to achieve the desired color and malt flavor. I discuss grist composition in further detail later in this chapter.

Compared to commercial alt beers, the commercial kölsch beers are fewer in number and less diverse in their character (see table 14.3). Overall, they are quite similar to

the alts in many respects. The original gravity is identical; esters and alcohol level are quite similar. Remarkable as it seems, the level of apparent attenuation is even higher for kölsch than for altbiers, with an average near 84 percent.

The biggest difference comes in color. Kölsch displays a pale character quite similar to that found in Pilseners. Indeed, the grain bill for commercial kölsch beers relies heavily on Pilsener malt and may even include up to 20 percent wheat malt.

Finally, there is the issue of bitterness. Overall, the bitterness of kölsch is nearly 25 percent lower than that for an authentic Düsseldorf alt. However, given the higher level of attenuation and lighter flavor of a Pilsener-plus-wheat-malt grist, the perceived bitterness may be quite similar to that found in an alt. Overall, the bitterness levels found in kölsch indicate a BU:GU range of 0.47 to 0.63, with the average firmly above 0.50.

One aspect of beer flavor that we have not discussed for alt and kölsch is hop flavor and aroma. In general, brewers of these styles reserve their hops for bittering purposes. The commercial examples typically have no hop aroma and very little hop flavor, if any at all.

Brewing Alt and Kölsch

Alt and kölsch share many common attributes (see table 14.4). Much of this results from the brewing process, which is unique among other ales and nearly identical for these two beers. These process differences relate primarily to the fermentation and conditioning of the beer, as I discuss below.

Table 14.3
Commercial Kölsch Characteristics

	SG	ABW	BU	Acetate Esters	%AA	Color (SRM)
Average	1.047	3.91	25	29	84	5
Min.	1.044	3.50	21	20	79	4
Max.	1.049	4.18	31	36	86	7

Table 14.4
Characteristics of Alt and Kölsch

Characteristic	Düsseldorf-Style Alt	Kölsch
Original gravity	1.045–1.050	1.044–1.049
Bitterness	26–50	20–30
BU:GU	0.70 Avg.	0.53 Avg.
Hop flavor	Very low	Low
Hop aroma	None	None
Color (SRM)	11–20	3.5–7
Apparent extract	1.008–1.010	1.006–1.010
Apparent attenuation	78–82%	80–85%
Alcohol (volume)	4.3–5	4.4–5
Esters	Low	Low
Diacetyl	None	None
Flavor profile	Medium to high maltiness with a dry, bitter finish. Some dark malt character.	Dry, winelike palate, with medium bitterness in finish.

The key differences between the styles of alt and kölsch come in the composition of the grain bill, so let us begin examination of the style with that subject.

Grains

Most of the available sources of information on commercial beers agree that Pilsener malt serves as the base for the alt and kölsch styles.[11] When Pilsener malt is not specified, then a European two-row malt is the alternative for the majority of the grist.[12]

The key debates with regard to production of these styles occur in consideration of the other grains that may be included. Many brewers believe that wheat is a common ingredient in both of these styles, but commercial practice does not bear this out. One of the most eminent authorities on German beer, Prof. Ludwig Narziss, summarized the use of wheat in these styles: "Sometimes in the case of kölsch, and rarely in the case of alt, 10 to 20 percent of wheat malt is blended in to give the beers slightly more body."

In the case of kölsch, the wheat can also help to achieve the pale color desired in the style. For alt, wheat seems counterproductive, because it may dilute the malt character and lighten the color. Thus, it seems wisest to limit the use of wheat to the occasional kölsch formulation.

Having discussed base malt and wheat, I have pretty much covered the grain bill for kölsch. In commercial practice, other ingredients are rarely included. In fact, one German brewmaster recently told me that he remembered kölsch being produced "exactly like (all-malt) Pilsener, except for the yeast."[13]

The grain bills for alts are slightly more complex, because they require some dark malts for color and character. After Pilsener malt, the primary ingredient of alt is usually Munich malt. One of the most popular alts in Germany, Diebels Alt, uses just two ingredients: 10 percent Munich malt and 90 percent base malt.[14] Other commercial German brewers add small quantities of black malt to achieve the desired color and, unfortunately, still others rely on caramel coloring for this purpose.[15]

From this data, it seems that an authentic all-malt alt formulation would rely entirely on Pilsener, Munich, and black malts. Some will argue that crystal malt has a place here as well, but I have found no evidence that such malts are actually used in the production of this style in Germany.

Having reviewed commercial approaches to the style, let us shift the focus to the formulations employed by those whose beers made it to the National Hombrew Competition (NHC) second round, looking, as usual, at the second-round recipes from 1993 and 1994.

As with commercial beers, two-row, Pilsener, and wheat malts are the dominant ingredients in NHC second-round kölsch formulations. Although Pilsener malt only appears in 27 percent of the recipes, two-row malt appears in all but one of the remaining entries. Wheat appears in most recipes. CaraPils or dextrin malt appears in only a third of the recipes, usually with wheat (see table 14.5).

The key difference between the commercial and the NHC second-round kölsch formulations is the use of what I sometimes call "character" malts — crystal, Munich, and other specialty malts that contribute color and flavor to the beer. Only three of the eleven kölsch recipes excluded such malts from their formulations. Of the remainder,

Table 14.5
Kölsch Grain Bill in NHC Second-Round Recipes

Grain Used (Range %)	Proportion	Incidence
Two-row (32–86)	72%	
Pilsener (56–91)	75%	
Wheat (3–22)	14%	
Crystal (1–7)	5%	
Munich (7–22)	13%	
CaraPils (3–11)	7%	
Other (3–4)	3%	

Key: This chart shows what proportion of the grain bill was provided by various grains in eleven kölsch recipes. The line next to each grain gives the range of values used by different brewers; this range is also listed below "Grains Used." The triangle above each line indicates the average proportion used across all recipes.

The icons in the column on the right show how often the eleven kölsch recipes included each grain. (Percentage figures indicate how many of the recipes included the grain.)

= rarely (30% or less)   = sometimes (30% to 60%)
= often (60% to 90%)   = usually (90% or more)

Table 14.6

The Use of Character Malts in NHC Second-Round Kölsch Formulations

No character malts used:	3
One character malt used:	6
Crystal only:	3
Munich only:	2
Specialty only (Biscuit):	1
Two character malts used:	2
Crystal plus Munich:	2

six used one addition of either Munich, crystal, or some other character malt. Only two recipes employed more than one character malt (see table 14.6).

Of course, Munich malt is still fairly light in color (usually 10 to 20 °L), and when crystal malt was used in these recipes, it was also generally pale, with a rating of 40 °L or lower. The biscuit malt provides some toasty malt character without much color addition — a fact I can vouch for, because the entry using this ingredient is mine!

The use of extract in kölsch formulations was fairly rare; it occurred in just two of the eleven recipes. In one instance, Alexander's Pale Syrup was used to supplement a small mash that included two-row malt; in the other, Williams Gold extract served as the base ingredient for the recipe.

In alt beer recipes, two-row malt was most often selected as the base. Pilsener malt was used in only two of twelve formulations. As would be expected for the style, more alt recipes used character malts than did the kölsch recipes. Here again, the patterns of usage depart somewhat from commercial practice (see table 14.7).

Where the commercial alts rely upon Pilsener, Munich, and black malts, the NHC second-round examples frequently use Munich or Vienna malt, with one or both appearing in two-thirds of the recipes. The use of small quantities (1 percent) of black malt is also common, although as an alternative, chocolate malt is sometimes used in similar amounts. Black and chocolate malt never appear in the same recipe.

We also find wheat in these alt formulations, although a bit more frequently than we would expect based upon commercial patterns of usage. But although more than half the recipes included wheat, the amounts were in line with commercial practice, accounting for 4 to 14 percent of the grist.

The greatest departure from commercial practice comes in the use of crystal malts. Every single NHC second-round alt recipe employed crystal malt for a portion of the grist. Furthermore, the amounts used were significant, with the average recipe including crystal malt for 10 percent of the grist. Though it is clear that good beers are being made this way, those who worry about the authenticity of the style should try brewing this beer without the use of crystal malt.

Only one alt recipe uses extract, but I can see no reason why extract brewers couldn't make an excellent example of this style. The recipe in question used Briess Light Dry Extract to supplement a mash that included two-row malt.

Mashing

According to the analysis of commercial beers, high levels of attenuation are expected in the commercial examples of both alt and kölsch. In the NHC second-round examples, attenuation levels cover a wide range, from a low of just 67 percent to a high of 87 percent for kölsch and 88 percent for alt. On average, however, the attenuation levels of the NHC second-round examples were about 5 percent lower than

Table 14.7
Alt Grain Bill in NHC Second-Round Recipes

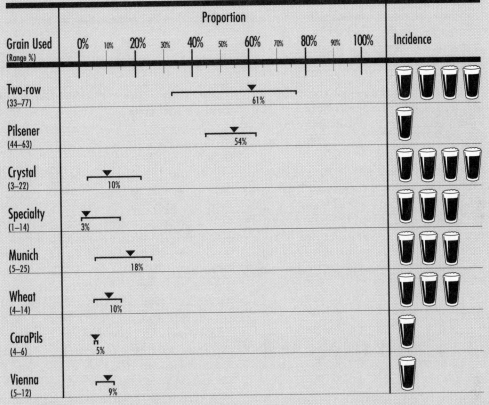

Grain Used (Range %)	Proportion	Average	Incidence
Two-row (33–77)		61%	🍺🍺🍺🍺
Pilsener (44–63)		54%	🍺
Crystal (3–22)		10%	🍺🍺🍺🍺
Specialty (1–14)		3%	🍺🍺🍺🍺
Munich (5–25)		18%	🍺🍺🍺
Wheat (4–14)		10%	🍺🍺🍺
CaraPils (4–6)		5%	🍺
Vienna (5–12)		9%	🍺

Key: This chart shows what proportion of the grain bill was provided by various grains in twelve alt recipes. The line next to each grain gives the range of values used by different brewers; this range is also listed below "Grains Used." The triangle above each line indicates the average proportion used across all recipes.

The icons in the column on the right show how often the twelve alt recipes included each grain. (Percentage figures indicate how many of the recipes included the grain.)

🍺 = rarely (30% or less)   🍺🍺 = sometimes (30% to 60%)
🍺🍺🍺 = often (60% to 90%)   🍺🍺🍺🍺 = usually (90% or more)

those seen in the commercial examples (see table 14.8).

Although yeast selection will have a certain impact on attenuation levels, the saccharification temperature used during the mash will have a greater effect. Higher mash temperatures (above 150 °F, 66 °C) produce more dextrinous worts that will not attenuate as much as those produced at lower temperatures. As I mentioned, one of the kölsch recipes from the NHC second-round beers is one that I brewed. As it

happens, this beer achieved a pretty good attenuation level for the style: 82 percent. Not surprisingly, the mash temperatures were low, starting out at 149 °F (65 °C) and sliding all the way down to 146 °F (63 °C) by the end of the mash.

On average, the mash temperatures used in the NHC second-round alts and kölschs were higher, at 153 °F (67 °C) and 151 °F (66 °C) respectively. Some brewers still believe that you must use a high mash temperature to increase the maltiness of

Table 14.8
Attenuation of Alt and Kölsch Beers

	Alt	Kölsch
Commercial examples	79%	84%
NHC second-round examples	74%	79%

the beer. But it is important to remember that there is no correlation between dextrin content and malt flavor. You can have lots of malt flavor in a beer that contains little dextrin.

To achieve the goals of alt and kölsch brewing with regard to both maltiness and attenuation, you can — and should — be looking at cooler mash temperatures, in the range from 145 to 149 °F (63 to 65 °C).

The literature contains little information about the waters used for brewing these beers.

Hops

It doesn't take long to cover the subject of hops with regard to kölsch and alt beers, for the styles typically display little, if any, hop flavor or aroma. Furthermore, I have already discussed the bitterness levels found in commercial examples. Before leaving the subject of bitterness, however, let's review the levels found in the NHC second-round examples.

On average, the IBUs calculated for second-round recipes showed bitterness levels a bit higher than those found in commercial beers. The kölsch beers come in 4 IBU higher than the commercial average mentioned earlier, while the alts are 6 IBUs higher. Given all the factors that influence actual bitterness, the effect achieved in the finished beers is probably pretty similar in both NHC second-round and commercial formulations. (See table 14.9.)

One point I haven't discussed yet is the selection of hop varieties. Although several different German hops are used in these beers, it appears that Spalt gets the nod as the favorite.[16] This is one of the finest varieties available, generally classified with Saaz, Tettnanger, and Hallertau as a fine aroma hop.

In the United States, Spalts are not always available to homebrewers — in part because they are less known than many other German varieties. Thus, Spalt is rarely used in NHC second-round German ales. Instead, most of the other German varieties are used, including those already mentioned, plus Perle, Northern Brewer, and Hersbruck. (See tables 14.10 and 14.11.)

In addition to the German varieties, some American hops are also used in the NHC second-round German ales. The most common is Mt. Hood — a selection that should be perfectly appropriate, because it was bred from Hallertau. Cascade, Chinook, and Cluster are a bit more off-beat and definitely lend an American character to these beers.

Although commercial examples of these styles generally avoid flavor and aroma hops, many of the NHC second-round interpretations include late hop additions. Still, in a partial concession to the style guidelines, the additions tend to be fairly modest in size (see table 14.12).

Fermentation and Aging

Compared to other styles of beer, production of alt and kölsch follows unique steps throughout fermentation and aging. Ale yeasts are used, but the temperatures and processing are more like those employed for lager production. To produce a product that

Table 14.9
IBU Levels in NHC Second-Round Kölsch and Alt Recipes

	Kölsch	Alt
Average	29	39
Maximum	69	58
Minimum	15	27

matches the desired flavor profile, you must first select an appropriate yeast and then plan and execute a suitable fermentation. Let's examine each of these issues in turn.

Even though alt and kölsch are viewed as fairly specialized products, there are a number of different yeast strains that may be used in them. The range of possibilities is indicated by the list of yeasts used by the NHC second-round beers, as shown in table 14.13.

Two special requirements in selecting a yeast for these beers are maximizing attenuation and minimizing ester production.

As I mentioned earlier, you want a high level of attenuation in both the alt and the kölsch styles, thus, medium- or low-attenuation yeast will not be appropriate. One of the most popular yeasts from the second-

round entries, the European ale yeast, is a poor attenuator, and I would recommend that you avoid it when making German-style ales. Among the other yeasts listed in table 14.13, good attenuators include American ale, Bavarian lager, and kölsch yeasts.

Yeast selection also has an impact on ester production, for some strains produce more fruity character than do others. In addition, your ability to control the fermentation temperature is important, because ester production generally increases at higher temperatures.

Lager yeasts yield low ester production, of course, but fermentation temperatures near 50 °F (10 °C) are generally required. Clean ale yeasts such as the American ale strains can also give good results, and I would recommend this type of selection if

Table 14.10
Hops Used in NHC Second-Round Kölsch Recipes

Type	Bitter	Flavor	Aroma	Dry	Total
Hallertau	5	3	4	0	12
Saaz	3	2	4	1	10
Cascade	3	2	1	0	6
Mt. Hood	1	1	1	0	3
Tettnanger	2	1	0	0	3
Hersbruck	0	1	1	0	2
N. Brewer	2	0	0	0	2
Perle	1	0	0	0	1
Spalt	1	0	0	0	1
Total	18	10	11	1	40

Note: The data show the number of times each hop was used across the eleven recipes analyzed.

Table 14.11
Hops Used in NHC Second-Round Alt Recipes

Type	Bitter	Flavor	Aroma	Dry	Total
Tettnanger	6	3	2	0	11
Perle	6	1	1	0	8
Hallertau	3	0	2	0	5
N. Brewer	4	0	0	0	4
Mt. Hood	1	2	0	0	3
Cascade	1	1	0	0	2
Chinook	2	0	0	0	2
Hersbruck	0	1	0	1	2
Saaz	0	1	1	0	2
Cluster	0	1	0	0	1
Total	23	10	6	1	40

Note: The data show the number of times each hop was used across the twelve recipes analyzed.

you must ferment at temperatures above 65 °F (18 °C).

The German ale and kölsch yeasts produce low levels of esters at temperatures of up to 64 to 66 °F (18 to 19 °C), but they also work down into the mid-50 °F range (about 13 °C). This leaves plenty of room for temperature fluctuations around an average fermentation temperature of 60 °F (16 °C), which is typical for these styles. Since both also produce high levels of attenuation, they are ideal for production of these beers according to traditional German brewing methods.

Among the NHC second-round beers, the fermentation temperatures ranged from 45 °F (7 °C) using a lager yeast up to a high of 70 ° F (21 °C) across all yeasts. But though the range stayed pretty low,

the average temperatures were still a bit higher than is typical during commercial production, at 65 °F (18 °C) for alt and 62 °F (17 °C) for kölsch. Based upon these data, it looks as though you can produce a nice product with many of these (ale) yeasts, even with fermentation temperatures in the mid- to upper 60s °F (about 20 °C).

Following fermentation, the German ale styles typically receive a period of cold storage, much like lager beers. Although temperatures near freezing might be employed, the few commercial discussions I found used temperatures that were rather warmer — in the range of 41 to 50 °F (5 to 10 °C).[17] This makes some sense when you consider that the objective is to slow the metabolic activity

Table 14.12
Late Hop Additions in NHC Second-Round Alt and Kölsch Recipes

	Alt Oz./Gal.	Alt Oz./5 Gal.	Kölsch Oz./Gal.	Kölsch Oz./5 Gal.
Flavor	0.13	0.65	0.07	0.36
Aroma	0.17	0.83	0.12	0.60

of the yeast rather than stop it altogether. Since the ale yeast's optimal fermentation temperature is 10 to 15 °F warmer than for a lager yeast, the cold-storage temperature may also need to be warmer.

Among the second-round beers, the practice of cold conditioning was far from consistent. A number of the entries indicated a conditioning period that amounted to little more that a prolonged secondary fermentation, since the temperature never dropped below 60 °F (16 °C). This practice was particularly common among kölsch producers, where fully 60 percent cited a conditioning temperature of 60 °F (16 °C) or higher. Alt brewers went to the opposite extreme; they cited an average conditioning temperature of just 35 °F (2 °C) — cold enough to frost even the heartiest ale yeast. The length of the conditioning period was relatively long in both cases, with an average of twenty-nine days for kölsch and forty-one days for alt.

From these data, you can see again that success can be achieved with procedures that differ from the commercial approach. At the same time, you can also see an opportunity for potentially improving homebrewed examples of these styles by more closely emulating the time-proven practices of the German brewmasters.

Conclusion

At the opening of this chapter I characterized alt and kölsch beers as enigmas for American brewers. The data presented in this chapter should enhance your understanding of the styles and improve your ability to produce authentic examples. Thus, even those who have brewed excellent beers in these styles in the past may find new ideas for refinement of their recipes. Those who have not attempted these styles previously can no longer use ignorance as an excuse for ignoring them.

Then, too, there is the romance of German ale brewing. These styles exist today only because many generations of brewers along the Rhine refused to abandon ales in the face of an overwhelming demand for lagers. As a small brewer, I think you can relate to that devotion to the "old" ways. And there is the opportunity to brew something a little different — something that the big industrial brewers would never make — or never make well. So pop a yeast pack and clean some fermenters, there are German ales to be brewed!

Table 14.13
Yeast Selection in NHC Second-Round Alt and Kölsch Recipes

Yeast	No. of Recipes
German ale (Wyeast 1007)	7
European ale (Wyeast 1338)	4
American ale (Wyeast 1056)	2
Düsseldorf ale (Yeast Labs)	2
Edme yeast	1
Weihenstephan Alt	1
Pilsener lager (Wyeast 2007)	1
Bavarian lager (Wyeast 2206)	1
Kölsch (Wyeast 2565)	1
Total	20

Key Success Factors in Brewing German Ales

- Select a quality Pilsener or two-row malt as the base for a full or minimash.

- Light-colored malt extract may be used to supplement a minimash.

- For kölsch, you may wish to add wheat malt for 10 to 20 percent of the grist. The remainder of the recipe should be base malt.

- For alt, supplement the base malt with 15 to 30 percent Munich malt and no more than 1 percent black or chocolate malt. Although crystal malt is often added to homebrewed recipes, the typical German examples exclude such grains. Wheat is occasionally added to alt beer grists.

- Select a saccharification temperature between 145 and 149 °F (63 and 65 °C) to ensure maximum fermentability of the wort.

- Use German aroma hop varieties, especially Spalt. Most or all of the additions should be made early in the boil to impart bitterness without contributing significant flavor or aroma.

- Bitterness levels should be 25 to 30 IBU for kölsch and 30 to 50 IBU for alt.

- For the most authentic results, do not make any hop additions during the last thirty minutes of the boil.

- Ferment at 60 °F (16 °C) using a highly attenuative German ale or kölsch yeast.

- Condition the beer for two to four weeks at 41 to 50 °F (5 to 10 °C).

15 BARLEY WINE

Barley wine is a style of ale that one could spend a lifetime exploring. These very strong ales mature and change with time, offering a rich complexity of subtly shifting flavors from year to year. Commercial examples are often dated by vintage to help the consumer manage his or her stock and appreciate the flavors wrought by age. A most memorable tasting event can be created by stockpiling these vintages and tasting several years' examples in sequence.

Current definitions of the style cut a broad swath at the high ends of the scale for gravity and bitterness, as shown in table 15.1.[1]

Despite the breadth of this definition, it is easy to find both commercial and homebrewed examples that fall outside the bounds of these parameters. To better understand this, let's examine the history of barley wine.

A Brief History of Barley Wine

For most of its history, barley wine has been a distinctly British creation. In most cases the term identifies the strongest member of a brewer's family of ales. Because barley wine shares the brewing traditions of its less robust siblings such as pale ale and bitter, it shares many common traits in the ingredients and techniques used for brewing.

Chief among these is the tradition of dry hopping, which is practiced by the vast majority of current and past producers of barley wines. It has long been traditional to add a measure of hops to a cask of ale before shipping it to the pub. Today this continues in many of the real ales served in England, and a similar practice of dry hopping is also practiced with many barley wines.

Pale ales and bitters are usually well attenuated, with 70 to 75 percent apparent attenuation being common. To reach similar levels of attenuation, barley wines often require some extra attention during the fermentation process. This may include extralong fermentations, multiple yeast pitchings, or rousing of the yeast.

One favored method of rousing was to take the large secondary fermentation casks for a "walk." Periodically, each cask would be taken out and rolled around the brewery courtyard a few times to achieve the necessary awakening of the yeast. Today of course, aging — when conducted at all by the brewery — takes place in fixed high-volume vessels. Such behemoths can hardly be taken out for a walk 'round the block!

Some other similarities between pale ales, bitters, and barley wines include the use of pale ale malt as a base and hopping to achieve firm levels of bitterness. All

Table 15.1
Characteristics of Barley Wine

Characteristic	Barley Wine
Original Gravity	1.090–1.120 (22.5–30 °B)
Bitterness	50–100 IBU
BU:GU	0.94 Average (range: 0.53–1.83)
Hop flavor	Low to high
Hop aroma	Low to high
Color (SRM)	14–22 °SRM
Apparent extract	1.024–1.032 (6–8 °B)
Apparent attenuation	56%–83%,
Alcohol (volume)	8.4%–12%
Esters	Medium to high
Diacetyl	Low to medium
Flavor profile	Malty sweet, full-bodied, alcoholic. Medium to high bitterness perception.

Source: C. Papazian, "Introducing: Beer Style Guidelines," The New Brewer (January-February, 1992): 10-16.

these common characteristics indicate not only the related nature of these products today but also the common heritage of these brews.

Although beers in the spirit of barley wine have been brewed for at least a couple of centuries, the use of the term "barley wine" is a much more recent innovation. Michael Jackson names the year 1903 as the first documented use of the term. In that year, Bass marketed a product called Bass No. 1 Barley Wine.[2]

Of course, barley wine is not a mass-production beer, and its history reflects this. Little can be found about its production or evolution that can provide us with clear guidance on the traditional methods for making this brew.

Still, beers that are like barley wine have certainly been around for a long time. Two schools of ale recipes that might qualify as barley wines can be found in a brewer's log from 1868.[3] The first group comes from Burton and the second from London.

The Burton ales (see table 15.2) were made exclusively with "pale" malt and generally with East Kent hops. They were always dry hopped at the rate of 1 pound per barrel or greater. Bittering hops were added at the rate of 4 to 6.5 pounds per British barrel, which works out to 1.4 to 2.3 ounces per U.S. gallon.

Table 15.2
Burton Ales, circa 1868

	OG	TG	Atten. (%)	Dry Hop (lb./bbl.)
Burton ale	1.122	1.063	48	3
Burton ale	1.086	1.037	57	1
Burton ale	1.086	1.031	64	1
Burton ale	1.077	1.032	58	1
Burton ale	1.083	1.035	58	1
Average	1.091	1.040	57	>1

These beers were not very highly attenuated, at least not when they left the brewery. Most were shipped to the trade less than two weeks after brewing; however, they were probably aged for several months before consumption. During this aging, carbonation would develop and some further attenuation may have taken place.

Quite a number of strong ales were also made in London at this time. Here, distinctions were drawn between different strengths of product using a nomenclature of K's and X's. The strongest products had the greatest number of letters, with K/XXXX reigning at the top of the heap. As shown in table 15.3, these ales were extraordinarily strong by any standard, with gravities as high as 1.139.

Working down the X and K rankings, we see that the gravities get progressively lower, although many of the XXX ales still weigh in at what is considered to be barley wine strength today.

This difference in labeling is not the only contrast with the strong Burton ales of the day. First, the malt used was "white" malt rather than the "pale" favored by Burton brewers. Attenuation levels were quite a bit higher, averaging 65 percent versus 57 percent for the Burton products. (Readings were taken at comparable times.)

Hopping rates were also somewhat lower, with 3 to 5 pounds of bittering hops used per batch. Most striking, however, is the fact that these ales received either no dry hops or only very small quantities. Finally, we know, of course, that the water character in Burton is quite different from that in London, where carbonate and sodium chloride favor the production of darker, sweeter beers.

As a result of all these differences, the London strong ales were no doubt quite different from their Burton cousins. Looking at these data, I'm inclined to believe it was the Burton strong ales that spawned the style we know today as barley wine. First, of course, it was the Burton brewer Bass who eventually coined the term "barley wine." In addition, the 150-year-old Burton strong ales resembled today's barley wines in all respects except for apparent attenuation — and that was soon to change.

By the end of the nineteenth century, analyses of some strong Burton ales appeared in the work published by Wahl and Henius (see table 15.4). In original gravity, these samples fall within the range reported in the 1868 analyses. At the same time, attenuation has increased. The higher attenuation in the oldest sample listed by Wahl and Henius may reflect the long, slow reduction in gravity that continues in these products over time. However, that one batch may have been less dextrinous to begin with.

Table 15.3
London Strong Ales, circa 1868

	OG	TG	Atten. (%)	Dry Hop (lb./bbl.)
London ale, K/XXXX	1.111	1.039	65	0.15
London ale, K/XXXX	1.139	1.039	72	1.00
London ale, K/XXX	1.100	1.033	67	None
London XXX	1.100	1.042	58	None
London ale, K/XXX	1.097	1.036	63	0.50
London XXX	1.097	1.028	71	None
London XXX	1.086	1.036	58	None
Average	1.104	1.036	65	0.23

Table 15.4
Strong Burton Ales, 1890–1896

	Year	OG	TG	AA%	ABV%	Notes
Bass strong ale	1896	1.102	1.035	64	8.6	
Worthington Burton ale	1890	1.102	1.030	69	9.8	18 months old
Worthington Burton ale	1890	1.110	1.030	71	10.8	90 years old (!)

Source: R. Wahl and M. Henius, The American Handy-Book of the Brewing, Malting and Auxiliary Trades (Chicago: Wahl-Henius Institute, 1908).

With the 1896 Bass product, we see the term "strong" ale used as a commercial name. This adds further support to Jackson's report that the phrase "barley wine" was not adopted until early in the twentieth century. Some sources also report use of the term "stingo"[4] in describing these strong ales.

After the dawning of the twentieth century, the various influences of taxes, war, and Prohibition exerted a downward pressure on the gravity of all beers, especially in England. The next report we find on strong ales comes from the work of H. L. Hind, in 1938.[5] He groups this style with mild and dark ales rather than with the pale ales. The formulation he reports is brewed to a gravity of 1.080 and includes 3 percent crystal malt and 3 percent amber malt. The fact that he fails to use the term "barley wine" probably tells us more about his focus on high-volume styles than about the commercial styles of his time.

Contemporary Examples

In today's commercial examples of barley wine, there is some confusion between barley wine and old ale. The classic barley wine cited by some observers is Eldridge Pope's Thomas Hardy's Ale, yet Michael Jackson consistently classifies this beer as an old ale.[6] Although the gravity is certainly high enough, the distinction appears to lie in the approach to formulation and production, with both attenuation and hopping rates running at lower old-ale levels in

Thomas Hardy's Ale. The presence of flavors attributable to *Brettanomyces* fermentation may be another basis for this classification.

Outside Britain, the most readily available classic barley wine is Young's Old Nick. Some consider this beer to be a "weakling" example of the style, with gravity at 1.084 and hopping at 50 to 55 IBU. Still, it provides an excellent example of one end of the barley wine spectrum.

The examples from Bass and Fuller's may be more in keeping with our U.S. notions of the style, although they are difficult to sample without crossing the Atlantic. Bass No. 1 Barley Wine was widely distributed within Britain,[7] but Fuller's Golden Pride (subtitled "Super Strength Ale") appears to have achieved better market share.

In the United States, a number of the early craft brewers developed barley wines with a passion for the extreme that is typical of the American psyche. Gravities are rarely less than 1.100, and the hop character is usually quite aggressive. Sierra Nevada's Big Foot may be the best example of the American style, showing high attenuation and a bountiful goodness of hop flavor and aroma brought on by late additions of Centennial and Cascade hops. Anchor's Old Foghorn, although less attenuated, strikes a similar balance through the use of higher hopping rates. Other examples include Rogue's Old Crustacean, Dock Street Barley Wine, and Bridgeport's Old Knucklehead (see table 15.5).

The Making of Barley Wine

The making of barley wine often turns into an exercise in logistics. Grain brewers will find the limits of their systems severely challenged if they try to produce a full-sized batch of barley wine. In general, everything will be bigger than you expect — the size of the mash, the amount of runoff, the length of the boil, and so on. Advance planning can make the brewing day more pleasant. Factors to consider include the possibility of making a smaller batch or adding extract for a significant portion of the gravity.

For extract brewers, the style can be a good one to make, but even they may find a few surprises when adding the vast amounts of extract and hops needed for these formulations.

Malt Bill

Unlike many other strong beers, the hallmark of the barley wine malt bill is simplicity. Overall, the malt profile is fairly similar to that of a bitter or pale ale. Pale malt or two-row malt makes up the majority of the malt bill, and specialty malts account for 10 to 15 percent of the total. Commercial brews generally use only pale, crystal, and perhaps a little dextrin or CaraPils in their formulations, but the barley wines that went on to the second round of the NHC include a wider variety of specialty malts (see table 15.6).

The common base malt is pale ale malt of English origin (Hugh Baird, Munton & Fisons, etc.), although North American two-row malt has also been used with success in the United States by both home and commercial brewers.

What is unique about the NHC second-round barley wine recipes is the extent to which malt extract is used. In a beer with this much malt, the use of a generous amount of extract won't detract at all from the overall recipe. In addition, extract makes production of the barley wine more practical by reducing the amount of grain you must mash as well as minimizing the volume of water you must evaporate during the boil.

Among barley wines sent on to the second round of the National Homebrew Competition, malt extract was used in 59 percent of the entries, where, on average, it accounted for half of the total gravity.

Note that, on average, pale malt and extract account for 86 percent of the raw weight of the ingredients included in the NHC barley wines. This means that you should keep the total content of specialty grains at or below 12 to 14 percent of the grain bill.

Only caramel malt was a more common addition to barley wine recipes than extract; it appears in nineteen out of

Table 15.5
Some Contemporary British and American Barley Wines

Brewer	Name	Gravity	Bitterness	Aroma Hops
Anchor	Old Foghorn	1.100	65 IBU	Cascade
Dock Street	Dock St. BW	1.106	60 IBU	Dry hopped with N. Brewer and Fuggle
Sierra Nevada	Big Foot	1.106	80 IBU[a]	Centennial and Cascade
Young's	Old Nick	1.084	50–55 IBU	Goldings and Fuggle

[a] P. Farnsworth, unpublished data, personal conversation, March 1996.

Table 15.6
Barley Wine Grain Bills in NHC Second-Round Recipes

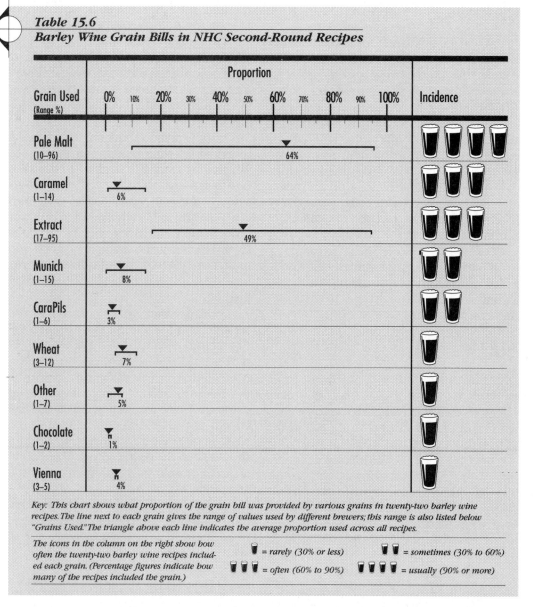

Key: This chart shows what proportion of the grain bill was provided by various grains in twenty-two barley wine recipes. The line next to each grain gives the range of values used by different brewers; this range is also listed below "Grains Used." The triangle above each line indicates the average proportion used across all recipes.

The icons in the column on the right show how often the twenty-two barley wine recipes included each grain. (Percentage figures indicate how many of the recipes included the grain.)

= rarely (30% or less) = sometimes (30% to 60%) = often (60% to 90%) = usually (90% or more)

twenty-two recipes. On average, it accounted for 6 percent of the grist — a rate similar to that found in bitters and pale ales.

After the base and crystal malts, no other single ingredient appears in more than half of the NHC second-round barley wine recipes. Still, specialty malts find fairly wide acceptance in barley wines as a way of contributing additional character to the beer.

Either CaraPils or wheat malt appears in eleven of the twenty-two recipes. These ingredients contribute residual body to the beer and aid in head retention. Though neither of these issues is likely to be of concern in an all-malt barley wine, such additions might aid a recipe that is heavily dependent upon extract.

Several other specialty malts were added to recipes to help increase the complexity of the malt profile, including Munich, Vienna, chocolate, Victory, aromatic, and toasted malt. At least one of these appeared in 60 percent of the barley wine recipes, and on average, specialty malts accounted for 8 percent of the grist when used. The overall pattern of these "character" malts is summarized in table 15.7.

Overall, the average attenuation shown by the NHC second-round barley wines was 71 percent — a value that is very much in line with historical and commercial examples. The average mash saccharification temperature employed was 153 °F (67 °C). To ensure adequate fermentability, I prefer to shoot for a slightly lower mash temperature of about 149 to 151 °F (65 to 66 °C). Traditional single-step infusion mashes work fine for this style.

Hopping of Barley Wines

An incredibly wide variety of hops are used in the making of barley wines, a fact that is probably attributable to the mixed English and American heritage of the style — at least as it is viewed in the United States.

The use of traditional English hops, especially East Kent Goldings (EKGs), define this style in some minds.[8] Certainly the modern commercial examples from Britain are likely to rely on EKGs for some of the late and dry hop additions, but other typical English ale hops, including Fuggle and Styrian Goldings, may also be found.[9]

In the United States, barley wine has come into being with the craft beer revolution of the 1980s and 1990s. As with many other styles, American commercial brewers have chosen to explore barley wine using their own distinctive domestic hops, such as Chinook, Centennial, and Cascade. They have not been shy about this, either. In addition to the traditional dry hops, they use substantial flavor hop additions to produce a hop profile that is assertive from beginning to end. The results, although distinctly different from the British examples, have nonetheless been outstanding.

As a result of the combined old and new influences, we find among the NHC second-round entries many barley wine formulations with a mixed heritage of hops. Chinook turns out to be the most common bittering hop, followed by Cluster, which is another old American favorite. For aroma applications Cascade takes the lead, but English Goldings is right behind. In among these, we find other English-style hops, such as Fuggle and Willamette, and also German favorites such as Hallertau and Tettnaner. In the vast universe that is barley wine, nothing seems out of place. (See table 15.8.)

The level of bitterness found in contemporary commercial barley wines tends toward the lower end of the range, with average BU:GU ratios of about 0.5 to 0.6. By contrast, most NHC second-round barley wines add enough hops to achieve higher

Table 15.7
The Pattern of Character Malts in NHC Second-Round Barley Wine Recipes

Grain Pattern	No. of Recipes
Crystal only, no character malts	8
Crystal plus one character malt	7
Crystal plus two character malts	4
No crystal, two character malts	2
No crystal, no character malts	1

levels of bitterness, in the range of 75 to 110 IBUs. A few are in the 50 to 75 range, and one or two attempt to break the bitterness barrier with calculated IBU values near 200. Thus, the average BU:GU ratio for NHC second-round barley wines was nearly 1.0.

You'll have to add a lot of hops to achieve these levels of bitterness, especially considering the high gravity of the wort being boiled. To avoid excessive hop mass in the boil kettle and a subsequent loss of wort, high-alpha hop pellets are recommended for bittering.

If you are brewing an American example of the style, you'll want to add flavor hops as well as aroma hops. Among those NHC second-round recipes that added hops between ten and twenty-nine minutes before the end of the boil, the average size of the addition was 0.87 ounces in 5 gallons.

Whether you use English or American varieties, you will want to add some aroma hops to your formulation. Among NHC second-round recipes, rates for dry hopping ranged from 1 to 6 ounces in a 5-gallon batch, with the average being 1.9 ounces. About half of the NHC second-round barley wines did not employ dry hopping but instead substituted a hot wort addition either during the last nine minutes of the boil or as a steep at the end of the boil. The quantity of hops used for these applications averaged about 1 ounce in 5 gallons. Occasionally a brewer will choose to add aroma hops as well as to dry hop. (See table 15.10.)

Fermentation and Yeast

Typically, barley wine fermentations are measured in weeks or months rather than days. Two to four months is a common duration for the completion of primary and secondary fermentation in NHC second-round barley wines. After this, they may be packaged and aged for an additional period of months or even years before consumption.

Table 15.8
Hops Used in NHC Second-Round Barley Wine Recipes

Type	Bitter	Flavor	Aroma	Dry	Total
Cascade	4	5	6	5	20
Goldings	3	2	5	2	12
Chinook	10	0	0	0	10
N. Brewer	4	1	1	0	6
Willamette	2	2	2	0	6
Cluster	5	0	0	0	5
Fuggle	4	0	1	0	5
Tettnanger	3	0	2	0	5
Hallertau	2	1	1	0	4
Centennial	2	0	1	0	3
Eroica	2	0	0	0	2
Galena	1	0	0	1	2
Mt. Hood	0	1	1	0	2
B.C. Kent	1	0	0	0	1
Bram. Cross	1	0	0	0	1
Bullion	1	0	0	0	1
Olympic	1	0	0	0	1

Note: The data in this chart show the number of times each hop was used across the twenty recipes analyzed.

Table 15.9
Hop Additions in NHC Second-Round Barley Wine Recipes

Hop Type	Avg. No. of Additions
Bitter	2.3
Flavor	0.6
Aroma	1.0
Dry	0.4
Total	4.3

Barley wines not only survive but thrive with this type of aging, and you should build it into your brewing plans.

As I mentioned earlier, various methods have been used by barley wine brewers to achieve an adequate level of attenuation for their products. Classically, the levels achieved were in the neighborhood of 70 percent apparent attenuation. Today we can generally achieve this level of attenuation, even in a beer of more than 1.100 gravity, by proper use of a moderate- to high-attenuation ale yeast.

Among the NHC second-round barley wines we find an incredible variety of yeasts used. In most styles some pattern emerges or some particular strain seems to be a favorite, but not so with barley wine. Thirteen different ale yeasts were used and only one (American ale) was found in more than one recipe. The yeasts that were used include American ale (3), Brewer's Resource CL18, British ale, Edme ale, European ale, Irish ale, M&F dry ale, Old Dominion ale, Sierra Nevada pale ale yeast, Special London ale, Whitbread, William's Burton ale.

The history of high-gravity brewing makes no mention of anything but ale yeast being used for fermentation. But since beer is no longer fermented in casks that can be "walked" for rousing, today's homebrewers, and some U.S. microbrewers, employ champagne or even wine yeast to help with attenuation. These yeasts may be used alone or in combination with a typical ale yeast and are sometimes added to the secondary fermenter.

Even though a champagne or wine yeast may help to improve attenuation, my examination of NHC second-round barley wine recipes does not bear this out. Regression analysis shows little, if any, correlation between the use of champagne yeast and higher attenuation, even when saccharification temperature is considered. In addition, several different ale yeasts produced attenuation higher than the best results achieved using champagne yeast (see table 15.11). Finally, some brewers report the production of off-flavors caused by champagne yeast.[10]

Of course, these conclusions are based upon a relatively small number of examples,

Table 15.10
Late Hop Additions in NHC Second-Round Barley Wine Recipes

Hop Type	Size of Late Additions (oz./gal.)	Size of Late Additions (oz./5 gal.)
Flavor	0.174	0.871
Aroma	0.215	1.076
Dry	0.388	1.938

Table 15.11

Champagne and Ale Yeast Fermentation in NHC Second-Round Barley Wines

Yeast	Number of Observations	Attenuation Range (%)	Mean (%)
Champagne (alone or with ale)	5	56–73	64
Ale Yeasts	15	63–83[a]	72

[a] One-third (five out of fifteen) of the ale-only fermentations achieved attenuation greater than 73 percent.

and your own experience may be different. In general, however, these data recommend the use of an ale yeast with medium to high attenuation properties. The American ale yeast is a popular favorite for this style, but quite a number of others have been used successfully. Whatever your choice, you may want to try repitching the beer with fresh yeast and rousing the yeast to drive attenuation to the highest level. If your first batch doesn't attenuate as much as you want, then you may want to lower the saccharification temperature used during mashing or reduce the amounts of crystal and Munich malts used in the recipe.

Two other factors should be considered when conducting the fermentation. First, you may want to take extra measures to maximize aeration of the wort before pitching. All that yeast will need additional oxygen to ferment properly, and a little time spent on aeration may pay off with better fermentation. Second, if you use extract for more than 50 percent of the gravity, you may want to add some yeast nutrients to ensure adequate levels of free amino nitrogen in the wort.

As for the amount of yeast you should pitch, conventional wisdom says that the quantity needed increases with the gravity of the wort you will ferment.[11] Since the starting gravities of barley wines are often double those of "normal" ales, you can count on needing twice as much yeast. To achieve this, I recommend that you repitch the yeast from a previous batch of ale. This not

only ensures that you will have enough yeast, it also allows you to use yeast that has been "warmed up" by a full, vigorous fermentation. If repitching is not possible, you may want to consider using packets of dry yeast to achieve the proper pitching quantities.

Water

The intense flavor profile created by the ingredients of barley wine leave little room for water to have a significant flavor influence. Traditional examples hail from London and Burton-on-Trent, but many excellent examples are made today from the waters of North America.

Many of the NHC second-round examples omit water treatment altogether, and others add only a teaspoon or two of gypsum or Burton salts to the mash to help with pH control. Only one of twenty-three recipes noted major water additions oriented toward emulation of the Burton water profile.

The recent British homebrewing guides don't make a big deal about water and mostly recommend the same type of water for all styles of beer.[12] The water treatments they recommend are designed to remove carbonate and add sulfate (using additions of both gypsum and Epsom salts), in effect mildly "Burtonizing" the water.

The older Dave Line text[13] specifies different waters based upon style, and for barley wines he recommends the same water as would be used for the making of bitter or pale ale — again pointing us in the direction of Burton-on-Trent.

The basic water treatment recommended by these sources applies to soft or carbonate water. It calls for precipitation of carbonate and the addition of one to two teaspoons of gypsum as well as one-half teaspoon of Epsom salts. (Note: Add the Epsom salts after carbonate removal.) These salt additions would *increase* ion concentrations in 6.6 U.S. gallons (25 liters) by the following amounts: calcium, 60 to 120 parts per million; magnesium, 8 parts per million; and sulfate, 165 to 300 parts per million.

Dedicated barley wine brewers may wish to explore the effects of water chemistry on various approaches to brewing this style. However, those who are brewing just a batch or two can opt for their regular water or the simple treatment outlined above, if it is appropriate for their water.

Final Thoughts

From the information presented in this chapter, it is clear that there are a number of different barley wine formulations to try, based on your choices of such key variables as U.S. or English hops, use or omission of flavor hop additions, and high or low attenuation levels. The breadth of opportunity offered by this style makes it one that could truly be explored for many years.

Key Success Factors in Brewing Barley Wine

- Use English pale ale malt or North American two-row as your base malt.

- Use malt extract to help achieve the desired original gravity. Consider the addition of yeast nutrients if extract accounts for more than 50 percent of the gravity.

- Limit specialty malts to no more than 15 percent of the total grain bill.

- Use high alpha acid hop pellets to achieve the majority of the 50 to 100 IBU of bitterness.

- For hop flavor and aroma, select either an American or an English hopping strategy, relying heavily on Cascade for the former and East Kent Goldings for the latter.

- Flavor hop additions are optional, being more typical of U.S. examples than of traditional English barley wines.

- Select a hardy ale yeast with good attenuation properties.

- Be prepared to pitch twice as much yeast as you would for a "normal" gravity beer. Repitch from another batch or use dry yeast.

- Aerate the wort aggressively. Rouse or repitch the yeast during secondary fermentation to ensure full attenuation.

- Dry hop in the secondary fermenter using 1.5 to 2 ounces of your selected hop per 5 gallons of beer. Alternatively, you may choose to steep a similar quantity of hops in the hot wort after completion of the boil.

16 BITTERS AND PALE ALES

Project	Designing Great Beers
	Brewers Publications
Project No.	61766

American brewers tend to think of bitters and pale ales as two distinct styles, in part because of the way our beer competitions are set up. In truth, however, the various entries for bitter and pale ale are more alike than are the substyles of many other categories, such as weizen, bock, and brown ale. (This is especially true if you omit the classic India pale ales.) Many writers and brewers who have studied the British beer scene conclude that bitter and pale ale are virtually the same.[1]

Although there are some differences between bitter and pale ale, the two are descended from the same lineage, and they share far more similarities than differences. Furthermore, recipe formulation for bitters and pale ales is almost identical — the recipes rely on the same malts and hops and the same brewing procedures.

In the end, the differences lie in slight shifts in gravity and bitterness or, for American interpretations, in the selection of hop varieties. Let's review the accepted (U.S.) characteristics for these styles (see table 16.1). These listings highlight just three areas of noticeable difference between these six "styles": gravity, bitterness, and hop flavor and aroma.

Gravity spans a range from 1.033 to 1.070, or nearly 37 gravity units. Though that is an appreciable range, it is a smaller one than what you will find within other styles such as old ale, stout, and bock. Thus, gravity serves as a primary distinction between the bitter and pale ale substyles.

With regard to bitterness, you will notice that it rises in relation to the gravity of the wort. Thus the BU:GU ratio for these styles stays relatively constant, with the exception of the two pale ales. Analysis of 216 commercial British bitters from Protz's *The Real Ale Drinker's Almanac* shows that the ordinary and best bitters both have BU:GU ratios of about 0.80, with a range of about 0.60 to 1.08. This is consistent with the data listed in table 16.1. Further, the data indicate similar values for the strong bitters and for the India pale ale style. Only the pale ales show appreciably lower values, with a range of 0.45 to 0.71.

Finally, there are some differences in hop flavor and aroma between bitters and pales ales. In England, most bitters are served on draft, and they are often dry hopped in the cask. Such beers will have a distinct fresh-hop aroma. Pale ales, on the other hand, are generally bottled, and therefore, dry hopping in the final container is not possible. To impart hop character in the beer, brewers of these styles are more likely to add hops late in the boil, at the end of the boil, or in a hop back. All of these methods can serve to impart hop aroma to the beer, but because they put hot wort in contact with the hops, they are also likely to impart hop flavor.

Table 16.1
Characteristics of Bitters and Pale Ales*

Bitters

	Ordinary	Best or Special	Strong or Extra Special
Original Gravity	1.033–1.037	1.038–1.045	1.046–1.060
Bitterness	20–35	23–48	30–55
Hop Flavor and Aroma	none to med.	none to med.	none to med.
Color (SRM)	4–12	8–14	8–15
Apparent Extract	70–80%	70–80%	70–80%
Alcohol (Volume)	3–3.7	4.1–4.8	4.8–5.8
Esters	low to med.	low to med.	low to med.
Diacetyl	low OK	low OK	low OK

Pale Ales

	Eng. Pale	Am. Pale	India Pale
Original Gravity	1.044–1.056	1.044–1.056	1.050–1.070
Bitterness	20–40	20–40	40–60
Hop Flavor and Aroma	med. to high	med. to high	med. to high
Color (SRM)	4–12	4–12	4–14
Apparent Extract	70–80%	70–80%	70–80%
Alcohol (Volume)	4.5–5.5	4.5–5.5	5–7.5
Esters	low to med.	low	low to med.
Diacetyl	low OK	low OK	low OK

* These style characteristics are based upon published data from the American Homebrewers Association and the Institute for Brewing Studies, as well as an evaluation of the current commercial offerings in these styles.
Source: Institute for Brewing Studies, The New Brewer, American Homebrewers Association 1995 National Homebrew Competition Guidelines.

Thus, differences in production methods dictated by the final package for the product may drive this difference in character.

The data in table 16.1 indicate:

- Three categories of bitters distinguished primarily by gravity.

- Two types of pale ale that have the same gravity as the strongest bitters but with less hop bitterness and more hop character.

- India pale ales, which present the maximum level of gravity, bitterness, and hop character found among the bitters and pale ales.

Although India pale ale is considered a subcategory of pale ale, it is in fact the granddaddy of the whole clan. To better understand how all these styles came into being and why they are so closely related in character, let's review the history of their development.

The Beer of an Empire

Imperialism and industry created the British Empire. Coincidentally, the same forces drove the development and popularization of the pale ales and bitters that still dominate the British brewing scene.

The Industrial Revolution came to England during the eighteenth and nineteenth centuries largely on the coattails of coal. Coal provided the efficient source of energy needed to power machines. In addition, the coke derived from coal allowed the production of steel that built all those wonderful industrial essentials like engines and bridges.

What does all this have to do with beer? Plenty. With the advent of coke, maltsters had an alternative to wood for fueling their kilns. In addition, better kilns could be built from steel. These influences made it possible to make malt that was not brown and smoky but pale and without any aroma imparted by the heat source. This "pale" malt begot pale ale, which first appeared during the reign of Queen Anne, from 1702 to 1714.[2]

Thus, the creation of pale ale preceded the development of porter as a distinct style. Nonetheless, porter would flourish and expand during the eighteenth century while pale ale would have to wait until the nineteenth century to realize its full potential. These events can also be linked to the political and social influences of the time. Porter's rise accompanied the growth of a laboring population in the cities that was in need of a rich, nutritional beverage. Thus porter — and its big brother, stout — soon came into prominence.

At the same time, the price of coal, increased in part by taxes, made the production of pale malt expensive. As a result, beers made exclusively from pale malt were available only to the well-to-do. Thus, pale ale was produced throughout the 1700s but it failed to find an extensive market such as existed for porter at the time.

One brewer of pale ales was George Hodgson of the Bow Brewery in East London. Although the brewery had produced pale products since the 1750s, it was an imbalance in foreign shipping rates that created a large new market for them outside of England.

In 1774 the British Empire appointed its first governor to India, and trade ships loaded with spices and silks traveled regularly back to England. But India was self-sufficient in virtually all goods, so the ships often returned to India empty. Thus, freight rates from England to India were quite low, a fact that Hodgson decided to exploit through the export of his products.

Hodgson's shipments to India began in the 1790s, and the market proved profitable. By 1800, shipments of beer to India totaled nine thousand barrels per year,[3] nearly all of it from the Bow Brewery.

The brewers of Burton — including Allsopp, Bass, and Ind — were exporters by nature, having built considerable trade with the Baltics and with Russia during the early to mid-eighteenth century, and many tried their hand in the Indian market after seeing Hodgson's success.[4] But Hodgson was not about to share "his" market, so he undercut their efforts with predatory pricing and other questionable business practices.[5]

It was not until the mid-1820s that Hodgson's greed finally caught up with him, turning his trade partners against him.[6] At the same time, the Burton brewers were feeling the pinch from the loss of export markets resulting both from the Napoleonic Wars and stiff import taxes in Russia.[7] This confluence of events created both motivation and opportunity for them to try the Indian market again.

One challenge faced by the Burton brewers was the poor suitability of their product to the rigors of the passage to India. Hodgson's India Ale was amber- to copper-colored, like his other pale ales, but it was quite different from other ales of the day. Specifically, two modifications were introduced to help ensure that the beer would not spoil during its long voyage through equatorial seas.

First, the beer was highly hopped in order to take advantage of the preservative qualities of the hop acids. This resulted, of course, in a very bitter beer. Second, the gravity of the India ale was actually reduced, compared to that of the average ale of the day.[8] This reduction helped to achieve a greater degree of fermentation by the yeast, thereby leaving less residual sugar that would attract spoilage organisms.[9]

At the time, the Burton brewers, descended from local monastic breweries of the thirteenth century, produced brown rather than pale ales.[10] Like most brewers in England, they produced very high gravity beers with apparent attenuation of 50 to 65 percent and reasonably moderate hop levels.

As a result of the differences between the traditional Burton brews and Hodgson's India Ale export, some recipe development was required. Various sources report that the Allsopp brewery developed its pale ale recipe by using a teapot as their pilot-scale mash tun.[11] Although shocked at the bitterness of Hodgson's product, they nonetheless followed suit. Today it is generally known that the sulfate and hardness of Burton water is ideally suited to the production of highly hopped ales, and that became an advantage to the Burton brewers.

The Burton brewers also pushed the style into a color range that was clearly pale, as it is known today. The skilled maltsters at Allsopp succeeded in making a light malt that produced a very pale golden ale even at high gravities.[12] This made the product lighter in color than Hodgson's — a fact that would eventually contribute to its attractiveness to drinkers both at home and abroad.

The hydrometer had become an accepted tool among brewers by this time, allowing them to measure and compare the relative extract produced by different types of malt.[13] Some believe that use of the hydrometer helped to bring pale malt into wider use by showing that its higher cost was overcome by higher extract yield compared to brown malt.[14] Improvements in the transportation system for coal and changes in the taxes levied on it probably also contributed to increased use of pale malt at this time.

As a result of these influences, India pale ale (IPA) took on what would become its classic characteristics. During the fourth decade of the 1800s, the market responded with attractive growth. In 1830, exports of IPA remained near turn-of-the-century levels at 9,708 barrels, but during the ensuing decade they more than doubled, rising to 20,350 barrels in 1840.[15]

At about this time, a thirst for the pale export ales developed in the home market as well.[16] One perspective on the increased interest is provided by the following:

The pale ale, prepared for the India Market, and therefore commonly known as India Pale Ale, is free from these objections (high levels of sugar). It is carefully fermented so as to be devoid of all sweetness, or in other words to be dry; and it contains double the usual quantity of hops; it therefore, forms a most valuable restorative beverage for invalids and convalescents.[17]

Compared to other ales of the day, IPAs were lighter in color, lighter in body, less filling, and less sweet. Although the thought seems odd by today's standards, IPAs were really the "light" beers of their day. Indeed, the public hankering for these products may have begun a trend toward minimalist beers that continues even today!

One factor that contributed to this interest in pale beer was the widespread availability of glass bottles and drinking vessels. In 1845 a heavy British tax on glass was removed, which fueled demand for mass-produced glass containers.[18] From this time on, consumers became more and more interested in evaluating the appearance of beers, as well as their flavor and aroma. Brewers began to increase their use of techniques that could contribute to product clarity, including the use of finings such as isinglass (patented in 1760[19]) and the addition of adjuncts such as sugar and maize.

The net result of all these changes was a tremendous increase in the size of the market for pale ales. Bass was among the Burton brewers who enjoyed this growth in both the Indian and domestic pale ale markets. By 1889, Bass was the largest producer of "ale and bitter beer" in the world.[20] Its maltings produced 7,600 quarters (2.5 million pounds) of malt per week to feed the twenty-one mash tuns that were kept in operation.[21] From this data and some conservative assumptions about the brewery's malting and brewing schedules, we can conclude that annual production must have been between 600,000 to 1 million barrels per year.

As for the formulation of this growth product, a Scottish brewer of the mid-nineteenth century records the character of India pale ales as having gravities between 1.044 and 1.070, with hop rates of 4 to 7 pounds per barrel.[22] However, by 1868 a more detailed account in Amsinck's writings sets the parameters more narrowly, as demonstrated by the nine recipes for "East India Pale Ale" in table 16.2.

By comparison to other recipes in Amsinck's publication, the IPA hop levels are quite high. A London ale with OG 1.111 calls for only 5 pounds of hops per barrel, and a "treble" stout at OG 1.097 calls for just 5.5 pounds per barrel. Dry hop rates for the IPAs are also at least 50 percent higher than for any other type of ale or porter.[23] For all

the recipes, East or Mid-Kent hops are specified. Pale malt was used to the exclusion of all other fermentable materials.

The apparent attenuation levels vary widely but many comply with the current understanding of the style as a highly attenuated one even by today's standards. Furthermore, the standards of the day may have been quite different, as indicated by a number of London and Burton ales recorded by Amsinck with low attenuation levels, ranging from 55 to 65 percent.[24]

As the popularity of pale ale rose, the word "India" was apparently dropped in many cases. By 1900, products — notably those from Bass — were labeled simply as "pale ale," though a few were still labeled as IPAs (see table 16.3). Note that these pale ales — as well as the IPA — have the same gravity as the original IPAs described in table 16.2.

Also at this time, a number of examples of IPA were being brewed in the United States, as shown in table 16.4. In these U.S.-made products, the gravity of IPA matches that of the traditional and contemporary English examples while many other American ales — including those sold as pale ale, sparkling ale, and cream ale — dropped to a lower gravity of about 1.052.

Table 16.2
Characteristics of Nine East India Pale Ales, circa 1868

OG	Hops[a]	Water	Dry Hops[a]	Apparent Atten. (%)
1.052	8.00	hard	1.5	68
1.058	6.25	hard	1.5	69
1.064	7.00	hard	1.5	78
1.064	5.75	hard	1.5	80
1.067	8.50	hard	1.5	78
1.067	8.125	hard	1.5	69
1.067	7.50	hard	1.5	65
1.067	7.25	hard	1.5	73
1.067	7.00	soft	1.5	62

Source: G. S. Amsinck, Practical Brewings: A Series of Fifty Brewings (London: George Stewart Amsinck, 1868), 94–101.
[a] Figures for hops are given in pounds per English barrel.

Twentieth Century Pale Ales

The first references to the significant use of sugar and adjuncts in English ales are found in literature from around the turn of the century. Parliament had passed a law allowing the use of sugar in the production of beer in 1847, but adoption of the practice came slowly.[25] Some fifty years later, in 1901, breweries were equally divided between those that used only malt and those that included sugar in their formulations.

Throughout the United Kingdom, the total weight of sugar and adjunct used in brewing in 1900 equaled nearly 25 percent of the weight of the malt employed.[26] This practice continues on a widespread basis today in England and influences the character of the bitter and pale styles.

In addition, original gravities have continued their gradual decline throughout the twentieth century. Even before the various economic and political upheavals that marked the first half of the century, other forces began to drive down the gravity of beer. In England, changes in taxation made lower gravities more attractive for all beer styles. In the United States, legislators did not bother with taxes; the voters preferred outright prohibition of all alcoholic beverages instead.

When the dust had settled after World War II, in England as well as the United States, beers were lighter, lower-gravity products across the board. A few breweries continued to produce IPAs, but adherence to the original style parameters fell by the wayside. One notable exception in the United States was Ballentine IPA, which until the early 1960s maintained a gravity near 1.070 and 60 IBU.[27] Sadly, that brewer has had to water down the recipe in order to keep the brand alive; better examples of the style can now be found from U.S. craft brewers.

Today the term IPA may appear on the label of virtually any light-colored ale. Even in England, products with this moniker may have gravities as low as 1.034, and among the ten I found in Protz's *The Real Ale Drinker's Almanac,* none had a gravity greater than 1.050.[28] BU:GU ratios are comparable to other bitters and pale ales at about 0.80.

This mongrelization of the term IPA has been accompanied by increasing use of other terms to describe similar beers, including the previously established "pale ale" and the now popular "bitter."

The twentieth century saw the first widespread use of "bitter" as a description for pale ales. A number of earlier references can be found back as far as 1857,[29] but it appears that the commercial significance of the name came to the fore in the period since World War II.

Table 16.3
Gravities of Pale Ales, circa 1890–1900

Year	Name/Brewer	OG
1879	Allsopp-Burton Ale	1.068
1887	Bass Pale Ale	1.063
1888	Bass Pale Ale	1.068
1896	Bass Pale Ale	1.060
1901	Bass Draught Ale	1.063
1901	Allsopp-Burton IPA	1.061

Source: R. Wahl and M. Henius, The American Handy-Book of the Brewing, Malting and Auxiliary Trades *(Chicago: Wahl-Henius Institute, 1908), 1284.*

Table 16.4
U.S.-made India Pale Ales, circa 1908

OG (B)	OG (SG)	AA%	Name and Source
16.1	1.065	78	Old India Pale Draught, Rochester, N.Y.
16.3	1.066	78	Old India Pale Primed, Rochester, N.Y.
16.6	1.067	69	New India Pale (bottled), Rochester, N.Y.
17.5	1.071	83	India Pale (bottled), Rochester, N.Y.
16.6	1.067	71	India Pale (bottled), Canandaigua, N.Y.
16.5	1.067	66	India Pale (bottled), Hudson, N.Y.
19.1	1.078	62	India Pale Draught, Philadelphia, Penn.

Source: R. Wahl and M. Henius, The American Handy-Book of the Brewing, Malting and Auxiliary Trades (Chicago: Wahl-Henius Institute, 1908), 1291.

One insight into this phenomenon may be provided by the 1938 brewer's guide written by the English brewer H. Loyd Hind.[30] In a table describing "Grists for Pale Ales," the lowest gravity example, at 1.040, is labeled as a "light pale ale."

The term "light" has become an accepted descriptor for beverages targeted at U.S. beer drinkers during the 1980s and 1990s, but I suspect it would have flopped in post–World War II Britain. Faced with this dilemma, a clever marketer may have decided that this low-alcohol, adjunct-diluted "light" pale ale might sell better if it were called something more manly. Something like "bitter."

Whatever the motivation, it is clear that most English and Welsh brewers today produce a beer they call bitter. Its character is generally defined in contrast to the other beer commonly produced at all these breweries, which is "mild."

Of the two, the bitter will be more dry and have more hop bitterness than the mild, but it needn't be particularly bitter or dry in its own right. This distinction between two popular products based on the brewer's frame of reference helps to create the broad range of bitterness values found in commercial bitters today. Thus, it is quite possible for one brewery's "bitter" to have less bitterness than another brewery's "mild."

In point of fact, one brewery in Central England reportedly renamed their mild (1.036 and 25 IBU) to bitter in the mid-1990s.[31] With a BU:GU ratio of 0.69, this beer falls well within the range found in English bitters as a group (0.58 to 1.09).

A Word About Real Ales

You can't read much about English beers without running into the term "real ale," which is defined as: "A name for a draught (or bottled) beer brewed from traditional ingredients, matured by secondary fermentation in the container from which it is dispensed and served without the use of extraneous carbon dioxide."[32]

A group called the Campaign for Real Ale (CAMRA) in Britain has been working since 1971 to revive and preserve this traditional type of ale. Fortunately, the group has been quite successful. Draft bitters and some pale ales may be real ales when you drink them in the United Kingdom these days. Indeed, a beer that the typical American tourist would describe as "warm and flat" most likely falls into this classification.

The distinction between real ale and normal draft comes as the result of activities by the brewer and the publican. Real ales are carbonated by secondary fermentation in the cask, then are fined or clarified before serving. To keep from disturbing the sediment before serving, these activities are conducted in the cellar of the pub rather than at the brewery. As a result, cellarmanship is an important skill of the publican because it affects many qualities of the product when it is served.

A common trait of real ale — and indeed of all bitters and pale ales — is a much lower level of carbonation than is usually found in American beers. Measured as volumes of CO_2 dissolved in one volume of beer, U.S. drinkers are accustomed to seeing values of 2.25 to 2.75.[33] As a result of cask conditioning, the typical bitter will have a value of just 0.75 to 1.0.[34]

Now anyone who has ever drawn beer from a keg knows that CO_2 is what forces the beer from the bottom of the keg to travel up the hose and into your glass. In bars, beer typically must travel quite a distance from the cooler to the tap head, and therefore quite a lot of CO_2 pressure must be applied to move the beer. With real ales, no external CO_2 pressure is applied to drive the beer. Instead, the beer must be "pumped" up to the bar using a traditional beer engine.

The long handle of the beer engine is used by the bartender to actually draw the beer from the cask through the hose and out the nozzle. The keg — or more properly, cask — containing the beer admits air to replace the volume of beer drawn. This interaction with the air of course changes the character of the beer from day to day and, in fact, from hour to hour as it is served. This drift in flavor is considered part of the charm of real ale. Of course, that charm can turn to vinegar if the publican doesn't manage his inventory to ensure rapid consumption of each cask.

Purists will also insist that the proper dispensing spout be used on the beer engine. They are very much against a device called a "sparkler," which has come into widespread use in recent years. This device forces the beer through very small holes as it enters the glass, thereby churning up a thick blanket of small CO_2 bubbles in the glass. When a pint poured in this fashion is set before you it looks like a swirling maze of foam — a bubbly typhoon in a glass. Then, in a minute or two the foam resolves into a creamy inch-high head riding on top of a beautiful, clear glass of beer.

Though this method produces a fine-looking beer, some brewers and drinkers complain about the resulting flavor effect. This dispensing method is said to remove CO_2 from the beer, leaving it less lively and, some would say, "flat." It is also said to force hop flavor components out of the beer and into the head, thereby changing the balance and character of the beer. Finally, that thick, creamy head is supposed to block aromas from the beer itself, which reduces enjoyment of the full character of the product. The flavor of the product dispensed in this manner is supposedly so different from that of the properly dispensed item that some pundits of the beer scene insist it no longer deserves to be called bitter.

Although I have not had the opportunity to taste sparkled and nonsparkled samples side by side, I do know that the sparkled version is quite different from that produced by a normal American CO_2 dispenser. I find that when the prickly, acidic bite of the CO_2 is stripped away, the resulting beer is softer, gentler, and usually much more interesting to drink.

Brewers who are working to brew bitters and pale ales should pay attention to carbonation and serving techniques. Although there are certainly a number of hard-core homebrewers and brewpubs who use beer engines for serving their bitters, this is not always possible. Those who do own beer engines should try removing the sparkler to evaluate the flavor differences.

Even without a beer engine, you can produce the style appropriately. The first option is to use bottle conditioning. When you do this, be careful not to over-carbonate; aim for values of 1.5 to 2.0 volumes of CO_2.[35] This will require smaller additions of priming sugar than are used for other beers.

A second (and perhaps the best) option is to use a keg without a beer engine. Although you could force carbonate to a low level with CO_2, it would be more traditional to carbonate by priming. In either case, when you dispense, you should keep the CO_2 pressure very low or work out some sort of gravity dispensing system. Purists may dislike this approach, but as a starting point it is not bad.

Finally, real ale cannot be served cold, and purists will insist that it should never be stored cold either. The proper temperature for a real-ale cellar is 55 to 57 °F (13 to 14 °C).[36] Though the first beer or two may register as being a bit warm at that temperature, you'll find that you get used to it. There can be no doubt that beer served at this temperature will reveal more of its flavor and character than those served in the frost zone of most American brews.

By following these techniques for priming, carbonation, and serving, you can produce English-style ales that emulate the classic examples of the style.

Commercial Examples

Finding good representative samples of English ales — especially bitters — is a real challenge for Americans. Your best bet is to visit a brewpub that specializes in reproducing these styles. I recall that Commonwealth Brewing in Boston had some very nice ales, and Jackson gives its Best Burton Bitter three stars.[37] In the Midwest, Sherlock's Home in Minneapolis serves a number of its ales at cellar temperature and from proper beer engines. It gets three-star ratings across the board from Jackson.[38]

Farther west, Coopersmiths in Fort Collins, Colorado, also uses beer engines, and their Albert Damn Bitter gets good reviews from various sources. In Portland,

Oregon, Bridgeport's ales get good marks. Farther north, in Seattle, the ales at both Pike Place and Redhook are generally impressive, and the latter can be found in bottles nationally these days.

Understandably, few people will have the advantage of visiting one of these cities in the short run, so bottled products will have to suffice to provide examples of the English styles. The following list gives at least one product for each style that can serve as a decent example.

Bitter. Bodington's Best Bitter (unusual for its pale color, but gravity, body, and flavor adequately illustrate the style).

Best Bitter. Fuller's London Pride (hop character is subdued in the bottled product, but it will be better if found on draft); Young's Special (occasionally seen on draft); Shepherd Neame's Master Brew Best Bitter (be sure to buy your six-pack from an unopened case to guard against skunkiness).

Strong or Extra Special Bitter (ESB). Fuller's ESB, Redhook ESB, Young's Ramrod, Brakespear's Henley Ale, Young's Special London Ale (or IPA), Shepherd Neame Spitfire, and Bishops Finger.

English Pale Ale. Bass Ale, Whitbread Pale Ale, Geary's Pale Ale, Sam Smith's Old Brewery Pale Ale.

American Pale Ale. Sierra Nevada Pale Ale, Pyramid Pale Ale, Bell's Amber, Pike Place Pale Ale.

India Pale Ale (IPA). Anchor Liberty Ale; Grant's IPA (lower gravity than the classic, but full of hop flavor and typically some diacetyl); Great Lakes Burning River.

Brewing Bitters and Pale Ales

Because of their many similarities, the brewing of bitters and pale ales, including

India pale ales, all follow similar patterns. Many of the differences between these individual styles will depend on your ability to control the original gravity of the beer as well as its bitterness levels. Let's begin examination of the brewing approach by looking at the bill of fermentable materials.

Fermentables

It goes without saying that the heart of a great bitter or pale ale is a great pale ale malt. The typical British pale ale malt is a well-modified two-row malt that is generally low in nitrogen content. Because they are kilned at higher temperatures during the final stage of drying, these malts have a bit more color (2.5 to 3 °SRM) than a typical lager or plain two-row malt (1.8 to 2.0 °SRM).

Writing about pale ale grists in 1938, British brewer H. Loyd Hind said: "The colour of the [pale ale] malt usually corresponds fairly well with its flavour and should, in most cases, be as high as the colour of the beer will permit."[39] As a result, I wouldn't fear the use of ale malts with color as deep as 4.5 in a bitter or pale ale, although any use of crystal malt should be reduced in such cases.

Because of the low nitrogen and high modification levels, pale malt can be mashed with a simple single-infusion mash. Most pale ale mashes are conducted at temperatures of 150 to 154 °F (66 to 68 °C),[40] although bitters may be mashed slightly lower, at 149 to 151 °F (65 to 66 °C).[41] These mashes are usually a bit thick, with a water-to-grain ratio of 1 quart per pound.[42]

The hop character and color of this style make it a good one for the use of malt extract. The middle of the color range for bitters and pale ales (8 to 10 °SRM) is about what you get from many light extracts. I have produced a number of excellent pale ales based upon 3 pounds of extract added to the proceeds of a small mash (4 to 5 pounds) of pale ale and crystal malts.

The other malt most commonly found in these recipes will be some sort of crystal or caramel malt, which is found in about three-quarters of all commercial products these days. In addition, many commercial examples include sugar, wheat, or maize. Very small portions of chocolate malt, black malt, or roast barley may be included, primarily as a coloring agent.

Table 16.5 shows the incidence and proportion of various fermentable materials listed in recipes for nearly two hundred commercial ordinary and best bitters with an average gravity of 1.038. As with several other analyses of commercial ale recipes in this book, the bulk of the raw data has come from Roger Protz's *The Real Ale Drinker's Almanac*.[43]

As you can see from table 16.5, the most common ingredient after pale and crystal malts is sugar, which is included in one-third of all bitter recipes. Among those recipes that included sugar, it accounts for more of the fermentable content than any other ingredient except pale malt.

In only one case did both chocolate malt and either black malt or roast barley appear in the same recipe together. Also, black malt and roast barley were less likely to be used in conjunction with crystal malt than was chocolate malt.

Homebrew writers who focus on bitters list the use of sugar in at least some recipes,[44] although it appears in only one of twenty-two (4.5 percent) of the National Homebrew Competition second-round beers.

In recipes coming from Britain, the type of sugar specified is often maltose. Because maltose is the main sugar in wort to begin with, adding additional quantities should not produce the ciderlike flavor impact often associated with sucrose or glucose sugars. Unfortunately, maltose syrup is generally impossible to find from U.S. brewing suppliers.

Cane and corn sugars are sometimes recommended in bitter recipes and may also

Table 16.5
English Commercial Bitter Grain Bills

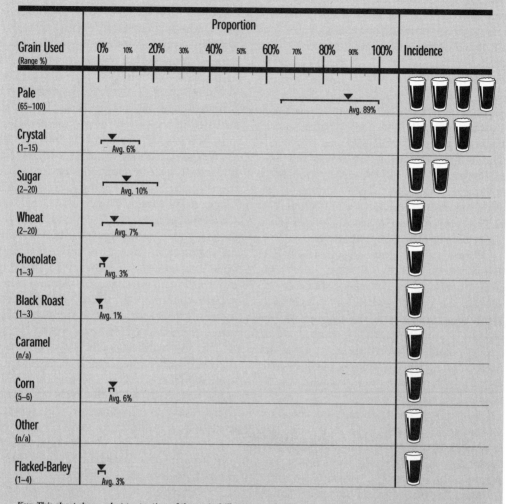

Grain Used (Range %)	Proportion	Incidence
Pale (65–100)	Avg. 89%	usually
Crystal (1–15)	Avg. 6%	often
Sugar (2–20)	Avg. 10%	sometimes
Wheat (2–20)	Avg. 7%	rarely
Chocolate (1–3)	Avg. 3%	rarely
Black Roast (1–3)	Avg. 1%	rarely
Caramel (n/a)		rarely
Corn (5–6)	Avg. 6%	rarely
Other (n/a)		rarely
Flacked-Barley (1–4)	Avg. 3%	rarely

Key: This chart shows what proportion of the grain bill was provided by various grains in 226 English commercial bitter recipes. The line next to each grain gives the range of values used by different brewers; this range is also listed below "Grains Used." The triangle above each line indicates the average proportion used across all recipes.

The icons in the column on the right show how often the 226 English commercial bitter recipes included each grain. (Percentage figures indicate how many of the recipes included the grain.)

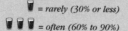
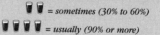

= rarely (30% or less)   = sometimes (30% to 60%)
= often (60% to 90%)   = usually (90% or more)

give desirable results as long as the quantity is not overdone.[45] A typical sugar addition would be 8 to 10 percent of the total weight of the raw fermentable materials.

The small number of bitters (fourteen) that I extracted from *The Real Ale Drinker's Almanac* in the "strong" or "extra special" range (average gravity of 1.049) showed few differences when compared to all the other bitters. These beers are less likely to use crystal and chocolate malt (50 percent and 0 percent respectively) and more likely to use roast barley or black malt, which appear in 21 percent of all such recipes. Although there were some changes in the incidence of wheat, sugar, flaked barley (all increased), and maize (decreased), the total proportion of the grist represented by these ingredients remained about the same at 20 to 25 percent.

The small number of pale ales and India pale ales (seventeen) identified in *The Real Ale Drinker's Almanac* showed only a few differences when compared to this analysis of bitters. The pale ales were slightly more likely to use wheat (29 percent versus 23 percent), although the amount used (7 percent) remained the same. None of the pale ales used chocolate malt, maize, or flaked barley. Although it seems a bit odd, the pale ales were more likely (18 percent versus 7 percent) to use caramel coloring.

Unlike commercial English products, American pale ales are highly unlikely to contain sugar or even maize. Although I have no data on commercial practice, experience indicates that there are a lot of pale ales being made at craft breweries these days, and ingredients such as sugar and flaked maize are rarely used in them.

In looking at the NHC second-round beers, I find that recipes for all six of these styles are essentially the same. They rely on base malts for an average of 87 percent of the grist and supplement this with specialty malts.

The base malts used by NHC second-round beers include British pale ale malts as well as American two-row malts and a good bit of malt extract (see table 16.6). From this data it doesn't appear that the selection of two-row American malts instead of English pale malts detracts from the character of these beers. Nearly 40 percent of the recipes included malt extract, and it generally accounted for more than half of the gravity in these cases. A couple of recipes used nothing but malt extract. Table 16.7 shows the various types of extract used in these recipes.

The portion of the grist devoted to specialty malts almost always contains some crystal or caramel malt. The Lovibond rating of the crystal malts used varies across the entire available range, but most additions were in the light to medium portion of the spectrum with an average of about 40 °L.

The body and head enhancers — CaraPils, wheat, and flaked barley — when combined, appeared in about half of all recipes. After this, no other ingredient appears in more than one-third of all recipes. Various character grains such as toasted, Victory, biscuit, aromatic, Munich, and Vienna malts appeared in a number of recipes. Although not found in the commercial examples, these grains add complexity and character to these recipes that may help propel them into the second round. One of the second-round entries was a bitter I brewed, and it is typical of this pattern. In addition to pale ale malt and crystal malt, it included 4 ounces of biscuit and 2 ounces of special "B."

Dark grains are not seen often in these styles, but they do make an occasional appearance in very small amounts. Fifteen percent of the recipes included chocolate malt, and it averaged just 0.5 percent of the grist. Roast barley appears in just two of fifty-six recipes, but it accounted for about 1 percent of the grist when used. Table 16.8 shows the incidence and proportions of specialty grains in these styles.

Based upon historical records of the IPA style, some sources suggest that contemporary IPAs should be made strictly from pale malt, as the original ones were, to achieve a golden-colored beer. Others, however, argue that the brewing processes of the time still produced IPAs that were amber to light copper in color.[46] Following this second argument, the malt bill for an IPA should be much the same as that for a pale ale; in fact, that is what I see in the homebrewed examples. Nonetheless, I know some judges who expect IPAs to be lighter in color than a regular pale ale.

Table 16.6
Base Malt Incidence and Proportion in NHC Second-Round Bitters and Pale Ales

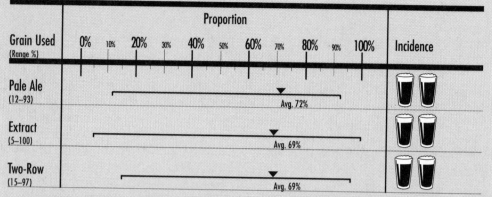

Key: This chart shows what proportion of the grain bill was provided by various grains in brewing fifty-six bitter and pale ale recipes. The line next to each grain gives the range of values used by different brewers; this range is also listed below "Grains Used." The triangle above each line indicates the average proportion used across all recipes.

The icons in the column on the right show how often the fifty-six bitter and pale ale recipes included each grain. (Percentage figures indicate how many of the recipes included the grain.)

🍺 = rarely (30% or less)   🍺🍺 = sometimes (30% to 60%)

🍺🍺🍺 = often (60% to 90%)   🍺🍺🍺🍺 = usually (90% or more)

Hop Bitterness

Hops form the soul of these styles both in their selection and their use. The finished beer may display every possible type of hop character, from assertive bitterness through a spectrum of hop flavors and aromas. Although no two beers are processed in exactly the same way, they do share some common characteristics. Let's look first at bitterness and then evaluate the use of flavor and aroma hop additions.

Bitterness is a defining characteristic for both the bitters and the pale ales. Among all the commercial bitters and pale ales selected from *The Real Ale Drinker's Almanac,* the average BU:GU ratio was 0.80, with a range from 0.58 to 1.09. To meet the average value, a 1.040 bitter would need 32 IBUs.

Table 16.7
Malt Extract Selection in NHC Second-Round Bitters and Pale Ales

Brand Used	No. of Recipes
Northwestern	8
Munton and Fison	4
Alexander's	3
John Bull	2
Geordie Light dry	1
Ireks Vienna	1
Unspecified brand	7
Total	26

Table 16.8
Incidence and Proportion of Specialty Malts in NHC Second-Round Bitters and Pale Ales

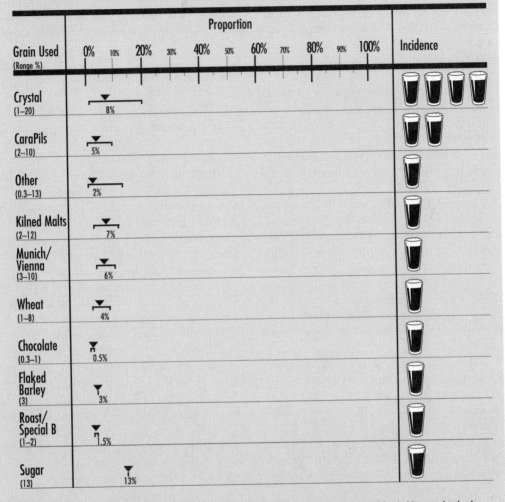

Grain Used (Range %)	Proportion	Incidence
Crystal (1–20)	8%	
CaraPils (2–10)	5%	
Other (0.3–13)	2%	
Kilned Malts (2–12)	7%	
Munich/Vienna (3–10)	6%	
Wheat (1–8)	4%	
Chocolate (0.3–1)	0.5%	
Flaked Barley (3)	3%	
Roast/Special B (1–2)	1.5%	
Sugar (13)	13%	

Key: This chart shows what proportion of the grain bill was provided by various grains in fifty-six bitter and pale ale recipes. The line next to each grain gives the range of values used by different brewers; this range is also listed below "Grains Used." The triangle above each line indicates the average proportion used across all recipes.

The icons in the column on the right show how often the fifty-six bitter and pale ale recipes included each grain. (Percentage figures indicate how many of the recipes included the grain.)

= rarely (30% or less); = sometimes (30% to 60%); = often (60% to 90%); = usually (90% or more)

Looking beyond this average value, I do find some variations in the BU:GU ratios by style. Both the ordinary (GU 30 to 37) and best (GU 38 to 45) bitters come in right at the average value, but the strong bitters (GU 46 to 60) show somewhat less bitterness, with a BU:GU ratio close to 0.70. These data are supported by a recent CAMRA survey that also found lower BU:GU ratios in strong bitters.[47]

The small number of pale ales (only four) from *The Real Ale Drinker's Almanac,* that offer bitterness data indicate a higher value of 0.89. This is not, however, consistent with the accepted style profiles as listed in table 16.2 at the beginning of this chapter, which indicate lower BU:GU ratios, in the range from 0.45 to 0.71. If one accepts these values, then one of the clear distinguishing factors between bitter and pale ale would be this difference in overall bitterness.

Just to prove how contrary people's views of styles can be, the data from the NHC second-round recipes show a relationship that is exactly opposite of what the style profiles assert, with pale ales having higher BU:GU ratios compared to the bitters (see table 16.9).

Because these IBU counts are calculated using the average utilization values listed in chapter 9, they cannot be compared to the commercial values with complete accuracy. Nonetheless, the average bitterness values for bitters by this method are quite close to those of the commercial examples, and the range of BU:GU values for each style pretty well matches those found in the commercial beers as well.

These calculated data make a good source for comparisons between styles within the NHC data. Excluding the data on ordinary bitter in table 16.9 because of the small sample size, you can see that as a group the bitters have a lower level of bitterness than do the pale ales and the IPAs. This is exactly opposite what is indicated by the style classifications.

For those who brew competitively, these values provide some idea of what level of bitterness has been succeeding in the national competition. By using the average utilization values in chapter 9, you should be able to match the level of bitterness in these beers fairly closely.

Hop Selection and Application

The selection of hops for bitters and pale ales raises the issues of patriotism and pragmatism. Although this book is written for distribution in the United States, those wishing to produce authentic English ales can not ignore the need for English hops. Yet if you wish to use English hops, you'll have a harder time finding them and you will pay more money than if you use domestic varieties. For homebrew, the extra time and expense should be well worth it. On the other hand, commercial brewers may have to stick with domestic hops to stay within budget constraints for these brews.

Finally, some Americanization does occur within these styles. American pale ale should certainly be made with U.S. hop varieties. In addition, one could argue that the best examples of IPA being made right now use domestic varieties like Cascade and Chinook. Even some brewers who would never dream of using anything but Fuggle and Goldings in a bitter tend to think of Cascade when IPA is mentioned.

Table 16.9
IBU Values for NHC Second-Round Bitters and Pale Ales

Type	BU:GU Average	Min.	Max.	No. of Recipes
Ordinary bitter	1.28	1.28	1.28	1
Special bitter	0.73	0.58	1.07	5
ESB	0.86	0.50	2.05	12
Pale ale	0.91	0.58	1.12	6
IPA	1.10	0.61	1.64	15
Total	0.95	0.50	2.05	39

In the end, you'll have to make your own decisions about this issue. When you do decide between English or American, you'll want to know exactly which varieties to choose. I turn to Protz's data for information on the former and then review the NHC second-round data for the latter.

As with most English ales, Goldings and Fuggle are the most popular varieties of hops used in bitters and pale ales. IPAs are a bit more likely to use these two to the exclusion of all others, while regular pale ales are a bit less likely to use them in favor of Target and other infrequently used types. Strong bitters also show some slight variations in usage: less Goldings, more Challenger and Progress (see table 16.10).

Data from the NHC show that among the extra special bitter (ESB) and English pale ale styles, Goldings and Fuggle make a good showing. Goldings are the most popular hop and Fuggle the second or third most popular, with Cascade taking the second position among the English pale ales (EPAs). In the ESBs, Goldings and Fuggle account for two-thirds of all aroma hop additions, and no other hop is used more than once for this purpose. In the EPAs, the Cascade hops are most often used for aroma, and they account for half of all aroma hop additions for the style.[48] Willamette, although

bred from Fuggle, seems to get little use in the English-style recipes (see tables 16.11 and 16.13).

Dry hopping was fairly unusual in these styles, occurring in about a third of all recipes in both cases, but aroma hops were often added instead (see tables 16.12 and 16.14).

The India pale ale recipes are dominated by Cascade and Chinook, which together account for more than half of all hop additions. Goldings makes an appearance, tied for the third most popular hop with Hallertau and Centennial. For aroma, Cascade dominates, accounting for 51 percent of all aroma hop additions. Goldings (12 percent of aroma additions) and Centennial (9 percent of aroma additions) also see duty as aroma hops in IPAs. These data demonstrate the extent to which American hops are accepted in IPA, even though it is supposed to be an English style.

As an indication of the pervasive influence of hops on this style, the IPAs average more than five hop additions per recipe. Dry hopping is nearly universal, and most recipes add hops during the aroma and flavor windows as well (see tables 16.15 and 16.16).

Not surprisingly, the American pale ales are dominated by Cascade hops. They

Table 16.10
Incidence of Hop Variety by Style in Commercial Bitters and Pale Ales

Style	Goldings (%)	Fuggle (%)	Challenger (%)	Target (%)	North-down (%)	Other* (%)	Progress (%)	No. of Recipes
Ordinary	79	52	36	14	10	10	5	124
Best	80	45	35	12	17	12	9	66
Strong	68	47	53	26	11	0	16	19
Pale	57	29	14	29	0	14	0	7
IPA	100	56	11	11	0	11	0	9
Total	79	49	36	15	12	10	7	225

Source: R. Protz, The Real Ale Drinker's Almanac (Glasgow: Neil Wilson Publishing, Ltd., 1993).
* Other includes Hallertau (8), Bramling Cross (7), Omega (3), Northern Brewer (3), Brewers Gold (2), Zenith (2), Tettnanger (1), Pride of Ringwood (1), Sunshine (1), and Yeoman (1).

Table 16.11
Hops Used in NHC Second-Round English Pale Ales

Hop	Bitter	Flavor	Aroma	Dry	Total
Goldings	5	2	1	1	9
Cascade	1	0	3	1	5
Fuggle	2	0	2	0	4
Cluster	2	0	0	0	2
Bullion	1	0	0	0	1
Galena	1	0	0	0	1
N. Brewer	1	0	0	0	1
Perle	1	0	0	0	1
Saaz	1	0	0	0	1

Note: The data in this chart show the number of times each hop was used across the seven recipes analyzed.

account for more than half of all hop additions and for more than two-thirds of all flavor and aroma additions. Other aroma varieties such as Hallertau, Fuggle, and Goldings take a secondary position along with Chinook, which mostly gets used for bittering (see table 16.17).

As with the IPAs, we find a fairly high number of hop additions per recipe, at 4.3. Almost all recipes included additions in each of the four classifications (bitter, flavor, aroma, and dry) established for this analysis (see table 16.18).

Although tables 16.10 through 16.18 give the varieties of hops used and the incidences of various additions, they do not tell the sizes of the additions made for flavor, aroma, and dry hopping. Table 16.19 provides this data for each of the four styles for which an adequate number of recipes was available.

Yeast

Selection of yeast for bitters and pale ales can be as easy or as involved as you would like it to be. On the easy side, simply pick up an example of either the British or London strain and give it a whirl. These two yeasts are used frequently in British-style ales, and the results are sure to be satisfactory. Those with more patience who want

Table 16.12
Hop Additions in NHC Second-Round English Pale Ale Recipes

Type	Avg. No. of Additions
Bitter	2.1
Flavor	0.3
Aroma	0.8
Dry	0.3
Total	3.6

Note: Total number of recipes analyzed = 7.

to search for the perfect yeast/wort combination can explore the dozen or so different British yeasts available these days.

The American ale yeast is an overwhelming favorite in these styles, dominating the picture for IPAs and American pale ales in NHC second-round recipes. It also sees considerable use in the production of bitters (see table 16.20). If you are setting out to produce a good bitter, I would strongly recommend you use something other than the American ale yeast. The character contributed by one of the more assertive British yeasts is a critical component of the overall flavor profile of the bitter styles.

When you consider that the grain bill and hop regimen vary only slightly between brands, it is often the yeast that accounts for much of the flavor difference between a passable bitter and a great one. Indeed, yeast has a major impact on the flavor profile of these styles, affecting the fruitiness, the hop presence, and the level of diacetyl that remains in the finished product. In fact, if you are looking for a unique taste in your bitter or English pale ale, you might want to go fishing for yeast in a pint of real ale the next time you get a chance to visit London. Another alternative is to seek out one of the many yeast banks maintained by homebrewers around the United States and acquire an interesting strain or two from them.

Water

The water of Burton-on-Trent established the standard for production of bitters and pale ales, because that is where pale ale came of age and grew in popularity to become the drink of an empire.

For most brewers, matching the water of Burton almost certainly means that you will have to add something to what comes out of your tap. Unfortunately, it also means that you'll probably have to take something out. This is true because Burton water is exceedingly hard but has no bicarbonate, as can be seen from the profile in table 16.21.

The presence of bicarbonate at significant levels in your brewing water can undermine the crisp, clean bitterness you are trying to achieve in these styles of beer. As a result, if carbonate levels exceed 50 parts per million in your water, you should take appropriate steps to remove it or dilute it before brewing these styles.

Once this is done, you can add gypsum (calcium sulfate) or Burton water salts (a

---

Table 16.13
Hops Used in NHC Second-Round ESB Recipes

Hop	Bitter	Flavor	Aroma	Dry	Total
Goldings	10	1	4	2	17
Fuggle	2	2	3	1	8
Centennial	2	1	0	1	4
N. Brewer	2	1	0	0	3
Mt. Hood	0	1	0	1	2
Target	1	0	1	0	2
Willamette	0	1	1	0	2
Other*	3	0	1	0	4

Note: The data in this chart show the number of times each hop was used across the thirteen recipes analyzed.
*Other includes one addition each of Cascade, Challenger, Chinook, and Hallertau.

Table 16.14
Hop Additions in NHC Second-Round ESB Recipes

Type	Avg. No. of Additions
Bitter	1.5
Flavor	0.5
Aroma	0.8
Dry	0.4
Total	3.2

Note: Total number of recipes analyzed = 13.

combination of minerals) to help achieve the mineral profile shown in table 16.21. Assuming that it weighs about 5 grams, 1 teaspoon of gypsum will add 61 parts per million of calcium and 148 parts per million of sulfate to 5 gallons of water.

If you are starting with 5 gallons of very soft water that contains little or no mineral ions, you could add 5 teaspoons of gypsum to achieve mineral concentrations that are near the Burton levels. In addition, you might want to add just a touch of salt (sodium chloride: 1/8 to 1/16 of a teaspoon, or 1 gram) and a touch of Epsom salts (mag-

nesium sulfate: 1/2 teaspoon or 2 to 3 grams). If you add the Epsom salts, you can add a little less gypsum, say 4 teaspoons.

Of course, the ideal solution is to get an analysis of your water and then devise an exact treatment and salt addition strategy to imitate the Burton profile. When you don't have the required information or time for this effort, the above treatment will work — assuming you have soft water as a starting point.

It is difficult to tell exactly how close NHC second-round bitters and English pale ales come to meeting the Burton profile

Table 16.15
Hops Used in NHC Second-Round India Pale Ale Recipes

Hop	Bitter	Flavor	Aroma	Dry	Total
Cascade	12	5	5	12	34
Chinook	7	2	1	0	10
Centennial	2	1	3	0	6
Goldings	2	1	2	1	6
Hallertau	2	3	1	0	6
Eroica	5	0	0	0	5
Mt. Hood	0	2	2	0	4
N. Brewer	4	0	0	0	4
Galena	2	0	0	0	2
Willamette	0	0	1	1	2
Other[a]	1	0	2	1	4

[a]Other includes one addition each of Bullion, Fuggle, Liberty, and Saaz.
Note: The data in this chart show the number of times each hop was used across the sixteen recipes analyzed.

Table 16.16
Hop Additions in NHC Second-Round India Pale Ale Recipes

Type	Avg. No. of Additions
Bitter	2.3
Flavor	0.9
Aroma	1.1
Dry	0.9
Total	5.2

Note: Total number of recipes analyzed = 16.

because we don't know the composition of their source water. What is clear is that the majority (60 percent) get away with no water treatment at all. Many of the rest use only 1 teaspoon of gypsum — an amount that will leave most drinking waters well short of appropriate mineral levels for the style. Only two of twenty-seven recipes indicated the kind of water treatment regimen designed to emulate the Burton style.

Among the IPAs brewed for the NHC, water treatment was more prevalent, with 60 percent of entries indicating some sort of water treatment. Furthermore, most of these (40 percent of the total) seemed to use quantities of gypsum and Burton salts that could come close to meeting the true Burton profile.

Conclusion

A good pale ale or bitter is a real pleasure to drink just about any day of the year. In addition, it is often the best way to test the wares of a brewer or pub. Just by drinking a pint of pale ale you can get an idea of the yeast character and bitterness levels that you are likely to encounter in other beers from the same brewer. And because pale ales (or in England, the bitters) move reasonably quickly, you can use them as a test of a pub's care for the beer by evaluating the freshness and conditioning of the pint it serves you.

For brewers, these styles serve as somewhat of a standard — a style that many people know and love. More specifically,

Table 16.17
Hops Used in NHC Second-Round American Pale Ale Recipes

Hop	Bitter	Flavor	Aroma	Dry	Total
Cascade	4	6	6	6	22
Hallertau	1	1	2	0	4
Chinook	3	0	0	0	3
Fuggle	0	1	0	1	2
Goldings	2	0	0	0	2
Other[a]	4	1	1	0	5
Total	14	9	9	7	39

[a] Other includes one addition each of Centennial, Mt. Hood, Northern Brewer, Perle, Saaz, and Willamette.
Note: The data in this chart show the number of times each hop was used across the nine recipes analyzed.

Table 16.18
Hop Additions in NHC Second-Round American Pale Ale Recipes

Type	Avg. No. of Additions
Boil	1.6
Flavor	1.0
Aroma	1.0
Dry	0.8
Total	4.3

Note: Total number of recipes analyzed = 9.

a standard is something that anyone who claims to be a practitioner of an art should be able to competently perform. Thus it is that your ability to brew a good pale ale or bitter can establish you as a great brewer among your friends and fellow brewers.

The huge diversity of commercial examples available in these styles both here and in the United Kingdom indicates the range of options you have for brewing a beer that is enjoyable but also unique. When you do this, you join nearly two centuries of brewers who have explored this style, and you touch a heritage that is nearly as old as civilization itself.

Table 16.19
Size of Late Hop Additions in NHC Second-Round Recipes, by Style

Style	Flavor	Aroma	Dry
APA	0.71	0.77	0.65
EPA	0.53	0.55	0.88
ESB	0.75	0.84	0.77
IPA	0.76	0.70	1.19

Note: All values are in ounces per 5 gallons.

Table 16.20
Yeast Used in NHC Second-Round Bitter and Pale Ale Recipes

Strain	Bitter	EPA	IPA	APA	Total
American	5	0	11	6	22
London	6	1	3	1	11
British	2	2	0	2	6
Other	2	2	1	1	6
Dry	4	1	0	0	5
ESB	1	0	0	0	1

Table 16.21
Burton Water Profile

Minerals	ppm[a]
Calcium	294
Magnesium	24
Sodium	24
Sulfate	801
Chloride	36
Bicarbonate	0

[a] ppm = parts per million

Key Success Factors in Brewing Bitters and Pale Ales

- Except in the case of American pale ales, brew using "Burtonized" water that is high in gypsum content.

- Choose a quality English pale ale malt or American two-row malt as the base for your recipe.

- Malt extract may be used to supply up to two-thirds of the gravity when supplementing a minimash.

- Include 5 to 8 percent crystal malt with a Lovibond rating of about 40.

- Up to 5 percent of the grist may include Munich, Vienna, aromatic, biscuit, Victory, or toasted malt to increase the malt complexity of the beer, especially in the American and English pale ale styles.

- For bitters, some sugar or flaked maize may be added, with each accounting for no more than 10 percent of the grist.

- Five to 15 percent wheat or 1 to 4 percent flaked barley may be added to any bitter or pale ale recipe.

- Conduct a thick mash (0.9 to 1 quarts per pound of grist) with temperatures in the range from 149 to 154 °F (65 to 68 °C).

- Select English or American hops according to the style you are trying to produce. Goldings, Fuggle, and Challenger are the English varieties used most often. The three Cs — Cascade, Centennial, and Chinook — are the most common American types.

- Add bittering hops to achieve a BU:GU ratio of 0.70 to 0.90.

- For bitters and English pale ales, you may elect to add flavor hops, with the average addition 0.5 to 0.7 ounces in 5 gallons. India and American pale ales should definitely have a flavor hop addition of 0.75 ounces or more.

- Most recipes will benefit from the addition of aroma hops and/or dry hops. See table 16.19 for addition amounts by style.

- For bitters and English pale ales, select a British-style yeast, such as the

Key Success Factors in Brewing Bitters and Pale Ales (continued)

British or London strains described in chapter 12. The American ale yeast continues to be a favorite for the production of India and American pale ales.

- Give the English styles less carbonation than you would other beers and, where possible, serve bitters through a hand-pumped English beer engine.

17 BOCK BEER

The mists of time veil the earliest days of most beer styles, but some circumstances of history give us a particularly clear view of the origins and development of the style that today is called "bock." It began not in Munich — although residents of this city probably gave it the name by which it is known today — but in northern Germany in a town called Einbeck.

The Beer of Einbeck

Einbeck began as a small estate not far from Hannover and was chartered as a city during the thirteenth century. Not long after, it joined a group of cities known as the Hanseatic League. Together, these metropolises of the Middle Ages controlled most trade both inside present-day Germany and between that area and other countries. The chief exports of the league included beer, wine, and linen.

Perhaps Einbeck was admitted to the Hanseatic League because of the quality of the beer produced there. At its height, brewing was the primary economic activity of Einbeck, and the mayor was the chief brewer. A portable brewpot was taken from home to home, with each household responsible for fermentation and maturation of the beer. Then, before beer could be sold, it was tested and poor-quality products were destroyed. This quality control

process helped to establish the renown of the Einbeck beers throughout Europe.

By 1325, Einbeck beer was being enjoyed in Hamburg and Bremen. Through the Hanseatic League, it was later exported to London, the Netherlands, Denmark, Norway, Sweden, and Russia; it is even reported to have gone to Jerusalem. Depots of the beer were established in most towns of any size, including Munich.[1]

Some information on the character of this beer has been preserved. The historian Arnold quotes two sources from that period regarding the beer of Einbeck. The first is J. Letzner from his "Chronicle." On the beer of Einbeck, this source reports:

This delicious, palatable, subtle, extremely sound and wholesome beer, which because of its refreshing properties and pleasant taste is exported to far-away countries, especially during summertime . . .

Now, all such Einbeck beer which shows the right hue, a wholesome odor and the proper savor is a delicious, famous and very palatable beverage and an excellent beer, wherewith a man, when partaken of in moderation, may save his health and his sound senses, and yet feel jolly and stimulated.[2]

Heinrich Knaust, who was a contemporary of Letzner says:

Of all summer beers, light and hoppy barley beers, the Einbeck beer is the most famed and deserves the preference. Each third grain to this beer is wheat; hence, too, it is of all barley beers the best . . . People do not fatten too much from its use; it is also very useful in fever cases.[3]

Another source reports that "The beer of Einbeck is thin, subtle, clear, of bitter taste, has a pleasant acidity on the tongue, and many other good qualities."[4]

Arnold further reports that the barley and wheat used were "but lightly kilned," and that Einbeck beer was brewed only in winter.[5] He also asserts that it was top-fermented and very strongly hopped — as would be consistent with the bitterness expressed in the description above.

The wide area to which this beer was shipped both within and outside Germany attests to its popularity. It is also said to have been consumed by Martin Luther on two occasions; the first was his wedding and the second was during the Diet of Worms in 1521.[6]

This success spanned at least three centuries, but Einbeck was not destined to become a permanent fixture in the world of brewing. The city was ravaged by fire twice during the sixteenth century. Not long after this the Thirty Years' War (1618–1648) is said to have ended completely the brewing trade in Einbeck[7] — and, indeed, it severely crippled much of Germany for nearly two hundred years.

The Munich Transformation

Anyone familiar with contemporary bocks realizes that the beers of Einbeck bear little relationship to the style as known today. Indeed, the term "bock" probably had not been coined before Einbeck's virtual demise during the Thirty Years' War. To bridge this gap in both brewing and linguistics required the people — and brewers — of Munich.

Prior to the sixteenth century, the beer made in Munich was not highly regarded, even by the local folk. Many imported

beers were enjoyed, and the beer from Einbeck was highly favored. During the 1500s, Munich tried to improve its beers with various ordinances, including a 1553 edict that required all beer to be made only of hops, barley, and water.[8]

As the seventeenth century dawned, the Munich brewers "bent all their energy to brewing a beer as good as that of Einbeck."[9] This effort failed until a brewer from Einbeck was drawn to Munich in 1612 and lent his skills to the cause.[10] Of course, the original recipe could not be reproduced precisely, for various reasons, as Darryl Richman explains:

The Munich version, however was different from the original. It was darker and, rather than the one-third wheat malt and two-thirds barley malt grist that the Einbeckers used, this version was made entirely from barley malt. Because hops were more dear in Munich, and because the water drawn from the chalky Isar River could emphasize an unpleasant bitterness, the beer was sweeter in balance.[11]

Although it is not explicit in any of the sources I have seen, it seems highly likely that this beer would have been made with a bottom-fermenting lager-type yeast. Lager brewing existed in Bavaria from the 1400s,[12] and this type of yeast and fermentation process would likely have been used to make such a prized beer.

When this first "knock-off" bock was finished, the resulting beer was named after the city of Einbeck, which in the Bavarian dialect was *Ainpoeckish Pier*.[13] The beer was enjoyed by the citizens of Munich and soon replaced the original. Not long after, brewing ceased in Einbeck as a result of the Thirty Years' War, and the name of the Munich-produced beer no doubt began to drift from *Ainpoeckish* to simply *Poeck* and ultimately to the "bock" we know today.[14]

Of course, this is not the only story told about the naming of bock beer. Those who spent hours on end enjoying this fine beverage no doubt used their uninhibited imaginations to create fanciful stories about its naming. One even attributes the naming to the Roman Emperor Julian (the Apostate) who lived in the fourth century A.D. — long before the advent of brewing in Einbeck.

These stories aside, the drift in Bavarian dialect seems to be the most likely and certainly the most linguistically rational explanation for the origin of the term. *Bock* means goat in German, and it's not surprising that someone drinking this beer would feel a "kick" and make the verbal connection forming a strong association between bock beer and goats — an association that continues even today.

Munich's initial success with the bock beer did not hold its ground for long. The need for economy (perhaps brought on by the Thirty Years' War, which destroyed 90 percent of the wealth of Germany) resulted in a weakening of the wort, and the beer lost favor for some time. It was not until 1799 or 1800 that history provides "facts and statistics showing Munich beer once more on the road to general favor."[15]

Salvator: The Second Coming

Those familiar with the evolution of stout as a strong version of porter would find it easy to accept that doppelbock had evolved as simply a stronger version of bock. However, this is not the case. Doppelbock has unique origins in monastic brewing, and it was only after this saintly beer was secularized that the term doppelbock evolved.

Monks from the order of St. Francis founded a community in Munich in 1634. These monks were known as Paulaners because they came from the city of Paula, Italy. Today, the brewery that bears their name — now secularized — still produces the special beer they created.

The beer, dubbed Salvator, or "the Savior," by the monks was an extrastrong brew intended to sustain them during the fasts of Advent and Lent. During these periods the monks were forbidden solid food, and so the beer was literally their "liquid bread."

The monks kept the beer to themselves until 1780, when they began to sell it to the public, presumably under the Salvator name. It was the consumers who found a similarity between it and the well-known bock beers. Noting the greater body and perhaps alcohol of the Paulaner's product, they dubbed it a *doppel*, or "double," bock.

This product proved quite popular, and other brewers rushed to copy it. Along with the beer, they copied the name as a style designator. As a result, nineteenth-century documents list a number of "Salvator" beers, the origins of which we cannot know for sure. In 1894 the name finally came under trademark protection, and the competing products had to find new names. To continue the imitation of the original product, most brewers still name their doppelbocks with words that end in -ator.

Nineteenth-Century Bock

Nearly two hundred years after the Thirty Years' War ended (in 1648), the German economy finally recovered the position it had held before the war started. With this came a general revival in economic growth, including brewing. Education and science also improved, and the thermometer and hydrometer were adopted from England, where they had been developed during the 1700s.

By this time, the bock beer style had reportedly spread well beyond Munich. A beer called Einbock was produced in the vicinity of Vienna during the eighteenth century,[16] and a bock brewery was also established in Berlin in 1839.[17] But despite this, Munich remained the home of bock as well as the home of most breweries that brewed the style.

By the latter half of the century, the style had settled into a fairly constant character wherever it was brewed. The original gravity was high, with values approximating those accepted today for both bock and doppelbock. Table 17.1 shows gravity levels displayed by bocks and doppelbocks during this time.

Despite these high gravities, the level of attenuation was somewhat low, and as a result the alcohol levels are lower than are commonly expected from twentieth-century fermentations (see table 17.2). Those accustomed to thinking of bock as a high-alcohol beer will be surprised to find that it was lower in alcohol than most English ale styles of the day (see table 17.3).

The color of the nineteenth-century bocks may have varied considerably, at least between bock and doppelbock. In general, however, bocks appear to have been somewhat darker than English ales, with doppelbock color falling closer to that of a porter. These conclusions are based upon data from 1882 (see table 17.4). The values given seem similar to the Lovibond scale, although Lovibond's work was not published until 1883. But even without knowing exactly what system of standards was being employed, these data provide comparisons with other beers.

Bock Comes to America

German immigrants dominated the brewing industry in the United States in the late 1800s. So much so, in fact, that the publication *American Brewer* was published only in German until Prohibition. These brewers brought lager fermentation to the United States soon after Pilsener was invented in Bohemia, and one of the styles they brought along was bock.

The earliest reference to bock in America I have seen comes from 1852. In this year, Best & Company (later Pabst) introduced their seasonal bock beer on the Fourth of July.[18] The ad they ran for the occasion explained little about the character of the beer except to note that it was "brewed according to the Munich fashion."[19]

The introduction of the product for the big American holiday was probably driven more by patriotism than by business sense. By 1860, the company was releasing bock beer in February and March,[20] which today is considered to be the traditional season for bock. However, the release of bock beer has come in many different seasons through the years.

Table 17.1
Nineteenth-Century Bock Beer Gravities

Beer	OG	TG	Year
Bock			
Münchener Bock[a]	15.5	1.021	1877
Kulmbacher[a]	15.4	1.023	1877
Bock[b]	16.0		1883
Doppelbock			
Salvator I[c]	17.8	1.028	1875
Salvator II[a]	18.5	1.032	1875
Salvator[b]	18–19		1883
Münchener, Salvator[d]	18.8		1897

Sources: [a] *Carl Lintner*, Lehrbuch der Bierbrauerei *(Brunswick: Friedrich Vieweg und Sohn, 1877), 556. J. E. Thausing, W. T. Brannt, A. Schwarz, A. H. Bauer*, The Theory and Practice of the Preparation of Malt and the Fabrication of Beer *(London: Henry Carey Baird & Co., 1882), 751.* [b] *Carl Michel*, Lehrbuch der Bierbrauerei *(München: Münchener praktischen Brauerschule, 1883), 170.* [c] *Lintner*, Lehrbuch der Bierbrauerei, *556.* [d] *R. Wahl and M. Henius*, The American Handy-Book of the Brewing, Malting and Auxiliary Trades *(Chicago: Wahl-Henius Institute, 1908), 1288.*

Table 17.2
Alcohol Content of Bock Beers

Year	% ABW	Name
1893	3.76	Einbecker Bock Export
1876	3.83	Schwechater
1884	4.03	Kieler Actien
1884	4.19	Budapester
1879	4.34	Dresdener Feldschlosschen
1876	4.39	Brunner
1879	4.75	Münchener, Hofbrau (Einbock)
1995	5 to 6	Contemporary bock
1878	5.08	Celzener Bock Export
—	5.3	Hamburger, Kopperhold
1878	5.39	Einbecker Bock

Source: R. Wahl and M. Henius, The American Handy-Book of the Brewing, Malting and Auxiliary Trades. (Chicago: Wahl-Henius Institute, 1908: 1288.
Note: Entries are sorted from lowest to highest alcohol content.

Under the Pabst brand, bock beer was once released in the fall rather than the early spring.[21] And even when the beers were released during the first quarter of the year, the exact date of the unveiling moved around quite a bit. Apparently, the brewers didn't like this. Following Prohibition, American brewers cooperated to set a specific date when they would all release their bock brews.[22]

In addition, there is ample evidence from Europe that bock is not confined to the mid-March release date so revered in the United States. A 1950 review of the subject in *American Brewer* (which by this time was being published in English) states:

. . . the dark heavy feast beer so prized by connoisseurs on both sides of the Atlantic generally makes its appearance on the Continent at the same time as does Old St. Nick and continues to be quaffed and enjoyed until the supply runs out . . .[23]

Table 17.3
Alcohol by Weight in Nineteenth-Century Beers

Beer Style	%ABW
Bockbier, München	4.2
Salvator, München	4.6
London porter (Barkley and Perkins)	5.4
Burton ale	5.9
London porter	6.9
Scotch ale, Edinburgh	8.5

Source: Carl Lintner, Lehrbuch der Bierbrauerei (Braunschweig: Friedrich Vieweg und Sohn, 1877), 562.
Note: Entries are sorted from lowest to highest alcohol content.

Table 17.4
Indications of Bock Color

Beer Style/Name	Color Rating
Pilseners and lagers	4–6
English ale	10.0
Munich bock	14.3
Kulmbach	16.7
English porter	40.0
Munich Salvator (doppelbock)	41.5

Source: J. E. Thausing, W. T. Brannt, A. Schwarz, A. H. Bauer, The Theory and Practice of the Preparation of Malt and the Fabrication of Beer (London: Henry Carey Baird & Co., 1882), 751.

The article goes on to relate the practices in various European countries where bock is sold either year-round (Norway) or starting at Christmas (Switzerland, Holland).

It is possible that Salvator is responsible for the seasonality of the bock beers. Recall that the monks drank it for fortification during Advent (leading up to Christmas) and Lent (in the weeks before Easter). These periods correspond to the widely accepted dates for bock consumption both in Europe and the United States. Today, of course, Salvator is sold year-round, but the first brew of the new season is still presented for ceremonial tapping in the traditional Lenten season.

The Paling of Bock

The twentieth century has seen many changes in bock brewing in the United States but few in Germany — until recently.

As early as 1905, U.S.-brewed bock beers had lost the potency that was their trademark in Europe. The Wahl-Henius *Handy-Book* reports that the average gravity of ten Milwaukee bock beers was just 12.96 °B (1.052 SG) at that time.[24]

This dilution of bock in America was almost certainly the result of Prohibitionist pressures. Even after Prohibition was lifted, brewers kept a wary eye on the still-active "drys" to keep the pendulum from swing-

ing their way once again. In addition, the shortages in materials and energy created by the two world wars hurt efforts to produce beer at all — much less rich, strong beers in the bock style.

Still, brewery consultant Nugey reported in 1948 that the original gravity of American bocks had risen somewhat, with examples cited at 13.5 and 14.3 °B (1.054 to 1.058 SG).[25] The finishing gravity of these beers was kept high so that the alcohol levels remained in the range of 3.4 to 3.6 percent (by weight).[26]

By 1970 the vast majority of the bock produced in the United States was virtually identical in formulation and taste to the adjunct lagers that were the flagship products of every brewery. We can be thankful that American craft brewers have rescued the style and restored it to its former glory.

In Germany, the style has remained true to its origins in terms of strength. Credit for this goes largely to labeling laws that mandate the original gravity of bocks (16 °B) and doppelbocks (18 °B). Even with labeling laws, it may be that German brewmasters are just more stubborn about sticking to tradition. In East Germany, where the labeling laws did not apply, the gravity of bock slipped only a little by 1988, to 15 or 15.5 °B.[27]

The primary shift in bock character in Germany during this century has been toward lighter-colored products. I found no references to pale-colored bock beers during the nineteenth century, but today such offerings are quite common. Positioned as a *maibock* (May bock), or perhaps as a *helles* (pale) bock, these beers may also carry a bit more bitterness and hop character than a dark bock. According to some observers, these paler products are fast becoming the most popular bock offering in Germany.

Finally, new taxes may do more to diminish the style than half a century of Prohibition and war were able to. In 1993, European Community beer tax harmonization took effect, hitting high-gravity beers extra hard. One of Germany's most revered observers of the beer scene, Prof. Ludwig Narziss, recently stated that "it could lead to a further reduction of Bockbier output. This is a pity, given that the stronger beer could be served on special occasions or on a seasonal basis instead of wine or stronger alcoholic beverages."

Present-Day Bocks

The commonly accepted style criteria for bocks today remain true to the style as it has been defined in Germany for the last hundred years or so. Specifically, a certain minimum gravity is required before the label "bock" or "doppelbock" can be displayed by a beer. See table 17.5 for the style guidelines based on those published by the Association of Brewers[28] (©C. Papazian, 1992).

In Germany, a beer must have an original gravity of at least 1.066 to be labeled a bock, thus alcoholic strength is a hallmark of the style. Traditional bock is deep copper to dark brown in color, and attenuation is 67 to 73 percent. Aroma and flavor are dominated by malt, which, depending upon the preferences of the brewer, may have a character relatively dry and toasty, richer and chocolaty, or fairly sweet and caramel-like. German "noble-type" hops are used sparingly for a subtle counterpoint to the malt, with very low levels of bitterness and hop flavor and no perceptible hop aroma.

Few regular bocks are imported from Europe into the United States, with Aass Bock from the Aass Brewery in Norway being the most widely available. However, some microbreweries are making good examples that fit the classic bock definition. One such example is Frankenmuth Bock, (Frankenmuth Brewing Company, Michigan)

Table 17.5
Association of Brewers Guidelines for Bock Characteristics

	Bock	Maibock	Doppelbock	Eisbock
Original gravity	1.066–74	1.066–68	1.074–80	1.092–116
Bitterness	20–30	20–35	17–27	26–33
BU:GU ratio	0.27–0.45	0.29–0.53	0.21–0.36	0.22–0.36
Hop flavor	Low	Low	Low	Low
Hop aroma	None	Low	None	None
Color (SRM)	20–30	4.5–6	12–30	18–50
Apparent extract	1.018–24	1.012–20	1.020–28	–
Alcohol (volume)	6–7.5	6–7.5	6.5–8	7.2–12
Esters	Very low	Very low	Low	Low to medium
Diacetyl	Very low	Very low	Very low	Very low

Doppelbock

The name of this style means double bock, but the gravity required for this labeling in Germany is 1.074 or 18 °P — just 0.008 or 2 °P above that required for a regular bock. Apparent attenuation is often less than the traditional bock, with a range of 65 percent to 72 percent. Alcoholic strength, while only nominally different in the statistics, is usually perceived to be greater than that found in regular bocks. Doppelbocks are often quite sweet with complex chocolate and caramel flavors. Color is generally on the dark end of the bock range, but some examples are lighter.

Commercial examples of doppelbock are usually easy to find. Salvator (Paulaner, Germany) and Optimator (Spaten, Germany) can be found widely; Andechs doppelbock dunkel (Klosterbraueri, Andechs, Germany) can also be found. In addition, U.S. brewer Samuel Adams makes a "double bock" that is worthy of the name.

Maibock

The first kegs of bock are often tapped with great ceremony in March each year, so by the time May rolls around, frequenters of the *Biergarten* are ready for some variety. Thus a batch of *maibock,* or May bock, may be rolled out. This subcategory of bock departs most dramatically from the rest of the family by being pale to amber in color and lacking the chocolate or caramel flavors common in the rest. Though still dominated in aroma and palate by malt, this style may be a bit hoppier than its brethren. The maltiness comes from lighter malts such as Pilsener and Munich and may result in the appellation *helles* — the German word meaning light or pale. Still, it maintains the gravity and alcoholic strength of the style.

Commercial examples from Europe can occasionally be found stateside, including a sample from Einbeck itself called Einbecker Mai-Ur-Bock (Einbecker, Germany.) From the United States, Sierra Nevada often offers a May bock, although it usually includes an assertive hop character that some find out of keeping with the traditions of the style.

Eisbock

This is the granddaddy of all bocks, with effective original gravities of 1.093 and higher. This beer may have inspired the fad in ice beers among North American brewers during the early to mid-1990s, but the two have little in common. The *eis* part of this beer's name stems from the fortification practiced by some breweries, which would freeze the fermented beer and remove the ice, leaving behind a very highly alcoholic and intensely malty brew. Because it is a method of fortification like distillation, this practice is, strictly speaking, illegal in the United States today. Nonetheless, passable eisbocks can be made without this step. Aside from higher gravity, eisbocks are essentially the same as traditional bock and doppelbock.

The beer labeled Eggenberger Urbock fits strictly into this category, because the label carries the notation "23°," indicating an original gravity of 23 °P or 1.096 SG. Other examples seen here are Kulmbacher Reichelbrau eisbock, with an original gravity of 24 °B or 1.101 SG, and EKU Kulminator, which weighs in at 28 °P and 13.5 percent alcohol by volume.

Another extremely high-gravity lager, although not labeled as a bock, generally fits the description of this style. This one, called Samiclaus, is produced in Switzerland with an original gravity of 27 °P or 1.108 SG and more than 13.5 percent alcohol by volume.

American Bock

Some mid-sized American brewers — most notably in the Midwest — have reintroduced bock beers into their product lines, but they generally fall short of the gravity required for a traditional bock. Nonetheless, some distinct and worthwhile beverages have been created. The most notable of these display the malt balance typical of bock while showing a definite increase in gravity over the regular Pilsener, with a range of 1.050 to 1.060.

Two good examples include Schell Bock (August Schell Brewing Company) and Garten Brau Bock (Capital Brewing Company). The Garten Brau Bock offers a notably rich palate with some chocolaty notes and very subtle hop flavoring.

Brewing Bocks

With the exception of the light-colored maibock or helles bock styles, recipe formulation for all bock styles is pretty consistent. The basic structure of the malt bill is the same for all dark bocks. The total quantity of grain and extract changes from style to style in order to achieve the original gravity desired. Let's review the various components of the malt bill to see how most bocks are structured.

Base Malt

Most beer recipes use a lightly kilned malt such as a Pilsener, lager, or pale ale malt for the majority of the grist, but bock can be something of an exception to this rule. Though many recipes rely on lager or Pilsener malt for the majority of the grist, one school of bock brewers (myself included!) looks to Munich malt to play the lead role.

Bock was created before the days of specialty malts, when chocolate malt, roast barley, and even crystal malt were unknown. As a result, most beers were made from a single type of malt. The flavor and color of the malt — and therefore the finished beer — were determined by conditions during malting, especially the kilning temperatures.

The Munich malt available today appears to be a direct descendant of the malts once used in all Munich beers, including the bocks created in that city. Thus, the use of Munich malt as the primary grain for a bock recipe is historically accurate. In addition, it provides a unique flavor and color contribution to the beer.

Like all malt production, the making of Munich malt today requires a sophisticated process. Steps taken in germination and kilning produce higher than normal quantities of amino acids and reducing sugars. During the final kilning of the malt at temperatures up to 220 °F (104 °C), these compounds combine to form many color and flavor compounds.[29] (See chapter 7 for further discussion of melanoidin formation.) Thus, when Munich malt is used as the primary grain, it provides a richness of color and flavor that cannot be duplicated by any pale malt.

In his recent book, *Bock,* Darryl Richman asserts that all beers in this style should use Munich malt for the majority of the grist. He makes a comparison to varietal wines, stating that bock is the varietal beer of Munich malt. The dunkel bock recipes he presents rely on Munich malt for 75 to 93 percent of their grists. Lager malt — when included — accounts for no more than 24 percent of the grain bill.

It is hard to ignore Richman's advice. Not only has he researched the subject in depth, but he has also used this approach to produce many award-winning beers. Nonetheless, in looking at the National Homebrew Competition second-round beers from 1993 and 1994 (Richman won the category in 1990),[30] I find only a few who follow his example.

Most NHC bock recipes (eleven of fifteen, or 73 percent) include Munich malt, but only two use it for more than 30 percent of the grist. Instead, they rely on lager or Pilsener malt for the majority of the grist and add Munich malt as a significant specialty malt. The average amount of

Munich in recipes that include this grain is 25 percent.

One factor that works against more extensive use of Munich malt is the poor quality of the product that is often found in U.S. homebrew stores. American maltsters often make Munich malt from six-row malt. When this product is used for the majority of the grist, it can produce an unpleasant astringent flavor in the finished beer.[31] This can be overcome by purchasing Munich malts made only from two-row malt — as is almost always the case with European products.

If you decide to use Munich as your bock base malt, keep in mind that you won't need quite as much crystal and dark malts in your formulation. These specialty malts should still be included, but the quantity can be reduced somewhat.

Malt Extract

Award-winning dunkel bocks are often brewed with malt extracts. In total, just under half of the NHC recipes included extract. Most used extract to supplement the gravity of a wort produced by mashing. This can be an effective way to reach the higher gravities required by bocks within the limitations of your current brewing equipment.

A portion of the recipes used extract to the exclusion of normal base malt grains. Three of fifteen, or 20 percent, excluded base malt altogether and relied upon extract for most of the gravity. The brands of extract used in these cases included John Bull, Laaglander, and Munton & Fisons. All but one of these recipes supplemented the extract with specialty malts, as discussed below.

Specialty Malts

All of the dunkel bock formulations I have ever seen or brewed have included specialty grains such as crystal and chocolate malt. Table 17.6 shows the incidence and proportion of these malts in the NHC recipes.

Regardless of base malt selection and extract use, virtually all dunkel bock recipes include crystal malt in the formulation. Richman recommends using a portion of dark crystal malts with Lovibond ratings in the range of 90 to 120 °L. These help to provide a richness of color and flavor desired in the style. Across his various recipes, crystal malt accounts for 6 to 9 percent of the total grist.

The increased proportion of crystal malt (average proportion of total grain bill, 14 percent) in the NHC recipes can be accounted for by observing that most brewers selected lager malt rather than Munich malt as the base for the grist. In a previous analysis of bock recipes, I found that the amount of crystal malt used was inversely related to the amount of Munich malt included in the formulation.[32]

Five out of fifteen, or one-third, of the dunkel bock recipes evaluated used no specialty malts other than Munich and crystal. Of the remaining ten recipes, chocolate malt was found in seven. In all cases, chocolate malt accounted for a small portion of the grist, ranging from 1 to 4 percent of the total. The three recipes that did not include chocolate malt did include some other specialty malt, such as home-toasted malt or commercial malts like Vienna, Special B, or Victory (see table 17.7).

In the NHC recipes, black malt was found in only one instance, where it was used in conjunction with chocolate and crystal malt. My earlier analysis found black malt to be more common in bock recipes, but brewers seem to be realizing that the other malts used in bock provide a more appropriate color and flavor profile.

Dextrin and wheat malts find some usage in bock as body and head enhancers. The two are rarely seen together in the same recipe and they usually account for 5 to 6 percent of the grist.

Table 17.6
Dunkel Bock Specialty Grain Bill in NHC Second-Round Recipes

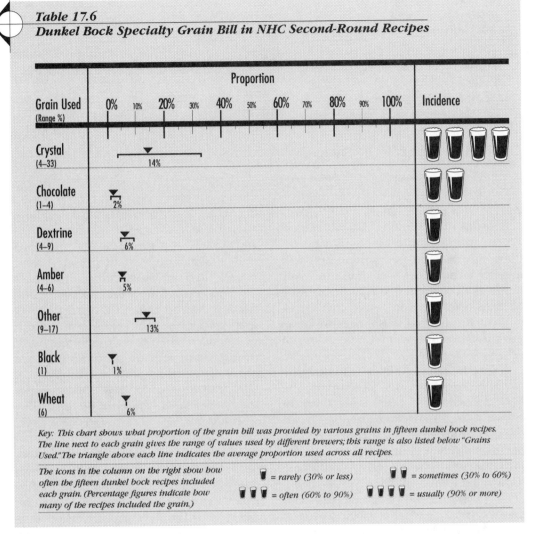

Key: This chart shows what proportion of the grain bill was provided by various grains in fifteen dunkel bock recipes. The line next to each grain gives the range of values used by different brewers; this range is also listed below "Grains Used." The triangle above each line indicates the average proportion used across all recipes.

The icons in the column on the right show how often the fifteen dunkel bock recipes included each grain. (Percentage figures indicate how many of the recipes included the grain.)

= rarely (30% or less) = sometimes (30% to 60%)
= often (60% to 90%) = usually (90% or more)

Pale Bock Grists

Helles bocks follow many of the patterns discussed for regular bocks except that they generally exclude grains darker than Munich malt. Richman's helles bocks still use Munich for 50 percent of the grist, but here again the NHC beers take a different tack. Munich malt appeared in all three recipes but only as 10 percent to 30 percent of the grist. Lager or Pilsener malt accounted for the majority of the remaining grain. Extract was not used in any of the NHC helles bocks.

Specialty malts play a very limited role in these pale bocks. CaraPils or dextrin and wheat malt are commonly included. Some sort of low-color character malt may also be added in small quantities, for instance home-toasted malt or Vienna malt.

Mashing Your Bock

If you have the ability (and the patience), decoction mashing is the ideal method for making a bock beer. In Europe, brewers still rely on decoction for making this style of beer. Some brewers go all the

Table 17.7
Specialty Malt Usage in NHC Second-Round Dunkel Bocks

Specialty Malt	Percentage of Total Recipe Base
Chocolate	47
With no other specialty malts (40%)	
With additional specialty malts (7%)	
No chocolate or other specialty malts	33
Other specialty malts without chocolate	20

Note: These figures are independent of crystal malt usage.

way to a triple decoction while others believe that a double decoction will suffice.

Regardless of the number of decoctions, this method of mashing serves a number of purposes, including the development of color and flavor as the result of Maillard reactions and melanoidin development. An infusion mash, because of its lower temperature, cannot come close to achieving this goal.

Nonetheless, good bocks can be made by infusion mash techniques. Among the NHC second-round beers, only three of eighteen used decoction mashing. When using an infusion mash, Richman recommends collecting extra wort and extending the boil time to allow additional melanoidin formation in the kettle.

If you normally do single-step infusion mashes, you might try a small stove-top decoction to help in achieving your mash-out temperature. You can pull the mash for

decocting just fifteen or twenty minutes after the saccharification rest begins, then add it back at the end of the rest along with boiling water to help you achieve your desired mash-out temperature.

The rest temperatures for bock production depend largely on the malt being used. If your base malt is European Munich or American two-row malt, a protein rest is probably not required because both are generally well modified. However, if European Pilsener or lager malts constitute more than a quarter of the grist, then a protein rest near 122 °F (50 °C) is probably a good idea.

The ideal saccharification temperature for a bock will be higher than for most other beers in order to help create a dextrinous wort and greater body in the finished beer. The average conversion temperature recorded among the NHC beers was 155 °F (68 °C).

Table 17.8
Average Gravity and Bitterness Levels in NHC Second-Round Bock Beers

	OG	BU:GU
Bock	1.073	0.34
Helles	1.066	0.36
Doppel	1.083	0.33
Eis	1.074	0.26
Average	—	0.33

Table 17.9
NHC Second-Round Bock Hop Selection and Use

Hop	Bittering	Flavor	Aroma	Dry	Total
Hallertau	15	6	4	1	26
Tettnanger	1	3	2	0	6
Hersbruck	4	1	0	0	5
Saaz	2	1	1	0	4
Perle	3	0	0	0	3
Eroica	2	0	0	0	2
Cascade	1	0	0	0	1
Goldings	1	0	0	0	1
Liberty	0	0	1	0	1
Mt. Hood	1	0	0	0	1
N. Brewer	1	0	0	0	1

Note: The data in this chart show the number of times each hop was used across the eighteen dunkel and helles bock recipes analyzed.

Bock Hopping

As I have mentioned a number of times, bock is a very malt-balanced style. As a result, the level of bitterness is typically rather low, with an average BU:GU ratio of 0.33 across all the NHC beers (see table 17.8). Commercial examples seem to fall in these same ranges. In both cases, the higher the gravity, the lower the bitterness level. Pale bocks carry a bit more bitterness than the dunkel styles, as shown in table 17.8.

As for hop selection, fine German varieties are used for all hop additions made to commercially brewed bocks. Hersbruck, Hallertau, Tettnanger, and Saaz lead the pack, with an occasional Northern Brewer and Perle. For the most part, the NHC second-round recipes follow this example, as shown in tables 17.9 and 17.10.

More than half of all bock hop additions are made with Hallertau hops. The top five hops, which account for nearly 85 percent of all additions, are German varieties. From these data it is rather clear which varieties should be selected for the hopping of your bock recipes.

Sixty percent of the hops added to bock are intended to increase bitterness more than flavor or aroma. Flavor and aroma additions account for 21 percent and 16 percent, respectively, of all hop additions.

Table 17.10
Average Number of Hop Additions per NHC Second-Round Recipe

Addition	Avg. No. per Recipe
Boil	1.7
Flavor	0.6
Aroma	0.5
Dry	0.1
Total	2.8

Table 17.11
Mineral Profile of Munich's Water

Mineral	ppm
Calcium	75
Magnesium	18
Sodium	2
Carbonate	180
Sulfate	120
Chloride	60

Note: ppm = parts per million

For these applications, only the low alpha acid aroma hops are used. The size of these later additions is also modest. Flavor additions average 0.63 ounces for 5 gallons; aroma additions average 0.70 ounces for 5 gallons. Furthermore, I have seen quite a number of published recipe guidelines for bock that specify just 0.25- to 0.5-ounce additions during the last twenty minutes of the boil.

Water

Because of its fame as a brewing center, many people expect Munich water to be quite soft. In truth, however, it is fairly hard, with a high amount of carbonate (see table 17.11). It is this carbonate content that has led Munich brewers to make dark, malt-balanced beers for most of their history. The acidity of the dark grains helps to counteract the alkalinity of the high carbonate content in the mash so that saccharification can take place at a normal rate. When it comes to hopping, however, carbonates can impart a soapy, harsh flavor to bitterness, and that prevents the use of high hop rates in the Munich beers.

Today, most homebrewers make bock beers without any changes to their brewing water. Many public sources have some carbonate in them. If you try to add chalk (calcium carbonate), you'll find that it doesn't dissolve readily unless your water is somewhat acidic, so adding carbonate rarely works out in practice.

Both the sulfate and the chloride levels are significant, but you'll want to avoid large additions of either gypsum or calcium chloride if you need to raise calcium levels. If calcium is called for, you might want to use a blend of these two sources to strike the right balance for this style.

Fermentation

Even more than most lagers, the fermentation of bock beers requires patience. The high-gravity worts of these styles take longer in every phase of fermentation, and they require extra care and attention to ensure a satisfying finished product. Fortunately for homebrewers, these steps can easily be accomplished at home.

Primary fermentation for a bock often runs three weeks, and the secondary and lagering phase can last as long as six months for a doppelbock or eisbock. This occurs both because of the low lager-fermentation temperatures used and because of the high gravities of the worts involved.

When it comes time for aeration, you should be especially aggressive to try to ensure an adequate oxygen level for the yeast. Whatever you normally do for aeration, consider doing it twice to achieve the desired effect.

The most popular yeast for brewing bocks (which appears in 42 percent of NHC second-round recipes) is that sold under the "Bavarian" name by several companies. This yeast produces a moderate level of attenuation and provides a clean, malty emphasis. I have used this yeast for a number of good beers, including bocks. I advise you to prepare the starter and pitch the wort only at the desired fermentation temperature, for this yeast has been known to stop working when started at room temperature and then cooled.

Another popular bock yeast is the "Munich" or "308" strain, available from more than one source these days. I have always been reluctant to use this strain due to its well-known fussy nature. It is a significant diacetyl producer and, therefore, requires that you raise the temperature of the fermentation when about two-thirds of the gravity has been fermented. In a commercial brewery where you can quickly and easily sample the fermenting wort through a valve at the bottom of the fermenter, this is easy to do. The logistics and potential for contamination that come with sampling from a glass carboy make this prospect far less attractive in the home brewery.

A few idiosyncratic yeasts are also found among the NHC beers, including Bohemian, 1; American, 1; Danish, 1; and California, 1. This indicates some possible areas for experimentation, but I would get the process down pat with one of the more popular yeasts before giving these a try.

In selecting an alternative, try to pick a yeast that provides low to medium attenuation or accentuates malt flavor. The apparent attenuation reported for the NHC second-round beers ranged from 62 percent for bocks to 72 percent for doppelbocks.

The proper fermentation temperature for most lagers is around 50 °F (10 °C). Of course, this can vary by 5 degrees or so, based on the characteristics of a specific strain. On average, however, the NHC beers reported a primary fermentation temperature of 48 to 50 °F (9 to 10 °C).

The lagering times and temperatures reported by the NHC second-round beers ranged widely, but the average values are consistent with recommended practice. Lagering should take place at or near the freezing point of water, that is, 32 °F (0 °C). On average, the NHC second-round bocks were lagered at 38 to 39 °F (3 to 4 °C). This average value reflects the fact that a few of these beers are "lagered" at temperatures as high as 50 °F (10 °C).

Regardless of temperature, the vast majority of successful bock beers receive prolonged periods of lagering before they are submitted for competition judging. Furthermore, the period of lagering increases with the original gravity of the beer, as shown in table 17.12.

Table 17.12
Lagering of Bocks

	Temp. °F (°C)	Time (days)
Bock	39 (4)	40
Helles	39 (4)	53
Doppel	38 (3)	69
Eis	38 (3)	116
Average	38 (3)	65

Conclusion

Bock is one of the grand styles of beer. Although centuries old, it has survived and even thrived through a variety of challenges and adversities. Even today, as increased taxation and concerns over alcohol consumption weaken its popularity in Europe, America's microbrewers have begun to produce these styles in both authentic and creative versions.

For the small brewer, bock is costly to produce. Not only is the wort of high gravity — thereby requiring a great deal of grain or extract for one batch — but it must be fermented and lagered for long periods. This demand can create the temptation to cut corners even among those blessed with generous cold storage capacity. Those who stick it out, however, will find themselves rewarded with a finished product that is both special and satisfying. Truly generous is the brewer who then shares such a patiently produced product with his friends and fellow brewers.

Key Success Factors in Brewing Bock

• Blend Pilsener or two-row malt with Munich malt to establish the base for any dunkel bock grist. Quality European Munich malts can be used for up to 90 percent of the bock beer grist.

• Add specialty grains, including crystal and chocolate malt, plus other character grains if you desire. These grains should constitute 10 to 20 percent of the total grist.

• Extract can be used effectively to supplement a small mash, especially when high-gravity styles are being prepared.

• Although decoction mashing is traditionally used for commercial production, infusion mashing can produce a good wort. Saccharification temperatures should be targeted for about 155 to 158 °F (68 to 70 °C).

• German-variety bittering hops should be added to achieve a BU:GU ratio of about 0.35.

• Though hop flavor and aroma are generally not desired, a 0.25- to 0.5-ounce (in 5 gallons) "noble-type" hop addition may be added about fifteen minutes before the end of the boil.

• Aerate aggressively and pitch generously with a low- to medium-attenuation lager yeast that emphasizes malt complexity.

• Following fermentation, lager at 32 to 35 °F (0 to 2 °C). The average lagering time across all styles is two months, but longer lagering periods may be employed with doppelbock and eisbock.

18 CALIFORNIA COMMON

Project	Designing Great Beers Brewers Publications
Project No.	61766

California common is the contemporary name for the style once known as "steam beer." Prior to Prohibition, a number of breweries in California (and some in other states) produced beers known by this name. After Prohibition, however, only one of these breweries, Anchor Steam Brewing Company, resumed production of "steam beer." Some thirty years ago, Anchor trademarked the term "steam beer" for its product, Anchor Steam Beer™, and so the alternate expression "California common" has been adopted to describe the broader style since Prohibition. To keep history and terminology clear, "California common" will be used to refer to the post-Prohibition style and "steam beer" will refer to pre-Prohibition brews.

Historically it is clear that "steam beer" existed as a distinct style produced by dozens of breweries between 1850 and 1920. The key distinguishing characteristic of the style was the production of lager beers without the use of ice or refrigeration. This resulted in fermentation temperatures between 60 to 65 °F (16 to 18 °C), and perhaps somewhat higher.[1] These temperatures resulted in a rapid fermentation and more than likely would have produced a distinct flavor profile as well.

The very first producer of "steam beer" is difficult to identify, but the style clearly has its origins in California. *One Hundred Years of Brewing* mentions several brewers who might have originated this method of brewing. The Hartmann & Scherrer brewery of San Jose was established in 1851 and made forty barrels of "steam beer" that year. By the turn of the twentieth century, its output had grown to 14,000 barrels annually.

Another possible creator of pre-Prohibition "steam beer" was J. F. Deininger. *One Hundred Years of Brewing* reports on his activities in 1870, when he established a brewery in Vallejo, California. But it notes that "twenty years before he had made the first steam beer [*sic*] in Los Angeles, contracting with the owner of the plant at $20 per brew and employing Indians to assist him."[2] Unfortunately, the phrasing of this sentence leaves us to wonder if he made the very first "steam beer" in 1850 or simply the first produced in Los Angeles. More clear is the indicated date of 1850, which would certainly make this the earliest brewing of the style that is unambiguously identified by this source.

Finally, the very first brewery of any kind in San Francisco was opened a year earlier, in 1849, by Adam Schuppert. Although *One Hundred Years of Brewing* does not say that this brewery made "steam beer," it would likely have been the first if it had done so.

I take it with a certain amount of faith that these pioneer brewers made beer that I would classify as being in the California common style today. Certainly, *One Hundred Years of Brewing* gives an accurate definition of the style before listing these parties as makers of "steam beer." Furthermore, there can be little doubt that refrigeration was unavailable at this time in California, and the brewers appear to be of German heritage, making it quite likely that they would have been using lager yeast.

Although many breweries eventually made "steam beer" before Prohibition, we have no record of which brewery first used the term commercially. *One Hundred Years of Brewing* lists twenty-five different California breweries as makers of "steam beer" during the period from 1850 to 1903. (See the sidebar on these breweries at the end of this chapter.) Another source indicates that there were fourteen breweries within San Francisco during the 1850s alone and that "most produced steam beer [*sic*]."[3] Furthermore, production was not limited to California, for breweries as far away as Idaho also produced beer in this style.[4]

Given the ubiquitous application of the term "steam" to the beer and breweries of the time, it seems likely that no one brewer first adopted the term. Instead, it may have arisen, much as other style names have, from popular jargon. Several sources report that the pressure inside the kegs was so extreme that they would "steam" when tapped. If true, this would no doubt grab the attention of bar workers and patrons alike, thus ensuring the beer's quick entry into the lore of the rapidly expanding California gold rush culture. Such widespread acceptance of this terminology is indicated by one source, which says that in the 1850s and 1860s a thirsty San Franciscan at the bar would simply order "a glass of steam."[5]

Despite the uncertainty about the exact origins of "steam," it is clear that the term was widely used and accepted by the time the Anchor Brewery happened upon the scene in 1894. Anchor appears to have been one of the last breweries built to make "steam beer," as mechanical refrigeration had by then become common in the region. Still, until Prohibition, a number of breweries including Anchor continued to make "steam beer." Only after Prohibition did Anchor emerge as the sole producer of the style.

From the repeal of Prohibition until the mid-1960s, the brewery continued a long, slow downhill slide that nearly ended in its demise. In a tale that is now legend among craft brewers, young appliance heir Fritz Maytag heard of the brewery's plight and decided to intervene. It took nearly a decade of struggle to return the brewery to profitability, but its success since that time has been a model for other small and struggling brewers. It was during this time that Anchor trademarked the term "steam."

From this chronology it is clear that Anchor's trademark claims to "steam" or "steam beer" come not as the result of origination but rather from long-term loyalty and post-Prohibition exclusive use.

Nineteenth-Century "Steam Beers"

The brewing of "steam beer" is described in a couple of sources from around the turn of the twentieth century. The first is an article on the subject written by a San Francisco brewer in the *Western Brewer* magazine in 1898.[6] The second comes from the detailed brewing manual produced by Wahl and Henius in 1908.[7] Together, these sources provide a good profile of the historical style (see table 18.1).

This composite description of "steam beer" paints a detailed account of the style as it was about one hundred years ago. On a number of points Buchner and Wahl-Henius diverge, creating some questions about actual practice — or at least pointing out the diversity of it. One of these points relates to the composition of the grain bill. Here Buchner indicates that all-malt was the most common approach, while Wahl and Henius imply that adjuncts may have been used. Both may have been editorializing a bit in their presentation of these facts, but I'm a bit more inclined to believe Buchner. He brewed beer in San Francisco and should have been in a better position to know the actual practices of local brewers. In addition, the Wahl-Henius book presents many pages of laboratory beer analyses, but not one for "steam beer" — another indication of how remote these beers must have been to these Chicago-based brewing scientists.

One of the most fascinating things about this beer is that it is "real beer" in the true CAMRA (the Britsh organization devoted to preserving true cask-conditioned beer) sense of the word. Secondary fermentation took place in the package, and the condition of the beer upon serving depended on the talent of the saloon-keeper for managing his stock.

Given the young age of the beer when delivered to the saloon, as well as the sometimes sizable increment of kraeusen, the flavor of these beers probably changed from day to day even before they were tapped. The elimination of acetaldehyde, diacetyl, and sulphur compounds that normally occurs during aging might often have been incomplete in these beers.[8] How interesting it would be to jump into a time machine to sample the "steam beers" offered by various breweries and publicans during that era.

The Contemporary Style: Anchor Steam

Jumping to the present, we can compare the current Anchor offering to the beers of old. What we find is a remarkable similarity. Table 18.2 lists the basic facts about the Anchor product.

Like many modern beers, this example has a higher attenuation level than those reported historically. In addition, the

kraeusening, though still used to carbonate the beer, now occurs during storage at the brewery instead of in the final trade packages. American-grown hops are still used, but the Northern Brewer variety is now employed,[9] with three separate additions made during the boil.[10]

Despite the tinkering that has taken place in the formulation and production of this beer over the past century, it is still very much in the mold set by the dozens of other brewers who first popularized the style during the nineteenth century. How wonderful it is that one example still exists; yet how unfortunate that others cannot be offered to the beer-drinking public with the historical style designation.

Brewing the Style

When brewing this style, it is easy to become fixated on Anchor Steam Beer because it is the only contemporary example. Nonetheless, the style encompasses a broader range of interpretations, both historically and within the competition guidelines, that are usually followed.

I have already discussed most of the details related to production of Anchor Steam Beer. In this section, I analyze the California common recipes from the National Homebrew Competition's second round.

Grain Bills

Historically, the California common–style beers may have been made from a single malt, but today virtually every recipe includes some specialty malt in addition to a base malt. Let's begin by reviewing the base malt selections.

The most popular base malt selection is two-row malt, but it still appears in less than half of all recipes (see table 18.3). Pale ale malt and extract account for the remainder of the base malt selections. Pale ale malt seems to be a good selection for this style, because it will add some

Table 18.1
Profile of "Steam Beer," circa 1900

Original gravity	1.044 to 1.050 (11 to 12.5 °P)
Apparent atten.	50 to 60 percent
Malt and grains	Buchner states that "raw grain or other substitutes are used but seldom"; however, Wahl and Henius allow for the use of "grits or raw cereals of any kind, and sugars, especially glucose, employed in the kettle to the extent of 33 percent."[a]
Mash technique	Infusion
Mash temp.	Wahl and Henius describe a three-step infusion program: 140 to 145 °F (60 to 63 °C); 149 to 154 °F (65 to 68 °C); then 158 °F (70 °C) until completely converted.
Hop level	¾ lb./bbl. Approximately 28 to 40 IBU
Hop additions	No specific pattern of additions is noted, and no mention is made of hop flavor or aroma characteristics. I do know that locally grown American varieties were used.
Wort cooling	Cooled to 60 to 62 °F (16 to 17 °C) through some combination of shallow holding tanks or Baudelot coolers.[b] Cooling would sometimes take place overnight.
Pitching	Once cooled, the wort was pitched with ⅓ to 1 pound of lager yeast per barrel. This step took place in a fermenting tub, which apparently had fairly traditional depth for a fermenter.
Fermentation	Twelve to eighteen hours after the yeast was pitched high kraeusen was reached, and the beer was run into long, wide, shallow vats called clarifiers. Buchner describes these as being about 12 inches deep and states that they had two purposes: (1) to prevent a high rise in temperature during fermentation by exposing a large surface of the beer to the surrounding air; (2) to accelerate the clarification of the beer by means of the shallowness of the clarifier. Under these circumstances, the beer generally fermented at temperatures between 60 to 70 °F (16 to 21 °C). The fermentation was complete within two to four days.
Packaging	From the clarifier, the beer was racked directly into kegs. Kraeusen was added at the rate of 15 to 40 percent of the package contents: e.g., a 15-gallon barrel would be dosed with 2.25 to 6 gallons of kraeusen and then filled with fully fermented beer from the clarifier. Finings were also added to the keg. The kegs were reportedly sealed with "iron screw bungs" and aged for two or three days before shipment to the trade.
Serving	At the saloon, the beers had to sit undisturbed for at least two days before tapping to allow the yeast and finings to settle. Very high levels of CO_2 pressure in the kegs were reported in written accounts from the turn of the century. Quoted values range from a low of 40 psi to a high of 70 psi. According to these sources, the bung or faucet would be manipulated to vent the excess pressure before serving.

Sources: R. Wahl and M. Henius, The American Handy-Book of the Brewing, Malting and Auxiliary Trades *(Chicago: Wahl-Henius Institute, 1908), 1235–36. J. Buchner, "Steam Beer,"* Western Brewer *23 (February 15, 1898), 278. R. Bergen, "California Steaming," Brewing in Styles column,* Brewing Techniques *(January/February 1994), 20–25.*
[a] *By modern reckoning, the use of sugar in these beers in any significant amount seems unlikely given the low apparent attenuations.*
[b] *A Baudelot cooler consists of a vertically ribbed surface over which hot beer is run. Cool water is run through pipes on the interior of the ribs. This device is cooled both by evaporation to the air and by transfer of heat to the water. The wort was also aerated during this process.*

Table 18.2
Contemporary Profile of Anchor Steam Beer

Gravity	1.048 to 1.051 OG
Final gravity	1.013, for an apparent attenuation of 74 percent
Grains	All-malt formulation that includes crystal malt
Mashing	Upward infusion, exact temperatures undisclosed
Bitterness	30 to 35 IBU
Yeast	Lager type
Fermentation Vessels	Two-foot-deep fermenters
Temperature	Pitched at 60 °F (16 °C), attemperated to ensure that it doesn't get too warm
Conditioning	Kraeusened and cellared for three weeks before packaging

Sources: M. Jackson, Michael Jackson's Beer Companion *(Philadelphia: Running Press Book Publishers, 1993), 235. F. Maytag, "California Common Beer,"* Zymurgy *(Special Issue 1991): 50–52.*

richness of flavor and some additional color, both of which are perfectly suited to this type of beer.

Extract was used in seven of twenty-two recipes. In three cases the extract supplemented a minimash with one of the above-mentioned base malts. In the remaining four cases, the beer was formulated on the "extract plus specialty malt" model. On average, when extract was used it accounted for 71 percent of the total grain bill weight. The most popular brand used was Alexander's Pale Malt Syrup, which appeared in four of the recipes. Other brands of extract that were used include John Bull Light, Steinbarts Light, Laaglander Light Dry, and Yellow Dog.

The most popular selection among specialty malts is crystal malt — a fact that is most likely attributable to the use of this grain in the Anchor formulation. More than 90 percent of the NHC second-round formulations included crystal malt. Furthermore, when it was used, crystal malt made up a significant portion of the grist, averaging 10 percent of the total grain bill. Although the crystal malts added color that ranged widely, from 15 to 120 °L, most (63 percent) fell within the range from 40 to 80 °L.

After crystal malt, no other grain appeared in more than about 40 percent of the recipes. Thus, many recipes included just base malt and crystal malt, or even base malt alone (see table 18.4).

Only about 55 percent of the recipes included some sort of "character" grain, such as Munich, Vienna, chocolate, biscuit, and toasted malt. Among these, Munich and toasted were the most popular, followed closely by chocolate malt. Biscuit and Vienna appeared in just one recipe each. More than a quarter of the recipes used just a single character malt, as shown in table 18.4; Munich was the most likely addition.

A slightly smaller number of recipes (23 percent) used two of the character malts. Munich and toasted malt were the most likely additions, each appearing in four of the five recipes. Chocolate malt appeared in just two of these formulations. Finally, one recipe included three character malts: Munich, chocolate, and toasted malt.

Although all these character grains increase the richness and complexity of the final beer, they don't always result in a winning brew. In the two years I have reviewed in detail, the winning beers in the AHA's California common category used simple formulations. One used no

Table 18.3
California Common Grain Bill in NHC Second-Round Recipes

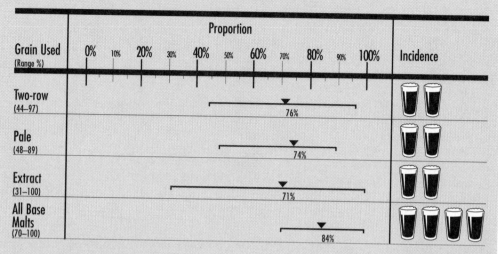

Grain Used (Range %)	Proportion	Incidence
Two-row (44–97)	76%	
Pale (48–89)	74%	
Extract (31–100)	71%	
All Base Malts (70–100)	84%	

Specialty Malts

Grain Used (Range %)	Proportion	Incidence
Crystal (5–20)	10%	
Munich/ Vienna (4–15)	9%	
Special (3–10)	6%	
Cara Pils (3–8)	4%	
Chocolate (0–6)	2%	

Key: This chart shows what proportion of the grain bill was provided by various grains in twenty two California common recipes. The line next to each grain gives the range of values used by different brewers; this range is also listed below "Grains Used." The triangle above each line indicates the average proportion used across all recipes.

The icons in the column on the right show how often the twenty-two California common recipes included each grain. (Percentage figures indicate how many of the recipes included the grain.)

= rarely (30% or less)   = sometimes (30% to 60%)

= often (60% to 90%)   = usually (90% or more)

crystal or specialty malts; the other used crystal and a small amount of biscuit malt.

Mashing for this style generally employs an infusion mash technique, often with just a single rest at the sacchar-ification temperature. Among the NHC second-round beers, the temperatures employed for this rest ranged from 150 to 158 °F (66 to 70 °C), with an average of 154 °F (68 °C).

Hops

As mentioned earlier, little information is available about the hop character of the "steam beers" produced a century ago. Lacking this, the style guidelines used today are, again, largely based on the Anchor product. The AHA criteria for California common beer are: "Medium to high hop bitterness. Hop flavor medium to high. Aroma medium."[11]

From this description it is clear that most beers in this style will include fairly generous hop additions at various times during the boil. Our only data from commercial practice comes from Anchor brewers, who reportedly make three hop additions during the boil.

The calculated bitterness found in the NHC second-round examples ranged from 22 to 94 IBU. The average value was 45 IBU — a level that is still a good bit higher than that used by Anchor. Based on this, the average BU:GU ratio is about 0.88.

As far as selection goes, we have just two pieces of information to guide us. First, we know that the style has traditionally been made with U.S.-grown hops. In the early days of the style, these were probably California-grown Cluster hops.[12] Our second data point again comes from the current Anchor Steam Beer, which is made using only Northern Brewer hops.

Hop data from the NHC second-round recipes are listed in table 18.5. Cascade is the number one hop in these recipes, although Northern Brewer runs a very close second. In looking at the data, it appears that many recipes chose the higher-alpha Northern Brewer for bittering purposes and then switched to Cascade for the flavor and aroma additions. Together, these two hops account for more than 70 percent of all hop additions for this style.

The average recipe included 4.25 hop additions (see table 18.5). The timing of these additions is indicated by the data in table 18.6, but it is important to remember the criteria for the "Bitter" and "Flavor" uses in this chart. For purposes of these analyses I have classified all hop additions boiled for thirty minutes or more as bittering hop additions. Of course, you do get some flavor impact with a thirty-minute addition, and in this case about 10 percent of all hop additions were made at the

---

Table 18.4
Grist Structure Analysis of NHC Second-Round California Common Beers

- No character malts used (10 recipes, 45%)
    - Base plus crystal (8 recipes, 36%)
    - Base alone (2 recipes, 9%)

- One character malt used (6 recipes, 27%)
    - Munich or Vienna (4 recipes, 18%)
    - Biscuit or chocolate (1 recipe each, 4.5% each)

- Two character malts used (5 recipes, 23%)
    - Munich plus toasted malt (3 recipes, 14%)
    - Chocolate plus toasted (1 recipe, 4.5%)
    - Munich plus chocolate (1 recipe, 4.5%)

- Three character malts used (1 recipe, 4.5%)

Note: Crystal malt appeared in 90 percent of all (twenty-two) recipes across all of these categories.

thirty-minute time interval. Thus, about half of all the hop additions — two for every recipe — were made during the last thirty minutes of the boil.

The size of the flavor and aroma additions was about what you would expect: 0.5-ounce per 5 gallons for flavor and 0.75-ounce per 5 gallons for both aroma and dry hop additions. Just for interest, I also checked the additions that were made at thirty minutes, and they averaged 0.60-ounce per 5 gallons.

Water

The water used for making Anchor Steam Beer appears to have been rather soft, historically, and this continues today as well.

One modern article on the style reports that the only notable feature of the current San Francisco water is a bit of calcium sulfate, giving a calcium content of 50 parts per million.[13] The same article reports that San Francisco brewers in the time of Wahl and Henius were supplied by the Hetch Hetchy water system, which that delivered very soft snow-melt water from the Sierra Nevada.[14]

Data from early in the twentieth century generally support these conclusions, although the quantity of carbonate indicated is higher than I would expect from "soft" water. The approximate values are provided in table 18.7.

From these reports it appears that most waters that lack a high mineral content should be suitable for the production of a San Francisco–style "steam beer." Accordingly, most of the homebrewed recipes showed no water treatment at all. The only exception was the curious addition of table salt (NaCl) in two of the recipes. Both added ¼ teaspoon for 5 to 6 gallons.

Fermentation

Probably the most important aspect of producing a beer in this style is management of the fermentation. I begin discussion of this process by reviewing issues in yeast selection, followed by discussions of the temperatures and conditions of fermentation itself.

Table 18.5
Hops Used in NHC Second-Round California Common Beers

Type	Bitter	Flavor	Aroma	Dry	Total
Cascade	9	7	13	6	35
N. Brewer	19	4	5	5	33
Hallertau	0	1	1	2	4
Centennial	1	1	1	0	3
Cluster	2	0	1	0	3
Fuggle	2	1	0	0	3
Perle	3	0	0	0	3
Chinook	2	0	0	0	2
Saaz	0	0	1	1	2
Tettnanger	0	2	0	0	2
Willamette	1	0	1	0	2
Brewer's Gold	1	0	0	0	1
Nugget	1	0	0	0	1

Note: The data in this chart show the number of times each hop was used across the twenty-two recipes analyzed.

Table 18.6
Hop Additions in NHC Second-Round California Common Beers

Addition	Avg. No. per Recipe	Size of Addition Oz./Gal.	Oz./5 Gal.
Boil	1.9	n/a	n/a
Flavor	0.7	0.10	0.50
Aroma	1.0	0.15	0.74
Dry	0.6	0.15	0.74
Total	4.3		

Only a few years ago, selection of the proper yeast for this style would have had to rely on experimentation. Today, however, a number of yeasts are available that are specifically intended for this style. Despite this, however, such yeasts are not universally used by brewers who make good California common beers.

Table 18.8 shows the yeasts used in the NHC second-round beers for the California common category. Although the specialized California lager yeasts were a strong favorite, almost 40 percent of the entries used some other yeast. Most of the alternatives relied upon lager yeasts, yet a couple opted for ale yeasts. Interestingly, neither of the two first-place beers from the two years I reviewed used the most widely available California lager yeast. Instead, one used a California lager yeast from another supplier, and the other relied on the Pilsen lager yeast.

In general, the yeast you select should give little ester character and little or no residual diacetyl. After this, the key question is one of attenuation. The most popularly available California lager yeast (Wyeast 2112) is actually a low attenuator intended to emulate the nineteenth-century style of "steam beer." By contrast, both of the NHC winners in this category used more highly attenuating yeasts that give a final body more similar to Anchor Steam Beer. Given the high proportion of crystal malt included in most formulations, these more attenuative yeasts may be in order. The less attenuative Wyeast strain might be better suited to less dextrinous formulations.

On average, the fermentation temperature used in making this style was right where you would expect it to be: 62 °F (17 °C). However, with all the different yeasts that were employed, it's not surprising that

Table 18.7
Water Profile for San Francisco, circa 1935

Mineral	ppm
Calcium	36
Magnesium	25
Sodium	17
Carbonate	80
Chloride	26
Sulfate	20

Source: The Treatment of Brewing Water in Light of Modern Chemistry (New York: Wallerstein Laboratories, 1935), 27.
Note: ppm = parts per million

some significant variations from this were seen. For instance, fermentations using ale yeast were generally a bit warmer, averaging 68 °F (20 °C). Those conducted with regular lager yeasts also might be a bit cooler, as in the case of the winning recipe, which used the Pilsen yeast with a primary fermentation temperature of 55 °F (13 °C).

From these data it seems clear that the proper strategy for setting your fermentation temperature will depend upon the yeast you have selected. In general, you should be using a temperature that is in the ideal range for the yeast. This means 65 to 70 °F (18 to 21 °C) for most ale yeasts, 60 to 65 °F (16 to 18 °C) for California lager yeast, and 50 to 55 °F (10 to 13 °C) for traditional lager yeast.

Following fermentation, some conditioning period may be used. Historically, "steam beers" were not conditioned before sale. After fermentation they were only held for a few days of warm storage to develop carbonation in the keg.

Today Anchor employs a conditioning rest for its Steam Beer, but it is different from traditional lagering. The difference lies in the temperature. The Anchor rest is conducted for three weeks at 50 °F (10 °C), whereas traditional lager conditioning occurs for a similar period but at a much colder temperature of 32 to 36 °F (0 to 2 °C).

A cool conditioning rest in the Anchor model seems to make a lot of sense for beers in this style. It should allow the yeast to finish the job of fermentation, including reduction of acetaldehyde, diacetyl, and some sulphur compounds. This will help to contribute the smooth, round lager character desired in the beer.

Among the NHC entries, only about 40 percent indicated the use of a conditioning period for their beers. But the average procedure followed by those who performed these rests was very similar to that at Anchor: twenty-two days at 47 °F (8 °C). This seems to support the use of a conditioning rest when making a California common–style beer.

One other consideration during conditioning is the use of kraeusening to carbonate the beer. Pre-Prohibition "steam beers" were kraeusened immediately after fermentation and warm-conditioned for just a few days before shipment to the saloons. Today, Anchor kraeusens during the conditioning rest so that the beer is conditioned, carbonated, and ready for packaging at the end of the three-week period. Although true kraeusening is a challenge to achieve in the homebrew setting, it would be an interesting authentic flourish to add if you are truly devoted to the style.

Conclusion

The California common style is one that every accomplished American brewer

---

Table 18.8
Yeast Selection in NHC Second-Round California Common Beers

No. of Recipes	Yeast
14	California lager
3	American lager
2	Pilsen lager
1	American ale
1	Bavarian lager
1	London ale
22	Total

should be able to brew. The current home-brewed examples tend to emulate Anchor Steam Beer, and a broader exploration of the style could help brewers to better understand what it must have been like during the San Francisco gold rush years.

As for commercial brewers, creativity is in order not only in the brewhouse but in the marketing department as well. Alternative terminology must be found that skirts Anchor's monopoly of the steam moniker while clearly communicating to the consumer that the product is brewed in the pre-Prohibition "steam-style." Without this, the style is destined to become an obscure specialty akin to German steinbier. Already, Anchor Steam Beer looms as a monolith that hampers the view of the broader character and history of the style. As this happens, diversity is lost in the contemporary selection of drinks; but more important, a part of the American brewing heritage is lost as well.

Key Success Factors in Brewing California Common Beer

- Formulate the base of the recipe using either two-row malt, pale ale malt, or extract. The extract can be used alone or as a supplement to a minimash. The base malts should account for about 85 percent of the grist.

- Include crystal malt for 5 to 20 percent of the grist. You may wish to include one, or at most two, of the following: Munich, Vienna, toasted, or chocolate malt to constitute 9 percent, 9 percent, 6 percent, or 2 percent of the grist, respectively.

- Use an infusion-mash program with a saccharification rest in the range from 150 to 154 °F (66 to 68 °C).

- Boil for one to two hours, making three to four hop additions.

- Hop primarily with Northern Brewer and Cascade hops. Other aroma varieties may occasionally be added.

- Hop to achieve a bitterness between 30 and 45 IBU, or a BU:GU ratio of 0.80 to 0.90.

- Add 0.10-ounce of hops per gallon (0.5-ounce for 5 gallons) between ten and thirty minutes before the end of the boil for hop flavor.

- Add 0.15-ounce of hops per gallon (0.75-ounce for 5 gallons) during the last nine minutes of the boil for hop flavor. (Alternatively, this addition can be steeped after the boil.)

- Dry hopping with 0.15-ounce of hops per gallon (0.75-ounce for 5 gallons) is practiced in some cases.

- Select a clean medium- to high-attenuation yeast based upon your ability to control fermentation. For temperatures in the range of 50 to 55 °F (10 to 13 °C), use Pilsen or Bavarian lager yeast; in the range of 60 to 65 °F (16 to 18 °C), use California lager yeast; and in the range of 65 to 68 °F (18 to 20 °C), use American ale yeast.

- Ferment according to the appropriate temperature for your yeast.

- Following fermentation, condition the beer for two to four weeks at approximately 50 °F (10 °C).

- For an authentic touch, kraeusen the beer during the conditioning rest so that it is both conditioned and carbonated when the rest is complete.

Sidebar: "Steam Beer" Breweries, circa 1850–1903

Year Opened	Name	City
1851	Hartmann & Scherrer	San Jose
1852	Wunder Brewing Co.	San Francisco
1855	El Dorado Brewery	Stockton
1855	F. Rechenmacher	Auburn
1856	Washington Brew & Malt	Oakland
1858	Schuster & Kroenke	San Francisco
1859	Frank Ruhstaller	Sacramento
1859	Claus Wreden Brew.	San Francisco
1861	National Brewing Co.	San Francisco
1862	Gambel & Weisgerber	Idaho
1867	Idaho Brewing Co.	Boise, Idaho
1868	Mrs. Nancy Muehlbach	Greenwood
1870	J. F. Deininger	Vallejo
1870	Redwood Brewing Co.	Redwood City
1870	H. F. Bader	Cherokee
1872	Anaheim Brewery	Anaheim
1873	Enterprise Brewing Co.	San Francisco
1873	Dennis F. Bernal	Livermore
1873	Grace Brothers Brewing Co.	Santa Rosa
1880	William Hoffmeier	Napa
1892	California Brewing Co.	San Francisco
1893	Ernst F. Hubler	Angels Camp
1893	Raspiller Brewing Co.	West Berkeley
1894	Big Trees Brewery	Santa Cruz
1894	Anchor Brewery	Oakland
1897	Mission Brewing Co.	San Francisco
1899	Charles Thomas	Truckee

Note: With the exception of the two Idaho breweries, these are all in California.
Source: Anon., One Hundred Years of Brewing (Chicago and New York: H. S. Rich and Co., 1903), 446.

19 FRUIT BEER

Because all of the other chapters in part two of this book focus on traditional beer styles, you may be surprised to find this entry for fruit beers. After all, most brewers from Germany and Britain would rather give up beer for a month than make a beer with fruit in it.

This abhorrence of fruit beers is the result of their checkered heritage. Anyone who has ever made a few batches of beer knows that the finished product can wind up with off-flavors that make it unsuitable for regular consumption. When this happens on a commercial scale, the brewer faces the prospect of dumping the batch at considerable cost. Another possible solution is to flavor the beer with something that will cover the off-flavors — something like fruit. Thus, many who despise fruit beers see them as a sign of failure or as a fraud.

Despite this lack of acceptance in most European brewing centers, fruit beers have become commonplace in America during the craft beer revolution. Although some of the early versions may have had their origins in off-flavored beer, most current examples are conceived and brewed as fruit beers. Most brewpubs and many microbreweries offer at least one beer that contains fruit or fruit flavoring. As a result of this popularity, many of today's beer drinkers can recall drinking at least one fruit beer.

Of course, we can probably trace the origins of craft-brewed fruit beers to the active imaginations of homebrewers. Fruit beers constitute one of the largest categories in the National Homebrew Competition each year. This volume shows the level of interest in crafting beers with fruit, and it probably also indicates untapped commercial potential for such beers.

From Belgium to Boston: A Brief Review of Commercial Fruit Beers

Fruit beers are so popular today that it's surprising they have so little precedent in recorded beer history. In other times and ages fruit was considered the province of wine and thus was ignored by brewers. One can imagine that it may have been considered wildly extravagant to combine grain and fruit in a single beverage. The cost of ingredients alone suggests this, and the extra time and effort required in processing add further to the burden.

The one legacy of fruit beer that we do have comes from the Belgians. Their lambic beers often contain fruit such as raspberries and cherries and occasionally peaches, bananas, pineapples, grapes, and currants. The cherry-based *kriek* beers may have been in production when Prohibition swept the globe early in the twentieth century[1] and were certainly available by the 1930s.[2] The use of raspberries followed not long after, but the use of other fruits seems to be a more modern innovation. Nonetheless, for at least a half century the Belgians have provided a model for fruit beer production.

Professional brewers from Germany, England, and America often scoff at the thought of including fruit in beer. By contrast, the Belgians have long been the iconoclasts of the beer world. Their methods, as well as their beers, defy categorization in any traditional taxonomy of zymurgy. Given this rebel image, its not surprising that the upstart American craft brewers would look to the Belgians for inspiration. Thus, when we look at American fruit beers, we find the telltale signs of Belgian ancestry.

Lambic beers are, at their heart, wheat beers. Typical formulations include 10 to 50 percent wheat — perhaps malted, but just as often unmalted. In contemporary American fruit beers, we often find wheat malt in similar proportions. At many breweries the fruit wheat beer has gone from seasonal novelty to flagship product.

Maryland's Oxford Brewing Company produces a raspberry wheat beer that accounts for more than half of its annual production. It contains one-third wheat malt and pureed real raspberries.[3]

The choice of raspberries by an American brewer echoes familiar patterns from Belgium, where raspberries and cherries are the fruits of choice. Among commercial examples these fruits are easily the most popular, accounting for 48 percent and 18 percent respectively of all U.S. commercial fruit brands (see table 19.1).

Thus, while it is clear that the Belgian lambics have inspired production of many American fruit wheat beers, the products being made today bear little relationship to true Belgian lambic.

Lambics are traditionally produced by fermentation with wild yeast and airborne bacteria. The resulting beer contains many flavors that brewers commonly regard as faults, such as acetic and lactic acid. The art of lambic comes in the use of fruit and the blending of batches to produce a product that strikes a winelike balance between various flavor components.

Table 19.1
Fruits Used in Commercial American Beers

Fruit	Number of Brands
Raspberry	39
Cherry	15
Blueberry	8
Chili	4
Cranberry	3
Passion fruit	3
Apple	2
Apricot	1
Blackberry	1
Huckleberry	1
Lemon/Lime	1
Marionberry	1
Orange	1
Peach	1
Total	81

Only one American brewer has been bold enough to wrongly appropriate the lambic title. Samuel Adams does this with its Cranberry Lambic, an interesting and refreshing fruit beer, but one utterly unrelated to classic lambic.

Though few other brewers have tried to closely match the fruit beers of Belgium, many have experimented and explored to move beyond the wheat beer styles and red fruits of Belgium.

Today, a number of stouts with fruit have been marketed, and other dark styles such as porter and bock have also been teamed with fruit. Whether dry and coffee-like or sweet like a *Schwarzwalder* cake, the marriage of dark grains with tart fruit is an enjoyable one. Most who have tasted a raspberry or cherry stout, such as that produced by Larry Bell at his Kalamazoo Brewing Company, find it to be a consuming passion. Given an avid following, I expect (and hope) to continue to find fine fruit-spiked stouts for many years to come.

In addition, American brewers have extended their exploration of fruit to include many species indigenous to the United States. This pioneering work has turned up some remarkable entries, such as passion fruit, pumpkin, and chili peppers. Perhaps most surprisingly, some of these novel additions seem to have struck a chord with beer drinkers and are now standard fare for the breweries that make them.

For example, take Cave Creek Chili Beer, made by Arizona's Black Mountain Brewing Company. In 1991, after two years of making "regular" beers, the brewery created a beer with a whole Serrano chili pepper in every bottle as a way of attracting business from area Mexican restaurants. The chili beer sent sales soaring, and today it accounts for about 95 percent of the brewery's output, reaching all fifty United States and a half-dozen other countries.[4]

A review of American beer brands reveals that more than 80 different fruit beers were sold in the United States in 1993

and 1994.[5] Just the names and style descriptions of these beers indicate the use of fourteen different fruits (see table 19.1). Furthermore, some brand names, while creative, leave the exact fruit — or combination of fruits — open to speculation. Names like Black Forest Ale, Paradisio Caribe, Razzleberry Ale, and Two-Berry Ale may stimulate mental images, but they do little to establish gustatory expectations.

Beyond the fruits used, we have the issue of the underlying beer style. As mentioned earlier, pub-brewed fruit beers often use a recipe containing wheat malt. These formulations give a base beer that is light in body, color, and flavor. With few beer flavors for competition, fruit flavor can come through even when relatively small amounts of fruit are used. Often, these beers employ raspberry as the fruit, in fact so much so that raspberry wheat beer may be on its way to becoming an established American style.

Despite this focus on making "accessible" beers for the craft beer novice, a number of brewers are producing products that display more complex fruit and beer flavors. At times these beers are designated with a specific style name (apple bock, blackberry porter), but others are simply labeled ale or lager. In fact, the vast majority of fruit beers carry no beer style indicator (see table 19.2).

Making Fruit Beers

Information on the formulation and production of commercial fruit beers in the United States is hard to come by. I know of no research or analysis of craft beers that reveals these details. Fortunately, we have good information on the formulations and methods employed by successful home-brewers from the National Homebrew Competition. Because many of the fruit beers in commercial production today started as basement brews, this is a good place to look for information on fruit beer production.

Table 19.2
Fruit Beer Styles

Wheat	16
Stout	6
Bock	2
Porter	2
Cream Ale	2
Unspecified	53

The making of a fruit beer can be divided into two parts. The first is production of the base beer. The second concerns addition of the fruit, including selecting the type of fruit, the amount, and the technique to be used.

Base Beer

These days, the National Homebrew Competition has two categories for fruit beers. The first is a generic fruit beer category where just about any gravity, bitterness, and color can be found. The second is the classic-style fruit beer. To enter a beer in this category, the brewer must specify the classic beer style of the base beer; for example, Bohemian Pilsener, Scottish light ale, and so on.

Most of the currently available commercial fruit beers specify no classic style and therefore fit into the generic fruit beer category. Because of this, and because I review production of the various classic beer styles elsewhere in this book, this chapter focuses on the formulations used for generic fruit beer entries.

In reviewing data from the NHC second-round beers in this subcategory, I find some characteristics that are unique among all the beer styles that are reviewed in this book. The most striking example of this is the fact that the vast majority of fruit beer brewers choose malt extract as the base for their beers. This certainly makes it easier to produce a fruit beer. It is also logical, because the fruit will often

make up for any flavor deficiencies that might be found in the malt.

Nearly three-quarters of the seventeen recipes I reviewed relied heavily on malt extract. All used extract for at least 73 percent of the fermentable materials, and five used no grains at all, only extract (see table 19.3).

Not surprisingly, a significant number of the recipes used wheat — or wheat extract — for a portion of the grist. In all, nearly half of the recipes included wheat, and in those recipes it accounted for an average of 20 percent of the fermentable materials. In the all-grain recipes, wheat was nearly universal, appearing in five out of six recipes. Here again, the average quantity was 20 percent of the grist.

Malts that would color the beer were used sparingly in these fruit beer formulations. Chocolate malt, black malt, and roast barley were almost unheard of; just one recipe included a small addition of dark malts.

Crystal malt was used a bit more frequently, but it, too, was used with restraint. Less than half of all the recipes included crystal malt, and in those where it appeared, it accounted for just 9 percent of the fermentable material on average. In all but one case where crystal malt was used, it supplemented an extract-based recipe to provide some malt body and character. Grain brewers were unlikely to use any crystal malt in their formulations.

The worts produced by these recipes had an average original gravity of 1.057, but this was heavily influenced by the one beer with an OG of 1.116. When this heavyweight is excluded from the calculation, the average OG drops to 1.052 (see table 19.4).

I should note that the OG readings for fruit beers can be misleading if used to determine alcohol content. When fruit is added to the beer, it adds fermentable sugar and therefore increases the alcohol in the finished product.

Table 19.3
Fruit Beer Bill of Key Fermentable Components in NHC Second-Round Recipes

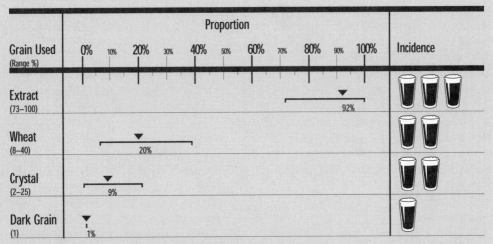

Key: This chart shows what proportion of the grain bill was provided by various grains in seventeen fruit beer recipes. The line next to each grain gives the range of values used by different brewers; this range is also listed below "Grains Used." The triangle above each line indicates the average proportion used across all recipes.

The icons in the column on the right show how often the seventeen fruit beer recipes included each grain. (Percentage figures indicate how many of the recipes included the grain.)

= rarely (30% or less)   = sometimes (30% to 60%)
= often (60% to 90%)   = usually (90% or more)

For most fruit beers, hops are a minor component of the overall recipe. The calculated average bitterness of the NHC fruit beers was 36 IBU, but this drops to 26 when the huge maximum value of 183 is dropped. Thus, I would expect bitterness in the range from 24 to 28 IBU for most fruit beers. Using the adjusted values for bitterness and gravity, the average BU:GU ratio of these beers was 0.50.

In addition to moderate bitterness, most fruit beers have only one late hop addition for flavor or aroma. Most often this will be an aroma addition made during the last nine minutes of the boil. Typical aroma hop varieties such as Saaz, Cascade, Hallertau, and Tettnanger account for more than two-thirds of all fruit beer hop additions during all parts of the boil. (see tables 19.5 and 19.6).

Table 19.4
Key Measurements in NHC Second-Round Fruit Beers

Measure	Avg.[a]	Min.	Max.
Gravity	1.057	1.043	1.116
BUs	36	10	183
BU:GU	0.56	0.15	1.58

[a] Each of these data sets includes one unusually high value. When the high values are dropped, the average gravity is 1.052, the BU is 26, and the resulting BU:GU ratio is 0.5.

Two general types of yeast are used for making fruit beers. By far the most common is a "clean" yeast that itself contributes little character to the beer. The American ale strains are the most popular example of this, but any lager strain used will generally produce this effect as well. The second type of yeast employed is one that produces a fruity character in normal use. These fruity notes may enhance perception of the fruit in your beer, or they may overwhelm it. Your own experience with the various fruits and yeasts will have to be your guide. The yeast strains that were used in the NHC second-round recipes are shown in table 19.7.

Using Fruit

Several issues must be considered when formulating fruit beer recipes. These issues include:

- Which fruit to use (raspberries, passion fruit, pumpkin, etc.)

- What form of fruit to use (whole, puree, extract, flavoring)

- When and how to add it to the beer

- How much to add (quantity per gallon of beer)

This section discusses each of these issues to help you in making these decisions and producing a wonderful fruit beer.

Selecting Fruit

Based on the variety of commercial beers that are available, at least a dozen different fruits can be used in making fruit-flavored beers. Despite this wide range of selections, raspberries are by far the favorite with homebrewers, just as they are with commercial brewers (see table 19.8). In general, raspberries seem easy and reasonably economical to use and they yield good results, so it is no surprise that they are so popular. In the NHC second-round entries,

Table 19.5
Hops Used in NHC Second-Round Fruit Beer Recipes

Type	Bitter	Flavor	Aroma	Dry	Total
Saaz	5	1	5	0	11
Cascade	3	1	1	1	6
Hersbruck	3	0	1	1	5
Tettnanger	3	1	1	0	5
Hallertau	2	1	1	0	4
CFJ-9	0	0	0	0	2
Eroica	2	0	0	0	2
Goldings	0	2	0	0	2
N. Brewer	1	0	1	0	2
Brewers Gold	1	0	0	0	1
Centennial	1	0	0	0	1
Chinook	1	0	0	0	1
Cluster	1	0	0	0	1
Nugget	1	0	0	0	1

Note: The data in this chart show the number of times each hop was used across the seventeen recipes analyzed.

Table 19.6
Hop Additions in NHC Second-Round Fruit Beers

	Average Number of Hop Additions per Recipe	Size of Late Additions (oz./gal.)	Size of Late Additions (oz./5 gal.)
Boil	1.5	n/a	n/a
Flavor	0.4	0.19	0.96
Aroma	0.6	0.14	0.70
Dry	0.1	0.15	0.75
Total	2.6	—	—

all of the dark beers (stout, porter, bock) and virtually all of the classic-style beers (Belgian ale, weizen, Scotch ale) used raspberries. This pairing occurs because raspberries can stand up to the richer flavors of these beers. In addition, raspberries tend to have plenty of acidity — a feature that often enhances the perception of fruit in the beer.

After raspberries, all the other fruits seem equally popular. Nine different fruits are found in the fourteen NHC beers that don't use raspberries. This total of ten fruits can be divided into two groups according to the assertiveness of their flavor. In the mild-flavored group are peaches, strawberries, apricots, and mangos. Each of these has a mild flavor that can be difficult to assert in the aroma and flavor of a beer. Generally, they are suited for pale, light-flavored beers,

although in large quantities or when added as extracts they can be suitable for slightly more flavorful styles. Other "mild" fruits that you might brew with include pumpkin, blueberries, and prunes.

The remaining fruits used in the NHC second-round beers can be classified as being more assertive in character. The strong-flavored group includes cherries, blackberries, passion fruit, and chili peppers. These four tend to be nearly as assertive in character as raspberries are, and they can still come through in beers that are more robust than a light wheat beer.

Cherries are highly favored by Belgian brewers, who add them, pits and all, to the secondary fermenter. Here, the beer will remain in contact with the fruit for several months. In addition to the regular fruit flavor, the beer will pick up a slightly bitter

Table 19.7
Yeast Selection in NHC Second-Round Fruit Beers

Yeast	No. of Recipes
American ale	8
Whitbread ale	2
Edme	1
European ale	1
German lager	1
Irish ale	1
Latrobe	1
Danish lager	1
Total	16

Table 19.8
Fruit Used in NHC Second-Round Fruit Beers

Fruit	Count	Percentage	Type
Raspberry	10	42	Assertive
Blackberry	2	8	Assertive
Cherry	2	8	Assertive
Passion fruit	2	8	Assertive
Peach	2	8	Mild
Strawberry	2	8	Mild
Apricot	1	4	Mild
Chili pepper	1	4	Assertive
Mango	1	4	Mild
Maraschino cherries	1	4	Assertive
Total	24	100*	

*Due to rounding, total of individual values does not equal 100%.

almondlike flavor from the pits during this time, which adds to the complexity of beers flavored with cherries.

I have no personal experience with blackberries or passion fruit in beer, but I hear and read from others that they are fairly strong-flavored. As you can see in table 19.8, the quantities used in the NHC beers bear this out.

Although it is technically a fruit, I have seen chili pepper beers entered in both the herb and specialty categories as well as the fruit category of the NHC. Of course, chili peppers can be quite strongly flavored, and for this reason they can be used with virtually any beer style. I once had a chili pepper–smoked beer that was wonderfully intense in both dimensions. And though they can be overwhelming, when used with a light touch chili peppers provide a subtle character to the overall flavor profile of a beer. I fondly remember a chili pepper Pilsener that was among the top beers when I judged at the NHC best-of-show competition one year.

Forms of Fruit

Every fruit starts out whole and fresh, but each can be preserved and used in different forms. Even with fresh fruit, ripeness can be an issue. Generally, fruit should be fully ripe when you use it in order to impart both the character and the quantity of flavor you desire. Some fruits, notably strawberries, do not ripen further after picking. Thus, they can be difficult to acquire in peak condition.

The use of frozen fruit for beermaking is perfectly acceptable and may, in fact, be desirable. Freezing helps to break open the fruit, making its sugars and flavors more accessible to the beer and the yeast. If you buy processed fruit, it may be pureed and frozen. This will change its appearance, but you should still be getting 100 percent pure fruit.

Whether it's fresh or frozen, whole or pureed, the amount of fruit your beer requires will not vary. All quantities quoted from recipes are for pounds of whole fruit per gallon of beer.

Other processed forms of fruit may include concentrates or syrups. These nearly always have a good portion of the sugars as well as flavor components. This means that they must be added sometime during fermentation — not at bottling time. Also, check the flavor before you use it, for it may be somewhat different from that of fresh fruit. These processed forms are easier and neater to use, but you will have to experiment to determine how much to use to achieve the flavor effect you want.

Finally, we have fruit-flavored extracts; the best — and those generally available to brewers — are made from the fruit and do not contain artificial flavors. These products contain no sugar, just highly concentrated fruit flavor. Generally, it takes just a few ounces to achieve the desired flavor effect. These extracts are very easy to use and can be added during bottling or kegging. By testing the amount you plan to add in a small sample of the beer beforehand, you should be able to achieve the exact balance you desire.

Although you may not choose to use fruit-flavored extracts as your primary method for adding fruit character, they are good products to keep in mind. If you add fruit early in the process and find that you still want more fruit character, extract may be a good way to achieve that. Under some circumstances, extract can also be a way to save a beer — especially if you need to have the beer ready for a special event, like a wedding.

Finally, extract may be the only effective way to achieve certain fruit flavors in a beer. Several sources comment that peaches do not produce good results when fermented. Not surprisingly, the two NHC beers with peach flavor both used extract to achieve this effect.

When to Add Fruit

Flavor extracts that contain no sugar can be added at any time, but most logically, they are added just before bottling. The question of when to add fruit is more critical when some form of whole fruit is used.

For some time, the standard wisdom has held that the best way to add fruit is during fermentation, usually after racking to a secondary fermenter. This approach has a number of advantages. First, it allows you complete control over the time that the fruit and beer are in contact. Second, it gives you an opportunity — if you want it — to taste the beer you have brewed without any fruit additions to make sure it doesn't have off-flavors that would make it unsuitable for combining with fruit. Finally, since the primary fermentation has produced alcohol in the beer, you can be less concerned about contamination from adding raw fruit, which undoubtedly contains bacteria.

Another strategy that is often discussed for adding fruit to beer occurs earlier in the brewing process, while the wort is still hot. This approach calls for steeping the fruit in the hot wort for fifteen to thirty minutes. At the end of this time the fruit is removed and the wort is chilled for fermentation.

The greatest advantage to this approach comes in reducing the likelihood of bacterial contamination from the fruit. The heat of the wort provides a pasteurization effect, and removal of the fruit before fermentation eliminates further transfers of bacteria.

Despite this, many accomplished homebrewers resist this approach. One reason is because fruits contain pectins that can cause haze in the finished beer. Heat extracts pectins from the fruit, especially at temperatures around boiling. Still, pectins need not be a problem, because the enzyme pectinase can be added to help clarify the beer during aging, if desired.

Some speculate that heating fruit may enhance its flavor, bringing out some of the compounds normally associated with cooked, rather than raw, fruit. Others believe the cooked flavors are not desirable and that the heat will drive off desirable aroma compounds and reduce the flavor impact of the fruit.

Perhaps the greatest argument against steeping is waste. Following normal proportions for most fruits, you will have 5 to 10 pounds of fruit for a 5-gallon batch. After thirty minutes of steeping, the fruit bulk you remove from the wort will be substantial.

Another question is the efficiency of the flavor transfer during a thirty-minute steep versus that obtained by weeks of contact in the fermenter. Based upon the limited data available from the NHC recipes, this does not appear to be a problem. In every comparison that I have done, the average amount of fruit added during steeping is equal to the average amount added to the fermenter.

Despite all these arguments, I don't know of any studies or data that support one approach or the other on the basis of either flavor or sanitation. I have always used the secondary fermentation method — but then I've never produced a fruit beer that won rave reviews. The NHC second-round recipes indicate that many successful fruit beers — 40 percent, in fact — are produced using the steeping method (see table 19.9).

Looking at these two methods, I found that when steeping was used, raspberries were involved in five recipes (71 percent), with cherries and strawberries making up the other two. Overall, the average steep time was twenty-four minutes, with a range from fifteen to thirty minutes.

Fermentation was used with a broader variety of fruits, including mangoes, maraschino cherries, raspberries (2); cherries, passion fruit (2); and blackberries.

The NHC recipe forms do not include space for reporting the length of time that the fruit and beer remain in contact. In general, however, the period of contact may last from a few weeks to a few months.

Quantities

The quantity of fruit you add to a beer recipe ultimately depends on all of the factors discussed so far in this chapter: The character of the beer, the character of the fruit, the form and method of addition, and certainly the overall effect you hope to achieve. If this seems hopelessly complicated, don't despair; in practice, few people consider these factors in any organized way.

In general, adding 1 to 2 pounds of fruit per gallon of beer will achieve the desired effect. The lower end of this scale generally applies to assertively flavored fruits, which among the NHC entries varied from 0.80 to 1.32 pounds per gallon. Cherries were somewhat of an exception to this, with both recipes showing high-quantity additions of 2 pounds per gallon (see table 19.10).

The quantities shown for raspberries may also be a little high for some applications. Using the secondary-fermenter approach, as little as 0.5-pound per gallon can

Table 19.9
Timing of Fruit Additions in NHC Second-Round Beers

When Added	Fruit[a]	Extract[b]
Steeped	7	0
Primary	5	0
Secondary	5	0
Aging	0	1
Bottling	0	3
Total	17	4

[a] Products that contain fermentable sugar
[b] Flavorings with no fermentable sugar

provide adequate raspberry character in a light-flavored beer. Even in heavy beers such as stout, I have found that 1 pound per gallon is adequate to produce a pronounced raspberry flavor. Mild fruits generally require greater quantities to achieve the desired effect, in the range from 1.6 pounds per gallon to 2.0 pounds per gallon.

To get pumpkin flavor (rather than nutmeg and cinnamon) in your beer, use three or four 8- to 10-inch-diameter pumpkins for 5 gallons of beer. Cook them for two hours at 325 °F (163 °C), then puree the pumpkin and add it to the mash. Blueberries should be considered a mild fruit, so you will need to add about 2 pounds per gallon, even in a light-flavored beer, to achieve a good blueberry character. (Note: "Blue" berries generally give beer a red color.)

If you are really worried about getting just the right balance of fruit, you might try a blending strategy. From one wort, make two batches of beer, adding a high concentration of fruit to one and no fruit to the other. When both are finished fermenting, take a sample of each and blend them in various proportions to find the ideal balance. You can then blend the bulk beers in the appropriate proportions.

One other tactic you might try to improve the character of your fruit beer is to add some food-grade acid to the finished beer. My colleague and fruit-beer maven, Randy Mosher, says that citric, malic, and even lactic acids can be added to adjust balance and enhance perception of the fruit.[6] Trial adjustments on a small sample are best before adding acid to a whole batch of beer.

Conclusion

Although many brewpubs and microbreweries make fruit beers today, they must do so in a way that is practical and profitable for their business. But much like wine, the flavors of fruit beer can take time to mature and develop. As a result, there are many opportunities for homebrewers to make wonderful beers that commercial brewers will never be able to replicate. If for no other reason than this, every homebrewer should devote some of his or her brewing energy to the making of fruit beers.

Table 19.10
Quantities of Fruit Used in NHC Second-Round Beers

Fruit Used	No. of Recipes	Avg. lb./gal.	Avg. OG
Cherry	2	2.00	1.064
Strawberry	2	1.80	1.050
Mango	1	1.60	1.047
Raspberry	7	1.32	1.053
Blackberry	2	1.00	1.068
Maraschino cherries	1	1.00	1.048
Passion fruit	1	0.80	1.046
Total	16	1.34	1.053

Key Success Factors in Brewing Fruit Beers

- For general fruit beers, use extract, wheat, and crystal malt to produce a pale to amber base beer with an original gravity of about 1.050.

- Hop using aroma varieties such as Cascade, Tettnanger, and Saaz. Target a BU:GU ratio of about 0.50 to achieve a moderate bitterness.

- Make just one late hop addition during the last nine minutes of the boil, again using aroma varieties. Make an addition of about 0.75-ounce in 5 gallons.

- Ferment using either a clean American ale strain or a lightly fruity British yeast.

- For each gallon of wort, add 1 pound of assertive fruit (raspberries, black-berries, passion fruit, chili peppers) or up to 2 pounds of mild fruit (strawberries, blueberries, peaches).

- Whole fruit (especially the assertive varieties) may be steeped in the hot wort after completion of the boil and then removed before fermentation. Fruit can also be added to the secondary fermentation, especially in cases where puree or mild fruit is being used.

- Fruit flavoring and extracts may be added to the finished beer before packaging to provide some or all of the fruit flavor.

- Long aging of beers made with real fruit often brings out the best flavor.

20 MILD AND BROWN ALES

Project	Designing Great Beers
	Brewers Publications
Project No.	61766

The words "mild" and "brown" are two of the oldest terms used to describe English beers — and they are still in use today. Not surprisingly, then, these terms can be the source of some confusion from a historical perspective. Fortunately, current commercial practice provides fairly clear definitions of these two styles for brewers and drinkers alike (see table 20.1). I will review the overall style definitions and some of the subclasses within them, but first, let's review a bit of the history of brown and mild beers in England.

A Brief History of English Mild and Brown Beers

Although they were probably known simply as ales, the earliest of English beers are believed to have been brown in color. The beverage of Robin Hood and Mary Queen of Scots would have been made from a malt that was brown and smoky as the result of kilning over a hardwood fire.[1] It was not until the development of coke (or coal) fires that this smoky flavor was removed. The smokiness derived from oak, beech, or hornbeam[2] was itself a prized characteristic of the day, just as hams and other smoked foods are often favored today.

The term brown malt is still seen, although it is rarely produced and no longer smoked. Nonetheless, beers made from a large percentage of brown malt have been consumed in the British Isles for parts of at least eight centuries.[3] Perhaps brown malt will reappear in commercial beers once again before another century has passed.

In looking for a beverage that was called "brown ale" prior to contemporary times, I find only one reference, which comes from *The London and Country Brewer*, published in 1750.[4] It provides a procedure for drawing several successively weaker worts from a single mash, listing the first as "Stout Beer," the second as "Stich or Strong Brown Ale," and the third as "Common Brown Ale." Into the early nineteenth century, porters and stouts were made with significant portions of brown malt. This early intimacy between brown ale and stout no doubt contributed to the use of the term "brown ales" to describe porters and stouts generally during much of their early history.

It appears that this type of "brown beer" may have been an early form of porter. What is certain is that porter was called "brown beer" in its early days. The *Private Brewer's Guide*, published in 1822, discusses this history as follows:

About this time much competition among the brewers appears to have taken place, and the introduction of brown beer became almost general . . . But may persons were so attached

Table 20.1
Commercial Mild and Brown Ale Characteristics

Characteristic	Mild	Brown
Original gravity	1.030–1.036	1.040–1.055
Bitterness	15–30	15–35 (higher for American versions)
Hop flavor and aroma	Low	low for English, high for American
Color (SRM)	8–50	8–50
Apparent extract	1.006–1.010	1.006–1.014
Alcohol (volume)	2.5–3.6%	4–5.5%
Esters	Low	Low
Diacetyl	Low	Low–medium
Flavor profile	Malty with toffee and chocolate notes.	Malt balanced, often with caramel or nutty tones. Some English examples may have a firmer bitterness and U.S. interpretations may be quite aggressively hopped.

to the pale beer, particularly in the country, that the consumption of brown beer became confined to London; however, even then the pale beer was drank, as the brown was considered heavy and glutinous; a mixture of stale, mild, and pale, which was called three-threads . . . as far back as 1720.

The Breweries now began to improve; the brown beer was started, well hopped, into butts, and was kept a considerable time to grow mellow. Being the beverage of labouring men, it obtained the name of porter, and was called intire butt beer . . .[5]

Thus we can see now that the terms "brown" and "mild" are both caught up with the history of porter. "Brown" was a generic term used to describe porter, and "mild" may have been one of the three beers initially used by the publican to prepare this popular London beverage. Furthermore, this quotation distinguishes mild ale from stale. Mild was most likely sold fresh, without aging that would have brought further attenuation and an acidic flavor. Thus, it no doubt tasted sweeter — and milder — than aged or stale beers.

This same early nineteenth-century treatise on brewing gives recipes for brown

stout[6] and brown porter,[7] which rely upon brown malt for a quarter to a half of their grist. These recipes harken back to a time when brown ale and stout were produced from the same mash. Together, these events led to the use of the umbrella term "brown beer," which can be found several times during the 1800s, to identify porters and stouts of all types and to distinguish them from pale beers.[8] It is unclear whether a product called "brown ale" was produced and sold during this period. However, it *is* clear that the term served to distinguish darker beers from those made with pale malt.

The quote above notes that the dark beers were "confined to London." This is most likely due to the realities of production, because the mineral profile of the water found in London and southern England was ideally suited to production of dark beers.[9] Also, the industry of England created a large laboring class in need of heavy, dark beers that provided sustenance and nutrition.

Later in the nineteenth century, the term "mild ale" can be found describing a number of products with gravities ranging from 1.055 to 1.080.[10] These milds were no doubt sold fresh, and this lack of aging may have been a key distinction between these beers and the other pub offerings of the day. By 1900 I find a fuller description of mild beer from the *Handy-Book of Brewing*: "The mild beers are distinguished from the stock beers by a more sweetish (mild) taste, containing more unfermented malto-dextrin and less acid ... Mild ales are usually brewed of a darker color than old ales, with less original gravity and less hops."[11]

In the United States, at least, the term "mild" was applied not only to ales but to porters and stouts as well, to indicate the young products that had not been aged. Contemporary with this, mild ales of more modest gravity were still being sold in England (see table 20.2).

The porter of the early 1900s displayed similar gravity and hop levels, showing the continuing relationship between these two styles. By that time, however, stouts and even pale ales were higher in gravity and more liberally hopped than the mild ales. Still, I cannot find a specific product called "brown ale" in any references from that period.

The Browns Continue

Today mild ale is in decline in England due to its working-class image. Micro-breweries are making the most popular examples of the style today, and a few brewers still make brown ale as well. In the United States an increasing number of brown ales can be found, while milds are quite scarce.

Since the start of the twentieth century, the average gravity of the mild style has dropped dramatically. The well-known English brewing author H. Loyd Hind offers mild recipes circa 1950 with gravities of 1.040 and 1.045.[12] Today the typical mild runs about 1.030 to 1.036. In general, hop levels are quite low, making these beers "mild" in comparison to the bitters of similar gravity often produced by the same brewery.

Milds are commonly quite dark, but a substantial number of pale examples can be found these days, with color as light as 6 °SRM.[13] My analysis of current milds shows that even those that exclude chocolate, roast, and black grains have an average color of 18 °SRM. Although some of the color comes from crystal malt, dark sugars and caramel coloring are often included to help deepen the hue. The darker milds have an average color of about 24 °SRM.

If you are in England, you should be able to try one of the sixty or so real ale milds available there.[14] In the United States, you'll have to look a bit harder for a brew-pub or microbrewery example, such as the PMD Mild made by Goose Island in Chicago and the Mariners' Mild offered at Pacific Coast Brewpub in Oakland, California.[15]

Though milds are far more plentiful than are brown ales in the United Kingdom, the reverse is true in the United States, with an increasing number of brown ales popping up in microbreweries and brewpubs.[16]

Table 20.2
Some Characteristics of Mild Ales in England, circa 1900

Style	°P (OG)	hops (lb.) per U.S. bbl. of wort
Burton Mild Ale	14–15 (1.056–1.060)	1.5–2
London Four Ale (mild)	13–14 (1.052–1.056)	0.8–1.25

Sources: R. Wahl and M. Henius, The American Handy-Book of the Brewing, Malting and Auxiliary Trades *(Chicago: Wahl-Henius Institute, 1908), 1253. P. Slosberg, "The Road to an American Brown Ale,"* Brewing in Styles *column, Martin Lodahl, ed.,* Brewing Techniques *(May/June 1995): 34.*

These commercial examples of brown ale define a broad range of style characteristics that include several substyles.

In the United Kingdom brown ale is generally a bottled product, although some cask-conditioned versions may be found.[17] In general, brown ales display starting gravities that are 0.010 to 0.020 higher than the milds, and depending upon the interpretation they may be more aggressively hopped both in the kettle and in the finish. Viewing both the Anglo and the American examples, we can identify three substyles: London or Southern English brown ale, Northern English brown ale, and American (or sometimes Texas) brown ale.

American sources don't distinguish between the English styles, but definitions from The (English) National Guild of Wine and Beer Judges,[18] as well as Jackson's writings,[19] clearly outline two separate styles. Here is a composite description of each:

London or southern brown ale. Gravity: 1.035–1.040; IBU around 20; generally dark brown but some pale examples exist; malty, caramel aroma; sweet in palate with malt and caramel flavor; low hop flavor. Examples include Mann's Brown Ale (1.035) and King and Barnes Dark Brown Ale (1.033). Because of their sweetness, these southern brown ales are sometimes derided as "learner beers" in the United Kingdom. Jackson suggests that some examples make suitable dessert-beer.[20]

Northern or Newcastle Brown. Gravity: 1.045–1.050; IBU 15 to 25; deep amber to reddish brown; aroma includes hops as well as caramel/malt. Although malt continues to dominate and contributes a noticeable sweetness, a medium level of bitterness is encountered. Newcastle Brown Ale is the obvious example, and Jackson cites the Strong Brown (1.046) and Extra Strong Brown (1.055) from Cornish Brewery, which is also known as Devenish of Redruth.

Even after subdividing their own brown ales, British brewers and writers mostly ignore the American interpretations of the style. In a sense, the category has been a beginner beer here, too. After all, I suspect that it was a group of overly hop-enthusiastic novice homebrewers down in Texas that pioneered the development of this style.[21] New to both hops and specialty grains in beer, they piled them on, giving rise to a beer that was big in both categories.

Today the primary definition for the U.S. version of brown ale comes from the American Homebrewers Association.[22]

American (or Texas) brown ale. It includes a gravity of 1.040 to 1.055 that provides medium maltiness and body; color ranges from dark amber to brown; bitterness ranges from 25 to 60 IBU. Along with this high hop bitterness, the style accommodates high levels of hop flavor and aroma — most always from American hop varieties. In keeping with English brewing traditions, low diacetyl levels are acceptable. Commercial examples of this style include Pete's Wicked Ale, Brooklyn Brown Ale, and Pyramid Best Brown Ale. Additional entries seem to be popping up regularly, so check out your local craft brewers for a taste.

Brewing Mild and Brown Ales

From a brewing perspective, there are five substyles to consider: pale mild, dark mild, southern brown, northern brown, and American brown. In some ways, of course, the differences between mild and brown are a matter of gravity. The malt bills of milds and browns follow the same patterns, even in America; the real distinctions lie in the gravity levels you hit and the hopping schedule you follow. In England, mild is both the oldest and most often encountered of these styles, so let's begin with an analysis of the malts found in English milds.

Malt Bill

The mild ales can be divided into pale and dark groups. The sixty-eight commercial examples I was able to analyze from Protz's *Almanac* fall nearly evenly into the two categories: 44 percent pale and 56 percent dark.[23]

Because color data are not always available, my distinction between the two groups takes a brewer's perspective and is based on the inclusion or omission of dark grains: chocolate malt, black malt, and roast barley. A portion of the pale examples (16 percent of all recipes) also omit crystal malt.

As a group, the pale examples are only a little lighter in color than the dark examples, with an average color of 18 °SRM versus 24 °SRM. One key difference between the two groups is that the pale examples are *more* likely to use caramel coloring to darken the wort or the finished beer. Caramel was listed as an ingredient in 45 percent of the pales versus just 21 percent of the darks.

Caramel is a food coloring agent. It appears to have no flavor impact in the quantities used in beer, so I can't imagine that it would be too popular with American craft brewers. Coloring beers made only from malt are also available and may be used instead of caramel in some U.S. breweries.

Beyond this difference in the use of caramel, the use of sugar (52 percent incidence in pale milds, 54 percent incidence in dark milds) and other individual adjuncts such as wheat, flaked barley, and maize were quite similar in both the pale and dark types of mild. Overall, the pale examples were slightly more likely to exclude adjuncts and sugar completely (31 percent versus 26 percent).

Among the dark formulations, most used crystal malt with one additional dark grain. Chocolate is the favorite, with black malt running a close second and roast a distant third. Smaller groups of recipes use dark malts without any crystal or doubled up on the dark malts (see table 20.3).

The data on grain proportion for these commercial examples (see table 20.4) show that when dark grains are used, they usually constitute 5 to 6 percent of the malt bill. At this concentration they will clearly have a flavor impact, although less so than in a stout, for example.

Table 20.3
Mild Ale Malt Bills

I. Pale milds (44%)[a]
 A. No Crystal (16%)
 B. With Crystal (28%)
II. Dark Milds (56%)
 A. Crystal + 1 Dark Grain (35%)
  1. Crystal + Chocolate (16%)
  2. Crystal + Black (14%)
  3. Crystal + Roast (5%)
 B. Dark Grain without Crystal (12%)
  1. Black (4.5%)
  2. Roast (4.5%)
  3. Chocolate (3%)
 C. Two Dark Grains (9%)
  1. Roast + Chocolate (6%)
  2. Other (3%)

Note: Total number of recipes analyzed = 68.
[a] No chocolate, black, or roast; color often obtained from brown sugars and caramel

Table 20.4
Specialty Grain Proportion by Weight in Commercial Mild Ale Recipes

Grain Used	Avg. (%)
Crystal	8
Chocolate	6
Black	5
Roast	6
Sugar	12
Corn	11
Wheat	5

Beyond these commonly used brewer's grains, most (70 to 75 percent) of the mild ales also use at least one nonmalt source of fermentable material. Chief among these is sugar, including cane sugar, dark or brown sugar, and syrups. Overall, more than half of the recipes in both the pale and dark groups include sugar. On average, sugar accounts for 14 percent of the contents in pale recipes that use sugar.[24] When sugar occurs in dark milds, it accounts for slightly less of the contents, 11 percent on average. Other adjuncts (wheat, flaked barley, maize) appear more often and account for a larger portion of the total gravity in the dark milds, as shown in table 20.5.

The impact of these additions will vary, depending on the exact ingredient used. Wheat and flaked barley should assist head retention while contributing a little gravity. Brown sugars may contribute a favorable flavor component as well as increase fermentability. Cane sugar, sugar syrups, and flaked maize will generally increase fermentability without having a significant flavor effect — although ciderlike flavors could occur.

Although craft brewing in the United States generally has no use for adjuncts such as sugar and maize, these additions are clearly used in a majority of the current English commercial examples of the style. Comparison of milds brewed with and without such additives should be an interesting exercise for those who wish to explore the style.

The two other factors you will want to consider in developing your mild ale malt bill are target gravity and color. Table 20.6 lists average values and ranges for gravity and color.

Brown Ale Malt Bills

Compared to the milds, relatively little data is available on commercial brown ales. What data is available shows that the sugars that are so popular with milds disappear from the brown ale recipes. One likely effect

Table 20.5
Nonmalt Ingredients in Commercial Mild Ale Recipes

| | Sugar | | Other Adjuncts | |
	Incidence (%)	Proportion (%)	Incidence (%)	Proportion (%)
Pale	52	14	44	12
Dark	54	11	47	21

Table 20.6
Average Gravity and Color for Commercial Milds

	Avg.	Min.	Max.	No. of Recipes
Gravity (GU)	34 –	30	39	64
Color (EBC)	85	22	200	24
Color (SRM)	43	11	102	24

of sugar in milds is a lightening of the malt flavors. Since the fuller-bodied browns don't seem to need such dilution, the sugar can be dropped. Beyond the exclusion of sugar, commercial brown ales seem to mimic the commercial mild ale grain bills (see table 20.7).

To summarize these data:

• Crystal and chocolate malt appear more often in the NHC brown ales than in the commercial milds. Indeed, virtually every recipe for brown ale that I have seen, whether commercial or homebrewed, has included these two malts.

• Black malt and roast barley appear with approximately the same incidence (20 to 25 percent) in the browns as the milds. However, the NHC second-round brewers seem to take a lighter touch with these grains,

Table 20.7
Profiles of Commercial Brown Ales

Name	Gravity	Malts	Color (SRM)	Hops	IBU
Pete's Wicked Ale	1.052	Pale, crystal, chocolate	40	Brewers Gold, Cascade	29
Brooklyn Brown	1.055	Pale, crystal, chocolate, biscuit, wheat	45	Northern Brewer, dry hopped with Willamette and Cascade	33
Pyramid Best Brown	1.052	Two-row, crystal Munich, roast	18	Nugget & Liberty flavor, post-boil	27
Newcastle Brown Ale	1.045	Blend of two beers	8	"English"	24
Double Maxim	1.044	—	11	Challenger, Fuggle, Target	22
Samuel Smith's Old Brewery Brown (aka Nut Brown)	1.048	—	16	—	34
Mann's Brown Ale	1.035	—	32	—	20

For more information about brown ales, tables 20.8 and 20.9 provide an analysis of the National Homebrew Competition second-round recipes. These tables divide the NHC browns into two categories, English and American, and compare them to the commercial milds evaluated in table 20.7.

Table 20.8
Grain Incidence in
Commercial Mild Recipes and NHC Second-Round Brown Ales

| Grain | Commercial English Mild* | NHC Second-Round Brown Ales | |
		English Style*	American Style*
Crystal	46 of 68 recipes	7 of 7 recipes	10 of 12 recipes
Chocolate	19 of 68 recipes	4 of 7 recipes	7 of 12 recipes
Black	17 of 68 recipes	2 of 7 recipes	4 of 12 recipes
Roast	13 of 68 recipes	0 of 7 recipes	3 of 12 recipes
Sugar	36 of 68 recipes	0 of 7 recipes	0 of 12 recipes
Corn	12 of 68 recipes	1 of 7 recipes	1 of 12 recipes
Wheat	19 of 68 recipes	2 of 7 recipes	3 of 12 recipes
Other	—	4 of 7 recipes	6 of 12 recipes

*These data show how many of the NHC recipes in each category included each grain.
Note: To accomodate the range of examples in the brown ale style category, tables 20.8 and 20.9 are presented in a modified format from other incidence and proportion tables in the book.

using them for just 1 to 2 percent of the total grist. This is true, in part, because they are usually added with chocolate malt rather than as an alternative to it, as is usually the case with commercially produced mild ales.

• Wheat appears in the same incidence (25 to 30 percent) and proportion (5 percent) in the NHC second-round browns as in commercial milds, but other adjuncts, such as corn and flaked barley, appear less often and account for less of the total homebrew recipe.

• Sugar is virtually unheard of in the NHC second-round brown ales, but other data indicate that this appears to be consistent with commercial practice.

• Other malts play a much bigger role in homebrewed brown ale recipes, as they do with other styles. Biscuit, aromatic,

Table 20.9
Average Grain Proportion by Weight in
Commercial Milds and NHC Second-Round Brown Ale Recipes

| Grain | Commercial Milds (%) | NHC Second-Round Brown Ales | |
		English (%)	American (%)
Crystal	8	15	10
Chocolate	6	3	2
Black	5	1	1
Roast	6	0	—
Sugar	12	0	0
Corn	11	4	4
Wheat	5	5	4
Other	—	7	14

Note: To accommodate the range of examples in the brown ale style category, tables 20.8 and 20.9 are presented in a modified format from other incidence and proportion tables in the book.

Special B, special roast, toasted malt, and other similar "character" malts appear in more than half of all the recipes. These malts account for the highest portion of the grain bill after pale and crystal malts.

With regard to gravity, the style definitions given at the beginning of the chapter hold true for both the commercial and the NHC examples. The average gravity of the commercial examples shown in table 20.7 is 1.047, while the average gravity of all the NHC second-round examples discussed above is 1.053.

The color of brown ales varies almost as widely as that of milds. Among the commercial examples the range runs from 8 to 45 °SRM, with an average of 25 °SRM.

Among the NHC second-round beers, extract was commonly used as the base for the recipes. Fully 42 percent of the recipes included just extract and specialty malts. Another 5 percent used some pale malt for a minimash but still relied upon extract for most of the gravity. The brands of extract used included the following: Munton & Fisons, 3; Northwestern, 2; Laaglander, 2; Williams, 2; Coopers, 1; and unspecified, 4.

Often, the homebrew approach to brewing darker styles such as mild and brown is to throw in a little bit of everything. One of these second-round beers is a mild I formulated to include five specialty malts: two types of crystal plus chocolate, Special B, and biscuit malts. Contrary to this kitchen-sink approach, the data in this section demonstrate that commercial brewers take a different tack, focusing on a single dark malt and using it for a substantial portion of the grist. It seems that brewers who combine this focus with careful evaluation of several possible yeast strains may have a better chance of achieving superior results.

Mashing for these styles is generally done on a single-infusion basis, especially when well-modified English malts are used as the base. Saccharification temperatures average 153 °F (67 °C) across all the NHC second-round examples. Within specific groups, the milds were slightly lower, at 150 °F (65.5 °C), and the English Brown ales a bit higher, at 155 ° F (68 °C).

Hopping

With the exception of the American-style brown ales, low bitterness is considered a hallmark of these styles. The commercial examples from Britain certainly demonstrate this, with IBU often dipping below 20 for the milds and below 25 for the brown ales. At the same time, however, these beers maintain a reasonable balance of bitterness for their gravities, generally showing BU:GU ratios of 0.50 to 0.70.

Table 20.10

Bitterness Levels (IBU) in Mild and Brown Ales

	No. of Recipes	Average	Low	High	BU:GU
Commercial Examples					
Mild	29	23	15	33	0.50–0.72
Brown	7	27	20	34	0.50–0.70
NHC Second-Round Examples					
Mild	5	23	8	43	0.64
Eng. Brown	6	30	15	52	0.54
Am. Brown	13	48	25	76	0.95

Among the American commercial brown ales, hopping follows a fairly similar pattern, with IBU values ranging from 20 to 33 (see table 20.7). This pattern of moderate bitterness carries through to the NHC second-round examples of mild and English brown ale, where the average IBU values are 23 and 30, respectively (see table 20.10).

Only in the NHC second-round examples of American brown ale do the IBU counts blast off the charts, with an average of 48 IBUs and a 0.95 BU:GU ratio. This dramatic increase in bitter hopping foreshadows the increased use of hops at all stages in the brewing process that is typical of American brown ales.

Flavor and aroma hopping are not widely practiced with the milds and English brown ales, but it does occur. In the published information on mild ales, fully 30 percent of the recipes indicate the use of either aroma or dry hops. The tasting descriptions for most of these mention a "light hop" aroma as a result.

In the NHC second-round examples of mild and English brown, we find virtually no dry hopping and very few flavor hop additions (see tables 20.11 and 20.12). Of the eleven recipes from the NHC second round, only one uses dry hops and three use flavor hops.

By contrast, aroma hops added during the last ten minutes of the boil are fairly common, as indicated by nine additions among these eleven NHC second-round recipes. So as not to go overboard, these additions tend to be fairly small, on the order of 0.5-ounce per 5-gallon batch, as shown in table 20.13.

Compared to these English styles, the American-style brown ales show a far more aggressive use of late hop additions. Overall, more than half of all hop additions are for flavor and aroma purposes, and the average recipe includes two additions in these categories (see tables 20.14

Table 20.11
Hop Types and Uses in NHC Second-Round Mild and English Brown Ales

Type	Bitter	Flavor	Aroma	Dry	Total
Mild Ales [a]					
Goldings	2	0	2	0	4
Fuggle	1	1	1	0	3
Eroica	1	0	0	0	1
N. Brewer	0	0	0	1	1
Willamette	1	0	0	0	1
English Brown Ales [b]					
Goldings	5	1	2	0	8
Tettnanger	3	0	2	0	5
Cascade	1	1	1	0	3
Perle	2	0	1	0	3
Fuggle	3	0	0	0	3
Willamette	2	0	0	0	2

[a] The data show the number of times each hop was used across the five recipes analyzed.
[b] The data show the number of times each hop was used across the six recipes analyzed.

Table 20.12
Average Number of Hop Additions
in NHC Second-Round Mild English and Brown Ales

Type	Boil	Flavor	Aroma	Dry	Total
Mild ales	1.0	0.2	0.6	0.2	2.0
English brown ales	2.7	0.3	1.0	0.0	4.0

and 20.15). The average recipe adds 0.5 ounce of hops during the last nine minutes of the boil or steeps them after the boil. In addition, the vast majority of recipes add more than 0.75-ounce of hops for flavor purposes. On top of all this, some recipes also dry hop during secondary fermentation.

Hop Selection

Fuggle seems to be a more dominant hop with commercial milds than with any other style of English ale. If a mild recipe contains only one hop, it will most likely be Fuggle. When more than one hop is used, the most popular combinations include Fuggle, as shown in table 20.16.

As always, Goldings varieties of various types also make a strong showing, and they are the most likely to be used for aroma or dry hopping — although Fuggle sees some duty in these applications as well. Challenger and Northdown are the other two hops seen with some frequency in commercial mild ales. As you can see from table 20.11, a similar pattern emerges in the NHC second round mild ales, where Goldings and Fuggle account for 70 percent of all hop additions.

When it comes to English brown ales, the information published for commercial examples includes little information on the hop varieties used. The data that is available fits with the patterns of usage established by the milds. Published homebrew recipes from U.K. sources list Fuggle (5) most often, followed by Northern Brewer (4), Goldings (2), and then Hallertau, Galena and Northdown (1 each).[25]

Homebrewed English brown ales from the NHC use English varieties in more cases than not, with Goldings, Fuggle, and the Fuggle descendent Willamette taking the lead (see table 20.11).

In both commercial and NHC second-round American brown ales, Cascade is clearly the favorite hop. Table 20.7 shows that two of the three commercial American brown ales include Cascade hops. Among

Table 20.13
Average Size of Late Hop Additions
in NHC Second-Round Mild and Brown Ales

	Flavor	Aroma	Dry
Mild	—	0.42	—
Eng. brown	0.60	0.58	—
Am. brown	0.82	0.51	0.82

Note: Values are in ounces per 5 gallons.

Table 20.14
Hop Types and Uses in NHC Second-Round American Brown Ales

Type	Bitter	Flavor	Aroma	Dry	Total
Cascade	9	6	9	3	27
N. Brewer	4	1	0	0	5
Tettnanger	1	0	1	1	3
Chinook	1	1	0	0	2
Hallertau	0	1	1	0	2
Mt. Hood	1	0	1	0	2
Perle	2	0	0	0	2
Hersbruck	0	0	0	1	1
Other*	4	0	0	0	1

* *Includes Bullion, Centennial, Eroica, and Fuggle.*
Note: The data show the number of times each hop was used across the thirteen recipes analyzed.

the NHC second-round beers shown in table 20.14, eleven of thirteen recipes use this variety. The English-type hops — Fuggle, Goldings, Willamette — are almost completely absent from these recipes, and no other variety occurs in more than three recipes. Other aroma hops, such as Hallertau, Mt. Hood, and Tettnanger, occasionally contribute to the character of these beers.

Yeast

Selection of yeast for the mild and brown ales will depend largely on whether you are making an American or an English interpretation. The American versions will typically be clean and balanced, while in the English versions the yeast may add substantially to the flavor profile.

The NHC second-round milds and browns relied upon a wide variety of yeasts. Two clear patterns emerge. First, when brewing American brown ales, most brewers choose an American ale yeast or a similar very clean strain such as the "dry" German ale. In two cases, lager yeasts were used and fermentation temperatures were kept cool (55 °F, 13 °C) to prevent excessive ester formation. For the milds and English browns, brewers used a variety of British-type yeasts, including Irish, London, and the full-bodied strains. Dry Edme and Kent ale yeasts were also used, as was the "sweet" type of German ale yeast.

By experimenting with these various yeasts, you should be able to create a unique flavor profile for your mild or brown ale — one that will please your palate, impress

Table 20.15
Average Number of Hop Additions in NHC Second-Round American Brown Ales

Boil	1.7
Flavor	0.7
Aroma	0.9
Dry	0.4
Total	3.7

Table 20.16
Hop Selections and Combinations in Commercial English Milds

No. of Varieties In Recipe	Percentage of Recipes Listing Each Variety			
	Fuggle	Goldings	Challenger	Northdown
One N=21	52	19	9	9
Two N=24	46	83	21	12
Three N=20	60	60	45	—

Note: N represents the total number of recipes in each group.

Water

These dark ales are a good style to brew if you have carbonate water. The carbonate works well with the malt character of the beers, so you can avoid treating the water before brewing.

Of course, London is the home of dark ales of all types, and London water is considered the prototype for this kind of brewing. The ion concentrations for London water are listed in table 20.17. Although relatively hard, this water is very different in composition from Burton water. It is high both in carbonate and in basic table salt — that is, sodium and chloride.

Regardless of your water source, the amount of salt needed will be very small. I typically use about ⅛ teaspoon. Among those NHC second-round beers that indicated water treatment, a portion added salt, usually on the order of ¼ teaspoon for 5 gallons. This addition can be made to the boil rather than at the time of mashing.

Finally, since you don't want a significant concentration of sulfate in this water, this is a good situation in which to add calcium chloride instead of gypsum to help with mash chemistry. However, if you use this in combination with sodium chloride, watch the total chloride levels.

Table 20.17
Profile of London Water

Mineral	ppm
Calcium	50
Magnesium	20
Sodium	100
Carbonate	160
Sulfate	80
Chloride	60

Source: T. Foster, Porter, Classic Beer Style Series, no. 5 (Boulder Colo.: Brewers Publications. 1992), 74.
Note: ppm = parts per million

Conclusion

It seems that milds and brown ales don't get much respect from brewers and beer drinkers these days — at least not in the United States. Maybe it is the public's aversion to dark beers or the relatively low alcohol levels offered by many examples of the style. But I would think that a good mild would be the perfect beer for those wanting something that's not bitter but still has some character.

For those who have not explored milds and browns, some interesting opportunities await. I have reviewed a number of possible strategies for development of a malt bill, including that big decision about the use of sugar. If your mash tun is big enough to get two batches of 1.032 wort from one mash, you might try adding sugar to the first and omitting it from its twin just to assess the effects. (Remember to adjust gravities beforehand so they'll be the same after addition of the sugar.)

Finally, when brewing these styles, try making a few batches that focus on just one or two dark malts, as the commercial milds generally do. The results may be cleaner and more focused than with the little-bit-of-everything approach. Furthermore, this approach will allow you to experiment with yeast strains in order to find one that contributes a distinct flavor profile that is perfect for the malt combination you have chosen.

Key Success Factors in Brewing Mild and Brown Ales

- Choose a well-modified two-row, pale ale, or mild ale malt as the base for your recipe. Extract may be used for a portion of the gravity.

- To produce a pale mild, exclude dark malts and add just a small portion of crystal malt. To produce a dark mild, use 10 to 15 percent crystal malt plus 2 to 3 percent chocolate malt or 1 percent black malt.

- For a brown ale, include 10 to 15 percent crystal malt and 2 to 3 percent chocolate malt. You may choose to use a small portion of black malt or about 5 percent wheat.

- Target a gravity of 1.035 to 1.040 for a mild, 1.050 to 1.055 for a brown ale.

- Mash using a single-step infusion process, with the saccharification rest at about 153 °F (67 °C).

- Use Fuggle and Goldings hops for all additions in milds and English brown ales and target a BU:GU ratio of 0.50 to 0.70. You may wish to include a 0.5-ounce aroma hop addition for these styles.

- For American brown ales, use Cascade or other American hops to hit a target BU:GU ratio of 0.90 to 1.0. Make at least two of the following using Cascade or other aroma hops: a 0.75- to 1.0-ounce flavor hop, a 0.5-ounce aroma hop addition, and a 0.75- to 0.5-ounce dry hop addition.

- Ferment milds and English brown ales with English style yeasts that will provide a distinct yeast character. Ferment American brown ales with clean ale strains such as the American ale yeast.

21 OLD ALE

Old ale is a somewhat ignored style these days, but it is rich in history and ripe with brewing opportunity. Though alcoholic strength is often associated with this style, many modern examples with modest alcohol content exist. (When old ales were created, they were actually *lower* in alcohol than many ales of the day.) As a result, you can make an old ale to suit almost any occasion.

Let's begin with a rundown of the style characteristics and then look back into history to learn more about how this style came to be. I've included an unusually long set of style characteristics in order to reflect the current commercial reality of the style as well as show the guidelines accepted for most homebrew competitions.

I recently examined published information on nearly seventy old ales produced primarily in the British Isles.[1] This information was used to establish the style characteristics listed in table 21.1.

For those who brew competitively, the style has been defined a bit more tightly. The 1995 National Homebrew Competition (NHC) guidelines are listed in table 21.2.

The Origins of Old Ale

One could plumb the history of English brewing for many years before developing a complete understanding of the terms "old ale," "strong ale," and "stock ale." The three terms have at times been used indiscriminately to describe the same cask of liquid.[2] Despite this confusion, their interesting history will provide a fuller understanding of these styles.

During the seventeenth century, it would have been redundant to say "strong" ale, because the word "ale" denoted strength and the word "beer" was reserved for "small malt liquors."[3] This continued to be true during the nineteenth century, when virtually all ale recipes had a starting gravity of greater than 1.060 — and many were above 1.090.

Chapter 15 includes many examples of these strong ales. The source that provided these examples also used the term "Old Ale" in presenting a couple of recipes. One was for London XXX Old Ale,[4] which has a starting gravity of 1.086 — lower than other XXX ale recipes in the same publication.

This old ale has only a slightly lower hopping level but significantly higher saccharification temperature than other XXX ales. The higher mash temperature produces a more dextrinous wort that results in a lower degree of apparent attenuation — 58 percent for the old ale versus 62 to 71 percent for others. In addition to these processing differences, the recipe notes make clear that the old ale was aged one full year before distribution.

Table 21.1
General Characteristics of Old Ales

Gravity	Mean: 1.057	Range: 1.040–1.125 (10–31 °B)	Malty, alcohol evident, medium- to full-bodied; nutty, fruity, vinous character possible
Bitterness	Mean: 33	Range: 15–75 IBU	Low to medium bitterness perception
BU:GU Ratio	Mean: 0.58	Range: 0.45 to 0.70	This measure gives the ratio of bitterness (in IBU) to gravity (in GU).
Hop flavor and aroma			Low to medium hop aroma and flavor
Color		7–30 °SRM	Amber to very dark brown
Other flavors			Low to medium esters, low diacetyl
Apparent extract		1.012–1.040 (3–10 °B)	Apparent attenuation: 56%–70%
Alcohol (volume)		3.75%–11.0%	

A second recipe from this source, labeled Dorset XXX Old Ale,[5] shows many similar characteristics, including a relatively high mash temperature that produced low attenuation at 58 percent. Aging is not explicitly stated, but after fermentation the beer was transferred to a "vat," which is the usual resting place for aging beers.

Like modern English old ales, both of these beers were brewed for low attenuation, and that seems to have been a key characteristic in distinguishing them from other ales brewed to a similar starting gravity. In addition, the extent of aging before distribution probably also set them apart from other products.

Another reference, this one from 1881, supports the fact that extensive aging may have been the chief trait of old ales. It lists two old ales aged two and three years (see table 21.3).

Table 21.2
NHC Guidelines for Characteristics of Old Ales

Gravity	1.055–1.075 (14–19 °B)
Bitterness	30–40 IBU
Hop flavor and aroma	Can be assertive
Color	10–16 °SRM, deep amber to copper
Apparent extract	1.008–1.020 (3–5 °B)
Alcohol (volume)	6%–8%

Source: American Homebrewers Association 1995 National Homebrew Competition Rules and Regulations *(Boulder, Colo.: American Homebrewers Association, 1995).*

According to other sources, aging was commonplace for porters and stouts at this time, and it is generally acknowledged that such aging played an important role in developing the flavor profile of ales as well. During aging, beers developed a distinctive flavor trait, an acidic and perhaps fruity character along with a horselike or leathery character and some solventlike notes. Many of these flavors are produced by the presence of *Brettanomyces* and various other microbes in the aging vats.[6] This phenomenon was described in 1890, in a report from a consultant to the English hop industry: "There was formerly a taste among English consumers for old ale, which had to be vatted for at least a year and probably more, before it was consumed, and acquired a sub-acid flavor, particularly relished by the consumer . . ."[7] Consistent with this, laboratory analyses from the late 1800s show that the aged beers from England displayed a rather high level of acidity.[8]

From this data it is clear that (1) old ales were aged before distribution, and (2) an acidic taste was part of the flavor profile. What remains unclear is the exact rationale for naming the beers "old ale." Use of this appellation may indicate the use of an old recipe or old brewing methods, as is seen with the German alt beers. However, given the aging employed, the term "old" may simply refer to the maturity of the product it describes. Still, it is clear that most beers were aged before consumption during the 1800s, so the old ales may have been unique only in the length of time they aged.

It appears that aging was indeed a distinguishing characteristic of old ales at least through the first few decades of the twentieth century. However, this issue is complicated somewhat by the production of another aged product, called stock ale. It appears that stock ale had the acidic character of old ale and was not intended for direct consumption but for blending with fresh beer to give it the flavor of ale that had been aged for several months.

English brewing scientist Horace Brown explained in about 1886 the operating cycle of many ale breweries at that time: "Burton breweries were almost completely shut down during the summer, the main brewing operations being carried on between the months of October and May. This practice of course, entailed the carrying of very large stocks of season-brewed beer for use in the summer."[9]

Infection and other "fetters" that affected beer flavor prevented warm-weather brewing. As an antidote for this, it was discovered that newly brewed summer beer could be "hardened" or "brought forward" by mixing it with a small portion of aged product from the brewery's stocks of winter-brewed beer.[10] This process quickly readied the summer beer for consumption so that it could be drunk before acquiring unpalatable flavors.

As this practice became widespread, the term "stock ale" was applied to the aged winter-brewed beer that was used as

Table 21.3
Differences in Gravity and Alcohol for Old Ales Aged Two and Three Years

Somerset Old Vat	OG	% Alcohol
2 years old	1.071	6.5
3 years old	1.085	8.6

Source: *H. S. Corran*, A History of Brewing *(London: David & Charles, 1975).*

the hardener. When fall came and brewing commenced again, any remaining stock ale might be sold whole as — you guessed it — old ale.[11]

There are many examples of stock ale in North America by the end of the nineteenth century. Their gravities were not unusually high by the standards of the time, but they often contained the high acidity previously noted in old ales. The Wahl-Henius *Handy-Book* reports the average values for nine American stock ales of 1896 with a gravity of 1.067 and lactic acid content of 0.256.[12] (Normal beers have lactic acid levels below 0.150, so this would have been a pretty acidic beer.) Other individual stock ale examples cited by Wahl-Henius were a bit tamer, with gravities between 1.058 and 1.065, with low levels of acidity.[13]

During the late nineteenth century the terms "old" and "stock" could be applied to either ale or porter, as shown in an 1890 handbill from Besley's Waukegan Brewing Co. (see figure 21.1). It shows the following listings: Pale Stock Ale, Old Stock Ale, and Old Porter, as well as "Present Use" ale and porter.

By the start of the twentieth century, two distinct styles had emerged. Old ale was defined as a high gravity ale (1.080 to 1.090) that is aged for a considerable period before distribution. High acidity, low apparent attenuation, and assertive hopping are typical of old ales. Stock ale, at least in North America, was a 1.055 to 1.070 gravity ale used for blending. It might be sold as old ale in late fall. Significant acidity is probably present in most samples. Like old ales, stock ales were probably made to be quite dextrinous. Across the Atlantic in England, the stock ales may have had a higher gravity, similar to the old ales I have mentioned.

Now I have identified old ale and stock ale, but what's missing is some sense of what strong ale might be.

Many ales were brewed to a high gravity and were therefore quite alcoholic in the

mid-1800s. Not long after that, India pale ale took over as the most popular style of beer in England. It was produced from a lower gravity — generally in the 1.055 to 1.065 range — and so had less alcoholic strength than the earlier London ales. It was only after this change in the marketplace that the "strong" label appeared on English ales.[14] Around 1895, I find the term "strong" applied to a beer with a gravity in excess of 1.100. Certainly this beer would have been a truly remarkable departure from the average 1.060 ale of that time.

Unfortunately, this one example, produced in Burton, seems to have been the precursor of barley wine rather than an offspring in the old ale tradition. Furthermore, I find no other significant historical references to strong ale.

Despite this, the term "strong" still finds some contemporary use in labeling ales. In England, where the normal gravity for a bitter ale tops out in the 1.040s, a "strong bitter" might have a gravity anywhere in the range from 1.043 to 1.060.[15] Above this, strong ales are also recognized with gravities of 1.060 to 1.080.[16]

The Modern Age of Old Ale

As the twentieth century got rolling, the combined effects of lager beer, refrigeration, and Prohibition wrought serious changes on the production of beer — and on the minds of brewers. By the time the Second World War wrapped up, lager was king and little was being written in the brewing literature about ales.

Yet, as I survey the scene today, I find dozens of products labeled "old" (or perhaps "owd") ale. They cover a huge range in gravity and bitterness, and only a handful seem at all related to the old ales known one hundred years ago.

In his *Beer Companion*, Michael Jackson outlines a three-part classification of old ale that he has come to appreciate as the result of tastings conducted by Mark Darber

Figure 21.1
Besley's Waukegan Brewing Company

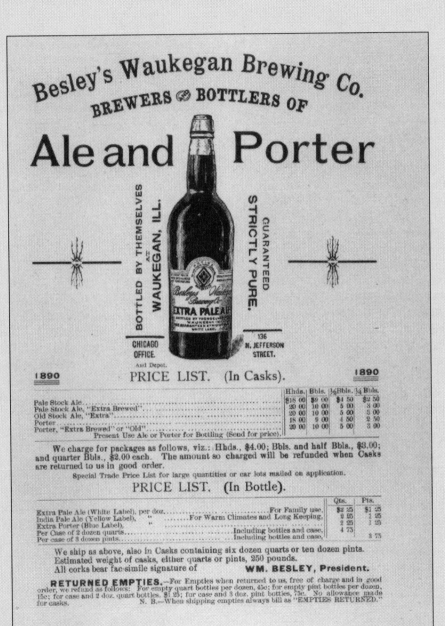

at the White Horse pub in London.[17] The three are (1) strong mild ales, >1.040 OG; (2) dark (and in some cases, strong) bitters; and (3) strong ales.

This combination of categories accommodates the broad range of examples found displaying the "old" moniker these days. But although their gravities and bitterness levels cover a broad range, the composition of their malts and hops is remarkably similar across these ranges.

Several classic examples of old ale can be readily obtained in the United States. The best known is Thomas Hardy's Ale. At 1.125, this beer has an original gravity well into the barley wine range, but Britain's best beer writers continue to classify it as an old or strong ale.[18] Between presentation and flavor impact, this beer is hard to forget. It is intensely malty and sharply alcoholic with a soft vinous character underneath that makes it very drinkable. This example is vintage dated, and additional aging by the consumer is recommended by the brewer.

The arrestingly named Old Peculier has a heritage dating to 1890, and Jackson says it is "arguably the definitive example" of the middle gravity (1.055 to 1.080) old ales.[19] Fruity and soft, it reminds some observers of black currants. With an original gravity of 1.057 and 28 IBU, this product is close to the median of all contemporary commercial examples.

Gale's Prize Old Ale is another example with a long heritage and widespread renown. It clocks in at 1.094 and 48 IBU and is quite fruity but intensely dry with hints of raisins and some acidic notes.[20] This beer fits the description once given by a nineteenth-century beer writer who described aged ale as being "racy but mellow."

I haven't seen the lower-gravity examples of the style in the United States, but those who travel might pick them up while visiting the British Isles. Three that I've enjoyed include:

• Old Buzzard (Cottleigh): 1.045 OG; light brown; nice caramel-like notes with some nuttiness and a slight fruitiness; very soft finish with lingering caramel and fruit notes.

• Old Thumper (Ringwood): 1.058 OG; pale to light amber; soft and fruity like peaches or apricots; on the sweet side — some would consider it cloying — with a lingering fruitiness in finish and a hazy appearance. Now brewed in the United States by the Shipyard Brewery in Portland, Maine, but quite different.

• Old Navigation (Hoskins and Oldfield): 1.071 OG; deep brown; a bit fruity; sweet with malt and alcoholic warmth; well attenuated.

Brewing Old Ales

Despite the wide range of gravities and BU levels found among contemporary old ales, they share considerable similarities. Specifically, the malt bills and hop varieties used across the style form a unique pattern that is valid at all points on the gravity continuum. Let's examine these two aspects of the style before trying to sort out the gravity and bitterness issues.

Malt Bill

As with most English ale styles, old ales are typically built around a well-modified pale ale malt. Occasional reference may be seen to mild or amber malt as a major component, but these days pale malt accounts for the majority of the grist in all commercial examples.

A wide variety of other ingredients may be found in old ales, including gravity enhancers such as malt extract, maize, and sugar, as well as character grains such as chocolate malt, roast barley, and black malt. The tables and accompanying notes listed below provide an analysis of old ale malt bills. The incidence data is based on the sixty-seven commercial recipes that listed their ingredients, while the proportion data is based on a subset of this group (twenty-seven recipes) that also listed proportion data (see table 21.4).

Further analysis of the recipe data allows classification of the malt bills into two major and five minor groups. The two major groups each account for about half of all the recipes, and they can be called "pale" and "dark." They are distinguished by whether the recipes include any chocolate malt, roast barley, or black malt.

Within the pale group, most recipes include crystal malt as well as some adjunct: wheat, maize, flaked barley, or sugar. A small number of recipes exclude crystal malt or rely solely on pale malt.

Within the dark group, the recipes are fairly evenly split between two camps. In the first, chocolate malt is used; in the second, black malt is preferred. It is extremely rare for these two color malts to be used together in an old ale recipe. When chocolate malt is used, crystal malt is included 80 percent of the time. When black malt is used, crystal is used slightly less often — only 67 percent of the time. Also, within the black malt group, wheat is included about half the time. The use of sugar in about one-third of the recipes is consistent across the major groupings of this analysis.

The analysis can be mapped in outline form, as shown in table 21.5. In all cases, the percentages refer to the total database of sixty-seven recipes.

The distribution of these major malt bill types is consistent across the range of gravities represented by current old ale styles. All recipe groups have examples below 1.045 and above 1.065, and each group's mean gravity falls between 1.052 and 1.062.

The one exception to this even distribution of gravity is above about 1.080. These high-gravity old ales are twice as likely to come from the pale-colored group as from a dark-colored group. This observation supports the distinction of a contemporary substyle of strong ale, as I mentioned earlier. It could be said that these strong ales generally are made without dark malts and possess a gravity of 1.080 or greater. One feature that further sets these strong ales apart from the other old ales is the lack of commercial old ales with gravities between 1.070 and 1.080.

Examination of NHC second-round old ale recipes shows both similarities and contrasts with current commercial practice. The use of crystal and chocolate malts, for instance, seems to be consistent between the two. However, the NHC second-round beers were brewed without the use of black malt and used roast barley, on occasion, instead. Sugar and other adjuncts are under-represented among the NHC beers, which is not surprising given the all-malt orientation of the hobby. At the same time, the use of wheat, flaked barley, and CaraPils is increased in the NHC brews compared to the commercial formulations. Finally, the NHC beers use several specialty malts, such as mild, brown, aromatic, Special B, and toasted malt (see table 21.6).

Generally, single-infusion mashes are ideal for this style, and a high rest temperature should be selected to produce a highly dextrinous wort. The NHC second-round beers used mash temperatures that averaged 155 °F (68 °C), although British home-brew books recommend slightly lower temperatures of 154 °F (68 °C), or even 152 °F (67 °C).[21] I would try to hit a temperature of 155 to 158 °F (68 to 70 °C).

As with barley wines and other high-gravity brews, malt extract can be used to advantage for a portion of the total gravity. You may have noticed that even some commercial brewers in Britain use malt extract to help hit the higher gravities demanded by some old ale recipes. If it works for them, it will certainly work for you! If you are able to do so, select a brand of malt extract that produces low attenuation

Table 21.4
Grain Incidence and Proportion in Commercial Old Ale Grain Bills

Grain Used (Range %)	Proportion	Incidence
Pale (74–100)	▼ at 89% (range 74–100)	🍺🍺🍺🍺
Crystal (3–17)	▼ at 7%	🍺🍺🍺
Chocolate (1–10)	▼ at 3%	🍺
Roast (3)	▼ at 3%	🍺
Black (1–5)	▼ at 3%	🍺
Wheat (1–10)	▼ at 6%	🍺
Sugar (2–18)	▼ at 8%	🍺🍺
Other (1–16)	▼ at 8%	🍺

Proportion scale: 0% 10% 20% 30% 40% 50% 60% 70% 80% 90% 100%

[a]Sugar includes invert sugar, cane sugar, maltose syrup, glucose syrup, and brown sugar.
[b]Wheat includes wheat malt, torrified wheat, wheat flour, and wheat syrup.
[c]Other includes flaked barley, flaked maize, amber malt, and malt extract.

Key: This chart shows what proportion of the grain bill was provided by various grains in sixty-seven commercial old ale recipes. The line next to each grain gives the range of values used by different brewers; this range is also listed below "Grains Used." The triangle above each line indicates the average proportion used across all recipes.

The icons in the column on the right show how often the sixty-seven commercial old ale recipes included each grain. (Percentage figures indicate how many of the recipes included the grain.)

🍺 = rarely (30% or less)   🍺🍺 = sometimes (30% to 60%)
🍺🍺🍺 = often (60% to 90%)   🍺🍺🍺🍺 = usually (90% or more)

levels so that the results will be in keeping with the demands of the style.

Hop Selection

The breadth and variety of malts used in old ale recipes contrasts with the simplicity and narrowness of the hop varieties employed.

As with many English ale styles, Goldings hops prove to be the most popular. Goldings varieties (primarily East Kent, but also some Whitbread or Styrian) are found in three-fourths of all old ales, often in combination with Challenger or Fuggle.

Those recipes that do not include Goldings varieties are most likely to be hopped with Challenger (19 percent) or with a less frequently used variety (9 percent) such as Northdown, Hallertau, or Progress. The overall incidence of the major hop varieties in British commercial

Table 21.5
Categorization of Commercial Old Ale Recipes

I. Pale Colored (48%)
    A. Pale & Crystal Malts + Adjuncts (35%)
    B. Pale Malt + Adjuncts (8%)
    C. Pale Malt Only (5%)
II. Dark Colored (52%)
    A. Chocolate Malt Based (28%)
        1. With crystal (20%)
        2. Without crystal (5%)
        3. With other dark malts, +/- crystal (3%)
    B. Black Malt Based (22%)
        1. With crystal, no wheat (10%)
        2. With wheat, no crystal (4.5%)
        3. With wheat and crystal (4.5%)
        4. No wheat or crystal (3%)
    C. Other Dark Malt Bills (2%)

old ales is: Goldings, 74 percent; Challenger, 47 percent; Fuggle, 42 percent; and others, 25 percent.

I find it interesting that Challenger is used more commonly than Fuggle. Challenger was bred from Northern Brewer stock to be disease-resistant and is reported to have good flavor and aroma characteristics. Some recipes report no other hops and may employ Challenger for all phases of production, including dry hopping. Old ale would be an interesting style with which to explore the use of Challenger hops, whether alone or in combination with Goldings, if you can acquire them through your supplier.

Other hops found in old ale recipes include: Northdown, 6 percent; Hallertau, 4 percent; Progress, 4 percent; Northern Brewer, 3 percent; Target, 3 percent; Pride of Ringwood, 3 percent; and Omega, 1 percent.

Not all of the commercial recipe descriptions offer detailed information on how the hops were processed, but it is clear that the use of dry hopping, hop backs, and kettle steeps to impart hop aroma is fairly common with this style. At least a quarter of all recipes specifically mentioned dry hopping.

Among NHC second-round brews, the main hops used in old ales are domestic varieties. Table 21.7 shows the incidence of the various hop varieties used by these brewers.

The average recipe included just three hop additions, with half of all hop additions made before the last twenty-nine minutes of the boil. Virtually all recipes included either an aroma or dry hop addition (see table 21.8).

Bitterness and Balance

Table 21.9 shows the spectrum of BU:GU ratios exhibited by the twenty-eight commercial old ales for which BU data were available. Although the range is vast — from 0.35 to 0.95 — 80 percent of the recipes fall between 0.45 to 0.70. The average value of 0.58 falls neatly in the center of this range.

Given the various malt bill approaches, you may wonder (as I did) if there is some difference in BU:GU ratio based on the character of the malt bill. Evaluation indicates that all but one of the malt bill groups seem similar with regard to bitterness balance.

Table 21.6
Old Ale Grain Bill in NHC Second-Round Recipes

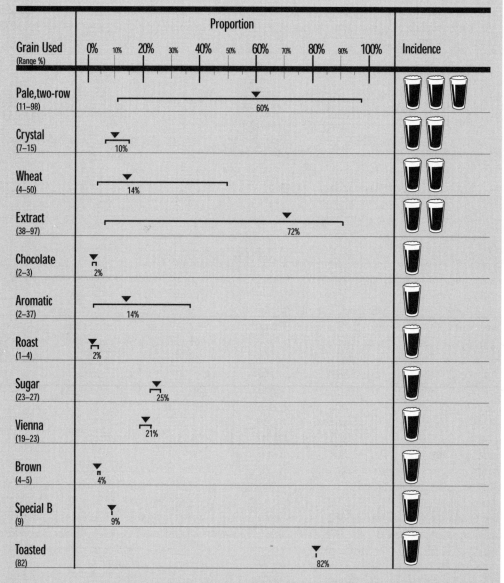

Grain Used (Range %)	Proportion	Incidence
Pale, two-row (11–98)	60%	🍺🍺🍺
Crystal (7–15)	10%	🍺🍺
Wheat (4–50)	14%	🍺🍺
Extract (38–97)	72%	🍺🍺
Chocolate (2–3)	2%	🍺
Aromatic (2–37)	14%	🍺
Roast (1–4)	2%	🍺
Sugar (23–27)	25%	🍺
Vienna (19–23)	21%	🍺
Brown (4–5)	4%	🍺
Special B (9)	9%	🍺
Toasted (82)	82%	🍺

Proportion scale: 0% 10% 20% 30% 40% 50% 60% 70% 80% 90% 100%

Key: This chart shows what proportion of the grain bill was provided by various grains in thirteen old ale recipes. The line next to each grain gives the range of values used by different brewers; this range is also listed below "Grains Used." The triangle above each line indicates the average proportion used across all recipes.

The icons in the column on the right show how often the thirteen old ale recipes included each grain. (Percentage figures indicate how many of the recipes included the grain.)

🍺 = rarely (30% or less)   🍺🍺 = sometimes (30% to 60%)

🍺🍺🍺 = often (60% to 90%)   🍺🍺🍺🍺 = usually (90% or more)

Table 21.7
Hops Used in NHC Second-Round Old Ales

Hop	Bitter	Flavor	Aroma	Dry	Total
Cascade	3	0	3	1	7
Chinook	3	1	1	0	5
Liberty	3	0	1	0	4
Perle	3	0	1	0	4
Willamette	0	2	0	2	4
Centennial	2	1	0	0	3
Fuggles	2	1	0	0	3
Goldings	1	0	1	1	3
Hallertau	1	0	0	1	2
Mt. Hood	0	1	0	1	2
Cluster	1	0	0	0	1
N. Brewer	1	0	0	0	1
Saaz	0	1	0	0	1

Note: The data in this chart show the number of times each hop was used across the fourteen recipes analyzed.

Using the categories presented in table 21.5, the pale-colored ales (I.A through I.C in table 21.5) and the two major dark-colored groupings (II.A and II.B) all show a wide range of BU:GU ratios, as well as mean BU:GU ratios that are quite similar (see table 21.9). The miscellaneous group of dark-colored ales (II.A.3 and II.C) has a notably lower range and mean.

The highly hopped examples (BU:GU >0.90) from groups 1, 2, and 3 may represent the "dark" or "strong bitter" substyle of the old ale family, while group 4 may come close to the "strong mild" substyle, as categorized by Darber and Jackson. Lesser hopped examples (BU:GU <0.50) from groups 2 and 3 might also fit into the "strong mild" classification. In the "strong ale" substyle, hopping levels also tend to be a bit lower, with a range from 0.38 to 0.60 and an average of 0.48 (based on analysis of four recipes).

From this analysis it seems clear that most old ales should be hopped to achieve a BU:GU ratio of about 0.58 and certainly in the range between 0.45 and 0.70.

Table 21.8
Hop Additions in NHC Second-Round Old Ales

	Average Number of Hop Additions per Recipe	Size of Late Additions (oz./gal.)	Size of Late Additions (oz./5 gal.)
Boil	1.4	—	—
Flavor	0.5	0.17	0.86
Aroma	0.5	0.12	0.61
Dry	0.4	0.21	1.04
Total	2.8	—	—

Note: Total number of recipes analyzed = 14.

Table 21.9
Old Ale BU:GU Ratios

Group	No. of Recipes	Min.	Max.	Average
1. All pale malts[a]	12	0.40	0.95	0.59
2. Chocolate malts[b]	4	0.45	0.94	0.62
3. Black malts[c]	7	0.49	0.91	0.61
4. Other dark malts[d]	5	0.36	0.67	0.47

[a] Pale and crystal malts and adjuncts (see table 21.5, group I).
[b] Chocolate malt with and without crystal malt (see table 21.5, group II, A1 and A2).
[c] Black malt with and without crystal and wheat malts (see table 21.5, group II, B1 thru B4).
[d] Other dark malts; chocolate malt with other dark malts, with or without crystal malt (see table 21.5, group II, A3 and C).

Darker, mild beer–like examples, as well as formulations with original gravities of 1.080 or higher, might go toward the less bitter end of the range, with an average BU:GU of 0.47 or 0.48 in a range from 0.36 to 0.60 or so. Guidelines for levels of bitterness in old ales are based on these conclusions (see table 21.10).

Yeast, Fermentation, and Maturation

The history of old ale makes clear the importance of fermentation and aging to this style. An old ale with a gravity of 1.060 or greater will probably be more drinkable and more interesting after at least two or three months of aging. As the gravity goes up, the period of aging that will produce improvement increases as well. The strong-ale types will improve over many years, making a wonderful addition to your cellar.

During maturation you have an excellent opportunity to dry hop the beer, as many English brewers do. Ideally, whole hops should be added to the secondary fermenter. One source says that the optimal length of contact between dry hops and the beer is twenty-eight days.[22]

If you want to emulate the acidic old ales of one hundred years ago, you might inoculate part of a batch with *Brettanomyces lambicus* and leave it to age for a year or more. The resulting product could be consumed straight as old ale or blended with a newer batch after the fashion of the stock ales.

As for yeast selection, little is mentioned in the descriptions of commercial old ales. Where information is included it usually indicates some unique feature. Old Peculier, for instance, uses a mixed strain that has been in use for more than thirty years.[23] In general, if you choose an English yeast with low to moderate attenuation properties, you will probably be happy with the results. Whitbread, London, and Irish strains have all been used by the old ales that advanced to the second round of the AHA's National Homebrew Competition. Of course, some brewers use the good old American ale yeast, and more than one has opted for the sweet German ale style.

Water

Old ales are made by brewers in many parts of the British Isles, and the water employed no doubt varies considerably from area to area. London, Burton, and Edinburgh waters probably all find their way into old ale products.

The only data on water treatment by commercial brewers comes from Michael Jackson, who notes that Eldridge Pope has "very hard, chalky water, which has to be softened slightly" and that Gale's uses well water "with some bicarbonate."

Table 21.10
Old Ale Bitterness Guidelines

| Gravity | Recommended Bitterness Units | | |
	Average (BU:GU=0.58)	Low (BU:GU=0.45)	High (BU:GU=0.70)
1.040	23	18	28
1.045	26	20	32
1.050	29	23	35
1.055	32	25	39
1.060	35	27	42
1.065	38	29	46
1.070	41	32	49
1.075	44	34	53
Gravity	Average (BU:GU=0.48)	Low (BU:GU=0.36)	High (BU:GU=0.60)
1.080	38	29	48
1.085	41	31	51
1.090	43	32	54
1.095	46	34	57
1.0100	48	36	60
1.0110	53	40	66
1.0120	58	43	72

As with barley wines, the British homebrewing guides recommend a mild burtonization of the brewing water for old ales.[24] The basic water treatment recommended by these sources applies to relatively soft or carbonate water. It calls for precipitation of carbonate and addition of 1 to 2 teaspoons of gypsum as well as ½ teaspoon of Epsom salts. (Note: Add the Epsom salts after carbonate removal.) These salt additions would *increase* ion concentrations in 6.6 U.S. gallons (25 liters) by the following amounts: calcium, 60 to 120 parts per million; magnesium, 8 parts per million; and sulfate, 165 to 300 parts per million.

Conclusion

If you like old ales, there is plenty of opportunity for exploration of the style. For starters, you could make a beer following each of the three major malt bill strategies at a range of specific gravities (say every 10 GU). What an interesting collection of beers that would be! Then, of course, there is the variation in bitterness allowed. At the very least, you'd have to choose between low, medium, or high bitterness for each recipe. You'd have more than fifty beers to brew just to explore these three variables, never mind the choices you have in hop variety, yeast selection, and aroma hop additions.

Given all these options, it may be that a full exploration of this style is a better project for a whole homebrew club rather than just one or two brewers. But however you choose to explore the style, it should be fun.

Key Success Factors in Brewing Old Ales

- Select a grain bill strategy: pale, dark with chocolate malt, or dark with black malt (see tables 21.4 and 21.5).

- Decide on your target gravity: between 1.055 to 1.075 for competition brews, or between 1.040 and 1.125 for general exploration of the style.

- Conduct a single-infusion mash with a rest temperature between 154 and 158 °F (68 and 70 °C).

- Aim for a BU:GU ratio of about 0.58 when gravities are below 1.075, and of about 0.48 when gravities are above 1.080 (see table 21.9).

- Select English hops such as East Kent Goldings, Challenger, or Fuggle for an English interpretation, or opt for U.S.-grown Cascade, Liberty, Willamette, or Fuggle hops.

- Aroma hopping is optional but fairly common. Add about 0.66 ounce for 5 gallons late in the boil, or 1 ounce in 5 gallons for dry hopping.

- Select a low to moderate attenuation English ale yeast.

- Mature the beer properly based on its starting gravity.

22 PILSENER AND OTHER PALE LAGERS

Probably everyone who drinks beer knows the Pilsener style. Its popularity spans the world, touching all continents and all countries. One might wonder if this widespread popularity comes from a long history of evolution that transplanted the style into each of the cultures where it thrives. In fact, just the opposite is true. Pilsener is very young as beer styles go, so young that history has recorded its exact birth date.

Even among the relatively young lagers, Pilsener is a newcomer. Lager brewing, using a bottom-fermentation yeast and cool fermentation temperatures, can be documented to the fifteenth century.[1] In fact, the famous Bavarian purity law, Reinheitsgebot, applied to the production of lager beers. Another Bavarian lager law established in 1553 set the times of year one could brew as running from September 29, in the fall to April 23, in the spring.[2]

By the dawn of the Pilsener age in the middle of the nineteenth century, the Bavarians had been making lagers for about four hundred years. Chief among these was what we today call a "dunkel" — that is, a deep copper or brown lager with a pronounced malt character. Bottom-fermented bock beer had also been developed in Bavaria.

A New Beer for Pilsen — and Posterity

The home of Pilsener is not Bavaria but rather Bohemia. In the modern Czech Republic one finds the city of Pilsen (or Plzeň in Czech). Both wheat and barley beers have been brewed in this city since 1295.[3] In addition, some exchange of beers and brewing techniques seems to have taken place with Bavaria over the years. Despite this, however, as recently as 1840 the Bohemians were still brewing ales.

Although Pilsen's ales were somewhat lackluster, destiny seems to have appointed the city to be the home of a great beer style. The largely agrarian Bohemian economy produced both barley and hops of the finest quality. The barley was two-row Moravian, or Bohemian, barley, long regarded and still revered as highly desirable for brewing.

The country's hops belonged to the "red" hop family, which was prized for its fine aroma. From the Zatec region in western Bohemia, these hops were known then as Zatec Red, but today we call them Saaz. Even then they were regarded as one of the finest hops in the world. To protect their value to the region, the king made it a crime punishable by death to smuggle the rhizomes (hop roots) out of the country.

Then, too, there was the water. Pilsen possesses remarkably soft water, with less than 50 parts per million of hardness. Today the value of this softness in making pale beers is widely appreciated by brewers, but in the nineteenth century the importance of the water was little understood.

As of 1840, Pilsen was a treasure trove of wonderful beer ingredients: the best barley, the finest hops, wonderful soft water. Unfortunately, the town's brewers were still fermenting their beers with ale yeast, and the product left something to be desired. In an effort to improve their beer, the townspeople decided to build a new brewery.[4]

A brewer named either Joseph or Felix Groll was hired to oversee the project.[5] The fact that his name has been lost to history indicates the small credit he receives for the beer that subsequently made the brewery famous. More noted is the contribution of a traveling monk who brought the Bavarian lager yeast to Pilsen and gave it to the new brewery. This yeast provided the final element needed for production of the beer we today call Pilsener Urquell.

The German word *Urquell* means "original spring," and the very first barrel of this original Pilsener was tapped on November 11, 1842.[6] Unfortunately, little was recorded about the flavor of that first beer. Nonetheless, it must have been similar to the flavor represented by the style today, given the rapid acceptance and widespread imitation the formulation experienced in the years to follow.

The Color of Pilsener

One aspect of the Pilsener style that caught everyone's attention was the pale color. The Munich beers of the time were brown, and Burton's pale ales displayed the amber to copper hues still known today. Using a measure that must have been similar to the Lovibond scale then in use, the Pilsener beers were given color ratings of 3.5 to 4.3 (see table 22.1). By contrast, most other lagers had values between 5 and 6.

The pale color of the Pilsners was remarkable for an all-malt beer. To understand this paleness, remember that most color comes from melanoidin formation, beginning with the drying and kilning of the malt. Historical data leave little doubt that the Pilsen malt was pale indeed.

Today, most lager malts achieve a final kilning temperature of 170 to 185 °F (70 to 85 °C). Of course, during the nineteenth century the kilning process was harder to control, so somewhat lower temperatures were targeted. One Austrian source from that time indicates that normal kilning temperatures were 145 to 167 °F (63 to 75 °C).[7] By comparison, the Pilsen malt wasn't really kilned at all, it was just dried, with typical final temperatures of 100 to 122 °F (38 to 50 °C).[8]

Today we know that such low kiln temperatures will remove 90 percent of the water, but without higher-temperature kilning the residual moisture in the malt will allow it to spoil after a time. The solution to that problem, of course, is to use the malt quickly once it is produced. The maltings that supply the Pilsener Urquell brewery are located at the brewery today, as they always have been. No doubt the proximity of the maltster to the brewer has allowed rapid consumption of the pale Pilsener malt to be a common practice.

The other common sources of melanoidin production during brewing come during the mash and during the boil. The process at Pilsen seems to have been quite similar to those employed at other breweries of the day, starting with a triple decoction mash that was at least as intense as those practiced elsewhere. Thus, the key difference in melanoidin production seems to have come in the production of the malt itself.

Water chemistry may also have played a role in the lighter-colored product — at least when compared to Munich beers.

Table 22.1
The Color of Pilsner Beer, circa 1882

Pilsen, Municipal Brewery	3.5
Pilsen export, Municipal Brewery	4.0
Pilsen lager, Joint-stock brewery	4.3
Other German and Austrian lagers*	5.5
Ale	10
Bock	14.7–16.7
Porter	40

Source: J. E. Thausing, W. T. Brannt, A. Schwarz, and A. H. Bauer, The Theory and Practice of the Preparation of Malt and the Fabrication of Beer (London: Henry Carey Baird & Co., 1882), 750-751.
* This value is an average of twenty-seven lagers.

Water analyses were just coming into vogue, and even then they showed differences in water between the great brewing centers of Europe. The values in table 22.2 show how very soft the Pilsen water was compared to brewing waters from Burton-on-Trent and Munich. Furthermore, much of the hardness in the Munich water is attributable to calcium carbonate.

The high carbonate levels (and accompanying high pH level) of Munich water most likely led to extraction of polyphenols from the husks during mashing. These compounds turn red when oxidized, so they probably played a role in the unshakable darkness of the Munich beers. In fact, evidence indicates that Munich brewers tried unsuccessfully to make pale lagers for several decades during the nineteenth century. Finally, around 1895 they issued a declaration that pale lager would never be made in Munich.[9]

The pale color of Pilsener — coming when it did — probably made the beer what it is today. By the mid-nineteenth century, glass containers were replacing stone, wood, and metal tankards for the serving and consumption of beer. Thus, consumers could see the beer. Clarity took on new importance, and the novelty of a tasty pale beer had instant appeal. On the continent as in England, this new pale style quickly became popular.

The Pilsener Decoction Mash

No discussion of historical brewing practices can bypass an assessment of mashing methods. Indeed, the brewers of Pilsen departed considerably from the

Table 22.2
Total Mineral Content of Some Brewing Waters, circa 1882

City	Parts per 10,000 parts of water
Pilsen	1.49
Burton-on-Trent	11.35
Munich*	5.60

Source: Thausing, et al., Preparation of Malt and the Fabrication of Beer, 124-125.
* The value for Munich is an average of seven different beer analyses.

routine decoction process practiced elsewhere in Europe.

According to one Vienna brewer writing in 1887, the Bohemians tended to use a greater number of smaller-sized decoctions during brewing.[10] This, it seems, is linked to the size of the brew kettle in which the decoctions are boiled as much as to any purposeful management of the mash temperatures.

The process this source describes utilizes three — or perhaps four — thick mashes for the main part of the mashing sequence. The brewer boils each decoction until "scum (or foam) no longer rises to the surface and the wort is a beautiful yellow-gold color."[11] Another source describing this same process gives the times for boiling each decoction as thirty minutes for the first, twenty-five for the second, and twenty for the third.[12]

After the third decoction is completed and the mash-out temperature is achieved, an unusual fourth step is described by both these nineteenth-century sources.[13] A small amount of water (equal to 3 percent of the original mash liquor) is added to the kettle and brought to a boil. Wort is run off from the lauter tun until it runs clear. The cloudy wort thus obtained, rather than being recirculated as is done today, was added to the boiling water in the kettle. Here it was boiled for a few minutes and then transferred back to the lauter tun without disturbing the grain bed. The apparent goal of this step was to denature the last active mash enzymes.

Twentieth-century brewing texts also credit Pilsen with a unique decoction mash process. It is still run in just two vessels, the mash/lauter tun and the kettle, but both seem to contain a portion of the mash throughout the process. As explained by the English brewer H. Lloyd Hind, a portion of the mash stays in the kettle at the end of each decoction.[14] This residual is kept at a boil in the kettle in order to quickly raise the next thick mash

up to its first rest temperature. Table 22.3 provides the details of such a mash.

To facilitate the decoction process, the Pilsen mash appears to be quite thin. Hind quotes a water-to-grist ratio of 6.0 to 6.3 hectoliters per 100 kilograms of grain. By comparison, Noonan recommends the equivalent of 2.3 to 3.9 hectoliters per 100 kilograms (36 to 60 ounces per pound) in *Brewing Lager Beer,*[15] and Hind gives a range of 3 to 4 hectoliters per 100 kilograms for dark lagers.[16]

DeClerck confirms the use of thin mashes at Pilsen, although he puts emphasis on the pulling of a thinner portion of the mash for the decoction itself.[17] It seems logical that a thinner decoction would most likely result from such a thin mash.

From the process described by Hind, we find that the rest temperatures for this mash occur at fairly commonly accepted points, specifically: 95 °F (35 °C), 110.5 °F (44 °C), 144.5 °F (63 °C), 162.5 °F (73 °C). The last two give us some pause. The saccharification temperature of 144.5 °F (63 °C) seems quite low given the full body generally exhibited by the classic Pilsener. Also, a final temperature of 162.5 °F (73 °C) is below that of 167 °F (75 °C) generally required at mash-out.

One possible explanation for this apparent paradox (high body, low mash temperature) may come from the overall chemistry of the mash. The very thin mash combined with the low calcium content of the Pilsen water undoubtedly reduces the resistance of the amylases to thermal breakdown.[18] Since alpha-amylase generally shows better heat resistance than beta-amylase, it may still be the more active of the two at 144.5 °F (63 °C) under these conditions.

Following this same hypothesis, enzyme activity may be effectively halted by the lower mash-out temperature. Even if this is true, however, the lower temperature will increase wort viscosity and may slow run-off times. Although no details are provided by these sources, it is possible

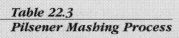

Table 22.3
Pilsener Mashing Process

Mash/Lauter Tun (main mash)	Kettle (mash water and decoctions)
	A portion of the mashing water is brought to a boil. Some boiling water transferred to mash, remaining water still at a boil.
Mix grain with cold water for doughing-in. Raise mash to 95 °F (35 °C) by addition of boiling water from kettle. Pull decoction, transfer to kettle. Mash rest at 95 °F (35 °C).	*First decoction:* Rises immediately to 126.5 °F (53 °C) due to combination with boiling water. Heat to 144.5 °F (63 °C) in thirteen minutes; raise to 167 °F (75 °C) in twenty minutes, rest for eight minutes; raise to boiling in twelve minutes, boil thirty minutes; return majority to mash. Total time: eighty-three minutes.
	Remaining portion of mash continues to boil.
Mash rises to 110.5 °F (43 °C). Brief rest, grain settles. Pull second decoction, transfer to kettle. Mash rest at 110.5 °F (44 °C).	*Second decoction:* Rises immediately to 144.5 °F (63 °C) when combined with boiling mash retained in copper from previous decoction. Raise in twenty minutes to 167 °F (75 °C), rest (time not specified, assume same as first decoction, eight minutes); raise rapidly (twelve minutes) to boil, boil fifteen minutes; return majority to main mash. Total time: fifty-five minutes.
	Remaining portion of mash continues to boil.
Mash rises to 144.5 °F (63 °C). Brief rest, grain settles. Pull third decoction, transfer to kettle. Mash rests at 144.5 °F (63 °C).	*Third decoction:* Rises immediately to 190.5 °F (88 °C) when combined with boiling mash retained in copper. Raise in twelve minutes to boiling, boil ten minutes. Return all contents of the kettle to the mash/lauter tun. Total time: twenty-two minutes.

Source: Adapted from H. L. Hind, Brewing Science and Practice (London: Chapman & Hall, Ltd., 1938), 582.

that hotter than normal sparge water might be used to counteract this effect.

Information on the brewery's operations in 1990 indicate that a slightly cooler final rest is now being used, at 158 °F (70 °C).[19] Although this helps to explain the body-producing dextrins found in the beer, it still indicates a mash program that lacks a conventional mash-out rest.

The Hopping of Pilsener Beers

As mentioned earlier, Zatec Red, or Saaz (the Czechs pronounce this *tzotz*), hops are reportedly the only variety ever found in Pilsener Urquell.[20] The quantity of hops used is about 400 grams per hectoliter[21] — and apparently this, too, has always been so.

Although hop utilization was not well understood by brewers during the nineteenth century, sources do quote the amount of hops used. The first reference I find to Pilsener hopping rates actually comes from an American source, the Wahl-Henius *Handy-Book of Brewing*, published in 1908. The authors quote specific hopping rates for Bohemian beers at various gravities, as outlined in table 22.4.

At 12 °B, Pilsener Urquell falls between the second and third lines in table 22.4, which calls for a hopping rate of 400 to 460 grams per hectoliter of wort. Given reasonable assumptions for alpha acid levels and kettle utilization rates, these additions would indeed give the 40 IBU commonly found in Pilsener Urquell. In American units, this hop quantity would be equal to just over 1 pound of hops per barrel, or 2.67 ounces in 5 gallons. Later in the twentieth century, DeClerk confirms this hop plan, noting that Pilseners have a "high hop rate (400g of Saaz/hL)."[22]

As for the timing of the additions, Richman's account of a visit to the brewery in 1990 provides some useful detail. He states that the wort is boiled for four hours to boil off the excess liquid. (Most likely, this is a result of the thin mash employed.) The hops are added in thirds, with the first charge added at the beginning of the boil, the second at the halfway point,

and the third about thirty minutes before the end.[23] This means that two-thirds of the hops added are boiled for an average of three hours — a fact that allows them to get high utilization out of the typically low alpha acid content of the Saaz hops.

Fermentation and Aging

The fermentation of most Pilseners is pretty much the same as for other lagers. A primary fermentation between 45 to 50 °F (7 to 10 °C) is followed by a period of lagering at 32 to 35 °F (0 to 2 °C).

At Pilsener Urquell, the fermentation is conducted using three different strains of yeast, which are reportedly quite similar to one another.[24] Today each batch that is brewed is split into three fermenters, each pitched with a different yeast. Up until about 1993, however, this was further complicated by the fact that both pitch-lined oak barrels and stainless-steel open fermenters were used. Here again, each batch was split between the two types.[25] In total, then, each batch was split six ways to cover both types of vat with all three types of yeast.

Although I found no direct mention of kraeusening in the current production of Pilsener Urquell, this practice was clearly commonplace in the past. Thausing's book from 1882 says that kraeusening was the

Table 22.4
Hopping Rates for Bohemian Beers, circa 1908

| Gravity (°B) | Hops Quantities (kg hops/hL wort) | | |
	Minimum	Average	Maximum
10.5	0.30	0.35	0.40
11.5	0.35	0.40	0.43
12.5	0.42	0.46	0.50
13.5	0.45	0.48	0.55

Source: R. Wahl and M. Henius, The American Handy-Book of the Brewing, Malting and Auxiliary Trades *(Chicago: Wahl-Henius Institute, 1908), 1241.*

standard practice in his time.[26] Furthermore, he provides the following information about the serving of beer "from the yeast" — a phrase most often used by the English to describe their real ales:

We should here mention a peculiar method of treating the beer which is customary in Austria, but especially in Bohemia (also in Pilsen). The very strongly attenuated beer is racked off from the fermenting tun directly into transport kegs, and is delivered to the saloon keeper as so called "yeast beer." The saloon-keeper opens the bung-holes of the barrels, fills them up with fresh water or beer, and bungs them again after the beer has become clear.

The beer is also filled from the fermenting tuns into transport kegs; these are allowed to "prick" for a few days in the brewery itself, are then filled up and delivered to the saloon-keeper, who then keeps them closed. Such beer foams strongly, and has an agreeable, refreshing taste. This method offers decided advantages during the cold season of the year, provided the saloon keeper treats the beer correctly and well.[27]

This passage makes it clear that cellar-manship — so important to the serving of English real ales even today — also played a critical role in the serving of authentic Pilsener at one time.

A Pilsener by Any Other Name

In the Czech Republic, the word "Pilsener" is considered an appellation — a term that can only be used on products brewed in the city of Plzeň.[28] As such, it applies only to Pilsener Urquell and to the beer of the Gambrinus brewery, which is located next door. Although most other Czech breweries also make a Pilsener-style beer, Michael Jackson says that they brand them with their own name and the number 12.[29]

Outside of the Czech Republic, of course, similar protections are not provided. Today many breweries offer products that carry the designation of Pilsener. In some cases the product is quite similar to that made in Pilsen — as is the case for some German beers — and in other cases, there is a vast gulf between the two — as in the case with the American "light" beers that carry this moniker.

To understand the evolution of the style, let's begin with the original. Fortunately, a number of analyses of the beers made in Pilsen during the nineteenth century are available for review. The beer brewed there appears to have settled into a very stable pattern by 1880, as shown in the nine analyses displayed in table 22.5.

On average, the Pilseners have an initial gravity of 1.048 (12.1 °B), with a terminal gravity of 1.014 (3.4 °B), which indicates an apparent attenuation of 71 to 72 percent. This attenuation level seems about right for the body displayed by the current examples from Pilsen. The alcohol level of 3.8 percent by weight (4.75 by volume) also matches the current specification.

Of course, Pilseners not made at Pilsen have been around for nearly as long as the original, and some of these also appear in the analyses from the 1800s, as shown in table 22.6. None of these examples closely matches the average values for the Pilsener products. In particular, note that the last two — with original gravities of 14.29 and 10.8 °B — fall well outside the range established by the twenty-five-year history of the style presented in table 22.5, even though they carry the name "Pilsener."

In addition to the imitations made by other breweries, some separate analyses are also provided for "keg" (Schank) and "export" products made by the Pilsen breweries during this time period. Some of these products fall outside the limits established by the regular Pilsener brewery products (see table 22.7).

Such special beers — mistaken for examples of the main product — along with the many imitators that have used the Pilsen name have probably helped to

Table 22.5
Pilsener Analyses, 1882–1907

Beer	Year	OG (°B)	TG (°B)	ABW (%)
Pilsen, Bürgerliches Brauhaus[a]	1882	11.91	3.25	3.47
Pilsen, Actien Brewery[a]	1882	12.27	3.25	3.72
Pilsener, Bürgerliches Brauhaus[b]	1883	—	3.55	4.6
Pilsener, Bürgerliches Brauhaus[b]	1883	11.95	3.55	3.46
Pilsener, Actien Brauhaus[b]	1883	—	2.75	4.6
Pilsener, Bürgerliches Brauhaus[b]	1886	11.2	3.55	2.98
Pilsener Lagerbier[c]	1893	12.45	4.0	3.43
Pilsener, Bürgerliches Brauhaus[b]	1901	12.83	3.43	3.95
Pilsener, Actien Brauhaus[b]	1907	12.2	—	3.82
Average		12.1 (1.048)	3.4 (1.014)	3.8

Sources: [a] *Thausing, et al.,* Preparation of Malt and the Fabrication of Beer, *750-51;* [b] *Wahl and Henius,* The American Handy-Book, *1286-87;* [c] *Thausing,* Malzbereitung und Bierfabrikation, *959, the German language version.*

expand the definition of the style over the years. Despite all this, the true original product, Pilsener Urquell, continues to target an original gravity of 1.048, or 12 °B, just as it did more than one hundred years ago.

Interestingly enough, the style definitions published by the Association of Brewers in the mid-1990s list a tighter specification for German Pilsener than for Bohemian. I suppose this makes sense, because the imitators are copying the Bohemian style. At the same time, I would bet that Germany's strict labeling laws help to narrow the parameters of what will be accepted as a Pilsener in that country.

In comparing the two, the German Pilsener is generally lighter in body because both the original and terminal gravities are usually lower than in the Bohemian. Still, the total extract fermented is about the same, so the alcohol levels are about equal between the German Pilsener and Bohemian Pilsener styles. Finally, hopping levels in the German Pilsener variety must be a bit lower because the lighter-bodied product cannot stand up to the same level of bitterness. For a comparison of these two Pilsener styles, try a side-by-side tasting of Pilsener Urquell with Germany's Warsteiner.

Table 22.6
Analyses of Other Pilsner-Style Beers, 1882–1901

Beer	Year	OG (°B)	TG (°B)	ABW (%)
Dreher's Bohemian Beer [a]	1882	12.74	4.25	3.60
Budweis Lager [a]	1882	11.34	2.75	3.55
Pilsener, Gennossenschafts [b]	1901	14.29	4.61	4.07
Pilsener, Anton Dreher [b]	1901	10.80	2.42	3.52

Sources: [a] *Thausing, et al.,* Preparation of Malt and the Fabrication of Beer, *750-51;* [b] *Wahl and Henius,* The American Handy-Book, *1286-87.*

Table 22.7
Analyses of "Keg" and "Export" Products Made by Pilsen Breweries, circa 1880-1900

Beer	OG (°B)	TG	ABW (%)
Pilsen export, Joint-stock brewery [a]	14.55	1.014	4.59
Pilsener (export), Burgerliches Brauhaus [b]	13.82	3.8 °B	4.20

Sources: [a] *Thausing, et al.*, Preparation of Malt and the Fabrication of Beer, 750–51; [b] *Wahl and Henius*, The American Handy-Book, 1286–87.

Dortmunder

In addition to the Pilseners, at least two other styles of pale lager are considered classics today: Dortmunder Export and Munich Helles. Both arose sometime after the development of Pilsener — most likely as an attempt at imitation or at least competition. Since then, each has developed into a specific style.

The Dortmunder style appears to have emerged during the latter third of the nineteenth century. I find no mention of it in the German brewing texts from that period, but it appears in many brewing books from the twentieth century.[30] The earliest, from 1907, offers the following description:"Dortmunder beer is very pale; brewed from low kilned malt; strongly hopped; and highly fermented."[31]

The same source provides the only early analysis I have found, as well as the earliest reference to the style, dated 1884. The analysis lists the source as the Dortmunder Victoria Brauerei, and the beer had an original gravity of 15.97 °B (1.064), terminal gravity of 4.75 °B, with alcohol by weight at 4.52 percent.[32]

This beer is clearly different from Pilsener; it was brewed from a much higher gravity and possessed considerably more alcohol. Furthermore, it appears that around 1907 Dortmunder lagers were actually lighter in color than the typical Pilsener.

Another source, from 1948, had this to say about the style: "Dortmunder Beer is a beer very light in color, not more than 8 °Lovibond, with neither malt nor hop flavor predominating, dry and bitter taste. The O.G. not less than 12.5 Balling."[33]

DeClerck, writing in the 1950s, provides another good description, as well as some important brewing details. He says that Dortmunder is a

pale beer like Pilsener, but with a less bitter and a finer, mellow palate. Germination is longer on the floor, but kilning is carried out as for the Pilsener. In other words, a fine, fully modified malt is used, but it is cured as for Pilsener.

The mashing liquor is highly charged with carbonates and calcium chloride. The two-mash decoction process is used. The hop rate is intermediate between that of Munich and Pilsener beer. Fermentation is carried out at low temperatures and attenuation is forced. Chips are often added at lagering.[34]

Today Dortmunder malt may be difficult, if not impossible, to find in the United States. One contemporary source indicates that this malt receives a short high-temperature (200 °F, 94 °C) session at the end of kilning.[35] This step sets it apart from normal Pilsener or even lager malt. To simulate this effect, John Mallett, who brewed the style at Old Dominion Brewing Company, suggests supplementing regular lager malt with 10 to 15 percent Munich malt.[36]

Hopping for the style can be anywhere from 20 to 29 IBU[37] — almost always with German hops or good American alternatives such as Mt. Hood or Liberty. A portion of the hops may be added about fifteen minutes before the end of the boil.

One of the most distinctive features of the Dortmunder style is the brewing water, which is quite hard (see table 22.8). Considerable levels of carbonate and sulfate are present and can accentuate bitterness. In addition, relatively high levels of sodium and chloride enhance the overall flavor of the beer. This is a good beer to brew if you have water with considerable carbonate content.

According to Jackson, the Dortmunder style was once quite popular in Germany under the name Export, but now its producers seem to downplay the style in favor of Pilseners.[38] Nonetheless, it is still produced as Export but it is rarely found in the United States. The products sold in the United States under the Dortmunder Actien Braueri (DAB) and Dortmunder Union Braueri (DUB) names are considered Pilseners rather than Export-style beers.

Americans who want to sample a Dortmunder Export should look out for other Jackson recommendations, including those from Gordon Biersch in Palo Alto, California, and Stoudt's brewery in Adamstown, Pennsylvania.[39] Those who can't find these examples might keep in mind the comment that the style is basically a pale Märzen beer. That seems to be a fitting way to think of it: a bit higher in alcohol and body than a Pils, but with somewhat less bitterness.

Table 22.8
Dortmund Brewing Water

Mineral	ppm
Calcium	225
Magnesium	40
Sodium	60
Chloride	60
Sulfate	120
Carbonate	180

Source: G. Noonan, Brewing Lager Beer (Boulder, Colo.: Brewers Publications, 1986), 55.
Note: ppm = parts per million

Munich Helles

While Dortmund brewers were busy popularizing their pale lager style, the brewers in Munich were frustrated by their efforts to develop a workable pale, or helles, formulation. One source tells that the Munich brewers declared the task impossible around 1894,[40] but Spaten now claims to have produced Munich's first pale lager in that year.[41]

If a pale Munich beer was available in the early 1900s, it certainly got little notice. Indeed, I have yet to find *any* brewing text that mentions Munich helles as a style prior to the 1990s. Apparently Paulaner claims to have developed the style in the post–World War I era, and at least one other source places development of the style in this time period.[42]

Today the style continues to live in the shadow of two beers: Pilsener and dunkel. Helles finds its main popularity in Bavaria, where many drink it as a daily beer. Outside Bavaria, however, the daily beer is generally a German-style Pilsener, and helles is not commonly found. In addition, of course, the pride of Bavaria for more than one hundred years has been, and continues to be, Munich dark, or dunkel, beer.

The only German-brewed example of helles that I find in the United States is the Spaten Premium Lager. Aside from this, you can sometimes find examples of helles at brewpubs or microbreweries that can provide you with a good idea of what defines the style. If you are lucky enough to get to Germany, be sure to sample the helles beers available from many of Munich's major brewers.

As for brewing helles, the style parameters (see table 22.9) are your best guide. A couple of years ago I brewed an example that won a few awards using Ayinger helles malt (77 percent), wheat malt (10 percent), CaraPils (10 percent), and Belgian biscuit malt (3 percent). The wort had an original gravity of 1.046. Another recipe I brewed included 9 percent Munich malt and 11 percent CaraPils in addition to Ayinger helles malt for an original gravity of 1.050. This recipe is similar to one published in *The New Brewer.*[43]

Both of my helles recipes employed infusion mashing with a protein rest at 120 °F (49 °C) and a saccharification rest at 148 °F (64 °C) for the first grain bill and at 152 °F (67 °C) for the second. The first batch (6 gallons) used an all-Hallertau hop schedule with 0.5-ounce for each of three additions at sixty, twenty, and five minutes before the end of the boil. The second batch was a bit more highly hopped, with 0.75-ounce Northern Brewer, 0.5-ounce Tettnanger, and 0.5-ounce Hallertau at the same time intervals as the first batch.

Carbonate water suits the Munich styles. For further discussion of water parameters, see chapter 17.

Brewing Pilsener

In the early days, Pilseners were quite simple. The grist bill contained just one ingredient: Pilsener malt. The hop bill also contained just one ingredient: Saaz hops. In those days, the making of beer was much more about the making of malt. The work of the maltster would drive the character of the finished beer through the character of the finished malt. As a result, brewers worked closely with — and often employed — the maltsters who supplied them.

In making a Pilsener today, similar attention should be paid to the malt. The most ideal malt for making a Pilsener comes from Moravian two-row barley. Although a great deal of this is grown in the United States, it is all controlled by Coors Brewing Company and generally is not available to other brewers.[44] Fortunately, this type of barely is grown in many regions of Europe; once malted, it is generally designated as Pilsener malt.[45] Malts so designated, from pretty much any European source, would be an excellent base for the making of your Pilsener.

The second choice is the use of American two-row malt such as that made from the Klages or Harrington varieties of barley. These are generally what you get when you buy American two-row malt. If you are shocked by the price of imported Pilsener malt — or simply find it unavailable — be assured that excellent and award-winning Pilseners are made from this American stock.

Table 22.9
Pale Lager–Style Parameters

	Bohemian Pilsener	German Pilsener	Dortmunder/Export	Munich Helles
Original gravity	1.044–56	1.044–50	1.048–56	1.044–52
Bitterness	35–45	30–40	23–29	18–25
BU:GU ratio	0.75–0.85	0.68–0.80	0.40–0.60	0.38–0.48
Hop flavor	Low–med.	Medium	Low	Low
Hop aroma	Low–med.	Medium	Low	Low
Color (°SRM)	3–5	2.5–4	4–6	3–5
Apparent extract	1.014–20	1.008–12	1.010–14	1.008–12
Alcohol (volume)	4–5	4–5	4.8–6	4.5–5.5
Esters	None	None	None	None
Diacetyl	Low–med.	Very low	None	Very low

Source: C. Papazian, "Introducing: Beer Style Guidelines: Part 2," The New Brewer, (March–April, 1992): 25–28.

Least desirable as a base for Pilsener is six-row malt. The higher proportion of husk to starch leads to a darker color and, often, a grainy or astringent flavor.

As for extract, I find only one beer out of twenty-three that advanced to the National Homebrew Competition second round that relied on extract alone for the base of the recipe. This particular recipe used Laaglander light and extra-light extract, supplemented with crystal malt and a pound of honey! Of the two other recipes that included extract, one used an unspecified brand of extract for the majority of the gravity but supplemented that with a minimash of two-row (1 pound) and crystal (0.5-pound) malts. The final extract recipe relied on a small mash (5.25 pounds total) for the majority of the gravity and supplemented that with one can of Alexanders Light malt extract.

Grist Composition

The recipes from the NHC second round were pretty evenly spilt between the use of Pilsener and two-row malts. A quarter of the recipes even combined the two. Little difference in the selection of base malt was seen between the German and Bohemian substyles. Six-row malt was seen in two cases as a supplement to two-row or extract — although I can see little reason for its use in either case.

Beyond the selection of base malt, many Pilsener recipes confine themselves to just two other ingredients: CaraPils or dextrin malt and crystal malt of some sort.

In looking at the NHC second-round recipes, I found that they differ somewhat, depending on whether a German- or Bohemian-style Pilsener was brewed. In general, the Bohemian-style Pilsener recipes were simpler, often confining themselves to the basic ingredients just mentioned. The German formulations, however, tended to include special ingredients such as Vienna or Munich malt.

Table 22.10 covers the most common approaches to the formulation of Pilsener grist bills. As presented, the table combines both the German and Bohemian approaches but provides some commentary on the breakdown of each.

Of the nine beers that included ingredients other than Pils, CaraPils, two-row, or crystal malt, only three were Bohemian style, and six were German style. Thus, three-quarters of the Bohemian-style Pilseners were simple in their construction, containing nothing but the three basic ingredients mentioned earlier: base malt, CaraPils, and crystal malt.

The incidence and approximate proportion of each grist element is shown, according to style, in tables 22.11 and 22.12.

Wort Production

Although some commercial breweries still practice decoction mashing for Pilsener,[46] many have gone to infusion methods

Table 22.10
Grist Formulations in NHC Second-Round Pilseners

No. of Recipes	Grist Bill	Style
6	Nothing but Pils/two-row + CaraPils	3 German, 3 Bohemian
6	Pils/two-row + crystal + other[a]	3 German, 3 Bohemian
4	Pils/two-row + CaraPils + crystal	1 German, 3 Bohemian
4	Pils/two-row, no crystal + other[b]	4 German
3	Nothing but Pils/two-row	1 German, 2 Bohemian

[a]Vienna, 2; six-row, 2; wheat, 1; honey, 1 [b]Vienna, toasted Pilsener, Munich, flaked maize

Table 22.11
German Pilsener Grain Bill in NHC Second-Round Recipes

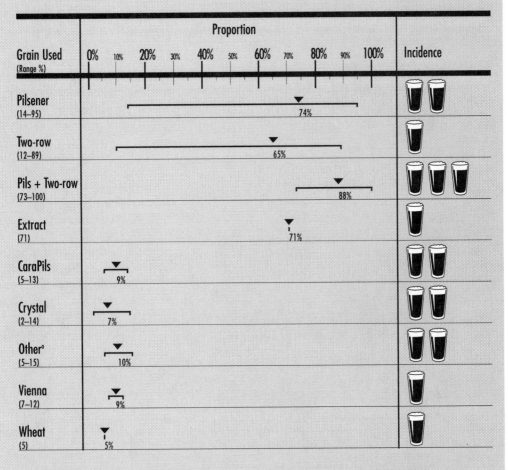

Grain Used (Range %)	Proportion	Incidence
Pilsener (14–95)	74%	🍺🍺
Two-row (12–89)	65%	🍺
Pils + Two-row (73–100)	88%	🍺🍺🍺
Extract (71)	71%	🍺
CaraPils (5–13)	9%	🍺🍺
Crystal (2–14)	7%	🍺🍺
Other^a (5–15)	10%	🍺🍺
Vienna (7–12)	9%	🍺
Wheat (5)	5%	🍺

[a] For German-style Pilseners, "Other" includes honey, six-row malt, flaked maize, and toasted Pils malts.
Key: This chart shows what proportion of the grain bill was provided by various grains in twelve German Pilsener recipes. The line next to each grain gives the range of values used by different brewers; this range is also listed below "Grains Used." The triangle above each line indicates the average proportion used across all recipes.

The icons in the column on the right show how often the twelve German Pilsener recipes included each grain. (Percentage figures indicate how many of the recipes included the grain.)

🍺 = rarely (30% or less)   🍺🍺 = sometimes (30% to 60%)
🍺🍺🍺 = often (60% to 90%)   🍺🍺🍺🍺 = usually (90% or more)

for this style of beer.[47] Among the NHC second-round beers, I found only one that used a decoction mash. The remainder used infusion techniques — although many included a protein rest.

Overall, 50 percent of the recipes that included mash data used a protein rest. In 80 percent of the cases the protein rest was applied to a grist based on European Pilsener malt. Most recipes based on U.S. two-row malts did not include such a rest.

The average saccharification temperature used during mashing was slightly higher in the production of Bohemian-

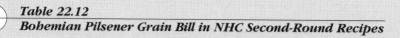

Table 22.12
Bohemian Pilsener Grain Bill in NHC Second-Round Recipes

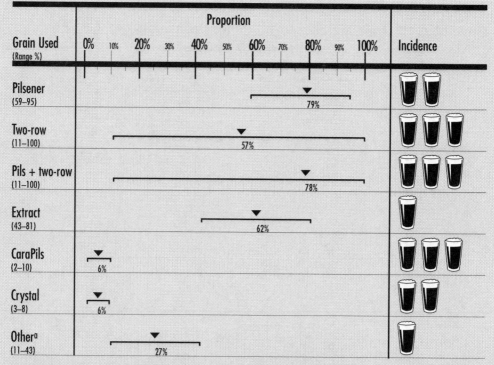

Grain Used (Range %)	Proportion	Incidence
Pilsener (59–95)	79%	
Two-row (11–100)	57%	
Pils + two-row (11–100)	78%	
Extract (43–81)	62%	
CaraPils (2–10)	6%	
Crystal (3–8)	6%	
Other[a] (11–43)	27%	

[a]*For Bohemian-style Pilseners, "Other" includes Munich and six-row malts.*

Key: This chart shows what proportion of the grain bill was provided by various grains in eleven Bohemian Pilsener recipes. The line next to each grain gives the range of values used by different brewers; this range is also listed below "Grains Used." The triangle above each line indicates the average proportion used across all recipes.

The icons in the column on the right show how often the eleven Bohemian Pilsener recipes included each grain. (Percentage figures indicate how many of the recipes included the grain.)

= rarely (30% or less)   = sometimes (30% to 60%)
= often (60% to 90%)   = usually (90% or more)

style Pilseners, at 153 °F (67.2 °C), than in the production of the German type, at 151 °F (66.1 °C). This fits with our general impression of these two styles, where the German style will be slightly thinner and the Bohemian style fuller bodied.

This difference between the two is also seen in the original and terminal gravities, as shown in table 22.13, where the Bohemian-style Pilseners — on average — are slightly higher on both counts. At the same time, attenuation — and therefore alcohol content — is identical between the two substyles.

Hop Selection

Not surprisingly, Saaz hops were the most popular variety of hop used in both German- and Bohemian-style Pilseners. In the Bohemian brews, where use of Saaz is clearly classic, this variety was used for most of the hop additions, accounting for 71 percent of the total. Hallertau and Tettnanger also found some favor with brewers but to a much lesser extent, and other varieties made only token appearances.

Table 22.13

Differences in Gravities and Attenuation Between NHC Second-Round German and Bohemian Pilseners

Style	OG	TG	Apparent Attenuation (%)
German	1.0488	1.0130	73
Bohemian	1.0504	1.0135	73

For German-style Pilseners, the traditional German aroma hops, including Hersbruck, Hallertau, and Tettnanger in total account for a much greater proportion of the hop additions than does Saaz alone. Aside from these four hops, however, other varieties are seen only infrequently and usually in bittering roles (see table 22.14). Thus, for those making Bohemian-style Pilsener, Saaz is clearly the way to go. Those making a German-style Pils can experiment a bit, as long as experimentation is limited to the proven German varieties.

Hop Usage

To the extent that nontraditional hops find a place in Pilsener recipes, they are usually relegated to a bittering role. The level of bitterness targeted is usually in the range of 30 to 50 IBU depending on the substyle. The Bohemian-style Pilseners generally have a little more original gravity and a little more residual body than the German-style ones, so they are hopped to a slightly higher BU level. As table 22.15 shows, the average Bohemian-style Pilsener recipe has a calculated bitterness level of 39 BU, while the average German-style Pilsener is a bit lower, at 37 BU.

As shown in table 22.16, only the varieties of Saaz, Hallertau, Tettnanger, and Hersbruck are used to any extent for flavor and aroma applications in Pilsener beers. Only two others, Mt. Hood — which is a U.S. Hallertau clone — and Styrian Goldings — an ale aroma hop — appear at

Table 22.14

Differences in Hops Used Between NHC Second-Round German and Bohemian Pilseners

German-style Pilseners[a]		Bohemian-style Pilseners[b]	
Type	Count	Type	Count
Saaz	13	Saaz	34
Hersbruck	9	Hallertau	6
Tettnanger	8	Tettnanger	3
Hallertau	7	N. Brewer	2
Perle	3	Centennial	1
Mt. Hood	2	Mt. Hood	1
Chinook	1	Willamette	1
Spalt	1		
Styrian Goldings	1	Total additions	48
Total additions	45		

[a] Total number of recipes analyzed = 12
[b] Total number of recipes analyzed = 11

Table 22.15
Differences in German and Bohemian Pilsener BU:GU Ratios

| | German-style Pilsener | | Bohemian-style Pilsener | |
	BU:GU	Calculated BU	BU:GU	Calculated BU
Average	0.74	37	0.80	39
Maximum	1.01	50	1.20	53
Minimum	0.35	17	0.28	20

all in these roles. For aroma and dry hopping, Saaz continues to be the overwhelming favorite, regardless of substyle, accounting for more than 70 percent of these additions.

The NHC Pilseners analyzed for this chapter included a total of twenty-three beers almost evenly split between German and Bohemian styles. On average, they included four hop additions (see table 22.17). Two of these are generally made before the last twenty-nine minutes of the boil, at ninety and forty-five minutes or sixty and thirty minutes before the end, for instance. The third is generally made between one and twenty-nine minutes before the end of the boil, and the last is

either steeped in the hot wort after the boil has ended or is dry hopped during fermentation. Table 22.18 shows the distribution of hop additions by time. The average size of the hop additions made for various applications is shown in table 22.19.

Water

As I have noted in previous chapters, a serious effort to match brewing water to that of the classic examples is pursued by only a minority of the NHC second-round beers. With Pilsener, this continues to be the case. Most of the second-round beers were brewed without any water treatment — at

Table 22.16
Hops Used in NHC Second-Round Pilseners

Type	Bitter	Flavor	Aroma	Dry	Total
Saaz	18	9	12	8	47
Hallertau	7	3	2	1	13
Tettnang	6	4	0	1	11
Hersbruck	4	2	2	1	9
Mt. Hood	2	0	1	0	3
Perle	3	0	0	0	3
N. Brewer	2	0	0	0	2
Centennial	1	0	0	0	1
Chinook	1	0	0	0	1
Spalt	1	0	0	0	1
Styrian Goldings	0	1	0	0	1
Willamette	1	0	0	0	1

Note: The data show the number of times each hop was used across the twenty-three recipes analyzed.

Table 22.17

**Hop Additions in All NHC
Second-Round Pilsener Recipes**

Boil	2.0
Flavor	0.8
Aroma	0.7
Dry	0.5
Total	4.0

Note: The data show the average number of hop additions across the twenty-three recipes analyzed.

least no treatment was indicated on the entry forms. Of course, some portion of these may have soft tap water that requires no adjustment for this style. But I doubt this is true in more than a few of the cases.

Among those entries with some water treatment, it was most often either minimal (acidification of sparge water) or inappropriate for the style (addition of gypsum).

Only three of twenty-three brewers clearly pursued water treatment strategies designed to emulate Pilsen water (see table 22.20). Two began with "pure" water

Table 22.18

**Hop Additions by Boil Time in
NHC Second-Round Pilseners**

Boil Time (min.)	Number of Additions
90	4
60	20
50	1
45	6
40	3
35	1
30	11
15	13
10	6
5	3
2	3
0	11
Dry	11
Total	93

— water that had either been distilled or run through a reverse osmosis (RO) filter. To this base the brewers added small amounts of chalk (calcium carbonate), Epsom salts (magnesium sulfate), and either table salt (sodium chloride) or calcium chloride. The amounts added were so small that each ion had a parts-per-million concentration of less than 15, and the total was still under 40 parts per million of total hardness.

Although this strategy produces a water profile that pretty well matches that of Pilsen with regard to the relevant brewing ions, other important trace minerals may be lost in the process. Zinc and copper, in small amounts, contribute to yeast metabolism. When these elements have been removed, the brewer needs to compensate in some way. One practical approach is to add yeast nutrient to the wort during boiling.

Another strategy for using distilled or RO water is to blend it with your regular tap water. By doing this in appropriate proportions, you will simply dilute your regular water so that the minerals are reduced to lower levels. This approach preserves low levels of trace minerals in the water so that there is less concern about proper support of yeast metabolism.

The third strategy used by the NHC beers for emulating Pilsen water simply used bottled, as opposed to distilled, water. The bottled water used was supposedly soft without being completely free of ions. The brewer who did this actually took first place one year, so this may be a pretty good strategy.

Finally, if you do nothing but adjust your mash chemistry through the addition of calcium when making a Pilsener, you should select calcium chloride rather than gypsum for the purpose. By this choice you avoid adding sulfate, which can give a sharper edge to the bitterness, and instead add chloride, which will provide a desirable roundness to the palate.

Table 22.19
Average Size of Hop Additions
in NHC Second-Round Pilseners

Type of Addition	oz./gal.	oz./5 gal.
Flavor	0.16	0.79
Aroma	0.18	0.90
Dry	0.13	0.60

Fermentation

Once you have produced a good Pilsener wort, you'll need a properly conducted fermentation in order to produce the finished beer you desire. Generally, the first issue in fermentation is yeast selection followed by primary fermentation and then secondary fermentation and lagering.

The most popular yeast used for making both German- and Bohemian-style Pilseners is the Bohemian lager (see table 22.21). These strains generally produce a smooth, full-bodied beer typical of the classic Pilsener style. Despite its typical connection to the Bohemian style of lager, it can also be used successfully for the production of German-style Pilsener.

Table 22.20
Typical Pilsen Water Profile

Mineral	ppm
Calcium	7
Magnesium	2
Sodium	2
Carbonate	15
Sulfate	5
Chloride	5
Total	36

Note: ppm = parts per million

Following the Bohemian strain in popularity is Pilsen, which generally produces a drier, crisper product. This strain seems more suited to the German-type Pilsener, but it has been used with equal success in making the Bohemian style.

Other lager yeasts that are occasionally used for Pilsener production include the Munich, Bavarian, and Danish strains. The Munich is a significant diacetyl producer and might be a good choice in reproducing the caramel-like Pilsener Urquell profile.

Primary fermentation of the award-winning Pilseners was conducted at an average temperature of 50 °F (10 °C) and lasted, on average, thirteen days. Following the primary fermentation, some included a brief secondary fermentation, usually near the same temperature as the primary. Lagering was conducted for most entries, and on average, this was conducted at about 40 °F (4 °C) for thirty-two days.

These averages fall relatively close to the expected program for a lager fermentation. What is of more interest is the fact that *some* of the beers that proceeded to the second round were the product of relatively warm fermentations and short lagering cycles. Table 22.22 shows that primary fermentation temperatures for some entries were as high as 63 °F (17 °C). Furthermore, some entries showed little or no cold conditioning, with times as short as two days and temperatures as high as 60 °F (16 °C).

Though I certainly can't recommend these offbeat fermentation and lagering strategies, this data does indicate that you can sometimes produce a good-quality product under less than ideal conditions. I certainly remember the process used for my first award-winning lager, which relied upon the cold weather of a Chicago winter for lagering.

Table 22.21
Differences in Yeast Selection
Between NHC Second-Round
German and Bohemian Pilseners

Yeast	German	Bohemian
Bohemian	5	7
Pilsener	3	4
Munich	2	0
Bavarian	2	0
Danish	1	1

Conclusion

Many people enjoy drinking a good Pilsener beer — in fact for many people this is the style that really got them started on quality beer. The making of a wonderful Pils is not simple, but it is certainly within the reach of any accomplished brewer. Those who really enjoy the style will find many ways to experiment with it, varying hop selection and application and altering the choice of base malts. Incredibly enough, these seemingly simple variations can and will produce beers that are remarkably different from one another.

Table 22.22
Fermentation Times and Temperatures for NHC Second-Round Pilseners

	Primary		Secondary	
	Days	°F (°C)	Days	°F (°C)
Average	13	50 (10)	32	40 (4)
Maximum	28	63 (17)	72	60 (16)
Minimum	4	40 (4)	2	30 (-1)

Key Success Factors in Brewing Pilsener Beers

- Select best-quality European Pilsener malt to constitute 80 to 90 percent of the grists for your recipe. A quality American two-row malt may also be used for this purpose.

- A Bohemian-style Pilsener *may* include CaraPils and/or light crystal malts; German-style Pilseners are even less likely to include these ingredients.

- Use relatively soft water for mashing and sparging.

- Mash with a decoction or step-infusion plan that includes a protein rest if you are using European malts. The saccharification rest should be conducted at 153 °F (67 °C) for Bohemian-style Pilsener and at 151 °F (66 °C) for German-style Pilsener.

- Target an original gravity of 1.048 for German-style Pilsener, 1.050 for Bohemian-style Pilsener.

- Select Saaz hops for a Bohemian-style Pilsener, and Saaz, Tettnanger, or Hallertau for a German-style Pilsener. Target a BU:GU ratio of 0.75 to 0.80.

- Make two hop additions for bittering and two for flavor and aroma. Make the first addition at sixty to ninety minutes before the end of the boil, the second at thirty to forty-five minutes, the third between ten and twenty-nine minutes, and the final addition should either be steeped in the kettle after the boil or dry hopped in secondary fermenter.

- Add 0.75- to 1.0 ounce of hops in 5 gallons of wort for each flavor or aroma addition.

- Ferment at 50 °F (10 °C) using a more full-bodied lager strain for Bohemian-style Pilsener and a drier, more highly attenuating strain for German-style Pilsener.

- Following fermentation, lager at 35 to 40 °F (2 to 4 °C) for three to five weeks.

23 PORTER

Home and craft brewers love the porter style in part, I think, because it can vary widely according to the interpretation of the brewer. In the past few years two subcategories of porter have been defined in an attempt to narrow the definitions a bit, but they are still rather wide, and by 1996 AHA once again combined them. Still, there are plenty of historical precedents for two substyles of porter, and this chapter will maintain the distinction.

Let's begin by looking at the style definitions (see table 23.1). About the only real departure these style definitions make from the historical character of the style is in gravity. The black porters of the nineteenth century were probably comparable to the upper end of the robust porter range. However, during the eighteenth century, when the porters truly would have been brown, the gravities were much higher, mostly in the range of 1.060 to 1.070.

Of course, it is not uncommon to find roast barley in both commercial and homebrewed porters despite the admonition against this practice contained in these descriptions. Although I agree that roast barley is best reserved for the making of stouts, a touch of it in a porter can be a wonderful thing.

The History of Porter

Porter was truly the first "industrial" beer. Rather than being a natural product of the brewing ingredients, it was "engineered" to meet specific consumer needs. Once established, it was subjected to the powers of the industrial revolution, giving rise to the first mammoth breweries known to society. Then, in its maturity, porter began to take the path of economy, sacrificing quality through the use of newfangled brewing ingredients, sugars, and adulterants. Finally, porter sired an offspring called stout, which would not only outlive it but would become the better known and more widely admired of the two.

Original Porter

Most beer styles evolve, but porter was created. A variety of accounts agree upon 1722 as the year in which the beer that would come to be known as porter was first brewed.[1] Although some sources credit George Harwood of Shoreditch Brewery with this development,[2] it seems likely that several brewers began this type of brewing in that same year.

In 1760, a veteran brewer writing under the nom de plume of Obadiah Poundage recounted the events of that era:

Table 23.1
Porter Style Definitions

Characteristic	Brown Porter	Robust Porter
Original gravity	1.040–1.050	1.044–1.060
Bitterness	20–30	25–45
BU:GU ratio[a]	0.55–0.72	0.61–0.93
Hop flavor and aroma	None to medium	None to medium
Color (SRM)	20–35	30+
Apparent extract	1.006–1.010	1.008–1.016
Alcohol (volume)	4.5–6%	5–6.5%
Esters	Low/OK	Low/OK
Diacetyl	Low–medium/OK	Low–medium/OK
Flavor profile	No roast barley or strong burnt	No roast barley. Sharp bitterness of black malt, without high burnt/character. Low charcoal-like flavor. Malty sweet to medium malt sweetness.

[a] *The higher values listed here come from the commercial and homebrewed examples examined later in the chapter.*
Source: *"American Homebrewers Association 1995 National Homebrew Competition Rules and Regulations" (Boulder Colo.: American Homebrewers Association, 1995). C. Papazian, "Introducing: Beer Style Guidelines," The New Brewer (January–February, 1992), 10–16.*

Some drank mild beer and stale mixed, others ale, mild beer and stale blended together at threepence per quart, but many used all stale at fourpence per pot.

On this footing stood the trade until about the year 1722 when the Brewers conceived there was a method to be found preferable to any of these extremes; that beer well brewed, kept its proper time, became racy and mellow, this is neither new nor stale, such would recommend itself to the public. This they ventured to sell for £1/3/- per barrel that the victualler might retail at threepence per quart. At first it was slow in making its way, but in the end the experiment succeeded beyond expectation.

The labouring people, porters etc. experienced its wholesomeness and utility, they assumed to themselves the use thereof, from whence it was called Porter or Entire Butt. As yet, however, it was far from being in the perfection which since we have had it. I well remember for many years it was not expected, nor was it thought possible to be made fine and bright, and four and five months was deemed to be sufficient age for it to be drunk at.

The improvement of transparency has since been added to it by means of more and better workmanship, better malt, better hops and the use of isinglass ...[3]

This passage begins by telling us that beer cocktails or blends were commonly consumed prior to the development of porter. In the decades preceding 1722, taxes on malt, hops, wort, and coal forced changes in the formulations of popular beers. To make up for these changes, the consumer began to blend the various beers (including the recently introduced and still expensive pale ale) to achieve his "ideal" pint.

These blends are a common element in the stories about porter's origins, although there is some disagreement about the exact number and identity of the beers used in such mixtures. I find the following:

- Mild beer and stale mixed[4]
- Ale, mild beer, and stale blended[5]
- Half-and-half (half ale and half two penny)[6]
- Three threads (ale, beer, and twopenny)[7]
- Mixture of two brown beers, one stale, one mild[8]

- Three threads: pale ale, new brown ale, and stale brown ale[9]
- Also: four threads and six threads (constituents not given)[10]

From these descriptions I suspect that several different mixtures were popular at the time. Many of them combined "stale" or aged products with "mild" or present-use beers to create an agreeable taste at an affordable price. Porter was formulated to meet these same needs while making life easier for the publican by allowing him to dispense from one cask rather than two or more. Thus, porter was intended as a prepackaged blend of beers, similar in a way to modern products like bottled Black and Tan or canned cocktails such as bourbon and cola. Thus, even in its birth, porter takes on the mantle of pragmatic industrialism.

Although the passage from Poundage states that porter was at first "slow in making its way," it was apparently well established just shortly after the year of its birth. Corran reports that the earliest written reference to porter is to be found in the letter of M. Cesar de Saussure to his family.

26 November 1726. Would you believe it, although water is to be had in abundance in London and of fairly good quality, absolutely none is drunk? . . . Another kind of beer is called porter . . . because the greater quantity of this beer is consumed by the working classes. It is a thick and strong beverage, and the effect it produces if drunk in excess, is the same as that of wine; this porter costs 3d the pot. In London there are a number of houses where nothing but this sort of beer is sold.[11]

A number of brewing authors agree that these original porters were made exclusively of brown malt. As you may recall, such malt was dried over a wood fire at fairly high heat. At least a portion of the kernels would torrify, that is, pop or blow up, during kilning. This led to the term "blown" malt as applied to this commodity. It later become so closely identified with porter that it is sometimes referred to as porter malt. Some sources draw a distinction between brown and blown malts, but it is not clear if it was widely observed.

The following passage gives some details about the production of brown malt.

For brown or porter malt, the grain is placed to the depth of about half an inch on the floor of the kiln, which, in this case, usually consists of perforated iron plates or wire network, while a strong, blazing fire, produced by the ignition of faggots of wood, is applied below. During the process, the temperature rapidly rises to 180 °F, or higher; a portion of the starch and sugar of the malt becomes carbonized, while, as some allege, the pyroligneous acid and other products evolved from the burning wood, impart to the malt that peculiar flavor so much esteemed by the porter drinker.[12]

The reference to "that peculiar flavor so much esteemed" is presumably a smokiness from the wood fire. Although it's not mentioned explicitly in any of the flavor descriptions of porter, some beer historians believe that porter would have had a distinctly smoky flavor.[13]

By 1750, the *London and Country Brewer* includes commentary on porter that indicates high hopping rates (3 pounds per hogshead) and blending of the three worts (from the first, second, and third mashes of the same grist) to form a single product.[14] Thus, the gravity of porter was probably less than strong ales of the day (made just from first mash runnings) but higher than common or table beers (usually made from third mash runnings). Foster concurs with this, stating, "It does seem likely that the original had OG somewhere in the range 1.050 to 1.070 with most brews probably falling in the range 1.060 to 1.070.[15]

Overall, the flavor of original porter was highly roasted, smoky, somewhat acidic (from the action of *Brettanomyces* during aging[16]), and well bittered. The product would have been translucent and probably ruby red rather than black or even brown in hue during the 1700s.[17] Brown-colored porter is not mentioned in the literature until after 1817, when formulations changed.

Modern brewers may be hard-pressed to find any brown malt, and when found it is certainly not smoked. Furthermore, you may find that producing a beer with nothing but brown malt is nearly impossible due to its low diastatic activity.

One solution is to roast pale malt to make your own brown malt. This gives you a commodity to work with but still does not address the issues of diastatic power or smoke flavor. You can, of course try the roasting over a wood fire, or simply add a quantity of smoked malt to the recipe. As another alternative, Dr. John Harrison and his colleagues at the Durden Park Beer Club suggest that middle-range crystal malts may have similar color and flavor effects.[18] Their recipe for original porter combines a base of pale malt with brown, black, and crystal malts. For information on roasting your own amber and brown malts, see the sidebar at the end of this chapter.

Industrial Porter

Once established, the production of porter blossomed with the Industrial Revolution taking place in England during the eighteenth century. To improve the economies of storing the product for many months while it aged, brewers took to building huge wooden storage vats secured with dozens of iron hoops, each weighing hundreds of pounds. These storage vessels were a matter of no small pride on the part of the brewers, and there was a competition of sorts to see who could build the biggest one. More than one was inaugurated by a dinner dance inside the vessel, with as many as two hundred guests accommodated.[19] The key players in this race were Whitbread, Thrale, and Meux. Table 23.2 shows some points in the progression of the biggest vat sizes.

By contrast, today the biggest aging tank found at the world's biggest single-site brewery (Coors in Golden, Colorado) is just 1,572 U.S. barrels, or 48,732 U.S. gallons.[20] The largest porter vat listed above was more than seventeen times bigger than the largest one in use today.

If the race of great vats had not already ended, it was put to rest by a disaster at Meux in 1814.[21] On October 16, a 22-foot-high vat ruptured, releasing a jet of porter that first wiped out an adjacent tank and then ravaged the surrounding neighborhood in a five-block radius. At least eight people (including women and children) were killed immediately, and a dozen others succumbed to injuries or were crushed by the crowds seeking to consume the fine porter that was running in the streets.[22]

The scope of this disaster, in terms of lives, money (the lost beer was valued at

Table 23.2
Progression of Vat Sizes, 1736–1795

Year	Size (bbl.)	Size (U.S. gal.)
1736	1,500	64,500
1745	4,000	172,000
1795	20,000	860,000

Source: T. Foster, Porter, Classic Beer Style Series, no. 5 (Boulder, Colo.: Brewers Publications, 1992), 21.

$15,000), and the impact on the surrounding community is one measure of the extent to which beer production had become highly industrialized. Another sign was the extensive capital required to enter into the porter-brewing business. One London business journal during this period said that only banking required a greater investment.[23]

This industrialization of porter resulted in phenomenal production capacity. By 1812 at least four London porter brewers — Whitbread, Truman, Meux, and Barclay Perkins — were producing more than 120,000 barrels of beer per year, with Barclay Perkins turning out 270,000 barrels. By contrast, the largest London ale brewer still produced only 20,000 barrels annually.[24]

Although the industrial brewing of porter allowed delivery of an economical product to the masses, it had some other effects on both beer and trade that were not entirely anticipated.

First, the large vats used for porter fermentation and aging had a high volume-to-surface area and so heated up considerably during fermentation. Sources from the mid-1800s give fermentation temperatures in the 75 to 79 °F (24 to 26 °C) range,[25] while ale fermentations rarely rose above 72 or 73 °F (22 or 23 °C). This high fermentation temperature in large fermenters is sure to have increased the presence of esters and fusel alcohols over what it would have been in the very first porters. One source credits the hot fermentations with producing the characteristic porter taste:

Porter owes much of its tart and astringent flavor to a high, rapid fermentation which lessens the density without diminishing the high flavor drawn from the materials. . . . The pitching temperature should be taken between 64 °F and 68 °F, except in summer, when it may be taken as low as possible; the heat of the gyle should be curbed between 74 °F and 78 °F . . .[26]

Another fact of life in industrial porter was the use of blending to achieve the flavors that come only with age. It seems that by blending a portion of aged porter with new porter, the new product would be "hardened" or "brought forward" into a mature tasting condition that would suit market demands. The source just quoted comments as follows:

A stock of old porter sufficient for staling twelve months' consumption, should be kept on hand. . . . The old porter should be mixed in the proportion of one-third with all sent out; it will produce a beverage of uniform strength, having the flavor of age, fine in summer, and full of tone in winter. . . . Never send out Mild Porter entire, as the admixture, if done by others, may spoil the article, and the fault be charged to your management.[27]

It is not clear how extensive this blending was among porter brewers during various times in the beer's history. Some claim that all porter was a blend of "soured" and new products[28] from the very beginning, and this may have been true. However, the description by Obadiah Poundage indicates that during the eighteenth century at least, all production was aged for a number of months before sale — a practice that would eliminate the need for blending.

Production practices clearly changed during the nineteenth century, and this may be when blending became commonplace. It is easy to understand the economic advantages of aging one-third of your production for twelve months versus aging all of your production for five months. Still, some recipes from the latter half of the 1800s indicate blending with aged product while many others clearly show that porter was being sold without any aging whatsoever.[29]

Whereas blending of old and new beer was one way to achieve the acidity desired by porter drinkers, another source notes a more insidious practice in this regard:
When new, as generally prepared at the present day, it is called "mild"; by keeping, a portion of

acid is developed in it and it is then denominated "hard." Formerly, when hard porter was in request, publicans were in the habit of rendering new beer hard, or as it was called, of bringing it forward, by the addition of sulfuric acid.[30]

Such "chemical brewing" was an unfortunate fact of life for porter. A long list of adulterants were used in porter at one time or another. These additions were generally made for marketing reasons, that is, to economically enhance the appeal of the beer to consumers. Such was the case with the sulfuric acid addition noted above. Another example is the use of colorants made from molasses or sugar.

Some sources note that taxation put economic pressure on brewers to reduce the amount of malt in their beers. This produced a decrease in color that was easily detected by the consumer. To overcome this, brewers began to color the beer using caramelized or burnt portions of sugar or molasses, as the following indicates:

Sugar is used in another form, for colouring Porter, it is termed colouring, but in fact for that purpose it is of little or no use, but it gives a pleasant and an agreeable flavour, it is made from Raw Sugar and burnt in an iron pan.[31]

A common coloring was molasses, boiled until it was dark, bitter and thick, and then set on fire and burned for a few minutes.[32]

Sugar and molasses were also sometimes used in quantity as a cheap substitute for malt. One source states that "twelve pounds of moist brown sugar is equal to a bushel of malt,"[33] and another source acknowledges production of a porter that was half malt and half sugar. Of this brew it was said, "It was not an improvement, at least as far as our own taste was concerned, but his customers made no remark, one way or the other, he did the same amount of business, which as it was considerable was pretty well tested in his case."[34]

When included in quantity, sugar produces the alcohol that would otherwise be lost from a recipe when the malt content is reduced. But such large quantities of sugar also cost a brewer money. Many of the other adulterants added to porter were designed to provide a stimulating or narcotizing effect that would give the drinker the impression of alcoholic potency without this cost. The most infamous of these additions was *Cocculus indicus*.

The *Oxford English Dictionary* lists *Cocculus indicus* as "the commercial name of the dried berries of a climbing plant found in Malabar and Ceylon; the berry is a violent poison, and has been used to stupefy fish, and in England to increase the intoxicating power of beer and porter."[35]

For a period during the late 1700s and early 1800s the use of this surprising addition to porter seems to have been commonly practiced but much debated. We are told of a porter recipe printed in the *Encyclopedia Britannica* that calls for *Cocculus indicus*,[36] but the author reporting this fact states, "It may be very well to give directions for two pounds of *Cocculus indicus Berries*, but I declare I should not like to drink the mixture."[37]

Another alludes to the effects of such additions, noting, ". . . in many houses a black sulky beverage being substituted in its stead, on the taste of which the stranger experiences a shake as sudden and electrical as that which seizes a spaniel when quitting the water."[38]

Eventually laws were passed prohibiting use of this poison in beer and penalizing any druggist who supplied it to a brewer.[39]

Other adulterants reportedly used in porter include "opium, Indian hemp, strychnine, tobacco, darnel seed, logwood, and salts of zinc, lead, and alum."[40] One can only wonder at the cornucopia of crud brewers saw fit to include in an otherwise healthful beverage during this time. Surely it is an "industrial" remoteness from the consumer that would lead to production of a beverage that the brewer himself probably would not drink.

Mature Porter

Many influences affected porter during its first one hundred years, from taxes to industrial production techniques to consumer tastes and even the development of brewing science. By the early 1800s porter was no longer formulated from brown malt alone but then included amber and pale malts as well.

Part of the reason for this appears to lie in the adoption of the hydrometer as a brewing tool. Studies with this tool revealed that the extract derived from brown malt was quite low when compared to that available from pale malt. Thus, although pale malt was more expensive, it was more cost-effective. As a result, brewers began to reduce the portion of brown malt in their grists. It's not hard to imagine that the use of artificial colorants as described above may have accompanied this switch. A text from 1818 provides formulations for a porter grist, as shown in table 23.3.

At this point, less than one hundred years after porter was born, brown malt had already lost its place as the style's predominant grain. And only in cases where a homebrewer wanted to make an authentic reproduction do we see a formulation where brown malt makes up as much as

half of the grist. The desire to abandon brown malt altogether seems apparent; the brown malt was retained only as an honest way to produce the color and character of the porter beer.

At this point in history there were effectively no other malts to use other than these three — although this situation was soon to change. Furthermore, the only malt common to all these recipes is one I haven't yet discussed that goes by the name of "amber." The following description from around 1850 gives us some idea of what this malt is all about:

Pale malt is usually made from the best barley, and occupies from two to three days in the drying, the temperature being slowly raised from about 90 °F to 120 °F, and the grain frequently turned. Amber malt is treated in a similar manner, until it is almost dry, when, to give it a slight scorching, the temperature is raised to 160 °F.[41]

By this description, this product sounds something like Munich malt or perhaps one of the lightly roasted character malts such as aromatic or biscuit.

As for the gravity and bitterness of these early-1800s porters, information is a bit sparse. By interpreting the text from which the above grist formulations were drawn, it appears that at least some of the recipes were intended to produce a beer with a gravity of about 1.057.[42] This is consistent with other data for this period,

Table 23.3
Formulations for Porter Grist, 1818

Title	Pale (%)	Amber (%)	Brown (%)
Porter — author's advice	33	33	33
Real Brown Beer[a]	50	50	—
Alternate	33	67	—
Gentleman's Family	50	25	25

Source: J. Tuck, The Private Brewer's Guide to the Art of Brewing Ale and Porter (Woodbridge, Conn.: ZymoScribe, 1995).
[a] The term "brown beer" was often used as a general description for porter or stout during this period.

which quotes gravities as being in the range of 1.054 to 1.065.[43]

However, bitterness seems lower than what is indicated by other sources. My calculations, based upon review of several sections of the text,[44] put the bitterness at 25 to 39 IBU.[45] As the author does not provide any description of the taste to be expected from these recipes, we cannot tell whether this was the level normally encountered at the time or not.

At about the time this text was written, a new development in malt kilning was patented that would completely change the production of porter. In 1817, Daniel Wheeler invented a cylindrical roasting drum that used water sprays to quench the heat and prevent malt from turning into charcoal when deeply roasted.[46] This invention allowed production of black patent malt. In addition, it prevented torrification, or popping, during roasting so that other deeply roasted commodities such as chocolate malt and roast barley could be produced. Wheeler's patent stated, in part, "A small quantity of malt thus prepared will suffice for the purpose of colouring beer or porter."[47]

This new type of malt gave porter brewers a way to achieve the color they wanted without having to be so dependent upon low-yielding brown malt for a significant portion of the grist. Whitbread and Barclay, two of the largest London porter brewers, adopted black malt for their porter recipes within a couple of years.[48] Roasting houses were also quickly established in Dublin quite close to the Guinness brewery.[49]

By the middle of the 1800s the grists for porter brewing had changed considerably, as indicated by a brewing text from that period:

Porter and stout are now prepared almost exclusively from pale and roasted malts, the use of brown and amber malt being confined to a few of the most extensive and best known porter breweries. But although on the score of economy and simplicity there is an advantage in brewing from pale and black malt only, it cannot be doubted, judging from the practice of the great porter-brewers, that to obtain the true porter flavor, a certain proportion of amber or slightly scorched malt should enter into the composition of the grist.

When pale and roasted malts are alone employed the grist is usually made up of 9 bushels or quarters of the former to 1 of the latter.

If brown and amber malts be introduced, the best proportions appear to be 9 of pale, 5 of brown, 5 of amber and 1 of black.[50]

This passage provides a great deal of general information about how the porters of the time were composed. We are fortunate to have available also the details from five different porter recipes brewed — presumably at different breweries — by the itinerant brewer Amsinck, as shown in table 23.4.

The first item of note in these recipes is that amber malt, which appeared in all of the recipes from forty years earlier, had been completely eliminated from use by 1868. Brown malt was still holding on, but it constituted an even smaller portion of the grist than it did earlier in the century. Black malt had clearly become a standard feature of porter recipes, which relied on pale malt for 70 to 80 percent of the grain bill.

Still, this brewer believed in the importance of brown malt, stating, "In Porter Brewings it is of the greatest consequence to have the best Brown, as the flavour depends a good deal on the quality of this part of the grist."[51]

The use of sugar in these recipes is of interest here and appears as a significant ingredient for the first time that I can find. Although short-term exceptions had been made previously, it was not until 1847 that sugar was routinely allowed to be used in beer as a fermentable material. Though still not the dominant practice at this date, it would appear that the use of sugar had clearly become accepted. Overall, the use of sugar in British beers continued to increase through the rest of the 1800s.[52]

The gravities for these beers are consistent with earlier projections of 1.054 to 1.065 and are also in agreement with other sources from this period.[53]

However, the bitterness units, calculated using similar assumptions, are much higher than the single data point I have from earlier in the century. Other sources agree with these higher levels for the porters of this period.[54]

Some descriptions of porter from the mid-1800s provide clues to how it must have looked and tasted:

The qualities which characterize what would be termed good porter or stout, in the present condition of the public taste, are — a light, brown color, fulness on the palate, pure and moderate bitterness, with a mixture of sweetness, a certain sharpness or acerbity without sourness or burnt flavor, and a close, creamy head, instantly closing in when blown aside.[55] . . . if much of the sugar be caramelized by the heat of the copper, there will be a disagreeable bitterness and a want of the soft fulness characteristic of a good porter.[56]

Porter owes much of its tart and astringent flavor to a high, rapid fermentation which lessens the density without diminishing the high flavor drawn from the materials. . . .[57]

[Porter has an] inviting brunette complexion and a mantling effervescence giving it a spurious "cauliflower head."[58]

All of the information available on porter from the middle of the 1800s was set down at a time when porter's dominance of the British beer scene was beginning to wane. By 1865 pale ale was the more popular of the two styles, and by the end of the century it was by far the dominant beer in Britain.

On the status of porter at the turn of the century, Corran states:"The dominant impression gained from a survey of the industry around 1900 is the surprising variety of products. Every medium-sized brewery produced a range of beers, including at least one stout or porter."[59] It is clear that during this period consumers had many styles of beer from which to choose.

Reflecting this reality, there is far less information available about the character and brewing practices related to porter around the turn of the twentieth century. The U.S.-published Wahl-Henius *Handy-Book* lists a number of analyses for British pale ale, but none for porters from the authors' homeland.[60]

The characterizations that are given for porter show similar to higher gravity levels (1.053 to 1.076) in beers with a very low acid content, which indicates a lack of aging at the brewery.

It seems that by this time porter was mostly regarded as the "little brother" of stout. Wahl and Henius state: "Porter is brewed less strong than the old beers. It stands in a similar relation to stout as does a mild to a stock ale."[61] Similarly, table 23.5 lists porter as part of the line of stout beers.

Finally, the directions given for brewing porter and stout are delivered as one parcel:

The principal requirements, as compared with ale, are greater palate-fulness, pronounced malt flavor and darker color. It is best to use mixed malts, i.e., a mixture of high and low kiln-dried malts. If this cannot be had, caramel malt, "black" malt, and sugar coloring to the required amount should be added."[62]

Further indication of the declining importance of porter can be seen in the fact that Whitbread — once the leading producer of porters — destroyed its last porter-aging vat in 1918.[63] During the 1930s, brewers in London ceased production of porter entirely,[64] thus ending its two-hundred-year presence in that metropolis.

In 1957, DeClerck said that porter was "the name given to a light gravity stout, but the name has fallen into disuse."[65] Despite this observation, the Guinness brewery, although better known for its stouts, continued to make a porter in Dublin until 1974.[66] When Guinness ceased production of the stout in that year, it seemed a death knell for porter. What had been the original industrial beer was overrun by the products of its success. Over a two-hundred-year period, the techniques of mass production that had launched porter led brewers to make only limited selection of products that could achieve acceptance in a mass market.

As a consequence, no porter was produced commercially in the British Isles for several years.[67]

Modern Porter

Today of course, porter is alive and well. This is so only because it has been revived by small brewers both in the United States and the United Kingdom. These newcomers to the brewing scene struggle to find a niche in a world dominated by the big industrial brewers. For the most part they succeed, and with them, porter seems to have a new lease on life.

Oddly enough, the popularity of the style seems much greater in the States than in the British Isles. I find only 31 porters listed in Roger Protz's catalog of U.K. real ales,[68] whereas 146 porter brands are listed for U.S. brewers in the *North American Brewers Resource Directory.*[69]

Unfortunately, we have very little information about the American examples other than the alcohol content that is given for most entries. Figure 23.1 shows the distribution of alcohol content for these U.S. porters. Mathematically, we can determine the likely original gravity of these beers by assuming a 72 percent rate of apparent attenuation. When this is done, we find an average gravity of 1.057, with a range from 1.040 to 1.085. It appears from these data that the U.S. porters are fairly close in gravity to many of the historical examples and generally a bit stronger than the average Pilsener or pale ale.

One of the nicest porters I've had comes from Catamount Brewing in Vermont, a chocolaty smooth black ale with a nice level of complexity. Sierra Nevada also

Table 23.4
Five Porter Recipes, circa 1868

| Type | Water | OG (GU) | TG(GU) | MALTS AND SUGAR | | | |
				Pale	Brown	Sugar	Black
Porter[1]	Soft	59.7	25.0	82.20%	14.50%	–	3.30%
Porter[2]	Mid-hard	59.7	21.1	78.30%	7.60%	8.70%	5.40%
Porter[3]	Mid-hard	61.1	20.8	78.10%	17.20%	–	4.70%
Porter[4]	Hard	63.8	13.9	73.00%	11.50%	7.70%	7.70%
Export Porter[5]	Soft	58.3	12.5	71.40%	25.00%	–	3.60%

Source: G. S. Amsinck, Practical Brewings: A Series of Fifty Brewings *(London: George Stewart Amsinck, 1868): 62-75.*
[1] *A July brew, fx temp as high as 77.5 °F; 4% stock ale or porter added before shipment.*
[2] *January brew, fx up to 75 °F. No blending or aging noted.*
[3] *September brew, fx up to 79 °F. No blending or aging noted.*
[4] *May brew, fx to 75 °F.*
[5] *November brew, fx to 77 °F. Dry hopped with 1.5 lb. new, 1 lb. spent hops per hogshead. Exported to India.*
Note: IBUs calculated assuming 4% alpha acid hops and 25% kettle utilization.

Table 23.5
Characterization of the Family of Stout Beers

Beer	°Balling	OG	lb. hops/U.S. bbl.
Porter	13–15	1.052–1.060	0.8–1.5
Single Stout	16–18	1.064–1.072	1.5–2.0
Double Stout	18–20	1.072–1.080	2.0–2.5
Imperial Stout	20–25	1.080–1.100	2.5–3.0
Russian Export	>25	>1.100	>3.25

Source: R. Wahl and M. Henius, The American Handy-Book of the Brewing, Malting and Auxiliary Trades (Chicago: Wahl-Henius Institute, 1908), 1253.

makes an excellent porter that is more assertive with a pronounced roasted character and a typical Sierra Nevada fondness for hops. The example that kept the style alive in the United States for many decades is Yuengling's, which displays a more subtle dark malt character.

The English porters have an average gravity of 1.045 with average bitterness of 31 IBU for an average BU:GU ratio of 0.69. The average color is 31 °SRM with a range from 18 to 74 °SRM. I have tasted a couple of examples in London, including RCH Old Slug Porter, which was very fruity in aroma with underlying roast malt flavors, and Harvey's Porter, which was made with brown malt and had a subdued roasted flavor with a smooth, slightly fruity character.

Brewing Porter

Based upon the English commercial examples and the second-round competitors in the National Homebrew Competition, we can get a pretty good profile of the grains, hops, and other ingredients required to develop an excellent porter.

	HOPS		
Type	(lb./bbl.)	IBU	First Mash Temp.
Kent	2.5	92	152
Belgian Sussex	1.5	55	154
Kent, Olds	2.0	73	154
Sussex, Olds	2.5	90	154
Kent	5.0	186	153

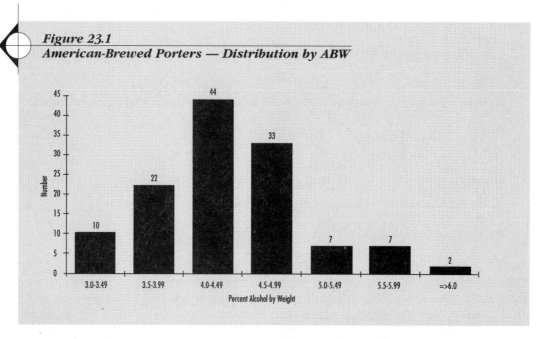

Figure 23.1
American-Brewed Porters — Distribution by ABW

Grain Bills

In examining the grain bills of the U.K. commercial porters, I find one or two that have revived the use of brown malt — although the quantities are small, just 14 to 20 percent. One of these is Whitbread, which made some of the original brown malt porters in the eighteenth century. If you should run across some Whitbread porter, be sure to give it a try.

For the grain bills of the rest of the English commercial porters, I find that the use of chocolate malt, roast barley, and black malt is pretty evenly split among the recipes. In general, most brewers use just one of these three dark grains, often in combination with crystal malt but sometimes without it. The thirty-one recipes examined break down as shown in tables 23.6 and 23.7 (see also table 23.8).

Chocolate is the most common dark grain, found in thirteen of thirty-one recipes. Next comes roast barley, which appears in eleven of the recipes, and finally black malt, which is in ten grain bills. I've always thought that roast barley was the grain that distinguished a stout from a porter, but in

contemporary English porter-brewing this grain is more common than black malt. Here's another way of looking at the dark grain breakdown:

- Ten use roast barley without black malt (two include chocolate)
- Nine use black malt without roast barley (one includes chocolate)
- Nine use chocolate without roast barley or black malt
- One uses roast barley, black malt, and chocolate malt

The homebrews entered in the National Homebrew Competition have been divided into the two categories of "brown porter" and "robust porter" for several years. Unfortunately, fifteen of twenty-one, or 70 percent, of the beers that made it to the second round fell into the "robust" category, so we can only get a glimpse of the differences between these two subgroups.

In general, gravities are not too different between the two, with 1.057 being the mean for robust porters and brown porters coming in just a bit lower at 1.054.

Table 23.6
Porter Recipes Analyzed for Malt Formulation

Formulation	Percent	No. of Recipes
One dark grain plus crystal	55	17
One dark grain, no crystal	26	8
Two dark grains plus crystal	10	3
Chocolate, roast, and black; no crystal	3	1
Crystal only	3	1
No dark or crystal grains	3	1
Total	100	31

The selection of malts between the substyles is quite similar, with crystal, chocolate, and black being the favorites. Despite this similarity, differences do exist between the robust and brown porters. These three grains are found in 80 to 90 percent of all robust porters while appearing in only about two-thirds of the brown porters. Roast malt, although prohibited by the style guidelines, appears in 40 percent of the robust porters.

Munich appears infrequently but accounts for more than 10 percent of the grist on average when it does. Wheat is a frequent minor ingredient in many other styles, but only rarely appears in porters (see table 23.8).

Overall, the grain bills for twenty-one NHC second-round porters break down as follows:

- Eleven use two dark grains plus crystal: nine are chocolate + black and two are chocolate + roast
- Four with everything: chocolate, black, roast, crystal
- Three with one dark grain plus crystal
- Two just one dark grain, no crystal
- Among these five: three black malt, two chocolate, no roast
- One uses all three dark grains, no crystal

The robust examples are more likely than the brown porters to include three dark grains (four of five recipes; or 26 percent of robust porters) and two dark grains (eight of ten recipes; 53 percent of dark porters).

One of the debates about porter grain bills is whether they should include roast barley. The AHA styles strictly prohibit it, but it appears in a number of commercial beers as well as some successful homebrewed examples.

Another factor that undermines this prohibition historically is the close relationship between porter and stout — so close that porter was often considered simply a lighter-gravity stout. In that case, it would not be surprising to find the same grains used in brewing both beers.

In his book *Porter*, Terry Foster confesses that he really does not like roast barley in porter, and that it can "easily put porter out of balance."[70] Still, he says that he thinks of porter as "one beer with a whole continuum of roasted malt flavors" that can include roast barley.[71] Only one of the seven recipes he gives includes roast barley, and that at a rate of 1 ounce in 5 gallons.[72]

About one-third of both the NHC second-round and commercial porters include roast barley. What is different in the homebrews is that roast is usually used in addition to chocolate and black malt for a robust porter, while in the commercial beers it is most often used instead of these other dark grains.

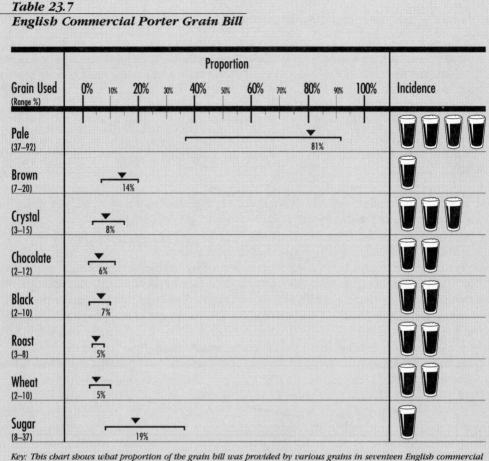

Table 23.7
English Commercial Porter Grain Bill

Grain Used (Range %)	Proportion	Incidence
Pale (37–92)	81%	🍺🍺🍺🍺
Brown (7–20)	14%	🍺
Crystal (3–15)	8%	🍺🍺🍺
Chocolate (2–12)	6%	🍺🍺
Black (2–10)	7%	🍺🍺
Roast (3–8)	5%	🍺🍺
Wheat (2–10)	5%	🍺🍺
Sugar (8–37)	19%	🍺

Key: This chart shows what proportion of the grain bill was provided by various grains in seventeen English commercial porter recipes. The line next to each grain gives the range of values used by different brewers; this range is also listed below "Grains Used." The triangle above each line indicates the average proportion used across all recipes.

The icons in the column on the right show how often the seventeen English commercial porter recipes included each grain. (Percentage figures indicate how many of the recipes included the grain.)

🍺 = rarely (30% or less)   🍺🍺 = sometimes (30% to 60%)

🍺🍺🍺 = often (60% to 90%)   🍺🍺🍺🍺 = usually (90% or more)

I'm more fond of the brown porter designation, and so, like Foster, I would prefer brewers save the roast barley for their stouts. Still, from time to time — especially in the Pacific Northwest — you get a really nice beer sold under the porter name that includes a healthy helping of roast barley. As with most issues related to the art of brewing, the final choice is up to the individual to select a grain combination that gives a beer he or she finds interesting and fulfilling.

Finally, a brief look at mash temperatures. The old recipes from 1863 list a very narrow range for the first mash temperature: 152 to 154 °F (67 to 68 °C). Similarly, the NHC second-round recipes show an average mash temperature of 153 °F (67 °C), although the range is much wider, from 147 to 160 °F (64 to 71 °C). Whether it is coincidence or some sort of brewer telepathy that creates this kind of congruence between old and new brewing methods, I don't know. But in any case, it

Table 23.8

Porter Grain Bill in NHC Second-Round Recipes

Robust Porters

Grain Used (Range %)	Proportion	Incidence
Pale (72–93)	80%	🍺🍺🍺🍺
Extract (6)	6%	🍺
Munich (9–16)	11%	🍺
Crystal (2–14)	8%	🍺🍺🍺
Chocolate (2–7)	4%	🍺🍺🍺
Black (2–9)	4%	🍺🍺🍺
Roast (2–6)	4%	🍺🍺
Wheat (2–4)	3%	🍺

Proportion scale: 0%, 10%, 20%, 30%, 40%, 50%, 60%, 70%, 80%, 90%, 100%

Key: This chart shows what proportion of the grain bill was provided by various grains in fifteen robust porter recipes. The line next to each grain gives the range of values used by different brewers; this range is also listed below "Grains Used." The triangle above each line indicates the average proportion used across all recipes.

The icons in the column on the right show how often the fifteen robust porter recipes included each grain. (Percentage figures indicate how many of the recipes included the grain.)

🍺 = rarely (30% or less)   🍺🍺 = sometimes (30% to 60%)
🍺🍺🍺 = often (60% to 90%)   🍺🍺🍺🍺 = usually (90% or more)

establishes a pretty clear target for those just starting to brew the porter style.

Hop Selection and Use

For the commercial porters brewed in Britain, hop selection follows pretty much the same patterns as with other English styles. Goldings varieties are the most popular, and Challenger, Fuggle, and Northdown account for the majority of the remainder. The incidence of each variety among the thirty-one recipes analyzed is shown in table 23.9.

Reported bitterness levels of the commercial British porters vary from 20 to 60 IBU, or BU:GU ratios of 0.40 to 1.11. The average values come in at 31 IBU and a BU:GU ratio of 0.69. Aroma hopping is fairly commonly practiced these days, with about

Table 23.8 *continued*
Porter Grain Bill in NHC Second-Round Recipes

Brown Porters

Grain Used (Range %)	Proportion					Incidence
	0% 10% 20% 30% 40% 50% 60% 70% 80% 90% 100%					
Pale (3–89)	55%					🍺🍺🍺
Extract (37–100)	71%					🍺🍺🍺
Munich (12)	12%					🍺
Crystal (5–16)	11%					🍺🍺🍺
Chocolate (3–6)	4%					🍺🍺🍺
Black (1–12)	5%					🍺🍺🍺
Roast (2)	2%					🍺
Wheat (3)	3%					🍺

Key: This chart shows what proportion of the grain bill was provided by various grains six brown porter recipes. The line next to each grain gives the range of values used by different brewers; this range is also listed below "Grains Used." The triangle above each line indicates the average proportion used across all recipes.

The icons in the column on the right show how often the six brown porter recipes included each grain. (Percentage figures indicate how many of the recipes included the grain.)

🍺 = rarely (30% or less)   🍺🍺 = sometimes (30% to 60%)

🍺🍺🍺 = often (60% to 90%)   🍺🍺🍺🍺 = usually (90% or more)

---

a quarter of all recipes specifically mentioning late additions of dry hops.

In the NHC second-round porters, a clear difference emerges in bitterness levels between the robust and brown subcategories. Robust porters have an average BU:GU ratio of 0.93 (53 IBU), versus a value of 0.72 (39 IBU) for the browns.

In the NHC examples of styles with a strong English heritage, such as IPA and English pale ale, I often find that U.S. varieties dominate the hop profiles. Here, where the majority of commercial examples come from the U.S., I find English hop varieties taking the lead in the NHC examples. Goldings, Northern Brewer, and Willamette account for three times as many additions as Cascade and Chinook. A number of different aroma hops, such as Hallertau and Saaz, see some duty for late hop additions. Table 23.10 presents the complete data on hops varieties and use in these beers.

Similar to the English commercial brews, I find that 25 percent of the hop additions are for aroma purposes (dry hopped, steeped, or boiled for less than ten minutes), and a similar portion is used for flavor (boiled for ten to thirty minutes). The average size of these late additions is shown in table 23.11.

Yeast

A fruity character is common in the British-brewed porters I have tasted, so selection of one of the British ale yeasts is particularly appropriate for the style. When selecting a yeast, keep in mind that porter is generally a well-attenuated style, with little residual sweetness.[73] Foster suggests the use of a yeast with good attenuation and medium flocculation characteristics.[74]

Accordingly, the homebrewed beers used mostly British yeasts (ten recipes) of various types, including London, Whitbread, Full-bodied, and Classic. Another popular yeast was the Irish strain (five recipes), although it was the sweeter, low-attenuating version. Although this strain is often recommended for all dark beers, the lower attenuation characteristic may not be the best for

porter. Check the attenuation level for the brand of Irish yeast available to you before using it in a porter.

As always, the standard American ale yeast (five recipes) gets some use as well. The clean, attenuated palate produced by this yeast is always safe, if a bit lacking in the fruitiness found in authentic English ales.

Water

If you have a reasonable level of carbonate or temporary hardness in your water, you probably won't need to do much other than add a bit of salt or calcium chloride when brewing porters.

The London water that nurtured the growth of porter has 160 parts per million of carbonate, 100 parts per million of sodium, and 60 parts per million of chloride. These last two contribute to palate fullness and help to provide a roundness or smoothness to the flavor. Further comments on adjustment of water to London quality are provided in chapter 20.

Among the NHC second-round recipes, only four (19 percent) added salts containing chloride (3) or carbonate (2) to the water. Most of the others simply added a bit of gypsum (typically 1 teaspoon) to the mash with no further adjustments to the water chemistry.

Table 23.9
Hop Incidence in Commercial British Porters

Hop	Percentage Incidence in Porter Recipes
Goldings	68
Challenger	39
Fuggle	32
Northdown	16
Target	6
Progress	6
Other	6

Note: Total number of recipes analyzed = 31

Table 23.10
Hops Used in NHC Second-Round Porters

Hop	Bitter	Flavor	Aroma	Dry	Total
Goldings	7	4	2	1	14
N. Brewer	10	0	1	0	11
Willamette	3	3	2	0	8
Cascade	0	5	2	0	7
Chinook	4	0	0	0	4
Eroica	4	0	0	0	4
Fuggle	0	1	3	0	4
Mt. Hood	0	1	2	0	3
Tettnanger	1	0	2	0	3
Hallertau	1	1	0	0	2
Saaz	0	1	0	1	2
Other[a]	3	0	1	0	4

[a] Other includes Centennial, Nugget, Ringwood, and Target, each of which appeared once.
Note: The data in this chart show the number of times each hop was used across the twenty-one recipes analyzed, which included fifteen robust porters and six brown porters.

Conclusion

You can still see advertisements for the position of "porter" in London today, but I imagine that the work is a bit different now than it was in 1722, when this fine beverage came into being. Still, even though modern tools may ease the process, I am sure that the fundamental need for a strong back to get the job done hasn't disappeared. Similarly, the brewing of porter now uses modern ingredients and processes, but the final effect brewers are trying to achieve hasn't changed all that much from the products of a century or two ago.

Porter is a wonderful style that is rich in history and variety. Whether you decide to make your own brown (and perhaps amber) malt in an effort to emulate the original porter, or whether you experiment with different proportions of chocolate, black, and roast grains in a contemporary formulation, you'll find there are many potential variations to explore.

Table 23.11
Hop Additions in NHC Second-Round Porters

Addition	Avg. No. per Recipe	Size of Addition[a] oz./gal.	Size of Addition[a] oz./5 gal.
Boil	1.6	–	–
Flavor	0.8	0.12	0.61
Aroma	0.7	0.16	0.78
Dry	0.1	–	–
Total	3.1		

[a] Only two porters were dry hopped.

You might add sugar or molasses to a batch or two. Alternatively, you might purchase a *Brettanomyces* culture and spike it into a batch for aging to that "racy and mellow" condition that was enjoyed more than two centuries ago.

If you are a competitive brewer, you'll want to heed the current guidelines, but you'll still have wide latitude for interpretation. Selection of yeast can give a pleasant fruitiness that is found in so many English ales. Selection and scheduling of your hop additions can produce a wide variety of effects and flavors — all well within the formal style guidelines.

Key Success Factors in Brewing Porter

- Select a good pale ale malt as the base malt for your recipe.

- Good quality pale extract can also be used as the base for a porter, providing you add the appropriate dark grains as listed below.

- Decide upon your dark grain strategy according to the type of finished product you wish to produce. For robust porter include black malt with chocolate and usually some crystal as well. A touch of roast malt may be included on an experimental basis. For brown porter, exclude black and roast malt and rely just on chocolate with some crystal. For experimental original porter, roast up some brown malt over a smoky wood fire.

- Water treatment should focus on achieving London-type water with medium-high levels of carbonate, sodium, and chloride. Choose calcium over calcium sulfate (gypsum) for mash calcium adjustment. A quarter-teaspoon or less of noniodized salt may be added to the boil.

- When mashing, conduct your saccharification rest in the range of 152 to 154 °F (67 to 68 °C).

- As a starting point, bittering hops should be added to achieve a BU:GU ratio of about 0.70 to 0.90 (35 to 50 IBU). Choose the lower end of the range for brown porters, the higher end for robust types.

- If you choose to add flavor and aroma hops, use English-type varieties (Goldings, Fuggle, Willamette), American Cascades, or continental aroma hops such as Hallertau, Tettnanger, or Saaz.

- Conduct a normal-length boil of sixty to ninety minutes.

- Ferment with a British ale yeast that gives good attenuation and produces some fruity character. Normal ale fermentation temperatures of less than 72 °F (22 °C) should be observed unless you want to experiment with the high-temperature fermentations (77 to 79 °F, 25 to 27 °C) seen in the industrial days of porter.

- For a special treat, lightly dry hop the porter in secondary fermenter with Goldings, as a small portion of modern British brewers do.

- For the truly experimental, age a batch of porter for six months after inoculating it with a *Brettanomyces* culture.

Sidebar: Roasting Your Own Amber and Brown Malts

Some of the malts traditionally used to make porter are no longer available commercially. To emulate the eighteenth- and nineteenth-century recipes, you will have to roast your own malts according to the following procedures, provided by Dr. John Harrison and the Durden Park Beer Circle.[75]

Procedure for Amber Malt

Place pale ale malt to a depth of ½ inch in a foil-lined cooking pan. Cook in the oven as follows:

1. Forty-five minutes at 230 °F (110 °C)
2. Twenty to sixty minutes at 300 °F (149 °C)
3. After the first twenty minutes, cut several kernels in half to inspect the color of the starchy endosperm. For amber malt, this area should be light buff in color when finished. Continue heating at 300 °F (149 °C) until this color is achieved, usually after forty-five to fifty minutes.

Procedure for Brown Malt

Follow the procedure for amber malt. After the proper endosperm color is achieved, raise the oven temperature to 350 °F and continue heating until the endosperm is a full buff color, or "about the color of the paler types of brown wrapping paper."

Alternative

As an alternative to these procedures, Randy Mosher[76] recommends filling a pan to a depth of no more than 1 inch. For amber malt, heat at 350 °F (176.5 °C) for twenty to thirty minutes; for brown malt, heat at 450 °F (232 °C) for thirty to forty minutes. As with the above procedures, evaluate the extent of roasting by periodically examining a cross section of the malt.

24 SCOTTISH AND SCOTCH ALES

With so many other kinds of ale, I sometimes find it a little hard to believe that the Scots could brew beers so distinct that they deserve recognition as a separate style. But anyone who has sampled a couple of Scottish ales will find that this is so.

In most taxonomies of beer the very strong beers (called Scotch ales) are classified separately from the lower-gravity Scott*ish* ales. In truth, however, all are brewed in much the same way, so it makes sense to treat them all together in one chapter.

The Scottish ales include three different subcategories, generally distinguished by gravity and called Scottish-style light, heavy, and export ales. The Scotch ales are sometimes called strong Scotch ales to clearly distinguish them from their Scottish ale brethren. The name "wee heavy" is also often used for these strong ales and should not be confused with the Scottish-style heavy ale.

An antiquated system of nomenclature for Scottish-style ales that is based on an obsolete unit of currency called the shilling is also seen from time to time. This system designates the four styles based on the nineteenth-century price charged for a barrel of each one. Light, heavy, and export are known as 60/-, 70/-, and 80/-, respectively, where "/-" is read as "shilling." The strong Scotch ales are designated with higher values, ranging from 90/- to 160/-.

Let's first review the parameters of the individual styles before we move on to see how these beers came to be unique among British ales (see table 24.1).

The Brewing of Ales in Scotland

Although Scotland harbors a population only one-tenth the size of England's, it has nurtured a unique brewing culture for much of its history. Like its neighbors (and sometimes competitors) to the south, Scottish brewers were active in exporting beer around the globe during the eighteenth and nineteenth centuries. They also produced a broad variety of styles, including those usually associated with England and Ireland, and they were the first brewers in the British Isles to make lagers.

Despite the variety of beers produced in Scotland over the last few centuries, one particular flavor profile emerged as the characteristic style of the land. As in other great brewing areas, this unique style is the result of geography and politics rather than of the will of the brewers. Let's review some of the factors that have led to the development of Scotch and Scottish-style ales.

Agriculture still occupies three-quarters of the land in Scotland, and grains constitute the leading crops.[1] Barley remains secondary, behind wheat, oats, and potatoes, but it is still widely grown. Barley

Table 24.1
Style Definitions of Scottish-Style and Scotch Ales

	60/- Light	70/- Heavy	80/- Export	90/- Strong
Original Gravity	1.030–35	1.035–40	1.040–50	1.072–85
Bitterness	9–20	10–19	15–25	25–35
BU:GU ratio	0.3–0.55	0.3–0.5	0.3–0.5	0.35–0.40
Hop flavor & aroma	None to low	None to low	None to med.	Low to med.
Color (SRM)	8–17	10–19	10–19	10–47
Apparent extract	1.006–10	1.010–14	1.010–18	1.020–28
Alcohol (volume)	3–4	3.5–4	4–4.5	6.2–8
Esters	None to low	None to low	None to med.	Medium
Diacetyl	Low to med.	Low to med.	Low to med.	Medium to high

Flavor Profile	All Scotch ales have a malt-balanced flavor profile, low carbonation, and little or no hop character. The classic fruity/estery aroma found in most ales is often undetectable due to low-temperature fermentations. A unique flavor that can be present in Scottish ale is a faint smoky character that is allowed in all four subtypes. The strong type will also have a distinct alcoholic character that helps to balance the sweetness of the style.

Note: Guidelines are based on the Institute for Brewing Studies and American Homebrewers Association's guidelines, and are modified slightly to conform to current commercial practice.

produced in the north of Scotland most often becomes Scotch whiskey, while that grown in the south is better suited to the making of beer.[2] As a result of these patterns, barley has been readily accessible to Scottish brewers throughout their history.

In contrast to barley, hops refuse to flourish in Scotland. As best I can tell, commercial hop production has never been established there. Long after the English had conceded to use hops, the Scots continued to prefer other bittering substances. There can be little doubt that a portion of this preference was born of economy, because hops had to be imported and were no doubt expensive. In addition, the Scots and the English have been far from friendly during much of their history, and Scottish brewers were most likely reluctant to adopt a practice embraced by their southern neighbors.

A variety of products were used instead of hops by Scottish brewers.

Bickerdyke reports that "ginger, pepper, spices and aromatic herbs" were used, perhaps as far back as the fifteenth century.[3] Later a substance called "quassia" became popular, and Noonan reports that it was used even into the nineteenth and twentieth centuries.[4] This bitter substance, derived from the wood of a tropical American plant, has also been used in medicine and as an insecticide.[5] One pound of quassia could be substituted for 12 pounds of hops.[6]

Like hops, quassia appears to have been an imported product. In both cases, economic pressures would no doubt favor minimal bittering of the Scottish ales. Thus, the patterns of agriculture and trade seem to have set the characteristic malt balance of Scottish ales long before brewers began to vary the style of product they produced.

A further encouragement of these pressures came when Scotland and England joined in 1707. An excise tax on malt had been imposed on English brewers ten years earlier. Because it was greater than the tax on hops, it encouraged an emphasis on hops in the making of English beers. The Treaty of Union that joined Scotland and England specifically excluded Scotland from the malt excise tax, thus sustaining the malt-oriented view of the Scottish brewers.[7]

During the century that followed this union, English brewing — led by the London porter producers — became industrialized. During the same century, Scottish ale production also expanded and changed.

At the beginning of the eighteenth century, most beer produced in Scotland was a fairly low-gravity type known as two-penny.[8] By contrast, nearly two-thirds of all English ale production was strong beer.[9] By 1800, the popularity of strong "Scotch" ale had risen, and these products accounted for more than a third of all Scottish brewery output.[10]

In the last half of the eighteenth century, the number of public breweries in Scotland rose from less than 50 to about 150.[11] Furthermore, established breweries expanded and began a campaign to sell more beer in England during this time.[12] The success of this effort may be marked by the fact that Scottish ale sold at a premium in London by around 1820.[13] This resurgence was relatively short-lived, however, with pale ale taking the foremost place with English ale drinkers within a few decades.

Despite these fluctuations in production, the Scottish strong ale appears to have held a place in the export market since prior to the union with England. Noonan reports that "well-aged and strong Scotch ales had gained an international reputation at least as early as 1578."[14] Furthermore, one historian of the eighteenth century reports that "despite the smallness of these quantities of Scotch ale involved, it may very well be that no inconsiderable proportion of the strong drink brewed in Scotland came to England."[15]

Then, during the nineteenth century, exports of strong beer are reported to have reached Jamaica, the West Indies, Canada, South America, Germany, the United States, Denmark, Russia, India, Australia, South America, and Africa.[16]

To ensure their success, however, the Scottish brewers were forced to brew other types of beer for export. In some cases they were aided by flukes of circumstance, in other cases by good old competitive capitalism. As an example of the former, it happens that certain wells in Edinburgh and Alloa produced hard water that proved suitable for the making of Burton ales. Still, the Scottish brewers lacked critical knowledge of how to brew the style, so they hired brewers away from established Burton breweries. With these resources in hand, the Scottish brewers set about to make India pale ale.

Apparently they met with great success in copying styles indigenous to other regions of Great Britain. Noonan reports that "by the late 1880s, Scottish brewers were exporting more India pale ale and export stout than Scotch ale."[17] Further evidence of this diversity comes from a practical Scottish brewing text from 1847, which includes a lengthy chapter devoted to the subject of brewing "India Ales."[18]

The revolution in lager brewing, although largely ignored in England, reached Scotland during the nineteenth century. The rapid adoption of lager brewing in Scotland may reflect the extent to which production of Scottish ales paralleled that of lagers.

Tennent was one of the first brewers to adopt lager brewing, and to this day its lager is better known in the United States than its ales. It began lager production in 1888 in a brewery that had been constructed more than a century before. Its success led to construction of a new brewery by 1906 that was "devoted to the manufacture of Lager, Munich and Pilsener beer."[19] In that same year, Corran reports,

"We find advertisements for Tennent's lager, Allsop's lager and a lager from Jeffrey's of Edinburgh."

Nineteenth-Century Brewing of Scottish Ales

Practical information on the classic techniques used in brewing Scottish ales is fairly scarce, but two sources provide some insight in this area. The first is a complete text on Scottish brewing published in 1847 by W. H. Roberts. This book, entitled *The Scottish Ale Brewer and Practical Maltster*, is a rare find that came to me through the generosity of master brewer and fellow book maven Steve Presley. This source covers the brewing process in detail and provides data on eighty different Scotch ales.

As a secondary source of information, I turn again to the itinerant brewer Amsinck, who describes two Scotch/Scottish ale brewings among the many recipes he published in 1868.[20] As I review his information, keep in mind that these recipes were brewed by English brewers trying to emulate the Scottish style of brewing.

On the selection of ingredients, the two sources generally agree. Amsinck's recipes call for "white" malt and Roberts makes the case for the use of malt "dried at the lowest instead of the highest temperature." Roberts emphasizes this malt selection by discussing the color achieved rather than the flavor:

The ale made from [this malt] will be of a paler and more delicate hue, and this peculiar colour, accompanied by a transparent clearness, has ever been considered an indispensable beauty. By strict attention to the rules prescribed, in regard to the quality of malt, the Scotch ales have justly acquired celebrity for their delicacy of colour.[21]

From this passage it is clear that Roberts considers Scotch ales to be beautifully pale, even though we generally think of them as darker in color than the English examples. Amsinck's records show a small portion of black malt added to one of the English-brewed Scottish ale recipes. This would, of course, darken the color of the finished beer. From this, we can deduce that the pale malts of England probably produced a lighter colored product than the pale malts of Scotland.

In conducting the mash, Amsinck's recipes, like most English brews of the day, show the use of more than one mash. The first mash would be conducted and run off into the copper before the lauter drain was closed and the second mash commenced. However, unlike most English brews at that time, which were mashed three or four times, both of Amsinck's Scottish recipes introduce sparging after the second mash.

Although sparging was rarely practiced in England, the brewers chronicled by Amsinck employed it in making Scottish ales in an effort to emulate the practices of Edinburgh. Still, they could not resist conducting at least two mashes before initiating the sparge.

In contrast to this, Roberts — writing a good twenty years earlier — notes only one mash followed by sparging as the standard practice in Scotland. He provides the following description of mashing and sparging:

The process of mashing in Scotland, by means of oars . . . is the same as in England. It is performed with the greatest care, until every ball or lump is broken, and the whole uniformly mashed. When this process is completed, about a bushel of grist is equally strewed upon the surface of the mash, which, by forming a temporary paste, retains the heat, and keeps up the temperature. The time generally employed in [mashing in] is from forty to fifty minutes. The mash-tun is then covered up, and allowed to remain in that state from two to three hours, accordant to the heat of the air. This being done, the tap is then set, and the wort allowed to run into the under-back . . .[22]

The practice of the Scottish brewer is to commence sparging very soon after the taps are set, or, as it is termed, slacked; others commence to sparge immediately upon the taps being set, and, indeed, some commence before they slack, and continue this operation without intermission until the desired quantity of extract has been obtained . . .[23]

As for the conditions of mashing, Roberts provides the greatest detail. He recommends a grist-to-liquor ratio equivalent to 1.33 pounds per quart. The strike temperature of the liquid is rather high by any standard, in the range from 180 to 190 °F (82 to 88 °C). Furthermore, he explains that, in Scotland, the liquor is added to the mash tun first and the proper temperature obtained before the grist is dumped in. This is the reverse of the English process, where the grist was dumped into the tun and then the liquor was added. Following the Scottish practice, the tun itself would have already been warmed, and so no heat would be lost to the metal during mash-in. Thus, even with comparable liquor temperatures, we would expect the Scottish mash to result in a slightly higher mash rest temperature.

Thus, as a result of both high liquor temperature and the methods employed in mashing, the rest temperature of the Scottish mash was no doubt quite high. Although Roberts supplies no data with regard to this measure, he does give a range for "tap heats." This is the temperature of the wort during runoff. Here, too, relatively high temperatures, with a range of 147 to 152 °F (64 to 67 °C), are quoted by Roberts.[24] Clearly, a wort having this temperature at the end of mashing will be fairly dextrinous — a feature that we shall see is characteristic of the Scotch and Scottish-style ales.

On the hop front, both Amsinck and Roberts indicate the use of Kent-grown products. Roberts mentions North-Clay and Worcester hops in passing but states that in Edinburgh, "nine-tenths of the hops which are used in brewing are grown in the county of Kent."

As is often the case with nineteenth-century recipes, the levels of bitterness actually achieved in these beers is the big question. Regarding the amount of hops used, Roberts is less than precise. He states, "In winter brewings, six pounds of hops for the best ale and four for the inferior kinds, may be considered a fair estimate." Given some reasonable assumptions about the conditions affecting utilization, I calculate additions of this size giving 40 to 60 IBU. Depending on the gravity of the ale produced, this would yield a BU:GU ratio of 0.40 to 0.70.

My calculations on Amsinck's English-brewed recipes gave higher BU:GU ratios, at 0.9 and 0.7. Several explanations may be found for this. First, since year-old hops are specified, their bittering power was no doubt greatly reduced, and the effective bitterness may be much lower than the calculations indicate. Second, being English, the brewers who formulated these recipes may have decided to increase the bitterness to their liking rather than to stick to an authentic Scottish recipe.

From both of our sources on Scottish ales, it appears that the hops were commonly added for the full duration of the boil. Roberts notes the only exception to this, explaining his own practice of adding 40 percent of the hops before the boil commences and the remaining 60 percent thirty to forty minutes before the end of the boil.[25] He notes, however, that this is not the general practice and that most Edinburgh brewers "put in the whole of the hops at the time when the wort is pumped into the copper."[26]

One of the greatest differences between English and Scottish brewing was the temperature of fermentation. Roberts provides commentary on this subject:

While the English brewers commence their fermentation at a high temperature, for the purpose of effecting a rapid attenuation; the [Scottish brewers] set out with a low temperature, and the process is consequently more protracted. These differences are very considerable; for, while the English brewers frequently set their worts as high as 75, or, according to some practical writers, occasionally 80, the Scottish seldom if ever exceed 58, and, in some cases, fall so low as 44. It must not be understood that 75 is a common temperature amongst the English, nor 44 amongst the Scottish brewers. These are extreme cases; but the average of the one may be taken at 65 and of the other at 50. These differences of heat necessarily cause corresponding differences in the time required to produce the same result; and accordingly, it is not uncommon in Scotland for brewers to have their gyles in the tun for twenty-one days, whilst in England, so long a period even as six days is considered as of rare occurrence.[27]

I am in a position to speak somewhat confidently on this point, having for a considerable time past been occupied in ascertaining, by every means in my power, the heats now employed by Scottish brewers; and from the information I have obtained, have been led to the conclusion that, when the atmosphere is tolerably cool, say about 42, the average temperature employed by the Scottish brewers may be considered as about 53 °F.[28]

In accordance with the Scottish practice, Amsinck's beers were fermented cool, and attemperators were used to keep the fermentation temperatures below 65 °F (18 °C) — a temperature that was indeed 7 to 10 degrees cooler than many of the other ale fermentations he documents.

Other fermentation issues related by Roberts include the fact that skimming the yeast was not generally practiced in Scotland, as it was in England. Furthermore, at the conclusion of fermentation Scottish brewers would transfer their ales to a second fermenter rather than fill the ale directly into barrels, as was the practice in England. The Scotch ales were allowed to sit in the secondary fermentor

for only a day or two, after which they were transferred to barrels. This practice probably helped to clear most of the yeast and haze from the beer, because Roberts observes that "Scottish brewers make no use of isinglass for finings."[29]

From Amsinck, we see that these beers were not extensively aged before delivery to the trade. The lighter-gravity product was shipped within two weeks of brewing, and the strong product received only six weeks' aging after fermentation was complete. Many ales and porters of the day were aged for longer periods or were blended with long-aged batches in order to give them a tart character derived from the action of *Brettanomyces* in the aging casks. One can only imagine that delivery of the sweetish, malt-accented flavor of a Scotch ale required brewers to avoid development of this tartness. This would explain the short aging before delivery. Roberts, unfortunately, is silent on this issue except as it relates to small beer, as shown at the end of this chapter in the sidebar on Scottish small beer, which is also known as Musselburgh Broke.

The final characteristic of these beers I will discuss is the degree of attenuation. As summarized in table 24.2, Roberts provides data on eighty ales brewed in Scotland, most coming from Edinburgh. This data shows that most of the Scotch ales were rather low in attenuation, with a range from 55 percent to 65 percent. According to Amsinck, most English ales of a similar gravity showed attenuation of 62 to 71 percent at the end of primary fermentation, and additional attenuation no doubt occurred during aging.

The low attenuation associated with Scotch ales results primarily from the high mash temperatures employed and perhaps, to a small extent, from the low fermentation temperature and short aging before consumption. Today, low attenuation and the full body that results are still characteristic of Scotch and Scottish-style ales.

Modern Examples

Many Scottish brewers still export a good portion of their strong ale production, and good examples can usually be found in the United States. Caledonian sends its strong ale to the United States under the label of MacAndrews Scotch Ale. Other examples of Scotch ale can be found as McEwan's Scotch Ale and Traquair House Ale. In addition, many brewpubs and some microbreweries make up a batch of wee heavy from time to time, and some are quite good.

It is fairly easy to find a representative sample of the strong Scotch ale style in the United States but a bit harder to find a good Scottish-style ale. I've recently enjoyed Belhaven's St. Andrews Ale, and it seems to be a pretty good example of the Scottish styles, even though at 1.046 it is a bit high in gravity even for an 80/-. McEwan's Export is sometimes seen here, and Caledonian's Golden Promise Ale has a bit of Scottish character to it. Washington State's Grant's produces a Scottish-Style Ale with a representative malt character but with more hop character than usual.

Brewing the Scottish Style

The need for cool fermentation and low attenuation in producing Scotch and Scottish-style ales is clear from the historic brewing practices I have reviewed.

Other practices that may be used to achieve the desired malt character in these ales include:

- Extensive cellaring at cold temperatures[30]
- Low hopping rates to produce a malt balance[31]
- Use of roast barley[32]
- Caramelization in the copper[33]
- No hop flavor or aroma[34]

With these common characteristics of the Scots ales in mind, let us review the basic brewing ingredients and procedures.

The Malt Bill

Although the base malt in most English-style ales is a good-quality pale ale malt with color of 2 to 3 °SRM, classic Scottish pale malt was reportedly darker, in the range of 3 to 4 °SRM.[35] Maltsters occasionally still make a mild ale malt in this approximate color range, but it is rarely available in the United States, and even Scottish brewers now rely primarily on standard pale malts. Although this slightly darker base malt can provide some of the color and character of Scotch and Scottish-style ales, roasted grains have become a part of the formulation.

It seems clear that most Scottish brewers traditionally did their own malting.[36] In addition to allowing greater control of

Table 24.2
Key Characteristics of Nineteenth-Century Scotch Ales

Type	Gravity in GUs			
	TG	OG	AA%	ABV%
140/- to 160/- ales	54.5	123.9	56.2	9.3
100/- to 120/- ales	40.2	108.6	63.0	9.0
60/- to 80/- ales	28.9	86.0	65.9	7.4
All examples	39.2	103.7	63.0	8.5

the finished product, this encouraged certain other practices that have influenced the evolution of Scottish ales. For instance, maltsters usually experience losses from poor-quality barley and from that portion of each batch that resists germination and floats to the top of the steep tank. Rather than lose this grain, Scottish brewers often roasted it so that it could be added in small quantities to contribute color and flavor to their ales.[37] This thrifty practice created a place for roast barley in the Scots' beers that continues even today.

One can make a superb Scottish-style ale using nothing but pale malt, a bit of dextrin malt, and a small quantity of roast barley. Noonan recommends this approach, at one point quoting Dr. David Brown, Scottish and Newcastle's technical director: "Keep in mind that this is oversimplified, but the use of roast barley, and residual sweetness, determines more what makes a Scotch ale than does the yeast."[38]

Furthermore, the mid-1800s recipes from Amsinck also support this approach. I have made a best-of-show quality Scottish-style export following this basic formulation; commercially, McEwan's uses it as the basis for its 70/- and 80/- products, adding only some sugar to the recipes.[39]

To get the best results using this simple grain bill, you should pay attention to the procedural steps outlined above to help emphasize the malt portion of the product: caramelization in the kettle with a long boil, cool fermentation temperature, low attenuation, and minimal hop flavor, aroma, and bitterness. A Scottish-style ale made this way should produce excellent results and will emulate the traditional Scottish ale product.

Other Approaches

Although historical, commercial, and homebrew evidence support this simple, pale-plus-roast-barley approach to the Scottish-style ale grain bill, many brewers —

both professional and amateur — follow other routes when making these styles.

Among the commercial brewers, a single approach is generally applied to all the Scottish products made by a specific brewery. When it comes to the dark roasted grains, black malt appears in more recipes than either chocolate malt or roast barley.

The brewers of Traquair House, Belhaven, and Caledonian all use black malt. Traquair House uses it alone, with no other dark or crystal malts. Belhaven generally supplements the black malt with some crystal malt. The Caledonian recipes always use chocolate and crystal malt with two out of three adding black malt as well.

After black malt, chocolate malt is most popular. In addition to the Caledonian recipes just mentioned, three Orkney ales use chocolate, supplemented with crystal malt.

Roast barley appears in just three commercial recipes, the two mentioned earlier from McEwan's, plus one from Harviestoun that includes crystal malt in the formulation.

In all cases, the amounts of these dark grains are very small, accounting for only 2 percent of the grist on average. One-third of the Scotch and Scottish-style ale recipes listed in Protz's *Real Ale Almanac* exclude the three dark roast grains altogether. Three products from Maclay use only pale malt and caramel coloring. A fourth Maclay ale, plus one product each from West Highland, Alloa, and Harviestoun, include crystal malt as the only color or character malt. Table 24.3 summarizes these findings.

Beyond the color grains, wheat — either malted or torrified — appears in 45 percent of Scottish-style ales. Sugar of some sort can also be found in 50 percent of all recipes. Only two recipes (both McEwan's) include both wheat and sugar; only five exclude them both (Traquair House and Maclay). Thus, nearly 80 percent of all Scottish-style ale recipes use one or the other of these nonbarley ingredients (see table 24.4).

NHC Second-Round Malt Bills

In the National Homebrew Competition second-round beers, the roles of roast barley and black malt are reversed. Roast barley appears in approximately 40 percent of both Scottish-style and Scotch ales, while black malt is completely absent from these recipes. Among the recipes using roast barley, most also include crystal malt. Only three recipes out of twenty-seven (11 percent) for Scottish-style and Scotch ale used roast barley without including crystal malt.

Chocolate malt occurs only slightly more often in NHC second-round beers than in the commercial examples, appearing in 35 percent of Scottish-style ale recipes and 40 percent of Scotch ale recipes. Chocolate malt rarely appears in the same recipe with roast barley (two of twenty-seven recipes), but it is nearly always accompanied by crystal malt (nine of ten recipes).

In general, crystal malt appears more frequently in the NHC second-round recipes (82 percent) than in commercial examples (64 percent). As a result, homebrew recipes based primarily on pale and crystal malts were more common, accounting for 30 percent of all recipes among both the low- and high-gravity formulations.

Unlike commercial recipes, the NHC second-round beers usually included some form of character malt. Munich malt appears in 35 percent of the recipes, and some sort of amber malt in another 47 percent. The amber designation includes home-toasted malt as well as special roast, biscuit, Victory, mild ale, aromatic, amber, and brown malts. One of these special malts or Munich malt appears in 78 percent of the Scottish-style and Scotch ale recipes.

In Scottish-style ales from the NHC second round, grains such as wheat, dextrin, and flaked barley occur at a rate similar to that found in commercial examples. Dextrin malt is the most popular alternative, followed by wheat and then flaked barley. The majority of strong Scotch ales included one of these three grains. By contrast with the commercial brews, only one recipe included sugar (see tables 24.5 and 24.6).

Smoked Malt

On the homebrew scene, smoked character is "allowed" in Scottish-style and Scotch ales at fairly subtle levels. In general, however, judges do not seem to expect this character, and only 15 percent of all the NHC second-round recipes included some sort of smoked malt.

Table 24.3
Commercial Approaches to Scottish-Style Ale

Malt Used	No. of Recipes	Commercial Brewers
Pale malt only (caramel coloring used)	3	All Maclay
Pale plus crystal	4	Maclay, West Highland, Alloa, and Harviestoun
Pale plus black	8 total	
Alone	3	Traquair House (2), Belhaven (1)
With crystal	3	All Belhaven
With chocolate plus crystal	2	Both Caledonian
Pale, chocolate, and crystal only	4	Orkney (3), Caledonian (1)
Pale with roast barley only	2	Both McEwan's
Pale, roast barley, and crystal	1	Harviestoun

Table 24.4
Commercial Scotch and Scottish-Style Ale Grain Bills

Grain Used (Range %)	Proportion	Incidence
Pale (84–99)	90%	🍺🍺🍺🍺
Crystal (2–10)	5%	🍺🍺🍺
Black (1–4)	2%	🍺🍺
Chocolate (1–3)	2%	🍺
Roast (2)	2%	🍺
Wheat* (2–5)	3%	🍺🍺
Sugar (5–12)	7%	🍺🍺

Proportion scale: 0% 10% 20% 30% 40% 50% 60% 70% 80% 90% 100%

*corn or flaked barley

Key: This chart shows what proportion of the grain bill was provided by various grains in thirteen commercial Scotch and Scottish-style ale recipes. The line next to each grain gives the range of values used by different brewers; this range is also listed below "Grains Used." The triangle above each line indicates the average proportion used across all recipes.

The icons in the column on the right show how often the thirteen commercial Scotch and Scottish-style ale recipes included each grain. (Percentage figures indicate how many of the recipes included the grain.)

🍺 = rarely (30% or less)   🍺🍺 = sometimes (30% to 60%)

🍺🍺🍺 = often (60% to 90%)   🍺🍺🍺🍺 = usually (90% or more)

Two types of smoked malt — with distinctly different flavors — are sometimes available commercially: rauch malt, which has been smoked over a hardwood fire, and distillers malt, which is smoked over a peat fire. Distillers malt is used in making Scotch whiskey, so you might expect the smoky character of a Scottish or Scotch ale to be similar. This is the case in two of the four NHC second-round examples. Of the remaining two, one recipe did not specify the type of smoke, and the final one used rauch malt. I prefer the flavor of hardwood smoked malts, and I have been successful competitively using rauch rather than distillers malt in Scotch ale.

Since the barley for making whiskey is quite different from that for making beer, it is likely that preparation of the two diverged long ago. Noonan relates that, even among Scots brewers, the old timers can only remember one ale that possessed the peat smoke flavor, or *reek,* as it is called. This beer was produced for several decades during the 1900s but was discontinued in the mid-1960s.

In his 1847 text on Scottish brewing and malting, Roberts specifies that malt kilns be fired with "coke, charcoal, culms, or wood."[40] This indicates that peat-smoked character would not have been a part of Scotch or Scottish-style ale flavor during the nineteenth century. Given this fact, I cannot help but wonder if the use of peat in malt kilns was an extreme measure adopted during the world wars early in the twentieth century.

Those who want to try a beer with a strong peat-smoked flavor should be on the lookout for the French-made Adelscott Malt Liquor, which is quite assertive in this regard.

If you choose to use smoked malt in your recipe, the big challenge is hitting the right balance of smoke in the finished product. If you can figure out the logistics, try blending smoked and nonsmoked batches to achieve the desired balance.

Mashing

With pale malt as a base, these beers can be mashed with a simple single-step infusion. To achieve the residual gravity and body desired, your rest temperature should be in the range of 154 to 158 °F (68 to 70 °C).

The average saccharification temperature used by second-round Scottish-style ales was 155 °F (68 °C), with a range from 150 to 158 °F (66 to 70 °C). For strong Scotch ale mash, temperatures are turned up a bit higher, in the range from 155 to 158 °F (68 to 70 °C) and averaging 156 °F (69 °C).

Hops and Scotch Ales

From the style descriptions onward, everything I have reviewed in this chapter about Scottish-style ales has emphasized their general lack of hop character.

Another anecdote supporting this conclusion comes from Noonan, who relates that "in 1834, Andrew Smith reported a 140 shilling ale being returned to the brewery because, presumably, the hops in it were too aromatic and too fresh."[41]

Since sweetness and maltiness are the hallmarks of this style, you are more likely to be criticized for having too much hop

---

Table 24.5
Grain Incidence in NHC Second-Round Scotch and Scottish-Style Ale Formulations

Grain Used	Scottish[a]	Scotch[b]
Pale	15	8
Extract	3	4
Roast	5	4
Black	0	0
Chocolate	6	3
Crystal	14	9
Munich	5	3
Amber	8	6
Smoked	3	1
Flaked	8	7
Sugar	1	0
Other	12	7

[a] Total number of recipes analyzed = 17
[b] Total number of recipes analyzed = 10

Table 24.6

Scotch and Scottish-Style Ale Grain Bill by Weight in NHC Second-Round Scotch and Scottish-Style Ale Beers

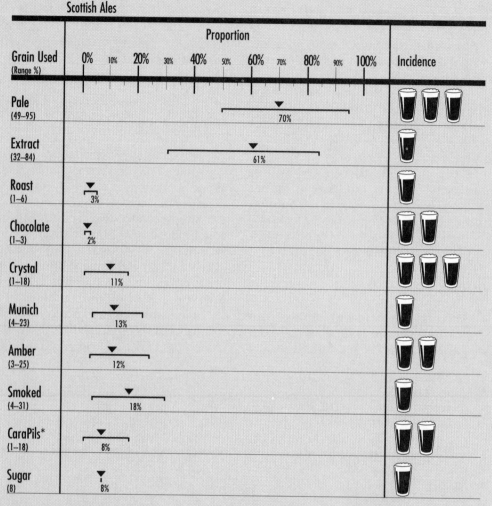

Scottish Ales

Grain Used (Range %)	Proportion	Incidence
Pale (49–95)	70%	
Extract (32–84)	61%	
Roast (1–6)	3%	
Chocolate (1–3)	2%	
Crystal (1–18)	11%	
Munich (4–23)	13%	
Amber (3–25)	12%	
Smoked (4–31)	18%	
CaraPils* (1–18)	8%	
Sugar (8)	8%	

*CaraPils, wheat, and flaked barley

Key: This chart shows what proportion of the grain bill was provided by various grains in seventeen Scottish-style ale recipes. The line next to each grain gives the range of values used by different brewers; this range is also listed below "Grains Used." The triangle above each line indicates the average proportion used across all recipes.

The icons in the column on the right show how often the seventeen Scottish-style ale recipes included each grain. (Percentage figures indicate how many of the recipes included the grain.)

= rarely (30% or less)   = sometimes (30% to 60%)
= often (60% to 90%)   = usually (90% or more)

character than too little. A Scottish-style ale that has too much bitterness will be harder for a knowledgeable drinker to accept than one that is too sweet.

Scotch and Scottish-style ales have some of the lowest BU:GU ratios seen in any style of ale. The commercial examples show an average BU:GU of 0.62 overall and

Table 24.6 *continued*
Scotch and Scottish-Style Ale Grain Bill by Weight in NHC Second-Round Scotch and Scottish-Style Ale Recipes

Scotch Ales

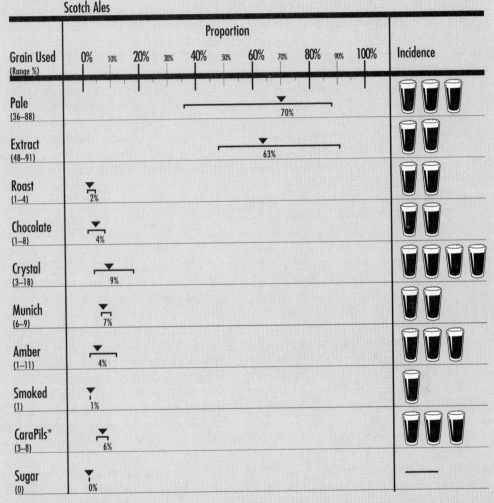

Grain Used (Range %)	Proportion	Incidence
Pale (36–88)	70%	
Extract (48–91)	63%	
Roast (1–4)	2%	
Chocolate (1–8)	4%	
Crystal (3–18)	9%	
Munich (6–9)	7%	
Amber (1–11)	4%	
Smoked (1)	1%	
CaraPils* (3–8)	6%	
Sugar (0)	0%	

*CaraPils, wheat, and flaked barley

Key: This chart shows what proportion of the grain bill was provided by various grains in ten Scotch ale recipes. The line next to each grain gives the range of values used by different brewers; this range is also listed below "Grains Used." The triangle above each line indicates the average proportion used across all recipes.

The icons in the column on the right show how often the ten Scotch ale recipes included each grain. (Percentage figures indicate how many of the recipes included the grain.)

= rarely (30% or less)   = sometimes (30% to 60%)
= often (60% to 90%)   = usually (90% or more)

0.50 for the strong ales alone. The range of values varies widely, from 0.25 to 0.83.

In the NHC second-round beers, we find even lower values, with an average of about 0.45 for both Scottish-style and Scotch ales. Again, however, the range of values varies widely, from 0.16 to 0.76. Because these beers were selected by beer judges from all over the country, these lower levels of bitterness would be a better target for anyone trying to please the critical American beer drinker.

As for flavor and aroma hopping, the commercial examples depart somewhat from the usual U.S. definition of the style. Fully 40 percent of the examples cited by Protz include aroma hop additions during the boil or as dry hops in the cask. As usual, Goldings and Fuggle are the varieties most often employed. Because of this departure, I have amended the "Hop flavor and aroma" entry of the style definitions table (see table 24.1) to read "None to medium" instead of "None to low" for the higher-gravity ales where this practice seems to occur.

The NHC second-round Scottish-style ales toe the line of the original definition more closely. Only two recipes (11 percent) include flavor hop additions, and only one (6 percent) includes an aroma or dry hop addition. By contrast, 70 percent of strong Scotch ales include flavor hop additions and nearly half include aroma hop additions. To ensure that such additions do not creep up over the threshold of "low" hop flavor or aroma, the average addition is smaller than I have seen with other styles: 0.48-ounce per 5 gallons for flavor additions and 0.25-ounce per 5 gallons for aroma.

Since there are no Scottish hop varieties, brewers can pretty much choose whatever hop they want for this style. The Scottish brewers themselves use traditional English hops because they are no doubt the least expensive to acquire. Goldings and Fuggle account for the vast majority of hops used in these ales; small quantities of Hallertau, Challenger, Progress, and Omega are also used.

United States homebrewers also show a preference for the most popular indigenous hops, with Cascade leading the way in the NHC recipes. Still, this variety accounts for only 23 percent of all hop additions for the style. The three next most popular hops are all English-related:

Fuggle, Goldings, and Willamette. Together, these three account for more than a third of all hop additions in Scotch and Scottish-style ales.

Other hops used in this style include Northern Brewer (8 percent), Chinook (7 percent), Perle (7 percent), Cluster (5 percent), Hallertau (5 percent), and Saaz (5 percent).

One final note on hopping Scotch ales: Because the aroma and flavor components are of little importance, this is a good place to use your older hops. Also, if they provide less bitterness than you expect, you should still be pleased with the outcome due to the malt-accented nature of these styles.

Water

The brewers of Edinburgh have been both blessed and cursed by the water available to them for brewing. Blessed because the geology of the area can yield various types of water, thus allowing brewers to adapt to changes in beer styles and consumer tastes. (Recall that Edinburgh became a great producer of pale ales thanks to the availability of hard water.) But the curse also comes in this variability. More than one brewery has observed changes in the character of its well water that required drilling of a new well or complete relocation of the brewery.

A consulting geologist explained this phenomenon in Noonan's work in Scotch ales:

Edinburgh lies in the center of a heavily faulted, generally north-dipping pile of Lower Carboniferous and Upper Old Red Sandstone strata. The juxtaposition of different rock types has meant that individual breweries have always had access to differing sources of water. Even boreholes in close proximity could produce waters with vastly different analyses. Thus the Edinburgh brewers have always blended waters to produce their characteristically wide range of beers, from milds to bitters and beyond.[42]

Given this variability, it is perhaps not surprising that published sources report differences in the chemistry of the water found in Edinburgh. Table 24.7 compares three sources, that differ and agree on various points.

Hind's presentation concludes with the statement that "Edinburgh is well known for its pale ales." This may indicate that the high-sulfate chemistry he presents was not intended for production of the malty Scottish styles of ale.

Noonan's work represents the most in-depth consideration of the subject, as reflected, in part, by the fact that he lists ranges for each of the ion concentrations. In this, he acknowledges the variability inherent in the source wells and provides us with general guidelines for use in preparing water treatment programs. His values are consistent with good brewing practice and with the flavor effects required in beers of this type.

Yeast

In the production of Scottish-style and Scotch ales, yeast plays a critical role not so much for the flavors it imparts but for the flavors it *doesn't*. The desired finished product lacks the esters traditionally produced by ale yeasts and should otherwise be clean and neutral to allow full exposition of the malt character.

Brewers conduct Scotch/Scottish ale fermentations following procedures that are quite unique compared to those for any other ale. The purpose is to produce the clean malty profile typical of the styles.

Most of us expect a good ale fermentation to take only a few days at a temperature between 65 and 70 °F (18 and 21 °C). When adequate yeast is pitched, commercial brewers expect the population of yeast to multiply five times during that period.

Scottish/Scotch ale fermentations are different in almost every respect. First, they are conducted at cooler temperatures

(50 to 60 °F, 10 to 16 °C) and as a result take much longer — up to three weeks — for primary fermentation. Following this, a period of cold-conditioning typically lasts six to twelve weeks. Finally, the growth of the yeast during fermentation is intentionally slowed, with commercial brewers shooting for a threefold growth of the yeast population rather than fivefold.[43]

The list of characteristics needed in a Scottish/Scotch ale yeast includes:

- Clean, neutral flavor character
- Ability to ferment below 60 °F (16 °C)
- Low apparent attenuation (65 to 70 percent)
- For Scotch ales, good alcohol tolerance

I know of at least three yeasts suitable for this style, and I have had very good results with two of them. The first is listed as "sweet European ale" in chapter 12, and it is the Wyeast European ale yeast, number 1338. I used this yeast in the strong Scotch ale that placed in the NHC one year. It reduced the 1.090 wort to a final gravity of 1.040, leaving it full-bodied and full of malt sweetness.

The second yeast is the low-attenuating Irish strain, again offered by Wyeast. I used this in several Scottish-style ales, one of which was a best-of-show contender at several regional competitions. This yeast gave me apparent attenuation of 64 to 67 percent following a mash at 156 °F (69 °C).

Finally, two companies (Wyeast and Yeast Culture) now offer a product called Scottish ale yeast, which I have yet to try. This yeast is supposed to be neutral with low attenuation, but unlike the other two I've mentioned, it has an optimal fermentation temperature that reaches all the way down to 55 °F (13 °C). Clearly worth a try.

Another yeast that can yield acceptable results for this style is American ale. Most examples of this strain produce a clean, neutral profile, even above 60 °F (16 °C), and some will ferment down into the 55 °F

Table 24.7
The Character of Edinburgh Water (mg/L)

Ion	Hind[a]	Noonan[b]	Papazian[c]
Ca	70	80–120	120
Mg	36	10–25	25
Na	92	10–30	55
SO₄	231	70–140	140
Cl	60	30–60	20
CO₃	210	120–200	225

Sources: [a] H. L. Hind, Brewing Science and Practice (London: Chapman & Hall, Ltd., 1938), 433; [b] G. Noonan, Scotch Ale, Classic Beer Style Series, no. 8 (Boulder, Colo.: Brewers Publications, 1993), 104; [c] C. Papazian, The Home Brewers Companion (New York: Avon Books, 1994), 83.

(13 °C) range. Their attenuation is a bit high for the style, so dextrin malt and high saccharification temperatures would definitely be in order.

These four yeast strains are the most widely used by brewers of Scotch and Scottish-style ales that made it to the second round of the NHC. The sweet Irish strain was most popular (in seven recipes), followed by the sweet European (four), the American ale (four), and finally, the Scottish ale strains (three).

Throughout this chapter I have mentioned the similarities of Scottish fermentation and conditioning to those used in lager production. With this in mind, a few brewers have successfully experimented with lager yeasts for production of their Scottish ales. Two lager yeasts, the Bavarian and the Pilsener, appeared in the second-round NHC beers. Both seem to fit the profile of the yeast required for the style, assuming that you can achieve the temperature control necessary to ensure that the ferment does not get warm enough to produce esters.

Conclusion

Production of a good Scottish-style or Scotch ale is an admirable accomplishment for any brewer. Although you can produce a passable imitation by following your regular brewing procedures, development of a truly great reproduction requires attention to nearly every aspect of the brewing process. Although some commercial brewers may lack the flexibility needed to do this, the necessary steps are well within the capabilities of most homebrewers.

Using the information in this chapter, you can develop a wide range of authentic Scottish-style and Scotch ale formulations with gravities ranging from 1.030 to 1.120. Each example you produce can be a wonderful adventure into the unique brewing culture of Scotland, so fire up the brew pot and enjoy.

Key Success Factors in Brewing Scottish-Style and Scotch Ales

- Use pale ale malt for the majority of the grist.

- Add roast barley, black malt, or chocolate malt for 0.5 to 2 percent of the grist.

- Consider adding wheat malt, dextrin malt, or flaked barley for 2 to 8 percent of the grist.

- You may exclude crystal malt, as the classic Scottish ales did, or follow the lead of many contemporary Scottish brewers who use it for 5 to 10 percent of the grist.

- Consider adding other character malts, such as Munich, biscuit, and Special Roast, for 1 to 5 percent of the grist.

- Use water that is high in calcium, sodium, carbonate, and chloride, but low in sulfate.

- Consider the addition of a small quantity of peat or hardwood smoked malt to provide a subtle complexity that is characteristic of the style.

- Mash at 154 to 158 °F (68 to 70 °C) to produce a thick, dextrinous wort.

- Boil over a direct gas flame or extend the boiling time to encourage caramelization during the boil.

- Use bittering hops to achieve a BU:GU ratio of 0.3 to 0.6. (Aged hops are OK.)

- Avoid flavor and aroma hop additions in Scottish-style ales and use only very small additions (0.25- to 0.5-ounce for 5 gallons) for strong Scotch ales.

- Select a neutral-flavor, low-attenuation yeast that will ferment at cool temperatures.

- Conduct the primary fermentation at 55 to 60 °F (13 to 16 °C). Primary fermentation may take up to three weeks.

- Cold-condition the beer for six weeks to three months at 35 to 45 °F (2 to 7 °C).

Sidebar: Small Scottish Beer

This passage is excerpted from W. H. Roberts' *The Scottish Ale Brewer and Practical Maltster*, third edition, published in 1847.[44]

About twelve years ago, it was customary with some of the small beer brewers in Edinburgh to make the small beer of considerable strength, and after the Exciseman had determined its quantity, and the duty to be paid on it, they diluted it largely with water, just when they were sending it out of the house. This fraud was easily put in practice, because the small beer is usually disposed of the moment it is mixed with the yeast, and before it has undergone any fermentation whatever. It ferments sufficiently in small casks, in which it is sent to the consumers. In Edinburgh it is customary to bottle this small beer, which makes it clear and very brisk, and, consequently, very agreeable to the palate.

If we may believe a tradition current in Scotland, this method of rendering table-beer brisk by the addition of cold water, arose from accident. A brewer's drayman going his usual round one day, accidentally spilt a considerable quantity of the beer contained in one of the casks. To prevent his master becoming acquainted with his carelessness, he filled up the cask with water, at the first stream he passed, on the road to Musselburgh, and left it at the nearest public-house, which was kept by an old woman, a regular customer, and a person whom he thought was less likely than others to discover the inferiority of the beer. Going some time afterwards to Musselburgh, he called for the old woman, expecting a severe rebuke for leaving her such sour, weak trash, and dreading its being returned. He was as much pleased as astonished to be informed, that it was the best beer she ever had, and that she hoped his master would always brew such, as her customers were much pleased with it — in fact, she never had had beer that took the bottle so soon, and was so fine, sharp, and brisk.

Upon his return home, the drayman told his master all the particulars of the accident and its consequences, who improved upon the hint for his future advantage. From this story, small beer, when it is very brisk, is often designated by, the vulgar "Musselburgh Broke." This small beer is very weak, which may be easily believed when we are informed that, when it is bottled and corked, it is sold for ninepence to one shilling a dozen.

25 STOUT

Project	Designing Great Beers
	Brewers Publications
Project No.	61766

An almost mystical character surrounds the stout style for some reason. Perhaps it is the blinding blackness of the brew as it sits in the glass — a sort of barroom black hole so intense that it might absorb everything around it. Of course, the flavor is just as striking. Those who finish their first glass often become converts, swearing allegiance and setting off on a sybaritic search for the perfect pint.

Before I go further, let's take a look at a breakdown of stout styles. The four are classic dry, foreign-style, sweet or cream stout, and imperial stout[1] (see table 25.1).

Each of the four stout styles has a distinct flavor profile.

Classic. Roasted barley character required, may be low-level. Slight sweetness or caramel character OK. Slight acidity/sourness OK. Medium to high bitterness.

Foreign. Slight acidity/sweetness OK. Slight sweetness or caramel character OK. Medium to high bitterness.

Sweet. Roasted barley character required, may be low-level. Sweet with mild roast barley character. Malt/caramel character evident. Low bitterness.

Imperial. Roasted barley character required, may be low-level. Rich, complex,

Table 25.1
Characteristics of Four Styles of Stout

	Classic	Foreign	Sweet	Imperial
Original gravity	1.038–48	1.052–72	1.045–56	1.075–95
Bitterness	30–50	30–70	15–25	50–80
BU:GU ratio	0.8–1.2	0.9 avg.	0.3–0.5	0.9 avg.
Hop flavor & aroma	None	None	None	Med.–high
Color (SRM)	40+	40+	40+	40+
Apparent extract	1.008–14	1.008–20	1.014–20	1.024–32
Alcohol (volume)	3.8–5	6–7.5	3–6	8.6–14.4
Esters	Low	Low	Low	High
Diacetyl	Very low	Very low	Low	Very low

Source: American Homebrewers Association 1995 National Homebrew Competition Rules and Regulations *(Boulder, Colo.: American Homebrewers Association, 1995).*

and generally intense maltiness. Alcoholic. Fruity/estery. Medium to high bitterness.

All of these beers are generally black, and they usually have a nice creamy head with real staying power. Recent research shows that melanoidin color compounds promote head retention,[2] so the deep color and long-lasting foam go hand in hand.

Son of a Porter

Compared to porter, stout is better known, more clearly defined, and more widely available. It seems odd, then, that stout should be the newcomer and odder still that porter should have the more illustrious and well-documented history. Nonetheless, it is so.

The earliest recorded use of the word "stout" to describe a beer comes in 1677 from a letter stating, "We will drink your health both in stout and best wine."[3] At this time, it appears that stout was a bit of jargon meaning simply "strong beer."[4] Still, the reference cannot be discounted, for the first stouts were indeed just strong porters.

In chapter 23 I traced the history of porter from its beginnings in 1722 as fuel for the throngs of workers who went to London during the Industrial Revolution. Then, after nearly 150 years of market dominance in Britain, porter waned as glass serving vessels and pale malt combined to launch pale ale to the height of popularity.

Somewhere along the line, porter drinkers began to distinguish stronger examples with the adjective "stout." A patron might enter a pub and say, "Give me a stout porter, bartender," in much the same way one might ask for a "hoppy pale ale." The label on the beer doesn't say "stout" or "hoppy," but if the server is familiar with the term, you'll get what you want.

Corran reports that the 1750 edition of *London and Country Brewer* contained instructions for making "stout butt beer,"[5] and this may be the earliest direct

forerunner of the beer we drink today. The term "butt beer" was sometimes used to describe porter, and "stout" can be taken for strong; therefore, the first evidence of a strong porter going under the name stout is as early as 1750.

For quite some time a stout porter would have looked about the same as a regular porter. Both would be made from brown malt, or from a mix of brown, amber, and pale malts. The stronger stout porters might have been a bit darker overall because it would take more malt per barrel to provide the requisite alcoholic strength. Indeed, some sources report that consumers of the time perceived a direct relationship between depth of color and alcoholic strength.

It was not until 1817 that a device for roasting barley and malt was patented, allowing the production of black patent malt and roast barley.[6] Thus, the earliest "stout porters" were probably brown and not black. After that date, it appears that the use of black malt in both porters and stouts became a widespread practice.

Other characteristics of old porter still survive in stout. First is the dry bitterness of the style. From the chapter on porter, you know that the early versions were highly hopped. Reflecting this, today's stouts display some of the highest bitterness levels of any style, as indicated by an average BU:GU ratio of about 0.90.

Another technique that originated with porter and survives in stout is the practice of "vatting." This is the term applied when aged beer and new beer are blended to give a finished product with an aged character.[7] Although it's not widely practiced these days, several sources report that vatting in wooden casks is still a part of the Guinness production process, at least in Ireland.[8]

Perhaps it is the history of adulteration we found in porter that has prompted some odd — although benign — additions to stout over the years. In the late 1800s there were novel additions to stout in the form of oatmeal, milk sugar,[9] and even oysters.[10] Oyster stouts actually contain oysters, and a few examples have been made of late by American microbrewers. Some contained the meat, others the juice, while still others used the shell, apparently as a fining agent.[11]

In contrast to the porter additives that were downright poisonous in many cases, the extras added to stout were often added to bolster the beer's position as a nutritional or health supplement. Nursing mothers in Victorian times were advised to drink 3 quarts a day of porter and stout![12] This health perception of stout was so strong that it continued into the middle of the twentieth century, when doctors prescribed a pint a day for the elderly and often had stout given to their hospital patients as well.[13]

The History of Stout Brewing

With all these similarities between porter and stout, we have difficulty defining a clear date for the origin of stout itself. It seems that the word "stout" was in common use by consumers before brewers began to use it as a label for their products.

Richardson reported on the gravities of various types of beer, including five porters, in 1788, but makes no mention of the word "stout."[14] During the period from 1775 to 1800, huge breweries were being built by Thrale (later Barclay Perkins), Whitbread, and others who were designated as porter brewers. Even Guinness was noted as a "porter specialist" during this period.[15]

From about 1820 we have evidence that stout was a commercial term for a product that was somewhat different from porter. The recipes provided by Tuck in 1822 draw a clear distinction between porter and "brown stout."[16] Porter was made from 50 percent amber, 25 percent brown, and 25 percent pale malts, with 6 pounds of hops used per quarter of malt. The brown stout relied more on brown malt and was

made from 50 percent brown and 50 percent pale malts. It was also hopped more heavily, with 8 pounds of hops per quarter of malt. In addition, it would appear that the stout was stronger, yielding just two worts from a quarter of malt versus three worts of porter from the same quantity.

About the time of Tuck's writing, black malt was invented and was fairly rapidly put to use by porter brewers, including Whitbread and Barclay Perkins.[17] Use of this product enabled brewers to create a product that was truly black for the first time. Since color had long been associated with alcoholic strength, it would make sense that all of these new black beers might be called stout.

Although we have no information about the recipes used, we know that Guinness began labeling one of their products as stout at about this same time. The product line included three porters, two designated as X and XX, with a stronger third product reserved for export to the Caribbean. In 1820, the XX was renamed Guinness Extra Stout Porter.[18] Although the formulation has no doubt changed since that time, the name remains largely the same today. Eventually the word porter became redundant and was dropped, so the name became simply Guinness Extra Stout.

The best information we have about the brewing of stout comes from the middle of the 1800s. At this time porter still reigned as the most popular beer in the land, so a number of writers discussed its production in detail. At the time, porter brewers might produce a porter as well as several different stouts. Original gravity was the primary factor distinguishing the various products.

Table 25.2 lists the original gravities reported for stout and porter at various times over a 120-year period. The first entry (1788) shows where porter started out. From there, the original porter gravity range (1.065 to 1.080) did not split but rather evolved into a new, lower-gravity range for porter (1.050 to 1.064). Stout simply takes over the gravity range once occupied by the original porters. This had clearly occurred by 1843, and the gravities of both then remained constant for the next sixty-five years.

In 1868, Amsinck published dozens of recipes from the many commercial breweries in which he had worked.[19] This provides a rich and detailed source of information on the composition and brewing of various styles. It is a particularly valuable source for comparison of two closely related styles since it was written entirely by the same individual and therefore eliminates the confusion that can arise in comparing data from different sources.

Table 25.3 shows the data presented by Amsinck for production of various stouts. The 1822 recipes discussed earlier did not include black malt because it had just been invented and was not yet in widespread use. In contrast, recipes from 1868 commonly use black malt for 2 to 6 percent of a stout grist. In addition, most remain true to the heritage of porter by including brown malt for a portion of the grist. The one exception to this is the Dublin Stout, brewed at Guinness. In 1868, the

Guinness brewers were making their stout solely from pale and black malt.

The hop rates for these stouts were universally high. Assuming 4 percent alpha acid content and 25 percent utilization, I calculate the average BU:GU ratio at a remarkably high rate of 1.86.

Three other factors related to porter production are found in these stout recipes. First, the fermentations were allowed to reach high temperatures, and this must have created high levels of esters and fusel alcohols. Second, note that vatting or aging was prescribed for most of these beers once primary fermentation was completed. Although aging does not appear to have been common at this time for porter brewing, it does harken back to the origins of porter, which did contain a portion of aged product. Finally, with the exception of Guinness, the apparent attenuation was relatively low (63 percent on average) — although this probably increased during vatting.

Compared to the porters, stouts across the board were higher in gravity, lower in attenuation, and somewhat higher in relative bitterness levels (see table 25.4). When the stouts are broken down by

Table 25.2
Porter and Stout Gravities, 1788–1908

Year	Porter	Stout
1788[a]	1.065–1.082	—
1843[b]	1.050	1.055–1.072
1857[b]	1.055–1.065	1.073
1860[c]	1.056–1.067	1.069–1.078
1868[d]	1.058–1.064	1.069–1.097
1881[e]	—	1.074–1.089
1899[e]	1.060–?	?–1.073
1908[f]	1.052–1.079	1.061–1.092

Sources: [a]J. Richardson, The Philosophical Principles of the Science of Brewing (London, 1788), 240. [b]H. S. Corran, A History of Brewing (London: David & Charles, 1975), 214. [c]W. R. Loftus, The Brewer (London, circa 1850). [d]G. S. Amsinck, Practical Brewings: A Series of Fifty Brewings (London: George Stewart Amsinck, 1868). [e]Corran, A History of Brewing, 224–226. [f]R. Wahl and M. Henius, The American Handy-Book of the Brewing, Malting and Auxiliary Trades (Chicago: Wahl-Henius Institute, 1908, 1284–85.

Table 25.3
Stouts, circa 1868

Type	OG	TG	AA%	Pale	MALTS Brown	Black	Hops lb./bbl.	Month	Water	High FX Temp (°F)	Disposition
Treble	1.097	1.031	68%	84%	14%	2%	5.5	March	soft	79	Vatted
Treble	1.094	1.033	65%	75%	22%	3%	5.75	Jan.	soft	76.5	Vatted
Double	1.086	1.032	63%	85%	13%	2%	5.75	Feb.	soft	78	Vatted
Double	1.081	1.031	62%	74%	22%	4%	4.5	Feb.	soft	77	Vatted
Double	1.081	1.033	59%	70%	25%	5%	4.25	Nov.	mid–hard	75	Present use
Single	1.074	1.028	62%	85%	13%	2%	4.5	Jan.	soft	76	Vatted
Single	1.069	1.021	70%	83%	12%	4%	5	Jan.	soft	75	Export
Single	1.069	1.03	57%	80%	14%	6%	3.25	June	mid–hard	75	Present use
Single	1.071	1.034	52%	75%	19%	6%	2.5	March	hard	75	Vatted
Single	1.072	1.017	76%	79%	13%	8%	2.5	May	hard	76	Into casks
Dublin	1.092	1.019	79%	97%	–	3%	5.5	March	soft	83	Vatted

designation, however, a porter and a single stout appear virtually identical except for the change in gravity. The higher-gravity stouts show some more pronounced differences, such as a greater reliance on brown malt over black malt and even higher hopping levels.

Despite these differences, it is clear that these four styles are very closely related. Just like today's bitters, they share a common heritage and flavor profile and can be divided only by technical values that are solely up to the brewer's discretion. Although porter and stout seem more clearly separate today, that may be more the result of artificial distinctions than real differences in the ways the community of available examples are produced commercially.

This faint distinction between porter and stout continued into the twentieth century, probably until the demise of porter in Britain around 1974. The Wahl-Henius *Handy-Book*, published in several versions between 1901 and 1908, draws little distinction between stout and porter. It describes the latter as: ". . . with a dark color, brewed like Stout, but not so strong."[20] Other data provide the gravity and hopping rates of porter and stouts, again showing porter as the lowest-gravity member of the stout family (see table 25.4).

The following is a general description of brewing techniques for "Stout and Porter" from the Wahl-Henius *Handy-Book*:

The principal requirements, as compared with ale, are greater palate-fulness, pronounced malt flavor and darker color. It is best to use mixed malts, i.e., a mixture of high and low kiln-dried malts. If this cannot be had, caramel malt, "black" malt, and sugar coloring to the required amount should be added.[21]

This passage seems to call for something like brown or amber malt as the "high kiln-dried malt" — a sort of retrospective harkening back at least fifty years. Without distinguishing between the two styles, this procedure stipulates that no dry hopping be conducted and that the product should be stored for three to four months.

In a similar vein, the well-known British brewing authority H. L. Hind writes the following under the title of "Grists for Stouts" in his 1938 book on brewing:

Table 25.4
Comparison of Average Values for Porters and Stouts, 1858

Type	O.G.	AA%	BU:GU	Grist Bill (%) Pale	Brown	Black
Porter	1.061	69	1.64	77	15	5
Stouts						
Single	1.071	63	1.75	80	14	5
Double	1.083	61	1.94	76	20	4
Treble	1.096	66	1.86	80	18	3

Source: G. S. Amsinck, Practical Brewings: A Series of Fifty Brewings (London: George Stewart Amsinck, 1868).

There are a number of distinct types of stout and porter, for which different blends of materials are used. On the one hand are the stouts brewed from malt only or from malt and roasted barley. On the other, are the sweeter stouts, for which a fairly high percentage of sugar is employed. The basis of the grists is a mixture of pale malt, not too fully modified, but with a moderate diastatic activity, and either roasted malt or roasted barley to give the requisite colour and flavour. Roasted barley gives a drier flavour than roasted malt and is preferred by many.[22]

The two sources I have just quoted, one British, one American, pretty much ignore porter in favor of stout, classifying porter as a mere subclass of stout. Another comment on this point comes from Belgium, a country where many British styles were brewed. Jean DeClerck's book on

brewing was translated into English and published in London in 1957. He, too, focuses on stout at the expense of porter.

Stout. This is prepared from a mixed grist of pale malt of moderate diastatic activity, plus 7 to 10% of roasted malt or roasted barley, and caramel is sometimes added as well. The grist is mashed by the infusion system and the striking heat is high. A high hop rate is used (600 to 700 g/hectolitre) [that's 98 IBU assuming 5% alpha acid and 30% utilization] and sugar and caramel are added in the copper, and attenuation is more or less forced during fermentation. The average gravity of stouts in Great Britain prior to the last War was 12% [12 °P or 1.048] and some stouts were as high as 20% [20 °P or 1.083] or even higher.

Porter. The name "Porter" was given to a light gravity stout, but the name has fallen into disuse.[23]

Table 25.5
Description of Porter and Stouts, 1908

Beer	Balling	lb. hops/U.S. bbl.
Porter	13–15	0.8–1.5
Single stout	16–18	1.5–2
Double stout	18–20	2–2.5
Imperial stout	20–25	2.5–3
Russian export	>25	>3.25

Source: R. Wahl and M. Henius The American Handy-Book of the Brewing, Malting and Auxiliary Trades (Chicago: Wahl-Henius Institute, 1908): 1253.

With this last comment about porter, DeClerck states finally what the earlier writers had implied: That porter is pretty much dead and, to the extent that it is still brewed, it is simply a light stout.

Finally, if we take the first of these three descriptions (Wahl-Henius) at face value, roast barley does not appear to have been widely used in stouts as of 1908. Just a few decades later both Hind and DeClerck mention its use, although as an option to black or roasted malt. These facts seem to indicate that black malt rather than roast barley was used as the coloring ingredient in stouts until the early twentieth century.

Further support for this conclusion is provided by the historical recipes from the Durden Park Beer Circle in England, whose publication lists seven different recipes for stouts with dates ranging from 1848 to 1909.[24] All include black malt; none include roast barley.

Earlier in the chapter I reviewed data from 1868 showing the use of black malt across the board, further supporting the twentieth century as the time of change. Perhaps shortages of fuel and other commodities during World War I caused this shift from the malted to unmalted roast grains. Whatever the case, we do know that roast barley is commonly included in many stouts today, the classic example of which is Guinness.

Classic of Classics

Today, more than almost any other major beer style, stout is defined by a single commercial producer. The name Guinness is synonymous with stout; its products are considered classics of the style.

One reason for this is longevity. Arthur Guinness purchased a derelict brewery at St. James Gate in Dublin in December 1759.[25] The company he founded there still exists today — nearly 250 years later — and his descendants have run the company, or helped to do so, for much of that time.

But the simple fact that you have been around for a couple of centuries does not mean that you will survive the next decade. Changes in consumer taste have bankrupted more than one brewery, and the vicissitudes of politics, economics, and war have ravaged brewers time and again. No brewer who hopes to pass his company on to the next generation in good health can simply sit and count the money as it comes in. Evidence suggests that Guinness has not only survived but thrived as the direct result of forethought and innovation.

We get the first sign of this forethought from the original Arthur Guinness himself. In a letter written about twenty-five years after the brewery was founded, he stated the value of the brewery at £10,000 but said, "I would not take £30,000 for it."[26] He clearly understood the potential of the business he had entered into and had big plans to achieve that potential.

The brewery had already been one of the first in Dublin to brew porter, and by 1799 Mr. Guinness discontinued production of all other types of beer, becoming a porter specialist like many of the London brewers.[27] The London product had proven popular in Ireland and was imported in great quantity. Although some thought that tax and transportation issues made it impossible for Irish brewers to compete with these imports, the move was to serve Guinness well. Corran states that "by 1804 Guinness's were brewing only porter and more beer was being exported from Ireland than was being imported."[28]

Corran goes on to say that

Guinness's porter was already being exported at the time of Waterloo (1815), and the firm had established an agency in Bristol by 1819. By 1836 a hotel in the Isle of Man was advertising "Barclay's London and Guinness's Dublin Porter." A little later a cask of Guinness made its appearance in one of the illustrations to Pickwick papers.[29]

Here, as in other areas, Mr. Guinness was an innovator:

The house of Messrs. Arthur Guinness Sons and Co. was the first to open the trade of exportation, and they have been successfully followed by several other respectable houses in Dublin.

Although some of these breweries also brewed ale, it is certain that the main bulk of the export trade was in stout and porter. Dublin Stout became as well established as Burton Ale, as may be seen from the legend engraved on stoneware bottles of the period.[30]

Corran concludes that by the middle of the 1800s, "the Dublin brewers, now porter and stout specialists [were] on the verge of a violent increase in trade."[31] Of course, Guinness was the largest of these, and none surpassed it as the business grew.

While perhaps not "violent" by contemporary standards, the growth of Guinness during this period was certainly impressive, as table 25.6 shows. Even more impressive is that fact that the sales curve shows no drops, only increases from about 1820 through to 1900.[32] That amounts to several generations of unmitigated prosperity.

During this period, a number of practices at the Guinness brewery provide further evidence of the management's willingness to change with the times and, where prudent, to be a leader in innovation. These include:

- Rapid adoption of black malt.[33]
- Use of Burton Union system fermenters until 1886.[34]
- The development of a skimming tank and mechanisms for removing yeast from the fermenting beer.[35]
- Conversion from wood to iron mash tuns.[36]
- Elimination of brown malt from porter and stout formulations.[37]
- Adoption of the practice of sparging.[38]

On this last item we are fortunate to have some contemporaneous detail provided by the itinerant brewer Amsinck. He visited the Guinness brewery during his travels and brewed with John G. Guinness Jr., who tried to demonstrate the value of sparging by showing that he could extract a yield of 130 brewers pounds per quarter of malt.[39]

Since most porter and stout grists of the day yielded an average of 82.3 brewers pounds per quarter,[40] Guinness was attempting to increase mash yield by nearly 60 percent. The experiment fell short of its goal, achieving just 101.4 pounds per quarter, but this was still 20 percent higher than average. Despite the significant improvement demonstrated, Amsinck was unimpressed. The following comments on the day's brewing tell us a good deal about his views.

This Gyle was carried out by Mr. John G. Guinness, Jr., for my instruction. The result was satisfactory, as to flavour, it closely represented the famous Dublin Stout. That peculiar sort of musty flavour, I imagine, is gained by carrying the fermentation, in the square, until the heat and head drop.

This Gyle should be kept in Vat six months, and then divided into another, and both filled up with a precisely similar Gyle, in six months longer, racked for sale.

This gentleman, I feel, was perfectly sincere in his operations and ideas. He came to instruct me on two points, one the Dublin Stout, the other, how to get 130 lbs. per quarter out of the Malt.

I wanted the first, the last I knew was chimerical, . . . the last 41 barrels' Return Wort only weighed 1.5 lb. per barrel, we had only reached 101 lbs. 4t. per quarter extract, he still persisted that a lot more was to be got by pursuing the same game [sparging] *ad infinitum*.[41]

This last paragraph indicates that the final runnings from the wort yielded forty-one barrels at 1.004 OG or 1 °P. As any experienced all-grain brewer knows, such runoff is nearly useless because of the very long boil that would

Table 25.6
Growth of the Guinness Brewery, 1800–1900

Year	Barrels Produced
1800	7,500
1820	15,000
1850	62,500
1881	1,000,000
1900	1,500,000

Sources: H. S. Corran, A History of Brewing (London: David & Charles, 1975), 222. One Hundred Years of Brewing (Chicago and New York: H. S. Rich & Co., 1903), 661.

be needed to concentrate this weak solution to a level that would be useful for beer production. Amsinck notes that Mr. Guinness had a unique solution for using such wort:

How did he propose to use all this Return Wort? [The low gravity last runnings] Thus: empty the Engine-boiler, take the Return therein, drive the engine with the steam generated therefrom, until it was reduced to a usable quantity.

It was certainly a genuine Irish idea, because, of course, the work must stand still, to do all this, for a considerable time during the brewing.

So much for practical information, which I was exceedingly pleased to obtain.[42]

Mr. John G. Guinness Jr. certainly had an inventive mind. He is the *only* brewer from dozens and dozens related by Amsinck to practice sparging. Furthermore, he has come up with a plan to use the weak last runnings as liquor for the steam engine in order to concentrate them to a usable level. No doubt this second idea — if ever attempted — failed. Sparging, on the other hand, was destined to become the dominant practice in brewing and, of course, it is still in use today.

This particular Mr. Guinness may have presided over the brewery during the latter portions of the 1800s, at a time when it was growing quite rapidly. By the end of the century it was the largest

porter brewery in the world.[43] By this time it was also a marvel of brewing technology, as reflected in this description from around 1903:

The property is situated on three principal levels, namely, the "upper level," about sixty feet above the quay, which includes the two breweries, fermenting rooms, vat houses, stables and hop and malt stores; the "second" or "middle level," where are located the maltings, grains department, a vat house and other buildings; and the "lower level" on Victoria quay, where are situated the cooperage shops, cask-washing sheds, racking and filling stores, and platforms for loading out goods to their various destinations, either by dray, boat or railway.

The different levels of the brewery are all connected by a narrow-gauge railway, over which small locomotives (of which there are fifteen) and trucks carry the goods of the company. A spiral tunnel . . . is the mode of ascent from the middle to the highest level.

Within the walls of the property are also a department for printing the required labels, a post office, a laboratory, electric plant and a telegraph and telephone office. Four systems of cooling machines are employed in St. James' Gate Brewery — [ether, ammonia absorption, carbonic acid, ammonia compression] — the total daily ice making capacity being 135 tons.[44]

Although Guinness was still regarded as a "porter" brewer at this date, it is clear that porter itself was nearly dead and that stouts were the product of the day. Guinness, in

Table 25.7
Comparison of Characteristics of Commercial Stouts, circa 1905

Type of Stout	OG	%AA	Lactic Acid (%)
Dublin Double Stout	1.082	86	0.364
Victoria Stout	1.062	85	0.055
Guinness Extra Bottled Foreign Stout	1.073	81	0.243
Allsopp Luncheon Stout	1.062	81	–
English Stout	1.073	80	0.151
Double Brown Stout (Barclay Perkins)	1.075	79	0.460
Guinness Extra Stout	1.070	74	–
American Brown Stout	1.073	70	–
Dublin Stout	1.092	69	0.252
Dublin Single Stout	1.061	60	0.222

Source: R. Wahl and M. Henius, The American Handy-Book of the Brewing, Malting and Auxiliary Trades (Chicago: Wahl-Henius Institute, 1908), 1285.

fact, continued to make a porter until 1974.[45] But it is the Guinness stouts that we find listed in the Wahl-Henius *Handy-Book*, along with a variety of other Dublin stouts and miscellaneous variations on this theme (see table 25.7).

By this time, the term Guinness Stout had become somewhat imprecise. Already we find two such products: Extra and Extra Bottled Foreign. Today, some nineteen different varieties of Guinness Stout are made in breweries around the world.[46] The gravities vary, and some are vatted, some bottled, and some exported. The grist may also vary depending on local availability of certain items.

According to Jackson, the draft and bottled products available in the United States are quite different. The draft product is brewed to a gravity of 1.039 with 45 BU of bitterness for a BU:GU ratio of 1.15.[47] This beer has an alcohol level of 4.2 percent by volume, making it lower in alcohol than Budweiser, which has 4.7 percent.[48] The bottled product, by contrast, is stronger on all fronts and has an alcohol content of 6 percent by volume.[49]

These two variations of Guinness available in the United States fall into two of the four stout styles introduced at the beginning of this chapter: the classic dry and the foreign-style. Other variations of Guinness, such as those sold in the Caribbean and in Europe, would appear to provide more dramatic examples of the foreign style, so be sure to try them if you get the opportunity. For additional examples of the classic dry, Jackson cites Murphy's Stout, Beamish Stout (both Irish), and Sheaf Stout from Australia,[50] although the latter may have changed somewhat in the intervening years.

Sweet Stout

Sweet stout is an odd specialty beer that mostly gets ignored by American craft brewers except for the occasional oatmeal stout. It is a much younger style than the classic dry, but it has endured the rollercoaster swings of the twentieth century beer market. One can imagine that this beer would be a nice mid-afternoon restorative, the perfect beer to drizzle over vanilla ice cream, and probably a good candidate for many cooking applications.

The various forms of sweet stout are completely absent from the literature during the 1800s and even from Wahl-Henius in 1908, because sweet stouts emerged as a recognizable commercial style between 1910 and 1940.

Jackson reports that Mackeson's made its first batch of milk stout in 1907.[51] After various mergers and acquisitions, the product finally became available nationally in 1936, and after that many breweries began to make a similar product.[52] This product is still available as of this writing and is considered the classic example of the style.

Evidence of the interest in Mackeson's pioneering work comes from H. L. Hind's book, published in 1938. He describes the changes to the basic stout recipe required to make the sweet product and includes a recipe:

Crystal and amber malts are commonly blended with [roast and pale malts] in the sweeter stouts. Milk stouts generally derive their name from the lactose or milk sugar added, with cane or other fermentable sugar, in the form of primings. The copper sugars are generally full flavoured and dark coloured.

Grist for sweet stout:

Ingredient	Quantity	% Extract
Pale malt	12 quarters	60.8
Roasted malt or barley	3 quarters	12.1
Crystal malt	2 quarters	8.4
Amber malt	2 quarters	8.5
Sugar	6 quarters	20.2

This will give 100 bbls. at 1.059 or 130 bbls. at 1.046.[53]

Some sweet stouts include oatmeal as a key ingredient, and some commercial examples can be found. These include Samuel Smith's Oatmeal Stout as well as a number of micro- and pub-brewed examples from around the United States.

Because of the oily nature of oats, the proportion added must be fairly small. The National Homebrew Competition second-round examples I have examined use 3 percent to 11 percent, with an average around 6 percent overall.

Jackson mentions that modern examples of sweet stout may be sweetened with sugar after fermentation and then pasteurized to inactivate the yeast and retain the sweet character in the final package.[54] This approach is dangerous, even on a commercial scale, and small brewers are better off controlling the balance of the recipe from the beginning. Under no circumstances should homebrewers put such products into bottles, because they could rapidly become randomly exploding hand grenades.

Of course, the one exception to this policy is the use of lactose. Assuming you use a pure form of this sugar, you shouldn't have any problem because it is not digestible by brewing yeasts — although some wild yeasts and bacteria may ferment it. This sugar doesn't contribute that much sweetness but will provide some body. Also, it is not easy to dissolve in beer, so boil it with a small amount of water first.[55] The quantity of lactose to be used in a sweet stout is about 3.3 ounces in 5 gallons.[56]

The classic sweet stouts listed by Jackson include: Tennent's Sweetheart Stout and Watney's Cream Stout (26 BU, 1.048).[57] Another commonly cited example is Whitbread's Mackeson Stout.

Imperial Stout

In the land beyond, foreign stout is a barley wine–strength stout known as imperial or Russian imperial stout. Wahl and Henius indicate that these appellations delineate different strengths of high-test stout, as shown in table 25.5.

Whether the terms imperial and Russian imperial have distinct meanings is quite difficult to tell because there is virtually nothing written about these styles in the literature. None of the historical sources that have proved useful to me in researching this book discuss this style. Neither do they discuss trade in stouts or porters with Russia or the Baltics, limiting such discussions instead to the activities of the ale brewers of Burton. The only available data come from contemporary sources.

Foster states that Barclay Perkins was the creator of imperial Russian stout, although he does not give a date.[58] This establishment was a prominent porter brewery founded in 1781 and continued to operate under that name until combined with Courage in 1955.[59]

The label on the Russian imperial stout currently marketed by Courage makes two claims: "Originally brewed for Catherine II, Empress of all the Russias," and "As brewed for over 200 years."

Catherine was Empress of Russia from 1762 until her death in 1796.[60] This latter date narrows the period when Barclay Perkins' product could have been appreciated by Catherine to just fifteen years, from 1781 to 1796.

The only other documentation supporting exportation of porter to Russia during this time comes from Michael Jackson. He states that ten London brewers once made this style and names Thrale (which became Barclay Perkins) as the best known of them.[61] Coincidentally, Jackson cites 1781 as a date when this product was being shipped to Bremen as well as to Nordic and Baltic ports.[62] This would indicate that imperial stout predated 1781 and that Thrale, rather than Barclay Perkins, might have created it. When asked, Courage could not provide any better information than this.

It appears that the trade in Russian stout continued a century later. Jackson reports that a shipload of Barclay's Stout en route from London sank in the Baltic in 1869.[63] Subsequent recovery of a few bottles leads Jackson down a trail of international trade that ends at the doorstep of a Russian brewery that served both the czarists and the marxists.

The Courage product survives today and is almost certainly the longest continuously marketed example of the style. The formulation includes pale, amber, and black malts as well as some sugar.[64] Of course,

the use of black malt discredits the label claim that it is "As Brewed for Over 200 Years," since black malt was not developed until 1817.

Despite this small shortcoming in labeling, the Courage product admirably represents the style with a gravity of 1.098 or better, 50 IBU, and 9.5 to 10.5 percent alcohol by volume.[65] The only other widely available example, from Samuel Smith's, has a gravity of just 1.072 — still short of imperial potency.

In the United States you'll find some craft-brewed examples with a good deal of potency, but few are bottled, so they rarely get the aging that yields the most interesting flavor profile. Herb Grant in Yakima, Washington, has bottled a product under the name of "Grant's Imperial Stout" since 1982.[66] Grant keeps the gravity at 1.066 (16.5 °P) to satisfy local distribution regulations but claims that it holds up well over time. This graceful aging may be assisted by honey, which is used for one-third of the total extract in his recipe.[67]

Bitterness levels, although not directly quoted by any of the commercial producers I examined, are generally thought to be lower than for dry and foreign-style stouts. One commercial recipe from Brooklyn Brewing brewmaster Garrett Oliver cites 40 to 45 IBUs at maturity in a 21.5 °P (1.088) wort.[68]

The Courage product claims hop rates "four times that of the average bitter,"[69] which could place it at about 96 IBU when corrected for the higher gravity of the wort. This places its bitterness — as brewed — at about that of a dry or foreign stout. However, since this is a vintage-aged product, the perceived bitterness of the beer several years after bottling may be lower than this calculated level.

Brewing Stouts

For brewers, the classic dry stout is a standard — a style that is so well known and so often requested that every brewer should be able to produce a good one practically without thinking about it. At its core, it is a very simple style to formulate and brew. Yet stout can be complex and involved as well. The four subcategories have room for exploration, and the roast palate of the style suggests it as a base for a number of fruit and novelty beers.

Dark Grains

For most brewers, roast barley is the focus of the stout grain bill. In both commercial examples and NHC second-round beers, this specialty grain is found more frequently than any other. Due in large part to the American Homebrew Association style definition, which virtually requires roast barley, twelve of thirteen dry and foreign stouts from the NHC second round include roast barley. On the commercial side, only 60 percent of the fifteen recipes examined showed roast barley as an ingredient. Some of the fifteen, however, excluded dark malts altogether.

Among the commercial brews that include roast barley, I find the following breakdown of dark grain usage:

4 Roast barley only
2 Roast plus crystal
1 Roast plus chocolate
1 Roast, crystal, plus chocolate
1 Roast, crystal, plus black

When roast barley is excluded, black malt most often takes its place, usually with a portion of crystal malt as well:

3 Black plus crystal
1 Chocolate plus crystal
1 Dark grains not specified
1 Crystal malt only

This demonstrates that the most popular commercial approach to stout brewing is simply to use pale malt plus roast barley.

I can tell you from experience that this will make an excellent stout. On the other hand, many variations of this have found success commercially, and some exploration of these other approaches may be of interest to devotees of the style.

One trait most of the commercial examples exhibit is simplicity. If possible, these use just one specialty grain, occasionally adding a second. Only two of fifteen, or 13 percent, used three color grains, and none used all four. By contrast, nearly 70 percent of all NHC second-round recipes use three or more color grains.

For competitive homebrewers, the use of roast barley is practically mandated by the style guidelines, so other additions are often included to distinguish an entry from the pack. As a result, we see a lot of "kitchen sink" beers. Here's how the thirteen NHC second-round dry and foreign stout recipes break down with regard to dark grains:

6 Crystal plus two dark grains
   4 Crystal, roast, and black
   1 Crystal, chocolate, and roast
   1 Crystal, chocolate, and black
3 Crystal, chocolate, roast, and black
2 Roast plus black
2 Roast only

Across both commercial and NHC second-round examples, the quantity of roast barley used was consistent at 10 percent of the grist for dry and foreign styles. Imperial stouts use a bit less at 7 percent on average; sweet stouts use less still, with an average of 5 percent for the two examples examined.

When it comes to black and chocolate malts, the NHC second-round brewers tend to use smaller amounts than commercial brewers, no doubt because these ingredients are almost always used in combination with roast barley. When crystal malt appears in either an second-round NHC or commercial stout, it averages 9 percent of the grist (see table 25.8).

Table 25.8
Average Percentage of Grains
in Addition to Roast Barley Used in Stout Recipes

	Black	Chocolate	Crystal
Commercial	7%	7%	9%
Homebrew	4%	4%	9%

Other Grains and Fermentables

A good number of stout recipes (Guinness among them) include another grain, such as oats, malted wheat, flaked barley, or CaraPils. These can all contribute to the body of the beer, and all but CaraPils will probably contribute to head retention as well. Flavor impact varies by grain and may be quite subtle.

About a quarter of all commercial stouts include wheat (three recipes) or flaked barley (one recipe). Guinness stout uses flaked barley for 10 percent of the grist.

Among NHC second-round beers, the body/head grains are more prevalent, with 61 percent of all recipes including one of the four ingredients. Flaked barley (6) is the favorite with homebrewers, followed by CaraPils (4), oatmeal (2), and wheat (1).

Some recipes actually include more than one of these four grains — one used three of them in the same formulation.

These grains form a small portion of the grain bill, ranging from 5 to 20 percent of the grist for the NHC second-round examples. Oatmeal is used in the smallest quantities (5 to 6 percent), while wheat may form a larger portion of the grist (10 to 20 percent). Flaked barley and CaraPils fall somewhere in the middle (5 to 10 percent).

Fully 20 percent of the commercial stouts listed by Protz include processed sugar of some sort. The usual variety of sugars appears to be used, although brown sugar seems to be slightly favored. The amounts used vary from 5 percent to 12 percent of the raw weight of the fermentables (see tables 25.9, 25.10, and 25.11).

In general, the NHC second-round stouts exclude sugar from their recipes. With regard to sweet stouts, neither of the examples from the NHC second-round entries included lactose or sugar of any other kind. These beers achieved their sweetness strictly through malt/hop balance.

Mashing Temperatures

The average mash temperature reported by NHC second-round brewers for stouts was 153 °F (67 °C), with 75 percent of all mashes conducted between 150 and 155 °F (66 and 68 °C). Some of the winning stouts used extract and steeped the grains at temperatures ranging from 150 to 200 °F (66 to 93 °C). Finally, three recipes

Table 25.9
Grain Incidence in
U.K.-Brewed Real Ale Stouts

Grain Used	No. of Recipes
Pale	15
Roast	9
Crystal	8
Chocolate	4
Black	4
Other	4
Wheat	3
Flaked	1
Caramel Color	2

Note: Total number of recipes analyzed = 15

Table 25.10
Grain Bill by Weight of U.K.-Brewed Real Ale Stouts

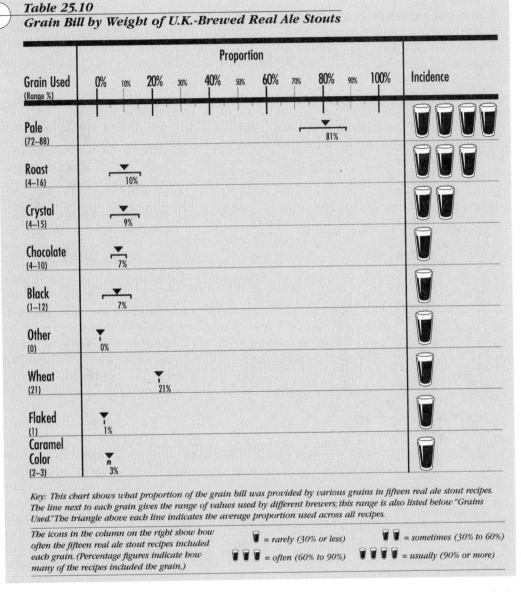

Grain Used (Range %)	Proportion	Incidence
Pale (72–88)	81%	usually
Roast (4–16)	10%	often
Crystal (4–15)	9%	sometimes
Chocolate (4–10)	7%	rarely
Black (1–12)	7%	rarely
Other (0)	0%	rarely
Wheat (21)	21%	rarely
Flaked (1)	1%	rarely
Caramel Color (2–3)	3%	rarely

Key: This chart shows what proportion of the grain bill was provided by various grains in fifteen real ale stout recipes. The line next to each grain gives the range of values used by different brewers; this range is also listed below "Grains Used." The triangle above each line indicates the average proportion used across all recipes.

The icons in the column on the right show how often the fifteen real ale stout recipes included each grain. (Percentage figures indicate how many of the recipes included the grain.)

= rarely (30% or less)   = sometimes (30% to 60%)
= often (60% to 90%)   = usually (90% or more)

called for boiling of dark grains for ten to thirty minutes. I have not encountered this practice previously and would be reluctant to try it myself, but obviously it has worked for some brewers.

Hops

Except for a pronounced bitterness in the dry and foreign styles, the effect of hops in most stouts is supposed to be largely in the background. Let's look at bitterness levels and then see what late additions are used by commercial and homebrewers.

Stout recipes call for most of the hops to be added near the beginning of the boil. For dry and foreign stouts, the additions are large enough to provide a BU:GU ratio of about 1.0. Imperial stouts will have similar to slightly lower bitterness levels. Sweet

Table 25.11
Stout Grain Bill in NHC Second-Round Recipes

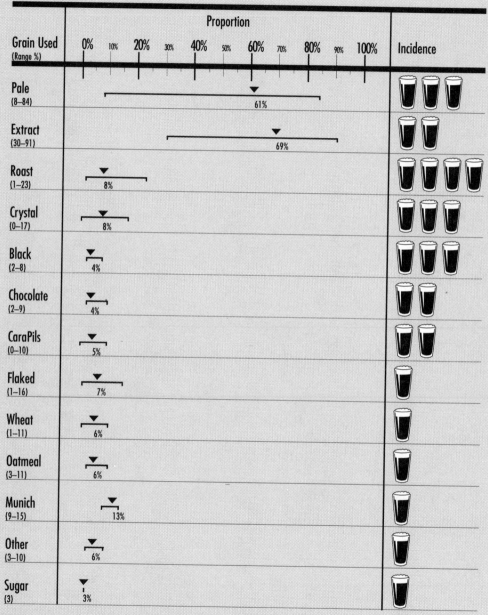

Grain Used (Range %)	Proportion	Average	Incidence
Pale (8–84)		61%	
Extract (30–91)		69%	
Roast (1–23)		8%	
Crystal (0–17)		8%	
Black (2–8)		4%	
Chocolate (2–9)		4%	
CaraPils (0–10)		5%	
Flaked (1–16)		7%	
Wheat (1–11)		6%	
Oatmeal (3–11)		6%	
Munich (9–15)		13%	
Other (3–10)		6%	
Sugar (3)		3%	

Key: This chart shows what proportion of the grain bill was provided by various grains in twenty-four stout recipes. The line next to each grain gives the range of values used by different brewers; this range is also listed below "Grains Used." The triangle above each line indicates the average proportion used across all recipes.

The icons in the column on the right show how often the twenty-four stout recipes included each grain. (Percentage figures indicate how many of the recipes included the grain.)

= rarely (30% or less)   = sometimes (30% to 60%)

= often (60% to 90%)   = usually (90% or more)

stouts are generally about half the dry/foreign rate (0.5), although some English stouts go as high as 0.7.

British brewers rely on tried-and-true English bittering hops in their stouts: Challenger, Target, and Northdown. Goldings and Fuggle are often seen in commercial stout recipes too, although the extent to which they are used for bittering is unclear.

American homebrewers are equally predictable in their selection of bittering hops, with Cascade topping the list and Chinook not far behind. Personally, I would never let a Chinook hop anywhere near a stout, but it appears to work for many who have found success competitively. Other popular choices are Northern Brewer, Bullion, Cluster, and Nugget.

Flavor and aroma hops do make appearances in both commercial and NHC second-round stouts, especially in the foreign and imperial styles. Wheeler and Protz list both Irish and English commercial examples with hop additions fifteen minutes before the end of the boil.[70] One uses Challenger and one uses Goldings.

In Protz's *Almanac*, 40 percent of the stout recipes include Goldings hops in addition to another type, indicating the likely use of Goldings for flavor or aroma purposes. Two recipes (13 percent) specify aroma hopping, both with Goldings varieties.

On the homebrew front, flavor hopping is fairly low across all styles, but aroma hopping is quite popular in the foreign and imperial styles, as shown in table 25.12. Dry hopping occurred only in the imperial stouts.

Among the NHC second-round brews, hop selection for late additions was again led by Cascade, which accounted for 40 percent of the flavor additions and 50 percent of the aroma additions. Northern Brewer was the second most popular in both applications, followed by a smattering of others, such as Goldings, Mt. Hood, Willamette, and Tettnanger. Dry hopping

was done with Cascade, Goldings, Mt. Hood, and Saaz hops.

The average size of these hop additions for 5 gallons of stout was: 0.88-ounces for flavor hops, 1.1 ounces for aroma hops, and 1.25 ounces for dry hops.

From these data you can see that although the style guidelines for stout specify that there should be no hop flavor or aroma, such additions are made both commercially and in competitively successful homebrewed beers. With all the roast malt that is present in this style, some hop character can furnish a welcome level of complexity and balance to the finished product.

Yeast

When producing stout, many brewers automatically select Irish yeast. Across the board, this yeast has produced more winning stouts than any other strain. Despite this, however, the most popular Irish yeast is not ideally suited to the making of all types of stout.

The classic dry Irish stout calls for a yeast that will deliver an apparent attenuation of 75 to 77 percent.[71] The most popular liquid Irish yeast generally results in about 71 to 75 percent apparent attenuation. As a result, those attempting to make a true classic dry stout may want to try an alternate yeast.

For dry stouts, NHC second-round brewers have preferred the more attenuative London strain and have also seen success with the somewhat dry Whitbread strain. In addition, other brands of Irish ale yeast may provide greater attenuation and can be investigated.

The popular Irish strain sees greater duty for production of foreign, imperial, and even sweet stouts (see table 25.13). The ever-popular American ale yeast also gets some use in this category. A variety of other dry or custom yeasts (including one Belgian Abbey yeast used for an imperial stout) accounts for the remainder of the recipes.

Table 25.12
Hop Additions in NHC Second-Round Stout Recipes

Style	Flavor (%)	Aroma (%)	Dry (%)
Dry	25	0	0
Foreign	33	78	0
Sweet	50	0	0
Imperial	55	78	55

Note: Total number of recipes analyzed = 24

Finally, two of eight imperial stout brewers added champagne yeast in addition to initial fermentation with a typical ale yeast. As discussed in the chapter on barley wine, champagne yeast appears to have little effect on apparent attenuation.

Water

The cities of London and Dublin gave birth to stout, so it is appropriate to look to them for guidance on water composition (see table 25.14).

Both are high in carbonate and relatively low in sulfate, but after that the similarities pretty much end. Starting with a relatively soft water, you would probably reach for the calcium carbonate when trying to duplicate Dublin water. London water is usually best approached using some cocktail of salts as discussed in chapter 20.

Classically, Dublin water would be more associated with the dry and foreign styles, while London's water would be better suited to the sweet and imperial styles. However, because of the assertive flavor of stouts, the water composition won't make a big difference in most instances. If your permanent hardness is less than 200 you are probably all set. If it is higher, you'll have to do some calculations to figure things out. Other than that, remember when you add calcium to the mash to opt for calcium chloride rather than gypsum to keep the sulfate content down.

Conclusion

The basic stout is so easy that the recipe can be written in less than twenty words: 90 percent pale ale malt, 10 percent roast barley, 1.042 gravity, 45 IBU at the start of the boil.

This recipe, brewed with almost any water, mashed at almost any temperature, and fermented with almost any yeast, should give an enjoyable product. You could screw it up by mashing at 120 °F (49 °C) and fermenting with a weizen yeast, but I'm willing to bet that anyone who has brewed more than a couple of beers would avoid such mistakes.

Despite the ease with which a basic recipe can be framed, the full dimensions of the style — including historical interpretations — provide fertile ground for innovation and exploration. Within them you can fiddle with grain bills, explore hop selection, and vary the gravity and bitterness across a wide range in your search for the perfect stout.

In your experimentation, don't forget to include some oatmeal — or perhaps some oysters! Later you can age a batch with *Lactobacillus* and then blend it with a newer batch in search of the authentic Guinness tang. When you're done with these variations, think about adding some coffee, raspberries, or smoked malt to your favorite stout formulation.

Clearly, there is a world of opportunity in stout brewing. Though examining the

Table 25.13
Yeast Selection in NHC Second-Round Stout Recipes

Yeast Used	% Apparent Attenuation[a]	No. of Recipes Using Yeast			
		Dry[b]	Foreign[c]	Sweet[d]	Imperial[e]
Irish	71–75	1	4	1	3
American	73–77	–	2	–	2
Whitbread	73–75	1	2	–	1
London	73–77	2	–	–	–

[a] These figures indicate the attenuation listed for the most popular yeasts sold under these designations as indicated by NHC second-round recipes.
[b] Number of recipes analyzed = 4
[c] Number of recipes analyzed = 8
[d] Number of recipes analyzed = 2
[e] Number of recipes analyzed = 8

information presented in this chapter, you'll encounter many options. Just remember that you can't test them all at the same time. Establish your basic simple recipe and experiment with one element at a time. I am sure you'll enjoy the results and learn more in the process.

Table 25.14
Water Profiles for London and Dublin

Minerals	London[a]	Dublin[b]
Calcium	50	115
Magnesium	20	4
Sodium	100	12
Carbonate	160	200
Sulfate	80	55
Chloride	60	19

Sources: [a] T. Foster, Porter, Classic Beer Style Series, no. 5 (Boulder, Colo.: Brewers Publications, 1992), 74. [b] C. Papazian, The Home Brewers Companion (New York: Avon Books, 1994), 83.

Key Success Factors in Brewing Stouts

- Use pale ale malt or pale extract for 70 percent to 90 percent of the grist.

- Use roast barley (or other dark grains) for about 10 percent of the grist.

- Consider addition of other specialty grains: up to 10 percent wheat, flaked barley, or CaraPils for a dry or foreign stout; 2 percent to 10 percent caramel or chocolate malt for sweet and imperial stouts; or 3 percent to 6 percent oatmeal.

- Mash at 150 to 155 °F (66 to 68 °C). Use calcium chloride for calcium addition.

- Make a single hop addition at the beginning of the boil that will provide a BU:GU ratio of about 1.0 for dry, foreign, and imperial stouts. Sweet stouts should have a BU:GU ratio of about 0.5.

- Late hop additions may be included for foreign and imperial stout recipes. Approximately 1.0 to 1.25 ounces should be added to 5 gallons as a dry hop or during the last few minutes of the boil.

- Ferment dry stouts using an attenuative British ale yeast such as London or Whitbread: Irish yeasts always produce good results, but some are low attenuators less suited to dry stout than to foreign, sweet, and imperial styles. American ale yeast can be used for a cleaner character in any stout.

Although it is easier to refer to this group of beers simply as the amber lagers, they seem more substantive and important when called by their proper names. Of course, the use of three words in describing them is a bit wasteful, especially since we generally regard this group as consisting of only two styles. To shorten things, people sometimes refer to this category as the VMOs.

The first style is Vienna, a beer with clear nineteenth-century origins in the city for which it is named. The second style may be referred to as either Märzen or Oktoberfest, and both terms are frequently used together. These two German words for the style contain the names of two months: March and October. Coming in opposite seasons, these months seem to have little in common, and the dual appellation sounds a bit confusing.

Most beer drinkers know Oktoberfest as a German beer festival held in late-September to mid-October each year. This celebration originated in 1810 not as a beer festival but as a wedding celebration for the Crown Prince of Bavaria.[1] The term "Oktoberfest" has evolved as the name applied to the special beers brewed for that celebration. To understand why the same beer might also be called a Märzen, we must better understand the origins of the word among German brewers.

The Beers of March

Whereas the origins of Oktoberfest can be traced to a specific year, the word "Märzen" has been used to describe some beers for hundreds of years. Before the advent of refrigeration, it was not possible to brew successfully in the summer months. When spring began to arrive, brewing would cease until fall, when cooler temperatures returned. Over the summer, beers that had been made and fermented in the cool months of the year would be consumed.

These summer beers were stored in cool cellars or caves in order to help preserve them during the nonbrewing months. Another tactic for preserving beers through the summer was to brew them to a higher gravity. As a result of these efforts, the last beers brewed each spring took on a special identity, and they were named Märzen, or March, beers, after the month in which most were brewed.

Because the Märzen designation arose from common brewing practices, we cannot tell exactly when or where it was first used. Today, Munich lays claim to creating the style, but it is clear that the term has strong ties to Vienna as well.

From its beginnings as a Roman outpost, Vienna struggled along for many centuries before becoming a city in its own right during the thirteenth century.[2] The first brewery — associated with a hospital — was noted not long after, in 1296.[3] For several centuries after this, beer was the underdog in a running battle with wine. Grapes grow well in the Vienna area, and the landed parties who produced wine demanded protection of their product from the competition posed by beer. It was not until the sixteenth century that brewing was widely licensed to convents, castles, towns, and marketplaces.[4]

By 1732, fourteen breweries operated near Vienna. They produced one or two types of oat beer, three varieties of wheat beer, and five varieties of barley beer.[5] One of the barley beers was known as Märzenbier. No doubt this beer bore little resemblance to the Märzen of today, but it demonstrates that the term was in use at an early date in Austria.

I find the first reference to Märzenbier in Munich just a few decades later. The history of the Hofbräuhaus München reports on the extensive cellars under that structure in the last half of the eighteenth century. These cellars, it notes, all became used for the storage of Märzen beers.[6]

Elsewhere, the same history reference names the brewery's early products, including two types of brown beer: Braunes Winterbier and Braunes Sommerbier.[7] The brown summer beer would logically be a Märzen: a beer brewed to a higher gravity and then cellared until needed during the hot months. The Hofbrauhaus book makes this clear by parenthetically adding "Märzen" after the Braunes Sommerbier notation.

It is fairly clear from these notations that the term Märzen was not actually applied to Munich beers at the time. The creation of a distinct Märzen style appears to have come from Vienna and was then adopted by Munich brewers to become the Oktoberfest style.[8] In the brewing literature, however, I find no references to a Munich Märzen style until the beginning

of the twentieth century. Furthermore, one source — published in Munich in 1883 — lists Märzen as a Viennese style, but names the Munich winter beers as Anstich Lagerbier, Doppelbier, Bock, and Salvator.[9] Thus, to understand the history of Vienna, Märzen, and Oktoberfest beers, the history of brewing in Vienna must be traced.

The city of Vienna clearly had a well-established Märzen style during the nineteenth century, as I discuss in detail below. But here again, the name of Munich brewer Gabriel Sedlmayr comes into play. Many sources believe it was the professional friendship between Sedlmayr and Vienna's Anton Dreher that gave rise to the Vienna lager style.[10]

Dreher came from a brewing family and studied with Sedlmayr in Munich as a young man before taking over the family brewery in Vienna. Early along, Dreher combined the Munich bottom-fermentation yeast with Vienna malts and brewing procedures to create the Vienna style of lager. The Märzen style produced in the same breweries was nothing more than a stronger version of the Vienna brew.

It appears that the Munich Oktoberfest style was an imitation of the Viennese Märzen beer. Interestingly enough, it was Gabriel Sedlymayr's son who is credited with brewing the first Vienna-style Oktoberfest beer.

The Original Vienna Beers

Prior to 1841, Vienna beer seems to have been fairly unremarkable. Little record exists of the ales that were commonly brewed, and nothing in the present catalog of beer styles can be traced to that time and place.

As mentioned above, it was Anton Dreher who revolutionized beer and brewing in Vienna. Sometime around 1841 — just a year before the creation of Pilsener — Dreher introduced lager brewing into his family brewery in Vienna.[11] From there, his career was one of the most dramatic and successful in the history of brewing. By the 1870s, the beers of Vienna were well known and carefully studied, even in Munich.

Although the various writings on Vienna brewing report some differences in the styles produced, three specific varieties of beer seem to have been commonplace, including Abzug, lager, and Märzen.

Abzug is a low-gravity (10 °P, 1.040 SG) lager brewed for quick consumption.[12] This beer was lagered before sale, but for a shorter period than the regular or Märzen beers. One source states that Abzug should be ready to drink within eight days of lagering, but that cold storage might be continued for up to two months.[13]

Lager refers to the Vienna lager upon which our current understanding of the style is based. Nineteenth-century sources consistently report that this beer had a gravity of 13 to 14 °P (1.052 to 1.056 SG).[14] Lagering ranged from four to ten months.

Märzen is a stronger version of the Vienna lager that would be cold-stored for up to twelve months before consumption.[15] The gravity of this style was generally reported to be in the range of 14 to 15 °P (1.056 to 1.060 SG).[16] One source also reports production of a Doppelmärzen to a gravity of 16.5 °P (1.066 SG).

Analyses of actual beers from the period suggest that the primary difference between the styles was a matter of gravity, as illustrated in table 26.1.

The scale for the color data reported in table 26.1 was not reported in the original sources, but it provides a basis for comparison of the styles. If we assume that this scale is at least related to that put forward by Lovibond at about this time, we would find these beers to be in the gold to amber range.

Despite the apparent similarities between these styles, one source suggests that the malts for the lager and Märzen beers may have been kilned differently, at least by some breweries.[17] The reported difference was in the final kilning temperature, where lager malt was finished at 176 °F (80 °C) and Märzen malt at 185 °F (85 °C). Although the temperature difference is not large, it certainly would have been sufficient — over the reported three-hour period of this stage — to change the flavor of the malt.

Another possible difference may have come in the relative bitterness of these styles. In general, Vienna beers are reported to have hop rates "30 percent less than those for Bohemian beers, about 30 percent more than those for Bavarian beers."[18] This midpoint distinguished the Vienna beers from those of its brewing neighbors, and it is also consistent with our contemporary perception of these styles.

Table 26.1
Nineteenth-Century Vienna Beer Styles

Style	OG	TG	%AA	%ABW	%ABV	Color
Abzug	10.3	1.014	67	2.8	3.6	5.3
Lager	13.4	1.017	68	3.8	4.7	5.4
Märzen	14.4	1.019	67	4.0	5.0	6.0

Sources: Carl Lintner, Lehrbuch der Bierbrauerei *(Brunswick, Germany: Friedrich Vieweg und Sohn, 1877). J. E. Thausing, W. T. Brannt, A. Schwarz, A. H. Bauer,* The Theory and Practice of the Preparation of Malt and the Fabrication of Beer *(London: Henry Carey Baird & Co., 1882).*

Note: All values are averages.

As would be expected, hop rates in the Vienna beers increased with the gravity of the style.[19] In some cases, however, it appears that the amount of hops added to the higher-gravity beers would have increased the BU:GU ratio and shifted the overall flavor balance of the product.[20] In general, however, BU:GU ratios appear to have been in the 0.40 to 0.50 range for most of the Vienna styles, with some of the higher-gravity beers perhaps reaching 0.6.[21]

The type of hop most commonly used in the Vienna beers appears to have been the Saaz variety grown in Bohemia.[22] One source suggests that other hops might have been used for Abzug, with Saaz being applied to the lager, and "finest Saaz" reserved for the Märzen.[23] Fix also reports that Dreher was fond of Styrian Golding hops.[24]

According to one source, half the hops were added at the beginning of the boil, and the other half thirty minutes before the end of the boil.[25]

Another view of the Vienna lager is provided through contrast with the beer of Pilsen. The Austrian brewer Thausing writes:

Schwechat[26] lager beer, and Pilsen lager beer, are placed beside each other, these Vienna and Bohemian beer, being the two principal representatives of the most important varieties of beer in Austria. The first (Vienna) is denser, richer in extract, in protein substances and carbonic acid, and more viscous, but contains less alcohol and is less attenuated than the Bohemia (Pilsen) beer.[27]

The analyses he refers to provide a number of chemical parameters, including the data in table 26.2.

This presentation provides a unique perspective on these two styles. Taking Pilsener Urquell as an example, the Pilsen style seems to have remained true to this profile over time. This comparison presents a good idea of what this Vienna lager must have been like.

Vienna Brewing Procedures

Like most continental brewers of the time, the Viennese used decoction mashing for the production of their beers. However, like their brethren in Pilsen and Munich, they had developed their own particular style of mashing that no doubt left its imprint on the finished beer.

Like others, the classic Vienna decoction used three boiling steps. The key difference came in the final decoction, where cloudy wort was boiled, rather than a thick portion of the mash.[28] After the second decoction was mixed back into the main mash, the entire mash was allowed to rest for some time, thereby creating a normal mash filter bed. Liquid was then drawn off

Table 26.2
Comparison of Characteristics of Lagers from Vienna and Pilsen

Characteristic	Vienna	Pilsen
OG (°P)	13.3	12.3
OG (SG)	1.053	1.049
TG (SG)	1.018	1.013
Alcohol (%ABW)	3.625	3.715
Color (SRM)	6.3	4.3

Source: J. E. Thausing, W. T. Brannt, A. Schwarz, A. H. Bauer, The Theory and Practice of the Preparation of Malt and the Fabrication of Beer (London: Henry Carey Baird & Co., 1882), 746–747.

from below the false bottom to make up the third decoction.

A considerable quantity of liquid must have been removed in this step in order to achieve the desired final temperature of 167 °F (75 °C). The boiling of this liquid decoction was apparently continued until "flakes" appeared and settled out from the clear wort in a sample tube.[29] Today's brewers would recognize these flakes as hot break material, and the brewers of that time referred to this procedure as "breaking" the mash.

The Austrian brewer Thausing also reports that two-step and even one-step decoctions were sometimes completed by dropping the lower temperature rests. The two-step procedure still used "one thick and one thin [clear] mash," but the single-step mash appears to have used only a thick mash.[30]

Sources differ on the exact rest temperatures for the main mash, although they are quite similar overall, as shown in table 26.3. I find it interesting that these mash schedules conducted their starch conversion rest at temperatures of 149 °F (65 °C) or lower. Based upon today's malts and procedures, the residual body seen in the style would seem to indicate a dextrin content consistent with a higher mash tempera-

ture. Here, as with Pilsener production, other parameters of the mashing process may come into play to create the needed dextrin content.

The length of boil for each decoction varied somewhat between sources, although the total time of boiling for all decoctions tended to be about equal.[31] One source suggests that different boil times would be used in making the higher-gravity beers, as shown in table 26.4.

Beyond the mashing procedure, most other aspects of brewing seem fairly consistent with well-known lager production methods. I discussed hopping practices earlier in this chapter; total boiling time appears to have been within the range of 1.5 to 2.5 hours.[32] I find coolships reported for wort chilling.[33] Thausing reports fermentation temperatures of 41 to 46 °F (5 to 7.5 °C)[34] and lager cellar temperatures of 34 to 41 °F (1.2 to 5 °C).[35]

In his discussion of fermentation and lagering, Thausing recommends blending different batches:

Beer from a brewery must not vary much in appearance and taste from week to week, or from month to month. If the brewer has attained favorable results by a certain method of brewing he should retain it . . . But this may

---

Table 26.3
Three Versions of Temperatures for Conducting Vienna Mashes

	°C			°F		
	1[a]	2[b]	3[c]	1[a]	2[b]	3[c]
First Rest *(First Decoction)*	35	30	30–37.5	95	86	86–99.5
Second Rest *(Second Decoction)*	47	50	44–53	117	122	111–127
Third Rest *(Third Decoction)*	60	65	56–65	142	149	133–149
Final Rest	75	75	71–75	167	167	160–167

Sources: [a] J. J. Mazger, "Das Wiener Brauverfahren," Der Banerische Bierbrauer (August 1871). [b] C. Lintner, ed., "Das Malz, Sud und Gabrverfahren in einer der ersten Brauereien Oesterreichs," Der Banerische Bierbrauer (March 1871): 34–35. [c] J. E. Thausing, W. T. Brannt, A. Schwarz, A. H. Bauer, The Theory and Practice of the Preparation of Malt and the Fabrication of Beer (London: Henry Carey Baird & Co., 1882).

Table 26.4
Decoction Boil Times — Vienna Brewing

	Lager	Märzen and Doppelmärzen
First decoction	30 mins.	45 mins.
Second decoction	30 mins.	45 mins.
Thin-mash decoction	45 mins.	60 mins.

Source: J. J. Mazger, "Das Wiener Brauverfahren," Der Banerische Bierbrauer (August 1871): 117.

be still further promoted by distributing the beer from different brewings into a larger number of barrels. For this reason every brewing is not stored by itself, but equal quantities of beer from one brewing are distributed, let us suppose, into 10 or 20 barrels, and these are then gradually filled with beer from later brewings. By doing this, after-fermentation is retarded, because, when a small quantity of beer is put into a large barrel, it cools quickly in the storing cellar, much quicker than if the barrel were filled at once.[36]

Thus blending — which we today associate only with the largest of breweries — was practiced more than one hundred years ago in the production of these classic beers. In addition to aiding uniformity, this procedure also appears to have had some practical benefits in terms of cooling.

Vienna Brewing Water

Although some sources indicate that Vienna brewing water may have been rather hard,[37] other sources claim that it is quite soft.[38] This confusion apparently springs from the fact that two or three different sources of water may have been available in Vienna over the past century or so.

The Danube River flows through Vienna, of course, and it would be a natural source of water for the city. More than likely, this is the hard-water source listed by some authors. In the 1950s, much of the city's drinking water was coming from mountains some forty miles away.[39] This water, used at the time by the Schwechat Brewery, was supposed to be quite soft, having only "eight points of hardness."[40]

Finally, I have seen references to the use of well water by Vienna brewers in both the nineteenth and twentieth centuries. Thausing lists an analysis of well water used for brewing at the Klein Schwechat Brewery near Vienna, circa 1882 (see table 26.5). This water has less than 150 parts per million of total hardness — not nearly as much as that quoted by twentieth-century brewing texts.

The 1950s article about Schwechat Brewery cited earlier also mentions the well water, saying that it is "somewhat harder than the drinking water." At that time the brewery actually used this harder well water for production of their dunkel beer. Given the nineteenth-century use of moderately hard well water in making classic Vienna lager, I'm inclined to believe that this is the proper source for authentic production of the style. It contains less than 100 parts per million of carbonate and about 50 parts per million of both calcium and sulfate. All other brewing-relevant ions are less than 20 parts per million. The carbonate should work well with the slightly colored Vienna malts, the calcium should be nearly sufficient for the needs of the mash, and the sulfate should be low enough to prevent the bitterness from becoming harsh.

The composition of this water fairly closely matches the recommendations

Table 26.5
Profiles of Vienna Water

Minerals	Well Water	Hard Water	Hard Water
Ca	48	225	200
Mg	20	90	60
Na	10	14	8
CO_3	76	270	120
SO_4	52	172	125
Cl	13	34	12

All measurements in milligrams/liter (parts per million).
Sources: J. E. Thausing, W. T. Brannt, A. Schwarz, A. H. Bauer, The Theory and Practice of the Preparation of Malt and the Fabrication of Beer (London: Henry Carey Baird & Co., 1882), 125. H. L. Hind, Brewing Science and Practice (London: Chapman & Hall, Ltd., 1938), 440. G. J. Noonan, Brewing Lager Beer (Boulder, Colo.: Brewers Publications. 1986), 55.

given by George and Laurie Fix in their book on these styles.[41]

Twentieth-Century Vienna, Märzen, and Oktoberfest Beers

The early twentieth century was not kind to the Vienna style of beer. War, prohibitionism, and economic depression pummeled all brewers during this period and virtually eliminated the classic Vienna-style beer from commercial production.

Despite all these challenges, the style survived, albeit in the unlikely environs of Mexico. A number of Austrian brewers had been transplanted there during the late nineteenth century, including one Santigo Graf.[42] He adopted the same uncompromising approach to brewing that had been exhibited by Anton Dreher in Austria. It is as a result of these immigrant brewers that we find today's most vital and popular examples of the Vienna style in Mexico.

The North American interpretations were largely ignored by the European brewing community, as indicated in 1957, when DeClerck reports on the Vienna style:"At one time a Vienna type of bottom fermentation beer was brewed. This had a colour intermediate between that of Munich and Pilsner. The palate was at the same time aromatic and bitter, qualities which are not compatible, and it has almost disappeared from the market."[43]

A report on the Schwechat Brewery is published in a 1955 edition of *American Brewer* magazine.[44] Schwechat was once a leader in the production of Vienna-style lagers, but the recipes reported in 1955 look more like pale American adjunct lagers. Although one of the two lead products has an original gravity of 1.054, both contain 15 percent rice. The only all-malt product is a "dunkel" at 1.048 OG that is described as being "very sweet" and thus probably not at all like the original Vienna-style beers.

While Vienna lager was on the decline, Märzen appears to have been on the rise. Today we find that both Vienna and Munich brewers produce beers designated as Märzen. Now it is the Munich version that provides our model for the style and the closest match to a nineteenth-century Vienna beer. I'm told that today's Austrian Märzen style, while still all-malt, is often quite pale, with gravities generally just above 12 °P (1.048 OG).[45]

The ascendancy of Munich appears to have followed Gabriel Sedlmayr's (the son) brewing of an Oktoberfest beer in the Viennese style around 1872. I find only one analysis of beer called a Märzen in the extensive work of Wahl and Henius during the first decade of the twentieth century.[46]

This beer is from the Munich Pschorr brewery, but the reported characteristics bear little resemblance to the well-established Vienna Märzen style (OG: 1.066, 16.42 °P; TG: 1.017, 4.35 °P; alcohol 4.93 percent by weight). This beer is higher in gravity and more highly attenuated than the various Vienna Märzens analyzed twenty years earlier — perhaps because it was being produced for export.

A photo caption in the history of the Hof Brau Haus indicates that this brewery, too, made a Märzen in 1898.[47] But neither this nor the Pschorr Märzen analysis provides much illumination of the history of this style.

The next reference I have been able to identify for Märzen comes much later, in the 1950s, when annual reviews of Märzen beer were published in *Brauwelt* for a number of years. Then, in the 1980s, in a series of articles titled "500 Beers of the Entire World," Professor Anton Piendl reports on the composition of German Märzens during the 1970s and 1980s.

These data show some interesting details about the evolution of the Märzen style during the twentieth century. The first data from the 1950s portray a Märzen that is still fairly close to the Vienna Märzen of the 1880s. The gravity is still near 14.0 °P, apparent attenuation has

risen some, to 71 to 72 percent, but the average alcohol level is still about the same, at 4.1 percent by weight. Thus, the body and malt character of the beer is probably quite similar to what it was nearly one hundred years before.

By the mid-1970s these same changes have been pushed even further: Gravity declines to as low as 12.7 °P while at the same time attenuation rises to about 78 percent (see tables 26.6 and 26.7). These two forces counteract each other somewhat with regard to alcohol production, but by 1975 to 1976 the average alcohol by weight has risen measurably. In total, this shift means that today's brew is a much thinner, slightly more alcoholic product that is probably beginning to lose the typical malt punch of the style. Further evidence of this is seen in the reported color of the beers, which were fairly pale at 4 to 5 °SRM.

The low average values for original gravity in the 1970s are surprising, especially given that the minimum gravity given by Piendl for a Munich Oktoberfest is 13.5 °P (1.054 SG) and the gravity for a Bavarian Märzen is 13.0 °P (1.052 SG).[48] Piendl's analysis of individual beers — probably done during the mid-1980s, when the article was published — show none with an OG below 13.0 °P (1.052 SG).[49]

There seems to have been a trend back

Table 26.6

Characteristics of German Märzen Beer, 1953–1968

	OG	TG	ABW (%)	ABV (%)	Brand Color*
1953	13.7	1.016	4.1	5.1	1.78
1954	13.8	1.016	4.1	5.1	1.93
1955	13.7	1.015	4.1	5.1	2.16
1956	13.9	1.014	4.3	5.4	2.21
1968	13.8	1.015	4.3	5.4	1.89

Sources: V. I. Bartek, "Die Wies'n-Märzen-Biere 1953 und 1954," Brauwelt 84, no. 19 (October 1954): 1266. Bartek, "Die Wies'n-Märzen-Biere 1955," Brauwelt 83, no. 14 (October 1955): 1418. Bartek, "Die Wies'n-Märzen-Biere 1956," Brauwelt 80, no. 5 (October 1956): 1428. P. Seidl, "Die Wies'n-Märzen-Biere 1968," Brauwelt 76/77, no. 20 (September 1968): 1421. Note: All values are averages.

*The correlation between Brand Color and SRM is unknown. These values provided for comparison between years only.

toward darker-colored Märzens in the early 1980s. Data on "the darker" Märzens of the 1980s show a range of 8 to 16.6 °SRM — quite a bit darker than the 4 to 5 °SRM range seen on average during the 1970s. Here again, the individual analyses in the article bear this out, showing colors that are generally in the range from 8 to 14 °SRM — values close to what we expect today.[50]

Two specific analyses are worth summarizing, for they represent contemporary examples made by traditional producers of this style (see table 26.8). The range illustrated by the characteristics of Spaten Urmärzen and Hof Brau Oktoberfest Märzen appears to be where the Märzen/Oktoberfest style has settled for the time being. A prominent expert on German beer, Professor Ludwig Narziss, commented in 1993 that the gravity of the Märzen/Oktoberfest style should fall in the range of 13 to 14 °P (1.052 to 1.057 SG) in order to maintain the character of the style.[51]

In comparing these modern Märzen/Oktoberfest beers to their 1880 counterparts, I find they are more similar in gravity to the Vienna lagers than to the so-called Märzens of that time. However, the level of apparent attenuation — and therefore the alcohol content — is significantly higher in the twentieth-century samples. Bitterness also seems to have declined somewhat — an observation that is echoed in the text of the Piendl article.[52]

From these data the current specifications of the style have been created and published by the Association of Brewers, as shown in table 26.9.

Examples of these beers are usually not difficult to find. The Märzen/Oktoberfest beers from Germany can be found seasonally each fall in most stores that carry imported beers. My favorites are the Hacker Pshorr Oktoberfest Märzen, which is toasty-rich and full-bodied with some residual sweetness, and the Paulaner Oktoberfest, which displays a similar malt complexity and toasted character but with less sweetness. Examples of the Vienna style can still be had from breweries in Mexico. Although Dos Equis is watered down for the North American market,[53] Negra Modelo retains its full character to provide a good model for the lighter-gravity member of this family.

Brewing Vienna and Märzen Beers

I began this chapter by explaining why three different words are used to name just two styles. Now that it's time to talk about

Table 26.7
German Märzen Beer, 1970–1976

Year	OG	TG	BU	BU:GU	ABW (%)	Color (EBC)	Color (SRM)
1970	13.0	3.0	20	0.38	4.2	10.8	4.5
1971	12.7	3.2	23	0.45	4.0	12.4	5.1
1972	12.8	3.2	20	0.39	4.0	10.9	4.5
1973	12.6	3.1	19	0.38	4.0	12.0	5.0
1974	12.7	2.8	22	0.43	4.1	9.6	4.1
1975	13.4	2.9	20	0.37	4.4	10.6	4.4
1976	13.1	2.9	19	0.37	4.3	11.9	4.9

Source: A. Piendl, "500 Bier Aus Aller Welt," Brauindustrie (1986): 1730.
Note: All values are averages.

Table 26.8
Characteristics of Two Contemporary Märzens

Name	OG	%AA	ABW (%)	SRM	BU	BU:GU
Spaten Urmärzen	13.5	75.3	4.24	16.6	16.5	0.31
Hof Brau Oktoberfest Märzen	13.6	72.9	4.12	11.0	20.0	0.37

brewing these beers, it becomes clear that virtually everything that can be said about the brewing of one applies to the other. Thus, this recipe formulation discussion will read as if I am discussing just one style rather than two or three.

The second-round VMO beers from the National Homebrew Competition showed a striking tendency toward the use of malt extract. Appropriately, this discussion of brewing methods will begin with a look at the formulations that used extract.

Extract Beers

Extract appeared in nearly 45 percent of the NHC second-round recipes. This was the highest proportion of extract beers in any classic style category of the NHC. Six of the eight extract recipes relied upon extract for the majority of the fermentable material. The remaining two used extract for about one-third of the total gravity. Table 26.10 shows the proportion of extract used in each recipe.

A half-dozen different extracts were used in these recipes, but Alexander's was the most popular, appearing in four of the eight extract-based formulations (see table 26.11). The four recipes that relied most heavily on extract all used more than one brand of extract in their formulations.

All but one of the extract-based VMO recipes included some grain in the

Table 26.9
Vienna and Märzen/Oktoberfest Style Characteristics

	Vienna	Märzen/Oktoberfest
Original gravity	1.048–55 (12–13.5 °P)	1.052–64 (13–16 °P)
Bitterness	22–28	22–28
BU:GU ratio	0.45–0.50	0.42–0.48
Hop flavor	Low-med.	Low
Hop aroma	Low-med.	Low
Color (SRM)	8–12	7–14
Apparent extract	1.012–18	1.012–20
Alcohol (volume)	4.4–6	4.8–6.5
Esters	None	None
Diacetyl	Low	Low
Other	Low malt sweetness; toasted malt aroma	Malty sweet, toasted malt aroma and flavor

Source: C. Papazian, "Introducing: Beer Style Guidelines: Part 2," The New Brewer (March–April 1992): 25–28.

Table 26.10
Distribution of Extract Proportion in NHC Second-Round VMO Recipes

Recipe	% Extract
1	100
2	93
3	92
4	84
5	67
6	57
7	35
8	31

Note: This table shows the percentage of total grain and extract weight that was made up of extract in eight recipes. Four were Vienna, four were Märzen/Oktoberfest.

formulation as well. Here two groups can be identified. The first group supplemented extract only with crystal malt. These beers are the ones that relied most heavily on extract in their formulation.

The second group performed a mini-mash using two-row malt plus additional specialty grains. These beers, which contained the lower proportions of extract, used two to three specialty grains in addition to the two-row malt. These additional grains and their overall incidence in the eight extract beers are shown in table 26.12. The chocolate malt that appeared in these recipes came in small amounts that could be as low as 1 ounce in a 5-gallon recipe.

Overall, two approaches are used in extract brewing of these amber lagers. In the first, several brands of extract are combined to account for 85 percent or more of the fermentable material. This extract base is then supplemented with crystal malt. Though some might ignore this approach as overly simple, a beer brewed on this model won the VMO category of the NHC just a couple of years ago.

The second group relies upon a mini-mash of two-row malt with several specialty grains for one-third to two-thirds of the total gravity. A single brand of extract is then used to make up the remaining gravity.

All-Grain Recipes

The all-grain recipes for the Vienna and Märzen/Oktoberfest styles generally relied on a blend of four grains for the majority of the grist. These four grains, in order of decreasing frequency, were Munich, two-row, Pilsener, and Vienna. In selection of each of these grains, Fix emphasizes the need to select products made from the finest two-row malt — usually European in origin — in order to ensure the fine malt character required of the style.[54]

Of course, the function of Pilsener and of two-row in a recipe are nearly the same, and this is also true for Munich and Vienna malts. If we look at the recipes using these combinations, we find that the average formulation contained 52 percent Pilsener plus two-row, and 30 percent Munich plus Vienna. As is often the case with averages, however, these figures are very misleading.

It is true that the total of these four ingredients usually accounted for 80 to 90 percent of the total grist. At the same time, however, the balance between Pils/two-row and Munich/Vienna varied widely across the recipes, as shown in table 26.13. Three recipes contain less than 10 percent Munich and Vienna, while another three contain about 60 percent of this combination.

Table 26.11
Extract Used in NHC Second-Round VMOs

Brand	No. of Recipes
Alexander's	4
Laaglander	2
Bierkeller	2
Mountain Springs	1
William's Vienna Extract	1
English Extract	1

Across the range of Munich/Vienna proportions, the amount of Pils/two-row generally varies inversely to keep the total for all four grains in the 77 to 92 percent range. There is only one exception to this rule, recipe #8, which relied on toasted two-row malt for nearly one-third of the total recipe.

Crystal malt appears in nearly all VMO formulations. I find no apparent pattern between the use or proportion of crystal malt and the amount of Munich/Vienna malt in a recipe. One recipe that excluded crystal contains only 5 percent Munich/Vienna, the other contains 64 percent.

Most recipes included 7 to 9 percent crystal or caramel malt regardless of the balance between the two groups of base malts. A number of recipes used more than one type of crystal malt, although most stayed in the light to medium color range (10 to 60 °L) for all additions.

Other or specialty malts appeared in the majority (55 percent) of the VMO recipes. These were generally amber malts of some sort, such as home-toasted malt, Victory, or aromatic malt. A very small amount of chocolate malt appears in one all-grain recipe.

We find CaraPils or wheat malt in seven of eleven, or 65 percent, of the all-grain recipes. The amounts average 7 percent and 3 percent of the grist, respectively. Most often CaraPils appears without wheat. Wheat appears in only three cases, twice with CaraPils and once without it (see table 26.14).

Mashing of these VMO grists usually followed a pretty simple process. None of the recipes I reviewed reported using decoction mash schedules. Very few indicated the use of protein rests and preferred instead the use of a simple infusion at the desired saccharification temperature. The average saccharification temperature reported by successful VMO brewers was 152.5 °F (67 °C). Fermentability of these worts averaged 71 percent across all recipes, with a slightly lower rate among the Vienna (69 percent) than among the Märzen/Oktoberfest beers (72 percent).

The average gravity of the worts produced was, of course, somewhat higher for the Märzen/Oktoberfest beers at 1.057 than for the Vienna beers at 1.052. The two American Homebrewers Association national winners from this group of beers represent the highest (1.065) and lowest (1.047) gravities reported for all the VMO recipes evaluated, even though both beers were judged in the Märzen/Oktoberfest style.

Hops

Compared to development of the malt bill, hopping these amber lagers is relatively straightforward. A moderate bitterness must be imparted through the use of traditional German or Bohemian hops. In addition, a low level of hop flavor and/or aroma may be included, again using fine continental hop varieties.

Table 26.12

Grain Bills in NHC Second-Round VMO Recipes That Include Extract

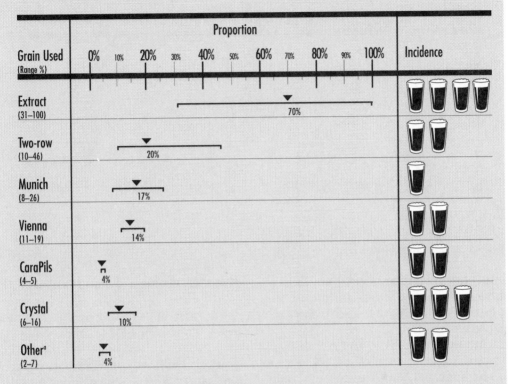

Grain Used (Range %)	Proportion	Incidence
Extract (31–100)	70%	
Two-row (10–46)	20%	
Munich (8–26)	17%	
Vienna (11–19)	14%	
CaraPils (4–5)	4%	
Crystal (6–16)	10%	
Other[a] (2–7)	4%	

[a]*Other includes chocolate (3) and toasted (1).*

Key: This chart shows what proportion of the grain bill was provided by various grains in eight VMO recipes. The line next to each grain gives the range of values used by different brewers; this range is also listed below "Grains Used." The triangle above each line indicates the average proportion used across all recipes.

The icons in the column on the right show how often the eight VMO recipes included each grain. (Percentage figures indicate how many of the recipes included the grain.)

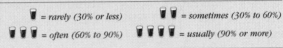

= rarely (30% or less)   = sometimes (30% to 60%)
= often (60% to 90%)   = usually (90% or more)

Data from the NHC second-round beers show BU:GU levels at about 0.50 for Vienna lager, with slightly higher levels, at 0.57, for Märzen/Oktoberfest. The calculated IBU values for these recipes range from 16 to 37 for Vienna and from 20 to 46 for Märzen/Oktoberfest.

Hop selection follows fairly traditional lines, with Hallertau, Saaz, and Tettnanger accounting for nearly 60 percent of all hop additions. The primary departure from this pattern comes in the use of newly developed Hallertau hybrids grown in the United States, including Liberty and Mt. Hood, which together accounted for nearly a quarter of all VMO hop additions. With the exception of one addition of Cascade hops for bittering, all of the remaining hops were traditional continental varieties. The pattern of these selections varied little across the various hop uses, as shown in tables 26.15 and 26.16.

Of course, all recipes included bittering hops, and the majority of the hop additions were dedicated to this use. Of more interest are the patterns of flavor and

Table 26.13
Proportions of Base Malts in NHC Second-Round All-Grain VMO Recipes

Recipe	2-Row + Pils	Munich + Vienna	Total of All Four Grains
1	92	0	92
2	81	7	88
3	77	5	82
4	69	22	91
5	61	15	77
6	48	32	80
7	42	42	83
8	36	22	58
9	33	56	88
10	23	64	86
11	10	69	79
Average	52	30	82

Note: All values are percentages.

aroma hop usage. In general, brewers of these styles tended to include at least one hop addition during the last twenty-nine minutes of the boil.

My analyses use the arbitrary division of zero to nine minutes of boiling for aroma hops and ten to twenty-nine minutes of boiling for flavor hops. Using these divisions, nearly all of the VMO recipes made either a flavor or aroma addition — but only a couple made both types of additions. Furthermore, I find the type of addition chosen differs by style, as shown in table 26.17.

Thus, the Vienna beers were much more likely to have a hop addition during the last nine minutes of the boil, while the Märzen/Oktoberfest beers were more likely to have a hop addition between ten and twenty-nine minutes before the end of the boil. Only one recipe made a dry hop addition.

The size of the late hop additions decreased as they neared the end of the boil. The average aroma hop addition was ½ ounce in 5 gallons, while the average flavor hop addition was ¾ ounce (see table 26.16).

Fermentation and Water Treatment

Brewers of Vienna/Märzen/Oktoberfest beers show remarkable consistency in their selection of yeast. Nearly three-quarters (thirteen of eighteen) used a Bavarian yeast strain suitable for the production of malt-accented beers. The only other yeast that was used by more than one brewer was the Munich style, also known as Weihenstephan 308. One brewer also used a Bohemian Pilsener yeast, which seems like it might be a good alternative for this style.

Average primary fermentation temperature was 50 °F (10 °C). According to the recipe sheets, some brewers succeeded in fermenting their lagers at temperatures as high as 57 °F (14 °C) using the Bavarian yeast, but lower temperatures are generally recommended.

In general, lagering seems to be fairly short for these styles, and a number of the recipe sheets reported no lagering at all. Among those who lagered their beers, temperatures of 33 to 38 °F (0.5 to 3 °C) were most common, and the average duration of lagering was four to five weeks.

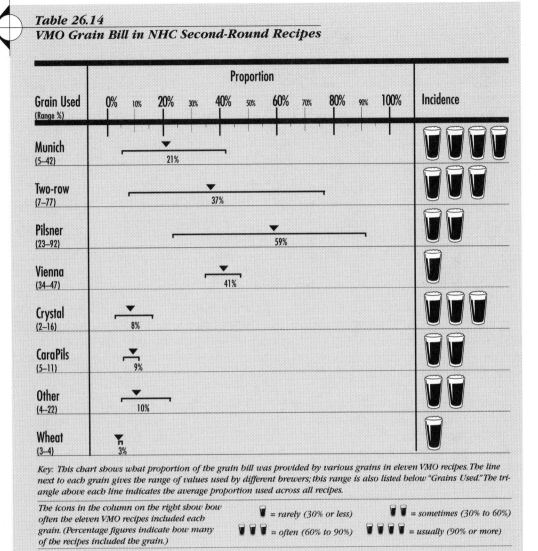

Table 26.14
VMO Grain Bill in NHC Second-Round Recipes

Grain Used (Range %)	Proportion	Incidence
Munich (5–42)	21%	
Two-row (7–77)	37%	
Pilsner (23–92)	59%	
Vienna (34–47)	41%	
Crystal (2–16)	8%	
CaraPils (5–11)	9%	
Other (4–22)	10%	
Wheat (3–4)	3%	

Key: This chart shows what proportion of the grain bill was provided by various grains in eleven VMO recipes. The line next to each grain gives the range of values used by different brewers; this range is also listed below "Grains Used." The triangle above each line indicates the average proportion used across all recipes.

The icons in the column on the right show how often the eleven VMO recipes included each grain. (Percentage figures indicate how many of the recipes included the grain.)

= rarely (30% or less)   = sometimes (30% to 60%)
= often (60% to 90%)   = usually (90% or more)

Nonetheless, Fix reports that "softness and elegance" can be imparted by extended lagering, and this approach may be considered by those interested in seriously exploring the style.[55]

Very few of the VMO recipes reported any treatment of the brewing water. As the earlier section on water indicated, there is some debate about the type of water actually used for this style. As a result, I do not believe that beer judges look for a specific water-chemistry character. This allows brewers to make good examples of these styles with just about any water.

For those who did include some water treatment in their recipe, gypsum was the most common additive. Of course, most brewers make such additions for the benefit of the mash chemistry rather than for any flavor impact. A single entry added not only gypsum but also chalk and salt. Generally I would recommend staying away from gypsum when making these styles because the sulfate can sharpen the bitter

Table 26.15
Hops Used in NHC Second-Round VMO Recipes

Variety	Bitter	Flavor	Aroma	Dry	Total
Hallertau	10	8	4	0	22
Liberty	8	1	3	0	12
Saaz	5	3	0	1	9
Tettnanger	1	1	3	0	5
Perle	2	1	1	0	4
Mt. Hood	1	1	1	0	3
N. Brewer	3	0	0	0	3
Styrian Goldings	4	0	0	0	4
Cascade	1	0	0	0	1

Note: The data in this chart show the number of times each hop was used across the nineteen recipes analyzed.

character. I prefer calcium chloride as a source for mash calcium when making malt-balanced beers.

Conclusion

There are a number of ways to produce a fine amber lager in the Vienna spirit. The final result should reflect what Fix calls "elegance and softness as well as a measure of complexity."[56] If one selects fine ingredients, this effect can no doubt be achieved with a variety of formulations, each quite distinct yet very satisfying.

Given the broad selection of fine malts and hops available to home and craft brewers today, I have no doubt that those devoted to these styles will be able to experiment for many years before finding the perfect expression of the style's elegance. In the meantime, they will no doubt produce many pleasing and enjoyable beers.

Table 26.16
Hop Additions in NHC Second-Round VMO Recipes

Addition	Avg. No. per Recipe	Size of Hop Additions	
		Avg. oz./gal.	Avg. oz./5 gal.
Boil	1.8	—	—
Flavor	0.8	0.15	0.77
Aroma	0.6	0.10	0.51
Dry	0.1	0.05	0.25
Total	3.3		

Note: Total number of recipes analyzed = 19

Table 26.17
Proportion of NHC Second-Round VMO Recipes Including Late Hop Additions

Style	Flavor	Aroma
Vienna	43%	71%
Märzen/Oktoberfest	67%	33%

Note: Total number of recipes analyzed = 19

Key Success Factors in Brewing Vienna, Märzen, and Oktoberfest

- The ideal water for this style is low in sulfate with moderate carbonate content. Mash calcification should be done with calcium chloride rather than gypsum in order to keep sulfate levels low.

- Malt extract may be used successfully in the making of amber lagers. Combine several varieties of extract with crystal malt, or use a single extract to supplement wort from a minimash that includes two-row plus specialty malts.

- For 80 to 90 percent of an all-grain grist blend two-row, Munich, Pilsener, and Vienna malts in virtually any proportion. High-quality European malts should be selected over products made from six-row malt.

- Crystal and toasted or commercial amber malts are included in most recipes.

- CaraPils or wheat malt is included in the majority of all recipes.

- A very small amount of chocolate malt (1 ounce for 5 gallons) may be added.

- Single-infusion mashing can be used with an average saccharification temperature of 152.5 °F (67 °C).

- Fine continental hops such as Hallertau, Saaz, and Tettnanger should be selected for all hop additions. American-grown Hallertau hybrids may also be used.

- Target a BU to GU ratio of 0.5 to 0.57. This generally means 25 to 35 IBUs.

- Add 0.75-ounce of aroma-type hops ten to twenty-nine minutes before the end of the boil for a Märzen/Oktoberfest, or 0.5-ounce of hops zero to nine minutes before the end of the boil for a Vienna-style beer.

- Ferment near 50 °F (10 °C) using Bavarian yeast, (or perhaps a Munich or Bohemian yeast.

- After fermentation, lager for thirty to forty days at a temperature between 34 and 40 °F (2 and 4 °C).

Project	Designing Great Beers
	Brewers Publications
Project No.	61766

Wheat is our most popular cereal grain, so it isn't surprising that it has been used to make beers for several millennia. In fact, the making of wheat beers has been abolished at certain times and in certain places because it consumed too much of the grain needed for making bread.

Barley has evolved as the grain of choice for most beers by a process of selection. The enzymes and husk of barley make it quite well suited to the brewing process that has been in use for many centuries now. In contrast, wheat, lacking a husk and having higher protein and fat content than barley,[1] tends to create problems when used for any significant proportion of a grist. Finally, barley provides more extract to the brewer per pound of grain than wheat does, and it is less suited to the making of bread than is wheat. Thus, given an equal supply of both grains, one can enjoy the greatest wealth of both beer and bread by dedicating the barley to brewing and the wheat to baking.

Of course the science needed to demonstrate the relative strengths and weaknesses of these grains for brewing and baking has only recently been developed. By contrast, the formulations and habits of brewers stretch back for centuries. Those involving wheat have proven not only successful, but also popular — at least at times — and so this fair grain continues to find a place in the production of beer today.

The History of Wheat Beers

The popularity of wheat beers has waxed and waned through the centuries. Along the way, at least two distinct styles evolved. The first is Bavarian (or south-German) weissbier, which is also called weizen. Today, this is the best known type of traditional wheat beer. But one hundred years ago weizen was nearly dead and virtually unknown. In those days, the phrase "weissbier" mostly referred to what is now called Berliner weisse. Today it is the Berliner weisse that seems moribund: a rare specialty that might disappear at any time.

The flip-flop in the popularity of these two styles over the past two hundred years makes tracing a comprehensive history of either style somewhat difficult. The resulting account leaves many questions unanswered but still presents an intriguing look at the brews of a bygone era. This section begins with a look at early wheat beer styles and then moves on to trace the brewing of these beers during the nineteenth and twentieth centuries.

Early Wheat Beers

The history of German (and Austrian) brewing is littered with references to wheat beers. Even early on, they were called weissbiers, or "white" beers to indicate their pale color. (Barley beers, by contrast, were called red or brown beers.) The following examples bear this out.

• Weissbier from the city of Hamburg is first noted in a 1410 decree stating that the beer must be "strong in corn [grain], not bitter of taste, yellow and not red of color."[2] Fifty years later a recipe for this brew shows that wheat made up only 10 percent of the grist. Nonetheless, sixteenth-century beer chronicler Dr. Henricus Knaustius proclaimed Hamburg beer the "queen of all Weiss beer."[3]

• Brunswick Mumme was a strong beer widely known in medieval days. Although it was made entirely from barley, the Brunswick brewers did make a wheat beer, and this apparently inspired one English brewer, who tried to copy the Mumme. The English Mumme recipe was based largely on wheat (7 bushels) with some oats and beans (one bushel each) and was well spiced with herbs of various kinds and "fined" with "ten new-laid eggs, not cracked or broken."[4]

• A white beer called Broyhan was brewed in 1526 as an attempt to copy the Hamburg wheat beer. It was "quite light in hue," and even the Duke gave it an enthusiastic reception.[5] It was reported that "Broyhan is all the better the more wheat in proportion to barley is used in its preparation." It appears that later on the approach to brewing Broyhan was changed to rely entirely upon barley malt.[6]

• A Dutch wheat beer is supposed to have inspired the opening of the first weisse beer brewery in Nurnberg in 1541.[7] The product of this brewery came to be known as Crazy Wrangel.[8] It was so popular that the red-beer brewers complained bitterly and took steps to limit the number of weisse beer breweries allowed to operate in their city.[9] This move probably

backfired by creating an artificial shortage of weissbier that no doubt heightened its popularity, increased its price, and greatly enriched the weissbier brewers.

• The famous Einbeck beer, one of the most widely heralded of German beers prior to 1618, included wheat to the proportion of one-third of the total grain.[10] It was this beer that eventually inspired the development of bock beer in Munich.

• In the year 1547 the city of Lubeck had two separate breweries, one for weisse beer, one for Rot (or red) beer.[11] The Lubeck beer was called Israel.

• Although somewhat later, wheat beer brewing was also popular in Vienna. Records from 1732 show that the fourteen breweries in the vicinity of Vienna produced three wheat beers: weisse beer, doppelbier (which might be a precursor of weizenbock), and weinbier (mixed with fermenting boiled wine).[12]

Weisse Beer in Munich

I have purposely omitted Munich — or more properly, Bavaria — from this listing of wheat beers because it has the most cohesive history of weisse beer brewing of any area in Germany. It seems that the first Bavarian weisse beers were brewed by a noble clan called Degenberger during the fifteenth century.[13] From that time on the brewing of weisse beer was possible only by license from royalty. The Degenbergers controlled this license until the last of the clan died out. Subsequently, the Bavarian house of dukes owned the rights.

Shortly after the dukes obtained these rights, Duke Maximilian I is said to have arranged for the construction of the first weissbier brew house in Munich.[14] The exact date of construction remains in doubt, but it would have occurred during the first decade or two of the 1500s if built under Maximilian's direction. Still, another source credits Duke William IV with the building of the Munich weissbier brewery,[15] perhaps in 1602, as indicated in this passage by the historian Arnold:

As far back as the 16th century, the brown beer of Munich had locally found a competitor in the Bohemian pale wheat beer, which became quite popular. Thereupon the Munich brewers began to imitate this beer, until the town authorities forbade its manufacture, in 1567, declaring that it used up too much wheat in the brewing, and also that "it is neither wholesome nor nourishing, nor gives strength and vigor, but merely incites to drinking unreasonably." However, in 1602 the "White Brewery" was fitted up on the same site where now stands the noted Hofbrauhaus, but the Munich brewers were forbidden to meddle with the brewing of such "white" beer, since the ruler of the land claimed and exercised this as his sovereign prerogative, and it was not until 1789 that this prerogative was relinquished in other parts of the country, but not in Munich.

As showing how popular this wheat beer was, it is mentioned that at the ducal brewery (the only place where it could be made), they brewed it in 1626 four times per week, but in 1648 already three brews daily; 1661, four brews daily; 1701 five times; and by 1705 six brews every 24 hours. However, this wheat beer, too, lost favor at last, and towards the end of the 18th century the brown beer gained complete supremacy.[16]

The brewery in Munich was just one of nearly two dozen breweries operated by the dukes while they controlled weissbier brewing in Germany. Various German and Austrian cities brewed weissbier during the sixteenth, seventeenth, and eighteenth centuries. Usually these breweries were operated "under privilege" granted by the ducal monopoly.

With the decline in popularity of weissbier in the late eighteenth century came a breakdown in the ducal monopoly on its brewing. As indicated in the above passage from Arnold, many of the ducal breweries were sold off and others were leased to private concerns.[17] The Munich Weissbier Brewery, standing at the site of today's Hofbräuhaus, continued to make weissbier, although in steadily declining volumes. In 1808 it appears that weissbier production was moved, although its production continued under a lease relationship.[18]

Still, it was not until 1872 that the royal rights to weissbier were relinquished to the public domain. This allowed all brewers to make weisse as well as lager beers and led to a modest revival in the Munich weissbier style. A brewer named Georg Schneider was apparently instrumental in ending royal control.[19] He subsequently purchased an old brewery in Munich to produce weissbier and tripled its output within a half-dozen years.[20] Schneider's descendants still operate a weissbier brewery near Regensburg, Germany, and their products (Schneider Weisse and the Aventinus Dunkel Weizenbock) are exported to the United States.[21]

Weissbier Brewing Techniques

Brewing science — notably the use of the thermometer and hydrometer — did not gain acceptance in Germany until weissbier was well into its decline. As a result, I find relatively little technical information about the brewing of Bavarian weissbier in the historical brewing literature. This is further complicated by the fact that the term weissbier is used by authors to designate both the Bavarian- and Berliner-style wheat beers.

The first specific reference I find to weizen states that it is "brewed like the weiss, from wheat malt, [but] dispenses altogether with hops."[22] Despite this description, I have yet to find any recipe for a weissbier that completely excludes hops from the formulation. Two references I have found to nineteenth-century Bavarian weisse (weizen) both include hops. They are both based on triple decoction mashes.

The first comes from Professor Lintner and is reported to be the technique used by "the former Weissbier brewery at the site of the Hofbräuhaus in Munich."[23] This recipe reports a grist that is 2 parts barley malt and 1 part wheat malt. These proportions are reversed from what we expect, but they may have been intentional, because Warner tells us that this ratio helps to maximize the production of the clove-flavored 4-vinyl guaiacol.[24]

The brewing process for Lintner's beer is described as follows:

1. The grist is doughed-in with cold water and allowed to stand for five hours to start. Then a triple decoction mash is performed.

2. Hot water is added to raise the temperature to 95 °F (35 °C); mix for five minutes.

3. Thick mash is pulled for decoction. The decoction is boiled for thirty minutes and then added back to the main mash, raising its temperature to 113 °F (45 °C). Mixed for two minutes.

4. Thick mash is pulled for decoction and boiled for forty-five minutes. When added back, this decoction raises the main mash to 136 °F (58 °C). Mixed two minutes.

5. Pull lauter mash (liquid, no grain) and boil for fifteen minutes. When added back to main mash, this decoction raised main mash to 160 °F (71 °C). Mixed for five minutes. Rest for one hour.

This recipe calls for "one half pound of hops per hectoliter of malt."

A second source, from the Munich-based *Der Banerische Bierbrauer* (edited by Lintner) of 1872, gives a different set of mash boil times and rest temperatures but still indicates the use of hops with a hop-to-malt ratio of 1.19 to 100 by weight quoted.[25] Other entries relate the hopping by weight of hops per hectoliter, with 0.2 kilogram per hectoliter given as the proper ratio. (That is equivalent to 0.5-pound per barrel, or 1.3 ounces in 5 gallons.) This article also provides information on the original gravity of the worts produced, showing that they ranged from 8.2 to 11 °B.[26]

After these two references on the production of Bavarian weizen beer, little additional information on this style can be found until the homebrewing literature of the 1990s. At the turn of the twentieth century Berliner weisse was considered the dominant wheat beer of Germany, and most discussions of weissbier ignore the existence of the Bavarian specialty altogether.

Berliner Weisse

The weissbier of Berlin appears to have been established in something like its current form by the beginning of the nineteenth century, when the soldiers of Napoleon's army dubbed it the "Champagne of the North."[27] Their description of this weisse was "wine-clear and sweetish-sour-like."[28]

Descriptions from later in the century bear this out, describing this weisse as "wan-yellow, strong foaming" with a "refreshing acidic taste."[29] The alcohol level given is near 2 percent.

The source of this description, from 1877, also provides details of the brewing process for Berliner weisse. Wheat malt accounts for three-quarters of the grist, and the mash is described approximately as follows:[30]

1. Mash-in at 35 °R (110 °F, 44 °C) with one-third of the mash water.

2. After thirty minutes, add the rest of the water to bring the mash to 40 to 45 °R (122 to 133 °F, 50 to 56 °C).

3. Pull one-third of the thin mash and cook with the hops in the kettle for fifteen minutes.

4. Pull another third, cook fifteen minutes, and return, hitting 60 to 65 °R (167 to 178 °F, 75 to 81 °C).

5. Run off the wort and chill in the coolship.

6. Add water to bring the mash bed to 66 to 68 °R (180 to 185 °F, 82 to 85 °C), run this wort off and cool it separately.

This procedure offers a dramatic departure from the normal brewing process because the wort is never boiled. This practice appears as a hallmark of the Berliner weisse style through quite a number of decades before boiling is adopted.[31]

With no boil, one might assume that these beers are not hopped. Such is not the case, however, as described in the Wahl-Henius *Handy-Book* of 1908: "The hot water for heating the mash is taken from the mash-pan where it was boiled with hops of which ½ pound per barrel is taken, and which are run with the last water into the mash, where they are stirred in and serve as a filtering material, this being important on account of the wheat malt being deficient in this respect."[32]

Even though the wort is never boiled, the hops are boiled with mash water, which allows alpha-acid isomerization to occur. Then both the water and the hops are mixed into the mash. The bitter iso-alpha acids thus enter the liquid, and the bulk from the whole hops improve the porosity of the mash bed to aid in lautering.

By not boiling the wort, brewers were apparently more successful in creating the tart, acidic flavor characteristic of the style. The souring takes place by lactic acid bacteria, which "thrive better in uncooked wort than in cooked" according to one source.[33]

Today, evidence shows that a number of yeast and bacteria were involved in production of the classic Berliner weissbier, including *Brettanomyces bruxellensis, Lactobacillus brevis,* and *Pediococcus* species, in addition to normal ale yeast.[34] This fermen-

tative biological cocktail indicates a surprisingly close relationship between this German classic and the Belgian gueuze and lambic beers.

Fermentations that rely on such a diverse cast of characters can produce unreliable results. The Belgians use blending to overcome this handicap, and the old German brewers had their techniques as well. Because the chief trait of the Berliner weisse style is an intense acidity, the brewers' primary tool was the addition of acid.

The recipe from 1877 listed earlier calls for the addition of 50 grams of tartaric acid for each 100 liters of beer.[35] The personal notebook of the American brewing scientist J. E. Siebel shows analysis of a number of weissbiers with the notations regarding the addition of acid (see table 27.1).

Under the industrialized brewing techniques of the twentieth century, the proper balance is achieved by splitting the wort into two separate fermentations: one by ale yeast and a smaller one by lactic acid bacteria.[36] Following fermentation, the two are blended and filtered before bottling. Although this method produces a more consistent product, traditionalists complain that the resulting beer is noticeably inferior to the classic bottle-conditioned Berliner weisse.[37]

As mentioned earlier, Berliner weisse was the dominant wheat beer style at the beginning of the twentieth century. Quite a number of different brands were produced, and their gravities and attenuation covered a fairly broad range, as related in a yearbook of Berlin breweries from 1913: "Weissbier has an O.G. between 5.48 and 8.01% Balling, attenuation of 47.1 to 84.6 percent and 0.66 to 2.49 percent alcohol (by weight)."[38]

Still, the basic parameters of the style were well established: low in gravity and alcohol and generally possessing a significant lactic acid character (see table 27.2). Although attenuation levels varied widely in the early part of the century, a very high

Table 27.1
J. E. Siebel's Notes on Weiss Beer Analysis

No.	ABW (%)	TG	Lactic Acid (%)	OG	Notes
14	3.35	3.33	0.17	10.0	Yeast and numerous bacteria
15	2.22	2.84	0.50	7.3	Ditto, acid used
16	2.78	3.82	0.39	8.4	Ditto, ditto
17	2.49	2.89	0.25	7.9	Yeast and little bacteria. Doubtful acid was added.
18	3.94	4.85	0.29	12.7	Yeast and little bacteria. Apparent addition of acid.

Source: J. E. Siebel Notebook. Unpublished.

level of attenuation came to be characteristic of the style later on.[39]

Wheat Beers Today

It seems that beer styles have cycles of popularity. A style embraced and loved by beer drinkers of one generation will be rejected in favor of an older, nearly forgotten style by the next.

Such shifts in zymo-demographics in Europe, along with the craft beer revolution in America, have shaped a wheat beer landscape that is quite different in the late twentieth century than it was even ten years earlier.

Right now, we can classify wheat beers into three families: Berliner weisse, Bavarian weizen, and American wheat. Although there are a number of distinguishing factors between each family, the ultimate defining characteristic is the fermentation.

As I discussed in the previous section, Berliner weisse uses a normal top-fermenting ale yeast as well as lactic acid bacteria and other organisms to create its distinct taste. The Bavarian weizen uses only yeast for fermentation, but it is a unique type of yeast that produces the distinctly clovelike character of the style. By contrast, the American wheat style uses normal yeast for fermentation, usually an ale strain.

Berlin's "Champagne of the North" seems to be at a low point in popularity today. Only one brand (Berliner Kindl Weisse) is commonly seen in the United States, and only one other (Schultheiss) appears to have been brewed in the past few decades. A Bremer weisse produced by the folks who make Beck's Beer is supposed to be in this style as well. My most recent tasting of the Kindl Weisse found it lacking in the tart acidity that it has possessed in the past, but I don't know whether this was the result of a purposeful change in formulation or simply the vagaries of multinational distribution.

Normally, the Berliner-style weisse is quite tart due to a high lactic acid content. When consumed, this beer is often dosed with a shot of either woodruff or raspberry-flavored syrup to cut the sourness and make it more palatable.

Bavarian weizen is the best-known German wheat beer today, and by all accounts it is the most popular in Germany as well as in the United States. As of 1992 it accounted for 22 percent of all beer produced in Bavaria,[40] and there were some two hundred weizen producers in Austria and southern Germany.[41] Part of the success of this "style" comes from its diversity, for there are several types, including the traditional hefeweizen, which is cloudy

343

Table 27.2
German and American Weisse Beers, circa 1900

Name	Year	TG	OG	AA (%)	ABW	Lactic Acid (%)
German Weissbiers						
Hannover Städtisch	1878	7.2	9.44	24	1.08	0.18
Hamburger Weissbier Brauerie	1884	2.45	8.3	70	2.38	0.578
Münchener v. Schramm	1888	4.05	13.23	69	3.75	0.44
Berliner Actien Brauerei	1887	4.95	5.77	14	0.94	0.363
Berliner G	1895	2.94	10.00	71	2.91	–
Berliner Export Bier	1895	2.54	10.88	77	3.52	–
Berlin	1895	1.85	10.26	82	3.53	–
Provinz Brauerie	1895	2.36	8.44	72	2.48	–
Münchener v. Schramm Weissbeer-Bock	1888	6.85	17.94	62	4.49	0.18
Lichtenhainer	1886	4.25	9.26	54	3.02	0.238
Lichtenhainer	1898	–	7.89	–	2.43	0.207
American Weisse Beers						
American weisse beer	1900	2.52	9.29	73	2.85	–
Weisse beer	1901	2.24	9.28	76	2.97	0.342

Source: R. Wahl and M. Henius, The American Handy-Book of the Brewing, Malting and Auxiliary Trades (Chicago: Wahl-Henius Institute, 1908), 1285, 1287.

and contains yeast, and its meticulous brother kristal, which is filtered and therefore as clear as any lager. Both present an estery profile with a more or less pronounced clove character. In addition to the regular weizens, there are also dunkel weizens and weizenbocks — both blends of the weizen character with traits found in other classic German styles.

A few U.S. microbreweries are making authentic German examples of these styles, such as the Tabernash weizen out of Denver. In addition, many imported examples are available and all are worth tasting. I would particularly recommend the Schneider products, which are Weisse, and the Aventinus Dunkel Weizenbock.

Finally, American wheat beers are the newcomers to this style. American craft brewers make wheat beers according to their own notions of what the style can be, typically using a clean American ale

yeast and more assertive hopping with American varieties. Still emerging, the style displays great variety in wheat content, product clarity, and bitterness levels. As we'll see later, this style often plays host to fruit in another emerging American style, the fruit wheat beer.

You can often find examples of the American style in your local bar these days, for instance, Widmer Hefe-Weizen, which originated in Portland but has achieved widespread distribution. In addition, many brewpubs make a wheat beer with a normal ale yeast that fits into this category.

For an analysis of the German styles, I turn to the excellent writings of Eric Warner as well as to the encyclopedic analysis performed by Prof. Anton Piendl during the 1970s and 80s.[42] For the American wheat, the listing comes from the American Homebrewers Association National Competition Guidelines (see table 27.3).[43]

Brewing Wheat Beers

Of the three families of wheat beers discussed above (Berliner, weizen, and American), I focus primarily on the brewing of weizens. The primary reason for this is their popularity with consumers and brewers at this time. From a practical perspective this popularity means that I have many examples to draw from in the weizen category among the National Homebrew Competition second-round beers. In fact, during the two years included in this analysis — 1993 and 1994 — not a single Berliner weisse has made it to the second round of the NHC. Similarly, the American wheat style has been grouped with American Pale Ale, and the popularity and intensity of this style makes it difficult for the American wheats to get into the second round.

Berliner Weisse

Before I jump into the weizens, I do want to comment on the making of Berliner weisse. As it happens, this style took both first and second place in the German wheat beer category in a recent Chicago Beer Society competition. A quick look at those recipes offers a good idea of how to go about formulating this style.

In both recipes, the amounts of wheat and base malt were nearly equal: 53 percent wheat, 47 percent barley in one; 47 percent wheat, 53 percent barley in the other. Both used a single German hop addition to establish a very low level of bitterness. The winning entry then simply fermented the wort with a clean American Ale yeast and spiked the finished beer with food-grade lactic acid (90 milliliters in 7 gallons) to achieve the required tartness. The original gravity of this beer was 1.035.

The second-place entry first fermented a normal weizen wort with weizen yeast and then added lactic acid bacteria. After several months, the brewer diluted the beer (to simulate the proper Berliner weisse OG) and added some more acid to achieve the desired flavor.

As you can see from these examples, a good Berliner weisse can easily be produced in a homebrew setting. In fact, when food-grade acid is used for all of the lactic acid production, there is nothing in this approach that would prevent a brewpub or microbrewery from making the same product. Let's hope that some adventurous brewers start to market a batch or two of this stuff each year in the near future.

Of course, those who really want to understand the style will heed the earlier

Table 27.3
Characteristics of Wheat Beers

	Berliner Weisse	Weizen	Dunkel Weizen	Weizen Bock	American Wheat
Original gravity	1.028–32	1.047–56	1.047–55	1.065–80	1.030–50
Bitterness	4–6	10–18	10–16	12–18	5–17
BU:GU ratio	0.14–0.18	0.21–0.32	0.21–0.29	0.20–0.23	0.16–0.34
Hop flavor	None	None	None	None	Low–high
Hop aroma	None	None	None	None	Low–high
Color (SRM)	2.0–3.5	3.5–9.5	10–23	10–29	2–8
Apparent extract	1.002–06	1.015–20	1.016–18	1.026–32	1.004–18
Alcohol (volume)	2.5–3.8	5–5.6	3.8–4.47	.0–8.1	3.5–4.5
Esters	Med.–high	High	Med.–high	Med.–high	Low–med.
Diacetyl	Very low	Very low	Very low	Very low	Very low

discussion of microorganisms found in Berliner weisse and begin to experiment with their effects on this style. I have every hope that we will soon taste a historically accurate Berliner weisse in homebrew circles.

Bavarian Weizens

For the most part, the successful homebrew approaches to brewing weizen have relied on a simple and consistent formula. This begins with the malt bill, where wheat malt and two-row or Pilsener malt account for 97 percent of the grain in the average recipe. In fact, 64 percent of the NHC second-round all-grain recipes included *only* these two malts. The four recipes that used other ingredients showed no pattern. Their additions included: 8 percent CaraPils, 3 percent 30 °L crystal malt, 11 percent rye malt, and 15 percent Vienna malt. One brewer added rice hulls to the mash to improve lautering.

The most surprising feature of the NHC weizens was the frequency with which extract was used — and not just as a supplement, but for the entire fermentable content. A bit more than one-quarter of the weizen recipes were extract-only formulations. Three used nothing but weizen extract — usually some mix of wheat and barley malts — and one included a small portion of regular barley malt extract in addition to weizen extract. (Table 27.4 shows the brands of extract included in these recipes.)

Among the traditional weizens there was no middle ground with regard to extract — the entries were either all grain or all extract. Although many would discard the all-extract approach, I must say that this has proven to be a viable route to the production of a good weizen. I once prepared a 3-gallon batch of weizen where 2.25 pounds of weizen extract supplemented a minimash consisting of 2 pounds of wheat malt and 1 pound of Pilsener malt. The resulting beer was entered in a competition

along with two other all-grain weizens I had made, and the extract beer actually beat the other two for first place.

Mashing details for the weizen grists shows a mix of infusion and decoction techniques, with an overall average saccharification temperature of 152 °F (67 °C). Among the nine brewers who provided mash details, five included at least one decoction step in their mashing process. The average original gravity of all the traditional weizens was 1.052 with an apparent attenuation of 77 percent.

Hopping of the weizens was also simple and predictable. Many recipes included just one hop addition for bittering. Only two recipes included more than three additions. Hallertau was by far the favorite hop, accounting for 57 percent of all additions and nearly three times as many uses as the next most popular hop, which was Saaz (see table 27.5).

The calculated bitterness units for weizens averaged 17 BUs for a BU:GU ratio of 0.35. The range around these values was quite wide, with the BUs varying from 10 to 30 and the ratio from 0.16 to 0.69.

Flavor and aroma hop additions were not uncommon, although fully 40 percent of the recipes used nothing but bittering hops. Among those employing late hop additions, one-third made only a flavor hop addition, one-third made only an aroma hop addition, and one-third used both. Thus, only 20 percent (one-third of 60 percent) of all the traditional weizen recipes included both aroma and flavor hops.

The varieties used for these additions are shown in table 27.5. The average number and size of the flavor and aroma additions was fairly small, as shown in table 27.6.

Dunkel Weizen and Weizenbock

Among the NHC second-round recipes for dunkel weizen and weizenbock, extract was used more commonly than in the traditional weizens. Nearly 60 percent of

Table 27.4
Brands of Extract Found in NHC Second-Round Weizens

Barley Malt Extracts

1	Australian Dry Pale Malt Extract
1	Laaglander Amber
1	John Bull Dark

Wheat Malt and Mixed Extracts

3	M&F Wheat Malt Extract (55/45)
2	Dry Wheat Extract
1	American Classic Wheat Syrup (60/40)
1	Briess Bavarian Wheat
1	Northwestern Weizen
1	Ireks Wheat Extract

these recipes include extract; the increased usage is in mash-extract recipes. Three weizenbocks included extract: one used extract only, while the other two used extract for one-third to two-thirds of the total gravity. An extract-only dunkel recipe mixed weizen extract with dark malt extract to achieve the desired effect.

Among the all-grain recipes, wheat consistently accounted for 53 to 55 percent of the grist. Unlike the traditional weizens, specialty grains played a bigger role, accounting for 15 to 25 percent of the grist. Grains used included Munich, crystal, chocolate and Special B malts.

Compared to traditional weizens, the average mash temperature was a bit higher, at 154 °F (68 °C), and apparent attenuation was lower, at 72 percent. The average OG for the weizenbocks was 1.069, and for the dunkels it was 1.051.

Hopping patterns followed those of the traditional weizens with regard to variety and use. Bitterness levels were similar on a relative basis with an average BU:GU ratio of 0.34.

Table 27.5
Hops Used in NHC Second-Round Weizen Recipes

Type	Bittering	Flavor	Aroma	Total
Hallertau	21	4	7	32
Saaz	6	3	2	11
Hersbruck	3	1	1	5
Tettnanger	2	1	0	3
Mt. Hood	2	0	0	2
Liberty	0	1	0	1
Perle	1	0	0	1
Styrian Goldings	1	0	0	1

Note: The data in this chart show the number of times each hop was used across the twenty-two recipes analyzed and includes all German wheat beer recipes: traditional, dunkel, and weizenbock

Fermentation

To a large extent, I believe it is the fermentation that differentiates a great weizen from a mediocre one. Although the selection of weizen yeasts is limited, the differences between them are quite significant. In addition, the temperature at which the fermentation is conducted will have a major effect on the flavor profile produced by each yeast. Finally, a good weizen can benefit from some conditioning to bring it to the peak of drinkability.

In his excellent book *German Wheat Beer*, Eric Warner introduces a rule of thumb for weizen fermentations. He says that the sum of the pitching temperature and the fermentation temperature — in Centigrade — should be equal to 30.[44] He says it is common to pitch at 12 °C (54 °F) and to ferment at 18 °C (64 °F).[45] Brewers of the NHC second-round beers seem to be heeding this advice, because the average primary fermentation temperature was 65 °F (18 °C) for the traditional weizens and 66 °F (19 °C) for the dunkels and bocks.

Of course, many of the brewers showed higher fermentation temperatures, with several around 70 °F (21 °C). At this higher temperature, some of the weizen yeasts will produce an excessive amount of esters, giving the beer a strong aroma of ripe banana or Juicy-Fruit gum. I prefer that this character be balanced with the malt and clove flavors of the style, and I find that this is best achieved at the lower temperatures recommended by Warner.

I have conducted Warner's recommended fermentation with the three most popular weizen yeasts available in the homebrewing channels. This includes the two from Wyeast (3056 and 3068), as well as the Bavarian weizen yeast from Yeast Labs. The resulting beers were markedly different from one another in their aroma and flavor. In a couple of competitions where all three beers were entered, the judges picked my favorite — produced by the Yeast Labs yeast — for first place, and in one case as best of show. Of course, both yeast strains and judges change over time, so you should experiment with several strains to find the one that gives you the results you desire.

As I look at the NHC second-round beers, I find quite a bit of diversity among the yeast strains selected (see table 27.7). No one yeast accounted for more than a third of all the entries, and fully 40 percent of the beers were made with yeasts other than those provided by the most popular sources.

When a weizen fermentation has reached terminal gravity, a number of different courses may be followed to finish the beer. The most traditional is to bottle the beer using speise and yeast to ensure bottle conditioning. The strictest definition of "speise" is unpitched wort, although Warner states that kraeusen and priming sugar may

Table 27.6

Hop Additions in NHC Second-Round Weizen Recipes

Addition	Avg. No. per Recipe	Avg. oz./gal.	Avg. oz./5 gal.
Boil	1.6	–	–
Flavor	0.5	0.09	0.47
Aroma	0.5	0.13	0.66
Total	2.5	–	–

also be used.[46] When this course is followed, commercial producers often filter the beer to remove all yeast and then add the speise along with a measured quantity of yeast.

Because it offers several advantages, the yeast used for priming a weizen is often a lager strain. Such strains will carbonate the beer even at cool temperatures. In addition, they tend to flocculate well, settling nicely on the bottom of the bottle. Finally, lager yeast may be less prone to the autolysis that can give the beer a yeast bite or bitterness.[47]

When this course is followed, the beer is generally warm conditioned (68 to 77 °F, 20 to 25 °C) for two to five days and then cold-conditioned for two to six weeks (39 to 46 °F, 4 to 8 °C).[48]

One alternative to this classic approach is to cold condition the beer prior to carbonation. Beer is held in tanks for five to twenty-eight days at 39 to 46 °F (4 to 8 °C). This improves the clarity of the beer, and isinglass may be used — even in Germany — at this stage to produce a beer in the kristal style. Hefeweizen is also made this way, however, and priming with speise and yeast may follow this type of cold-conditioning phase.

Calculation of the exact amount of speise to add for priming is a somewhat involved process that is covered well in Warner's *German Wheat Beer* for those who wish to pursue it.[49]

For the most part, the NHC second-round recipes stick to proven priming methods, with the vast majority (fifteen out of twenty-two) simply adding corn sugar. Another group (three recipes) forced carbonation in a keg: two used speise, one used kraeusen, and one primed with extract.

Nearly all of the NHC second-round recipes seemed to aim for normal carbonation levels. Warner suggests weizen CO_2 levels at 3.6 to 5.1 volumes —one and one-half to two times that found in most other beers.[50] Yet most of the recipes that used corn sugar stuck to the proven formula of ¾ cup for 5 gallons. Clearly, increased carbonation levels would lead to a more authentic product.

Few of the recipes (four of twenty-two) noted any lagering of their weizens, and two of those that did used short cold-conditioning rests of seven to ten days. Two others used longer periods of cold conditioning, in one case in conjunction with the use of a lager yeast for priming. Of course, recipe forms do not always note the unintentional lagering that often occurs when kegs or bottles are kept refrigerated for serving or while waiting to be entered into a competition.

Conclusion

The variety of both yeasts and extracts available for the making of good weizens has expanded opportunities for home and pub brewers alike. I can easily imagine making nothing but weizens for many months on end in order to explore the variety offered by the style. After you have perfected hefeweizen and kristal, you might try substituting rye for the wheat to make an imitation of a German specialty called Roggenbier, which has recently been available in the United States.

The potential of Berliner weisse seems underrecognized by both brewers and consumers alike, and I suspect we will soon see some spectacular beers produced in this style. Although most commercial producers will shy away from the use of lactic acid bacteria and *Brettanomyces* homebrewers who are experienced in their use from making lambics have an exciting opportunity to use these organisms for the production of historically correct Berliner beers.

Finally, a number of good examples of American wheat beer — the New World's poor relation to these classics — are already being produced. The coming years will show which ones become the classics of our time as they are widely appreciated by consumers and widely imitated by other brewers.

Table 27.7
Weizen Yeast Selection and Fermentation Temperatures in NHC Second-Round Recipes

Yeast Used	No. of Recipes	Avg. Fermentation Temperature in °F (°C)
Wyeast 3056	7	66 (19)
Wyeast 3068	6	65 (18)
Special[a]	4	60 (16)
GW Kent Weihenstephan	2	69 (21)
Brewers Resource CL62	1	62 (17)
Wyeast 1214[b]	1	67 (19)
Yeast Labs W51	1	70 (21)
Total	22	65 (18)

[a] *Yeasts that are not commercially available (acquired from a commercial brewery or cultured from a bottle).* [b] *Used in combination with W3056.*

Key Success Factors in Brewing Weizens

- Use one-half to two-thirds wheat malt, with the balance being two-row barley malt. Wheat/barley malt extract may be substituted for all or part of this.

- For dunkel weizen and weizenbock, add dark grains such as crystal, Munich, chocolate, and Special B to account for 15 to 30 percent of the total grist.

- For a regular weizen, mash at approximately 152 °F (67 °C) to produce a wort with an original gravity of about 1.052 (13 °B). Dunkels and bocks mash at a higher temperature, of 154 ° F or more (68 °C), with average gravities at 1.051 and 1.069, respectively.

- Hop with Hallertau, Saaz, or other continental aroma varieties to achieve a low level of bitterness, usually about 15 to 17 IBUs or a BU:GU ratio of about 0.35.

- The same hop varieties may be used for flavor and aroma hop additions, with the average addition being about 0.5-ounce for 5 gallons.

- For all weizens, select a proper German weizen yeast and ferment at a temperature between 62 and 67 °F (17 and 19 °C).

- To make an American wheat beer, ferment with a regular ale yeast instead of a German weizen strain.

- Carbonate to 3.6 to 5.1 volumes of CO_2 — nearly twice the level found in most lagers.

- Cold condition the beer for five days after carbonation.

This book focuses on the development of recipes for brewers of all skill levels and does not cover the details of the brewing process in any depth. Despite this, every brewer needs certain essential skills to brew successfully. This chapter provides a list of primary brewing skills and a bibliography of sources that you can use to expand your knowledge of brewing techniques. This literature primarily addresses homebrewing, but much of it is applicable to small-scale commercial brewing as well. If you want more in-depth coverage of the theory and science of brewing as well as more in-depth coverage of commercial brewing, I recommend that you pick up a copy of the two-volume *Malting and Brewing Science*.

It is not necessary for you to have mastered the techniques listed in this chapter before reading and using the contents of *Designing Great Beers*. However, at various points throughout this text, reference will be made to techniques such as minimashes or decoction mashing, which require an in-depth presentation that is not possible during discussion of recipe formulation. This appendix serves as a reference to allow the brewer to efficiently research these techniques.

The listings are divided into two groups. The first covers the basics; the second gets into more advanced techniques.

The Basics

Sanitizing Equipment

Most books offer a few comments, but two really cover the issue in detail and are worth review if you have not read them recently. The article from *Brewing Techniques* is also worth tracing.

Papazian. *The New Complete Joy of Home Brewing*, 34–41, 121–127.
Raines, Maribeth. "Methods of Sanitization and Sterilization," *Brewing Techniques* 1, no. 2.

Boiling Wort

Miller. *The Complete Handbook of Homebrewing*, 140–147.
Noonan. *New Brewing Lager Beer*, 153–160.
Papazian. *The Homebrewer's Companion*, 136–142.

Chilling Wort

Miller. *The Complete Handbook of Homebrewing*, 148–151.
Noonan. *New Brewing Lager Beer*, 161–163.
Papazian. *The Homebrewer's Companion*, 152–159.

Aerating Wort before Pitching

Miller. *Brewing the World's Great Beers*, 43.
Mosher. *The Brewer's Companion*, 191.
Papazian. *The Homebrewer's Companion*, 169.
Papazian. *The New Complete Joy of Home Brewing*, 113.

Preventing Aeration during Transfers and Bottling

Miller. *The Complete Handbook of Homebrewing*, 181–182.
Mosher. *The Brewer's Companion*, 248 (under "Stale, cardboardy").

Papazian. *The Homebrewer's Companion*, 20-21, 179, 188.

Papazian. *The New Complete Joy of Home Brewing*, 138 (under "bottling").

Priming and Carbonating Finished Beer

These sources include discussions of kegging and kraeusening.

Miller. *Brewing the World's Great Beers*, 22-24, 115-124.

Miller. *The Complete Handbook of Homebrewing*, 168-171.

Mosher. *The Brewer's Companion*, 199-206, 248-249.

Noonan. *New Brewing Lager Beer*, 245-248.

Papazian. *The Homebrewer's Companion*, 181-201.

Papazian. *The New Complete Joy of Home Brewing*, 325-332.

Intermediate and Advanced Techniques

Use of Hops for Bittering, Flavor, and Aroma

Mosher. *The Brewer's Companion*, 153-155.

Noonan. *New Brewing Lager Beer*, 81-88, 156.

Papazian. *The Homebrewer's Companion*, 57-69.

Papazian. *The New Complete Joy of Home Brewing*, 59-73.

Use of Specialty Grains to Supplement Extract Beers

Burch. *Brewing Quality Beers*, 6 (provides a concise procedure for the use of specialty or small amounts of grains).

Papazian. *The New Complete Joy of Home Brewing*, 130-131.

Conducting a Minimash

Miller. *Brewing the World's Great Beers*, 61-66.

Miller. *The Complete Handbook of Homebrewing*, 102-106.

Papazian. *The New Complete Joy of Home Brewing*, 226-229.

Conducting All-Grain Mashes: Infusion and Decoction

Miller. *Brewing the World's Great Beers*, 85-94 (brief practical overview).

Miller. *The Complete Handbook of Homebrewing*, 110-139 (thorough discussion of home mashing techniques, with focus on infusion mashing).

Mosher. *The Brewer's Companion*, 171-186 (compares five different techniques; charts provide the required strike-temperature for various rests), 258 (brief discussion of equipment approaches).

Noonan. *New Brewing Lager Beer*, 126-146, 227-233, 298-305 (focus on decoction mashing but also includes a good discussion of principles governing all mashes) (practice).

Owens. *How to Build a Small Brewery*, 1-13 (great pictures and diagrams with advice on how to build your own mash tun, lauter tun, etc.).

Papazian. *The Homebrewer's Companion*, 112-135 (includes basic discussion of equipment).

Papazian. *The New Complete Joy of Home Brewing*, 250-264, 282-306 (a thorough introduction to the subject, but familiarization with other sources is also recommended).

Proofing and Starting Dry Yeast

Mosher. *The Brewer's Companion*, 190.

Papazian. *The New Complete Joy of Home Brewing*, 82.

Yeast Management/Starters/ Pitching an Adequate Quantity of Yeast

Miller. *Brewing the World's Great Beers*, 33-39.

Miller. *The Complete Handbook of Homebrewing*, 86-95.

Mosher. *The Brewer's Companion*, 188-194.

Noonan. *Brewing Lager Beer*, 69-78, 137-141.

Papazian. *The Homebrewer's Companion*, 86-96, 163.

Papazian. *The New Complete Joy of Home Brewing*, 275-281.

Rajotte, Pierre. *First Steps in Yeast Culture*: Part One (an illustrated manual on the techniques of proper yeast handling).

Water Chemistry Basics: How to Adjust the Faults in Your Water

Miller. *The Complete Handbook of Homebrewing*, 62-76 (good discussion of practical treatment options).

Mosher. *The Brewer's Companion*, 163-170 (reference charts, worksheets, map of U.S. municipal water types).

Noonan. *New Brewing Lager Beer*, 35-74 (a thorough review of the theory and practice of water chemistry).

Papazian. *The Homebrewer's Companion*, 73-85 (adequately detailed, practical approach).

Papazian. *The New Complete Joy of Home Brewing*, 267-274 (good review of the basics).

Use of Irish Moss and Other Clarifying Agents

Miller. *The Complete Handbook of Homebrewing*, 191-193 (haze causes and reduction).

Mosher. *The Brewer's Companion*, 144 (summary chart).

Noonan. *New Brewing Lager Beer*, 195-196 (fining and beech chips).

Papazian. *The Homebrewer's Companion*, 202-211 (filtering).

Papazian. *The New Complete Joy of Home Brewing*, 100-104.

Bibliography

Burch, Byron. *Brewing Quality Beers*. Fulton, Calif.: Joby Books, 1986.

Miller, Dave. *Brewing the World's Great Beers*. Pownal, Vt: Storey Publishing, 1992.

Miller, Dave. *The Complete Handbook of Homebrewing*. Pownal, Vt: Storey Publishing, 1988.

Mosher, Randy. *The Brewer's Companion*. Seattle: Alephenalia Publications, 1994.

Noonan, Gregory J. *New Brewing Lager Beer*. Boulder, Colo.: Brewers Publications, 1996.

Owens, Bill. *How to Build a Small Brewery*. Ann Arbor, Mich.: G. W. Kent, 1992.

Papazian, Charlie. *The Homebrewer's Companion*. New York: Avon Books, 1994.

Papazian, Charlie. *The New Complete Joy of Homebrewing*. New York: Avon Books, 1991.

Rajotte, Pierre. *First Steps in Yeast Culture: Part One*. Montreal: Alliage Editeur, 1994.

When maltsters deliver malt to a brewery, they usually supply an analysis of the malt. One figure included in this will be the potential extract. If you get a malt analysis, one or several of four different extract numbers may be given. The extract procedure can be run using either a "fine grind" or a "coarse grind" of the malt. In addition, the resulting extract may be reported on either an "as is" or on a "dry" basis. Generally speaking, the *coarse grind "as is"* figure is the one that most realistically represents the potential extract for a small brewer.[1]

The extract analysis is reported as a percentage (e.g., 78.5 percent), representing the portion of the original malt weight that was recovered as extract. To find out what this figure would mean in specific gravity when 1 pound is added to 1 gallon, simply consult the conversion chart shown below.

Converting Extract Analyses to Coarse Grind, As Is

If the malt analysis you have gives extract figures on a "fine grind" or "dry" basis, it may be possible to estimate the "coarse grind, as is" number with reasonable accuracy.

Fine Grind to Coarse Grind

For this conversion, you need to know the actual number for fine/coarse difference. (Common notations include "F/C Diff," or just "F/C.") Good malt should have a fine/coarse difference of less than 2 percent and, unfortunately,

many malt specification sheets just say "<2%." If this is the case, or if the F/C number is not supplied at all, you will have to make an assumption. For most two-row malts a value of 1.7 would probably not be off by more than two- or three-tenths. Six-row malts generally have a lower difference, so a slightly lower figure of 1.5 would probably be more appropriate.

Once you have the F/C difference, the conversion is easy:

Coarse Grind (%) = Fine Grind (%) − F/C Diff. (%)

Dry to As Is

Converting from a "dry" to "as is" basis requires that you know the moisture content of the malt. This is always given when a complete malt analysis is provided but may not be included on a summary report. Unfortunately, the moisture range found in finished malt can vary considerably. I have found values in the range of 3.25 percent to 4.75 percent, but some sources give a narrower range of 3.8 to 4.2 percent.[2] Obviously, all the values are centered at 4 percent moisture, and this is the figure you should use if you must make an assumption. Be aware, however, that the value you get for "as is" extract could be off by as much as plus or minus ½ percent.

Once you have the moisture figure, the calculation is easy:

As Is = Dry Basis × [(100 − Percent moisture)/100]

Reading the Chart

Once you have a figure for course grind "as is" extract, you can determine the potential extract in specific gravity or gravity units by reading from the chart below. For instance, if course grind, as is extract is 75.25 percent, then potential extract is about 1.035, or 34.8 GU.

Coarse Grind "as is" (%)	GU[a]	1 lb./gallon Yields SG	Coarse Grind "as is" (%)	GU[a]	1 lb./gallon Yields SG
50	23.11	1.0231	75.25	34.77	1.0348
51	23.57	1.0236	75.50	34.88	1.0349
52	24.03	1.0240	75.75	35.00	1.0350
53	24.50	1.0245	76.00	35.11	1.0351
54	24.96	1.0250	76.25	35.23	1.0352
55	25.42	1.0254	76.50	35.34	1.0353
56	25.88	1.0259	76.75	35.46	1.0355
57	26.34	1.0263	77.00	35.57	1.0356
58	26.80	1.0268	77.25	35.69	1.0357
59	27.27	1.0273	77.50	35.80	1.0358
60	27.73	1.0277	77.75	35.92	1.0359
61	28.19	1.0282	78.00	36.03	1.0360
62	28.65	1.0287	78.25	36.15	1.0362
63	29.11	1.0291	78.50	36.27	1.0363
64	29.57	1.0296	78.75	36.38	1.0364
65	30.03	1.0300	79.00	36.50	1.0365
66	30.50	1.0305	79.25	36.61	1.0366
67	30.96	1.0310	79.50	36.73	1.0367
68	31.42	1.0314	79.75	36.84	1.0368
69	31.88	1.0319	80.00	36.96	1.0370
70	32.34	1.0323			
71	32.80	1.0328			
72	33.27	1.0333			
73	33.73	1.0337			
74	34.19	1.0342			
75	34.65	1.0347			

[a] $GU = (S.G - 1) \times 1{,}000$

For descriptions of specific malts, hops, and yeasts, see the chapters covering these ingredients.

acrospire. The germinal plant-growth of the barley kernel.

ad-humulone. The third (or sometimes second) most prevalent of the three alpha acids, which, when isomerized during boiling of the wort, provide most of the bittering characteristic that comes from hops.

adjuncts. Sources of fermentable extract other than malted barley. Principally corn, rice, wheat, unmalted barley, and glucose (dextrose).

aerate. To force atmospheric air or oxygen into solution. Introducing air to the wort at various stages of the brewing process.

aerobic. In the presence of or requiring oxygen.

agar. Agar-agar. A non-nitrogenous, gelatinous solidifying agent, more heat-stable than gelatin. A culture medium for microbial analysis.

agglutination. The grouping of cells by adhesion.

airlock. See *fermentation lock*.

airspace. See *ullage*.

albumin. Intermediate soluble protein subject to coagulation upon heating. Hydrolyzed to peptides and amino acids by proteolytic enzymes.

alcohol by volume (v/v). The percentage of volume of alcohol per volume of beer. To calculate the approximate volumetric alcohol content, subtract the final gravity from the original gravity and divide the result by 75. For example: 1.050 − 1.012 = .038/0.0075 = 5% v/v.

alcohol by weight (w/v). The percentage weight of alcohol per volume of beer. For example: 3.2% alcohol by weight = 3.2 grams of alcohol per 100 centiliters of beer. Alcohol by weight can be converted to alcohol by volume by multiplying by 0.795.

aldehyde. An organic compound that is a precursor to ethanol in a normal beer fermentation via the EMP pathway. In the presence of excess air this reaction can be reversed, with alcohols being oxidized to very complex, unpleasant-tasting aldehydes, typically papery/cardboardy/sherry notes.

ale. 1. Historically, an unhopped malt beverage; 2. Now a generic term for hopped beers produced by top fermentation, as opposed to lagers, which are produced by bottom fermentation.

aleurone layer. The enzyme- and pentosan-bearing layer enveloping, and inseparable from, the malt endosperm.

all-extract beer. A beer made with malt extract as opposed to one made from malted barley or from a combination of malt extract and malted barley.

all-grain beer. A beer made with malted barley as opposed to one made from malt extract or from malt extract and malted malted barley.

all-malt beer. A beer made with barley malt, with no adjuncts or refined sugars.

alpha acid, α-acid. The principle source of bitterness from hops when isomerized by boiling. These seperate but related alpha acids come from the soft alpha resin of the hop.

alpha acid unit (AAU). The number of AAUs in a hop addition is equal to the weight of the addtion in ounces times the alpha acid percentage. Thus 1 ounce of 5 percent alpha acid hops contain 5 AAUs. AAU is the same as HBU.

alt. The German word for old. This is a top-fermenting style of beer that undergoes a cold lagering for maturation.

ambient temperature. The surrounding temperature.

amino acids. The smallest product of protein cleavage; simple nitrogenous matter.

amylodextrin. From the diastatic reduction of starch; α-limit dextrin; the most complex dextrin from hydrolysis of starch with diastase. Mahogany (red-brown) color reaction with iodine.

amylolysis. The enzymatic reduction of starch to soluble fractions.

amylopectin. Branched starch chain; shell and paste-forming starch. Unable to be entirely saccharified by amylolytic enzymes; a-limit dextrins, or amylodextrins, remain.

amylose. Straight chain of native starch; a-D-glucose (glucose dehydrate) molecules joined by a-(1-4) links. Gives deep blue-black color with iodine.

anaerobic. Conditions under which there is not enough oxygen for respiratory metabolic function. Anaerobic microorganisms are those that can function without the presence of free molecular oxygen.

analyte. A chemical compound that is the target of a particular assay or test system.

anion. An electronegative ion.

apparent attenuation. A simple measure of the extent of fermentation that a wort has undergone in the process of becoming beer. Using gravity units (GU), Balling (B), or Plato (P) units to express gravity, apparent attenuation is equal to the original gravity minus the terminal gravity divided by the original gravity. The result is expressed as a percentage and equals 65 percent to 80 percent for most beers.

apparent extract. A term used to indicate the terminal gravity of a beer.

aqueous. Of water.

ash. The residue left behind after all the organic matter of a substance has been incinerated. It consists of mineral matter and serves as a measure of the inorganic salts that were in the original substance.

attemper. To regulate or modify the temperature.

attenuate. Fermentation, reduction of the extract/density by yeast metabolism.

attenuation. The reduction in the wort's specific gravity caused by the transformation of sugars into alcohol and carbon-dioxide gas.

autolysis. Yeast death due to shock or nutrient-depleted solutions.

bacteriostatic. Bacteria-inhibiting.

Balling, degrees. A standard for the measurement of the density of solutions, calibrated on the weight of cane sugar in solution, expressed as a percentage of the weight of the solution (grams per 100 grams of solution).

beerstone. Brownish gray mineral-like deposits left on fermentation equipment. Composed of calcium oxalate and organic residues.

blow-off. A single-stage homebrewing fermentation method in which a plastic tube is fitted into the mouth of a carboy, with the other end submerged in a pail of sterile water. Unwanted residues and carbon dioxide are expelled through the tube, while air is prevented from coming into contact with the fermenting beer, thus avoiding contamination.

body. A qualitative indicator of the fullness or mouthfeel of a beer. Related to the proportion of unfermentable long-chain sugars or dextrins present in the beer.

Brettanomyces. A genus of yeasts that have and do play a role in the production of some beers, such as modern lambics and Berliner weisse and historical porters.

brewer's gravity. SG. See *gravity.*

buffer. A substance capable of resisting changes in the pH of a solution.

BU:GU ratio. The ratio of bitterness units to gravity units for a specific beer or group of beers. International bitterness units (IBU) are used for bitterness, and gravity units (GU) are used for the gravity component. For most beers and beer styles the resulting ratio has a value between 0.3 and 1.0.

carbonates. Alkaline salts whose anions are derived from carbonic acid.

carbonation. The process of introducing carbon dioxide gas into a liquid by: injecting the finished beer with carbon dioxide; adding young fermenting beer to finished beer for a renewed fermentation (kraeusening); priming (adding sugar to) fermented wort prior to bottling, creating a secondary fermentation in the bottle; finishing fermentation under pressure.

carboy. A large glass, plastic, or earthenware bottle.

caryophylline. A secondary component of hop oil found in varying proportions in different varieties of hops.

cation. Electropositive ion.

cellulose. A polymer of sugar molecules that plays a structural rather than storage role. The sugars that make up cellulose cannot be liberated by the enzymes found in most plant systems.

chill haze. Haziness caused by protein and tannin during the secondary fermentation.

chill-proof. Cold conditioning to precipitate chill haze.

closed fermentation. Fermentation under closed, anaerobic conditions to minimize risk of contamination and oxidation.

co-humulone. The second (or sometimes third) most prevalent of the three alpha acids, which, when isomerized during boiling of the wort, provide most of the bittering characteristic that comes from hops.

coliform. Waterborne bacteria, often associated with pollution.

colloid. A gelatinous substance in solution.

decoction. Boiling, the part of the mash that is boiled.

density. The measurement of the weight of a solution, as compared with the weight of an equal volume of pure water.

dextrin. Soluble polysaccharide fraction from hydrolysis of starch by heat, acid, or enzyme.

diacetyl. See *diketone*.

diastase. Starch-reducing enzymes; usually alpha- and beta-amylase, but also limit dextrinase and a-glucosidase (maltase).

diastatic malt extract. A type of malt extract containing the diastatic enzymes naturally found in malt and needed for conversion of starch into sugar. This type of extract is sometimes used in recipes that contain grain adjuncts such as corn or rice.

diketone. Aromatic, volatile compound perceivable in minute concentration, from yeast or *Pediococcus* metabolism. Most significantly the butter flavor of diacetyl, a vicinal diketone (VDK). The other significant compound of relevance to brewing is 2,3-pentanedione.

dimethyl sulfide (DMS). An important sulfur-carrying compound originating in malt. Adds a crisp, lagerlike character at low levels and corn or cabbage flavors at high levels.

disaccharides. Sugar group; two monosaccharide molecules joined by the removal of a water molecule.

dry hopping. The addition of hops to the primary fermenter, the secondary fermenter, or to casked beer to add aroma and hop character to the finished beer without adding significant bitterness.

dry malt. Malt extract in powdered form.

EBC (European Brewery Convention). See *SRM*.

enzymes. Protein-based organic catalysts that effect changes in the compositions of the substances they act upon.

erythrodextrin. Tasteless intermediate dextrin. Large α-limit dextrins. Faint red reaction with iodine.

essential oil. The aromatic volatile compounds from the hop.

esters. "Ethereal salts" such as ethyl acetate; aromatic compounds from fermentation composed of an acid and an alcohol, such as the "banana" ester. Formed by yeast enzymes from an alcohol and an acid. Associated with ale and high-temperature fermentations, although esters also arise to some extent with pure lager yeast cultures, though more so with low wort oxygenation, high initial fermentation temperatures, and high-gravity wort. Top-fermenting yeast strains are prized for their ability to produce particular mixes of esters.

extract. Soluble constituents from the malt, including sugars and proteins.

extraction. Drawing out the soluble essence of the malt or hops.

farnescene. A secondary component of hop oil found in varying proportions in different varieties of hops.

fecal bacteria. Coliform bacteria associated with sewage.

fermentation lock. A one-way valve that allows carbon dioxide gas to escape from the fermenter while excluding contaminants.

final specific gravity. The specific gravity of a beer when fermentation is complete.

fining. Clarifying beer with isinglass, gelatin, bentonite, silica gel, or polyvinyl pyrrolidone.

flocculation. The tendency of yeast to clump together at the end of fermentation. The greater the tendency for the yeast to flocculate, the faster it will drop out of the solution, creating clear beer.

germination. Sprouting of the barley kernel, to initiate enzyme development and conversion of the malt.

glucophilic. An organism that thrives on glucose.

gravity (SG). Specific gravity as expressed by brewers; specific gravity 1.046 is expressed as 1046. Density of a solution as compared to water; expressed in grams per milliliter (1 mL water weighs 1 g, hence sp gr 1.000 = SG 1000; sp gr 1.046 = SG 1046).

gravity units (GU). A form of expressing specific gravity in formulas as a whole number. It is equal to the significant digits to the right of the decimal point (1.055 SG becomes 55 GU and 1.108 SG becomes 108 GU).

green malt. Malt that has been steeped and germinated and is ready for kilning.

hexose. Sugar molecules of six carbon atoms. Glucose, fructose, lactose, mannose, galactose.

homebrewers bittering units (HBU). A formula adopted by the American Homebrewers Association to measure bitterness of beer. Example: 1.5 ounces of hops at 10 percent alpha acid: $1.5 \times 10 = 15$ HBU. Same as AAU.

homofermentive. Organisms that metabolize only one specific carbon source.

hop pellets. Finely powdered hop cones compressed into pellets. Hop pellets are less subject to alpha acid losses than are whole hops.

humulene. A primary component of the essential oil of the hop cone. Although rarely found in beer in this native form, it is processed into a number of flavor-active compounds that are significant in beer. The quantity of humulene found in a hop varies by variety, year, and growing region.

humulone. The most prevalent of the three alpha acids, which, when isomerized during boiling of the wort, provide most of the bittering characteristic that comes from hops.

hydrolysis. Decomposition of matter into soluble fractions by either acids or enzymes, in water.

hydrometer. A glass instrument used to measure the specific gravity of liquids as compared to water, consisting of a graduated stem resting on a weighed float.

hydroxide. A compound, usually alkaline, containing the OH (hydroxyl) group.

inoculate. The introduction of a microbe into surroundings capable of supporting its growth.

international bitterness unit (IBU). This is a standard unit that measures the concentration of iso-alpha acids in milligrams per liter (parts per million). Most procedures will also measure a small amount of uncharacterized soft resins, so IBUs are generally 5 to 15 percent higher than iso-alpha acid concentrations.

isinglass. A gelatinous substance made from the swim bladder of certain fish and added to beer as a fining agent.

isomer (Iso). Organic compounds of identical composition and molecular weight, but having a different molecular structure.

kilning. The final stage in the malting of barley that prepares it for use by the brewer. Kilning reduces the moisture contained by the grain to approximately 4 percent and also roasts the malt to some extent. The degree of roasting affects the flavor and color of the malt as well as of the beer it produces.

kraeusen. The period of fermentation characterized by a rich foam head. Kraeusening describes the use of actively fermenting beer to induce fermentation in a larger volume of wort or extract-depleted beer.

lactobacillus. Species of bacteria that ferments wort sugars to produce lactic acid. Although considered undesirable in most breweries and beer styles, it plays a significant role in the production of some beers, such as Berliner weisse and lambics.

lactophilic. An organism that metabolizes lactate more readily than glucose.

lager. A long, cold period of subdued fermentation and sedimentation subsequent to active (primary) fermentation.

lauter. The thin mash after saccharification; its clear liquid. From the German adjective for "pure."

lauter tun. A vessel in which the mash settles and the grains are removed from the sweet wort through a straining process. It has a false, slotted bottom and spigot.

lipids. Fatlike substances, especially triacylglycerols and fatty acids. Negatively affect ability of beer to form a foam head. Cause soapy flavors; when oxidized contribute stale flavors.

liquefaction. The process by which alpha-amylase enzymes degrade soluble starch into dextrin.

malt. Barley that has been steeped in water, germinated, then dried in kilns. This process converts insoluble starches to soluble substances and sugars.

malt extract. A thick syrup or dry powder prepared from malt.

maltodextrin. Isomaltose; also amylodextrin, or an impure mixture of glucose with compounds formed of it.

maltose. A disaccharide composed of two glucose molecules, and the primary sugar obtained by diastatic hydrolysis of starch. One-third the sweetness of sucrose.

mash, mashing. The process of enzymatically extracting and converting malt solubles to wort, in an aciduric aqueous solution.

melanoidins. Color-producing compounds produced through a long series of chemical reactions that begin with the combination of a sugar and an amino acid.

modification. The degree to which the malt endosperm is converted, manifested by the solubilization of malt protein.

mole. A unit of measure for chemical compounds that is equal to 6.02×10^{23} molecules. the weight, in grams, of a mole of any compound is the atomic weight of the substance.

monosaccharides. Single-molecule sugars.

myrcene. A primary component of the essential oil of the hop cone. Although rarely found in beer in this native form, it is processed into a number of flavor-active compounds that are significant in beer. The quantity of myrcene found in a hop varies by variety, year, and growing region.

original gravity (OG). The specific gravity of wort prior to fermentation. A measure of the total amount of dissolved solids in wort.

oxidation. The combination of oxygen with other molecules, oftentimes causing off-flavors, as with aldehydes from alcohols.

pectin. Vegetable substance, a chain of galacturonic acid that becomes gelatinous in the presence of sugars and acids.

pentosan. Pentose-based complex carbohydrates, especially gums.

pentose. Sugar molecules of five carbon atoms. Monosaccharides from the decomposition of pentosans, unfermentable by yeast. Xylose, arabinose.

peptonizing. The action of proteolytic enzymes upon protein, successively yielding albumin/proteoses, peptides, and amino acids.

pH. A logarithmic measure of acidity or alkalinity of a solution, usually on a scale of one to fourteen where seven is neutral.

phenols. Aromatic hydroxyl precursors of tannins/polyphenols. "Phenolic" describes medicinal flavors in beer from tannins, bacterial growth, cleaning compounds, or plastics.

phosphate. A salt or ester of phosphoric acid.

pitching. Inoculating sterile wort with a vigorous yeast culture.

Plato, degrees. Commercial brewers' standard for the measurement of the density of solutions, expressed as the equivalent weight of cane sugar in solution (calibrated on grams of sucrose per 100 grams of solution). Like degrees Balling, but Plato's computations are more exact.

polymer. A compound molecule formed by the joining of many smaller identical units. For example, polyphenols from phenols, polypeptides from peptides.

polyphenol. Complexes of phenolic compounds involved in chill haze formation and oxidative staling.

polysaccharides. Carbohydrate complexes, able to be reduced to monosaccharides by hydrolysis.

ppm. Parts per million. Equal to milligrams per liter (mg/L). The measurement of particles of matter in solution.

precipitation. Separation of suspended matter by sedimentation.

precursor. The starting materials or inputs for a chemical reaction.

primary fermentation. The first stage of fermentation, during which most fermentable sugars are converted to ethyl alcohol and carbon dioxide.

priming solution. A solution of sugar in water added to aged beer at bottling to induce fermentation (bottle conditioning).

priming sugar. A small amount of corn, malt, or cane sugar added to bulk beer prior to racking or at bottling to induce a new fermentation and create carbonation.

protein. Generally amorphous and colloidal complex amino acid containing about 16 percent nitrogen with carbon, hydrogen, oxygen, and possibly sulphur, phosphorous, and iron. True protein has a molecular weight of 17,000 to 150,000; in beer, protein will have been largely decomposed to a molecular weight of 5,000 to 12,000 (albumin or proteoses), 400 to 1,500 (peptides), or amino acids. Protein as a haze fraction ranges from molecular weight 10,000 to 100,000 (average 30,000), and as the stabilizing component of foam, 12,000 to 20,000.

proteolysis. The reduction of protein by proteolytic enzymes to fractions.

racking. The transfer of wort or beer from one vessel to another.

reagent. A substance involved in a reaction that identifies the strength of the substance being measured.

real ale. A style of beer found primarily in England, where it has been championed by the consumer rights group called the Campaign for Real Ale (CAMRA). Generally defined as beers that have undergone a secondary fermentation in the container from which they are served and that are served without the application of carbon dioxide.

resin. Noncrystalline (amorphous) plant excretions.

rest. Mash rest. Holding the mash at a specific temperature to induce certain enzymatic changes.

ropy fermentation. Viscous gelatinous blobs, or "rope," from bacterial contamination.

rousing. Creating turbulence by agitation; mixing.

ruh beer. The nearly fermented beer, ready for lagering. Cold secondary fermentation.

saccharification. The reduction of malt starch into fermentable sugars, primarily maltose.

saccharometer. An instrument that determines the sugar concentration of a solution by measuring the specific gravity.

solubilization. Dissolution of matter into solution.

sparge. The even distribution or spray of water over the saccharified mash to rinse free the extract from the grist.

sparging. Spraying the spent grains in the mash with hot water to retrieve the remaining malt sugar.

specific gravity. Density of a solution, in grams per milliliter.

SRM (Standard Reference Method) and EBC (European Brewery Convention). Two different analytical methods of describing color developed by comparing color samples. Degrees SRM, approximately equivalent to degrees Lovibond, are used by the ASBC (American Society of Brewing Chemists), while degrees EBC are European units.

starch. A polymer of sugar molecules, starch is the chief form of energy storage for most plants. It is from starch that the relevant sugars for brewing are derived.

starter. A batch of fermenting yeast, added to the wort to initiate fermentation.

steeping. The initial processing step in malting where the raw barley is soaked in water and periodically aerated in order to induce germination.

strike temperature. The target temperature of a mash rest, the temperature at which a desired reaction occurs.

substratum. The substance in or on which an organism grows.

tannin. Astringent polyphenolic compounds, capable of colliding with proteins and either precipitating or forming haze fractions. Oxidized polyphenols form color compounds relevant in beer.

terminal extract. The density of the fully fermented beer.

titration. Measurement of a substance in solution by addition of a standard disclosing solution to initiate an indicative color change.

trisaccharide. A sugar composed of three monosaccharides joined by the removal of water molecules.

trub. Precipitated flocks of haze-forming protein and polyphenols.

turbidity. Sediment in suspension; hazy, murky.

ullage. The empty space between a liquid and the top of its container. Also called airspace or headspace.

viscosity. Of glutinous consistency; the resistance of a fluid to flow. The degree of "mouthfeel" of a beer.

volatile. Readily vaporized, especially esters, essential oils, and higher alcohols.

v/v. See *alcohol by volume*.

water hardness. The degree of dissolved minerals in water.

wort. Mash extract (sweet wort); the hopped sugar solution before pitching (bitter wort).

w/v. See *alcohol by weight*.

References

Chapter 3: Malt Extracts

1. D. Edgar (Director, Institute of Brewing Studies), personal communication, March 28, 1996.
2. Wayne Waananen, "Winner's Circle: Best of the Best, 1988," *Brewers and Their Gadgets, Zymurgy*® 11, no. 4 (Special Issue 1988): 53; David Edgar, "Winner's Circle: Best of 1989," *Yeast and Beer, Zymurgy* 12, no. 4 (Special Issue 1989): 64; David Edgar, "Winner's Circle: America's Best, 1990," *Hops and Beer, Zymurgy* 13, no. 4 (Special Issue 1988): 61-62; Dan Fink, "Winner's Circle: America's Best, 1991," *Traditional Beer Style, Zymurgy* 14, no. 4 (Special Issue 1988): 69-70; James Spence, "Winner's Circle: 1992 Brewing Champions," *Gadgets and Equipment, Zymurgy* 15, no. 4 (Special Issue 1988): 94; James Spence, "Winner's Circle," *Traditional Brewing Methods, Zymurgy* 16, no. 4 (Special Issue 1988): 104; James Spence, "Winner's Circle," *Special Ingredients and Indigenous Beers, Zymurgy* 16, no. 4 (Special Issue 1988): 112.
3. James Spence, "Winner's Circle," *Special Ingredients and Indigenous Beers, Zymurgy* 16, no. 4 (Special Issue 1988): 111-121.
4. J. Paik, N. H. Low, and W. M. Ingledew, "Malt Extract: Relationship of Chemical Composition to Fermentability," *ASBC Journal* 49, no. 1 (1991): 8-13.
5. J. R. Heron, "Some Observations on Commercial Malt Extracts," *Journal of the Institute of Brewing* 2 (1966): 456.
6. J. S. Hough, D. E. Briggs, R. Stevens, and T. W. Young, "Adjuncts and Industrial Enzymes," in *Malting and Brewing Science,* 2d ed. vol. 1, (London: Chapman and Hall, 1982), 245.
7. Heron, "Some Observations," 452. Hough, et al., "Adjuncts and Industrial Enzymes," 245.
8. J. M. Ames, "Control of the Maillard Reaction in Food Systems," *Trends in Food Science & Technology* (December 1990): 151.
9. Heron, "Some Observations," 256; G. Fix, *Principles of Brewing Science* (Boulder, Colo.: Brewers Publications, 1989), 117.
10. Ames, "Maillard Reaction in Food," 152. T. Pasechke (consulting food technologist), personal communication, December 8, 1994.
11. J. M. Ames, "Maillard Reaction in Food"; S. Laufer, "Factors Influencing Color of Beer and Ale," *The American Brewer* 74, no. 5 (May 1941): 20-24.
12. Laufer, "Factors Influencing Color of Beer and Ale," 23.
13. Fix, *Principles of Brewing Science,* 117.
14. R. Mosher, *The Brewers Companion* (Seattle: Alephenalia, 1994).

Chapter 4: Flavor and Aroma from Fermentables

1. G. Wheeler, *Home Brewing: The CAMRA Guide* (Herts, U.K.: The Campaign for Real Ale, 1993).
2. Wheeler, *Home Brewing.*
3. M. Matucheski, "Oats: The Right Grain to Brew," *Zymurgy* (Special Issue 1994).
4. Wheeler, *Home Brewing.*
5. B. Ridgely, "African Sorghum Beer," and "Sorghum," *Zymurgy* (Special Issue 1994).

6. P. Farnsworth, personal communication, February 1996.

7. J. Bourbonnais, "Brew with Wild Rice," *Zymurgy* (Special Issue 1994).

8. J. De Clerck, *A Textbook of Brewing,* translated by Kathleen Barton-Wright (Chapman & Hall Ltd., 1957).

9. L. W. Aurand, A. E. Woods, and M. R. Wells. *Food Composition and Analysis* (New York: Van Nostrand Reinhold Company, 1987).

10. J. Frane, "How Sweet It Is — Brewing with Sugar," *Zymurgy* 17, no. 1 (Spring 1994).

11. Aurand, et al., *Food Composition and Analysis.*

12. C. Bailey, "Make Mine with Molasses," Special Ingredients & Indigenous Beer, *Zymurgy* 17, no. 4 (Special Issue 1994): 102–103.

13. Frane, "How Sweet It Is — Brewing with Sugar," 38–41.

14. Aurand, et al., *Food Composition and Analysis.*

15. Thomas J. Payne Market Development, "Honey Potential in Beer: Preliminary Research" (San Francisco: National Honey Board, 1993).

Chapter 5: Calculating the Malt Bill

1. Portions of the grain such as the husk do not contain starch. In addition, the portion of the starch that is convertable during brewing will vary according to malting conditions.

Chapter 7: Beer Color

1. W. Swistowicz, "Interpretation of Laboratory Analysis," in *The Practical Brewer: A Manual for the Brewing Industry*, 2d ed. (Madison, Wis.: Master Brewers Association of the Americas, 1977): 328.

2. ASBC Beer Analysis Check Service, sample 91-B; 50(4), 1992, as reported in K. D. Zastrow, "Quality Control & Quality Assurance," lecture notes from Siebel Institute of Technology, 1995.

3. L. R. Bishop, "Proposed Revision of the Lovibond '52 Series' of Glass Slides for the Measurement of the Colour of Worts and Beers," *Journal of the Institute of Brewing* 56 (1950): 373; G. F. Beyer, "Spectrophotometric Determination of Lovibond Number in Brown Lovibond Glasses Series No. 52, Brewer's Scale,"

Association of Official Agricultural Chemists 26, no. 1 (1943): 164–171.

4. Bishop, "Proposed Revision of the Lovibond '52 Series,'" 373.

5. Ibid.

6. Ibid.

7. J. D. Reynolds, University of Arkansas School of Medicine, Health USA database.

8. I. Stone and P. P. Gray, "Photometric Standardization and Determination of Color in Beer," *Proceedings,* American Society of Brewing Chemists (1946): 40–49.

9. J. van Strien and B. W. Drost, "Photometric Determination of Beer and Wort Colors," *ASBC Journal* 37, no. 2 (1979): 84–88.

10. Stone and Gray, "Photometric Standardization and Determination," 40–49. American Society of Brewing Chemists, "Report of Subcommittee on Color in Beer," *Proceedings* (1950).

11. D. A. Skoog and D. M. West, *Analytical Chemistry: An Introduction*, 2d ed. (New York: Holt, Rinehart and Winston, 1974): 470.

12. American Society of Brewing Chemists, "Report of Subcommittee," 193.

13. J. C. Seaton and I. C. Cantrell, "The Determination of Beer Colour — Collaborative Trial," *Journal of the Institute of Brewing* 99 (January–February 1993): 21–23. F. R. Sharpe, T. B. Garvey, and N. S. Pyne, "The Measurement of Beer and Wort Colour — A New Approach," *Journal of the Institute of Brewing* 98 (July–August 1992): 321–324.

14. *EBC Analytica*, 4th ed. of the Analysis Committee of the EBS 1987 Supplement (1989): E131–E132.

15. K. Thomas (Brewlab, University of Sunderland), personal communication, May 1995.

16. J. R. Hudson, et al., "Institute of Brewing: Analysis Committee Measurement of Colour in Wort and Beer," *Journal of the Institute of Brewing* 75: 164–168.

17. F. Eckhardt, *The Essentials of Beer Style;* C. Papazian, *The New Complete Joy of Home Brewing* (New York: Avon Books, 1991): 49; G. Fix, "A Simple Technique for Evaluating Beer Color," in *Evaluating Beer* (Boulder, Colo.: Brewers Publications, 1993); G. Smith, *The Beer Enthusiast's Guide: Tasting and Judging Brews from Around the World* (Pownal, Vt.: Storey Publishing, 1994).

18. AHA "1994 NHC Guidelines," *Zymurgy* 16, no. 5.
19. D. Davison, *Homebrew Color Guide* (Greenfield, Wis.: Dennis Davison, 1993).
20. Fix, "Evaluating Beer Color," 133-141.
21. Skoog and West, *Analytical Chemistry*, 471.
22. This phenomenon is not entirely understood. While some suggest that it is the result of instument error, other evidence points to a true physical cause.
23. Joe Power (Siebel Institute of Technology), telephone conversation with author, December 16, 1994.
24. Power, telephone conversation.
25. Power, personal communication; M.A. Gruber (Briess Malting), personal communication, December 1994.
26. A. Holtermand, "Recent Chemical Aspects of the Browning Reaction," in EBC *Proceedings* (Brussels, 1963): 146-147; S. Laufer, "Factors Influencing Color of Beer and Ale," *The American Brewer* 74, no. 5 (May 1941): 20-24.
27. J. A. Ames, "The Maillard Browning Reaction — An Update," *Chemistry and Industry* (September 5, 1988): 558-561.
28. Ibid. Hough, et al., *Malting and Brewing Science*, 462-469.
29. H. B. Heath, and G. Reineccius, *Flavor Chemistry and Technology* (Westport, Conn.: AVI Publishing, 1986): 71-72.
30. Ibid. J. M. Ames, "Maillard Browning Reaction — Update," 558-561; J. M. Ames, "Control of the Maillard Reaction in Food Systems," *Trends in Food Science & Technology* (December 1990): 150-151; F. A. Lee, *Basic Food Chemistry*, 2d ed. (Westport, Conn.: AVI Publishing, 1983).
31. J. M. Ames, "Maillard Reaction in Food," 150-151.
32. Heath and Reineccius, *Flavor Chemistry and Technology*, 75.
33. N. Hashimoto, "Amino-Carbonyl Reaction During Wort Boiling in Relation to Flavor Stability of Beer," Report of Research Labs of Kirin Brewery Co. Ltd., no. 16 (1973): 1-9; N. Hashimoto, *Journal of the Institute of Brewing* 78, no. 43 (1972); G. Fix, "The Detriments of Hot-Side Aeration," *Zymurgy* 15, no 5: 34-40; K. Ohtsu, N. Hashimoto, K. Innoue, S. Miyaki, "Flavor Stability of Packaged Beer in Relation to Oxidation of

Wort," *Brewers Digest* 61, no. 6 (June 1986): 21.
34. Hough, et al., *Malting and Brewing Science*, 462-469; Fix, "Hot-Side Aeration," 34-40.
35. Hashimoto, "Amino-Carbonyl Reaction," 1.
36. Hough, et al., *Malting and Brewing Science*, 840.
37. E. Sandegren, L. Enebo, H. Guthenberg, and L. Ljungdahl, *Proceedings of the Annual Meeting of the American Society of Brewing Chemists* (1954): 63; M. Jones and J. S. Pierce, *Journal of the Institute of Brewing* 73 (1967): 342.
38. Hashimoto, "Amino-Carbonyl Reaction."
39. Holtermand, "Chemical Aspects of the Browning Reaction," 146-147.
40. J. M. Ames, "Maillard Reaction in Food," 150-151.
41. S. Laufer, "Color of Beer and Ale," 20-24; Lee, *Basic Food Chemistry*.
42. J. M. Ames, "Maillard Reaction in Food," 152.
43. Ibid. Pasechke (consulting food technologist), personal communication, December 12, 1994.
44. J. M. Ames, "Maillard Reaction in Food," 150-51.
45. Holtermand, "Chemical Aspects of the Browning Reaction," 146-147.
46. Laufer, "Color of Beer and Ale," 20-24.
47. Holtermand, "Chemical Aspects of the Browning Reaction," 146-147; Laufer, "Color of Beer and Ale," 20-24.
48. Fix, *Principles of Brewing Science*, 119-125, 135-138; Ohtsu, et al., "Flavor Stability of Beer," 21.
49. Laufer, "Color of Beer and Ale," 20-24; Fix, *Principles of Brewing Science*; 119-125, 135-138; Hough, et al., *Malting and Brewing Science*, P. R. Smith, "The Control of Beer Color," lecture notes, Chicago: Siebel Institute of Technology, 1995.
50. Laufer, "Color of Beer and Ale," 20-24; Lee, *Basic Food Chemistry*, 290-291.
51. Holtermand, "Chemical Aspects of the Browning Reaction," 146-147.
52. Lee, *Basic Food Chemistry*.
53. Hough, et al., *Malting and Brewing Science*, 462-469; Laufer, "Color of Beer and Ale," 20-24.
54. Lee, *Basic Food Chemistry*, 291.
55. Laufer, "Color of Beer and Ale," 20-24.

56. R. Mosher, *The Brewer's Companion* (Seattle: Alephenalia, 1994): 34.

57. Laufer, "Color of Beer and Ale," 20-24.

58. Ibid.

59. D. Richmond, *Bock*, Classic Beer Style Series, no. 9 (Boulder, Colo.: Brewers Publications, 1994), 55, 86-87.

60. Fix, "Hot-Side Aeration," 34-40; Fix, "Evaluating Beer Color."

61. Hough, et al., *Malting and Brewing Science*, 462-469.

62. G. J. Noonan, *Scotch Ale*, Classic Beer Style Series, no. 8 (Boulder, Colo.: Brewers Publications, 1993), 92-93.

63. Fix, "Evaluating Beer Color"; Laufer, "Color of Beer and Ale," 20-24.

64. Fix, "Evaluating Beer Color."

65. Laufer, "Color of Beer and Ale," 20-24.

66. Fix, "Evaluating Beer Color."

Chapter 8: Water

1. This assumes 70 percent efficiency of extraction on a grain with laboratory course grind, as is, extract of 80 percent, moisture content of 4 percent.

2. "Brewhouse Calculations," Chicago: Siebel Institute of Technology.

3. P. Kolbach, *Wschr. Brauerei,* no. 44 (1941); P. Kolbach, *Mschr. Brauerei.* 6, No. 5 (1953): 49.

4. G. J. Noonan, *Brewing Lager Beer* (Boulder, Colo.: Brewers Publications, 1986): 44; G. Fix, presentation at 1995 Microbrewers Conference; K. D. Zastrow, "pH in Brewing," lecture notes, Chicago: Siebel Institute of Technology, 1995.

Chapter 9: Using Hops and Hop Bitterness

1. K. Zastrow, "Hops," lecture, Chicago: Siebel Institute of Technology, February 1995.

2. Ibid.

3. Ibid.

4. G. B. Nickerson, "Better Bitter Beer: Quality Control of Flavors Introduced by Hops," *Brewers Digest* (June 1992): 24-26.

5. T. Foster, *Pale Ale,* Classic Beer Style Series, no. 1 (Boulder, Colo.: Brewers Publications, 1990): 28.

6. J. Helmke (Siebel Institute of technology), personal communication, May 17, 1995.

7. I. Shelton (Siebel Institute of Technology), personal communication, May 16, 1995.

8. I know this from my personal experience in taste panels conducted at the Siebel Institute. Although I could detect most beer faults at or near the threshold value in blind trials, I generally missed the samples where the IBU had increased from 10 to 20!

9. Dry-hopping refers to the practice of adding hops to the beer during fermentation, aging, or packaging rather than during the kettle boil.

10. F. Palmer, "The Determination of Pitching Yeast Concentration," *MBAA Technical Quarterly* 6, no. 2: 141-145.

11. A. Korzonas, personal communication, December 28, 1994.

12. J. Rager, "Calculating Hop Bitterness in Beer," *Zymurgy* 13, no. 4 (Special Issue 1990): 53

13. Ibid.

14. M. Garetz, *Using Hops: The Complete Guide to Hops for the Craft Brewer,* (Danville, Calif.: HopTech, 1994): 156.

15. R. M. Kenber, "Hop Products and Their Usage — A Review" (from Siebel notebook, Hops section).

16. Nickerson. "Better Bitter Beer," 24-26.

17. Garetz, *Using Hops,* 137.

18. Ibid.

19. Zastrow, "Hops."

20. S. T. Likens, G. B. Nickerson, C. E. Zimmermann, "An Index of Deterioration in Hops," *ASBC Journal* (1970): 68-74.

21. A. L. Whitear, "Changes in Resin Composition and Brewing Behaviour of Hops During Storage," *Journal of the Institute of Brewing* 72 (1966): 177-183.

22. A. J. Rehberger and L. H. Bradee, "Hop Oxidative Transforms and Control of Beer Bitterness," *MBAA Technical Quarterly* 12, no. 1 (1975): 1-8.

23. Garetz, *Using Hops,* 103-115.

Chapter 10: Flavor and Aroma Hops

1. G. Fix, *Principles of Brewing Science,* (Boulder, Colo.: Brewers Publications, 1989), 52.

2. J. Haley and T. L. Peppard, "Differences in Utilisation of the Essential Oil of Hops During the Production of Dry-hopped and Late-hopped Beers," *Journal of the Institute of Brewing* 89 (1983); R. T. Foster and G. B. Nickerson, "Changes in Hop Oil Content

and Hoppiness Potential (Sigma) during Hop Aging," *ASBC Journal* 43, no. 3 (1985).

3. V. E. Peacock and M. L. Deinzer, "Chemistry of Hop Aroma in Beer," *ASBC Journal* 39, no. 4 (1981); V. E. Peacock and M. L. Deinzer, "Fate of Hop Oil Components in Beer," *ASBC Journal* 46, no. 4 (1988); Foster and Nickerson, "Changes in Hop Oil Content."

4. T. L. Peppard, S. A. Ramus, C. A. Witt, and K. J. Siebert, "Correlation of Sensory and Instrumental Data in Elucidating the Effect of Varietal Differences on Hop Flavor in Beer," *ASBC Journal* 47, no. 1 (1988).

5. Ibid.

6. Fix, *Principles of Brewing Science*, 52.

7. Haley and Peppard, "Differences in Utilization of the Essential Oil," 87.

8. Peacock and Deinzer, "Chemistry of Hop Aroma"; Haley and Peppard, "Differences in Utilisation"; G. B. Nickerson and E. L. Van Engel, "Hop Aroma Component Profile and the Aroma Unit," *ASBC Journal* 50, no. 3 (1992).

9. Foster and Nickerson, "Changes in Hop Oil Content."

10. Peacock and Deinzer, "Chemistry of Hop Aroma."

11. K. C. Lam, R. T. Foster, and M. L. Deinzer, "Aging of Hops and Their Contribution to Beer Flavor," *Journal of Agricultural Food Chemistry* 34 (1986): 763-770.

12. Peppard, et al., "Correlation of Sensory and Instrumental Data."

13. Ibid.

14. Peacock and Deinzer, "Chemistry of Hop Aroma in Beer."

15. Ibid.

16. Lam, Foster, and Deinzer, "Aging of Hops," 763-770.

17. Peppard, et al., "Correlation of Sensory and Instrumental Data."

18. Nickerson and Van Engel, "Hop Aroma Component Profile," 77.

19. There is some bickering among hop experts about the meaning of the term "noble-type" hops. Some say there are only three varieties, others say only four. Still others say the term applies to *all* aroma hops that meet the characterisitics specified in this section. As a result of this confusion, the term itself is falling into disuse and may soon be obsolete.

20. Foster and Nickerson, "Changes in Hop Oil Content," 127-135.

21. Ibid.

22. Lam, Foster, and Deinzer, "Aging of Hops," 763-770; Nickerson and Van Engel, "Hop Aroma Component Profile," 77-88; Peacock and Deinzer, "Chemistry of Hop Aroma," 136-141; A. Forster and R. Schmidt, "Characterisation and Classification of Hop Varieties," *Brauwelt International* (1994/II): 108-124.

23. K. T. Westwood and I. S. Daoud, "A New Technique to Control Hop Flavor," *EBC Congress Proceedings, 1985*: 579-586.

24. Haley and Peppard, "Differences in Utilisation," 87-91.

25. Westwood and Daoud, "A New Technique."

26. Nickerson and Van Engel, "Hop Aroma Component Profile," 77-88; Westwood and Daoud, "A New Technique," 579-586.

27. Peppard, et al., "Correlation of Sensory and Instrumental Data," 18-26.

28. Nickerson and Van Engel, "Hop Aroma Component Profile," 77-88.

29. Ibid. Haley and Peppard, "Differences in Utilisation," 87-91.

30. Lam, Foster, and Deinzer, "Aging of Hops," 763-770.

31. Haley and Peppard, "Differences in Utilisation," 87-91.

32. Lam, Foster, and Deinzer, "Aging of Hops," 763-770.

33. Westwood and Daoud, "A New Technique," 579-586.

34. Nickerson and Van Engel, "Hop Aroma Component Profile," 77-88.

35. Ibid.

36. Haley and Peppard, "Differences in Utilisation," 87-91.

37. Peacock and Deinzer, "Fate of Hop Oil Components in Beer," 104-107.

38. J. X. Guinard, R. D. Woodmansee, M. J. Billovits, L. G. Hanson, M. J. Gutierrez, M. L. Snider, M. G. Miranda, and M. J. Lewis, "The Microbiology of Dry-Hopping," *MBAA Technical Quarterly* 27 (1990): 83-89.

39. Ibid.

40. Nickerson and Van Engel, "Hop Aroma Component Profile," 78-88; Forster and Schmidt, "Characterisation and Classification of Hop Varieties," 108-124; Westwood and Daoud, "A New Technique," 579-586;

Foster and Nickerson, "Changes in Hop Oil Content," 127-135.

41. Westwood and Daoud, "A New Technique," 579-586.

Chapter 11: Hop Variety Characteristics

1. T. L. Peppard, S. A. Ramus, C. A. Witt, and K. J. Siebert, "Correlation of Sensory and Instrumental Data in Elucidating the Effect of Varietal Differences on Hop Flavor in Beer," *ASBC Journal* 47, no. 1 (1988): 18-26.
2. Ibid.
3. Ibid.
4. D. Miller, *The Complete Handbook of Home Brewing* (Pownal, Vt.: Storey Communications, 1988), 81.
5. T. L. Peppard, et al., "Correlation of Sensory and Instrumental Data in Elucidating the Effect of Varietal Differences on Hop Flavor in Beer," 18-26.

Chapter 12: Yeast and Fermentation

1. The brewer can use any portion of the ingredients in the kit and usually has the option of adding one or two specific additional ingredients (honey, for instance).
2. G. P. Casey, "Yeast Identification," lecture, Chicago: Institute of Technology, 1995.
3. M. G. Barker and K. A. Smart, "Changes in the Cell Surface of Brewing Yeast During Cellular Ageing," abstract, ASBC Newsletter (Spring 1995); G. P. Casey, "Chromosome Fingerprinting Investigations Regarding the Origin and Stability of Lager and Ale Brewers Yeasts," abstract, ASBC Newsletter (Spring 1995).
4. Some microbiologists tell me that there can be metabolic diversity even within the same strain.
5. G. Casey, "Yeast Identification."
7. Ibid.
6. Ibid.
7. C. Boulton, "Yeast Management and the Control of Brewery Fermentations," *Brewers' Guardian* (April 1991): 25-29.
8. J. S. Hough, D. E. Briggs, R. Stevens, and T. W. Young, *Malting and Brewing Science*, vol. 2, *Hopped Wort and Beer* (London: Chapman and Hall, 1982), 646.
9. Hough, et al., *Malting and Brewing*, 635.
10. Unk, "Wort Aeration," Siebel Course in Brewing Technology, 1995.

11. Hough, et al., *Malting and Brewing Science*, 646.
12. C. Boulton, "Yeast Management," 25-29.
13. Hough, et al., *Malting and Brewing Science*, 635.
14. Ibid.
15. Boulton, "Yeast Management."
16. Unk, "Pitching Rate," Siebel Course in Brewing Technology, 1993.
17. Hough, et al., *Malting and Brewing*, 668; H. L. Hind, *Brewing Science and Practice*, vol. 2, *Brewing Processes* (London: Chapman and Hall, 1948), 809.
18. G. J. Noonan, *Brewing Lager Beer* (Boulder, Colo.: Brewers Publications, 1986), 138.
19. Unk, "Pitching Rate."
20. Fifty milliliters of liquid from a Wyeast packet pitched into approximately 1 quart of 1.044 wort and incubated until high kraeusen yields a solution with about 20 x 106 cells per milliliter.
21. Unk, "Pitching Rate"; D. McConnel (Yeast Culture Kit Company), personal communication, May 30, 1995.
22. P. Farnsworth, personal communication, February 1996.
23. Unk, "Pitching Rate."
24. G. J. Noonan, *Brewing Lager Beer*, 139; C. Papazian, *The Home Brewer's Companion* (New York: Avon Books, 1994), 91.

Chapter 13: Introduction to Part Two

1. R. Protz, *The Real Ale Drinker's Almanac*, (Glasgow: Neil Wilson Publishing, Ltd., 1993).
2. A. Piendl, "500 Bier Aus Aller Welt," *Brauindustrie* (1986).

Chapter 14: The Barley Ales of Germany

1. F. Schönfeld, *Obergärige Biere und ihre Herstellung* (Berlin: Paul Parey, 1938).
2. Schönfeld, *Obergärige Biere,* 185.
3. N. Hardy, ". . . on Altbier," in *Brewing in Styles,* Martin Lodahl, ed., *Brewing Techniques* (January/February 1995): 36-41.
4. Schönfeld, *Obergärige Biere,* 135-138.
5. R. Wahl and M. Henius, *The American Handy-Book of the Brewing, Malting and Auxiliary Trades* (Chicago: Wahl-Henius Institute, 1908), 1289.
6. *One Hundred Years of Brewing* (Chicago and New York: H. S. Rich & Co., 1903), 27.

7. J. P. Arnold, *Origin and History of Beer and Brewing* (Chicago: Alumni Association of the Wahl-Henius Institute of Fermentology, 1911), 304.

8. Ibid. 236.

9. Ibid. 304–306.

10. Ibid.

11. H. Kieninger, "Altbiere: Zusammenhange zwischen Rohstoffen, Herstellung und analytischen Kennzahlen," *Brauwelt* (1980): 560–569; F. Eckhardt, "German Style Ale: Kölschbier," *Zymurgy* (Special Issue 1991): 42–44; R. Deschner, "The Regal Altbiers of Düsseldorf," *Zymurgy* (Winter 1994): 52–56.

12. Hardy, ". . . on Altbier," 36–41.

13. K. Zastrow, personal communication, November 1995.

14. Hardy, ". . . on Altbier," 36–41.

15. Kieninger, "Altbiere," 560–569.

16. M. Jackson, *Michael Jackson's Beer Companion* (Philadelphia: Running Press, 1993), 146; Deschner, "The Regal Altbiers of Düsseldorf," 52–56; Hardy, ". . . on Altbier," 36–41.

17. Hardy, ". . . on Altbier," 36–41; Deschner, "The Regal Altbiers of Düsseldorf," 52–56.

Chapter 15: Barley Wine

1. C. Papazian, "Introducing: Beer Style Guidelines," *The New Brewer* (January–February 1992): 10–16.

2. Unfortunately, Bass discounted this product in 1995.

3. G. S. Amsinck, *Practical Brewings: A Series of Fifty Brewings* (London: George Stewart Amsinck, 1868), 94–101.

4. M. Jackson, *Michael Jackson's Beer Companion* (Philadelphia: Running Press, 1993).

5. H. L. Hind, *Brewing Science and Practice*, vol. 2, *Brewing Processes* (London: Chapman and Hall, 1948), 545.

6. Jackson, *Beer Companion*; M. Jackson, *The New World Guide to Beer* (Philadelphia: Running Press, 1988).

7. Jackson, *Beer Companion*.

8. T. Buchman, "Barley Wine," *Zymurgy* (Fall 1993): 45–51.

9. Jackson, *Beer Companion*.

10. P. Farnsworth, personal communication, February 1996.

11. The standard rule of thumb is one million yeast cells per milliliter of wort per °Plato of wort gravity. (See chapter 12 for additional discussion of pitching rates.)

12. G. Wheeler and R. Protz, *Brew Your Own Real Ale at Home* (Herts, England: CAMRA Books, 1993); Wheeler, *Home Brewing: The CAMRA Guide* (Herts, England: CAMRA Books, 1993).

13. D. Line, *Brewing Beers Like Those You Buy* (Herts, England: Argus Books, Ltd., 1984).

Chapter 16: Bitters and Pale Ales

1. T. Babinec and S. Hamburg, "Confessions of Two Bitter Men," *Zymurgy* 18, no. 2: 36–44. T. Foster, *Pale Ale*, Classic Beer Style Series, no. 1 (Boulder, Colo.: Brewers Publications, 1990); M. Jackson, *Michael Jackson's Beer Companion* (Philadelphia: Running Press, 1993).

2. *One Hundred Years of Brewing* (Chicago and New York: H. S. Rich & Co., 1903).

3. T. Tomlinson, "India Pale Ale, Part I: IPA and Empire — Necessity and Enterprise Give Birth to a Style," *Brewing in Styles*, Roger Bergen, ed., *Brewing Techniques* (March/April 1994): 24.

4. *One Hundred Years of Brewing*.

5. Tomlinson, "India Pale Ale," 20–27.

6. W. L. Tizard, *Theory and Practice of Brewing*, 4th ed. (London, 1857), 459–460; Tomlinson, "India Pale Ale," 24.

7. Foster, *Pale Ale*, 11.

8. H. S. Corran, *A History of Brewing* (London: David & Charles, 1975), 140, 153.

9. Ibid., 140.

10. Tomlinson, "India Pale Ale," 24.

11. Tomlinson, "India Pale Ale," 24; G. Oliver, "East India Pale Ale," *All About Beer* 16, no. 1 (March 1995): 62–63.

12. Oliver, "East India Pale Ale," 62–63.

13. Corran, *A History of Brewing*, 135.

14. Foster, *Pale Ale*, 8.

15. Tizard, *Theory and Practice of Brewing*, 461.

16. Tomlinson, "India Pale Ale," 20–27.

17. J. Pereira, "Treatise of Food and Diet" (London, 1934), as quoted in Corran, *A History of Brewing*, 214.

18. Foster, *Pale Ale*, 13.

19. Corran, *A History of Brewing*, 123.

20. Ibid., 218.

21. Ibid., 218.
22. W. H. Roberts, *The Scottish Ale Brewer* (Edinburgh and London, 1837, 1849), as quoted in Corran, *A History of Brewing,* 217.
23. G. S. Amsinck, *Practical Brewings: A Series of Fifty Brewings* (London: George Stewart Amsinck, 1868).
24. Ibid.
25. *One Hundred Years of Brewing,* 684.
26. Ibid., 654.
27. Jackson, *Michael Jackson's Beer Companion,* 84.
28. R. Protz, *The Real Ale Drinker's Almanac* (Glasgow: Neil Wilson Publishing, Ltd., 1993).
29. R. Wahl and M. Henius, *The American Handy-Book of the Brewing, Malting and Auxiliary Trades* (Chicago: Wahl-Henius Institute, 1908); Foster, *Pale Ale,* 17; Tizard, *Theory and Practice of Brewing,* 452.
30. H. L. Hind, *Brewing Science and Practice* (London: Chapman & Hall, Ltd., 1938), 544.
31. S. Hamburg, personal communication, July 1995.
32. *Cellarmanship* (Herts, England: Campaign for Real Ale, 1992), 4.
33. C. Papazian, "Introducing Beer Style Guidelines," *The New Brewer* (January–February 1992): 10-16; C. Papazian, "Introducing: Beer Style Guidelines: Part 2," *The New Brewer* (March–April 1992): 25-28.
34. Foster, *Pale Ale,* 28.
35. Ibid.
36. *Cellarmanship,* 17.
37. M. Jackson, *Pocket Guide to Beer* (New York: Simon & Schuster, Inc., 1994).
38. Ibid.
39. H. L. Hind, *Brewing Science and Practice,* 544.
40. Foster, *Pale Ale,* 110-118.
41. G. Wheeler, and R. Protz, *Brew Your Own Real Ale at Home* (Herts, England: Campaign for Real Ale, 1993).
42. Foster, *Pale Ale,* 87; Wahl and Henius, *The American Handy-Book,* 1253.
43. Protz, *The Real Ale Drinker's Almanac.*
44. Wheeler and Protz, *Brew Your Own Real Ale at Home;* Foster, *Pale Ale,* 115.
45. Wheeler and Protz, *Brew Your Own Real Ale at Home;* Foster, *Pale Ale,* 115.
46. T. Tomlinson, "India Pale Ale, Part II: The Sun Never Sets," *Brewing in Styles,* Roger Bergen, ed., *Brewing Techniques* (May/June 1994): 20-26.
47. "Beer Style Assessment," CAMRA Technical Report, no. 27/95, 1-2.
48. From this data it seems clear that judges are either not able to discriminate between Cascade hops and English varieties or that they are perfectly willing to allow the use of American hops in a style that is supposed to have only English varieties.

Chapter 17: Bock Beer

1. J. P. Arnold, *Origin and History of Beer and Brewing* (Chicago: Alumni Association of the Wahl-Henius Institute of Fermentology, 1911), 292.
2. Ibid.
3. Ibid.
4. *One Hundred Years of Brewing* (Chicago and New York: H. S. Rich & Co., 1903), 28.
5. Arnold, *Origin and History of Beer and Brewing,* 293.
6. D. Richman, "Bock and Doppelbock," in *Brewing in Styles,* Martin Lodahl, ed. *Brewing Techniques* (March/April 1995): 36-41.
7. Arnold, *Origin and History of Beer and Brewing,* 293.
8. Ibid., 313.
9. Ibid., 313.
10. Richman, "Bock and Doppelbock," 36-41.
11. Ibid.
12. K. D. Zastrow, *History of Brewing,* (Chicago: Siebel Institute of Technology, 1995), 6.
13. Arnold, *Origin and History of Beer and Brewing,* 313; Richman, "Bock and Doppelbock," 36-41.
14. *One Hundred Years of Brewing,* 30.
15. Arnold, *Origin and History of Beer and Brewing,* 313.
16. Ibid., 350.
17. *One Hundred Years of Brewing,* 681.
18. T. C. Cochran, *The Pabst Brewing Company: The History of an American Business* (New York: New York University Press).
19. Ibid.
20. Ibid.
21. Ibid., 216.

22. F. J. Wetzel, "Bock Beer," *The Brewers Technical Review* (February 1937): 54–55.

23. "Fanfare for Bock . . . in Europe," *American Brewer* (January 1950): 44–46.

24. R. Wahl and M. Henius, *The American Handy-Book of the Brewing, Malting and Auxiliary Trades* (Chicago: Wahl-Henius Institute, 1908): 1283.

25. A. L. Nugey, *Brewers Manual* (Self-published, 1948), 3.

26. Ibid.

27. M. Siebert, "The Development of the Brewing Industry in the German Democratic Republic," *Brauwelt International* 4 (1988): 419–422.

28. C. Papazian, "Introducing: Beer Style Guidelines: Part 2," *The New Brewer* (March–April, 1992): 25–28.

29. D. Richman, *Bock,* Classic Beer Style Series no. 9. (Boulder, Colo.: 1994), 60–61.

30. D. Edgar, "Winners Circle: America's Best, 1990," *Hops and Beer, Zymurgy* 13, no. 4 (Special Issue): 65.

31. D. Miller, "Recipe Formulation: Experimenting with Munich Malt," *Beer and Brewing: 1990 National Conference on Quality Beer and Brewing,* Tracy Loysen, ed. (Boulder, Colo.: 1990): 77–84.

32. R. Daniels, "Bock Talk," *Beer and Brewing,* 12 (Boulder, Colo.: Brewers Publications, 1992), 215–238.

Chapter 18: California Common

1. J. Buchner, "Steam Beer," *Western Brewer* 23 (February 15, 1898): 278. R. Wahl and M. Henius, *The American Handy-Book of the Brewing, Malting and Auxiliary Trades* (Chicago: Wahl-Henius Institute, 1908), 1236.

2. *One Hundred Years of Brewing* (Chicago and New York: H. S. Rich & Co., 1903), 446.

3. W. L. Downard, *Dictionary of the History of the American Brewing and Distilling Industries* (Westport, Conn.: Greenwood Press, 1980), 165.

4. *One Hundred Years of Brewing,* 446.

5. B. Yenne, *Beers of North America* (New York: Gallery Books, 1986), 69–70.

6. Buchner, "Steam Beer," 278.

7. Wahl and Henius, *The American Handy-Book,* 1235–37.

8. This same effect occurs with the cask-conditioned real ales found in England.

9. F. Maytag, "California Common Beer," *Zymurgy* (Special Issue 1991): 50–52.

10. M. Jackson, *Michael Jackson's Beer Companion* (Philadelphia: Running Press, 1993), 235.

11. "*American Homebrewers Association 1995 National Homebrew Competition Rules and Regulations,*" (Boulder, Colo.: American Homebrewers Association, 1995).

12. R. Bergen, "California Steaming," *Brewing in Styles, Brewing Techniques* (January/February 1994): 20–25.

13. Ibid.

14. Ibid.

Chapter 19: Fruit Beer

1. J. X. Guinard, *Lambic,* Classic Beer Style Series no. 3 (Boulder, Colo.: Brewers Publications, 1990), 19.

2. R. Mosher, "Sweetness and Light — Fruit Beer Today," *Brewing in Styles,* Martin Lodahl, ed., *Brewing Techniques* (September/October 1995): 48–52.

3. Mike Jaeger (General Manager, Oxford Brewing Company), personal communication, December 21, 1995.

4. Scott Chilleen (Brewmaster, Black Mountain Brewing Co.), personal communication, December 21, 1995.

5. D. S. Edgar, ed., *North American Brewers Resource Directory* (Boulder, Colo.: Brewers Publications, 1994), 304–350.

6. R. Mosher, "Sweetness and Light."

Chapter 20: Mild and Brown Ales

1. G. Wheeler, *Home Brewing — The CAMRA Guide* (Herts, England: CAMRA Books, 1993), 127.

2. Ibid.

3. Ibid., 127.

4. *The London and Country Brewer* (Dublin, 1750), quoted in H. S. Corran, *A History of Brewing* (London: David & Charles, 1975), 106.

5. J. Tuck, *The Private Brewer's Guide to the Art of Brewing Ale and Porter* (Woodbridge, Conn.: ZymoScribe, 1995), 3–4.

6. Ibid., 137, 162, 171.

7. Ibid., 128, 170.

8. G. S. Amsinck, *Practical Brewings: A Series of Fifty Brewings* (London: George Stewart Amsinck, 1868), 157.

9. P. Slosberg, "The Road to an American Brown Ale," *Brewing in Styles,* Martin Lodahl, ed., *Brewing Techniques* (May/June 1995): 35.

10. C. Graham, research paper (London: University College, 1881), as reported in H. S. Corran, *A History of Brewing* (London: David & Charles, 1975).

11. R. Wahl and M. Henius, *The American Handy-Book of the Brewing, Malting and Auxiliary Trades* (Chicago: Wahl-Henius Institute, 1908), 1251-1252.

12. H. L. Hind, *Brewing Science and Practice* (London: Chapman & Hall, Ltd. 1938), 395.

13. M. Jackson, *Michael Jackson's Beer Companion,* (Philadelphia: Running Press, 1993).

14. R. Protz, *The Real Ale Drinker's Almanac* (Glasgow: Neil Wilson Publishing, Ltd., 1993).

15. Jackson, *Michael Jackson's Beer Companion,* 69.

16. *Barley Corn* (June/July 1995).

17. Slosberg, "The Road to an American Brown Ale," 34.

18. Ibid., 35.

19. Jackson, *Michael Jackson's Beer Companion,* 68-69; M. Jackson, *The New World Guide to Beer* (Philadelphia: Running Press, 1988), 169.

20. Jackson, *Michael Jackson's Beer Companion,* 91.

21. In fact, I'm told that Texas brown ale originated as a catch-all category in the Dixie Cup Homebrew Competition held each year in Houston.

22. *1995 Category Descriptions, National Homebrew Competition* (Boulder, Colo.: American Homebrewers Association, 1995).

23. Protz, *The Real Ale Drinker's Almanac.*

24. Because of the way the data is published, I cannot be sure if this is the percentage of gravity contributed or the percentage of raw ingredient weight.

25. D. Line, *Brewing Beers Like Those You Buy* (Herts, England: Argus Books, Ltd., 1984); Wheeler, *Home Brewing.*

Chapter 21: Old Ale

1. R. Protz, *The Real Ale Drinker's Almanac* (Glasgow: Neil Wilson Publishing, Ltd.,
1993.); R. Protz, *The European Beer Almanac* (Moffar, Scotland: Lochar Publishing, 1991); G. Wheeler and R. Protz, *Brew Your Own Real Ale at Home,* (Herts, England: CAMRA Books, 1993); D. Line, *Brewing Beers Like Those You Buy* (Herts, England: Argus Books, Ltd., 1984); M. Jackson, *Michael Jackson's Beer Companion* (Philadelphia: Running Press, 1993).

2. M. Lodahl, "Old, Strong and Stock Ales," *Brewing Techniques* (September/October 1994): 22-29.

3. J. Bickerdyke, *The Curiosities of Ale and Beer* (London: Spring Books, 1965).

4. G. S. Amsinck, *Practical Brewings: A Series of Fifty Brewings* (London: George Stewart Amsinck, 1868), 94-101.

5. Amsinck, *Practical Brewings,* 112-113.

6. Lodahl "Old, Strong and Stock Ales," 22-29.

7. H. S. Corran, *A History of Brewing* (London: David & Charles, 1975).

8. R. Wahl and M. Henius, *The American Handy-Book of the Brewing, Malting and Auxiliary Trades* (Chicago: Wahl-Henius Institute, 1908), 1284.

9. Corran, *A History of Brewing.*

10. Wheeler and Protz, *Brew Your Own Real Ale at Home.*

11. Ibid.

12. Wahl and Henius, *The American Handy-Book.*

13. Ibid.

14. Ibid., 1284.

15. "Beer Style Assessment," CAMRA Technical Report No. 27/95: 1-2.

16. "Beer Style Descriptions," National Guild of Wine and Beer Judges, 1995.

17. Jackson, *Michael Jackson's Beer Companion.*

18. Wheeler and Protz, *Brew Your Own Real Ale at Home;* Jackson, *Michael Jackson's Beer Companion;* Jackson, *The New World Guide to Beer* (Philadelphia: Running Press, 1988).

19. Jackson, *Michael Jackson's Beer Companion.*

20. Wheeler and Protz, *Brew Your Own Real Ale at Home.*

21. Wheeler and Protz, *Brew Your Own Real Ale at Home;* G. Wheeler, *Home Brewing: The CAMRA Guide* (Herts, England: CAMRA Books, 1993).

22. A. L. Nugey, *Brewing Formulas Practically Considered* (Rahway, N.J.: A. L. Nugey, 1937), quoted in Lodahl, "Old, Strong and Stock Ales," 22–29.

23. Jackson, *Michael Jackson's Beer Companion.*

24. Wheeler and Protz, *Brew Your Own Real Ale at Home;* G. Wheeler, *Home Brewing;* Line, *Brewing Beers Like Those You Buy.*

Chapter 22: Pilsener and Other Pale Lagers

1. K. D. Zastrow, "History of Brewing" (Chicago: Siebel Institute of Technology, 1995).

2. Ibid.

3. M. Jackson, *Michael Jackson's Beer Companion* (Philadelphia: Running Press, 1993), 211.

4. Miller, *Continental Pilsener,* Classic Beer Style Series no. 2 (Boulder, Colo., Brewers Publications, 1990), 6; Zastrow, "History of Brewing."

5. Zastrow, "History of Brewing."

6. Ibid.

7. J. E. Thausing, W. T. Brannt, A. Schwarz, A. H. Bauer, *The Theory and Practice of the Preparation of Malt and the Fabrication of Beer* (London: Henry Carey Baird & Co., 1882), 348–350.

8. Ibid.

9. Zastrow, "History of Brewing."

10. H. Rudinger, *Die Bierbrauerei und die Malzextract-Fabrication* (Wien: A. Hartleben's Verlag, 1887), 179–180.

11. Ibid.

12. Thausing, et al., *Preparation of Malt and the Fabrication of Beer,* 419.

13. Thausing, et al., *Preparation of Malt and the Fabrication of Beer,* 419; Rudinger, H. *Die Bierbrauerei and Die Malzextract-Fabrication,* 179–180.

14. H. L. Hind, *Brewing Science and Practice* (London: Chapman & Hall, Ltd., 1938), 582.

15. G. J. Noonan, *Brewing Lager Beer* (Boulder, Colo.: Brewers Publications, 1986), 186.

16. Hind, *Brewing Science and Practice,* 580.

17. J. DeClerck, *A Textbook of Brewing* (London: Chapman & Hall Ltd., 1957), 273.

18. G. Fix, *Principles of Brewing Science* (Boulder, Colo.: Brewers Publications, 1989), 97.

19. D. Richman, "Pilsener Urquell: The Brewery — Uncovering the Unusual," *Zymurgy* (Summer 1991): 30–36.

20. During a recent visit to the Pilsener Urquell brewery, my colleague Randy Mosher saw both hop pellets and hop extract in the brewhouse, apparently about to be added to a batch of beer. Pehaps these other forms of hops are used only for the lower-gravity beer and not for the classic Pilsener.

21. Richman, "Pilsener Urquell: The Brewery — Uncovering the Unusual," 30–36.

22. DeClerck, *A Textbook of Brewing,* 554.

23. Richman, "Pilsener Urquell," 30–36.

24. Ibid.

25. Ibid.

26. Thausing, et al., *Preparation of Malt and the Fabrication of Beer,* 673.

27. Ibid.

28. Jackson, *Michael Jackson's Beer Companion,* 212.

29. Ibid.

30. R. Wahl and M. Henius, *The American Handy-Book of the Brewing, Malting and Auxiliary Trades,* (Chicago: Wahl-Henius Institute, 1908), 1287; A. L. Nugey, *Brewers Manual* (Self-published, 1948). DeClerck, *A Textbook of Brewing.*

31. Wahl and Henius, *The American Handy-Book,* 1238.

32. Ibid., 1286.

33. Nugey, *Brewers Manual,* 2.

34. DeClerck, *A Textbook of Brewing,* 555.

35. J. Mallett, "Dortmunder Export," *The New Brewer* (September–October 1994), 27–28.

36. Ibid.

37. Mallett, "Dortmunder Export." D. Norton, "Dortmund, Export," *Zymurgy* (Special Issue, 1991), 33.

38. Jackson, *Michael Jackson's Beer Companion,* 220.

39. Ibid.

40. Zastrow, "History of Brewing."

41. J. Dorsch, "Münchner Helles: The Everyday Refresher," *The New Brewer* (March–April, 1995), 35–36; M. Jackson, *The New World Guide to Beer* (Philadelphia: Running Press, 1988), 46.

42. Jackson, *The New World Guide to Beer;* Dorsch, "Münchner Helles," 35–36.

43. Dorsch, "Münchner Helles," 35–36.

44. G. Fix and L. Fix, *Märzen-Oktoberfest-Vienna,* Classic Beer Style Series, no. 4 (Boulder, Colo.: Brewers Publications, 1991), 32.

45. Ibid.

46. Richman, "Pilsener Urquell," 30–36.

47. E. Warner, "Malting Techniques," ***Zymurgy*** (Special Issue 1993), 13; D. Miller, "Classic Pilsener," ***Zymurgy*** (Special Issue: 1991), 50.

Chapter 23: Porter

1. H. S. Corran, *A History of Brewing* (London: David & Charles, 1975), 112–113.

2. J. Bickerdyke, *The Curiosities of Ale and Beer* (London: Spring Books, 1965), 366; *One Hundred Years of Brewing* (Chicago and New York: H. S. Rich & Co., 1903), 35; *The Compact Edition of the Oxford English Dictionary* (Oxford: Oxford University Press, 1971), 2245.

3. Corran, *A History of Brewing,* 112–114.

4. Ibid., 113.

5. Ibid.

6. *One Hundred Years of Brewing,* 35.

7. Ibid.

8. G. Wheeler, *Home Brewing — The CAMRA Guide* (Herts, England: CAMRA Books, 1993), 128.

9. Corran, *A History of Brewing,* 110.

10. T. Foster, *Porter,* Classic Beer Style Series no. 5 (Boulder, Colo.: Brewers Publications, 1992), 6.

11. Corran, *A History of Brewing,* 111.

12. W. R. Loftus, *The Brewer* (London: circa 1850), 79.

13. G. Wheeler and R. Protz, *Brew Your Own Real Ale at Home* (Herts, England: CAMRA Books, 1993), 141.

14. Corran, *A History of Brewing,* 116.

15. Foster, *Porter,* 12.

16. Ibid., 15.

17. Ibid., 11.

18. J. Harrison, et al., *An Introduction of Old British Beers and How to Make Them* (London: Durden Park Beer Circle, 1991), 8.

19. Foster, *Porter,* 21.

20. Vincent Wright (Adolph Coors Co.), personal communication, August 14, 1995.

21. Foster, *Porter,* 21.

22. A. D. Eames "Death by Drowning in Beer . . .," *All About Beer* (August/September 1991): 10–11.

23. Foster, *Porter,* 20.

24. Ibid., 22.

25. G. S. Amsinck, *Practical Brewings: A Series of Fifty Brewings* (London: George Stewart Amsinck, 1868), 62–75; Loftus, *The Brewer,* 124–125.

26. Loftus, *The Brewer,* 126.

27. Ibid.

28. Wheeler and Protz, *Brew Your Own Real Ale at Home,* 139.

29. Amsinck, *Practical Brewings,* 62–75.

30. Corran, *A History of Brewing,* 215, quoting J. Pereira, *Treatise on Food and Diet* (London, 1843).

31. Amsinck, *Practical Brewings,* 27.

32. Wheeler, *Home Brewing,* 130.

33. J. Tuck, *The Private Brewer's Guide to the Art of Brewing Ale and Porter* (Woodbridge, Conn.: ZymoScribe, 1995), 174.

34. Amsinck, *Practical Brewings,* 26.

35. *Oxford English Dictionary,* 451.

36. Tuck, *Private Brewer's Guide,* 134.

37. Ibid., 176.

38. W. L. Tizard, *Theory and Practice of Brewing* (London, 1857).

39. *Oxford English Dictionary,* 451.

40. Wheeler, *Home Brewing,* 130.

41. Loftus, *The Brewer,* 79.

42. Tuck, *Private Brewer's Guide,* 129.

43. R. Mosher, "Brewing Porter" (handout from Chicago Beer Society style meeting, November 20, 1992), 2.

44. Tuck, *Private Brewer's Guide,* 159.

45. This assumes hop alpha acids of 4 to 5 percent and utilization of 20 to 25 percent.

46. Harrison, et al., *Old British Beers,* 7.

47. Corran, *History of Brewing,* 174.

48. Ibid.

49. Ibid., 174.

50. Loftus, *The Brewer,* 124.

51. Amsinck, *Practical Brewings,* 20.

52. *One Hundred Years of Brewing,* 654.

53. Corran, *History of Brewing,* 215; Loftus, *The Brewer,* 125.

54. Harrison, et al., *Old British Beers,* 40; Corran, *History of Brewing,* 215; Loftus, *The Brewer,* 125.

55. Loftus, *The Brewer,* 124.

56. Ibid.

57. Ibid.

58. Tizard, *Theory and Practice of Brewing.*

59. Corran, *History of Brewing,* 225.
60. R. Wahl and M. Henius, *The American Handy-Book of the Brewing, Malting and Auxiliary Trades* (Chicago: Wahl-Henius Institute, 1908).
61. Wahl and Henius, *The American Handy-Book,* 1252.
62. Ibid., 1275.
63. Wheeler, *Home Brewing,* 131.
64. Foster, *Porter,* 1.
65. J. DeClerck, *A Textbook of Brewing,* trans. Kathleen Barton-Wright (London: Chapman & Hall Ltd., 1957), 555.
66. M. Jackson, *Michael Jackson's Beer Companion* (Philadelphia: Running Press, 1993), 172.
67. Ibid.
68. R. Protz, *The Real Ale Drinker's Almanac* (Glasgow: Neil Wilson Publishing, Ltd., 1993).
69. D. S. Edgar, ed., *North American Brewers Resource Directory* (Boulder, Colo.: Brewers Publications, 1994).
70. Foster, *Porter,* 68.
71. Ibid., 52.
72. Ibid., 104–110.
73. C. Papazian, "Introducing: Beer Style Guidelines," *The New Brewer* (January – Feburary 1992): 10–16.
74. Foster, *Porter,* 68–69.
75. Harrison, et al., *Old British Beers,* 45.
76. Mosher, "Brewing Porter," 138.

Chapter 24: Scottish and Scotch Ales

1. "Scotland," Microsoft® Encarta, Microsoft Corporation and Funk & Wagnall's Corporation, 1994.
2. R. Protz, *The Real Ale Drinker's Almanac* (Glasgow: Neil Wilson Publishing, Ltd., 1993), 16.
3. J. Bickerdyke, *The Curiosities of Ale and Beer* (London: Spring Books, 1965), 129.
4. G. Noonan, *Scotch Ale,* Classic Beer Style Series no. 8 (Boulder Colo.: Brewers Publications, 1993), 71.
5. *The American Heritage Dictionary of the English Language,* 3d ed., Houghton Mifflin Company, electronic version licensed from InfoSoft International, Inc. 1992.
6. Noonan, *Scotch Ale,* 71.
7. *One Hundred Years of Brewing* (Chicago and New York: H. S. Rich & Co., 1903), 650.
8. Ibid.
9. Ibid.
10. Ibid., 650.
11. I. Donnachie, *A History of Brewing in Scotland* (Edinburgh: John Donald Publishers Ltd., 1979), quoted in Noonan, *Scotch Ale,* 11.
12. P. Mathias, *The Brewing Industry in England, 1700-1830* (Cambridge: University Press, 1959), 151.
13. Noonan, *Scotch Ale,* 18.
14. Ibid., 10.
15. Mathias, *Brewing Industry in England,* 151.
16. Noonan, *Scotch Ale,* 17.
17. Ibid., 21.
18. W. H. Roberts, *The Scottish Ale Brewer and Practical Maltster,* 3d ed. (Edinburgh: A & C Black, 1847), 155-174.
19. H. S. Corran, *A History of Brewing* (London: David & Charles, 1975), 228.
20. G. S. Amsinck, *Practical Brewings: A Series of Fifty Brewings* (London: George Stewart Amsinck, 1868), 102, 122.
21. Roberts, *Scottish Ale Brewer,* 41.
22. Ibid., 72.
23. Ibid., 75.
24. Ibid., 55.
25. Ibid., 89.
26. Ibid., 92.
27. Ibid., 108.
28. Ibid., 109.
29. Ibid., 150.
30. Ibid.
31. Corran, *History of Brewing,* 217; Noonan, *Scotch Ale,* 74–75; Roberts, *Scottish Ale Brewer.*
32. Noonan, *Scotch Ale,* 43; Amsinck, *Practical Brewings.*
33. Noonan, *Scotch Ale,* 93.
34. Noonan, *Scotch Ale,* 71, 75; W. H. Roberts, *Scottish Ale Brewer,* 88–89.
35. Noonan, *Scotch Ale,* 64.
36. Roberts, *Scottish Ale Brewer,* 175; Noonan, *Scotch Ale,* 60.
37. Noonan, *Scotch Ale,* 66.
38. Ibid., 43.
39. Ibid.
40. Roberts, *Scottish Ale Brewer,* 200.
41. Noonan, *Scotch Ale,* 71.
42. S. Cribb, "Beer and Rocks," **Zymurgy** 13, no. 3 (Fall 1990): 36.

43. Noonan, *Scotch Ale,* 95.

44. Roberts, *Scottish Ale Brewer,* 86–87.

Chapter 25: Stout

1. *"American Homebrewers Association 1995 National Homebrew Competition Rules and Regulations,"* (Boulder, Colo.: American Homebrewers Association, 1995).

2. L. T. Lusk, H. Goldstein, and D. Ryder, *Independent Role of Beer Proteins, Melanoidins and Polysaccharides in Foam Formation, ASBC Journal* 3, no. 53: 53.

3. H. S. Corran, *A History of Brewing* (London: David & Charles, 1975), 102.

4. Ibid., 102.

5. Ibid., 102.

6. Ibid., 174.

7. R. Wahl and M. Henius, *The American Handy-Book of the Brewing, Malting and Auxiliary Trades* (Chicago: Wahl-Henius Institute, 1908); 1267.

8. R. Bergen, "A Stout Companion," *Brewing in Styles, Brewing Techniques* (November/December 1993): 18–21; M. Jackson, *Michael Jackson's Beer Companion* (Philadelphia: Running Press, 1993), 182.

9. H. L. Hind *Brewing Science and Practice* (London: Chapman & Hall, Ltd., 1938), 546.

10. G. Wheeler *Home Brewing: The CAMRA Guide* (Herts, England: CAMRA Books, 1993), 133; Jackson, *Michael Jackson's Beer Companion,* 179–180.

11. Jackson, *Michael Jackson's Beer Companion.*

12. Wheeler, *Home Brewing,* 133.

13. Wheeler, *Home Brewing;* Jackson, *Michael Jackson's Beer Companion,* 179–180.

14. J. Richardson, *The Philosophical Principles of the Science of Brewing* (London, 1788), 240.

15. Corran, *A History of Brewing,* 212.

16. J. Tuck, *The Private Brewer's Guide to the Art of Brewing Ale and Porter* (Woodbridge, Conn.: 1995), 159–163.

17. Corran, *A History of Brewing,* 174.

18. Jackson, *Michael Jackson's Beer Companion,* 177.

19. G. S. Amsinck, *Practical Brewings: A Series of Fifty Brewings* (London: George Stewart Amsinck, 1868).

20. Wahl and Henius, *The American Handy-Book,* 1100.

21. Ibid.

22. Hind, *Brewing Science and Practice,* 546.

23. J. DeClerck, *A Textbook of Brewing,* trans., Kathleen Barton-Wright vol. 1 (London: Chapman & Hall Ltd., 1957), 555.

24. J. Harrison, et al., *An Introduction of Old British Beers and How to Make Them* (London: Durden Park Beer Circle, 1991), 39–43.

25. Corran, *A History of Brewing,* 147; *One Hundred Years of Brewing* (Chicago and New York: H. S. Rich & Co., 1903), 661.

26. Corran, *A History of Brewing,* 150.

27. Ibid., 212.

28. Ibid., 150.

29. Ibid., 218.

30. Ibid.

31. Ibid.

32. Ibid., 222.

33. Ibid., 174.

34. Ibid., 210.

35. Ibid.

36. Ibid., 188.

37. Amsinck, *Practical Brewings,* 55.

38. Ibid., 56–59.

39. Ibid.

40. Ibid., 36–59.

41. Ibid., 58.

42. Ibid., 58–59

43. *One Hundred Years of Brewing,* 661.

44. Ibid. This description makes quite a contrast to the inventory of the property that Arthur Guinness purchased at this site in 1759: "3 Marble chimney pieces, one kitchen grate and rack and shelves, two small fixed grates, eleven troughs, one float, very bad; one kieve, very bad, and two brass cocks; one underback quite decayed; one copper and seventy barrels with a large brass cock; two underback pumps; one tun; six oars; one strike; one horse mill; one hopper and pan of stones; box of draws and desk in the office." From Corran, *A History of Brewing,* 147.

45. Jackson, *Michael Jackson's Beer Companion,* 172.

46. Ibid., 182.

47. Ibid., 182.

48. F. Eckhardt, *The Essentials of Beer Style: A Catalog of Beer Styles for Brewers and*

Beer Enthusiasts (Portland, Ore.: Fred Eckhardt Associates, 1989), 52.

49. Jackson, *Michael Jackson's Beer Companion*, 182.

50. Ibid.,181-183.

51. Ibid., 184-185.

52. Ibid.

53. Hind, *Brewing Science and Practice*, 546.

54. Jackson, *Michael Jackson's Beer Companion*, 184-186.

55. C. Papazian, *The New Complete Joy of Homebrewing* (New York: Avon Books, 1991), 87; Wheeler, *Home Brewing*, 28.

56. Wheeler, *Home Brewing*.

57. Jackson, *Michael Jackson's Beer Companion*, 184-188.

58. T. Foster, *Porter*, Classic Beer Style Series no. 5 (Boulder, Colo.: Brewers Publications, 1992), 25.

59. Foster, *Porter*, 25; "Courage: Imperial Russian Stout," news release (The Courage Brewery, February 1995): 1.

60. "Catherine the Great," Microsoft Encarta. Microsoft Corporation® and Funk & Wagnall's Corporation, 1994.

61. Jackson, *Michael Jackson's Beer Companion*, 189.

62. Ibid.

63. Ibid., 190.

64. R. Protz, *The Real Ale Drinker's Almanac* (Glasgow: Neil Wilson Publishing, Ltd., 1993), 73.

65. Jackson, *Michael Jackson's Beer Companion*, 195.

66. J. Dorsch, "Imperial Stout: Something Bold, Something New," *The New Brewer* (May-June 1995): 67-68.

67. Ibid.

68. Ibid.

69. Protz, *The Real Ale Drinker's Almanac*, 73.

70. G. Wheeler and R. Protz, *Brew Your Own Real Ale at Home* (Herts, England: CAMRA Books, 1993), 143, 148.

71. Ibid., 143-148.

Chapter 26:
Vienna, Märzen, and Oktoberfest

1. M. Jackson *The New World Guide to Beer* (Philadelphia: Running Press, 1988), 47.

2. J. P. Arnold, *Origin and History of Beer and Brewing* (Chicago: Alumni Association of the Wahl-Henius Institute of Fermentology, 1911), 347.

3. Ibid., 349.

4. Ibid.

5. Ibid., 350.

6. *Hofbrauhaus München 1589-1989: 400 Jahre Tradition Festschrift* (Munich: Carl Gerber Verlag GmbH, 1989), 33.

7. Ibid., 44.

8. Jackson, *The New World Guide to Beer*, 47.

9. C. Michel, *Lehrbuch der Bierbrauerei*, (Munich: Münchener praktischen Brauerschule, 1883), 170.

10. Jackson; *The New World Guide to Beer*, 47. G. Fix and L. Fix, *Oktoberfest, Vienna, Märzen*, Classic Beer Style Series no. 4 (Boulder, Colo.: Brewers Publications, 1991), 6.

11. Fix and Fix, *Oktoberfest, Vienna, Märzen*.

12. Michel, *Lehrbuch der Bierbrauerei*, 170; J. E. Thausing, *Die Theorie und Praxis der Malzbereitung und Bierfabrikation* (1893), 959; C. Lintner, ed., "Das Malz, Sud und Gahrverfahren in einer der ersten Brauereien Oesterreichs," *Der Banerische Bierbrauer* (March 1871): 34.

13. J. E. Thausing, W. T. Brannt, A. Schwarz, A. H. Bauer, *The Theory and Practice of the Preparation of Malt and the Fabrication of Beer* (London: Henry Carey Baird & Co., 1882), 670.

14. Michel, *Lehrbuch der Bierbrauerei*, 170; Thausing, *Malzbereitung und Bierfabrikation*, 959. J. J. Mazger, "Das Wiener Brauverfahren," *Der Banerische Bierbrauer* (August 1871): 116; C. Lintner, ed., "Das Malz, Sud und Gahrverfahren," 34; Thausing et al., *Preparation of Malt and the Fabrication of Beer*, 746-747.

15. "Malting, Brewing and Fermentation in One of the Best Breweries in Austria," *Der Banerische Bierbrauer*, no. 3 (March 1871): 34-35.

16. Michel, *Lehrbuch der Bierbrauerei*, 170; Thausing, *Malzbereitung und Bierfabrikation*, 959; Lintner, "Das Malz, Sud und Gahrverfahren," 34; Thausing, et al., *Preparation of Malt and the Fabrication of Beer*, 746-747; Mazger, "Das Wiener Brauverfahren," 116.

17. Mazger, "Das Wiener Brauverfahren," 115.

18. R. Wahl and M. Henius, *The American Handy-Book of the Brewing, Malting and*

Auxiliary Trades (Chicago: Wahl-Henius Institute, 1908), 1248.

19. Mazger, "Das Wiener Brauverfahren," 117; Lintner, "Das Malz, Sud und Gahrverfahren," 34–35.

20. Lintner, "Das Malz, Sud und Gahrverfahren"; Thausing et al., *Preparation of Malt and the Fabrication of Beer,* 458.

21. Thausing, et al., *Preparation of Malt and the Fabrication of Beer.*

22. Fix and Fix, *Oktoberfest, Vienna, Märzen,* 11; Mazger, "Das Wiener Brauverfahren," 117; Lintner, "Das Malz, Sud und Gahrverfahren," 34–35.

23. Lintner, "Das Malz, Sud und Gahrverfahren," 34–35.

24. Fix and Fix, *Oktoberfest, Vienna, Märzen,* 11.

25. Lintner, "Das Malz, Sud und Gahrverfahren," 34.

26. Schwechat is the name of a town near Vienna. It has long been a home for breweries and continues to be so this day.

27. Thausing, et al., *Preparation of Malt and the Fabrication of Beer,* 745.

28. Mazger, "Das Wiener Brauverfahren," 117; Thausing, et al., *Preparation of Malt and the Fabrication of Beer,* 413–419.

29. Ibid., 413–419.

30. Ibid.

31. Lintner, "Das Malz, Sud und Gahrverfahren," 34; Mazger, "Das Wiener Brauverfahren," 117.

32. Thausing et al., *Preparation of Malt and the Fabrication of Beer,* 462; Lintner, "Das Malz, Sud und Gahrverfahren," 34.

33. Mazger, "Das Wiener Brauverfahren," 117.

34. Thausing, et al., *Preparation of Malt and the Fabrication of Beer,* 573.

35. Ibid., 606.

36. Ibid., 668–669.

37. G. J. Noonan, *Brewing Lager Beer* (Boulder, Colo.: Brewers Publications, 1986), 55; H. L. Hind, *Brewing Science and Practice* (London: Chapman & Hall, Ltd., 1938), 440.

38. "Beer Boom in Austria: A Visit to Austria's Largest Brewery," *American Brewer* (January 1955), 38–41.

39. Ibid.

40. Ibid.

41. Fix and Fix, *Oktoberfest, Vienna, Märzen,* 40–41.

42. Ibid., 18–19.

43. J. DeClerck, *A Textbook of Brewing* trans. Kathleen Barton-Wright (London: Chapman & Hall Ltd., 1957), 555.

44. "Beer Boom in Austria," 38–41.

45. Conrad Siedl (Austrian beer writer), personal communication, Denver, October 6, 1995.

46. Wahl and Henius, *The American Handy-Book,* 1293.

47. *Hofbrauhaus München,* 70.

48. A. Piendl, "500 Bier Aus Aller Welt," *Brauindustrie* (1986).

49. Ibid.

50. Ibid.

51. L. Narziss, "Beer Quality 1993," *Brauwelt International* (1994/I): 20–28.

52. Piendl, "500 Bier Aus Aller Welt," 1723–31.

53. Fix and Fix, *Oktoberfest, Vienna, Märzen,* 78.

54. G. J. Fix, "Vienna, Oktoberfest and Märzen," *Zymurgy* (Special Issue, 1991): 41–42.

55. Ibid., 41–42.

56. Ibid.

Chapter 27: Wheat Beers

1. Y. Pomeranz, ed., *Wheat: Chemistry and Technology,* vol. 1 (St. Paul, Minn., American Association of Cereal Chemists, Inc., 1995), 12.

2. J. P. Arnold, *Origin and History of Beer and Brewing* (Chicago: Alumni Association of the Wahl-Henius Institute of Fermentology, 1911), 282.

3. Ibid., 284.

4. Ibid., 300.

5. Ibid., 301–302.

6. Ibid., 303.

7. Ibid., 318.

8. *One Hundred Years of Brewing* (Chicago and New York: H.S. Rich & Co., 1903), 676.

9. Arnold, *Origin and History of Beer and Brewing,* 318.

10. Ibid., 293.

11. Ibid., 290.

12. Ibid., 349–350.

13. E. Warner, *German Wheat Beer,* Classic Style Series no. 7 (Boulder, Colo.: Brewers Publications, 1992), 13.

14. Ibid.

15. F. Schonfeld, *Obergärige Biere und ihre Herstellung* (Berlin: Paul Parey, 1938), 161.

16. Arnold, *Origin and History of Beer and Brewing,* 314.

17. Warner, *German Wheat Beer,* 15; *One Hundred Years of Brewing,* 31.

18. *Hofbräuhaus München 1589-1989: 400 Jahre Tradition Festschrift* (Carl Gerber Verlag GmbH, 1989), 33.

19. Warner, *German Wheat Beer,* 15-16.

20. Ibid.

21. M. Jackson, *Michael Jackson's Beer Companion* (Philadelphia: Running Press, 1993), 56-57, 62.

22. *One Hundred Years of Brewing,* 681.

23. C. Lintner, *Lehrbuch der Bierbrauerei* (Brunswick, Germany: Friedrich Vieweg und Sohn, 1877), 372-374.

24. Warner, *German Wheat Beer,* 45.

25. C. Brandtl, *Der Banerische Bierbrauer* no. 6 (March 1872): 90-92.

26. Ibid.

27. H. Schulze-Besse, *Aus der Geschichte des Berliner Brauwesens und seiner Braumeister* (Berlin: Institute für Garungsgewerbe, 1927), 37.

28. Ibid.

29. H. Rudinger, *Die Bierbrauerei und die Malzextract-Fabrication* (Wien: A. Hartleben's Verlag, 1887), 193.

30. Ibid.

31. Schonfeld, *Obergärige Biere und ihre Herstellung,* 150-151; R. Wahl and M. Henius, *The American Handy-Book of the Brewing, Malting and Auxiliary* Trades (Chicago: Wahl-Henius Institute, 1908), 1278-1280.

32. Ibid.

33. Schonfeld, *Obergärige Biere und ihre Herstellung,* 150-151.

34. K. Wackerbauer and F. J. Methner, "The Microorganisms of 'Berliner Weissbier' and Their Influence on the Beer Flavor," *Brauwelt International* 4 (1988): 382-388.

35. Rudinger, *Die Bierbrauerei und die Malzextract-Fabrication,* 193.

36. K. Wackerbauer and F. J. Methner, "On the Formation of Acids and Esters in 'Berliner Weissbier,'" *Brauwelt International* 1 (1989): 68-74.

37. Ibid.

38. M. Delbruck and W. Rommel, *Jahrbuch Versuchs und Lehranstalt für Brauerei in Berlin* (Berlin: Verlagsbuchhandlung Paul Parey, 1913), 104.

39. A. Piendl, "500 Bier Aus Aller Welt," *Brauindustrie* (1986).

40. Warner, *German Wheat Beer,* 5.

41. Ibid., 17.

42. Warner, *German Wheat Beer,* 21-37. Piendl, "500 Bier Aus Aller Welt."

43. "*American Homebrewers Association 1995 National Homebrew Competition Rules and Regulations*" (Boulder, Colo: American Homebrewers Association, 1995).

44. Warner, *German Wheat Beer,* 73.

45. Ibid.

46. Ibid., 29.

47. Ibid., 80.

48. Ibid., 83.

49. Ibid., 78-79.

50. C. Papazian, *The Home Brewers Companion* (New York: Avon Books, 1994), 183.

Appendix 2: Calculating Potential Extract from Malt Analysis

1. D. J. Lubert, "Interpretation of Malt Analyses," *MBAA Technical Quarterly* 13, no. 4 (1976): 203-207.

2. W. J. Pitz, "An Analysis of Malting Research," *ASBC Journal* 48, no. 1 (1990): 34.

About the Author

Ray Daniels is an award-winning author and craftbrewer. He has won numerous awards from the North American Guild of Beer Writers, and is a regular contributor to leading beer and brewing magazines. Recently, he became editor-in-chief of *Zymurgy* and *The New Brewer*, published respectively by the American Homebrewers Association, and the Institute for Brewing Studies.

His achievements include founding the Real Ale Festival, which celebrates annually America's largest collection of British-style, cask-conditioned ales outside of Great Britain. He has won nearly 100 homebrewing awards, and travels the world teaching brewing and beer appreciation courses. Every year he is a judge in homebrewing and commercial beer competitions, including the Great American Beer Festival, World Beer Cup, and World Beer Championships.

He also knows whereof he speaks. He is a top graduate of Siebel Institute's diploma course in brewing, holds an MBA from Harvard's Graduate School of Business, and earned a B.S. degree in Biochemistry from Texas A&M. He is also author of *101 Ideas for Homebrew Fun*, and coauthor of *Smoked Beer* and *Brown Ale*, both part of the Classic Beer Style Series published by Brewers Publications.

He lives with his family in Chicago, where he writes, brews, and looks at life through beer-colored glasses.

Index